June 11–13, 2014
Salzburg, Austria

Association for
Computing Machinery

*Advancing Computing as a Science & Profession*

# IH&MMSec'14
## Proceedings of the 2014 ACM
## Information Hiding and Multimedia
## Security Workshop

*Sponsored by:*
**ACM SIGMM**

*Supported by:*
**Technicolor, Authentic Vision, Secure Business Austria,
DENUVO, Digimarc, & University of Salzburg**

**Association for Computing Machinery**

*Advancing Computing as a Science & Profession*

**The Association for Computing Machinery**
2 Penn Plaza, Suite 701
New York, New York 10121-0701

**ISBN:** 978-1-4503-2647-6

Additional copies may be ordered prepaid from:

**ACM Order Department**
PO Box 30777
New York, NY  10087-0777, USA

Phone: 1-800-342-6626 (USA and Canada)
+1-212-626-0500 (Global)
Fax: +1-212-944-1318
E-mail: acmhelp@acm.org
Hours of Operation: 8:30 am – 4:30 pm ET

**ACM Order Number:** 433149

Printed in the USA

# Chairs' Welcome

It is our great pleasure to welcome you to the 2nd ACM Workshop on Information Hiding and Multimedia Security, Salzburg, Austria, June 11-13, 2014.

For over a decade, two workshops have been shaping the landscape of research in multimedia security. On the one hand, Information Hiding (aka. IH) was created in 1996 and focused on digital watermarking, steganography and steganalysis, anonymity and privacy, hard to intercept communications and covert/subliminal channels. On the other hand, the ACM Workshop on Multimedia and Security (aka. ACM MM&Sec) was initiated in 1998 and focused on data hiding, robust/perceptual hashing, biometrics, video surveillance and multimedia forensics. Key seminal works have been published in these two workshops and papers accepted for publication there attracted over 9,000 citations in total. Year after year, the two communities grew closer and the overlap between their respective scopes got bigger. As a result, after 14 successful editions each, IH and ACM MMSec decided to merge into a single event in an attempt to establish synergies between the two communities while, at the same time, building upon the reputation obtained over the years.

After the successful 1st edition being held Montpellier, France, June 17-19, 2013, the 2nd ACM Workshop on Information Hiding and Multimedia Security is being held here in Salzburg, Austria, June 11-13, 2014. We hope that this second edition of the workshop, resulting from merging two long standing sustainable events, successfully continues to be an attractive research forum that facilitates cross-fertilization of ideas among key stakeholders from academia, industry, practitioners and government agencies around the globe.

The call for papers attracted 64 submissions from Asia, South America, the United States, and Europe. The program committee accepted 24 papers (which corresponds to an acceptance rate of 37.5%) that cover a variety of interesting topics.

Throughout the review process, we obtained 190 reviews in total which equals 3 reviews per paper on average. Reviews either came from members of the PC, or from one of 33 external reviewers. In case of conflicting reviews, the reviewers were encouraged to engage in discussion, adjust their scores, and reach a consensus decision. During two PC chair meetings, these discussions as well as the initial reviews served as the basis for final acceptance or rejection. 11 full and 13 short papers, distributed over 1 main track and 4 special sessions, were eventually selected for presentation at the conference.

The program includes two invited talks (on JPEG security standardization and the EU FP7 FastPass project), four special sessions (Security and Privacy Technologies for Intelligent Energy Networks, Security and Robustness in Biometrics, Forensic and Biometric Challenges in Information Hiding and Media Security, and HEVC, H.264, and JPEG Security), and two industrial presentations by local Salzburg media security companies (Authentic Vision and Denuvo).

We would like to thank the program committee members for providing high-quality reviews in a timely manner which enabled us to compile an attractive program. We further thank the members of the local organizing team for their tremendous work to make the workshop a smoothly running event worth to be remembered. Last but not least, we would like to thank our sponsor and supporters (ACM, Technicolor, Authentic Vision, SBA Research, Denuvo, Digimarc, and Universität Salzburg) to provide organizational and financial help to conduct the workshop in a decent manner.

We hope that these proceedings will serve as a valuable reference for researchers.

**Andreas Uhl**
*IH&MMSec'14 General Chair*

**Stefan Katzenbeisser**
**Roland Kwitt**
**Alessandro Piva**
*IH&MMSec'14 Program Chairs*

# Table of Contents

## Keynote Address
Session Chair: Roland Kwitt *(University of Salzburg)*

## Special Session on HEVC, H.264, and JPEG Security
Session Chairs: Jan De Cock *(University of Ghent)*, Thomas Stütz *(Salzberg University of Applied Sciences)*

## Session: Software Security
Session Chair: Stefan Katzenbeisser *(Technische Universität Darmstadt)*

## Session: Watermarking
Session Chair: Gwenaël Doërr *(Technicolor)*

## Keynote Address
Session Chair: Andreas Uhl *(University of Salzburg)*

## Session: Forensic and Biometric Challenges in Information Hiding and Media Security
Session Chairs: Claus Vielhauer *(Brandenburg University of Applied Sciences)*,
Chang-Tsun Li *(University of Warwick)*, Klimis Ntalianis *(Technological Educational Institute of Athens)*,
Nicolas Tsapatsoulis *(Cyprus University of Technology)*

## Session: Steganography

## Session: Fingerprinting

Session Chair: Alessandro Piva *(University of Florence)*

## Session: Security and Privacy Technologies for Intelligent Energy Networks

Session Chairs: Dominik Engel *(Salzburg University of Applied Sciences)*, Zekeriya Erkin *(TU Delft)*

## Session: Digital Forensics

Session Chair: Rainer Böhme *(University of Münster)*

## Session: Security and Robustness in Biometrics

Session Chairs: Christian Rathgeb *(Hochschule Darmstadt)*, Peter Wild *(University of Reading)*

# IH&MMSec 2014 Workshop Organization

**General Chair:** Andreas Uhl (*University of Salzburg, Austria*)

**Local Organizing Chair:** Andreas Unterweger (*University of Salzburg, Austria*)

**Program Chairs:** Stefan Katzenbeisser (*TU Darmstadt, Germany*)
Roland Kwitt (*University of Salzburg, Austria*)
Alessandro Piva (*University of Florence, Italy*)

**Steering Committee:** Patrizio Campisi (*University of Roma TRE, Italy*)
George Danezis (*Microsoft Research Cambridge, UK*)
Jana Dittmann (*Otto-von-Guericke University, Germany*)
Jessica Fridrich (*SUNY Binghamton, USA*)
Stefan Katzenbeisser (*TU Darmstadt, Germany*)
Balakrishnan Prabhakaran (*University of Dallas, USA*)

**Program Committee:** Boris Assanovich (*University of Grodno, Belarus*)
Florent Autrusseau (*Polytech'Nantes, France*)
Morgan Barbier (*École Polytechnique, France*)
Johann Barbier (*Novetix, France*)
Mauro Barni (*University of Siena, Italy*)
Patrick Bas (*LAGIS, France*)
Federica Battisti (*University of Rome, Italy*)
Rainer Böhme (*University of Münster, Germany*)
Adrian Bors (*University of York, UK*)
Patrizio Campisi (*University of Rome, Italy*)
Marco Carli (*University of Rome, Italy*)
François Cayre (*University of Grenoble, France*)
Ee-Chien Chang (*University of Singapore, Singapore*)
Christophe Charrier (*University of Caen, France*)
Marc Chaumont (*University of Montpellier, France*)
Rémi Cogranne (*University of Troyes, France*)
Christian Collberg (*University of Arizona*)
Ingemar J. Cox (*University College London, UK*)
Scott Craver (*University of Binghamton, UK*)
George Danezis (*University College London, UK*)
Claude Delpha (*University of South Paris, France*)
Jana Dittmann (*Otto-von-Guericke University, Germany*)
Gwenaël Doërr (*Technicolor, France*)
Jean-Luc Dugelay (*EURECOM, France*)
Karen Egiazarian (*University of Tampere, Finland*)
Dominik Engel (*Salzburg University of Applied Sciences, Austria*)
Zekeriya Erkin (*Telft University of Technology, Netherlands*)
Wen-Pinn Fang (*University of Yuanpei, Taiwan*)

**Program Committee**
**(continued):** Hany Farid *(University of Dartmouth, USA)*
Tomáš Filler *(Digimarc Corporation, USA)*
Caroline Fontaine *(Télécom Bretagne, France)*
Jessica Fridrich *(SUNY Binghamton, USA)*
Bernhard Guillemin *(University of Auckland, New Zealand)*
Chad Heitzenrater *(Department of Defense, USA)*
Heinz Hofbauer *(University of Salzburg, Austria)*
Yongjian Hu *(University of Warwick, UK)*
Neil F. Johnson *(Johnson & Johnson Technology Consultants, LLC, USA)*
Johnatan Katz *(University of Maryland, USA)*
Stefan Katzenbeisser *(TU Darmstadt, Germany)*
Andrew Ker *(University of Oxford, UK)*
Matthias Kirchner *(International Computer Science Institute, Berkeley, USA)*
Jan Kodovsky *(Binghamton University, USA)*
Vladimir Kolesnikov *(University of Toronto, Canada)*
Christian Kraetzer *(Otto-von-Guericke University, Germany)*
Deepa Kundur *(University of Toronto, Canada)*
Patricia Ladret *(University of Grenoble, France)*
Xuejia Lai *(University of Shanghai, China)*
Patrick Le Callet *(University of Nantes, France)*
Heung-Kyu Lee *(Korea Advanced Institute of Science, Korea)*
Chang-Tsun Li *(University of Warwick, UK)*
Chih-Yang Lin *(University of Asia, Taiwan)*
Qingzhong Liu *(Sam Houston State University, USA)*
Chun-Shien Lu *(Academia Sinica, Taiwan)*
Valdimir Lukin *(University of Kharkiv, Ukraine)*
Emanuele Maiorana *(University of Rome, Italy)*
B. S. Manjunath *(University of California, USA)*
Wojciech Mazurczyk *(Warsaw University of Technology, Poland)*
Klimism Ntalianis *(Technical University of Athens, Greece)*
John McHugh *(University of North Carolina and RedJack, LLC., USA)*
Fernando Péréz-González *(University of Vigo, Spain)*
Mathieu Perreira Da Silva *(University of Nantes, France)*
Dijana Petrovska *(TELECOM SudParis, France)*
Tomáš Pevný *(Czech Technical University, Czech Republic)*
Nikolay Ponomarenko *(University of Ukraine, Ukraine)*
Balakrishnan Prabahakaran *(University of Dallas, USA)*
Wiliam Puech *(LIRMM / University of Montpellier, France)*
Christian Rathgeb *(University of Darmstadt, Germany)*
Ajita Rattani *(Michigan State University, USA)*
Amy Reibman *(AT&T Labs, USA)*
Vincent Rijmen *(University of Leuven, Belgium)*
Claudia Rinaldi *(University of Aquila, Italy)*

**Program Committee**
**(continued):**    Christophe Rosenberger *(University of Caen, France)*
Thomas Schneider *(TU Darmstadt, Germany)*
Yun-Quing Shi *(New Jersey Institute of Technology, USA)*
Kaushal Solanki *(Eyenuk, LLC, USA)*
Thomas Stütz *(Salzburg University of Applied Sciences, Austria)*
Neeraj Suri *(TU Darmstadt, Germany)*
Massimo Tistarelli *(University of Sassary, Italy)*
Claus Vielhauer *(FH Brandenburg, Germany)*
Sviatoslav Voloshynovskiy *(University of Geneva, Switzerland)*
Ran-Zan Wang *(Yuan Ze University, Taiwan)*
Peter Wild *(University of Reading, UK)*
Min Wu *(University of Maryland, USA)*

**Additional reviewers:**

Alireza Farrokh Baroughi

Thomas Bergmüller

Moazzam Butt

Lulu Chen

Hermann de Meer

Günther Eibl

Javier Franco-Pedroso

Javier Galbally

Dalila Goudia

Yongjian Hu

Yun Huang

Muhammad Kamarudin

Klaus Kasper

Finian Kelly

Sarra Koudier

Yue Li

Peter Meerwald

Christian Neureiter

Martin Aastrup Olsen

Petru Radu

Kai Samelin

Neyire Deniz Sarier

Pascal Schöttle

Qi Shi

Vassilios Solachidis

Benjamin Tams

Juan R. Troncoso-Pastoriza

Andreas Unterweger

Matthieu Urvoy

Feng Zhao

Xi Zhao

Michael Zohner

Jinyu Zuo

# IH&MMSec 2014 Sponsor & Supporters

Sponsor:

Supporters:

DIGIMARC | ⓓ

# Image Security Tools for JPEG Standards

Peter Schelkens
Vrije Universiteit Brussel - iMinds
Peter.Schelkens@vub.ac.be

## ABSTRACT

Image privacy and security are receiving increasingly more attention these days though their impact is still underestimated. Every day billions of digital pictures are generated and distributed via social media, news sites and photo sharing applications. These images tend to carry quite some information that can be regarded to be private for the photographer and/or the pictured individuals. Furthermore, this information is not solely constrained to the visible information carried by the picture. For instance, the sensor noise that is embedded in the picture provides information related to the camera used to take the photo. Besides the picture essence also metadata is signaled in the image file containers, providing geospatial information, camera settings, photographer related information, etc. Hence, it is evident to understand that to protect the privacy of the persons that can be associated with the picture, the necessary security precautions need to be taken. Since many pictures are represented in JPEG image formats, it is evident that the JPEG committee is also investigating how it can integrate better support for privacy and security requirements in its suite of standards. In this presentation, an overview will be given of standardized solutions, where we will particularly focus on JPEG 2000 JPSEC framework, but will also discuss how the committee plans to further improve the support for these requirements in the context of the legacy JPEG standard.

### Categories and Subject Descriptors

E.4 CODING AND INFORMATION THEORY (H.1.1) - Data compaction and compression; H.3.2 Information Storage - File organization; H.3.7 Standards; K.6.5 Security and Protection (D.4.6, K.4.2) - Authentication

### Keywords

JPEG, JPEG 2000, JPSEC, security, image coding, metadata protection

## Bio

Peter Schelkens obtained an electrical engineering degree (MSc) in applied physics, a biomedical engineering degree (medical physics), and, finally, a PhD degree in applied sciences from the Vrije Universiteit Brussel (VUB).

Peter Schelkens currently holds a professorship at the Department of Electronics and Informatics (ETRO) at the Vrije Universiteit Brussel (VUB). Peter Schelkens is research director at the iMinds

institute founded by the Flemish government to stimulate ICT innovation. Additionally, since 1995, he has also been affiliated to the Interuniversity Microelectronics Institute (Imec), Belgium, as scientific collaborator. Since 2010, he became a member of the board of councilors of the same institute. From 2002 till 2011, Peter Schelkens has held an FWO postdoctoral fellowship and since 2014, he holds an ERC Consolidator Grant focusing on digital holography.

The research interests of Peter Schelkens are situated in the field of multidimensional signal processing encompassing the representation, communication, security and rendering of these signals while especially focusing on cross-disciplinary research. Peter Schelkens has published over 200 papers in journals and conference proceedings, and he holds several patents and contributed to several standardization processes. His team is participating in the ISO/IEC JTC1/SC29/WG1 (JPEG) and WG11 (MPEG) standardization activities. Peter Schelkens is the Belgian head of delegation for the ISO/IEC SC29 and JPEG standardization committees, editor/chair of part 10 of JPEG 2000: ''Extensions for Three-Dimensional Data'' and PR Chair of the JPEG committee. From 2012 onwards he is acting as rapporteur/chair of JPEG Coding and Analysis Technologies, overlooking image processing technologies embedded in all JPEG standards. He is co-editor of the books, ''The JPEG 2000 Suite'' and ''Optical and Digital Image Processing'', published respectively in 2009 and 2011 by Wiley. He is a member of the IEEE, SPIE, and ACM, Belgian EURASIP Liaison Officer and elected committee member of the IEEE Image, Video, and Multidimensional Signal Processing Technical Committee (IVMSP TC) (Term 2013-2015) and the IEEE Multimedia Signal Processing Technical Committee (MMSP TC) (Term 2014-2016). Peter Schelkens is associate editor of IEEE Transactions on Circuits and Systems for Video Technology.

In 2011, he was acting as General (co-)Chair of the following conferences: IEEE International Conference on Image Processing (ICIP), Workshop on Quality of Multimedia Experience (QoMEX) and Workshop on Image Processing for Art Investigation (IP4AI). Peter Schelkens is also co-founder of the spin-off company, Universum Digitalis. His team is also member of the Intel Exascience Lab in Leuven, Belgium.

*IH&MMSec'14*, June 11–13, 2014, Salzburg, Austria.
ACM 978-1-4503-2647-6/14/06.
http://dx.doi.org/10.1145/2600918.2600943

# Detection of JSteg Algorithm Using Hypothesis Testing Theory and a Statistical Model with Nuisance Parameters.

Tong Qiao
ICD - LM2S - UMR CNRS 6281
Troyes University of
Technology (UTT)
tong.qiao@utt.fr

Cathel Zitzmann
ICD - LM2S - UMR CNRS 6281
EPF Graduate School of
Engineering
cathel.zitzmann@epf.fr

Rémi Cogranne
ICD - LM2S - UMR CNRS 6281
Troyes University of
Technology (UTT)
remi.cogranne@utt.fr

Florent Retraint
ICD - LM2S - UMR CNRS 6281
Troyes University of
Technology (UTT)
florent.retraint@utt.fr

## ABSTRACT

This paper investigates the statistical detection of data hidden within DCT coefficients of JPEG images using a Laplacian distribution model. The main contributions is twofold. First, this paper proposes to model the DCT coefficients using a Laplacian distribution but challenges the usual assumption that among a sub-band all the coefficients follow are independent and identically distributed (i. i. d.). In this paper it is assumed that the distribution parameters change from DCT coefficient to DCT coefficient. Second this paper applies this model to design a statistical test, based on hypothesis testing theory, which aims at detecting data hidden within DCT coefficient with the JSteg algorithm. The proposed optimal detector carefully takes into account the distribution parameters as nuisance parameters. Numerical results on simulated data as well as on numerical images database show the relevance of the proposed model and the good performance of the ensuing test.

## Categories and Subject Descriptors

H.1.1 [**Mathematics of Computing**]: Probability and Statistics—*Detection methodology*; I.4.10 [**Image Processing**]: Image Representation—*Statistical modelling*; H.1.1 [**Models and Principles**]: Systems and Information Theory—*Information theory*; D.2.11 [**Software Engineering**]: Software Architectures—*Information hiding*

## Keywords

Steganography, Steganalysis, Hypothesis Testing Theory, Optimal Detection, Statistical Modelling, DCT coefficients.

## 1. INTRODUCTION

Steganography nowadays refers to the technologies that exploit a covert channel to hide secret data within innocuous looking digital objects, without any perceptual modifications. Potentially a wide range of digital objects can be used to hide information such as images [16], videos [5], or network packets [1, 33]. On the opposite, passive steganalysis aims at discovering the use of such covert channel or at retrieving some information on hidden data, such as estimating the size of hidden data, the key or the algorithm used for embedding, for instance. During the last decade, steganographic algorithms and detection methods have been considerably improved, the reader is referred to [6] and [14] for detailed review of existing methods in steganography and steganalysis respectively.

However, as detailed in [16], a wide range of problems, theoretical as well as practical, remains uncovered and some prevent the moving of "steganography and steganalysis from the laboratory into the real world". This is especially the case in the field of Optimal Detection, see [16, Sec. 3.1], in which this paper lies. Roughly speaking, the goal of optimal detection in steganalysis, is to exploit an accurate statistical model of cover source, usually digital images, to design a statistical test which properties can be established; typically, in order to guarantee a false alarm probability and to calculate the optimal detection performance one can expect from the most powerful detector.

This optimal detection approach has been studied for the detection of data hidden within spatial domain of digital images since [13] and has been then considerably improved with more accurate statistical model of cover images [8, 31, 12]. For the detection of data hidden within the DCT coefficients of JPEG images, the application of hypothesis testing theory for designing optimal detectors, that are efficient in practice, is facing the problem of accurately modelling the statistical distribution of DCT coefficients. It can be noted that several models have been proposed in the literature to model statistically the DCT coefficients; among those models, the Laplacian distribution is probably the most widely used due to its simplicity and its fairly good accuracy [19]. More accurate models such as the Generalised Gaussian [23] and, more recently, the Generalised Gamma model [7] have been shown to provide much more accuracy at the cost of higher complexity. Some of those models have been exploited in the field of steganalysis, see [27, 4] for instance. In the framework of optimal detection, a first attempt has been made to design a statistical test modelling the DCT coefficient with the Laplacian distribution, see [34]. While the performance of this test has been analytically established and a threshold has been theoretically calculated to guarantee a prescribed false-alarm probability, a dramatic loss of performance has been empirically observed [34]. This can be explained by the inaccuracy of the Laplacian model that prevents the detection of such small changes as the embedding of hidden data cause.

It should be noted that other approaches have been proposed for the detection of data hidden within DCT coefficients of JPEG images, to cite few, the structural detection [18], the category attack [20], the WS detector [3], and universal or blind detectors [22, 26]. However, establishing the statistical properties of those detectors remains a difficult work which has not been studied yet. In addition, the most accurate detector based on statistical learning is sensitive to the so-called cover source-mismatch [2]: the training phase must be performed with caution.

In this paper, a novel approach is proposed to model the DCT coefficients of JPEG image and is exploited to design a powerful statistical test based on the concept of nuisance parameters. The key idea of this approach is to consider that all the DCT coefficients of a sub-band do not have the same distribution parameters which act as nuisance parameters for the detection of hidden data.

In fact most of the proposed model of DCT coefficients are based, or have at least their accuracy verified, on observations of histograms of all the DCT coefficients of a sub-band. This method implicitly assumes that, among a sub-band, all the DCT coefficients follow the same statistical distribution. In practice, it makes sense to consider that the content of the digital image will largely influence the distribution of those coefficients. This implies that the DCT coefficients may not all follow the same distribution because their distribution parameters depend on the local content of the image.

For simplicity and clarity, it is proposed in this paper to apply this methodology with the Laplacian model. A simple approach is proposed to estimate the expectation of each coefficient by denoising the image in spatial domain and transforming the denoised image back into the DCT domain. Then it is proposed to exploit the framework of hypothesis testing theory to design an optimal detector based on this model that takes into account the Laplacian distribution parameters as nuisance parameters .

The contributions of this paper are summarised below:

- First, a novel model that does not assume that all the DCT coefficients of a same sub-band are i. i. d. is proposed, contrary to almost every statistical model of DCT coefficients .

- Second, this statistical model of DCT coefficients is used to design an accurate test to detect data hidden within JPEG images with the JSteg algorithm. This statistical test takes into account distribution parameters of each DCT coefficient as nuisance parameters.

- Numerical results show the sharpness of the theoretically established results and the good performance that the proposed statistical test achieves. A comparison with the statistical test based on the Laplacian and on the assumption of i. i. d. coefficient, see [34], shows the relevance of the proposed methodology.

This paper is organised as follows. Section 2 formalises the statistical problem of detection of information hidden within the DCT coefficients of JPEG images. Then, Section 3 presents the optimal Likelihood Ratio Test (LRT) for detecting the JSteg algorithm based on the Laplacian distribution model. Section 4 presents the proposed approach for estimating the nuisance parameter in practice. Finally, Section 5 presents comparisons with other detector and Section 6 concludes the paper.

## 2. PROBLEM STATEMENT

In this paper, a grayscale digital image is represented, in the spatial domain, by a single matrix $\mathbf{Z} = \{z_{i,j}\}, i \in \{1, \ldots, I\}, j \in \{1, \ldots, J\}$. The present work can be extended to colour image by analysing each colour channel separately. Most of the digital images are stored using the JPEG compression standard. This standard exploits the linear Discrete Cosine Transform (DCT), over blocks of $8 \times 8$ pixels to represent an image in the so-called DCT domain. In the present paper, we avoid the description of the imaging pipeline of a digital still camera; the reader is referred to [24] for a description of the whole imaging pipeline and to [25] for a detailed description of the JPEG compression standard.

Let us denote the DCT coefficients by the matrix $\mathbf{V} = \{v_{i,j}\}$. An alternative representation of those coefficients is usually adopted by gathering the DCT coefficients that corresponds to the same frequency sub-band. In this paper, this alternative representation is denoted by the matrix $\mathbf{U} = \{u_{k,l}\}, k \in \{1, \ldots, K\}, l \in \{1, \ldots, 64\}$ with $K \approx I \times J/64^1$.

The coefficients from the first sub-band $u_{k,1}$, often referred to as DC coefficients, represent the mean of pixels value over $k$-th block of $8 \times 8$ pixels. The modification of those coefficients may be obvious and creates artifacts that can be detected easily, hence, they are usually not used for data hiding. Similarly, the JSteg algorithm does not use the coefficients from the others sub-bands, referred to as AC coefficients, if they equal 0 or 1. In fact, it is known that using the coefficients equal to 0 or 1 modifies significantly the statistical properties of AC coefficients; this creates a flaw that can be detected.

The JSteg algorithm embeds data within DCT coefficients of JPEG images using the well-known LSB (Least Significant Bit) replacement method, see details in [32]. In brief, this method consists in substituting the LSB of each DCT coefficient by a bit of the message it is aimed to hide. The number of bit hidden per coefficient, usually referred to as the payload, is denoted $R$. Since the JSteg algorithm does not use every DCT coefficient, the payload will in fact be measured in this paper as the number of bits hidden per *usable* coefficients (that is the number of bits divided by the number of AC coefficients that differ from 0 and 1).

---

[1]In this paper we assume, without loss of generality, that both the width and the height of the inspected image are multiple of 8.

4

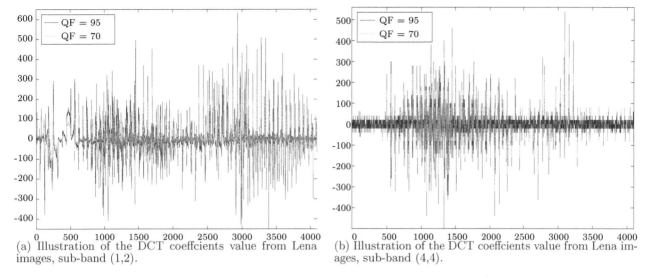

(a) Illustration of the DCT coeffcients value from Lena images, sub-band (1,2).

(b) Illustration of the DCT coeffcients value from Lena images, sub-band (4,4).

Figure 1: Illustrative examples of the value of the DCT coefficients of two sub-bands from *lena* image. Those examples show that the assumption that DCT coefficients are i. i. d. within a sub-band hardly holds true in practice.

Let us assume that the DCT coefficients are independent and that they all follow the same probability distribution, denoted $\mathcal{P}_\theta$, parametrised by the parameter $\theta$ which may change among the coefficients. Since the DCT coefficients can only take value into a discrete set, the distribution $\mathcal{P}_\theta$ may be represented by its probability mass function (pmf) denoted $P_\theta = \{p_\theta[u]\}$; for simplicity[2], it is assumed in this paper that $u \in \mathbb{Z}$. Let us denote $\mathcal{Q}_\theta^R$ the probability distribution of *usable* DCT coefficients from the stego-image, after embedding a message with payload $R$. A short calculation shows that, see [13, 15, 35], the stego-image distribution may be represented with following the pmf $Q_\theta^R = \{q_\theta^R[u]\}_{u \in \mathbb{Z}}$ where

$$q_\theta^R[u] = (1 - {}^R\!/_2)p_\theta[u] + {}^R\!/_2\, p_\theta[\bar{u}], \qquad (1)$$

and $\bar{u} = u + (-1)^u$ represents the integer $u$ with flipped LSB. For the sake of clarity, let us denote $\theta_{k,l}$ the distribution parameter of $k$-th DCT coefficient from $l$-th sub-band and let $\boldsymbol{\theta} = \{\theta_{k,l}\}, k \in \{1, \dots, K\}, l \in \{2, \dots, 64\}$ represents the distribution parameter of all the AC coefficients.

When inspecting a given JPEG image, more precisely its DCT coefficients matrix $\mathbf{U}$, in order to detect data hidden with the JSteg algorithm, the problem consists in choosing between the two following hypotheses $\mathcal{H}_0$: *"the coefficients $u_{k,l}$ follow the distribution $\mathcal{P}_{\theta_{k,l}}$"* and $\mathcal{H}_1$: *"the coefficients $u_{k,l}$ follow the distribution $\mathcal{Q}_{\theta_{k,l}}^R$"* which can be written formally:

$$\begin{cases} \mathcal{H}_0 : \left\{ u_{k,l} \sim \mathcal{P}_{\theta_{k,l}}, \forall k \in \{1, \dots, K\}, \forall l \in \{2, \dots, 64\} \right\}, \\ \mathcal{H}_1 : \left\{ u_{k,l} \sim \mathcal{Q}_{\theta_{k,l}}^R, \forall k \in \{1, \dots, K\}, \forall l \in \{2, \dots, 64\}, R > 0 \right\}. \end{cases} \qquad (2)$$

A statistical test is a mapping $\delta : \mathbb{Z}^{I \cdot J} \mapsto \{\mathcal{H}_0, \mathcal{H}_1\}$ such that hypothesis $\mathcal{H}_i$ is accepted if $\delta(\mathbf{U}) = \mathcal{H}_i$ (see [21] for details on hypothesis testing). As previously explained, this paper focuses on the Neyman-Pearson bi-criteria approach: maximising the correct detection probability for a given false-

alarm probability $\alpha_0$. Let:

$$\mathcal{K}_{\alpha_0} = \left\{ \delta : \sup_{\boldsymbol{\theta}} \mathbb{P}_{\mathcal{H}_0}[\delta(\mathbf{U}) = \mathcal{H}_1] \le \alpha_0 \right\}, \qquad (3)$$

be the class of tests with a false alarm probability upper-bounded by $\alpha_0$. Here $\mathbb{P}_{\mathcal{H}_i}(A)$ stands for the probability of event $A$ under hypothesis $\mathcal{H}_i, i = \{0, 1\}$, and the supremum over $\boldsymbol{\theta}$ has to be understood as whatever the distribution parameters might be, in order to ensure that the false alarm probability $\alpha_0$ can not be exceed.

Among all the tests in $\mathcal{K}_{\alpha_0}$, it is aimed at finding a test $\delta$ which maximises the power function, defined by the correct detection probability:

$$\beta_\delta = \mathbb{P}_{\mathcal{H}_1}[\delta(\mathbf{U}) = \mathcal{H}_1], \qquad (4)$$

which is equivalent to minimising the missed detection probability $\alpha_1(\delta) = \mathbb{P}_{\mathcal{H}_1}[\delta(\mathbf{U}) = \mathcal{H}_0] = 1 - \beta_\delta$.

In order to design a practical *optimal detector*, as referred to in [16], for steganalysis in spatial domain, the main difficulty is to estimate the distribution parameters, that is the expectation and the variance of each pixel. On the opposite, in the case of DCT coefficients, the application of hypothesis testing theory to design an optimal detector has previously being attempted with the assumption that the distribution parameter remains the same for all the coefficients from a same sub-band. With this assumption, the estimation of the distribution parameters is not an issue because thousands of DCT coefficients are available. However which distribution model to choose remains an open problem.

The hypothesis testing theory has been applied for the steganalysis of JSteg algorithm in [34] using a Laplacian distribution model and using the assumption that DCT coefficients of each sub-band are i. i. d. However, this pioneer work does not allow the designing of an efficient test because a very important loss of performance has been observed when comparing results on real images and theoretically established ones. Such a result can be explained by the two following reasons: 1) the Laplacian model might be not accurate enough to detect steganagraphy and 2) the assumption that the DCT coefficients of each frequency sub-

---

[2]In practice, DCT coefficients belong to set $[-1024, \dots, 1023]$, see [34].

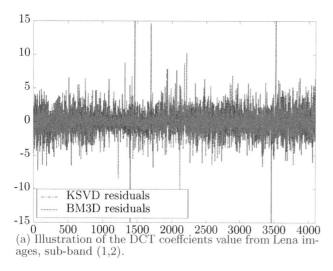

(a) Illustration of the DCT coeffcients value from Lena images, sub-band (1,2).

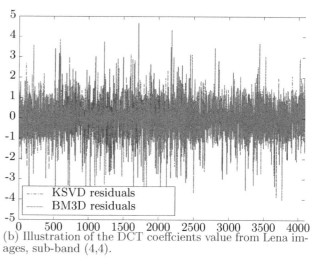

(b) Illustration of the DCT coeffcients value from Lena images, sub-band (4,4).

Figure 2: Illustrative examples of the DCT coefficients of the residual noise, obtained by denoising image. The same two DCT sub-bands, as in Figure 1 are extracted the residual noise of *lena* image. On those examples the assumption of i. i. d. distribution seems to be more realistic.

band are i. i. d. may be wrong. Recently, it has been shown that the use of Generalised Gamma model or even more accurate model [28, 29] allows the designing of a test with very good detection performance. On the opposite, in this paper it is proposed to challenge the assumption that all the DCT coefficients of a sub-band are i. i. d.

A typical example is given by Figures 1 and 2. Figure 1a (resp. Figure 1b) represents the DCT coefficients of the sub-band (1,2) (resp. sub-band (4,4)) extracted from the image *lena*. Observing those two graphs, it is obvious that the assumption of all those coefficients being i. i. d. is doubtful. However, if it is assumed that each coefficient has a different expectation, one can estimate this expected value and compute the "residual noise", that is the difference between the observation and the computed expectation. Such results are shown in Figure 2, with two different models for estimating the expectation of DCT coefficients of the same two sub-bands from *lena*. Obviously, residual noises look much more i. i. d. than the original DCT coefficients.

In the following section, we detail the statistical test that takes into account both the expectation and the variance as nuisance parameters and we study the optimal detection when those parameters are known. A discussion on nuisance parameters is also provided in Section 4.

## 3. OPTIMAL DETECTION FRAMEWORK

When the payload $R$ and the distribution parameters $\boldsymbol{\theta} = \{\theta_{k,l}\}, k \in \{1, \ldots, K\}, l \in \{2, \ldots, 64\}$ are known, problem (2) is reduced to a statistical test between two simple hypotheses. In such a case, the Neyman-Pearson Lemma [21, theorem 3.2.1] states that the most powerful test in the class $\mathcal{K}_{\alpha_0}$ (3) is the LRT defined, on the assumption that DCT coefficients are independent, as:

$$\delta^{\mathrm{lr}}(\mathbf{U}) = \begin{cases} \mathcal{H}_0 \text{ if } \Lambda^{\mathrm{lr}}(\mathbf{U}) = \sum_{k=1}^{K} \sum_{l=2}^{64} \Lambda^{\mathrm{lr}}(u_{k,l}) < \tau^{\mathrm{lr}}, \\ \mathcal{H}_1 \text{ if } \Lambda^{\mathrm{lr}}(\mathbf{U}) = \sum_{k=1}^{K} \sum_{l=2}^{64} \Lambda^{\mathrm{lr}}(u_{k,l}) \geq \tau^{\mathrm{lr}}, \end{cases} \quad (5)$$

where the decision threshold $\tau^{\mathrm{lr}}$ is the solution of the equation $\mathbb{P}_{\mathcal{H}_0}\left[\Lambda^{\mathrm{lr}}(\mathbf{U}) \geq \tau^{\mathrm{lr}}\right] = \alpha_0$, to ensure that the false alarm probability of the LRT equals $\alpha_0$, and the log Likelihood Ratio (LR) for one observation is given, by definition, by:

$$\Lambda^{\mathrm{lr}}(u_{k,l}) = \log\left(\frac{q_{\theta_{k,l}}^{R}[u_{k,l}]}{p_{\theta_{k,l}}[u_{k,l}]}\right). \quad (6)$$

In practice, when the rate $R$ is not known one can try to design a test which is locally optimal around a given payload rate, named Locally Asymptotically Uniformly Most Powerful (LAUMP) test, as proposed in [11, 35] but this lies outside the scope of this paper.

From the definition of $p_{\theta_{k,l}}[u_{k,l}]$ and $q_{\theta_{k,l}}^{R}[u_{k,l}]$ (1), it is easy to write the LR (6) as:

$$\Lambda^{\mathrm{lr}}(u_{k,l}) = \log\left(1 - \frac{R}{2} + \frac{R}{2}\frac{p_{\theta_{k,l}}[\bar{u}_{k,l}]}{p_{\theta_{k,l}}[u_{k,l}]}\right), \quad (7)$$

where, as previously defined, $\bar{u}_{k,l} = u_{k,l} + (-1)^{u_{k,l}}$ represents the DCT coefficient $u_{k,l}$ with flipped LSB.

Accepting, for a moment, that one is in this most favourable scenario, in which all the parameters are perfectly known, we can deduce some interesting results. Due to the fact that observations are considered to be independent, the LR $\Lambda^{\mathrm{lr}}(\mathbf{U})$ is the sum of random variables and some asymptotic theorems allow the establishing of its distribution when the number of coefficients become "sufficiently large". This asymptotic approach is usually verified in the case of digital images due to the very large number of pixels or DCT coefficients.

Let us denote $E_{\mathcal{H}_i}(\theta_{k,l})$ and $V_{\mathcal{H}_i}(\theta_{k,l})$ the expectation and the variance of the LR $\Lambda^{\mathrm{lr}}(u_{k,l})$ under hypothesis $\mathcal{H}_i, i = \{0, 1\}$. Those quantity obviously depend on the parametrised distribution $\mathcal{P}_{\theta_{k,l}}$. The Lindeberg's central limit theorem (CLT) [21, theorem 11.2.5] states that as $L$ tends to

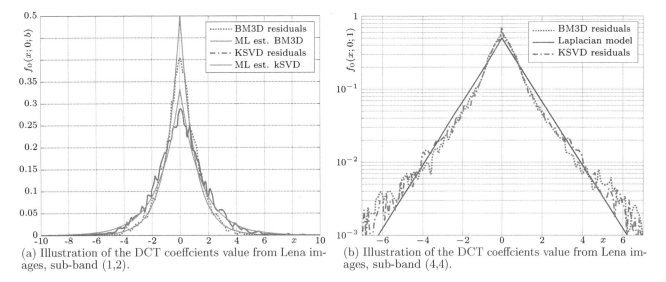

(a) Illustration of the DCT coeffcients value from Lena images, sub-band (1,2).

(b) Illustration of the DCT coeffcients value from Lena images, sub-band (4,4).

Figure 3: Statistical distribution of the DCT coefficients of the residual noise plotted in Figure 2. For comparison, the Laplacian pdf, with parameters estimated by the Maximum Likelihood Estimation are also shown. Note that for a meaning comparison, Figure 3b show the results after normalisation by the estimated scale parameter $\widehat{b}$.

infinity it holds true that[3]:

$$
\frac{\sum_{k=1}^{K}\sum_{l=2}^{64} \Lambda^{\mathrm{lr}}(u_{k,l}) - E_{\mathcal{H}_i}(\theta_{k,l})}{\left(\sum_{k=1}^{K}\sum_{l=2}^{64} V_{\mathcal{H}_i}(\theta_{k,l})\right)^{1/2}} \xrightarrow{d} \mathcal{N}(0,1) , \ i = \{0,1\}, \quad (8)
$$

where $\xrightarrow{d}$ represents the convergence in distribution and $\mathcal{N}(0,1)$ is the standard normal distribution, *i.e.* with zero mean and unit variance.

This theorem is of crucial interest to establish the statistical properties of the proposed test [8, 10, 31, 34]. In fact, once the moments have been calculated under both $\mathcal{H}_i, i = \{0,1\}$, one can normalise under hypothesis $\mathcal{H}_0$ the LR $\Lambda^{\mathrm{lr}}(\mathbf{U})$ as follows:

$$
\begin{aligned}
\overline{\Lambda}^{\mathrm{lr}}(\mathbf{U}) &= \frac{\Lambda^{\mathrm{lr}}(\mathbf{U}) - \sum_{k=1}^{K}\sum_{l=2}^{64} E_{\mathcal{H}_i}(\theta_{k,l})}{\left(\sum_{k=1}^{K}\sum_{l=2}^{64} V_{\mathcal{H}_i}(\theta_{k,l})\right)^{1/2}}, \\
&= \frac{\sum_{k=1}^{K}\sum_{l=2}^{64} \Lambda^{\mathrm{lr}}(u_{k,l}) - E_{\mathcal{H}_i}(\theta_{k,l})}{\left(\sum_{k=1}^{K}\sum_{l=2}^{64} V_{\mathcal{H}_i}(\theta_{k,l})\right)^{1/2}}. \quad (9)
\end{aligned}
$$

Since this essentially consists in adding a deterministic value and scaling the LR, this operation of normalisation preserves the optimality of the LRT.

It immediately follows from Lindeberg's CLT (8) that $\overline{\Lambda}^{\mathrm{lr}}(\mathbf{U})$ asymptotically follows, as $L$ tends to infinity, the normal distribution $\mathcal{N}(0,1)$. Hence, it is immediate to set the decision threshold that guarantee the prescribed false alarm probability:

$$
\overline{\tau}^{\mathrm{lr}} = \Phi^{-1}(1 - \alpha_0), \quad (10)
$$

where $\Phi$ and $\Phi^{-1}$ respectively represent the cumulative distribution function (cdf) of the standard normal distribution

[3]Note that we refer to the Lindeberg's CLT, whose conditions are easily verified in our case, because the random variable are independent but are not i. i. d.

and its inverse. Similarly, denoting

$$
m_i = \sum_{k=1}^{K}\sum_{l=2}^{64} E_{\mathcal{H}_i}(\theta_{k,l}) \ \text{ and } \ \sigma_i^2 = \sum_{k=1}^{K}\sum_{l=2}^{64} V_{\mathcal{H}_i}(\theta_{k,l}), i = \{0,1\},
$$

it is also straightforward to establish the detection function of the LRT given by:

$$
\beta_{\overline{\delta}^{\mathrm{lr}}} = 1 - \Phi\left(\frac{\sigma_0}{\sigma_1}\Phi^{-1}(1 - \alpha_0) + \frac{m_0 - m_1}{\sigma_1}\right). \quad (11)
$$

Equations (10) and (11) emphasise the main advantage of normalising the LR as described in relation (9): it allows to set a threshold that guarantee a false alarm probability independently from any distribution parameters and, this is particularly crucial because digital images are heterogeneous, their properties vary for each image. Second, the normalisation allows to easily establish the detection power which again, is achieved, for any distribution parameters and hence, for any inspected image.

## 3.1 Application with the Laplacian Distribution

In the case of the Laplacian distribution, the framework of hypothesis testing theory has been applied for the steganalysis of JSteg in [34] in which the moments of LR are calculated under the two following assumptions: 1) all the DCT coefficients from the same sub-band are i. i. d. and 2) the expectation of each DCT coefficient is zero.

The continuous Laplacian distribution has the following probability density function:

$$
f_{\mu,b}(x) = \frac{1}{2b}\exp\left(-\frac{|x - \mu|}{b}\right) \quad (12)
$$

where $\mu \in \mathbb{R}$, sometimes referred to as the location parameter, corresponds to the expectation, and $b > 0$ is the so-called scale parameter. During the compression of JPEG images, the DCT coefficients are quantised. Hence, let us defined the discrete Laplacian distribution by the following pmf, see details in Appendix A:

$$f_{\mu,b}[k] \overset{def.}{=} \mathbb{P}\Big[x \in [\Delta(k - \tfrac{1}{2}), \Delta(k + \tfrac{1}{2})[\Big]$$

$$= \begin{cases} \exp\left(-\frac{|\Delta k - \mu|}{b}\right)\sinh\left(\frac{\Delta}{2b}\right) & \text{if } \frac{\mu}{\Delta} \notin [k - \tfrac{1}{2}; k + \tfrac{1}{2}[ \\ 1 - \frac{1}{2}\exp\left(-\frac{\Delta(k+1/2)-\mu}{2b}\right) - \frac{1}{2}\exp\left(-\frac{\Delta(k-1/2)-\mu}{2b}\right) & \text{otherwise} \end{cases}$$
(13)

where $\Delta$ is the quantisation step.

From the expression of the discrete Laplacian distribution (13) and from the expression of the LR (7), one can express the LR for the detection of JSteg under the assumption that DCT coefficients follow a Laplacian distribution, as follows, see Appendix B:

$$\log\left(1 - \frac{R}{2} + \frac{R}{2}\exp\left[\frac{\Delta}{b}\text{sign}(\Delta k - \mu)(k - \bar{k})\right]\right). \quad (14)$$

It can be noted that this expression (14) of the LR is almost the same as the one obtained in [34] assuming that all DCT coefficients have a zero-mean, only the sign term $\text{sign}(\Delta k - \mu)$ becomes $\text{sign}(k)$ when assuming a zero-mean. It should also be noted that the log-LR equals 0 for every DCT coefficient whose value is 0 or 1 because the JSteg algorithm does not embed hidden data in those coefficients. In the present paper, the moments of the LR (14) are not analytically established, the reader interested is referred to [34].

## 4. DEALING WITH NUISANCE PARAMETERS

As already explained, most of the statistical model of DCT coefficients assume that within a sub-band the coefficients are i.i.d. However, as illustrated in Figure 1 and 2 this assumption is doubtful in practice. Another way to explain why the DCT coefficients may not be i.i.d. is to consider a block of $8 \times 8$ pixels in spatial domain, say the first, $\mathbf{z} = z_{i,j}, i \in \{1, \ldots, 8\}, j \in \{1, \ldots, 8\}$. The value of those pixels can be decomposed as:

$$z_{i,j} = x_{i,j} + n_{i,j},$$

where $x_{i,j}$ is a deterministic value that represents the expectation of pixel at location $(i, j)$ and $n_{i,j}$ is the realisation of a random variable representing all noises corrupting the inspected image. Clearly, this decomposition can be done for the whole block $\mathbf{z} = \mathbf{x} + \mathbf{n}$, where $\mathbf{x} = \{x_{i,j}\}$ and $\mathbf{n} = \{n_{i,j}\}$. Since the DCT transformation is linear the DCT coefficient of any block may be expressed as:

$$\text{DCT}(\mathbf{z}) = \mathbf{D}^T \mathbf{z}\mathbf{D} = \mathbf{D}^T(\mathbf{x} + \mathbf{n})\mathbf{D}$$
$$= \mathbf{D}^T \mathbf{x}\mathbf{D} + \mathbf{D}^T \mathbf{n}\mathbf{D} = \text{DCT}(\mathbf{x}) + \text{DCT}(\mathbf{n}), \quad (15)$$

where DCT represents the DCT transform and $\mathbf{D}$ is the change of basis matrix from spatial to DCT basis, often referred to as the DCT matrix.

It makes sense to assume that the expectation of the noise component $\mathbf{n}$ has a zero-mean in the spatial and in the DCT domain. On the opposite, it is difficult to justify that the DCT of pixels' expectation $\mathbf{x}$ should necessary be around zero. Actually, this assumption holds true if and only if the expectation is the same for of all the pixels from a block: $\forall i \in \{1, \ldots, 8\}, \forall j \in \{1, \ldots, 8\}, x_{i,j} = x$, see [30, 28, 29] for details.

On the opposite, in the paper, it is mainly aimed at estimating the expectation of each DCT coefficient. To this end, it is proposed to decompress a JPEG image $\mathbf{V}$ into the spatial domain to obtain $\mathbf{Z}$, then to estimate the expectation of each pixel $\widehat{\mathbf{Z}}$. Then this denoised image, which corresponds to estimated expectation of pixels in spatial domain, is transformed back into the DCT domain to finally obtain the estimated value of all DCT coefficients, denoted $\mathbf{V} = \{v_{i,j}\}, i \in \{1, \ldots, I\}, j \in \{1, \ldots, J\}$. Several methods have been tested to estimate the expectation of pixels in the spatial domain $\widehat{\mathbf{Z}}$, namely, the BM3D collaborative filtering, kSVD sparse dictionary learning and non-local weighted averaging method from NL-means.

In addition, the proposed model also assumes that the scale parameter $b_{k,l}$ is different for each DCT coefficient. The estimation of this parameter, for each DCT coefficient, is based on the WS Jpeg method to locally estimate the variance; that is, for coefficients $v_{i,j}$, it simply consists of the sample variance of the DCT coefficients of the same sub-band from neighbouring blocks:

$$\widehat{\sigma}_{i,j}^2 = \frac{1}{7}\sum_{\substack{s=-1 \\ (s,t)\neq(0,0)}}^{1}\sum_{t=-1}^{1}\left(v_{i+8s,j+8t} - \bar{v}_{i,j}\right)^2, \quad (16)$$

where $\bar{v}_{i,j}$ is the sample mean: $\frac{1}{8}\sum_{\substack{s=-1 \\ (s,t)\neq(0,0)}}^{1}\sum_{t=-1}^{1} v_{i+8s,j+8t}$.

Let us recall that the Maximum Likelihood Estimation (MLE) of the scale parameter of Laplacian distribution from realisations $x1, \ldots, x_N$ is given by $\hat{b} = N^{-1}\sum_{n=1}^{N}|x_n - \mu|$. The local estimation of the scale parameter it is proposed to use in this paper is given by:

$$\hat{b}_{i,j} = \frac{1}{8}\sum_{\substack{s=-1 \\ (s,t)\neq(0,0)}}^{1}\sum_{t=-1}^{1}|v_{i+8s,j+8t} - \bar{v}_{i,j}|, \quad (17)$$

where $\bar{v}_{i,j}$ is the sample mean previously defined. As in the WS Jpeg algorithm, this approach raises the problem of scale parameter estimation for blocks located on the sides of the image. In the present paper, as in the WS Jpeg method, it is proposed not to use those blocks in the test.

### 4.1 Design of the Proposed Detector

In Section 3 the framework of hypothesis testing theory has been presented assuming that distribution parameters are known for each DCT coefficient. To design a practical test, a usual solution consists in replacing the unknown parameter by its ML estimation. This leads to the construction of a Generalised LRT. A similar construction is adopted in this paper, using the *ad hoc* estimators presented at the beginning of section 4, instead of using the ML method to estimate the distribution parameters of each DCT coefficient. The proposed test is thus defined as:

$$\widehat{\delta}(\mathbf{U}) = \begin{cases} \mathcal{H}_0 \text{ if } \widehat{\Lambda}(\mathbf{U}) = \sum_{k=1}^{K}\sum_{l=2}^{64}\widehat{\Lambda}(u_{k,l}) < \widehat{\tau}, \\ \mathcal{H}_1 \text{ if } \widehat{\Lambda}(\mathbf{U}) = \sum_{k=1}^{K}\sum_{l=2}^{64}\widehat{\Lambda}(u_{k,l}) \geq \widehat{\tau}, \end{cases} \quad (18)$$

where the decision statistic $\widehat{\Lambda}(u_{k,l})$ for a single DCT coefficient is given by, see Equation (14):

$$\widehat{\Lambda}(u_{k,l}) = \log\left(1 + \frac{R}{2} + \frac{R}{2}\exp\left[\frac{\Delta}{\widehat{b}_{k,l}}\mathrm{sign}(\Delta k - \widehat{\mu}_{k,l})(k - \bar{k})\right]\right),$$
(19)

and, in order to have a normalised decision statistic for the whole image, $\widehat{\Lambda}(\mathbf{U})$ is defined as:

$$\widehat{\Lambda}(\mathbf{U}) = \frac{1}{S_L}\sum_{k=1}^{K}\sum_{l=2}^{64}\widehat{\Lambda}(u_{k,l}) - E_{\mathcal{H}_0}(\widehat{\mu}_{k,l}, \widehat{b}_{k,l}) \quad (20)$$

with
$$S_L^2 = \sum_{k=1}^{K}\sum_{l=2}^{64} V_{\mathcal{H}_0}(\widehat{\mu}_{k,l}, \widehat{b}_{k,l}).$$

Finally, note that in practice the direct use of the estimated scale parameter $\widehat{b}_{k,l}$ may cause numerical instabilities because this term may be close to zero. A simple, yet efficient, technique to avoid this problem is to replace $\widehat{b}_{k,l}$ by the following term $\min(\widehat{b}_{k,l}, b_{\min})$. That is when the estimate $\widehat{b}_{k,l}$ is smaller that than the fixed constant $b_{\min}$, the estimated is replaced by the constant. This technique is similar to the adding of a constant to the estimated variance used in the WS [15, 17].

## 4.2 Comparison with Prior-Art

The WS Jpeg, as well as the WS for spatial domain, is based on the underlying assumption that the observations follow a Gaussian distribution. As recently shown [11, 35], the WS implicitly assumes that the quantisation step is negligible. Let us rewrite the LR test for JSteg detection based on a Gaussian distribution model of DCT coefficients. Let $X$ be a random variable following a quantised Gaussian distribution. Exploiting the assumption that the quantisation step is negligible compared to noise standard deviation allows the writing of:

$$\mathbb{P}[X = k] = \int_{\Delta(k-1/2)}^{\Delta(k+1/2)} \frac{1}{\sigma\sqrt{2\pi}}\exp\left(-\frac{(x-\mu)^2}{2\sigma^2}\right) dx$$

$$\approx \frac{\Delta}{\sigma\sqrt{2\pi}}\exp\left(-\frac{(\Delta k - \mu)^2}{2\sigma^2}\right) \quad (21)$$

Putting this expression of the pmf under hypothesis $\mathcal{H}_0$ into the LR (2), and assuming that the quantisation step is negligible compared to the noise standard deviation, $\Delta << \sigma$, it is immediate to obtain the following expression of the LR under the assumption of Gaussian distribution of DCT coefficient

$$\log\left(1 + \frac{R}{2} + \frac{R}{2}\frac{\exp\left(-\frac{(\Delta\bar{k}-\mu)^2}{2\sigma^2}\right)}{\exp\left(-\frac{(\Delta k-\mu)^2}{2\sigma^2}\right)}\right)$$

$$\approx \underbrace{\frac{R\Delta}{\sigma^2}}_{w_\sigma} \underbrace{(k - \bar{k})}_{\pm 1} \underbrace{(\Delta k - \mu)}_{(\Delta k - \mu)} \quad (22)$$

see details in Appendix C.
This expression highlights the well known fact the WS consists in fact of three terms: 1) the term $w_\sigma$ which is a weight so that pixels or DCT coefficients with highest variance have a smallest importance, 2) the term $(k - \bar{k}) = \pm 1$ according the LSB of $k$ and 3) the term $(\Delta k - \mu)$.

In comparison, the expression of the LR for a Laplacian distribution model (14), as well as the expression of the proposed test with estimates (19) only depends on the term

$$\underbrace{\frac{\Delta}{b}}_{=~w_b} \underbrace{(k - \bar{k})}_{\pm 1} \underbrace{\mathrm{sign}(\Delta k - \mu)}_{\mathrm{sign}(\Delta k - \mu)} \quad (23)$$

which is also made of three terms; the two first are roughly similar to the two first terms of the WS : 1) the term $w_b$ is a weight so that DCT coefficients with highest "scale" $b$ have a smallest importance, note that the variance is proportional to $b^2$, 2) the term $(k - \bar{k}) = \pm 1$ according to the LSB of $k$. However, in the expression of the LR based on the Laplacian model the term $(\Delta k - \mu)$ of the WS is replaced with its sign. This shows that the statistical tests based on Laplacian model and based on Gaussian model are essentially similar.

## 5. NUMERICAL RESULTS

To verify the relevance of the proposed methodology, it is proposed to compare the proposed statistical test with two other detectors. The first chosen competitor is the statistical test proposed in [34] as it is also based on the Laplacian model but does not take into account the distribution parameters as nuisance parameters; it considers that DCT coefficients are i.i.d., following a Laplacian distribution with zero-mean. The comparison with this test is meaningful as it allows us to measure how much the detection performance is improved by removing the assumption that the DCT coefficients of each sub-band are i. i. d. The second chosen competitor is the WS [3] due to its similarity with the proposed statistical test, see details in Section 4.2.

For a large scale verification, it is proposed to use the BOSS database, made of 10 000 grayscale images of size $512 \times 512$ pixels, used with payload $R = 0.05$. Prior to our experiments, the images have been compressed in JPEG using the linux command convert which uses the standard quantisation table. Note also that all the JSteg steganography was performed using a Matlab source code we developed based on Phil Sallee's Jpeg Toolbox[4]. Three denoising methods have been tested to estimate the expectation of each DCT coefficient, namely the k-SVD denoising, the BM3D and the NL-means algorithms. The codes used for those three denoising methods have been downloaded from the Image Processing On-Line website[5].
Figure 4 shows the detection performance obtained over the BOSS database compressed with quality factor (QF) 70. The detection performances are shown as ROC curves, that is the detection power is plotted as a function of false-alarm probability. The Figure 4a particularly emphasises that the statistical test based on the Laplacian model does not perform well while the proposed methodology which takes into account the Laplacian distribution parameters as nuisance parameters allows us to largely improve the performance. Similarly the WS detector achieves overall good detection performance. However, it can be shown on Figure 4b, which presents the same results using a logarithmic scale, that for low false-alarm probabilities, the performance of the WS significantly decreases. On the opposite, the proposed statistical test still performs well.

---

[4]Phil Sallee's Jpeg Toolbox is available at : http://dde.binghamton.edu/download/jpeg_toolbox.zip
[5]Image Processing On-Line journal is available at: http://www.ipol.im

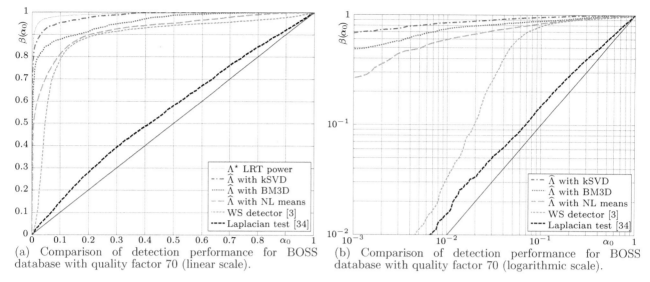

(a) Comparison of detection performance for BOSS database with quality factor 70 (linear scale).

(b) Comparison of detection performance for BOSS database with quality factor 70 (logarithmic scale).

Figure 4: Comparison of detection performance for BOSS database with quality factor 70

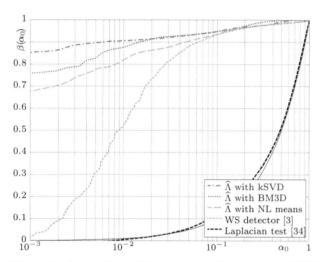

Figure 5: Comparison of detection performance for BOSS database with quality factor 85 (logarithmic scale).

Among the three denoising algorithms that have been tested, the k-SVD achieves the best performance but it can be observed on Figure 4 that the performance obtained using the BM3D and using the NL-means denoising methods are also very good.

To extend the results previously presented, a similar test has been performed over the BOSS database using the quality factor 85. The detection performance obtained by the proposed test and by the competitors are presented in Figure 5. Again, this figure shows that the statistical test based on the Laplacian model and assuming that DCT coefficients of a sub-band are i. i. d. has an unsatisfactory performance. It can also be noted that even though the WS performs slightly better for low false-alarm probability, compared to the results obtained with quality factor 70, it performs much worse than the proposed statistical test.

## 6. CONCLUSIONS

This paper aims at improving the optimal detection of data hidden within the DCT coefficients of JPEG images. Its main originality is that the usual Laplacian model is used as a statistical model of DCT coefficients but, opposed to what is usually proposed, it is not assumed that all DCT coefficients from a sub-band are i. i. d. This leads us to consider the Laplacian distribution parameters, namely the expectation $\mu$ and the scale parameter $b$, as nuisance parameters as they have no interest for the detection of hidden data, but must be carefully taken into account to design an efficient statistical test. Numerical results show that by estimating those nuisance parameters, the Laplacian model allows the designing of an accurate statistical test which outperforms the WS. The comparison with the optimal detector based on the Laplacian model and on the assumption that all DCT coefficients of a sub-band are i. i. d. shows the relevance of the proposed approach.

A possible future work would be to apply this approach with state-of-the-art statistical model of DCT coefficients, such as the Generalised Gaussian or the Generalised Gamma model. This could provide improvements in the detection performance at the cost of a higher complexity.

## Acknowledgements

The work of R. Cogranne, F.Retraint and C. Zitzmann is funded by Troyes University of Technology (UTT) strategic program COLUMBO. The PhD thesis of Tong Qiao is funded by the China Scholarship Council (CSC) program.

## 7. REFERENCES

[1] V. Anantharam and S. Verdu. Bits through queues. *Information Theory, IEEE Transactions on*, 42(1):4–18, 1996.

[2] P. Bas, T. Filler, and T. Pevný. Break our steganographic system — the ins and outs of organizing boss. In *Information Hiding International Workshop*, LNCS vol.6958, pages 59–70, 2011.

[3] R. Böhme. Weighted stego-image steganalysis for jpeg covers. In *Information Hiding*, pages 178–194. Springer, 2008.

[4] R. Böhme and A. Westfeld. Breaking cauchy model-based jpeg steganography with first order statistics. In *Computer Security-ESORICS 2004*, pages 125–140. Springer, 2004.

[5] U. Budhia, D. Kundur, and T. Zourntos. Digital video steganalysis exploiting statistical visibility in the temporal domain. *Information Forensics and Security, IEEE Transactions on*, 2006.

[6] R. Böhme. *Advanced Statistical Steganalysis*. Springer Publishing Company, Incorporated, 1st edition, 2010.

[7] J.-H. Chang, J.-W. Shin, N. S. Kim, and S. Mitra. Image probability distribution based on generalized gamma function. *Signal Processing Letters, IEEE*, 12(4):325–328, 2005.

[8] R. Cogranne and F. Retraint. An asymptotically uniformly most powerful test for LSB matching detection. *Information Forensics and Security, IEEE Transactions on*, 8(3):464–476, 2013.

[9] R. Cogranne, F. Retraint, C. Zitzmann, I. Nikiforov, L. Fillatre, and P. Cornu. Detecting hidden information using decision theory: Methodology, results and difficulties. *Digital Signal Processing*, 24:144 – 161, 2014.

[10] R. Cogranne, C. Zitzmann, L. Fillatre, I. Nikiforov, F. Retraint, and P. Cornu. A cover image model for reliable steganalysis. In *Information Hiding International Workshop*, LNCS vol.6958, pages 178 – 192, , 2011, Springer-Verlag, New York.

[11] R. Cogranne, C. Zitzmann, L. Fillatre, F. Retraint, I. Nikiforov, and P. Cornu. Statistical decision by using quantized observations. In *IEEE International Symposium on Information Theory*, pages 1135 – 1139, August 2011.

[12] R. Cogranne, C. Zitzmann, F. Retraint, I. V. Nikiforov, P. Cornu, and L. Fillatre. A local adaptive model of natural images for almost optimal detection of hidden data. *Signal Processing*, 100:169 – 185, 2014.

[13] O. Dabeer, K. Sullivan, U. Madhow, S. Chandrasekaran, and B. Manjunath. Detection of hiding in the least significant bit. *Signal Processing, IEEE Transactions on*, 52(10):3046 – 3058, oct. 2004.

[14] J. Fridrich. *Steganography in Digital Media: Principles, Algorithms, and Applications*. Cambridge University Press, 1st edition edition, 2009.

[15] J. Fridrich and M. Goljan. On estimation of secret message length in LSB steganography in spatial domain. In Proc. SPIE, volume 5306, pages 23–34, 2004.

[16] A. D. Ker, P. Bas, R. Böhme, R. Cogranne, S. Craver, T. Filler, J. Fridrich, and T. Pevný. Moving steganography and steganalysis from the laboratory into the real world. In *Proceedings of the first ACM workshop on Information hiding and multimedia security*, IH&MMSec '13, pages 45–58, 2013.

[17] A. D. Ker and R. Böhme. Revisiting weighted stego-image steganalysis. In *Proc. SPIE 6819*, pages 501–517, 2008.

[18] J. Kodovsky and J. Fridrich. Quantitative structural steganalysis of JSteg. *Information Forensics and Security, IEEE Transactions on*, 5(4):681–693, 2010.

[19] E. Lam and J. Goodman. A mathematical analysis of the DCT coefficient distributions for images. *Image Processing, IEEE Transactions on*, 9(10):1661 –1666, oct 2000.

[20] K. Lee, A. Westfeld, and S. Lee. Category attack for lsb steganalysis of JPEG images. In *Digital Watermarking*, pages 35–48. Springer, 2006.

[21] E. Lehmann and J. Romano. *Testing Statistical Hypotheses, Second Edition*. Springer, 3rd edition, 2005.

[22] S. Lyu and H. Farid. Steganalysis using higher-order image statistics. *Information Forensics and Security, IEEE Transactions on*, 1(1):111 – 119, march 2006.

[23] F. Muller. Distribution shape of two-dimensional dct coefficients of natural images. *Electronics Letters*, 29(22):1935–1936, 1993.

[24] J. Nakamura. *Image sensors and signal processing for digital still cameras*. CRC Press, 2005.

[25] W. B. Pennebaker. *JPEG: Still image data compression standard*. Springer, 1992.

[26] T. Pevny and J. Fridrich. Multiclass detector of current steganographic methods for jpeg format. *Information Forensics and Security, IEEE Transactions on*, 3(4):635–650, 2008.

[27] P. Sallee. Model-based methods for steganography and steganalysis. *International Journal of Image and Graphics*, 5(1):167–189, jan. 2005.

[28] T. H. Thai, R. Cogranne, and F. Retraint. Steganalysis of Jsteg algorithm based on a novel statistical model of quantized DCT coefficients. In Proc. of IEEE*International Conference on Image Processing (ICIP)*, pages 4427 – 4431, 2013.

[29] T. H. Thai, R. Cogranne, and F. Retraint. Statistical model of quantized DCT coefficients : Application in the steganalysis of jsteg algorithm. *Image Processing, IEEE Transactions on*, 23(5):1980–1993, 2014.

[30] T. H. Thai, F. Retraint, and R. Cogranne. Statistical Model of Natural Images. In Proc. of IEEE *International Conference on Image Processing (ICIP)*, pages 2525 – 2528, 2012.

[31] T. H. Thai, F. Retraint, and R. Cogranne. Statistical detection of data hidden in least significant bits of clipped images. *Signal Processing*, 98:263 – 274, 2014.

[32] D. Upham. Jsteg. *Software available at http://zooid.org/~paul/crypto/jsteg/*, 2002.

[33] L. Yao, X. Zi, L. Pan, and J. Li. A study of on/off timing channel based on packet delay distribution. *Computers & Security*, 28(8):785–794, 2009.

[34] C. Zitzmann, R. Cogranne, L. Fillatre, I. Nikiforov, F. Retraint, and P. Cornu. Hidden information detection based on quantized Laplacian distribution. In IEEE *International Conference on Acoustics, Speech, and Signal Processing*, pages 1793–1796, 2012.

[35] C. Zitzmann, R. Cogranne, F. Retraint, I. Nikiforov, L. Fillatre, and P. Cornu. Statistical decision methods in hidden information detection. In *Information Hiding International Workshop*, LNCS vol.6958, pages 163 – 177, 2011.

# APPENDIX

## A. QUANTIZED LAPLACIAN PMF

Let $X$ be a Laplacian random variable with expectation $\mu$ and variance $b$. Its pdf is thus, see (12):

$$f_{\mu,b}(x) = \frac{1}{2b} \exp\left(-\frac{|x-\mu|}{b}\right),$$

and a straightforward calculation shows that its cdf is given by:

$$F_{\mu,b}(x) = \frac{1}{2} + \frac{1}{2}\text{sign}(x-\mu)\left(1-\exp\left(-\frac{|x-\mu|}{b}\right)\right), \quad (24)$$

$$= \begin{cases} \frac{1}{2}\exp\left(\frac{x-\mu}{b}\right) & \text{if } x < \mu, \\ 1 - \frac{1}{2}\exp\left(-\frac{x-\mu}{b}\right) & \text{if } x \geq \mu. \end{cases} \quad (25)$$

Now consider the result from quantisation of this random variable $Y = \lfloor X/\Delta \rfloor$, it is immediate to establish the pmf of this random variable. Let us first consider the case $\Delta(k + 1/2) < \mu$ (due to the symmetry of Laplacian pdf, the case $\Delta(k-1/2) > \mu$ is treated similarly).
The pmf of $Y$ is given by:

$$\mathbb{P}[Y=k] = \mathbb{P}[\Delta(k-1/2) \leq X < \Delta(k+1/2)],$$

$$= \frac{1}{2}\exp\left(\frac{\Delta(k+1/2)-\mu}{b}\right) - \frac{1}{2}\exp\left(\frac{\Delta(k-1/2)-\mu}{b}\right),$$

$$= \frac{1}{2}\exp\left(\frac{\Delta k-\mu}{b}\right)\exp\left(\frac{\Delta}{2b}\right)$$

$$- \frac{1}{2}\exp\left(\frac{\Delta k-\mu}{b}\right)\exp\left(\frac{-\Delta}{2b}\right),$$

$$= \exp\left(\frac{\Delta k-\mu}{b}\right)\sinh\left(\frac{\Delta}{2b}\right),$$

Applying similar calculations for case $\Delta(k-1/2) > \mu$, one gets:

$$\mathbb{P}[Y=k] = \exp\left(-\frac{|\Delta k-\mu|}{b}\right)\sinh\left(\frac{\Delta}{2b}\right), \quad (26)$$

which corresponds to the pmf given in Eq. (13). The case $\Delta(k-1/2) < \mu < \Delta(k+1/2)$ is treated similarly.

## B. LOG-LIKELIHOOD RATIO CALCULATION

By putting the expression of quantised Laplacian pmf (26) into the expression of the LR (7), it is immediate to write:

$$\Lambda^{\text{lr}}(u_{k,l}) = \log\left(1 - \frac{R}{2} + \frac{R}{2}\frac{\exp\left(-\frac{|\Delta\bar{k}-\mu|}{b}\right)\sinh\left(\frac{\Delta}{2b}\right)}{\exp\left(-\frac{|\Delta k-\mu|}{b}\right)\sinh\left(\frac{\Delta}{2b}\right)}\right).$$

Let us study the term:

$$\frac{\exp\left(-\frac{|\Delta\bar{k}-\mu|}{b}\right)\sinh\left(\frac{\Delta}{2b}\right)}{\exp\left(-\frac{|\Delta k-\mu|}{b}\right)\sinh\left(\frac{\Delta}{2b}\right)} = \frac{\exp\left(-\frac{|\Delta\bar{k}-\mu|}{b}\right)}{\exp\left(-\frac{|\Delta k-\mu|}{b}\right)},$$

$$= \frac{\exp\left(-\frac{|\Delta k+\Delta(\bar{k}-k)-\mu|}{b}\right)}{\exp\left(-\frac{|\Delta k-\mu|}{b}\right)},$$

$$= \frac{\exp\left(-\frac{|\Delta k-\mu|}{b}\right)\exp\left(\frac{\text{sign}(\Delta k-\mu)(k-\bar{k})}{b}\right)}{\exp\left(-\frac{|\Delta k-\mu|}{b}\right)}, \quad (27)$$

$$= \exp\left(\frac{\text{sign}(\Delta k-\mu)(k-\bar{k})}{b}\right).$$

From this Eq. (27), it is immediate to establish the expression (14):

$$\log\left(1 - \frac{R}{2} + \frac{R}{2}\exp\left(\frac{\text{sign}(\Delta k-\mu)(k-\bar{k})}{b}\right)\right).$$

## C. LR BASED ON THE GAUSSIAN MODEL (WS)

Let $X$ be a Gaussian random variable with expectation $\mu$ and variance $\sigma^2$. Define the quantized Gaussian random variable as follows $Y = \lfloor X/\Delta \rfloor$, its pmf is given by $P_{\mu,\sigma} = \{p_{\mu,\sigma}[k]\}_{k=-\infty}^{\infty}$ with:

$$p_{\mu,\sigma}[k] = \mathbb{P}[Y=k] = \int_{\Delta(k-1/2)}^{\Delta(k+1/2)} \frac{1}{\sigma\sqrt{2\pi}}\exp\left(-\frac{(x-\mu)^2}{2\sigma^2}\right)dx.$$

Assuming that the quantisation step $\Delta$ is "small enough" compared to the variance $\Delta \ll \sigma$, it holds true that [11, 9]:

$$p_{\mu,\sigma}[k] \approx \frac{\Delta}{\sigma\sqrt{2\pi}}\exp\left(-\frac{(\Delta k-\mu)^2}{2\sigma^2}\right), \quad (28)$$

and

$$p_{\mu,\sigma}[k] + p_{\mu,\sigma}[\bar{k}] \approx \frac{2\Delta}{\sigma\sqrt{2\pi}}\exp\left(-\frac{(\Delta(k+\bar{k}/2)-\mu)^2}{2\sigma^2}\right). \quad (29)$$

Let us rewrite the LR for the detection of JSteg (7) as follows

$$\Lambda^{\text{lr}}(u_{k,l}) = \log\left(1 - \frac{R}{2} + \frac{R}{2}\frac{p_{\mu,\sigma}[\bar{k}]}{p_{\mu,\sigma}[k]}\right),$$

$$= \log\left(1 - R + \frac{R}{2}\frac{p_{\mu,\sigma}[\bar{k}] + p_{\mu,\sigma}[k]}{p_{\mu,\sigma}[k]}\right). \quad (30)$$

Using the expressions (28) and (29) let us study the following ratio:

$$\frac{p_{\mu,\sigma}[\bar{k}] + p_{\mu,\sigma}[k]}{p_{\mu,\sigma}[k]} = 2\frac{\exp\left(-\frac{(\Delta(k+\bar{k}/2)-\mu)^2}{2\sigma^2}\right)}{\exp\left(-\frac{(\Delta k-\mu)^2}{2\sigma^2}\right)},$$

$$= 2\frac{\exp\left(-\frac{(\Delta k-\mu+\Delta/2(\bar{k}-k))^2}{2\sigma^2}\right)}{\exp\left(-\frac{(\Delta k-\mu)^2}{2\sigma^2}\right)},$$

$$= 2\frac{\exp\left(-\frac{(\Delta k-\mu)^2}{2\sigma^2}\right)\exp\left(\frac{\Delta(\Delta k-\mu)(k-\bar{k})}{2\sigma^2}\right)\exp\left(-\frac{\Delta^2}{8\sigma^2}\right)}{\exp\left(-\frac{(\Delta k-\mu)^2}{2\sigma^2}\right)},$$

$$= 2\exp\left(\frac{\Delta(\Delta k-\mu)(k-\bar{k})}{2\sigma^2}\right)\exp\left(-\frac{\Delta^2}{8\sigma^2}\right). \quad (31)$$

Putting the expression (31) into the expression of the log-LR (30) immediately gives:

$$\Lambda^{\mathrm{lr}}(u_{k,l}) = \log\left(1 + R\left(\exp\left(\frac{\Delta(\Delta k - \mu)(k - \bar{k})}{2\sigma^2}\right)\exp\left(\frac{\Delta^2}{8\sigma^2}\right) - 1\right)\right)$$

from which a Taylor expansion around $\Delta/\sigma = 0$, this results from the assumption that $\Delta \ll \sigma$, and finally gives the well-known expression of the WS:

$$\Lambda^{\mathrm{lr}}(u_{k,l}) = \frac{R\Delta}{\sigma^2}(k - \bar{k})(\Delta k - \mu) \tag{32}$$

# Slice Groups for Post-Compression Region of Interest Encryption in SVC

Andreas Unterweger
University of Salzburg
Department of Computer Sciences
Jakob-Haringer-Straße 2
Salzburg, Austria
aunterweg@cosy.sbg.ac.at

Andreas Uhl
University of Salzburg
Department of Computer Sciences
Jakob-Haringer-Straße 2
Salzburg, Austria
uhl@cosy.sbg.ac.at

## ABSTRACT

In this paper, we assess the adequacy of slice groups for the reduction of drift which occurs in bit-stream-based region of interest encryption in SVC. For practical surveillance camera applications, we introduce the concept of all-grey base layers which simplify the encryption of regions of interest while obeying all standard-imposed base layer restrictions. Furthermore, we show that the use of slice groups is possible with relatively low overhead for most practical configurations with two or three spatial layers. In addition, we analyze the effect of spatial resolution on overhead, showing that an increase in resolution decreases the relative overhead.

## Categories and Subject Descriptors

I.4.2 [**Image Processing and Computer Vision**]: Compression (Coding)—*SVC, Slice groups*; E.3 [**Data**]: Data Encryption—*Selective encryption*

## General Terms

Experimentation, Measurement, Verification

## Keywords

SVC, Slice groups, Selective encryption, Region of Interest, Overhead

## 1. INTRODUCTION

In video surveillance and other applications, there is often the need to disguise people's identities in order to protect their privacy. A common approach to achieve this is the selective encryption of people's faces (also called region-based selective [15] or Region of Interest (RoI) encryption), i.e. encrypting all picture areas which contain a face, while leaving all other picture areas untouched.

This allows for reversible de-identification, i.e., the disguise

**Figure 1: Examples for spatial and temporal drift: The first, second and tenth frame (from left to right) of the *foreman* sequence (top: original, bottom: encrypted) where one macroblock block row around the eyes in the first frame (left) has been encrypted.**

of identities with the possibility to restore them by undoing the encryption. Restoring is typically only possible with a correct key which is possessed, e.g., by law enforcement authorities in case suspects of a crime need to be identified. Although several techniques for reversible de-identification exist, RoI encryption is one of the most common ones in video surveillance.

While RoI encryption can be applied before (e.g., [2, 3, 7]), during (e.g., [23, 20, 11]) or after compression (e.g., [24, 4, 6]), each with its own advantages and disadvantages [14], most approaches proposed so far focus either on encryption before or during compression. Although this makes drift, i.e., the propagation of parts of encrypted picture areas into non-encrypted ones through spatial and temporal prediction as depicted in figure 1, easier to manage, it does not allow using existing surveillance infrastructure whose input images and/or encoder cannot be modified.

Typically, surveillance cameras have compression hardware built in (as of 2013, Motion JPEG and H.264 are very common) which is used to reduce the bandwith of the captured and transmitted video footage. Although this saves time and computational resources by not requiring additional encoding hardware, it makes modifications (like an additional encryption step) to the built-in compression hardware quasi impossible due to the often hard-wired encoder.

In order to be able to reuse this infrastructure notwithstanding, applying RoI encryption after compression has to be considered, reviving the drift issue. Therefore, in this paper, we try to assess the fitness of the slice group coding tool of Scalable Video Coding (SVC) [17] for allowing to selectively encrypt picture areas and containing drift.

For the sake of applicability, we consider a state-of-the-art video surveillance system which delivers SVC bit streams. We assume that the surveillance system detects faces (or other regions of interest) and places them in slice groups which are to be encrypted after compression. The main reason for using slice groups is their ability to contain drift to a certain extent, thereby simplifying RoI encryption. Note that slice groups have other uses as well, thereby extending the results of our investigations to scenarios which are not encryption-specific.

By evaluating the limitations and possibilities of slice group coding, we aim at determining whether or not the aforementioned setup simplifies the encryption process in terms of drift. Furthermore, we evaluate the overhead induced by this approach in order to determine whether or not it is of practical use, i.e., for example to be included into existing and/or future surveillance systems to simplify RoI encryption after compression.

Related work on RoI encryption in SVC is sparse. Two approaches are proposed in [21] and [10], albeit without considering or compensating for the effects of drift, which is an important matter. [11] deals with drift by imposing restrictions on the encoding process in terms of a limited motion estimation range as well as interpolation and upsampling constraints. Besides the reported significant increase in bit rate, this method cannot be applied on a bit stream level without recompression. Similarly, [19] proposes separate RoI coding by restricting motion estimation and inter-layer prediction, albeit without the explicit intention to do so for the sake of encryption. However, all of these approaches are in-compression encryption methods and cannot be applied at bit stream level.

Apart from RoI-related experiments and analyses of SVC, the encryption of certain Network Abstraction Layer (NAL) units has been proposed in [13]. However, their proposed encryption approach yields bit streams which are no longer format compliant and can hence not be decoded anymore by a regular decoder. This is not desirable in surveillance applications as the background without the encrypted RoI should be visible and therefore decodable. Furthermore, the optimization of RoI across multiple layers to lower the total bit rate has been analyzed in [8].

Although slice groups have been used to deal with drift in a number of encryption approaches (e.g., [23, 5]), a detailed examination of its actual usefulness to contain different causes of drift has not been done so far. The overhead induced by some of the aforementioned encryption approaches has been analyzed, but this is not true for the general overhead introduced by slices groups which change from frame to frame to cover RoI. This is especially true for SVC.

This paper is structured as follows: In section 2, the key concepts of video coding with slice groups in SVC are described, followed by an analysis of their limitations in section 3. After evaluating several scenarios in terms of feasibility for video surveillance with encrypted RoI in section 4, we conclude our paper.

## 2. Scalable Video Coding

SVC is specified as the scalable extension of H.264, specified in its Annex G [9]. It allows for multiple so-called

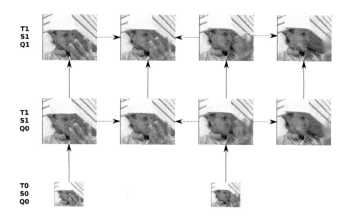

**Figure 2: SVC with multiple layers: The base layer with half the frame rate and a quarter of the picture size can be used to predict the first spatial enhancement layer, which itself can be used to predict a second temporal and subsequently a third SNR enhancement layer. Adopted from [17]**

layers within one bit stream, which can be accessed or extracted depending on the capabilities of the device decoding the stream. Each layer differs from the others either by frame rate (temporal scalability), resolution (spatial scalability) or quality (Signal-to-Noise Ratio (SNR) scalability). The bottom-most layer is referred to as base layer and coded in a way that is compatible with (non-scalable) H.264.

All layers but the base layer can exploit inter-layer redundancies by using coded information of lower layers for prediction. The basis of this prediction for spatial and SNR scalability can either be filtered intra-coded samples (inter-layer intra prediction), motion vectors (inter-layer motion prediction) or inter-coded difference signal samples (inter-layer residual prediction), with details for each prediction type to be found in [18]. In contrast, temporal scalability is achieved through hierarchical inter prediction as explained in detail in [17].

Figure 2 shows an example of a scalable bit stream with multiple layers. The base layer (temporal layer 0 (T0), spatial layer 0 (S0) and SNR layer 0 (Q0)) has the lowest possible frame rate, resolution and quality and is used to predict the first spatial enhancement layer (T0, S1, Q0; not labeled) which doubles both, picture width and height. This enhancement layer is further used to predict an enhancement layer of the same resolution, but a doubled frame rate (T1, S1, Q0) as well as an enhancement layer with higher quality (T0, S1, Q1; not labeled) and subsequently a doubled frame rate (T1, S1, Q1).

In each layer, a coded picture is split into slices which can be summarized to slice groups of specific forms, depending on the so-called slice group map type. As RoI encryption requires a background left-over, i.e., a region of the picture which does not belong to any encrypted region of interest, only slice group map types 2 (foreground slice groups with left-over background) and 6 (explicit slice group specification) will be considered, as only they allow this. Since slice group map type 6 is practically identical to slice group map type 2 in this use case, we will only consider slice group map type 2 henceforth.

To exploit spatial and temporal redundancy, samples can be

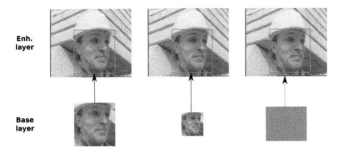

Figure 3: Alternatives to slice groups in the base layer: Left and middle: Extended spatial scalability; right: all-grey base layer

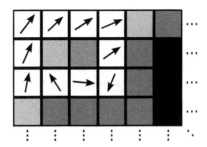

Figure 4: Constrained intra prediction: In a P slice, intra blocks may not use inter blocks for prediction. The grey level of the depicted intra blocks denotes the number of allowed intra modes

predicted from neighboring samples around the block to be predicted (in the same picture) as well as from samples of arbitrary blocks in previously coded pictures. In the former case, predictions over slice borders are forbidden, thereby allowing all slices to be decoded independently and preventing spatial drift.

# 3. STANDARD-IMPOSED LIMITATIONS

The H.264 standard imposes restrictions on coding tools and parameter values by specifying profiles. As this paper discusses slice groups, we only consider profiles which allow the use of multiple slice groups in the first place. In this section, we investigate other relevant limitations imposed by those profiles.

For scalable bit streams, only the Scalable Baseline profile supports slice groups. Although it allows using up to eight slice groups in total, one slice group is considered to be the background, i.e., the remainder of what the other seven slice groups encode. In addition, entropy coding is limited to CAVLC, the number of slice groups cannot exceed seven (plus background) and B slices are not allowed. Furthermore, the base layer may not contain more than one slice group.

This is a severe limitation in an encryption scenario because this means that the regions of interest cannot be in separate slice groups in the base layer. Thus, either a different drift compensation approach for the base layer is required or an alternative to slice groups in the base layer has to be found. As the former is hard to achieve, we consider three additional alternatives to slice groups in the base layer as depicted in Figure 3.

One possibility is to use extended spatial scalability, depicted on the left and in the middle of Figure 3, where the base layer only contains the region of interest and the enhancement layer adds the rest of the video frame. Due to the limitations of the Scalable Baseline profile, the width and height ratios between the base layer and the corresponding region of interest in the enhancement layer have to be either 1 (Figure 3, left), 1.5 (not depicted) or 2 (Figure 3, middle). However, this setup is only useful if there is exactly one region of interest. Since this would impose a severe practical limitation, it is not considered in the remainder of this paper. Alternatively, we propose adding a base layer which is all-grey ($Y = C_b = C_r = 128$) as shown in Figure 3, right. Since intra DC prediction and skip modes allow encoding such an artificial layer very compactly, its overhead is relatively small when using the maximum possible width and

height ratios of 2, i.e., a base layer with half the width and height of the enhancement layer.

However, it effectively reduces the number of usable spatial layers, which is limited to three in the Scalable Baseline profile, by one. This allows for a maximum of two non-grey spatial layers for actual video content. Depending on the use case, these two remaining layers may be sufficient to provide spatial scalability.

Despite the loss of one usable spatial layer, the grey base layer simplifies encryption by containing drift. Although the unavailability of slice groups in the base layer (see above) would normally make encryption harder (without the possibility of using slice groups to contain drift), the fact that the base layer is all grey does not require any encryption and does therefore not induce any drift.

Although there have been multiple proposals for region-of-interest support through slice groups in all layers [1, 22], the final version of the standard does not allow this. Similarly, the technique proposed in [12] to alternatively support regions of interests as enhancement layers is not supported. This paper limits the available options to the ones supported by the standard, i.e., the all-grey base layer introduced above as well a regular (i.e., full-content) base layer for comparison.

Regarding further limitations imposed by the standard, we will focus on the combination of constrained intra prediction and constrained inter-layer prediction, which ensure single-loop decoding [16]. Since these two limitations severely limit the number of possibilities for prediction and therefore drift, they are crucial for the RoI encryption use case.

Constrained intra prediction limits the blocks which can be used for intra prediction. Figure 4 illustrates this in a P slice which contains inter (depicted by motion vectors) and intra (depicted by grey levels) macroblocks. Although the black intra blocks may use all possible intra prediction modes, the dark- and light-grey ones may not. For example, the light-grey macroblock at the top left may only use DC prediction since all other prediction directions would require predicting from one of the surrounding inter macroblocks.

SVC enforces constrained intra prediction in all layers which are used for inter-layer prediction so that inter-layer predicted samples do not require additional motion compensation in the base layer. Additionally, constrained inter-layer prediction ensures that inter-layer-predicted intra samples are not used for intra prediction themselves, as illustrated in Figure 5.

Inter-layer prediction allows using information from the base

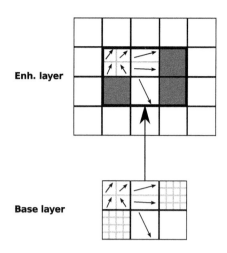

Figure 5: Constrained inter-layer prediction: Up-sampled intra blocks (grey) must be reconstructed from base layer intra samples

Figure 6: Moving slice groups: Frames 1, 11 and 21 of the *foreman* sequence with one moving foreground slice group around the face (green) and one background slice group (remainder, turquoise)

Figure 7: Encrypted RoI: Frames 1, 11 and 21 of the *foreman* sequence. The RoI in this example is the actor's face

layer in the enhancement layer. If blocks are upsampled through inter-layer intra prediction (grey blocks in Figure 5), the corresponding reference block in the base layer has to be an intra block as well. Constrained inter prediction in the base layer ensures that no additional motion compensation loop is required. Furthermore, if the enhancement layer is used for further inter layer prediction, the upsampled blocks may not be used for further intra prediction due to the constrained intra prediction requirement to avoid multi-loop decoding.

## 4. EXPERIMENTAL EVALUATION

In this section, we describe our experimental setup and results. We refer to the term of "moving slice groups" for RoI herein since the position of RoI may change from frame to frame, thereby changing the slice group positions accordingly, as illustrated in Figure 6. Recall that our use case is encryption, i.e., we assume that the moving slice groups will be encrypted at some point, as illustrated by example in figure 7.

## 4.1 Setup

In order to evaluate the effect of slice-group-based RoI for encryption, we added support for moving slice groups to the SVC reference software (*JSVM*) since it does not support this by itself.

In the *JSVM*, slice group coding is implemented partially, but not used. Therefore, it is enabled separately for all spatial layers but the base layer which does not support slice

group coding (see section 3). This is done by setting the slice group map type to 2 using the current layer's Picture Parameter Set (PPS) in *LayerEncoder::process*.

In each layer, the RoI coordinates are calculated depending on the picture size and the corresponding slice group settings (number of slice groups, top-left and bottom-right coordinates) in the PPS are adapted accordingly. In order to determine the absolute frame number in the layer being processed, a helper variable is introduced which counts the number of processed Group Of Pictures (GOP). Together with the frame index of the current GOP (which is provided by the encoder), an absolute frame number can be calculated so that the corresponding RoI coordinates can determined. In order to signal the slice groups, one additional PPS per frame and enhancement layer is needed. Although the PPS changes described above take effect in the encoder immediately, the decoder needs to take notice of them by a PPS update. This requires inserting one PPS per frame per enhancement layer into the bit stream using the corresponding functions provided by the *NalUnitEncoder* class. Note that it is essential to use the *LayerEncoder::xAppendNewExtBinDataAccessor* and *LayerEncoder::addParameterSetBits* functions to assign the PPS NAL unit and its corresponding overhead to the correct layer.

We use three test sequences with 300 frames each to simulate typical surveillance senarios. *akiyo* has one RoI and very little motion, while *foreman* has a significant amount of motion and also one RoI. Conversely, the *crew* sequence has a changing number of RoI. Since a maximum of seven slice groups (RoI) is supported in SVC (see section 3), only the first top-left-most faces are considered, i.e., placed in a separate slice group. All faces were segmented manually by enclosing them in rectangles. The corresponding coordinates were rounded to the nearest macroblock border.

We use both, Common Intermediate Format (CIF) and 4CIF resolution, in order to determine the impact of spatial resolution on the measurements. While the following section gives a detailed description of the results for CIF resolution, section 4.3 describes the differences when using 4CIF resolution.

## 4.2 Overhead (CIF)

We use the GOP size of the default JSVM configuration, i.e., four. Since GOP structures with B frames are not allowed in combination with slice groups (see section 3), we use P frames instead. Thus, an $(IPPP)*$ GOP structure, i.e., a repeated sequence of one I frame and followed by three P frames, is used.

We encode the test sequences with a constant Quantization Parameter (QP) for both frame types and default settings with two and three dyadic spatial layers. The base layer is all grey (see section 3), although we test "classical" base

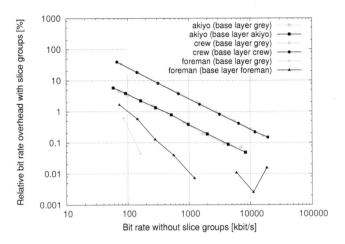

Figure 8: Overhead with slice group coding for different CIF sequences when using two dyadic spatial layers

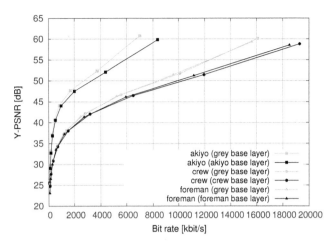

Figure 9: Rate-distortion plot for SVC with two dyadic spatial layers and slice groups. Different base layers (depicted in grey and black) result in significantly different enhancement layer Y-PSNR.

layers (with the actual down-sized input video) as well for comparison. Inter-layer prediction is set to adaptive to allow for optimal coding efficiency.

We encode the test sequences with a constant QP for all frame types and default settings. Using QPs between 3 and 51 with a step size of 6 to double the quantizer step size with each run allows covering the whole QP range. Each QP-sequence combination is encoded with and without slice groups. Since the difference in terms of distortion between the encoded sequences with and without slice groups is very small ($< 0.15$ dB), we approximate the overhead introduced by slice group coding by comparing the corresponding bit rates directly.

As depicted in Figure 8, it is obvious that the *crew* sequence (depicted by circles in figure) exhibits the highest overhead in quasi all scenarios, since it requires the highest number of slice groups. Conversely, the *foreman* sequence exhibits the lowest overhead, since it requires only one additional slice group (apart from the background) for the first half of the sequence. It profits from scalability more than the other sequences, resulting in some very small negative overhead values ($< 0.1\%$ absolute). Note that these values cannot be depicted properly due to the logarithmic Y axis.

In general, the overhead decreases with the bit rate, i.e., it increases with the QP. For low bit rates, slice group coding adds an unacceptable overhead of up to nearly one hundred per cent. Conversely, for bit rates which are higher than 500 kbit/s, all sequences but *crew* exhibit a small overhead of approximately 1% or less.

Using an all-grey base layer does not affect the overhead significantly due to the use of slice groups, except for very low bit rates, which are impractical. Compared to the classical base layer configuration, however, an all-grey base layer allows using slice-group-based encryption for SVC in the first place, since slice groups cannot be used in the base layer (see section 3).

Figure 9 shows a rate-distortion plot for the two-layer case with slice groups, where the Y-PSNR values are those of the enhancement layer. The plot allows comparing the all-grey base layer with a classical base layer. It is obvious that the all-grey base layer results in significantly better rate-

distortion performance (up to 5 dB) for medium and high bit rates.

Since an all-grey base layer greatly improves rate-distortion performance avoiding the need for additional drift compensation due to encryption in the base layer, it can be considered a better solution than a classical base layer for this use case. As the overhead due to slice groups is similar in both, the all-grey and the classical base layer scenario (see above), this is also true for other potential use cases in which the base layer does not have to be the downsampled input sequence.

Note that an all-grey base layer in a scenario with two spatial layers defies the purpose of scalable video coding, since one of the two layers becomes unusable for content. However, it allows establishing a baseline for comparison in terms of overhead and allows assessing the usefulness of the concept. In order for all-grey base layers to be practically useful, a scenario with three spatial layers has to be considered so that two spatial layers remain for actual content.

When increasing the number of spatial layers to the maximum of three (see section 3), the overhead due to slice groups increases, as depicted in Figure 10. The overall overhead is significantly higher than in the two-layer case (see Figure 8) for low to medium bit rates. This is due to the fact that slice groups introduce prediction borders which reduce coding efficiency and the three-layer case (with two enhancement layers with slice groups) uses double the amount of slice groups than the two-layer case (with one enhancement layer with slice groups). However, for high bit rates, the overhead is still relatively small and therefore practically negligible for most use cases.

Compared to the two-layer case, the all-grey base layer configuration in the three-layer case allows for an overhead which is approximately as low as the overhead in the classical base layer configuration. Although the all-grey base layer configuration exhibits a higher overhead for medium-to-high bit rates, the actual overhead is only insignificantly higher.

However, in the three-layer case the rate-distortion performance improvement of the all-grey base layer is only very small, as depicted in Figure 11. Although there are still

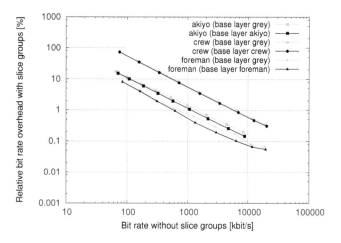

Figure 10: Overhead with slice group coding for different CIF sequences when using three dyadic spatial layers

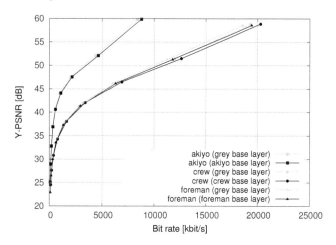

Figure 11: Rate-distortion plot for SVC with three dyadic spatial layers and slice groups. Different base layers (depicted in grey and black) result in similar enhancement layer Y-PSNR.

differences of up to 1 dB between an all-grey and a classical base layer in terms of enhancement layer Y-PSNR, but the performance improvement is nowhere near the improvements of the two-layer case (see above).

This is mainly due to the fact that there are two enhancement layers, which use most of the bit rate and the fact that the first enhancement layer can be used to predict parts of the second one through inter-layer prediction. This makes the three-layer case with an all-grey base layer similar to a two-layer case with an additional all-grey bit stream, which is very likely not used at all for inter-layer prediction. However, an all-grey base layer still has advantages compared to a classical base layer for the use case in this paper, since base layer encryption cannot rely on slice groups due to base layer limitations (see above). Thus, an all-grey base layer is still to be preferred over a classical base layer in the three-layer case.

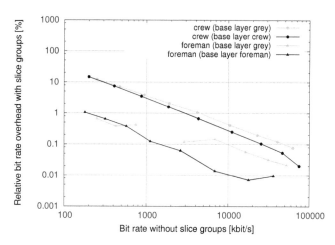

Figure 12: Overhead with slice group coding for different 4CIF sequences when using two dyadic spatial layers

## 4.3 Overhead (4CIF)

In order to analyze the influence of spatial resolution on overhead, we repeat the experiments of the previous section with sequences in 4CIF resolution. Note that a 4CIF version of *akiyo* could not be obtained, which is why the following paragraphs only describe results for the *foreman* and the *crew* sequences.

Figure 12 shows the overhead induced by moving slice groups with two spatial layers, like in the previous section. As expected, the decrease of the relative overhead with increasing bit rate is quasi identical, while the overhead values are mostly smaller. Due to the higher spatial resolution, the percentage of macroblocks which are affected by the slice-group-induced prediction borders is smaller, thereby increasing coding efficiency compared to the CIF case depicted in figure 8.

The overhead for the *foreman* sequence (triangles) is 1% or lower for all QP. Although the use of an all-grey base layer introduces a larger overhead than in the CIF case depicted in figure 8, it can still be considered insignificantly small for most QP.

The overhead for the *crew* sequence (circles) is about two to three times lower than in the CIF case depicted in figure 8 when comparing equal QP, and quasi identical when comparing equal bit rates. This is due to the high number of slice groups in the *crew* sequence which induce a significant number of prediction borders. At 4CIF resolution, these have a smaller effect than at CIF resolution, as described for the *foreman* sequence above.

When the *crew* sequence is encoded with an all-grey base layer (grey circles), the overhead is slightly higher than in the regular base layer case (black circles). Although this deviates from the behavior at CIF resolution, where both curves overlap quasi completely, the difference can still be considered to be insignificantly small.

Figure 13 shows the overhead induced by moving slice groups with three spatial layers. As in the two-layer case, the overhead for the *foreman* sequence (triangles) is about 1% or lower. The overhead for the *crew* sequence (circles) is about two to four times lower than in the CIF case depicted in figure 10 when comparing equal QP, and quasi identical when

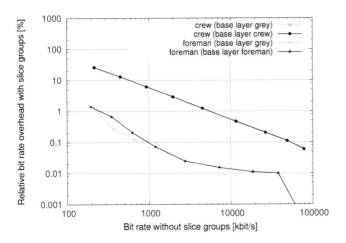

**Figure 13: Overhead with slice group coding for different 4CIF sequences when using three dyadic spatial layers**

comparing equal bit rates.

When using an all-grey base layer (grey circles), the overhead is quasi indistinguishable from the regular base layer case (black circles). Consequently, using all-grey base layers at higher resolutions is recommended for two and three layers, as in the CIF resolution case.

Regarding the overhead results for higher resolutions in general, it can be concluded that equal bit rates yield quasi equal overhead values. Since the overhead decreases with bit rate, the relative overhead decreases with increasing resolution. Thus, at higher resolutions than 4CIF, it is to be expected that the overhead with moving slice groups becomes so small that it can, for most use cases, be ignored.

## 5. FUTURE WORK

This paper shows that slice groups help containing drift in SVC. Although this result can be extended to (non-scalable) H.264 for the most part (since SVC is built upon H.264), a detailed analysis of the overhead induced by slice groups in (non-scalable) H.264 bit streams is desired. Furthermore, the use of B frames and other GOP structures on both, the overhead and the ability to contain drift has to be investigated.

In addition, the detailed effects of SNR scalability have to be studied. Although SNR scalability can be considered as a special case of spatial scalability where width and height remain the same, the overhead of slice groups in SNR layers may be significantly lower due to the more restricted inter-layer prediction mechanisms. This would make SVC encryption yet more feasible, since SNR layers are identical to spatial layers in terms of drift as analyzed in this paper.

## 6. CONCLUSION

We showed the impact of slice group coding on post-compression encryption for a typical surveillance use case. We analyzed the slice-group-induced bit rate overhead as well as the usefulness of slice groups for the containment of drift. For medium and high bit rates, configurations with two and three spatial layers can be used to reduce drift with slice groups with relatively low overhead. For low bit rates, the overhead is too large for practical use at CIF resolution, but

moderate at 4CIF and higher resolutions since the relative overhead decreases with increasing resolution. Furthermore, we introduced the concept of all-grey base layers which simplifies encryption significantly in the two- and three-layer case, albeit at the cost of losing one spatial scalability layer.

## 7. ACKNOWLEDGMENTS

This work is supported by FFG Bridge project 832082.

## 8. REFERENCES

[1] T. M. Bae, T. C. Thang, D. Y. Kim, J. W. K. Yong Man Ro, and J. G. Kim. Multiple Region-of-Interest Support in Scalable Video Coding. *ETRI Journal*, 28(2):239–242, Apr. 2006.

[2] T. E. Boult. PICO: Privacy through invertible cryptographic obscuration. In *IEEE/NFS Workshop on Computer Vision for Interactive and Intelligent Environments*, pages 27–38, Lexington, KY, USA, Nov. 2005.

[3] P. Carrillo, H. Kalva, and S. Magliveras. Compression Independent Reversible Encryption for Privacy in Video Surveillance. *EURASIP Journal on Information Security*, 2009:1–13, Jan. 2009.

[4] F. Dufaux and T. Ebrahimi. Video surveillance using JPEG 2000. In *Proceedings of the SPIE Applications of Digital Image Processing XXVII*, volume 5588, pages 268–275, Aug. 2004.

[5] F. Dufaux and T. Ebrahimi. H.264/AVC video scrambling for privacy protection. In *Proceedings of the IEEE International Conference on Image Processing, ICIP '08*, pages 47–49, San Diego, CA, USA, Oct. 2008. IEEE.

[6] F. Dufaux and T. Ebrahimi. Scrambling for privacy protection in video surveillance systems. *IEEE Transactions on Circuits and Systems for Video Technology*, 18(8):1168–1174, 2008.

[7] F. Dufaux and T. Ebrahimi. A framework for the validation of privacy protection solutions in video surveillance. In *Proceedings of the IEEE International Conference on Multimedia & Expo, ICME '10*, pages 66–71, Singapore, July 2010. IEEE.

[8] D. Grois, E. Kaminsky, and O. Hadar. Roi adaptive scalable video coding for limited bandwidth wireless networks. In *2010 IFIP Wireless Days (WD)*, pages 1–5, Oct. 2010.

[9] ITU-T H.264. Advanced video coding for generic audiovisual services, Nov. 2007. http://www.itu.int/rec/T-REC-H.264-200711-I/en.

[10] Y. Kim, S. Jin, and Y. Ro. Scalable Security and Conditional Access Control for Multiple Regions of Interest in Scalable Video Coding. In Y. Shi, H.-J. Kim, and S. Katzenbeisser, editors, *International Workshop on Digital Watermarking 2007 (IWDW 2007)*, volume 5041, pages 71–86. Springer Berlin / Heidelberg, 2008.

[11] Y. Kim, S. Yin, T. Bae, and Y. Ro. A selective video encryption for the region of interest in scalable video coding. In *Proceedings of the TENCON 2007 - IEEE Region 10 Conference*, pages 1–4, Taipei, Taiwan, Oct. 2007.

[12] J.-H. Lee and C. Yoo. Scalable ROI algorithm for H.264/SVC-based video streaming. In *2011 IEEE*

*International Conference on Consumer Electronics (ICCE)*, pages 201–202, Jan. 2011.

[13] C. Li, X. Zhou, and Y. Zhong. NAL level encryption for scalable video coding. In *Advances in Multimedia Information Processing, PCM'08*, pages 496–505. Springer-Verlag, Dec. 2008.

[14] A. Massoudi, F. Lefèbvre, C. D. Vleeschouwer, B. Macq, and J.-J. Quisquater. Overview on selective encryption of image and video, challenges and perspectives. *EURASIP Journal on Information Security*, 2008(Article ID 179290):doi:10.1155/2008/179290, 18 pages, 2008.

[15] Y. Ou, C. Sur, and K. H. Rhee. Region-based selective encryption for medical imaging. In *Proceedings of the International Conference on Frontiers in Algorithmics (FAW'07)*, Lecture Notes in Computer Science, pages 62–73, Lanzhou, China, Aug. 2007. Springer-Verlag.

[16] H. Schwarz, T. Hinz, D. Marpe, and T. Wiegand. Constrained inter-layer prediction for single-loop decoding in spatial scalability. In *IEEE International Conference on Image Processing (ICIP) 2005*, volume 2, pages II–870–873, Sept. 2005.

[17] H. Schwarz, D. Marpe, and T. Wiegand. Overview of the scalable H.264/MPEG4-AVC extension. In *Proceedings of the IEEE International Conference on Image Processing, ICIP '06*, pages 161–164, Atlanta, GA, USA, Oct. 2006. IEEE.

[18] C. A. Segall and G. J. Sullivan. Spatial scalability within the H.264/AVC scalable video coding extension. *IEEE Transactions on Circuits and Systems for Video Technology*, 17(9):1121–1135, Sept. 2007.

[19] S. S. F. Shah and E. A. Edirisinghe. Evolving Roi Coding in H.264 SVC. In *VISAPP 2008: Proceedings of the Third International Conference on Computer Vision Theory and Applications – Volume 1*, pages 13–19, 2008.

[20] Z. Shahid, M. Chaumont, and W. Puech. Selective and scalable encryption of enhancement layers for dyadic scalable H.264/AVC by scrambling of scan patterns. In *16th IEEE International Conference on Image Processing*, pages 1273–1276, Cairo, Egypt, Nov. 2009.

[21] H. Sohn, E. Anzaku, W. D. Neve, Y. M. Ro, and K. Plataniotis. Privacy protection in video surveillance systems using scalable video coding. In *Proceedings of the Sixth IEEE International Conference on Advanced Video and Signal Based Surveillance*, pages 424–429, Genova, Italy, Sept. 2009.

[22] T. C. Thang, T. M. Bae, Y. J. Jung, Y. M. Ro, J.-G. Kim, H. Choi, and J.-W. Hong. Spatial Scalability of Multiple ROIs in Surveillance Video. http://wftp3.itu.int/av-arch/jvt-site/2005_04_Busan/JVT-O037.doc, Jan. 2005.

[23] L. Tong, F. Dai, Y. Zhang, and J. Li. Prediction restricted H.264/AVC video scrambling for privacy protection. *Electronic Letters*, 46(1):47–49, Jan. 2010.

[24] T.-L. Wu and S. F. Wu. Selective encryption and watermarking of MPEG video (extended abstract). In H. R. Arabnia, editor, *Proceedings of the International Conference on Image Science, Systems, and Technology, CISST '97*, Las Vegas, USA, Feb. 1997.

# What's the PointISA?

Sudeep Ghosh[*]
Microsoft Corporation, One Microsoft Way,
Redmond, WA-98052, USA
sugho@microsoft.com

Jason D. Hiser, Jack W. Davidson
Computer Science Department, Univ. of Virginia
Charlottesville, VA-22903, USA.
{hiser, jwd}@virginia.edu

## ABSTRACT

Software watermarking, fingerprinting, digital content identification, and many other desirable security properties can be improved with software protection techniques such as tamper resistance and obfuscation. Previous research has demonstrated software protection can be significantly enhanced using a Process-level Virtual Machine (PVM). They can provide robust program protections, particularly at run time, which many other software protection techniques lack. PVMs have been used to provide tamper detection, dynamic code obfuscation, and resistance to static disassembly. Overall, the presence of PVMs makes it more difficult for the adversary to achieve their goals.

Recently, a new attack methodology, called Replacement Attacks, was described that successfully targeted PVM-protected applications. This methodology circumvents execution of the protective PVM instance through the use of another virtual machine to execute the program. The replacement occurs dynamically and allows execution of the application without any PVM-based protections.

In this work, we formalize the notion of a replacement attack using a novel model. We then present a defense against such attacks. To the best of our knowledge, this technique is the first defense against replacement attacks. The technique relies on software interpretation of instructions, which forms the basis of PVMs. By carefully modifying the semantics of some individual instructions, it is possible to make the application unusable without the presence of the protective PVM instance. The technique is called PointISA, named after a point function—a function which returns true for only one given input. We provide a formal description of PointISAs and an evaluation of the strength of the approach.

---

[*]This work was completed when the author was a graduate student at the University of Virginia.

## Categories and Subject Descriptors

D.3.4 [**Programming languages**]:  Processors – Run-time Environments; D.4.6 [**Operating Systems**]: Security and Protection

## Keywords

Process-level Virtual Machines; Tamper detection; Replacement Attack

## 1. INTRODUCTION

Software protection techniques, such as tamper resistance and obfuscation, are commonly used and important techniques to provide a variety of real-world software security properties, such as watermarking, fingerprinting, or digital content identification [2, 19, 26, 6, 8, 16]. In recent years, process-level virtual machines (PVM) have been shown to support a variety of robust software protections [2, 32, 15]. There are several reasons for the growing success of PVMs in the area of software protections.

- Process-level virtualization provides a platform for enhanced run-time security.

- Protection techniques are largely separated from the application development process.

- Static protection schemes can be strengthened when the application is virtualized.

Compared to other techniques, PVM-based protections have demonstrably increased the effort required by the adversary to reverse engineer applications. Commercial PVM-based obfuscation tools, such as VMProtect [32] and Code Virtualizer [23], are increasingly used by software developers to protect applications. We have also previously discussed the dynamic nature of the protections offered by PVMs [15]. Overall, PVMs provide robust dynamic protection against reverse engineering and tampering.

Recently, an attack technique was proposed and demonstrated against PVM-protected applications. The attack replaces the protective PVM with an attack PVM so that the application executes without mediation by the protective PVM instance [14]. This attack was possible because the application is not bound tightly to the protective PVM instance, and therefore, these two components can be sundered. Subsequently, the application can be executed under control of an attack PVM. The result of this attack can be seen in Figure 1(d); the application is separated from its protective PVM and instead runs under control of a potentially malicious VM. Section 3 discusses the attack in more detail and formally defines a replacement attack.

Currently, applications are not adequately bound to the protective PVM. One possible binding technique involves the creation of a secret Instruction Set Architecture (ISA), which can only be interpreted by a protective PVM instance. The application's instructions are then converted to the secret ISA. At run time, the protective PVM instance interprets the application's instructions. This methodology is adopted by tools such as VMProtect and Themida [32, 22].

In theory, this scheme appears resistant to attack because innumerable ISAs can be created for the purpose of program protection. However, in practice, researchers have discovered that obfuscation tools that use secret ISAs are much more restricted. Rolf Rolles demonstrated that VMProtect typically generates secret ISAs from the same generic template [27]. An adversary can analyze a few different outputs generated by VMProtect and reverse engineer any protected application. Consequently, PVM-protected applications that use secret ISAs are susceptible to collusion attacks which can lead to a successful replacement attack.

To combat this type of replacement attack methodology, we present a technique called *PointISA*. This technique seeks to bind the application to its associated protective PVM instance. This novel relationship is achieved by inserting instructions into the application, whose semantics are interpreted *uniquely* by the associated protective PVM instance. Any other interpreter attempting to execute the protected application will interpret these instructions according to their original semantics, and the deviation can be detected.

The major contributions of the paper are:

- We provide a formal description of the replacement attack using a novel model.

- We formally describe the PointISA technique and demonstrate its effectiveness at thwarting replacement attacks.

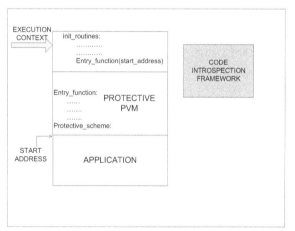

(a) The virtualized application, $TR(P)$, is run under an introspection framework.

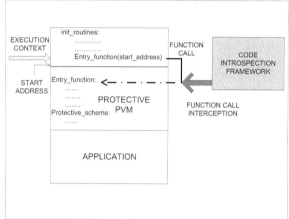

(b) The CIF intercepts the call to the entry function of the protective PVM.

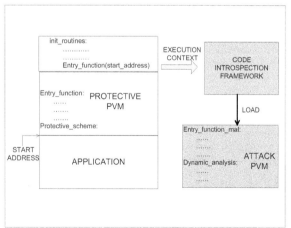

(c) The CIF proceeds to load an attack PVM.

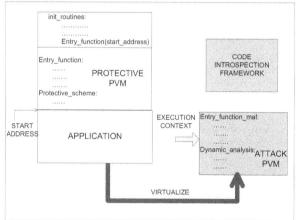

(d) Control is then transferred to the entry function of the attack PVM, which proceeds to run $P$ without any dynamic protections.

Figure 1: Steps illustrating the attack methodology on virtualized applications.

- We design and evaluate a prototype PointISA system that makes a compelling case for using PointISA to prevent replacement attacks.

- Finally, we provide an in-depth discussion of possible security vulnerabilities in PVM-protected applications.

The remainder of this paper is organized as follows: Section 2 describes the threat model in which our techniques must operate. Section 3 defines a replacement attack, and Section 4 formally defines an application, PVM protections, and replacement attacks. Section 5 presents the PointISA technique in detail and includes a formal description of the technique. Section 7 gives a thorough evaluation, and potential security issues are discussed in Section 8. Finally, Section 9 discusses related work, while Section 10 provides a conclusion and a summary of our findings.

## 2. THREAT MODEL

We begin by describing the trusted environment used to create software applications. The software developer uses various trusted tools (compilers, optimizers, and assemblers) to convert high-level source code or specifications into applications. To safeguard the application's static image, the developer applies static code obfuscations and tamper-detection mechanisms to the application. At this point, we assume the application is safe from static, dynamic or hybrid static/dynamic tampering attacks. While such an assumption is likely not reasonable in practice, we make this assumption to focus on PVM replacement attacks against the application.

The application is then released for public use. An attacker can use various tools (e.g., debuggers, simulators, and emulators, etc.) to run, observe and modify the program in a number of ways. For example, Skype, the popular VoIP tool, was reverse engineered by researchers using a debugger [5]. Even the operating system can be modified to return incorrect information, thereby thwarting any protection features that depend on the OS [34]. Furthermore, hardware can be emulated to return forged results to the application. Consequently, we consider all hardware and other software on the host machine as potentially malicious, and the entire protected application (including any virtual machine distributed with said application) is a target of attack.

In essence, the adversary is mounting a white-box attack [21]. The adversary can inspect, modify, or forge any information in the system. Given enough time and resources, the adversary can succeed in understanding the ISA of the protected application. However, human adversaries have difficulty directly solving large problems. As such, they rely on algorithmic solutions to perform analyzes on the application packages, such as trying to determine the secret ISA of a protected application. Our goal is to make such analyses less effective so that replacement attacks are not successful.

## 3. REPLACEMENT ATTACKS

This section describes and explores the loose connection between an application and a protective PVM instance when using a PVM to protect software. The only requirement on the part of the PVM involves the ability to interpret (using hardware, or any software technique) designated portions of the application's instruction sequence. This weak binding stems from the need to make applications platform-independent, which was one of the initial goals behind virtualization. The application is compiled once and should be runnable on any platforms. This adaptability is facilitated by the virtual machine, which is implemented according to the specifics of the native platform. In this paradigm it is essential that the application and the PVM be unbound. However, this does not hold true for protective PVMs that we wish to keep bound to the application.

It has been shown that such adaptability leads to a serious weakness when PVMs are utilized in program protection [14]. An able adversary can replace the protective PVM instance with a non-protective VM, and proceed to analyze the application unhindered. The adversary can apply standard reverse engineering techniques to study the application.

The replacement attack methodology targets the surface of the application that is most vulnerable to attack (i.e., when protections are at their weakest). More specifically, this attack methodology targets the application just after start up (when static protections are not as effective), but before the PVM assumes control and begins applying protections to the application. If successful, the attack disengages the protective PVM and disables the run-time protections.

To craft a successful replacement attack against PVM-protected applications, certain requirements need to be met:

- The attacker must be able to locate the entry function (EP) of the protective PVM in a protected application. The entry function is defined as the function of the PVM which initiates software virtualization. The entry function often takes the starting address location of the application's code as an argument.

- The attacker must be aware of the guest application's instruction set architecture. The code of the guest application, is typically obscured using a secret ISA. To analyze and run the application after the protective PVM has been disabled, the attacker needs to be cognizant of the ISA, which involves analyzing and understanding the secret ISA.

Such needs are discussed in more detail in earlier work [14].

Replacement attacks occur in two stages. In the first stage, the attack PVM has to be extended to decode the protected application, which involves understanding the guest ISA. If the ISA is encrypted, the decryption keys and algorithms must also be obtained and used to further extend the attack PVM by including the decryption algorithm and keys. For the discussion of PointISA, we assume that the ISA has not been encrypted. For a discussion on techniques for deciphering an encrypted ISA see Ghosh [14, 13].

Figure 1 illustrates the second stage of the attack on the protected application. In Figure 1(a), the attacker invokes the program under a *code introspection framework* (CIF), which is capable of monitoring and instrumenting the code being executed, allowing instructions to be observed as they execute. Well known examples of CIFs include Pin [20] and QEMU [4]. The attacker modifies the CIF to locate the call to the entry function of the protective PVM.

The initialization routine then proceeds to prepare the PVM's internal structures. As the entry function of the protective PVM is invoked, the CIF intercepts this call and extracts the start address, depicted in Figure 1(b).

The CIF then proceeds to load and initialize the attack PVM, shown in Figure 1(c). The CIF then invokes this attack PVM with $P$'s start address which has been extracted from the initial call.

Thus, $P$ now runs under the mediation of the attack PVM (shown in Figure 1(d)). The protective PVM is circumvented and fails to provide dynamic protection to $P$. The attack PVM can be used to perform tasks that helps the attacker understand $P$ (e.g., dump information, identify function locations, trace instructions, etc.).

# 4. FORMAL MODEL

To describe a replacement attack formally, we start by describing applications and their protection schemes.

## 4.1 Modeling an Application

Consider a generic software application that has been compiled to run on a machine. Any machine is acceptable and the formulas will not rely on the details of any particular machine. Equation 1 describes such an application.

$$P_{APP} = < I_{APP}^{mach}, IN_{APP}, OUT_{APP}, A_{APP} > \qquad (1)$$

Where $I_{APP}^{mach}$ refers to its instruction sequence in the target machine's ISA. $IN_{APP}$ and $OUT_{APP}$ refer to its input and output set, respectively. Finally, $A_{APP}$ refers to its assets, that is information contained in the program that should remain secret.

The software defender applies several transformations that are designed to protect the application. These transformations are represented by the operator, $TR$, which can be applied to an application. Equation 2 describes the protected application.

$$P_{TR(APP)} = < I_{TR(APP)}^{mach}, IN_{APP}, OUT_{APP}, A_{APP} > \qquad (2)$$

$I_{TR(APP)}^{mach}$ refers to the transformed instruction sequence. The rest of the variables have the same meaning as in Equation 1. In our research, an example of a transformation could be to encrypt the instruction sequence, which is then decrypted at run time by the protective PVM.

## 4.2 Modeling a Protective PVM

Next, we model the protective PVM (PPVM), which runs the protected application. Equation 3 describes the protective PVM.

$$P_{ppvm} = < I_{ppvm}^{mach}, IN_{ppvm}, OUT_{ppvm}, A_{ppvm} > \qquad (3)$$

$I_{ppvm}^{mach}$ represents the instruction sequence of the protective PVM in the machine's ISA. The input set for the PVM is a subset of $\rho_{APP} \times IN_{APP} \times C_{ppvm}$, where $\rho_{APP}$ refers to all applications. In this example, we assume that the applications have been compiled for the machine's architecture and subsequently protected. $IN_{APP}$ represents the input set to the applications. Finally, $C_{ppvm}$ refers to the configurations for the protective PVM, to enable executing the application. Similarly, the output set for PPVM, $OUT_{ppvm}$, consists of $OUT_{APP} \times O_{ppvm}$, where $OUT_{APP}$ refers to the outputs generated by the application, and $O_{ppvm}$ represents the outputs generated by the protective PVM. $A_{ppvm}$ refers to the assets of the PVM.

## 4.3 Modeling Runtime Behavior

We now focus on the run time. This application is interpreted by the PVM, which applies dynamic protections

techniques, similar to those described in previous work [32, 22, 15]. The interpretation by the PVM can be modeled as:

$$\phi_{ppvm}(P_{TR(APP)}, in_{APP}, m_{ppvm}^{in}) \longrightarrow < out_{APP}, m_{ppvm}^{out} > \qquad (4)$$

In Equation 4, $\phi_{ppvm}$ is to the interpretation operation under the PVM. $P_{TR(APP)}$ refers to the protected application, the operation $TR()$ indicating that the application can also be protected by techniques independent of the protective PVM (e.g., static protections) [8, 26] The input variable, $in_{APP}$ consists of the application inputs. $m_{ppvm}^{in}$ represents the initial memory state (including registers, conditions codes, etc.) At the conclusion of interpretation, $out_{APP}$ is generated, and the final memory state is denoted by $m_{ppvm}^{out}$.

The protective PVM is itself an application that is interpreted by the machine's platform. Equation 5 represents the interpretation of the PVM on the machine's architecture.

$$\phi_{mach}(P_{ppvm}, in_{ppvm}, m_{mach}^{in}) \longrightarrow < out_{ppvm}, m_{mach}^{out} > \qquad (5)$$

The interpreter takes as input the protective PVM software application, $P_{ppvm}$, and an input, $in_{ppvm}$, while generating output $out_{ppvm}$. The memory state is transformed from $m_{mach}^{in}$ to $m_{mach}^{out}$.

Expanding the variables in Equation 5 to include the representation of the protected application, $P_{TR(APP)}$, we obtain Equation 6, which shows the full nested interpretation.

$$\phi_{mach}(P_{ppvm}, < P_{TR(APP)}, in_{APP}, c_{ppvm} >, m_{mach}^{in}) \longrightarrow$$
$$<< out_{APP}, o_{ppvm} >, m_{mach}^{out} > \qquad (6)$$

The input to the interpreter is composed of a tuple, comprising the protected software application $P_{TR(APP)}$, the input to the original application, $in_{APP}$, and $c_{ppvm}$, the configuration settings for the PVM to run the application. For example, if the application is encrypted, $c_{ppvm}$ can represent the decryption key. The memory is in its initial state, which can be broken down into the memory state for the protective PVM, $(m_{mach}^{in})^{ppvm}$, and the state for the application, $(m_{mach}^{in})^{APP}$. On successful completion, the output, $out_{APP}$ is generated, and memory is in its final state, denoted by $(m_{mach}^{out})^{ppvm}$ and $(m_{mach}^{out})^{APP}$.

## 4.4 Modeling Replacement Attacks

Next, we describe the replacement attack using our model. To remove PVM-enabled protections and to execute and analyze the application unhindered, the adversary replaces the protective PVM with a non-protective instance. We refer to such a PVM instance as the *attack PVM*. This PVM can also interpret any application that has been compiled to run on the PVM, but enables the adversary to perform analysis. The attack PVM can be represented by:

$$P_{attack} = < I_{attack}^{mach}, IN_{ppvm}, OUT_{ppvm}, A_{attack} > \qquad (7)$$

Comparing Equations 3 and 7, we observe that the attack VM has the same input set, and generates the same output set as the PPVM. $I_{attack}^{mach}$ denotes the instruction sequence for the attack PVM on machine. Finally, $A_{attack}$ represents the assets of the attack PVM.

We now model the attack, by modifying Equation 6:

$$\phi_{mach}(P_{attack}, < P_{TR(APP)}, in_{APP}, c_{attack} >, m_{mach}^{in})$$
$$\longrightarrow << out_{APP}, o_{attack} >, m_{mach}^{out} > \qquad (8)$$

Equation 8 illustrates the replacement attack. The machine interpreter operates on the attack PVM, $P_{attack}$. The inputs consist of a 3-tuple comprised of the protected application, $P_{TR(APP)}$, the input to the application, $in_{APP}$, and a configuration setting for the PVM, $c_{attack}$. During interpretation, the memory state is transformed from $m_{mach}^{in}$ to $m_{mach}^{out}$. On conclusion, the interpreter outputs a tuple consisting of $out_{APP}$, which is the output of the application, and $o_{attack}$, which is the output specific to the attack PVM. The adversary can configure the attack PVM to generate additional information that could facilitate analysis. An example of $o_{attack}$ could be the run-time trace of the application, which enables dynamic control flow analysis.

# 5. POINT ISAS

The replacement attack succeeds because the application can be virtualized by any PVM that can interpret the ISA of the protected application, $P$. This section proposes a solution that thwarts replacement attacks by semantically binding $P$ with a specific instance of the protective PVM (i.e., $P$ can only be interpreted by a unique PVM instance.)

We apply this property in the context of software virtualization to ensure that the protective PVM is not replaced. Traditionally, each instruction of an ISA possesses a unique semantics. In our proposed solution, certain instructions are selected from the ISA of the application, $P$. We refer to this set as $I^{PI}$, and each individual member of this set by $i^{PI}$. These instructions are inserted into the application at appropriate locations. Consequently, the PVM is configured to handle these instructions uniquely as follows: At run time, when the protective PVM encounters any of these select instructions, it interprets them in a custom manner, *different* from the semantics specified by the platform documentation, i.e., the protective PVM instance will interpret these instructions using customized semantics, whereas other interpreter instances will interpret it in the conventional manner (e.g., according to the platform documentation). When run under the protective PVM, the transformed application should generate outputs which are identical to the unprotected version, for any input combination.

The set of instructions is not unique, but varies for each application. Implemented correctly, a replacement attack and subsequent interpretation on a generic interpreter can cause the application to behave in an undefined manner and either lead to failure, or trigger an appropriate response mechanism. Thus, the replacement attack will fail in its objective of successfully executing the application without the protective PVM. This solution methodology is termed *PointISA*[1].

There are several components of this solution that require investigation. Some of the primary areas of research include identifying the set $I^{PI}$, and designing mechanisms to detect and seamlessly respond to a replacement attack. Care must also be taken to ensure that the transformed application running on the PVM instance generates outputs that are

---

[1] *PointISA* has been derived from the term, *point functions* in cryptography. Point functions return `true` for only one input, and false otherwise. In our case, $i^{PI}$ corresponds to its correct value (i.e., $f^{-1}$) in only one context (i.e., when it is interpreted by the associated protective PVM instance.) In all other contexts, $i^{PI}$ is interpreted according to the architectural ISA.

identical to those of the original application. The next few sections discuss these issues in detail. First, however, we formalize the PointISA protection technique.

## 5.1 Formalizing PointISA

In Section 3, we formalized replacement attacks. We now extend this formalization to characterize the PointISA scheme. We recall Equation 5, which describes the execution of the protected application on the protective PVM. The PPVM itself is running on an arbitrary machine.

$$\phi_{mach}(P_{ppvm}, < P_{TR(APP)}, in_{APP}, c_{ppvm} >, m_{mach}^{in}) \longrightarrow$$
$$<< out_{APP}, o_{ppvm} >, m_{mach}^{out} > \quad (9)$$

In Equation 9, the input to the interpreter is composed of a tuple, comprising the protected software application $P_{TR(APP)}$, the input to the original application, $in_{APP}$, and $c_{ppvm}$, the configuration settings for the PPVM to run the application. For example, if the application is encrypted, $c_{ppvm}$ can represent the decryption key. The memory is in its initial state, which can be broken down into the memory state for the PPVM, $(m_{mach}^{in})^{ppvm}$, and the state for the application, $(m_{mach}^{in})^{APP}$. On successful completion, the output, $out_{APP}$ is generated, and memory reaches its final state, denoted by $(m_{mach}^{out})^{ppvm}$, and $(m_{mach}^{out})^{APP}$.

The replacement attack results in the substitution of the protective PVM with an attack PVM, which can then be used to analyze the application without any hindrance. Recalling Equation 8, The machine interpreter operates on the attack PVM, $P_{attack}$. The inputs consist of a 3-tuple comprised of the protected application, $P_{TR(APP)}$, the input to the application, $in_{APP}$, and a configuration setting for the PVM, $c_{attack}$. During interpretation, the memory state is transformed from $m_{mach}^{in}$ to $m_{mach}^{out}$. On conclusion, the interpreter outputs a tuple consisting of $out_{APP}$, which is the output of the application, and $o_{attack}$, which is the output specific to the attack PVM. The adversary can configure the attack PVM to generate additional information that could facilitate analysis.

We now introduce the $\Psi$ operator, which represents the PointISA protection scheme. This operator is applied to the software application, and results in a transformed application, $\Psi(P_{TR(APP)})$. Now, the application can only be successfully executed under the mediation of its associated protective PVM, $ppvm_{APP}$. This protection scheme is orthogonal to other protection schemes, allowing it to be used in conjunction with other techniques.

Equation 10 describes the interpretation of a PointISA protected application on the native platform.

$$\phi_{mach}(P_{ppvm^{APP}}, < \Psi(P_{TR(APP)}), in_{APP}, c_{ppvm^{APP}} >,$$
$$m_{mach}^{in}) \longrightarrow << out_{APP}, o_{ppvm} >, m_{mach}^{out} > \quad (10)$$

The application has a unique PVM associated with it, denoted by $ppvm^{APP}$. The interpreter function, $\phi_{mach}$, operates on the PVM application, $P_{ppvm^{APP}}$. The inputs consist of the protected application, $\Psi(P_{TR(APP)})$, the application input $in_{APP}$, and the configuration setting for the PVM $c_{ppvm^{APP}}$. The outputs consists of the output from the application $out_{APP}$, and the output from the PVM itself, $o_{ppvm}$. The memory state changes from $m_{mach}^{in}$ to $m_{mach}^{out}$.

The interpretation of this PointISA protected application on the associated protective PVM is identical to the interpretation of the original application (represented by Equation 9). However, if this application is subjected to a replacement attack, the interpretation fails. This scenario is represented by the following equation.

$$\phi_{mach}(P_{attack}, < \Psi(P_{TR(APP)}), in_{APP}, c_{attack} >, m_{mach}^{in})$$
$$\longrightarrow << (out_{APP})^{error}, o_{attack} >, m_{mach}^{out} > \quad (11)$$

In Equation 11, the machine interpreter ($\phi_{mach}$) operates on the attack PVM, $P_{attack}$. The inputs to the attack PVM consist of the protected application, $\Psi(P_{TR(APP)})$, the application input $in_{APP}$, and the configuration for the PVM $c_{attack}$. In this case, the application fails to execute correctly, and an error message is generated ($(out_{APP})^{error}$), along with any output from the attack PVM, $o_{attack}$. The memory state changes from $m_{mach}^{in}$ to $m_{mach}^{out}$.

### 5.1.1 Modeling PointISA Instructions

The previous set of equations described the solution methodology at a conceptual level. We now proceed to expand our model to describe PointISA at a finer level of granularity. To begin, we need to represent the interpretation of a sequence of instructions on the host machine via our model. Described in a simple form, interpreting an instruction (or a sequence of instructions) implies transforming memory of the computing machine from one state to another. To express this action in our model, we introduce a new operation, $\Phi_H$. We describe the interpretation of a sequence of instructions in Equation 12.

$$\Phi_H(i_1^H, i_2^H, i_3^H .., m_H^{in}) \longrightarrow < m_H^{out} > \quad (12)$$

The operator, $\Phi_H$ denotes the interpretation of an instruction sequence on the host $H$. The sequence is denoted by $i_1^H, i_2^H, i_3^H ...$ The initial memory state is denoted by $m_H^{in}$, and the final state by $m_H^{out}$.

We can now utilize Equation 12 to represent PointISA instructions. As we described, the semantics of the PointISA instruction depend on the instance of the interpreter. We consider an instruction belonging to the machine's ISA, and its interpretation by a standard machine interpreter, and the protective PVM running on an arbitrary machine. Equation 13 describes these two scenarios.

$$\Phi_{mach}(i_{mach}^{PI}, m_{mach}^1) \longrightarrow < m_{mach}^2 > \quad (13)$$
$$\Phi_{ppvm}(i_{mach}^{PI}, m_{mach}^1) \longrightarrow < m_{mach}^3 > \quad (14)$$

When the instruction, $i_{mach}^{PI}$, is interpreted by a generic machine interpreter, the memory state is transformed from $m_{mach}^1$ to $m_{mach}^2$. When that same instruction is interpreted by the $ppvm$ instance, the memory state is transformed from $m_{mach}^1$ to $m_{mach}^3$. The premise behind PointISA is that this behavior of $i_{mach}^{PI}$ (which leads to memory states $m_{mach}^2$ and $m_{mach}^3$) can be differentiated programmatically enabling detection of the replacement attack.

We are now ready to design the PointISA solution. For this purpose, we utilize two functions $f$ and $f^{-1}$, which are defined as follows.

$$f(m) \longrightarrow n \quad (15)$$
$$f^{-1}(n) \longrightarrow m \quad (16)$$

As Equations 15 and 16 represents, the function $f$ takes an input $m$ and transforms it to $n$, while the function $f^{-1}$ transforms $n$ back to $m$, (i.e., the pair are the inverse of each other.)

These functions are inserted into the application in the following manner. The function, $f$ is implemented via a sequence of instructions. The function $f^{-1}$ is implemented via a PointISA instruction, $i_{mach}^{PI}$. The PVM is configured such that, when it encounters $i_{mach}^{PI}$ at run time, it implements the semantics of the PointISA instruction, $f^{-1}$. Equations 17 and 18 illustrate these scenarios.

$$\Phi_{ppvm}((f = \{i_{mach}^1, i_{mach}^2 ... i_{mach}^k\}), m_{mach}^1)$$
$$\longrightarrow < m_{mach}^2 > \quad (17)$$

$$\Phi_{ppvm}(i_{mach}^{PI}, m_{mach}^2)) \longrightarrow < m_{mach}^3 > \quad (18)$$

During software creation, the instruction sequence implementing $f$ (i.e., $i_{mach}^1, i_{mach}^2 ... i_{mach}^k$), is inserted at a suitable location in the application's CFG, followed by the insertion of $i_{mach}^{PI}$ at a second location. The two locations are chosen such that both of them are guaranteed to be reached during program execution. Dominator analysis can be used to make the arrangement less predictable. The protective PVM instance is configured such that $i_{mach}^{PI}$ is interpreted according to the semantics of $f^{-1}$.

Under normal circumstances, this arrangement guarantees that protected applications produce outputs identical to those of the original application, for the same set of inputs (we define this scenario as *output equality*). If a replacement attack occurs, the execution of a PointISA instruction leaves memory in an undefined state. We now proceed to describe appropriate response mechanisms to an attack.

### 5.1.2 Response to Replacement Attacks

During application execution, after instructions representing Equations 17 and 18 have been interpreted, $m^1$ and $m^3$ should be equal. This scenario is necessary for PointISA to maintain output equality. If the protective PVM instance is replaced, the attack interpreter will interpret $i_{mach}^{PI}$ according to the ISA specifications, and not the semantics of $f^{-1}$. Consequently, output equality will no longer be achieved. We can respond to this event in two ways.

The first response mechanism, termed the *Value Modification* mechanism, involves letting the application continue execution. Since the memory of the application is no longer in a predictable state (due to the execution of the actual semantics of $i_{mach}^{PI}$, as opposed to $f^{-1}$), there is a probability that the program will execute an incorrect path and fail. Such a failure is likely to be obscure due to the fact that the path taken may not be predictable. The downside to this technique is that the modification may be ineffectual, resulting in unmodified execution on the replacement PVM.

The second response technique, termed the *Auditor* mechanism, involves the use of a guarding mechanism to check that output equality has been maintained. If the checks detect that output equality is not satisfied, appropriate measures are taken. The downside of this scheme is that a knowledgeable adversary might be able to detect these checks and disable them. Therefore, to obtain a robust defense mechanism, a probabilistic mix of both schemes should be employed. Equation 19 describes functionality of the auditor function, which checks the memory, and triggers an attack response if they are not equal.

$$f_{audit} \longrightarrow \begin{cases} \text{if } m^3 \equiv m^1 \text{ continue execution} \\ \text{if } m^3 \neq m^1 \text{ respond to attack} \end{cases} \quad (19)$$

$m^1$ denotes the state of memory prior to execution of the PointISA solution. $m^3$ denotes the state of memory after PointISA has successfully executed. If the two states are equal, it indicates that the execution has proceeded as expected. If the states are not equal, it indicates an attack, and an appropriate response is generated.

For the remainder of this discussion, the components represented by Equations 17, 18, and the optional part, 19 are referred to as the *components* of the PointISA methodology. In the next section, we describe the implementation of these components in greater detail. Section 8 discusses the security of such the technique.

# 6. DESIGNING POINTISA

There are several factors that can determine the effectiveness of PointISA. We address these issues in this section.

## 6.1 PointISA Instruction Identification

The protective PVM instance interprets the redefined semantics of selected instructions. To enable such custom interpretation, the PVM must be able to distinguish the PointISA instructions, $I_{PI}$, from regular instructions that form part of the application. A straightforward manner to obtain such classification is to analyze the original, unprotected application, and choose an instruction that is not in the application.

Consequently, the protective PVM instance is modified such that, on encountering the PointISA instruction, $i_{PI}$, it implements the semantics of an inverse PointISA component, $f^{-1}$. Each application to be protected via a PVM will possess its own PointISA instructions.

An adversary may be able to perform frequency analysis on the application, and decipher which instructions form part of $I_{PI}$. To thwart such analyses, instead of choosing a unique instruction, a unique combination of opcode and operands can be chosen. The opcode may be present in the original application, but the combination of the opcode and its operands is not. In this case, the protective PVM instance will have to decode the instruction completely (opcode and operands) before deciding whether to trigger the semantics of $f^{-1}$.

The next design issue involves devising techniques to insert the various PointISA components into the application such that they are executed in the correct order.

## 6.2 PointISA Component Insertion

To recall, our semantic-binding scheme involves the insertion of a function, $f$, and a PointISA instruction, $i_{PI}$, into the control flow of the application, such that the output of the transformed application matches the original version, for all inputs. To achieve this property, $i_{PI}$ is interpreted by the protective PVM instance as $f^{-1}$.

To implement PointISA, the control flow of the application needs to be adjusted such that its components are scheduled for execution in correct order. For the purposes of our proof-of-concept, we inserted the PointISA components in sequential order at appropriate locations in the application. We describe our prototype in greater detail in Section 7.1.

Maintaining output equality of the components is essential for correct functioning of PointISA. Reducing performance overhead is also critical, because a large increase is undesirable and makes the protection scheme impractical. To reduce excessive overhead, the point of insertion must be on a path that is executed, but not too frequently. The issue is similar to that of placing checksumming guards in executables, as described in previous work [6]. In the case of checksumming guards, one must establish a balanced trade-off between execution rate and overhead to maintain constant protection. In the case of PointISA, we believe that the rate of execution of its components is not as relevant, because any one of them can trigger a response in the event of an attack. Furthermore, the PointISA concept is significantly less expensive than performing a checksum over a range of code or data. Consequently, we used profile information to guide the insertion process. (That is, the application was run in profiled mode to obtain frequently-executing paths. Then, PointISA components are randomly inserted based on a probability which is inversely proportional to path's frequency of execution.)

## 6.3 Replacement Attack Response

If an adversary attempts to replace the protective PVM instance and execute the application on a different interpreter (software or hardware), the semantics of the $i_{PI}$ will revert to its original and this event can be detected. We have devised two mechanisms to respond to such an attack.

### 6.3.1 Auditors

In the first case, we employ the use of an *auditor* to detect the attack and take appropriate action. Recalling Section 5.1, the function, $f$ updates a memory location's from, $m^1$, to $m^2$, whereas the protective PVM interprets the PointISA instruction, $i_{PI}$, such that the memory location's value reverts back to $m^1$. The auditor is placed further along the same program path, and checks that the value of the memory location is indeed $m^1$. In case there is a mismatch, the auditor will trigger a response (e.g., stopping application execution or forcing control along an incorrect path). Assuming that all the components ($f$, $i_{PI}$, and the auditor) run correctly and in order, this technique ensures that replacing the protective PVM instance will cause the application to fail.

### 6.3.2 Value Modification

The use of an auditor leads to the creation of another point of attack. If the adversary is able to disable the auditor (e.g., by replacing it with no-op instructions), a replacement attack will not be detected. To obfuscate PointISA, we modify the function, $f$, to update a value belonging to the application (e.g., modify a register). The protective PVM instance is also updated such that the interpretation of $i_{PI}$ reverts the value of the variable.

The basic premise behind this response scheme is that if the application is run under an attack PVM, $f$ will be invoked as usual, but the interpretation of $i_{PI}$ will not revert the program variable. Further along this program path, the update caused by $f$ could lead to program failure, although the final result is non-deterministic.

# 7. EVALUATING POINTISA

This section discusses the creation and evaluation of a prototype implementing PointISA on an Intel x86 platform. Some of the design decisions included techniques to select candidate instructions, identifying locations in the application control flow graph where the PointISA instruction could be inserted and appropriate response mechanisms to detected replacement attacks.

## 7.1 Prototype Design and Implementation

The PointISA implementation depends on the complementary functions $f$ and $f^{-1}$. Any number of such functions can be designed. For the purposes of our implementation, we defined $f$ and $f^{-1}$ in two ways, corresponding to the Value Modification and the Auditor mechanisms. Equation 20 describes the semantics of the functions in the case of the Value Modification Mechanism:

$$f, f^{-1}: \ \sim \texttt{reg} \longrightarrow \texttt{reg} \qquad (20)$$

In this scheme, $f$ modifies an application value residing in a hardware register. $\texttt{reg}$ can be any standard hardware register such as $\texttt{eax}$, $\texttt{ebx}$, etc., on the Intel x86 platform.

Equation 21 describes the semantics of the functions in the case of the Auditor mechanism:

$$
\begin{aligned}
[MEM_1] &= INIT \\
f, f^{-1}: \ &\sim [MEM_1] \longrightarrow [MEM_1] \qquad (21) \\
f_{audit}: [MEM_1] &== INIT = \\
&\begin{cases} \text{do nothing} & \text{if } \texttt{true} \\ \text{respond to attack} & \text{if } \texttt{false} \end{cases}
\end{aligned}
$$

In this scheme, the memory location, $[MEM_1]$ refers to the contents of a global memory variable that is created during the software protection process (i.e., this location is not a part of the original application). This variable is initialized to a randomly selected value. $f$ and $f^{-1}$ consist of **negating** this variable. Finally, the audit function, $f_{audit}$ checks whether the value of the variable has been reverted. For the sake of simplicity, we have provided only one version of $f$ and $f^{-1}$. A robust implementation of PointISA should possess different versions of these functions for most PointISA protection locations.

In both these equations, **negation** ($\sim$) is the primary logical operator. This operator was chosen because:

- On the 32-bit Intel x86 platform, the **negation** operator does not change any processor flags. Consequently, the flag register does not need to be preserved, which is beneficial for reducing overhead.

- The **negation** operator possesses the property of *involution* (i.e., the function is its own inverse), making the implementation of $f$ and $f^{-1}$ identical [33].

The prototype is created using the link-time optimizer, *Diablo* [11]. The inputs to Diablo consist of the original, unprotected application ($P$), a set of PointISA instructions $(I_{PI})^2$, and an instance of the protective PVM (in this case, the Strata PVM) [28]. The logic of Strata has been modified

---

2 Selection criteria for these instructions is described in Section 7.2.

such that, during execution, when it encounters a PointISA instruction, it implements the semantics of $f^{-1}$.

During software creation, we use Diablo to generate a flow graph of $P$. The nodes in this flow graph consist of basic block data structures (i.e., instruction sequences with a single entry point and a single exit point). The edges in this graph correspond to control flow branches (direct jumps, conditional jumps, calls, etc.) An edge connects a *predecessor* block (i.e., the source block of the control transfer) to a *successor* block (i.e., the destination block of the transfer) [1].

Once the flow graph information is obtained, PointISA is ready to be implemented. First, we consider the Value Modification mechanism, specifically Equation 20. Based on a selection criteria (described in Section 7.2), a target basic block, $X_P$, belonging to the application is identified. This block is subjected to liveness analysis in isolation [1], and registers are identified that contain live values exiting this block. An instruction sequence **negating** one of these registers is inserted into a basic block data structure, $BB_f$. Next, an instruction is randomly selected from $I_{PI}$, and inserted into another basic block structure, $BB_{I_{PI}}$. The protective PVM is modified such that it interprets $i_{PI}$ as $f^{-1}$. The CFG is then modified such that $X_P$ becomes the new direct predecessor of $BB_f$, and $BB_f$ becomes the new direct predecessor of $BB_{I_{PI}}$. All the previous successors of $X_P$ becomes the new successors of $BB_{I_{PI}}$. This modification ensures that any program path that contains $X_P$ is guaranteed to execute $BB_f$ and $BB_{I_{PI}}$, enabling the Value Modification scheme.

Thus, if $N_{succ}$ is the set of successors of $X_P$, the relationship is denoted by:

$$X_P \xrightarrow{pred} \{N_{succ}\}$$

We modify the CFG such that:

$$X_P \xrightarrow{pred} BB_f \xrightarrow{pred} BB_{I_{PI}} \xrightarrow{pred} \{N_{succ}\} \qquad (22)$$

The Auditor mechanism can also be implemented in a similar way, however the function $F_{audit}$, in Equation 21, needs to be handled as well. The instructions corresponding to $F_{audit}$ are stored in a new basic block, $BB_{audit}$. $BB_{audit}$ is inserted into the CFG such that it becomes the new immediate successor of $BB_{I_{PI}}$, and the new predecessor of all the original successors of $X_P$. Thus, the modified CFG would look as follows:

$$X_P \xrightarrow{pred} BB_f \xrightarrow{pred} BB_{I_{PI}} \xrightarrow{pred} BB_{audit} \xrightarrow{pred} \{N_{succ}\} \qquad (23)$$

where $\{N_{succ}\}$ is the set of successors to $X_P$ in the original application, $P$.

Both these schemes are applied multiple times to blocks selected based on profiled information to obtain a distributed protection mechanism.

## 7.2 PointISA Instruction Selection

Selecting the set of PointISA instructions, $I_{PI}$, is crucial to the success of PointISA. These instructions should belong to the set of commonly used instructions of most applications. Such unobtrusiveness provides a natural cover from techniques such as frequency analysis. For our prototype, we created the set $I_{PI}$, based on unique instruction opcodes. We statically analyzed a collection of applications binaries (SPEC CPU2000 and $\texttt{binutils}$ package), and stored their

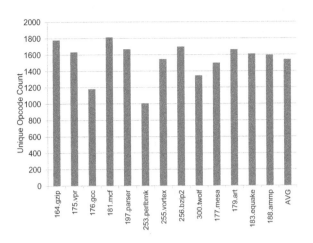

**Figure 2: Number of opcodes in the database that can form part of $I_{PI}$, for each benchmark.**

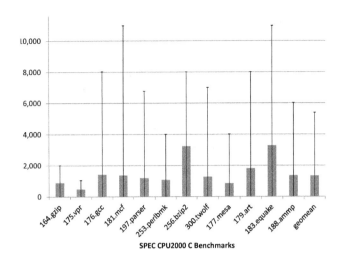

**Figure 3: Number of instructions before failure becomes visible. Error bars indicate the maximum and minimum for 10 random protections.**

instruction opcodes in a database. Let this set be denoted by $I_D$ Subsequently, while processing a benchmark $b$, its unique opcodes are collated. This set is denoted by $I_b$. The set of PointISA instructions can be obtained by calculating the set difference between $I_D$ and $I_b$. This equation can be represented as follows:

$$I_{PI} = I_D \setminus I_b$$

where $\setminus$ denotes the set difference operation. Any opcode in the database that does not occur in $b$, can be used to form $I_{PI}$. Once $I_{PI}$ has been identified for a particular application, an instance of the protective PVM is created that handles each member instruction, $i_{PI}$ accordingly.

Figure 2 displays the number of opcodes that can be used to form the set $I_{PI}$, for each benchmark of the SPEC CPU2000 suite. As the figure illustrates, each benchmark has enough options such that even large benchmarks can be sufficiently protected. Because all these opcodes occur in standard applications, their presence in the protected application should be well camouflaged. The options for $I_{PI}$ can be further increased by considering instruction operands in addition to the opcodes. In this case, the number of options increased by several orders of magnitude.

During the software creation process, Diablo randomly selects one instruction at a time. This instruction is then inserted in basic block $B$, and the process continues as described in Section 7.1.

### 7.3 Replacement Attack Detection

We tested two modes of operation. The first mode exclusively uses the auditor mechanism. We randomly insert just one auditor and have verified that it can detect replacement attacks.

In the second mode, we use only the value modification scheme and randomly insert just one value modification component which is set to randomly modify one register if a replacement attack is detected. We repeat this process ten times. Most of the time when a replacement attack is attempted, the program fails with some type of fault, such as a segmentation fault. In four of the 120 cases, the program ran to completion without generating a fault. In one version of 177.mesa, the program exited but produced dif-

ferent results. We believe this is a suitable (and especially subtle!) way to respond to a replacement attack. In 3 other cases, the auditor failed to modify the program. This failure is likely because the auditor's randomly chosen register was not live. Simple dataflow analysis could prevent this situation [1]. However, even with random insertion of just one auditor, we can successfully detect and respond to 97.4% of the replacement attacks in our tests.

Figure 3 shows the average number of instructions between the execution of the value modification component and the detected failure. Error bars show the minimum and maximum for the runs where a fault was detected. In general, we see that a large number of instructions execute, effectively providing temporal and spatial camouflage for the auditor. Further, the range of failure times is quite large, further hindering an attacker's ability to isolate the PointISA instruction.

In both cases, we show that a single PointISA component can successfully detect replacement attacks. In a real system, additional auditors would be important to stop an adversary from finding the singleton auditor and removing it before attempting the replacement attack. But for our purposes, having just a single auditor demonstrates that they can detect replacement attacks. The next section explores the performance overhead associated with having many PointISA components in a system.

### 7.4 Performance

As with any other protection scheme, low overhead is an important factor in the design of PointISA. High overhead could limit the adoption of this technique.

The selection of a basic block to insert the PointISA component is directly related to the overhead associated with PointISA. Because all the inserted blocks are predecessors of this particular node, a high execution frequency for this node will translate into a high execution frequency for the newly inserted nodes. A high frequency adds to the overhead. Therefore, a judicious arrangement to select blocks to protect is needed As long as the PointISA components execute, protection will be achieved, as shown in Section 7.3.

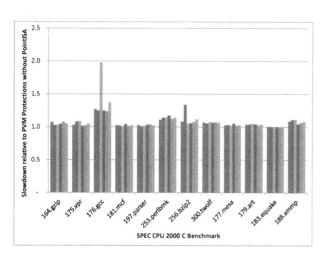

**Figure 4: Performance overhead for PointISA, normalized to the PVM protected application. Individual bars represent separate randomly protected binaries.**

Therefore, we select basic blocks that have low frequency based on profiling information. We use the inverse of the execution count to generate a probability for each basic block of the program. During software creation, the selection of the block to protect depends on its assigned probability. We insert guards into 1% of the blocks based on this random selection. Figure 4 shows the performance overhead for five runs of the SPEC CPU2000 benchmarks. On average, this technique adds an overhead of 8% over the PVM protected application. The various protections, including the PVM execution time, yields a 19% slowdown. Of course, if a particular application requires more protection or lower performance overhead, the insertion rate of protections can be altered. We selected 1% of blocks to be protected to demonstrate that adequate protection can be achieved with low overhead.

Because the placement method is probabilistic, there is a non-zero probability that the PointISA components will be placed in a hot path. The result can be seen in one data point in each `177.gcc` and `256.bzip2`. In such cases, it is judicious to rerun the protection process to get a more favorable binary.

We further note that the `177.gcc` benchmark shows the highest overhead for PointISA. We believe this overhead to be due to profiling input not yielding realistic frequency counts for the reference inputs.

# 8. SECURITY DISCUSSION

This section discusses the impact of PointISA on program protection. Specifically, we consider the robustness of this scheme against particular attack methodologies. We also examine the presence of any weaknesses that an adversary might exploit and offer alternate schemes.

## 8.1 Reverse Engineering

Section 7.1 presented a straightforward mechanism to implement PointISA, which consisted of inserting the PointISA components in a predictable order into the CFG of $P$. Such a naive implementation can be disabled by a knowledgeable adversary.

Data-flow analyses can be used to make PointISA more robust against reverse-engineering attacks. Calculating `def-use` chains is commonly used to identify instructions that define and use the variables in an application. The sequence of instructions that mark the *definition* and *use* of a variable are termed *chains*. In the Value Modification Scheme, `def-use` chains can be used to identify multiple locations to insert the PointISA components. Value Modification components can be inserted randomly at any site within the confines of the `def-use` chain associated with the live value being modified. This additional obfuscation makes it harder for the adversary to identify and disable these PointISA components as they are harder to separate from the dataflow of the application. Applying this scheme multiple times should give sufficiently camouflaged PointISA components.

To increase the robustness of the Auditor mechanism, we utilize dominator analysis [1]. In any directed graph (e.g., the CFG of an application), a node $d$ is called the dominator of node $e$ if all paths from the graph entry point (i.e., program entry point) to $e$ pass through $d$ [1]. Similarly, the node $e$ post-dominates $d$ if the paths from $d$ to the graph exit point pass through $e$. Referring to Equation 23, the PointISA components ($BB_f$, $BB_{I_{PI}}$, and $BB_{audit}$) can be placed on the post-dominator path of the block to be protected, $X_P$, to application exits. Care must be taken to ensure that the components all execute the same number of times. This restriction can be enforced trivially by avoiding their placement in any loops.

$$1_{P..} \xrightarrow{sdom} BB_f.. \xrightarrow{sdom} BB_{I_{PI}} \xrightarrow{sdom} 2_{P..}$$
$$\xrightarrow{sdom} BB_{audit}.. \xrightarrow{sdom} X_P \quad (24)$$

The blocks $1_P$, $2_{P..}$ refer to basic blocks of the original application. Equation 24 implies that the components are inserted at random locations in the dominance tree of the block to be protected. Thus, this scheme makes PointISA more unpredictable and thus, harder to reverse engineer.

## 8.2 Protective PVM Tampering

A knowledgeable adversary can attempt to uncover the special semantics of the PointISA instructions by investigating the instruction handling logic of the protective PVM instance and comparing with the instruction reference manual. Instruction handling is one of the most complicated components of any PVM implementation. Applying traditional program protection techniques to the PVM can make reverse engineering even harder. Thus, while it is theoretically possible to analyze the PVM and discover the PointISA instructions, we do not see a trivial way to achieve this task. The adversary will have to manually investigate the handling of each possible instruction. By expanding the domain of PointISA instructions to include instruction operands as well, this task can be made still harder.

## 8.3 Collaborative applications

The use of PointISA instructions can be extended for applications with protective PVMs. During software creation, large sequences of code (e.g., a function block) of the application can be replaced by a PointISA instruction. At run time, when the PVM encounters this instruction, it will interpret it according to the semantics of the replaced block.

In this scenario, further analysis is required to ensure that, in the case of a replacement attack, the interpretation of the PointISA instruction actually leads to a successful detection of the attack. This topic is a source of further research.

## 8.4 Overall Protection Synopsis

PointISA is designed to be used in conjunction with static protections and a protective PVM. The static protections safeguard the application and the PVM from analysis and tamper. At run time, the associated PVM instance continuously applies tamper-resistance techniques, making dynamic analysis harder. PointISA ensures that this protective PVM instance is not replaced by another PVM instance by an adversary attempting to obviate security measures. Thus, such a protective configuration lays the foundation for a robust tamper resistance execution environment.

## 9. RELATED WORK

Software applications are increasingly being used to perform critical tasks and their protection against malicious modifications is of paramount important. Much research has been done in the area of tamper resistance. Significant work in this area is based on the seminal research by Aucsmith [3]. Many hardware and software techniques are based on this work in some way [6, 16, 17, 19, 34, 8, 9, 25, 29, 10, 24, 18, 31], but all have a variety of drawbacks such as insufficient protections in real-world threat models, unreasonable performance overhead, or excessive hardware requirements.

Consequently, researchers have started using virtualization to improve program protections. A number of commercial PVMs have been created, such as VMProtect [32] and Themida [22]. These tools obscure the application using a secret instruction set architecture and at run time, execute the code using the just-in-time interpretation model [30].

System-level virtual machines have also been utilized to provide tamper resistance. The Terra system implements a trusted virtual machine monitor that can be used to create closed-box platforms where the developer tailors the software stack to meet security requirements [12]. However, this scheme requires hardware support to validate the software stack. Chen et al. discuss Overshadow, a system that uses a VMM to cryptographically isolate the application from the OS it is running on. This system offers another layer of tamper resistance, even in the case of OS compromise [7]. However, none of the systems mentioned thoroughly describe a replacement attack nor how to prevent them.

## 10. CONCLUSIONS

This paper has described a new technique, called PointISA, to prevent adversaries from carrying out replacement attacks against software that is protected using process-level virtual machines. PointISA tightly binds the application to be protected to the protective PVM by creating a new and unique meaning for certain instructions in the instruction set of the application. This mechanism is formally defined and thoroughly evaluated. We find that PointISA is capable of adequately protecting an application against replacement attacks while providing low overhead: only 8% slowdown over a typical PVM-protected application and can be tuned to meet the performance/security tradeoffs of the application.

## Acknowledgements

This research is supported by National Science Foundation (NSF) grant CNS-0811689, the Army Research Office (ARO) grant W911-10-0131, and the Air Force Research Laboratory (AFRL) contracts FA8650-10-C-7025 and FA8750-13-2-0096. The views and conclusions contained herein are those of the authors and should not be interpreted as necessarily representing the official policies or endorsements, either expressed or implied, of the NSF, AFRL, ARO, or the U.S. Government.

## 11. REFERENCES

[1] AHO, A. V., SETHI, R., AND ULLMAN, J. D. *Compilers: principles, techniques, and tools.* Addison-Wesley Longman Publishing Co., Inc., Boston, MA, USA, 1986.

[2] ANCKAERT, B., JAKUBOWSKI, M., AND VENKATESAN, R. Proteus: virtualization for diversified tamper-resistance. In *DRM '06: Proceedings of the ACM Workshop on Digital Rights Management* (New York, NY, USA, 2006), ACM Press, pp. 47–58.

[3] AUCSMITH, D. Tamper-resistant software: An implementation. In *Proceedings of the 1st International Workshop on Information Hiding* (London, U.K, 1996), Springer-Verlag, pp. 317–333.

[4] BELLARD, F. QEMU, a fast and portable dynamic translator. In *ATEC '05: Proceedings of the USENIX Annual Technical Conference* (Berkeley, CA, USA, 2005), USENIX Association, pp. 41–41.

[5] BIONDI, P., AND FABRICE, D. Silver needle in the skype. In *Black Hat Europe* (Amsterdam, the Netherlands, 2006).

[6] CHANG, H., AND ATALLAH, M. J. Protecting software code by guards. In *DRM '01: Revised Papers from the ACM CCS-8 Workshop on Security and Privacy in Digital Rights Management* (London, UK, UK, 2002), Springer-Verlag, pp. 160–175.

[7] CHEN, X., GARFINKEL, T., LEWIS, E. C., SUBRAHMANYAM, P., WALDSPURGER, C. A., BONEH, D., DWOSKIN, J., AND PORTS, D. R. Overshadow: A virtualization-based approach to retrofitting protection in commodity operating systems. In *ASPLOS XIII: Proceedings of the 13th International Conference on Architectural Support for Programming Languages and Operating Systems* (New York, NY, USA, 2008), ACM Press, pp. 2–13.

[8] COLLBERG, C., THOMBORSON, C., AND LOW, D. A taxonomy of obfuscating transformations. *University of Auckland Technical Report* (1997), 170.

[9] COLLBERG, C., THOMBORSON, C., AND LOW, D. Manufacturing cheap, resilient, and stealthy opaque constructs. In *POPL '98: Proceedings of the 25th ACM SIGPLAN-SIGACT Symposium on Principles of Programming Languages* (New York, NY, USA, 1998), ACM, pp. 184–196.

[10] COMPUTING GROUP, T. TCG TPM specification version 1.2 revisions 62-94.

[11] DE BUS, B., DE SUTTER, B., VAN PUT, L., CHANET, D., AND DE BOSSCHERE, K. Link-time optimization of ARM binaries. In *LCTES '04: Proceedings of the 2004 ACM SIGPLAN/SIGBED Conference on Languages, Compilers, and Tools for Embedded*

*Systems* (Washington D.C., U.S.A, 7 2004), ACM Press, pp. 211–220.

[12] GARFINKEL, T., PFAFF, B., CHOW, J., ROSENBLUM, M., AND BONEH, D. Terra: a virtual machine-based platform for trusted computing. In *SOSP '03: Proceedings of the 19th ACM Symposium on Operating Systems Principles* (New York, NY, USA, 2003), ACM Press, pp. 193–206.

[13] GHOSH, S. *Software Protection via Composable Process-level Virtual Machines*. PhD thesis, University of Virginia, Charlottesville, VA, USA, 2013.

[14] GHOSH, S., HISER, J., AND DAVIDSON, J. W. Replacement attacks against VM-protected applications. In *VEE '12: Proceedings of the 8th ACM SIGPLAN/SIGOPS Conference on Virtual Execution Environments* (New York, NY, USA, 2012), ACM, pp. 203–214.

[15] GHOSH, S., HISER, J. D., AND DAVIDSON, J. W. A secure and robust approach to software tamper resistance. In *IH '10: Proceedings of the 12th International Conference on Information Hiding* (Berlin, Heidelberg, 2010), Springer-Verlag, pp. 33–47.

[16] HORNE, B., MATHESON, L. R., SHEEHAN, C., AND TARJAN, R. E. Dynamic self-checking techniques for improved tamper resistance. In *Digital Rights Management Workshop* (London, U.K., 2001), pp. 141–159.

[17] JACOB, M., JAKUBOWSKI, M. H., AND VENKATESAN, R. Towards integral binary execution: Implementing oblivious hashing using overlapped instruction encodings. In *MM&Sec '07: Proceedings of the 9th Workshop on Multimedia & Security* (New York, NY, USA, 2007), ACM Press, pp. 129–140.

[18] LIE, D., THEKKATH, C., MITCHELL, M., LINCOLN, P., BONEH, D., MITCHELL, J., AND HOROWITZ, M. Architectural support for copy and tamper resistant software. In *ASPLOS '00: Proceedings of the 9th International Conference on Architectural Support for Programming Languages and Operating Systems* (New York, NY, USA, 2000), vol. 35, ACM Press, pp. 168–177.

[19] LINN, C., AND DEBRAY, S. Obfuscation of executable code to improve resistance to static disassembly. In *CCS '03: Proceedings of the 10th ACM Conference on Computer and Communications Security (CCS)* (Washington D.C., U.S.A, 2003), ACM Press, pp. 290–299.

[20] LUK, C.-K., COHN, R., MUTH, R., PATIL, H., KLAUSER, A., LOWNEY, G., WALLACE, S., REDDI, V. J., AND HAZELWOOD, K. Pin: Building customized program analysis tools with dynamic instrumentation. In *PLDI '05: Proceedings of the 2005 ACM SIGPLAN Conference on Programming Language Design and Implementation* (New York, NY, USA, 2005), ACM Press, pp. 190–200.

[21] OORSCHOT, P. C. v. Revisiting software protection. In *Information Security*, C. Boyd and W. Mao, Eds.,

vol. 2851 of *Lecture Notes in Computer Science*. Springer Berlin Heidelberg, 2003, pp. 1–13.

[22] OREANS TECHNOLOGIES. Themida. http://oreans.com/themida.php, 2009.

[23] OREONS TECHNOLOGY. Codevirtualizer. http://oreans.com/codevirtualizer.php, 2009.

[24] PEINADO, M., P.ENGLAND, AND Y.CHEN. An overview of NGSCB. *Trusted Computing, Chapter 4* (2005).

[25] PHIPPS, J. Physical protection devices. In *The protection of computer software—its technology and applications* (New York, NY, USA, 1989), Cambridge University Press, pp. 57–78.

[26] POPOV, I. V., DEBRAY, S. K., AND ANDREWS, G. R. Binary obfuscation using signals. In *SSYM '07: Proceedings of 16th USENIX Security Symposium-Volume 18* (Berkeley, CA, USA, 2007), USENIX Association, pp. 19:1–19:16.

[27] ROLLES, R. Unpacking virtualization obfuscators. In *WOOT '09: Proceedings of the 3rd USENIX Conference on Offensive Technologies* (Berkeley, CA, USA, 2009), USENIX Association, pp. 1–10.

[28] SCOTT, K., KUMAR, N., VELUSAMY, S., CHILDERS, B., DAVIDSON, J. W., AND SOFFA, M. L. Retargetable and reconfigurable software dynamic translation. In *CGO '03: Proceedings of the International Symposium on Code Generation and Optimization* (Washington D.C., U.S.A, 2003), IEEE Computer Society, pp. 36–47.

[29] SHIMIZU, K., NUSSER, S., PLOUFFE, W., ZBARSKY, V., SAKAMOTO, M., AND MURASE, M. Cell Broadband Engine: Processor security architecture and digital content protection. In *MCPS '06: Proceedings of the 4th ACM International Workshop on Contents Protection and Security* (New York, NY, USA, 2006), ACM, pp. 13–18.

[30] SMITH, J., AND NAIR, R. *Virtual Machines: Versatile Platforms for Systems and Processes (The Morgan Kaufmann Series in Computer Architecture and Design)*. Morgan Kaufmann Publishers Inc., San Francisco, CA, USA, 2005.

[31] SUH, G. E., CLARKE, D., GASSEND, B., VAN DIJK, M., AND DEVADAS, S. AEGIS: Architecture for tamper evident and tamper resistant software. In *SC '03: Proceedings of the 17th Annual International Conference on Supercomputing* (2003), ACM Press, pp. 161–171.

[32] VMPROTECT SOFTWARE. VMProtect. http://vmpsoft.com/, 2008.

[33] WHITEHEAD, A., AND RUSSELL, B. *Principia Mathematica*. No. v. 2 in Principia Mathematica. University Press, 1912.

[34] WURSTER, G., OORSCHOT, P. C. v., AND SOMAYAJI, A. A generic attack on checksumming-based software tamper resistance. In *SP '05: Proceedings of the 2005 IEEE Symposium on Security and Privacy* (Washington D.C., U.S.A, 2005), IEEE Computer Society, pp. 127–138.

# Gradient Based Prediction for Reversible Watermarking by Difference Expansion

Ioan-Catalin Dragoi
Electrical Engineering Dept.
Valahia University of
Targoviste, Romania
dragoi@valahia.ro

Dinu Coltuc
Electrical Engineering Dept.
Valahia University of
Targoviste, Romania
coltuc@valahia.ro

Ion Caciula
Electrical Engineering Dept.
Valahia University of
Targoviste, Romania
caciula@valahia.ro

## ABSTRACT

This paper proposes a novel predictor, EGBSW (Extended Gradient Based Selective Weighting), and investigates its usefulness in difference expansion reversible watermarking. EGBSW is inspired by GBSW, a causal predictor previously used in lossless image compression and known to outperform well-known predictors as the median edge detector (MED) or the gradient-adjusted predictor (GAP). The proposed predictor operates on a larger prediction context than the one of GBSW, namely a rectangular window of $4 \times 4$ pixels located around the pixel to be predicted. Similar to GBSW, the extended predictor computes the gradients on horizontal, vertical and diagonal directions and selects the smallest two gradients. Opposite to the classical predictor, EGSBW uses a set of four simple linear predictors associated with the four principal directions and computes the output value as a weighted sum between the predicted values corresponding to the selected gradients. The reversible watermarking scheme based on EGBSW appears to outperform not only the ones based on GBSW, MED or GAP, but also some recently proposed schemes based on the average on the rhombus context. Experimental results are provided.

## Categories and Subject Descriptors

D.2 [**Software Engineering**]: Software Arhitectures — *Information hiding*

## Keywords

reversible watermarking, difference expansion, adaptive predictors, MED, GAP, GBSW

## 1. INTRODUCTION

Reversible watermarking extracts the embedded data and recovers the original host signal/image without any distortion. Among the approaches developed so far for reversible watermarking on discrete images, much attention has been

devoted to histogram shifting (HS) and difference expansion (DE) based schemes.

The HS schemes use the histogram of a pixel based image feature (graylevel [1], prediction error [2], etc.,). A histogram bin is selected and the space for data embedding is created into an adjacent bin by shifting a part of the histogram. The embedding is performed into the pixels with the feature value equal to the selected bin. When the bit to be embedded is "0", the pixel is left unchanged, while for "1" the pixel is changed in order to move the feature into the free bin.

The DE schemes consider for embedding certain pixel based differences like the difference between pairs of pixels [3, 4], the prediction error [5, 6], etc. The pixels are modified in order to double the computed difference. This expansion clears the least significant bit of the difference and, implicitly, creates space for embedding one bit of data.

For both DE and HS reversible watermarking schemes, the most interesting results are obtained by using the prediction error. More precisely, the prediction error histogram is used in HS schemes and the prediction error is expanded for data embedding in DE schemes. The choice between a HS or a DE scheme is guided by the amount of data to be embedded. Thus, if one needs less space than the maximum of the prediction error histogram, the most efficient solution is the use of HS. It should be noticed that for embedding an amount less than the maximum histogram bin, both the shifting of the histogram and the embedding introduce errors of up to one graylevel. If more data should be embedded, the solution is the use of prediction error expansion.

This paper considers the prediction-error embedding reversible watermarking. Since the expansion is done by adding to the current pixel its prediction error, it clearly appears that the distortion introduced by watermarking depends on the prediction error. The lower the prediction error, the lower the distortion introduced by the reversible watermarking scheme.

As explained in the above paragraph, the improvement of the prediction is of great interest for reversible watermarking. The problem of prediction is also of great importance for lossless compression. Since a lot of research has already been devoted to prediction improvement for lossless compression, the reversible watermarking schemes have taken advantage of the results obtained so far. Such an example is the median edge detector (MED) predictor. MED is a nonlinear predictor that detects horizontal and vertical edges by using a context of three neighbors and estimates the value of the current pixels accordingly. MED was previously used in JPEG-LS [7] and then it was introduced in reversible watermarking in [5] and it is currently used in many schemes [6, 8] etc.

Improved results (i.e., lower distortions for the same embedding bit-rates) are obtained by using the gradient-adjusted predictor (GAP) instead of the MED predictor. The GAP algorithm, known from CALIC [9] (context based, adaptive, lossless image coding), outperforms MED. It uses a context of 7 pixels and selects the output based not only on the existence of a horizontal/vertical edge, but also on its strength. GAP is used in reversible watermarking in [8, 10], etc.

Lower estimation errors than the ones of MED and GAP and implicitly, better results are provided by the simple average on the rhombus composed of the four horizontal and vertical neighbors. The rhombus predictor is usually used in a two-stage embedding scheme [11]. The image pixels are split in two equal sets, diagonally connected, as the black and white squares of a chessboard. The watermark is embedded in two stages. The pixels of a set are marked by using for prediction the pixels of the other set. The prediction of the first set is done with original pixels, while the one for the second set uses already modified pixels. The overall very good performances of the simple average on the rhombus context are due to the fact that the prediction is performed on an entire neighborhood surrounding the pixel and not only on a part of it like for the normal causal or anticausal predictors. Most of the recent reversible watermarking schemes are based either on the rhombus predictor or an improved versions of the rhombus predictor ([12]-[14]). Two exceptions are [15] and [16]. In [15], the embedding is performed by shifting the interpolation error histogram. In [16], the embedding is performed into the interpolation error of [15] by using some specially designed binary codes.

This paper starts from a predictor previously proposed for lossless compression, GBSW (Gradient Based Selective Weighting) [17, 18]. The original GBSW is a causal predictor that estimates the current pixel by using a context of 10 neighbors. Since noncausal predictors are expected to provide better results, we define a noncausal GBSW predictor by extending the prediction context to a $4 \times 4$ window (15 pixels around the predicted pixel). Besides the enlargement of the context, the final stage of the prediction algorithm is modified as well. The usefulness of the newly defined predictor in DE reversible watermarking is investigated.

The outline of the paper is as follows. The standard GBSW predictor, the proposed EGBSW predictor and the corresponding DE reversible watermarking scheme are presented in Section 2. Experimental results and comparisons with other DE reversible watermarking schemes are presented in Section 3. Finally, the conclusions are presented in Section 4.

## 2. EXTENDED GBSW BASED DE REVERSIBLE WATERMARKING

### 2.1 The GBSW predictor

The gradient based selective weighting (GBSW) predictor was introduced in [17]. The intention of the authors was to develop a rather low cost predictor more efficient than other adaptive predictors like GAP, MED, etc. For instance, while MED and GAP compute the predicted value after the estimation of the edges in two directions, GSBW estimates four

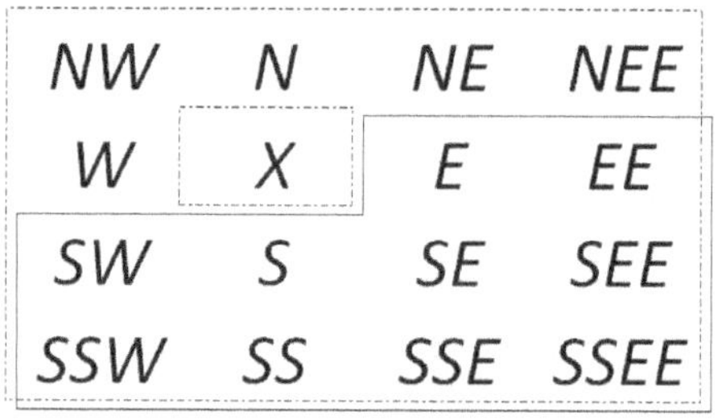

Figure 1: Prediction context for the anticausal GBSW (solid line) and the noncausal EGBSW (dashed line).

directions. Thus, GBSW can adapt to more complex edges or texture orientations than GAP or MED. More precisely, the average gradients on the four directions are first estimated. Then, the weights of the predictor are computed by considering only the contribution of the two smallest in rank gradients.

Next we present the anticausal version of GBSW. The predictor estimates the current pixel ($X = x_{i,j}$) by using a context of 10 pixels (Fig. 1) as follows. Pixel differences in horizontal ($d_h$), vertical ($d_v$), diagonal ($d_d$, 45°) and antidiagonal ($d_a$, 135°) directions are first computed:

$$d_h = 2\,|E - EE| + 2\,|S - SE| + 2\,|SE - SEE| \qquad (1)$$
$$+ 2\,|S - SW| + |SS - SSE| + |SS - SSW|$$

$$d_v = 2\,|S - SS| + 2\,|E - SE| + 2\,|SE - SSE| \qquad (2)$$
$$+ 2\,|SW - SSW| + |EE - SEE| + |SEE - SSEE|$$

$$d_d = 2\,|E - SEE| + 2\,|S - SSE| + |SE - SSEE| \qquad (3)$$
$$+ |SW - SS|$$

$$d_a = 2\,|EE - SE| + 2\,|S - SSW| + |S - E| \qquad (4)$$
$$+ |SS - SE|$$

The gradients in horizontal, vertical, diagonal and antidiagonal directions ($g_h$, $g_v$, $g_d$ and $g_a$) are further computed by averaging and rounding the differences computed above:

$$g_h = \left\lfloor \frac{d_h}{10} + 0.5 \right\rfloor, \quad g_v = \left\lfloor \frac{d_v}{10} + 0.5 \right\rfloor,$$
$$g_d = \left\lfloor \frac{d_d}{6} + 0.5 \right\rfloor, \quad g_a = \left\lfloor \frac{d_a}{6} + 0.5 \right\rfloor \qquad (5)$$

where $\lfloor x \rfloor$ represents the greatest integer less than or equal to $x$.

Only two gradients out of the four computed above are further considered, namely the two smallest ones. The directions of the two smallest gradients are used to select the two neighbors that participate in the computation of the predicted value, the gradients are also used as weights. More precisely, let $g_{(0)} \leq g_{(1)} \leq g_{(2)} \leq g_{(3)}$ be the set of gradients sorted in ascending order and let $x_0$, $x_1$, $x_2$ and $x_3$ be corresponding close neighbors of the predicted pixel, where $x_i$ corresponds to $g_{(i)}$. For the prediction context of the anticausal GBSW, the set of four close neighbors is $\{E, S, SE, SW\}$, where $E$ is the close neighbor of $X$ for horizontal, $S$ for vertical, $SE$ for diagonal and $SW$ for antidiagonal direction. For instance, if the minimum gradient $g_{(0)}$ is $g_h$, one has $x_0 = E$ and so on. With the above notations, the predicted value $\hat{x}$ is computed as a weighted average of $x_0$ and $x_1$:

$$\hat{x} = \left\lfloor \frac{g_{(0)}x_1 + g_{(1)}x_0}{g_{(0)} + g_{(1)}} + 0.5 \right\rfloor \qquad (6)$$

Since $g_{(0)} \leq g_{(1)}$, the weight corresponding to $x_0$ (the neighbor on the direction with the smallest average gradient) is larger than the the weight corresponding to the other neighbor, $x_1$.

## 2.2 Extended GBSW

The proposed extended noncausal GBSW predictor, EGBSW, operates on a context of 15 pixels placed in a rectangular window of $4 \times 4$ pixels as shown in Fig. 1. The prediction algorithm is similar to the original GBSW one: the gradients on the four directions are determined and the two smallest gradients are considered. Besides the enlargement of the prediction context, the proposed EGBSW scheme uses four linear predictors. The predicted value is computed by weighting not the two selected close neighbors but the results of the linear predictors corresponding to the selected directions.

In order to determine the gradients, for each direction, the differences between pairs of adjacent pixels with the considered orientation are first accumulated. As for the classical GBSW, the pairs close to the predicted pixel and with a good match of the orientation at hand are accumulated twice. Compared with equations (1)-(4), the computation of $d_h$, $d_v$, $d_d$ and $d_a$ is slightly different due to the extension of the prediction context:

$$d_h = 2|W - E| + 2|E - EE| + |NW - N| \qquad (7)$$
$$+ |N - NE| + |NE - NEE| + |SW - S|$$
$$+ |S - SE| + |SE - SEE|$$

$$d_v = 2|N - S| + 2|S - SS| + |NW - W| \qquad (8)$$
$$+ |W - SW| + |SW - SSW| + |NE - E|$$
$$+ |E - SE| + |SE - SSE|$$

$$d_d = 2|NW - SE| + 2|SE - SSEE| + |W - S| \qquad (9)$$
$$+ |S - SSE| + |N - E| + |E - SEE|$$
$$+ |SW - SS| + |NE - EE|$$

$$d_a = 2|NE - SW| + |W - N| + |S - E| \qquad (10)$$
$$+ |SS - SE| + |SE - EE| + |SSE - SEE|$$

The gradients $g_h$, $g_v$, $g_d$ and $g_a$ are immediately computed by averaging and rounding the differences computed above:

$$g_h = \left\lfloor \frac{d_h}{10} + 0.5 \right\rfloor, \quad g_v = \left\lfloor \frac{d_v}{10} + 0.5 \right\rfloor,$$
$$g_d = \left\lfloor \frac{d_d}{10} + 0.5 \right\rfloor, \quad g_a = \left\lfloor \frac{d_a}{7} + 0.5 \right\rfloor \qquad (11)$$

Each direction is next associated with a linear predictor. The predictors for the horizontal, vertical and diagonal directions are defined as follows:

$$\hat{x}_h = \left\lfloor \frac{W + E}{2} + 0.5 \right\rfloor, \quad \hat{x}_v = \left\lfloor \frac{N + S}{2} + 0.5 \right\rfloor \qquad (12)$$

$$\hat{x}_d = \left\lfloor \frac{2(NW + SE) + N + S + W + E}{8} + 0.5 \right\rfloor \qquad (13)$$

$$\hat{x}_a = \left\lfloor \frac{2(NE + SW) + N + S + W + E}{8} + 0.5 \right\rfloor \qquad (14)$$

The set of gradients is sorted and the resulting ordered set is associated with the predictions computed as above. Let $\hat{x}_0$, $\hat{x}_1$, $\hat{x}_2$ and $\hat{x}_3$ be the set of predicted values after reindexing. Finally, the two smallest values of the gradients, $g_{(0)}$ and $g_{(1)}$, and the predicted values in their directions, $\hat{x}_0$, $\hat{x}_1$, take part in the computation of the final result:

$$\hat{x} = \left\lfloor \frac{g_{(0)}\hat{x}_1 + g_{(1)}\hat{x}_0}{g_{(0)} + g_{(1)}} + 0.5 \right\rfloor \qquad (15)$$

For images that have perfectly uniform areas (not very common for natural images) $g_{(1)}$ must be replaced in (15) with $g_{(1)} + 1$ in order to prevent the case where both the weights are 0. This problem is also somewhat mitigated by the prediction context which uses both original and embedded pixels as it will be seen in Sect. 2.3.

The major difference between the classical GBSW and the newly proposed EGSBW is the use of predicted values corresponding to the selected directions instead of simple neighbors. The rhombus context (introduced in [11]) offers excellent prediction and it was shown in [12] that the results can be improved by only using the horizontal or vertical neighbors according to the corresponding gradients. Based on this, (12) appears as a natural extension from using the closest neighbor. The diagonal ($NW$, $SE$) and antidiagonal neighbors ($NE$, $SW$) are farther away from the central pixel and thus they offer a weaker prediction. The use of the rhombus neighborhood in (13) and (14) improves the prediction on all tested images.

We have tested several noncausal extensions of GBSW. The EGBSW appeared to provide the best results. In Section 3, results for two other extensions will be presented.

## 2.3 Reversible watermarking scheme

The proposed predictor is further integrated into a basic difference expansion reversible watermarking scheme with threshold control and flag bits. Let integer $T > 0$ be the threshold.

### 2.3.1 Marking

The embedding proceeds in raster-scan order, pixel by pixel, starting from the upper left corner. The pixels that do not have a full prediction context, namely the ones of the first row/column and the last two lines/columns are not considered for embedding. For each pixel $x_{i,j}$, the predicted value, $\hat{x}$, is computed by using the EGBSW predictor and the prediction error $p_e$ is calculated:

$$p_e = x_{i,j} - \hat{x}_{i,j} \qquad (16)$$

If $-T \leq p_e < T$ the data bit $b$ is embedded in $x_{i,j}$ as follows:

$$x'_{i,j} = x_{i,j} + p_e + b \qquad (17)$$

If the prediction error does not fulfill the conditions for pixel embedding, $x_{i,j}$ is shifted:

$$x'_{i,j} = \begin{cases} x_{i,j} + T & \text{if } p_e \geq T, \\ x_{i,j} - T + 1 & \text{if } p_e < -T. \end{cases} \qquad (18)$$

The pixel values are limited to the domain $[0, L - 1]$, where $L$ is the number of graylevels. For 8 bit images, $L = 256$. The flag bit scheme introduced in [5] is used in order to prevent overflow and underflow errors. $x'_{i,j}$ replaces $x_{i,j}$ in the host image only if $x'_{i,j} \in [0, L - 1]$. Also,

**Figure 2: Test images:** *Lena, Mandrill, Jetplane, Barbara, Tiffany* and *Boat*.

if $x'_{i,j} \in [0,T] \cup [255-T, 255]$, the flag bit "1" is inserted in the next embeddable pixel instead of $b$. If $x'_{i,j} \notin [0,255]$ the flag-bit "0" is inserted in the next embedded pixel.

### 2.3.2 Decoding

At decoding stage, pixels are processed in reverse raster-scan order. The first decoded pixel is the last one processed at embedding stage.

The scheme identifies the pixels that have not been modified because of overflow/underflow by using the flag bits. Thus, if $x'_{i,j} \in [T, L-1-T]$, the current pixel was modified (either embedded or shifted). Otherwise the data bit previously extracted is a flag bit. More precisely, if the flag-bit is "1" the current pixel was modified and if the flag-bit is "0" the current pixel was not modified by the watermarking scheme. The flag-bit is removed from the extracted data stream.

The scheme distinguishes between embedded and shifted pixels by checking the prediction error: if $p'_e \in [-2T, 2T]$ the pixel was embedded, otherwise it was shifted. The data bit $b$ is extracted from the prediction error of the embedded pixel:

$$b = p'_e \bmod 2 \qquad (19)$$

and the embedded pixel is restored to its original value:

$$x_{i,j} = x'_{i,j} - \left\lfloor \frac{p'_e}{2} \right\rfloor - b \qquad (20)$$

The shifted pixels are recovered by shifting into the opposite direction:

$$x_{i,j} = \begin{cases} x'_{i,j} - T & \text{if } p_e > 0, \\ x'_{i,j} + T & \text{if } p_e < 0. \end{cases} \qquad (21)$$

After the entire image is processed and all the pixels are restored, the embedded data is obtained by reversing the elements of the extracted bit stream. Finally we mention that a two step embedding scheme similar to the one of [11] was also tested, but failed to bring any improvement of the results.

## 3. EXPERIMENTAL RESULTS

In this section, experimental results for the proposed reversible watermarking scheme based on EGBSW prediction are presented. Six standard graylevel test images of $512 \times 512$

pixels are used. The test images (*Lena, Mandrill, Jetplane, Barbara, Tiffany* and *Boat*) are presented in Fig. 2.

The first experiment considers the zero-order entropy of prediction errors for the test images of Fig. 2. Besides MED, GAP, GBSW and the average on rhombus, three extensions of GBSW are investigated. The first predictor is SGBSW, namely a direct extension of GBSW that uses the close neighbors in the gradient directions in the computation of the final prediction results. The second version is AGBSW, a slightly more complex extension of GBSW that uses the average of the two close neighbors in the gradient directions (predictors similar to (7) are used for the diagonals) in the computation of the predicted value. The third version is the proposed EGBSW of Sect. 2.2. The results are presented in Table 1. From Table 1, one can see that the EGBSW predictor outperforms the standard causal predictors (MED, GAP, GBSW), the noncausal rhombus as well as the two other noncausal extensions of GBSW.

The second experiment presents results obtained for the scheme of Section 2.3 (with both the proposed EGBSW and the standard GBSW) and the well-known two-stages rhombus based scheme of [11] (Fig. 3). Let us first compare the results for the EGBSW with the ones for the GBSW predictor. As it can be seen in Fig. 3, EGBSW outperforms the GBSW predictor on all the six test images. The average improvement on the entire image set is of 1.7 dB. The largest average improvement on a single image is 2.63 dB (*Jetplane*) and the smallest one is 1.25 dB (*Boat*). The use of the appropriate neighbors for prediction is the key in obtaining a small prediction error. This can be seen on *Jetplane*, where the large uniform areas have caused a significant drop in prediction quality for GBSW. The GBSW predictor needs a clear direction to be detected in order to properly select the neighbors for prediction. While the ideal context for a uniform area is composed of the four nearest neighbors, GBSW uses at most two of these pixels. EGBSW does not have this weakness. If no horizontal or vertical direction with $g_{(0)} = 0$ is detected, all four rhombus neighbors take part in prediction. Notice that the uniform areas of *Jetplane* have a smaller variation between neighboring pixels, but are not perfectly uniformed.

Next, the EGBSW predictor is compared with the rhombus average of [11]. On two of the six test images, EGSW provides a significant gain in PSNR over [11]: 1.23 dB on *Barbara* and 1.25 dB on *Boat*. Both images have strong edges and textures with strong linear features easily detectable by the proposed predictor. An easily noticeable gain over the rhombus average is also obtained on *Mandrill* (an average of 0.7 dB) and *Tiffany* (0.69 dB). For the textures of *Mandrill* and *Tiffany* (formed of hair in both cases) the selection of the appropriate predictor is more difficult, since edges are not so well defined as the ones found into the previous images. The uniform nature of the last two images limits the effectiveness of EGBSW with respect to the rhombus average. Thus, the average gain is 0.41 dB on *Lena* and 0.3 dB on *Jetplane*. For the entire set of images, EGBSW outperforms the rhombus average with an average gain in PSNR of 0.76 dB.

We also compared the results of the proposed EGBSW prediction scheme with the ones published in some more recent papers [10], [12], [13], [14], [15], [16]. The results for three test images are presented in Table 2. EGBSW appears to outperform the other methods on textured images. This

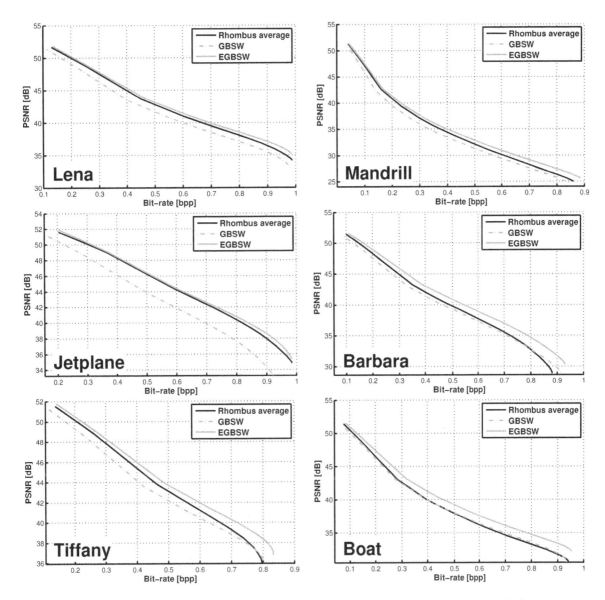

Figure 3: **Experimental results for the rhombus average of [11], the GBSW predictor of [17] and the proposed EGBSW predictor.**

can be easily noticed on *Mandrill*, where most of the schemes start with similar results (41.3 dB at 0.2 bpp), but the gap in performance between EGBSW and the other watermarking schemes becomes larger as the bit-rate increases (0.16 dB at 0.4 bpp, 0.41 dB at 0.6 bpp and 1 dB at 0.8 bpp). For images having large uniform areas, EGBSW provides improvement at large bit-rates.

## 4. CONCLUSIONS

A novel adaptive predictor, EGBSW, has been proposed and its usefulness in reversible watermarking has been investigated. The proposed predictor is a noncausal version of GBSW, a causal predictor previously proposed for lossless image compression. Beside the extension of the prediction context, the final stage of the prediction is modified as well. The use of EGSBW in reversible watermarking provides promising results. The difference expansion reversible watermarking based on EGBSW clearly outperforms its coun-

terparts based on GBSW, MED or GAP. Mainly on images with large textured areas, the DE scheme based on EGBSW appears to outperform some recently proposed schemes based on the average on the rhombus context.

## 5. ACKNOWLEDGMENTS

This work was supported by UEFISCDI Romania, project PN-II-PT-PCCA-2011-3.2-1162.

## 6. REFERENCES

[1] Z. Ni, Y. Q. Shi, N. Ansari, and W. Su. Reversible data hiding. *IEEE Trans. Circuits Syst. Video Technol.*, 16(3):354–362, 2006.

**Table 1: Prediction error entropy**

| Test image | MED | GAP | GBSW | Rhombus | SGBSW | AGBSW | EGBSW |
|---|---|---|---|---|---|---|---|
| Lena | 4.55 | 4.39 | 4.38 | 4.11 | 4.19 | 4 | 3.98 |
| Mandrill | 6.27 | 6.21 | 6.18 | 5.97 | 6.05 | 5.87 | 5.82 |
| Jetplane | 4.19 | 4.13 | 4.24 | 3.87 | 4.1 | 3.83 | 3.75 |
| Barbara | 5.48 | 5.39 | 5.09 | 5.14 | 4.95 | 4.81 | 4.83 |
| Tiffany | 4.43 | 4.3 | 4.24 | 4.13 | 4.07 | 3.91 | 3.9 |
| Boat | 5.1 | 4.98 | 4.95 | 4.81 | 4.8 | 4.62 | 4.59 |

**Table 2: PSNR versus bit-rate: comparison with some recent results.**

| Test image | Bit-rate [bpp] | [10] [dB] | [12] [dB] | [13] [dB] | [14] [dB] | [15] [dB] | [16] [dB] | EGBSW [dB] |
|---|---|---|---|---|---|---|---|---|
| Lena | 0.2 | 49.96 | 50.03 | 50.51 | 50.86 | 49.08 | - | 50.2 |
| | 0.4 | 44.23 | 45.11 | 44.8 | 45.27 | 43.59 | 44.58 | 45.32 |
| | 0.6 | 40.67 | 41.17 | 41.27 | 41.54 | 39.66 | 40.6 | 41.45 |
| | 0.8 | 37.56 | 38.14 | 38.18 | 38.48 | 36.74 | 36.88 | 38.51 |
| Mandrill | 0.2 | 39.78 | 41.31 | 41.06 | 41.62 | 40.33 | 39.72 | 41.33 |
| | 0.4 | 33.8 | 34.84 | 34.68 | 34.64 | 33.42 | 33.5 | 35 |
| | 0.6 | 29.43 | 30.51 | - | 30.03 | 29.21 | - | 30.92 |
| | 0.8 | 26.24 | 26.3 | - | 26.18 | 25.76 | - | 27.36 |
| Barbara | 0.2 | 48.86 | 48.7 | 49.41 | 48.54 | 47.9 | 43.49 | 48.94 |
| | 0.4 | 43.42 | 42.54 | 42.87 | 43.67 | 41.51 | 39.59 | 42.99 |
| | 0.6 | 37.78 | 38.29 | 38.61 | 39.03 | 37.47 | 36.05 | 38.9 |
| | 0.8 | 34.75 | 33.75 | 32.93 | 32.13 | 34.29 | 32.97 | 34.66 |

[2] H.-T. Wu and J. Huang. Reversible image watermarking on prediction errors by efficient histogram modification. *Signal Processing*, 92(12):3000–3009, 2012.

[3] J. Tian. Reversible data embedding using a difference expansion. *IEEE Trans. Circuits Syst. Video Technol.*, 13(8):890–896, 2003.

[4] D. Coltuc and J.-M. Chassery. Very fast watermarking by reversible contrast mapping. *IEEE Signal Processing Lett.*, 14(4):255–258, 2007.

[5] D. Thodi and J. Rodriguez. Expansion embedding techniques for reversible watermarking. *IEEE Trans. Image Processing*, 16(3):721–730, 2007.

[6] Y. Hu, H.-K. Lee, and J. Li. De-based reversible data hiding with improved overflow location map. *IEEE Trans. Circuits Syst. Video Technol.*, 19(2):250–260, 2009.

[7] M. Weinberger, G. Seroussi, and G. Sapiro. The loco-i lossless image compression algorithm: Principles and standardization into jpeg-ls. *IEEE Trans. Image Processing*, 9(8):1309–1324, 2000.

[8] D. Coltuc. Improved embedding for prediction-based reversible watermarking. *Trans.Inf. Forensics Security*, 6(3):873–882, 2011.

[9] X. Wu and N. Memon. Context-based, adaptive, lossless image coding. *IEEE Trans. on Commun.*, 45(4):437–444, 1997.

[10] X. Li, B. Yang, and T. Zeng. Efficient reversible watermarking based on adaptive prediction-error expansion and pixel selection. *Trans. Image Processing*, 20(12):3524–3533, 2011.

[11] V. Sachnev, H.-J. Kim, J. Nam, S. Suresh, and Y.-Q. Shi. Reversible watermarking algorithm using sorting and prediction. *IEEE Trans. Circuits Syst. Video Technol.*, 19(7):989–999, 2009.

[12] C. Dragoi and D. Coltuc. Improved rhombus interpolation for reversible watermarking by difference expansion. In *EUSIPCO'2012 Signal Processing Conference*, August 2012.

[13] B. Ou, Y. Zhao X. Li, and R. Ni. Reversible data hiding based on pde predictor. *Journal of Systems and Software*, 86(10):2700–2709, 2012.

[14] X. Li, B. Li, B. Yang, and T. Zeng. General framework to histogram-shifting-based reversible data hiding. *IEEE Trans. on Image Process.*, 22(6):2181–2191, 2013.

[15] H.-T. Wu and J. Huang. Reversible image watermarking on prediction errors by efficient histogram modification. *Signal Process.*, 92(12):3000–3012, 2012.

[16] W. Zhang, B. Chen, and N. Yu. Improving various reversible data hiding schemes via optimal codes for binary covers. *IEEE Trans. on Image Process.*, 21(16):2991–3003, 2012.

[17] J. Knezovic and M. Kovac. Gradient based selective weighting of neighboring pixels for predictive lossless image coding. In *25th International Conference on Information Technology Interfaces*, June 2003.

[18] R. M. Rad, A. Attar, and A. Shahbahrami. A predictive algorithm for multimedia data compression. *Multimedia Systems*, 19(2):103–115, 2013.

# On the Combination of Randomized Thresholds and Non-Parametric Boundaries to Protect Digital Watermarks against Sensitivity Attacks

Erwin Quiring
Dept. of Information Systems
University of Münster
Leonardo-Campus 3
48149 Münster, Germany
erwin.quiring@wwu.de

Pascal Schöttle
Dept. of Information Systems
University of Münster
Leonardo-Campus 3
48149 Münster, Germany
pascal.schoettle@wwu.de

## ABSTRACT

With unlimited access to a watermark detector, an attacker can use sensitivity attacks to remove the watermark of a digital medium. Randomized detectors and non-parametric decision boundaries are two ways of defending the watermark against these attacks. However, both approaches have their vulnerabilities when used individually. The first enables working with the randomized region boundary. The second still provides reliable information. This paper presents a combination of these two approaches to overcome their shortcomings. We develop a detector that has a randomized region with non-parametric outer boundaries. To empirically evaluate our combination, we apply two attack algorithms: Kalker's attack and Blind Newton Sensitivity Attack. The combination is more effective than the non-parametric boundary alone and comparable with using only the randomized threshold. In addition, we increase security by preventing attacks against the outer boundaries.

## Categories and Subject Descriptors

D.2.11 [**Software Architectures**]: Information hiding

## General Terms

Security, Algorithms, Theory

## Keywords

Digital Watermarks; Sensitivity Attacks; Randomized Decision Boundaries; Security

## 1. INTRODUCTION AND MOTIVATION

The need to protect digital media against unauthorized distribution or manipulation has led to digital watermarks being imperceptible and inseparable information [5]. Watermarks are applicable to various media like image, video or audio files and ideally survive unintentional changes and intentional attacks. For example, a DVD player can recognize copyrighted content due to a watermark and refuse the unauthorized playback.

In this example, the DVD player represents a black box watermark detector, giving only a binary decision on watermark presence by accepting or refusing the playback [4]. Internally, we can view the detection process as a geometrical process. Each medium corresponds to a point in a high-dimensional space [5]. The detector differentiates between unwatermarked and watermarked media by dividing this space into two subspaces – one for the watermark's absence, one for its presence. As both subspaces represent a different detector decision, we call the dividing area between them decision boundary. By determining which subspace a medium is in, the detector decides on watermark absence or presence and finally returns a binary decision [5].

However, this binary output – together with an unlimited access to the watermark detector – still provides a sufficient information leakage for an attack, called sensitivity attack [4]. In this case, an attacker aims at the decision boundary. If a medium is slightly changed in this area, it possibly crosses that boundary and causes a different detector decision. The information through the respective changes – combined with the detector outputs – are still enough to calculate an unwatermarked medium. Note that the attacker can easily remove the watermark with large modifications, but in the example of the DVD player, this might produce an unwatchable film. Therefore, the attacker tries to find a position on the decision boundary with the smallest possible changes [4].

A randomized detector is one countermeasure. As sensitivity attacks exploit the decision boundary, the detector can distort the calculations, for example, by returning random decisions in a region along that boundary [13]. Despite this randomized region, an attacker can remove the watermark. But now it is not guaranteed anymore that the resulting medium has the smallest possible changes [13].

Another way of defending the watermark is to complicate the decision boundary by a non-parametric curve. Thereby, for example, gradient descent based attacks do not necessarily converge to the minimal changes [3]. Furthermore, an attacker cannot estimate the boundary itself [15].

However, both approaches have their vulnerabilities. Although a randomized region disturbs attack algorithms with misinformation, a weak point still remains: the outer boundaries. In this area, the detector again returns deterministic decisions. Thus, an attacker can move to these boundaries and, for example, estimate their course. Also, a detector with a non-parametric decision boundary still returns deterministic decisions, so that the attacker can adapt an algorithm to exploit the envelope of the non-parametric boundary [3].

By combining both countermeasures, we overcome their shortcomings and reduce the attack surface. We develop a detector that has a randomized region with non-parametric outer boundaries. Inside the randomized region, the detector only returns unreliable information. The non-parametric outer boundaries complicate the attempt to circumvent the randomized region by attacking these boundaries.

The paper is organized as follows: Section 2 reviews related work. Section 3 introduces the watermark model and explains the randomized threshold as well as the non-parametric decision boundary. On this basis, Section 4 introduces our proposed combination. Section 5 presents the experimental results and a discussion of these. Finally, Section 6 draws a conclusion and gives directions for future research.

## 2. RELATED WORK

Different approaches to create randomized detectors are discussed in the literature: Linnartz and van Dijk use a randomized threshold to create a randomized region [13], whereas Choubassi and Moulin randomly divide the medium into subsets and aggregate different detector functions on the respective subsets [6]. Also, Venkatesan and Jakubowski randomly divide the medium into subsets, but calculate a correlation over each subset and return their median [16]. Venturini records previous medium inputs with a hash table and returns a random decision in the case of a re-entered similar or equal input [17]. Recently, Barni et al. also propose a stateful detector [1]. This so-called smart detector analyses the sequence of inputs to determine whether the detector is currently subject to an oracle attack. Then, the detector has different reaction possibilities, for example, switch to a more convoluted detection function or the output of random decisions.

Different watermarking techniques complicate the decision boundary: the asymmetric watermarking technique in [10] creates quadratic boundaries. Through the detector function for generalized Gaussian distributions from [11], the watermark detection region consists of several areas as long as the right parameters are used [3]. The watermarking technique JANIS [9] applies $N$-th order polynomial detector functions. All theses approaches have in common that an attacker can estimate the boundary from a finite number of known points [15]. Mansour and Tewfik prevent this attack by using non-parametric decision boundaries [15].

Both randomized detectors and complex boundaries are vulnerable. For instance, the attack by Kalker [12] circumvents a randomized region. The algorithm creates a circle of vectors starting in a centre in the randomized region and for the most part ending outside this region. Then, it averages the vectors and estimates the normal vector to the decision boundary. The Blind Newton Sensitivity Attack (BNSA) [3] attacks complex boundaries by using iterative methods such as Newton's method or gradient descent to find the minimum distance to the decision boundary. We briefly describe both attacks in Appendix A.

In order to reduce that attack surface, we choose the randomized threshold as basis for our combination, since it initially provides the easiest model to randomize detector decisions, but also complicates the attack, as the other strategies do. We combine this with non-parametric boundaries, since they are not calculable due to their complexity.

Note, Furon and Bas also apply randomized detectors and complex boundaries for their watermarking technique "broken arrows" [8], but we present a more general technique which is also suitable to expand existing watermarking schemes.

## 3. MODEL AND BASIC COUNTER-MEASURES

This section introduces the background to develop our combination: the watermark model and its notation, randomized thresholds, and non-parametric boundaries.

### 3.1 Notation and Watermark Model

We denote the original media $\boldsymbol{x}$, the watermark $\boldsymbol{w}$ and the watermarked media $\boldsymbol{y}$ as column vectors in $\mathbb{R}^n$ with $n$ as the number of medium samples. To highlight column vectors, we use bold face symbols.

For embedding, we use the additive spread spectrum technique [5] and add $\boldsymbol{w}$ with a strength parameter $\lambda$ to $\boldsymbol{x}$, resulting in $\boldsymbol{y} = \boldsymbol{x} + \lambda\boldsymbol{w}$. Furthermore, the vector $\boldsymbol{t}$ represents the unintentional and intentional changes on $\boldsymbol{y}$. This results in the final vector $\boldsymbol{z} = \boldsymbol{y} + \boldsymbol{t}$.

For the detection of the watermark, we apply a correlation-based detector using the following detector function to map the $\mathbb{R}^n$ vector $\boldsymbol{z}$ to an index in $\mathbb{R}$:

$$f(\boldsymbol{z}) = \frac{1}{n}\,\boldsymbol{w} \bullet \boldsymbol{z}. \tag{1}$$

Comparing this function value with a detector threshold $\eta$, the watermark detector decides on watermark presence and returns a binary decision. Geometrically, the different constellations of vector components mapping to $\eta$ form a decision boundary in $\mathbb{R}^n$. Thus, the boundary course depends on the detector function and divides $\mathbb{R}^n$ in two subspaces, the rejection region $R_0$ (watermark absence) and detection region $R_1$ (watermark presence):

$$R_0 = \{\boldsymbol{z} \in \mathbb{R}^n \mid f(\boldsymbol{z}) \leqslant \eta\}, \tag{2}$$
$$R_1 = \{\boldsymbol{z} \in \mathbb{R}^n \mid f(\boldsymbol{z}) > \eta\}. \tag{3}$$

In our model, we get a linear hyperplane as decision boundary which is orthogonal to $\boldsymbol{w}$ and divides $\mathbb{R}^n$ into two half-spaces. Finally, by determining the position of $\boldsymbol{z}$, the detector decides on the absence ($\boldsymbol{z} \in R_0$) or presence ($\boldsymbol{z} \in R_1$) of the watermark.

An attack tries to find a vector $\boldsymbol{t}$ with the smallest possible length to reach an unwatermarked position on the boundary. The next sections briefly introduce two countermeasures against this attack.

### 3.2 Randomized Threshold

To distort the attack calculations with misinformation, the detector can randomize the threshold where the detector decides on watermark presence or absence. For example, Linnartz and van Dijk create an interval $I = [\eta - a, \eta + b]$ with $a, b > 0$ [13]. Given that $f(\boldsymbol{z}) \in I$, the detector returns a random binary decision. This interval and the detector function in Equation (1) form a linear randomized region in the $n$-dimensional space (Figure 1(a)).

The binary decision depends on a monotonically increasing probability function $p$ assigning each $f(\boldsymbol{z})$ value in $I$ a probability that the detector assumes the watermark's presence. Hence, the closer the medium lies to $R_1$, the higher the probability that the detector assumes the presence. This reduces the false positives [13]. Linnartz and van Dijk derive such a function $p$ that also minimizes the information leakage by the detector output [13].

## 3.3 Non-Parametric Decision Boundaries

The complexity of the decision boundary has an influence on attack success. For example, the BNSA cannot ensure the global optimum without a convex boundary [3]. In the worst case, the attacker can estimate the boundary itself and calculate the shortest projection out of $R_1$ for each medium with the same watermark key [15]. A non-parametric boundary prevents this attack, since the boundary cannot be estimated from a finite number of known boundary points [15].

We create a new detector function which uses a fractal as non-parametric decision boundary. We choose fractals due to their simple recursive generation. However, even in our simple watermark model, we have to replace an $(n-1)$-dimensional linear hyperplane with a matching multidimensional fractal. To decrease the complexity, Mansour and Tewfik map the hyperplane to a new one-dimensional decision boundary by splitting the detector function in Equation (1) in two parts [15]. The first part calculates the function value of the even indices, the second one of the uneven indices. As a result, we get the following new correlation-based detector function [15]:

$$T_1(\boldsymbol{z}) = \frac{2}{n} \sum_i \boldsymbol{z}[2i] \cdot \boldsymbol{w}[2i] \qquad (4)$$

$$T_2(\boldsymbol{z}) = \frac{2}{n} \sum_i \boldsymbol{z}[2i+1] \cdot \boldsymbol{w}[2i+1]. \qquad (5)$$

The different constellations of $T_1(\boldsymbol{z})$ and $T_2(\boldsymbol{z})$, whose arithmetic value yields the old detector threshold $\eta$, form the coordinates of the new boundary. If the resulting point $T(\boldsymbol{z}) = (T_1(\boldsymbol{z}), T_2(\boldsymbol{z}))$ lies above this boundary, we assume the watermark's presence, otherwise its absence.

Next, a fractal like the Triadic Koch Curve [14] can replace the boundary, which is computationally easier than the replacement by a higher-dimensional fractal. And this also leads to a non-parametric course of the previous $(n-1)$-dimensional boundary [15]. Figure 1(b) shows this process: We replace the newly created one-dimensional linear boundary with an adapted Triadic Koch Curve such that the linear boundary is tangent to the Koch Curve's midpoint. Thus, the Koch Curve oscillates near the linear boundary, permitting a fair comparison of the attack results between the fractalized boundary and the linear hyperplane introduced earlier.

## 4. COMBINATION OF EXISTING COUNTERMEASURES

This section illustrates how both countermeasures can be combined to overcome their shortcomings. First, we explain the gained security advantages and then describe the necessary changes to the detector function.

## 4.1 Security Advantages

Even if a non-parametric boundary complicates the attack, it still provides reliable detector decisions. Thereby, for example, the attacker can adapt the BNSA to concentrate on the boundary's envelope [3]. Although this does not guarantee the global optimum, the BNSA can still find a short path out of $R_1$ [3].

A randomized region prevents this attack, since the detector distorts the attack calculations by returning misinformation. But now, its outer boundaries are the weak point. In this area, the detector again returns deterministic decisions, so that an attacker can move to these boundaries. By slightly changing the medium and comparing the detector decisions, the attacker can limit the boundary's position.

Therefore, its estimation might still be possible. As the randomized decisions distort the estimated boundary points, many more of them are needed compared to the boundary estimation with a deterministic detector. However, for example, in the case of a linear outer boundary, the number of necessary points still remains linear in $n$. Thus, the attacker calculates the shortest projection to this boundary and scales this direction to a position in $R_0$. Although the decisions are random, the result is still a position in $R_0$ with the smallest possible medium changes.

Therefore we employ non-parametric curves as outer boundaries. By this combination, the attacker cannot use the outer boundary instead of the previous decision boundary to perform a sensitivity attack.

## 4.2 Practical Realization

In order to apply the proposed combination, we map the $(n-1)$-dimensional decision boundary to a new one-dimensional boundary and replace it with an adapted triadic Koch Curve, as described in Section 3.3. To use the fractal as a decision boundary, we save only the fractal coordinates such that, when connected by line segments, the coordinates describe the complete route of the fractal.

Then, we create the randomized region around the Koch Curve by defining the outer boundaries. For reasons of simplicity, we derive them from the decision boundary which is diagonally shifted upwards or downwards to create each outer boundary. Figure 1(c) shows the resulting randomized region.

To compare the attack results between the randomized threshold and our combination in Section 5, we need to adjust the area of both randomized regions. When using the randomized threshold, we add $b$ to the detector threshold $\eta$ to create the random interval $I$. With the combination, we divide $f(\boldsymbol{z})$ into two parts $(T_1(\boldsymbol{z}), T_2(\boldsymbol{z}))$. Therefore, we need to add $b$ to $\eta$ on both axes to create a comparable random area. Hence, we shift the upper outer boundary exactly so far that the point $(\eta + b, \eta + b)$ lies on that boundary. As we shift diagonally, if the midpoint of the decision boundary is $(\eta, \eta)$, we only have to ensure that the midpoint of the upper outer boundary is $(\eta + b, \eta + b)$ and the one of the lower outer boundary is $(\eta - a, \eta - a)$. Thereby, the fractalized outer boundaries in $n$-dimensional space are located near the corresponding outer boundaries of the randomized threshold.

In order to decide on watermark presence, we calculate $T(\boldsymbol{z})$ and determine its position relative to the fractalized outer boundaries. We propose a change of basis of the coordinate system, so that the one-dimensional linear boundary and the Koch Curve's envelope run parallel to the x-axis. Thereby, we can often restrict the detection process to the coordinates of one axis, simplifying the computation drastically. Figure 1(d) shows the randomized region with the new basis.

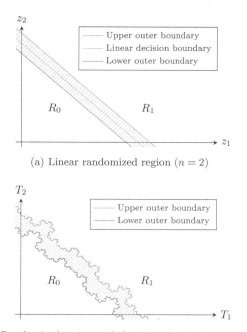

(a) Linear randomized region ($n = 2$)

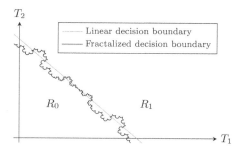

(b) Newly created one-dimensional decision boundary replaced by an adapted Triadic Koch Curve

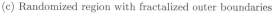

(c) Randomized region with fractalized outer boundaries

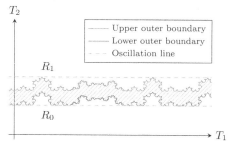

(d) Randomized region with fractalized outer boundaries and with new basis

Figure 1: The creation process of a randomized region with non-parametric outer boundaries.

At first, we verify whether $T(\boldsymbol{z})$ lies outside the area where the outer boundaries of the randomized region oscillate [15] – illustrated by the two dashed lines in Figure 1(d). Comparing the $y$ coordinates between $T(\boldsymbol{z})$ and the dashed lines leads to a simple decision about the position.

Inside the area between the dashed lines, we determine whether $T(\boldsymbol{z})$ lies above or below the respective outer boundaries. In doing so, we ascertain whether $T(\boldsymbol{z})$ lies in $R_1$, the randomized region or $R_0$. Based on the intersection idea of [15], we begin with the upper outer boundary and count its intersections with a vertical line segment which joins $T(\boldsymbol{z})$ to a reference point in $R_0$. Using a vertical line accelerates detection because we can focus on the line segments having an x-coordinate in the immediate vicinity of $T_1(\boldsymbol{z})$. Only these can intersect with the vertical line. If the number of intersections is uneven, $T(\boldsymbol{z})$ lies above the upper outer boundary and therefore in $R_1$. In the even case, the detector repeats the process with the lower outer boundary. If this intersection count is uneven, the detector deduces a position in the randomized region. Otherwise, $T(\boldsymbol{z})$ lies in $R_0$.

In the case of a randomized region position, the detector employs a pseudorandom number generator (PRNG) with Bernoulli distribution to get the binary random output. In order to still use the probability function $p$ from Section 3.2, we pass a function value specifying the position of $\boldsymbol{z}$ in the randomized region, for example the relative position of $T(\boldsymbol{z})$ on a vertical line segment joining the outer boundaries.

In addition, a seed is required to initialize the PRNG. By using a hash value of $\boldsymbol{z}$, the detector always returns the same decision for a respective medium [13]. This prevents, for example, the attack by Choubassi and Moulin creating a "p-boundary" through repeated input of the same medium [7].

Overall, the resulting detection process shows that the complexity in implementing and using the combination does not strongly increase – compared to the countermeasures

used individually. Once the outer boundaries are calculated, the detector can store them for reuse. And due to the change of basis, only a few fractal coordinates in each detector call are necessary to determine the position of $T(\boldsymbol{z})$.

## 5. EXPERIMENTAL RESULTS

This section practically examines the influence of each presented countermeasure – both the individual use of a randomized threshold or a non-parametric boundary and their combination – against two selected attack algorithms. Kalker's algorithm successfully attacks a randomized threshold [12], whereas the BNSA is applicable against a non-parametric boundary [3]. Hence, we verify our proposed combination with an attack scenario aiming at both individual parts.

Our set-up is as follows: We employ an adapted version of Kalker's attack which estimates the normal vector to the decision boundary (see Appendix A.1 for more details). Besides, we use the gradient-based version of BNSA (as described in Appendix A.2) whose number of iterations is limited to four, since its attack results converge after a few iterations or already indicate the countermeasure's influence. The experiments are carried out on 225 128x128 pixel natural grayscale images ($n = 16384$) cropped from 512x512 pixel images of the BOSS image database [2].

We use the Peak Signal To Noise Ratio (PSNR) to measure the quality changes on the original image due to the watermarking (ratio between $\boldsymbol{x}$ and $\boldsymbol{y}$) and due to the attacks (ratio between $\boldsymbol{x}$ and $\boldsymbol{z}$). A higher value indicates a stronger match.

Table 1 shows the average value over all images for the different constellations of attacks and countermeasures (including values for no defence mechanism). The increase for each constellation is attributable to the watermarking

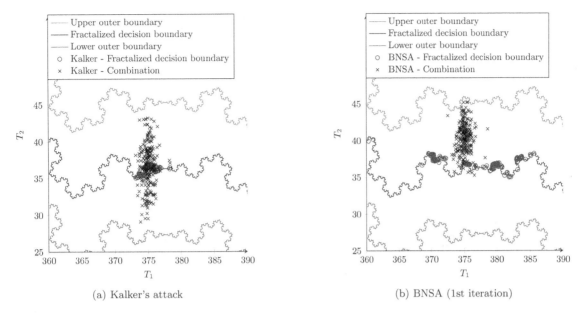

| | (a) Kalker's attack | (b) BNSA (1st iteration) |

Figure 2: Distribution of detector function values $T(z)$.

| | $\varnothing$PSNR($x$,$y$) | $\varnothing$PSNR($x$,$z$) | | | | |
|---|---|---|---|---|---|---|
| | | Kalker's | BNSA - Iterations | | | |
| Countermeasure | | attack | 1. | 2. | 3. | 4. |
| No counterm. | 14.826 | 15.869 | 16.047 | 16.101 | 16.158 | 16.172 |
| Random. thresh. | 14.826 | 15.864 | 15.615 | 15.572 | 15.596 | 15.606 |
| Fractaliz. bound. | 14.826 | 15.868 | 15.933 | 15.924 | 15.953 | 15.965 |
| Combination | 14.826 | 15.847 | 15.647 | 15.609 | 15.598 | 15.602 |

Table 1: The average PSNR($x$, $y$) and PSNR($x$, $z$) of all images for each attack and each countermeasure

model, as an attack reverses the changes during the watermarking, leading to a closer position to $x$. As the sensitivity attack's aim is to create an unwatermarked medium with the smallest possible changes, the increase is small. While the BNSA performs worse in the case of a randomized threshold or a combination, the results of Kalker's algorithm remain constant for each countermeasure.

In addition, Figure 2(a) and 2(b) show the distribution of $T(z)$ with the respective attacks. When using fractalized boundaries, the BNSA positions are widely spread horizontally, whereas the positions of Kalker's attack are not. This is because the BNSA explores the decision boundary with various step lengths during the gradient descent. In contrast, Kalker's attack is based on the normal vector and therefore tests and uses a single boundary position.

When employing random decisions additionally, the function values are also spread vertically, indicating the calculation errors of the attack algorithms. Most of the BNSA results lie in the upper part of the randomized region, because the algorithm tries, with various step lengths, different positions in the assumed descent direction. Random decisions distort the following bisections scaling each position to the supposed decision boundary, so that the results are spread vertically. As soon as the algorithm obtains a result in the upper part of the randomized region with a smaller distance to $y$ than the current solution, the attack will choose this new solution. Thus, the BNSA results are closer to $R_1$.

| | BNSA - Iterations | | | |
|---|---|---|---|---|
| Countermeasure | 1. | 2. | 3. | 4. |
| No counterm. | 615013 | 624066 | 631675 | 633262 |
| Random. thresh. | 633174 | 741891 | 859030 | 951677 |
| Fractaliz. bound. | 613995 | 620283 | 622892 | 624249 |
| Combination | 633431 | 763363 | 876989 | 978486 |

Table 2: Average detector calls of all images by BNSA

Furthermore, for BNSA, Table 2 shows the average detector calls over all images, highlighting the increase in attack effort when randomized decisions are used. In contrast, Kalker's algorithm has a fixed number of detector calls – one call for each circle vector (which is in our case one order of magnitude less than the number of calls of BNSA).

Taking all results into account, the attack results for the randomized threshold and the combination are comparable. Slight differences between the results are due to the different course of their outer boundaries, although these are close to each other due to the adjustment in Section 4.2. Compared to the fractalized boundary or linear hyperplane (no defence mechanism), they perform best – with lower PSNR values and higher detector calls.

Examining the attacks, the BNSA is most affected by random decisions, since it calculates the gradient within the randomized region which results in permanently incorrect interval bisections. In this way, the calculation errors add up. The gradient is no longer reliable. More interval bisections and therefore more detector calls are necessary.

Kalker's attack creates a vector circle around the randomized region and as the largest part is outside this region, the attack estimates a nearly correct normal vector to the decision boundary. Only the attempt to subtract the normal vector with a scaling factor from $z$ to obtain a boundary position leads to errors – the direction is approximately correct.

Together with our simple watermarking model, this attack provides useful insights into how a watermarking scheme should be designed to increase its security with our combination. The success of Kalker's attack depends on the envelope of the randomized region. Even if we employ non-parametric outer boundaries, the envelope remains linear so that a large vector circle is not influenced. This motivates a watermarking scheme with a more complex boundary course, e.g. a polynomial of degree $N$ [9] which then will be replaced by the randomized region. Thus, the normal vector from a starting position does not necessarily correspond to the shortest possible path from $z$ out of $R_1$.

## 6. CONCLUSION AND OUTLOOK

This paper explores how combining a randomized threshold and a non-parametric boundary influences sensitivity attacks. To gain first important findings, we use a simple watermark model: a correlation-based detector which results in a linear decision boundary. On this basis, we develop our combination: We map the higher-dimensional linear boundary to an one-dimensional linear boundary, since the non-parametric boundary creation and the detection process are easier in this projected region than in the previous space. Finally, this linear boundary is replaced by a randomized region with non-parametric outer boundaries.

We use Kalker's attack [12] (in a slightly adapted version [5]) and the Blind Newton Sensitivity Attack [3] to examine the individual use of the two countermeasures as well as their combination. To our knowledge, there are no other works so far which precisely compare the individual use with the combination. When one of the individual countermeasures is used, the attack performs worse, but the randomized threshold is more effective than the non-parametric boundary; when the two countermeasures are used in combination, the decrease in attack performance is comparable to the individual use of the randomized threshold. Therefore, combining the countermeasures does not decrease attack performance further, but it increases security by preventing attacks against the outer boundaries, without being significantly more difficult to implement and use.

As an attacker can aim at the envelope of the randomized region, future work may include the examination of our combination with extended watermarking schemes to achieve a complex envelope of the randomized region. Another open question is the possibility to combine more elaborate randomized detectors with non-parametric boundaries.

As can be seen by these examples, our paper is only the first step. In contrast to Choubassi and Moulin, we do not write off randomized detectors, yet. Furthermore, the choice by Furon and Bas to use randomized thresholds and complex boundaries for "broken arrows" [8] gives us confidence that future work on this topic can help to increase the security of watermarks.

## Acknowledgement

We thank Patrick Bas for helpful advice and Deutsche Forschungsgemeinschaft (DFG) for financial support.

## 7. REFERENCES

[1] M. Barni, P. Comesaña-Alfaro, F. Pérez-González, and B. Tondi. Are you threatening me?: Towards smart detectors in watermarking. In A. M. Alattar, N. D. Memon, and C. D. Heitzenrater, editors, *Media Watermarking, Security, and Forensics 2014*, volume 9028 of *Proceedings of SPIE*, pages 902806–902806. 2014.

[2] P. Bas, T. Filler, and T. Pevný. Break our steganographic system — the ins and outs of organizing BOSS. In T. Filler, T. Pevný, S. Craver, and A. Ker, editors, *Information Hiding*, volume 6958 of *Lecture Notes in Computer Science*, pages 59–70. Springer, 2011.

[3] P. Comesaña, L. Pérez-Freire, and F. Pérez-González. Blind newton sensitivity attack. *IEE Proceedings on Information Security*, 153(3):115–125, 2006.

[4] I. J. Cox and J.-P. M. G. Linnartz. Public watermarks and resistance to tampering. In *IEEE International Conference on Image Processing*, pages 26–29, 1997.

[5] I. J. Cox, M. Miller, J. Bloom, J. Fridrich, and T. Kalker. *Digital watermarking and steganography.* The Morgan Kaufmann Series in Multimedia Information and Systems. Morgan Kaufmann, 2002.

[6] M. El Choubassi and P. Moulin. On the fundamental tradeoff between watermark detection performance and robustness against sensitivity analysis attacks. In E. J. Delp III and P. W. Wong, editors, *Security, Steganography, and Watermarking of Multimedia Contents VIII*, volume 6072 of *Proceedings of SPIE*, pages 1–12. 2006.

[7] M. El Choubassi and P. Moulin. Sensitivity analysis attacks against randomized detectors. In *IEEE International Conference on Image Processing*, volume 2, pages 129–132, 2007.

[8] T. Furon and P. Bas. Broken arrows. *EURASIP Journal on Information Security*, 2008:1–13, 2008.

[9] T. Furon, B. Macq, N. Hurley, and G. Silvestre. JANIS: Just another N-order side-informed watermarking scheme. In *IEEE International Conference on Image Processing*, volume 3, pages 153–156, 2002.

[10] T. Furon, I. Venturini, and P. Duhamel. Unified approach of asymmetric watermarking schemes. In E. J. Delp III and P. W. Wong, editors, *Security and Watermarking of Multimedia Contents III*, volume 4314 of *Proceedings of SPIE*, pages 269–279. 2001.

[11] J. R. Hernandez, M. Amado, and F. Pérez-González. DCT-domain watermarking techniques for still images: Detector performance analysis and a new structure. *IEEE Transactions on Image Processing*, 9(1):55–68, 2000.

[12] T. Kalker. Watermark estimation through detector observations. In *IEEE Benelux Signal Processing Symposium*, pages 119–122, 1998.

[13] J.-P. M. G. Linnartz and M. van Dijk. Analysis of the sensitivity attack against electronic watermarks in images. In D. Aucsmith, editor, *Information Hiding*,

volume 1525 of *Lecture Notes in Computer Science*, pages 258–272. Springer, 1998.

[14] B. B. Mandelbrot. *Die fraktale Geometrie der Natur.* Birkhäuser Verlag, 1987.

[15] M. F. Mansour and A. H. Tewfik. Improving the security of watermark public detectors. In *14th International Conference on Digital Signal Processing*, volume 1, pages 59–66, 2002.

[16] R. Venkatesan and M. H. Jakubowski. Randomized detection for spread-spectrum watermarking: Defending against sensitivity and other attacks. In *IEEE International Conference on Acoustics, Speech, and Signal Processing*, volume 2, pages 9–12, 2005.

[17] I. Venturini. Oracle attacks and covert channels. In M. Barni, I. J. Cox, T. Kalker, and H.-J. Kim, editors, *4th International Workshop on Digital Watermarking*, volume 3710 of *Lecture Notes in Computer Science*, pages 171–185. Springer, 2005.

# APPENDIX

## A. ATTACK ALGORITHMS

To understand the purpose of the countermeasures, we explain (with the notation from Section 3.1) the idea behind Kalker's attack and BNSA.

### A.1 Kalker's attack

In [12], Kalker introduces an attack against a normalized correlation detector with a bipolar watermark. With slight modifications, this attack is applicable to a larger class of watermarking schemes [5]. The idea is to calculate the normal vector $m$ to the decision boundary in order to find the shortest path out of $R_1$. Figure 3 exemplifies this attack which we divide into three phases [12, 5]:

1. The starting position is any random medium on or near the decision boundary. Note that the resulting medium $z_s$ must not resemble $y$ [4]. For example, using an image, we reduce the contrast until the image crosses the boundary and the detector changes the detector output [4]. Alternatively, we can employ a bisection algorithm to find a scalar $\gamma^*$, such that $\gamma^* y$ lies on the decision boundary [3]:

$$z_s = \gamma^* y. \tag{6}$$

2. The attacker creates a zero-mean random vector $v$ with components $\{-k, +k\}$. By adding $v$ to $z$, the resulting vector ends either in $R_0$ or in $R_1$. If the detector returns the watermark's presence, we assume a positive correlation between $v$ and the normal vector $m$ and use $v$ to estimate $m$. If the detector returns the watermark's absence, $v$ points to the opposite direction of $m$ (negative correlation) and we use $-v$ to estimate the normal vector.

   The attacker repeats this process to generate a certain number of such random vectors. As each vector has only two possible component values, all random vectors have equal length. Thus, we create a circle of vectors around the starting position $z_s$.

3. By averaging over all random vectors, the attacker estimates $m$. In the case of a linear decision boundary, $(-m)$ represents the direction of the shortest path out of $R_1$. Thus, we subtract $m$ with a scaling factor $\alpha$

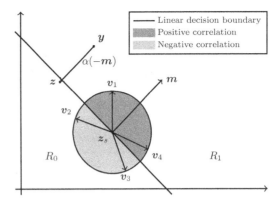

Figure 3: Geometric view of Kalker's attack ($n = 2$). Based on [12].

from $y$ such that we obtain a position on the boundary. In doing so, we obtain an unwatermarked medium with minimal distortion.

Originally, Kalker interprets the normal vector as watermark vector. To estimate a bipolar watermark, he scales $m$ such that its quantized components are in the target set $\{-1, 0, 1\}$.

However, using the normal vector interpretation, this attack also deals with other watermarking schemes, for which the normal vector provides information about the shortest path out of $R_1$ [5]. Furthermore, this attack circumvents a randomized threshold by creating a vector circle whose largest part is outside of the randomized region.

### A.2 Blind Newton Sensitivity Attack

In [3], Comesaña et al. introduce the BNSA which interprets the watermark removal as non-linear optimization problem:

$$\min \quad d(t) \tag{7}$$
$$\text{subject to} \quad f(z) = f(y + t) = \eta. \tag{8}$$

The objective function $d : \mathbb{R}^n \to \mathbb{R}$ measures the intentional changes of $y$ through the attacking vector $t$. For example, $d(t) = \|t\|_2^2$, the squared Euclidean norm of $t$, minimizes the length of $t$ and therefore the changes of the final vector $z$.

Simultaneously, the optimal solution $t^*$ must satisfy the constraint that the detector does not detect the watermark in $z$. It is sufficient to reach a position on the boundary to obtain an undetectable version. Thereby, we restrict the detector function in Equation (8) to $\eta$.

Nevertheless, the attacker does not know the function in Equation (8) (as $\eta$ is part of secret key) and can only record the binary detector output. Thus, Comesaña et al. rewrite the optimization problem into:

$$\arg \min_{t \in \mathbb{R}^n} d(h(t)). \tag{9}$$

The function $h(t)$ reflects the constraint function by mapping $t$ to the decision boundary. For example, a bisection algorithm can find a scalar $\alpha^*$ such that $\alpha^* t$ is on the decision boundary.

Thereby, we obtain an unconstrained optimization problem in Equation (9). However, a direct method to solve this problem is not applicable, since the complete decision boundary – represented by $h(t)$ – is still unknown. Instead, we employ numerical iterative methods such as gradient descent or Newton's method. Thus, the attack begins with any random medium $z_s$ on the decision boundary (as in Kalker's attack) and calculates a start vector $t_0 = z_s - y$. Based on the current position, the attack finds the direction in which $d(t)$ decreases fastest. Next, it calculates the step length to a better solution $t_1$.

For example, using the gradient-based version, we can summarize an update step with the following equation:

$$t_{k+1} = t_k - \underbrace{\xi_k}_{\text{step length}} \cdot \underbrace{\nabla d(h(t_k))}_{\text{descent direction}} \quad . \tag{10}$$

As an analytic calculation of the gradient $\nabla d(h(t_k))$ is not possible, Comesaña et al. present a solution by numerically approximating the gradient.

Then, either a new iteration starts in the current position, or the attack terminates based on a certain criterion. Note, the iterative methods of BNSA can only ensure the global optimum for convex problems. This is the case for a linear boundary, for which the attacker obtains an unwatermarked medium $z$ with minimal distortion. However, when attacking non-linear boundaries, the BNSA may only ensure a local optimum.

# Application of Grubbs' Test for Outliers to the Detection of Watermarks

Matthieu Urvoy
LUNAM Université, Université de Nantes
IRCCyN UMR CNRS 6597, Polytech Nantes
Rue Christian Pauc BP 50609 44306, Nantes,
France
matthieu.urvoy@univ-nantes.fr

Florent Autrusseau
LUNAM Université, Université de Nantes
IRCCyN UMR CNRS 6597, Polytech Nantes
Rue Christian Pauc BP 50609 44306, Nantes,
France
florent.autrusseau@univ-nantes.fr

## ABSTRACT

In an era when the protection of intellectual property rights becomes more and more important, providing robust and efficient watermarking techniques is crucial, both in terms of embedding and detection. In this paper, the authors specifically focus on the latter stage. Most often, the detection consists in the comparison of a fixed and non-adaptive decision threshold to a correlation coefficient. This threshold is usually determined either theoretically or experimentally. Here, it is proposed to apply Grubbs' test, a simple statistical test for outliers, on the correlation data in order to take a binary decision about the presence or the absence of the searched watermark. The proposed technique is applied to three algorithms from the literature: the correlation data generated by the detector is fed to Grubbs' test. The obtained results show that Grubbs' test is efficient, robust and reliable. Above all, it automatically adapts to the searched watermark and can be easily applied to most types of watermarking approaches.

## Categories and Subject Descriptors

I.4.9 [**Computing Methodologies**]: Image Processing and Computer Vision—*Applications*

## General Terms

Watermarking, detection, Grubbs test

## Keywords

Watermarking, detection, Grubbs test

## 1. INTRODUCTION

During the past two decades, watermarking has proven to be a practical and efficient solution to secure all kinds of digital documents. Typically, a watermarking scheme features two separate stages. On the one hand, the embedding step inserts an information, called watermark, within a host signal, in such a way that it cannot be perceived (*e.g.* invisible in images and video contents). On the other hand, the detection step assesses the presence or the absence of the watermark within the processed content. For optimal performances, it is crucial that both the embedding and the detection steps are jointly designed. Eventually, the detection results are binarized into a positive/negative output; the performances of this decision mechanism critically affect the efficiency of the overall watermarking chain.

In this study, a new decision mechanism is proposed. It can only be applied to correlation-based techniques, that is – as pointed out in [1] – most techniques: "*The example system we have used in our investigations, however fall into the class of correlation-based watermarking systems. Although this class does not include all possible watermarking systems, it does include the majority of example systems presented in this book, and, we believe, the majority of systems proposed in the literature.*"

Three kinds of correlation techniques can be encountered: the Linear Correlation (LC), the Normalized Correlation (NC) and the Correlation Coefficient (CC). Typically, the resulting values are compared to a decision threshold whose determination is often delicate and complex, but critical when it comes to ensure best performances, that is lowest False Positive (FP) and False Negative False Negative (FN) rates. Three scenarios (or hypotheses) are typically assessed to best determine the decision threshold. The detection is performed either (1) on a set of un-watermarked images, or (2) on a set of watermarked images, or (3) on a set of watermarked images but with mismatching watermarks. In this paper, notations $\mathcal{H}0$, $\mathcal{H}1$ and $\mathcal{H}2$ will respectively denote the first, second and third scenarios.

Numerous methodologies, of varying complexities, have been employed to determine the detection threshold. A common and simple practice is based on the "detector response", a diagram showing the correlation value obtained in a large number of contents, of which a single one has been watermarked. The resulting plot is used to empirically derive a threshold value. In [2], the detection threshold is set to the highest correlation value (0.23) obtained in a set of un-watermarked images. A similar approach is proposed in [3], where a large number of images (1000) are assessed under $\mathcal{H}0$ and $\mathcal{H}1$ hypotheses. The Probability Density Functions (PDFs) of the obtained correlation under $\mathcal{H}0$ and $\mathcal{H}1$ are then plotted. The threshold is set approximately halfway between $\mathcal{H}0$ and $\mathcal{H}1$ distributions, that is 0.17 in [3].

More rigorous approaches often consider the statistical properties of the PDF of the correlation under $\mathcal{H}0$, $\mathcal{H}1$ and $\mathcal{H}2$ hypotheses. These distributions are typically assumed to be Gaussian. The obtained statistical models may then be used to determine the threshold that maximizes the True Positive (TP) rate while limiting the False Positive (FP) rate to the desired value [4, 5, 6]. This is known as the Neyman-Pearson criterion.

No matter how complex are these methodologies, they all provide a fixed detection threshold. Yet, numerous factors may influence the correlation, including the host signal as well as the embedded watermark (dimensions, statistical properties, etc). A given threshold might be optimal for a given set of host signals and watermarks but may not be suited to other contents. Moreover, the recurrent assumption that processed signals are normally distributed may not hold in practice, thus inducing further detection mismatches. Besides, any variation in the embedding method (domain, equation) requires for the detection threshold to be re-estimated; in [7], for instance, a detection threshold is used for additive embedding, while another threshold is used for multiplicative embedding. When equations for the threshold are proposed, they only hold within the context of their study, that is for a particular watermarking scheme. In [4], for instance, the proposed equation (their Eq. 15) only applies to additive embedding within the Discrete Wavelet Transform (DWT) domain. In [6], a similar equation is available for multiplicative embedding in the Discrete Cosine Transform (DCT) domain. As an alternative, an adaptive detector was proposed in [8]; the detector, for each correlation peak, computes the probability that it does not belong to scenario $\mathcal{H}0$, based on a folded-normal distribution whose parameters may be estimated at detection.

In this study, a fast, universal and efficient decision method used to assess the presence or the absence of a watermark is proposed. It is based on Grubbs' test for outliers, a test that searches for eventual outlying observations in the cross-correlation data. Therefore, there is no need for a detection threshold anymore. Provided that the detection is correlation-based, the proposed method can be applied to all embedding domains and equations (additive, multiplicative, substitutive, etc), whatever the correlation is (linear or normalized, 1D or 2D). Methods computing a CC can also be easily adapted to the proposed technique. This stands in contrast with classical threshold estimation techniques, such as in [4], where derived equations solely apply to the proposed watermarking scheme. Moreover, in most previous works, several assumptions on the statistics of the host signal and the watermark coefficients are necessary. Instead, the proposed technique solely requires for the cross-correlation values to be approximately normally distributed.

In this study, the proposed method is adapted to three algorithms of the literature [9, 10, 3] that operate in different embedding domains and feature various embedding equations. This paper is organized as follows: section 2 first describes the proposed decision method; section 3 then briefly reviews the watermarking techniques in which the proposed method was evaluated. Section 4 then presents experimental results and thoroughly assesses the performances of the proposed method. Finally, section 5 concludes this work.

## 2. PEAK DETECTION: GRUBBS' TEST FOR OUTLIERS

According to [11], *"an outlier is an observation which deviates so much from the other observations as to arouse suspicions that it was generated by a different mechanism"*. When viewing cross-correlation plots such as the ones from Fig. 1, it makes sense to consider the detection peak as an outlying value with respect to the surrounding correlation noise. For this reason, it is proposed here to apply outlier detection theory to the problem of watermark detection decision.

The literature provides a large range of outlier detection techniques [12], whether they rely on data indicators (*e.g.* samples depth, deviation, distance, density, etc) or make assumptions on the statistical properties of the input data and perform statistical tests. In this study, it is proposed to use Grubbs' test [13] as it is robust, reliable and computationally inexpensive. In some of our earlier experiments, the Extreme Studentized Deviate (ESD) test [14] showed equivalent performances to those of Grubbs'. However, alternatives could be considered, such as Dixon's test [15] or Tietjen-Moore's test [16]. In this paper, we only focus on Grubbs' test.

Typically, Grubbs' test is used to detect the presence of a single outlier in a univariate dataset whose distribution is approximately Gaussian. Both one-sided and two-sided variants have been proposed; here, the proposed watermark detection method is based on the latter. Grubbs' test two-sided statistic writes as

$$\mathcal{T}_G = \frac{\max |s(n) - \mu_s|}{\sigma_s} \quad (1)$$

where $s(n)$ denotes the input samples, $\mu_s$ and $\sigma_s$ respectively being the samples mean and standard deviation. The hypothesis that there is an outlier is accepted if $\mathcal{T}_G$ exceeds its critical value, that is

$$\mathcal{T}_G > \frac{N-1}{\sqrt{N}} \sqrt{\frac{(t_{\alpha_G/(2N), N-2})^2}{N-2+(t_{\alpha_G/(2N), N-2})^2}} \quad (2)$$

where $N$ denotes the number of samples and $t_{\alpha_G/(2N), N-2}$ the critical value of Student's $t$-distribution with $N-2$ degrees of freedom and a significance level of $\alpha_G/(2N)$.

How does this apply to watermark detection? Let us now consider a typical still image watermark detection scheme: the searched watermark and the possibly marked signal are cross-correlated. The obtained cross-correlation (be it 1D or 2D) is input to Grubbs' test. Figure 1 shows an example of 2D cross-correlation data obtained with a modified version of the algorithm in [10] that was used to watermark the image Lena. Instead of using LC or Rao's detectors, as proposed in the original work, a normalized 2D cross-correlation [17] was computed between the watermarked sub-band and the watermark. Despite variations in correlation amplitudes due to two different sets of watermarking parameters (see section 3.3 for further details), the cross-correlation data features a central peak surrounded by a correlation noise of (much) lower amplitude. Provided that (1) the embedded watermark exhibits good auto-correlation properties and (2) the cross-correlation noise is (approximately) normally distributed, the detection is positive if Grubbs' test cannot reject the hypothesis that the central peak is an outlier.

Grubbs' test only takes two parameters as inputs, the correlation data and the significance level $\alpha_G$. The latter cor-

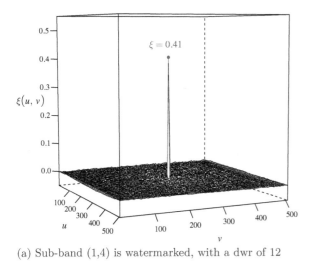

(a) Sub-band (1,4) is watermarked, with a dwr of 12

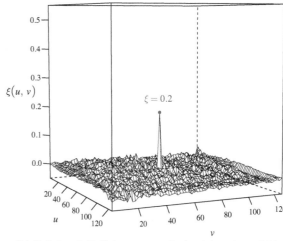

(b) Sub-band (3,4) is watermarked, with a dwr of 20

Figure 1: Cross-correlation 2D data obtained with [10] for image Lena for two sets of embedding parameters.

responds to the maximum probability that the occurrence of the correlation peaks is due to chance alone, in other words the maximum probability that the detected correlation peaks are not outlying values. Therefore, $\alpha_G$ can be used to control the tradeoff between the True Positive (TP) and the FP detection rates: high (resp. low) values bring higher (resp. lower) TP and FP rates. Practical experiments will further detail the role of $\alpha_G$ in section 4. The proposed watermark detection decision technique features an iterated version of Grubbs' test which discards outliers one at a time until no more outliers are found.

## 3. APPLICATION TO EXISTING WATER-MARKING SCHEMES

Three watermarking schemes [9, 10, 3] were selected from the literature in order to evaluate the performances of the proposed Grubbs-based decision technique. All three schemes exhibit various characteristics: different embedding domains and equations, various watermark dimensions and multiple detection algorithms. Table 1 summarizes the main features and characteristics of the three experimented algorithms. Section 3.1 briefly reviews the selected algorithms and Section 3.2 details the modifications which were made to incorporate Grubbs' test. Section 3.3 presents preliminary detection results, and Section 3.4 describes the process by which it was made sure that tested cross-correlation data is approximately Gaussian. More complete and detailed results are available in Section 4.

### 3.1 Description of experimented algorithms

**Lin *et al.*, 2008** [9] – The watermark is embedded within the 3rd Low-High (LH3) sub-band of the DWT decomposition. The targeted sub-band is split into blocks of 7 consecutive coefficients. Each block is used to hold one bit of watermark information, by quantization of its two largest coefficients. At the detection, the difference between the two largest DWT coefficients of every block is compared to a threshold to retrieve the binary watermark information. The detection score is then given by the NC coefficient, which is

eventually compared to a fixed detection threshold of 0.23 in order to ensure a FP probability of $1.03 \times 10^{-7}$. In a later publication [18], it was shown that this technique may present security issues; this is of no concern for the current study as it purely focuses on detection performances.

**Kwitt *et al.*, 2009** [10] – Here, additive spread spectrum embedding is performed in the Dual Tree Complex Wavelet Transform (DT-CWT) domain. A perceptual mask is used to weight the watermark prior its embedding. Their study mostly focuses on various detection methods, and concludes that the Rao detector performs better than the simple LC.

**Solachidis and Pitas, 2001** [3] – Multiplicative embedding is performed within the modulus of the Discrete Fourier Transform (DFT) domain, at mid-frequencies of the Fourier spectrum. The watermark is shaped as concentric rings, arranged into angular segments that each carry a watermark coefficient, for a total of 2300 coefficients arranged into 115 concentric rings and 20 sectors. The detection computes a CC between the searched watermark and the information retrieved in the Fourier magnitude.

### 3.2 Adaptation to Grubbs

As explained in section 2, Grubbs' test takes cross-correlation data as an input. However, the selected watermarking schemes do not feature such an information. Therefore, all three schemes were modified accordingly for Grubbs' test to be successfully incorporated.

**Lin *et al.*, 2008** [9] – Instead of computing the CC between the searched watermark and the retrieved information from the DWT domain, the 1D normalized CC is used to obtain a detection vector whose length is $2 \times 512 - 1$, that is 1023. Grubbs' test is then conducted on the resulting cross-correlation vector.

**Kwitt *et al.*, 2009** [10] – Instead of Rao's test, the 2D normalized CC (from [17]) is computed between the extracted sub-band and the searched watermark (both being $128 \times 128$ matrices for a level 1 embedding process applied on a $256 \times 256$ image). Grubbs' test is then applied to the resulting $255 \times 255$ cross-correlation data.

**Solachidis and Pitas, 2001** [3] – The hidden infor-

Table 1: **Principal features and characteristics of experimented watermarking techniques.**

| | Embedding | | Detection | | Watermark |
| --- | --- | --- | --- | --- | --- |
| | *Domain* | *Method* | *Method* | *Correlation* | dimensions |
| [9] | DWT | Quantization | Blind | CC | $1 \times 512$ |
| [10] | DT-CWT | Additive | Blind | LC, Rao's test | $128 \times 128$ |
| [3] | DFT | Multiplicative | Blind | CC | $20 \times 115$ |

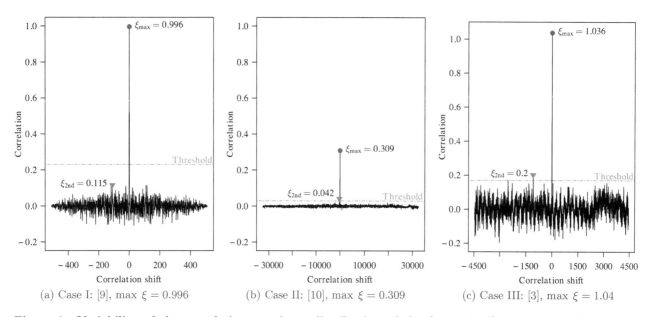

(a) Case I: [9], max $\xi = 0.996$    (b) Case II: [10], max $\xi = 0.309$    (c) Case III: [3], max $\xi = 1.04$

Figure 2: **Variability of the correlation matrices: distribution of the (vectorized) inter-correlation values obtained in three algorithms from the literature. The highest and second highest correlation peaks are respectively depicted by a round symbol (●) and a triangular symbol (▼).**

mation is first retrieved by averaging, for each frequency-angular segment, the modulus of the corresponding Fourier coefficients. The 2D normalized CC (from [17]) is then performed between the retrieved matrix and the searched watermark, both of which featuring $20 \times 115$ coefficients. The resulting $39 \times 229$ CC data is then input to Grubbs' test.

### 3.3 Preliminary results and remarks

Before delving into large experiments and substantial results, it is proposed to first experiment all three modified watermarking schemes [3, 9, 10] on the Lena $512 \times 512$ image. The detection is applied to the watermarked image, without any attacks. Fig. 2 plots the (vectorized) cross-correlation data obtained; in each case, the highest ($\xi_{max}$) and second highest ($\xi_{2nd}$) correlation peaks are respectively depicted by a round and a triangular symbol. From now on, the sliding position of the cross-correlation is called *correlation shift* (see $x$-axes in Fig. 2).

In all three algorithms, the detection peak occurs at the center of the cross-correlation data, that is when the searched watermark and the retrieved information fully overlap and therefore best match. This peak, and its amplitude $\xi_{max}$, correspond to the correlation value of the original scheme; in [10], this corresponds to the output of the simple LC detector, not Rao's test whose output cannot be compared to a correlation value. In each plot of Fig. 2, the dashed line represent the detection threshold $\tau$ of the original algorithm. The detection is thus positive in all three techniques as the cross-correlation peak is higher than the threshold. Moreover, the amplitudes of the cross-correlation noise – in sliding positions other than the center – are mostly below the threshold, thus indicating that the searched watermark is only detected at its exact location.

As mentioned earlier, the length of the vectorized cross-correlation data depends on the experimented algorithm, respectively 1023, $255 \times 255 = 65025$ and $39 \times 229 = 8931$ in [9], [10] and [3]. As can be seen in Fig. 2, the amplitude of the cross-correlation peak significantly varies amongst experimented algorithms. Similarly, the average amplitude of the cross-correlation noise shows strong variations as well. For instance, the second highest cross-correlation peak in [3] (Fig. 2c) is equal to the cross-correlation peak in [10] (Fig. 1b). Another striking observation is that the second highest cross-correlation peak in [3] is higher than the advised detection threshold, thus indicating that that the advocated threshold (0.17) may not be optimal.

Table 2 lists the values of the CC's highest and second highest peaks in all three experimented algorithms on image Lena, as well as correlation gaps between the peaks and the threshold. Here, it can be seen that the cross-correlation gap $\Delta^{\tau}_{2nd}$ between the original detection threshold and the second highest peak shows a large variability amongst algorithms. The same observation can be made on the gap $\Delta_{2nd}^{max}$ between the highest and second highest detection peaks.

**Table 2: Variability of the correlation peaks obtained on image Lena.**

| Alg. | $\tau$ [a] | Peaks[b] | | Corr. gaps[c] | |
|---|---|---|---|---|---|
| | | $\xi_{max}$ | $\xi_{2nd}$ | $\Delta_{2nd}^{\tau}$ | $\Delta_{2nd}^{max}$ |
| [3] | 0.170 | 1.036 | 0.201 | -0.031 | 0.835 |
| [9] | 0.230 | 0.996 | 0.115 | 0.766 | 0.881 |
| [10] | 0.029 | 0.309 | 0.042 | -0.013 | 0.267 |

[a] $\tau$ is the detection threshold.
[b] $\xi_{max}$ and $\xi_{2nd}$ are respectively the highest and second highest correlation peaks.
[c] $\Delta_{2nd}^{\tau}$ is the correlation gap between $\tau$ and $\xi_{2nd}$, and $\Delta_{2nd}^{max}$ is the gap between $\xi_{max}$ and $\xi_{2nd}$.

Besides, even the same embedding algorithm can produce very different cross-correlation data with varying parameters. Such a scenario is illustrated in Fig. 1 for the modified algorithm [10] – see previous Section 2 –. In Fig. 1a, the DT-CWT sub-band (1,4) was watermarked with a dwr of 12, whereas in Fig. 1b the sub-band (3,4) was watermarked with a dwr of 20. The cross-correlation noise (that is the correlation values located around the central peak) exhibit a standard deviation of $1.66 \times 10^{-3}$ in the first case, and $1.11 \times 10^{-2}$ in the second case, that is a variation close to one order of magnitude.

Naturally, these variations in cross-correlation are to be expected with such different embedding techniques and parameters. This emphasizes the fact that the detection threshold must be derived for each embedding technique and parameter set. Moreover, the methodology used to derive the threshold also needs to be adapted to the considered embedding scheme, which makes the matter even more difficult.

When applying Grubbs' test to the cross-correlation data shown in Fig. 2 ($\alpha_G = 10^{-6}$), only the highest peak is positively detected as an outlier in each case. Such a detection performance is especially valuable when considering the large differences between the experimented watermarking schemes and the resulting cross-correlation data. Therefore, these preliminary tests tend to show that Grubbs' test provides a universal method for taking the decision whether a watermark is present or absent.

### 3.4 Gaussianity of the cross-correlation data

Most statistical methods for estimating the detection threshold make several assumptions on the statistical properties of processed signals. As mentioned earlier, Grubbs' test stands in contrast to such approaches as it solely requires for the cross-correlation data to be normally distributed, even approximately [13, 19]. According to [20], the sample size should be greater than 6, another requirement that is obviously met in the studied context where the cross-correlation data is likely to hold thousands of coefficients.

In the preliminary experiments of previous section, Grubbs' test successfully detected the cross-correlation peaks as outlying values. However, it was not ensured whether the cross-correlation data could be reasonably approximated to a Gaussian distribution. It was thus proposed to bin the cross-correlation data into histograms that were fitted to a Gaussian distribution. Fig. 3 shows the obtained histograms for

preliminary cases I (see Fig. 2a) and III (see Fig. 2c). Histograms are superimposed onto the fitted Gaussian curves.

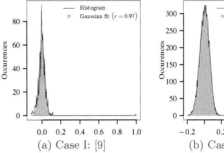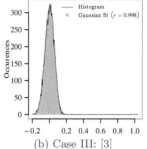

(a) Case I: [9]    (b) Case III: [3]

**Figure 3: Application of [9] and [3] to image Lena: distribution of the cross-correlation data.**

In [3] (Fig. 3b), the cross-correlation histogram fits very well a Gaussian distribution – the correlation (Pearson's $r$) between the histogram and the fitted curve reaches 0.998. In [9] it is best fitted by a Laplacian distribution, yet the Gaussian fit still provides a reasonable approximation. Table 3 provides goodness of fit for the estimated distributions in terms of Pearson's $r$ and Root Mean Square Error (RMSE). Overall, the distribution of the obtained cross-correlation data are close enough to a Gaussian distribution and therefore can be input to Grubbs' test. It is important to note that the distributions of the cross-correlation data in Fig. 3 are not centered due to the outlying correlation peaks (respectively 0.996 and 1.036 in [9] and [3]).

**Table 3: Goodness[a] of fit for cross-correlation data in [9] and [3] on image Lena**

| | Gaussian fit | | Laplacian fit | |
|---|---|---|---|---|
| | *Pearson's r* | *RMSE* | *Pearson's r* | *RMSE* |
| [9] | 0.970 | 0.203 | **0.986** | **0.168** |
| [3] | **0.998** | **0.174** | 0.979 | 0.633 |

[a] Bold values designate best fitting parameters.

Now focusing on preliminary case II (see Fig. 2b), the observation of the signals processed in algorithm in [10] revealed various kinds of distributions. Figure 4 shows the distribution of four successively processed signals: (1) the DT-CWT sub-band (Fig. 4a), (2) the watermark (Fig. 4b), (3) the watermarked sub-band (Fig. 4c) and (4) the cross-correlation data (Fig. 4d). Again, the distribution of the cross-correlation data in Fig. 4d is not centered due to the outlying correlation peak with amplitude 0.309. Each of these distributions were fitted to both Gaussian and Laplacian models; the resulting goodness of fit is listed in Table 4.

As can be seen, the distributions of both the original and watermarked sub-bands are rather Laplacian, whereas the watermark is normally distributed. In the end, it appears that the cross-correlation data still follows a Gaussian distribution (Pearson's $r$ of 0.997), despite the Laplacian behavior of the sub-band values. Here, typical estimation techniques for the detection threshold – that assume Gaussian distributions of both the host signal and the watermark – may

**Table 4: Gaussianity of the signals processed in [10]: goodness[a] of fit for Gaussian and Laplacian model.**

|  | Gaussian fit | | Laplacian fit | |
|---|---|---|---|---|
|  | $r$[b] | RMSE | $r$[b] | RMSE |
| Subband | 0.934 | 0.0030 | **0.980** | **0.0018** |
| Watermark | **0.996** | **0.0146** | 0.972 | 0.0541 |
| Marked subb. | 0.990 | 0.0012 | **0.995** | **0.0007** |
| Cross-corr. | **1.000** | **0.1015** | 0.987 | 0.5463 |

[a] Bold values designate best fitting parameters.
[b] $r$ denotes Pearson's correlation coefficient.

provide erroneous values. On the contrary, the requirements for Grubbs' are all met, therefore ensuring that the detected outlying values indeed correspond to cross-correlation peaks for which the detection is positive.

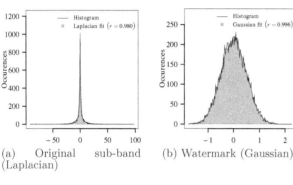

(a) Original sub-band (Laplacian)  (b) Watermark (Gaussian)

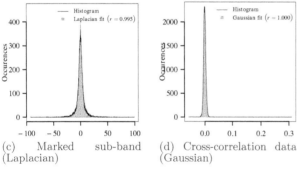

(c) Marked sub-band (Laplacian)  (d) Cross-correlation data (Gaussian)

**Figure 4: Application of [10] to image Lena: distribution of the host signal, the watermark, the marked signal and the cross-correlation.**

# 4. RESULTS

Preliminary results tend to show that Grubbs' test is capable of locating watermark detection peaks in different scenarios. Large scale experiments are now conducted in order to systematically assess Grubbs' test ability to detect the presence or the absence of a watermark from cross-correlation data.

## 4.1 Experimental apparatus and parameters

Hereon, two main datasets are used for the experiments: dataset $\mathcal{D}_a$ contains 1000 gray level images from the BOWS-

2 contest[1]; dataset $\mathcal{D}_b$ contains 10 color images from the Kodak Database[2]. The second dataset $\mathcal{D}_b$ serves in scenarios that involve a large number of detections, so as to keep the experimental scale within reasonable bounds. The datasets are listed and detailed in Table 5.

Three main experimental hypotheses are considered. One of them ($\mathcal{H}1$) should ideally lead to positive detections, contrary to the other two ($\mathcal{H}0$ and $\mathcal{H}2$) in which detection should conclude in the absence of the searched watermark.

- In scenario $\mathcal{H}0$, original – therefore un-watermarked – images from dataset $\mathcal{D}_a$ are input to detection.

- In scenario $\mathcal{H}1$, watermarked images from dataset $\mathcal{D}_a$ are first attacked and then input to detection, which searches for the initially embedded watermark.

- In scenario $\mathcal{H}2$, watermarked images from dataset $\mathcal{D}_b$ are input to detection, which searches for 1000 erroneous watermarks.

When necessary, that is in scenario $\mathcal{H}1$, four types of attacks are simulated: (1) attack *Blur 3* applies Gaussian blur with standard deviation $\sigma = 3$; (2) attack *Pois. 120* inserts Poisson noise with parameter $\lambda = 120$; attack *Pois. 140* inserts Poisson noise with parameter $\lambda = 140$; (4) attack *Med. 5* performs $5 \times 5$ median filtering.

**Table 5: Datasets used in the experiments**

| Name | Description | Type | Size | Resolution |
|---|---|---|---|---|
| $\mathcal{D}_a$ | BOWS-2 | Gray level | 1000 | $512 \times 512$ |
| $\mathcal{D}_b$ | Kodak | Color | 10 | $512 \times 768$ |

## 4.2 A first glance at cross-correlation data

The whole concept of the present study relies on the assumption that cross-correlation data should behave differently depending on the presence or the absence of a watermark. To be more precise, it is expected in scenario $\mathcal{H}1$ that a visible peak emerges at the center of the cross-correlation data, whereas this should not happen in scenario $\mathcal{H}0$. In some cases, however, and notably when geometric distortions are undergone, the correlation peak may move away from the center (provided that the watermarking algorithm is resilient against geometric distortions). Alternatively, the correlation data may contain several peaks (either by design or due to geometric distortions); the iterative implementation of Grubbs' test (see Section 2) is expected to detect them one at a time. To verify this, the modified algorithm [10] was evaluated against the dataset $\mathcal{D}a$ under both $\mathcal{H}0$ and $\mathcal{H}1$ hypotheses.

In each scenario, the 2D cross-correlation data was collected and averaged over the 1000 experimented images. The resulting averages are plotted in Fig. 5. The obtained results show that, over a large number of images, there is indeed a clearly visible cross-correlation peak for the $\mathcal{H}1$ scenario (Fig. 5a). This stands in contrast with scenario $\mathcal{H}0$ (Fig. 5b) in which the central peak of the cross-correlation barely emerges from the surrounding cross-correlation noise.

---

[1] http://bows2.ec-lille.fr
[2] http://r0k.us/graphics/kodak/

The averaged cross-correlation data of Fig. 5 were input to Grubbs' test for outlier, with $\alpha_G = 10^{-6}$. In Fig. 5a, five outliers are detected, including the central peak and four others in its vicinity. In Fig. 5b, no outliers are detected at all. Similar results were obtained in [9] and [3]. Therefore, this study's underlying assumption holds in practice.

## 4.3 Gaussianity of the cross-correlation over experimental datasets

Similarly to what was done in section 3.4, it is proposed here to ensure the normality of the collected cross-correlation data over the entire datasets $Da$ and $Db$. The modified algorithms [9] and [3] were evaluated under hypotheses $\mathcal{H}0$ (dataset $Da$), $\mathcal{H}1$ (dataset $Da$) and $\mathcal{H}2$ (dataset $Db$) – see section 4.1 for their definitions –. This resulted in 1000 cross-correlation data under hypothesis $\mathcal{H}0$, 4000 under hypothesis $\mathcal{H}1$ and 10000 under hypothesis $\mathcal{H}2$.

The collected cross-correlation data were then binned into histograms, which in turn were fitted to a Gaussian distribution. The goodness of fit was evaluted in terms of Pearson's $r$ and RMSE between the experimental histogram and the fitted curve. For each algorithm and hypothesis, Table 6 lists the average, minimum and maximum figures for both indicators.

**Table 6: Gaussian fits goodness of fit**

|  | Pearson's $r$ | | | RMSE | | |
|---|---|---|---|---|---|---|
|  | Mean | Min | Max | Mean | Min | Max |
| **Solachidis *et al.* [3]** | | | | | | |
| $\mathcal{H}0$ | 0.9977 | 0.9555 | 1.0000 | 0.0296 | 0.0043 | 0.1560 |
| $\mathcal{H}1$ | 0.9952 | 0.9367 | 0.9999 | 0.0387 | 0.0068 | 0.1609 |
| $\mathcal{H}2$ | 0.9988 | 0.9650 | 0.9999 | 0.0236 | 0.0072 | 0.1456 |
| **Lin *et al.* [9]** | | | | | | |
| $\mathcal{H}0$ | 0.9883 | 0.9631 | 0.9987 | 0.0856 | 0.0270 | 0.1438 |
| $\mathcal{H}1$ | 0.9897 | 0.9588 | 0.9998 | 0.0814 | 0.0109 | 0.1551 |
| $\mathcal{H}2$ | 0.9916 | 0.9189 | 0.9998 | 0.0720 | 0.0127 | 0.2094 |

In [3], the cross-correlation data fits very well a Gaussian distribution; Pearson's $r$ never falls below 0.9555 and averages at 0.9977. In [9], the goodness of fit is reasonably high as well, high enough to justify the use of Grubbs' test; Pearson's $r$ reaches 0.9189 at its minimum. This can be explained by the fact that, as was already seen in Fig. 3 and Table 3, the cross-correlation data in [9] is best approximated by a Laplacian distribution. Still, such a distribution is well handled by Grubbs' test, provided that its standard deviation is high enough not to present heavy tails – which is the case here.

## 4.4 True Positive and False Positive rates

Properly setting the value of Grubbs' significance level $\alpha_G$ is crucial as it drives detection performances. High values of $\alpha_G$ (*e.g.* $10^{-2}$) are very likely to detect outlying values, but on the other hand are also likely to detect non-outlying values with respect to the considered context. Inversely, on the same input data, low values of $\alpha_G$ (*e.g.* $10^{-8}$) ensure not to detect these false outliers, but are also likely to miss truly outlying values. Transposed to watermarking, this means that both TP and FP rates are likely to increase with $\alpha_G$.

Grubbs' test detection output was collected in modified algorithms [9] and [3] for all three scenarios $\mathcal{H}0$, $\mathcal{H}1$ and $\mathcal{H}2$, for varying $\alpha_G$ ($10^{-8}$ to $10^{-2}$). Under $\mathcal{H}0$, none of the 1000 original images of dataset $Da$ led to false detections. As for hypotheses $\mathcal{H}1$ (TP) and $\mathcal{H}2$ (FP), the obtained evolution in FP and TP rates as a function of $\alpha_G$ is plotted in Fig. 6. Note that the values for the plotted TP rates correspond to *Pois. 120* attacks only.

As expected, the experimental results show that both TP ($\mathcal{H}1$) and FP ($\mathcal{H}2$) rates increase with $\alpha_G$. Still, in [3], the TP rate barely increases and remains rather stable over the entire experimented values of $\alpha_G$. The two modified algorithms present rather opposite behavior. Algorithm [3], on the bright side, displays a high TP rate (around 95%), but on the downside a high FP rate as well (up to 50% for low values of $\alpha_G$). As for [9], both its TP rates and FP rates are rather low; the first range from 30 to 50% while the second remains below 15%.

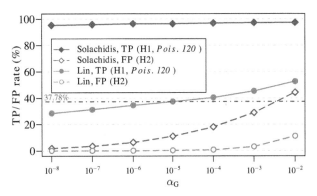

Figure 6: TP and FP rates against Grubbs' significance level $\alpha_G$ in [3] and [9]. TP rates correspond to $\mathcal{H}1$ scenarios featuring the attack *Pois. 120*; FP rates correspond to scenarios $\mathcal{H}2$.

For comparison purposes, we also experimented the original algorithm [3] under hypothesis $\mathcal{H}2$. Interestingly, it features an FP rate of 37.78% (see dotted-dashed line in Fig. 6), meaning that Grubbs' test outperforms the original detection algorithm, in terms of FPs, for significance levels below $\alpha_G = 10^{-3}$. In addition, we will see later that the method in [3] presents abnormally high detection rates. Still, the main objective of this study is to investigate whether the proposed detection decision mechanism is competitive, that is how much better or worse it performs in comparison to the original detection schemes.

## 4.5 Comparison of original and proposed detection schemes

As was just pointed out, the main objective of our study is to compare the proposed Grubbs-based detection scheme to the initial threshold-based detection scheme. To this end, the modified algorithms [9] and [3] were evaluated under hypothesis $\mathcal{H}1$, a scenario which features four types of attacks (see Section 4.1 for full details). Based on TP and FP experimental rates obtained in previous section, Grubbs' significance level $\alpha_G$ will be set to $10^{-6}$, which provides a proper tradeoff between the ability to retrieve a watermark and the ability to distinguish between different watermarks. Corresponding values for TP and FP rates are listed in Table 7.

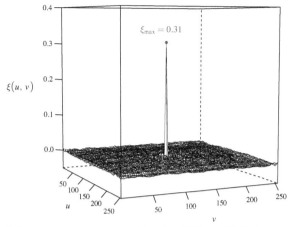

(a) Average cross-correlation for [10] on 1000 images (from $\mathcal{D}a$) - True positives

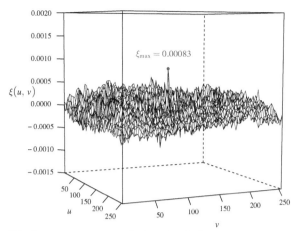

(b) Average cross-correlation for [10] on 1000 images (from $\mathcal{D}a$) - False Positives

**Figure 5: Average 2D cross-correlation data obtained with [10] against 1000 marked images (a), and against original images (b).**

**Table 7: FP and TP rates: operating values for a Grubbs significance level of $\alpha_G = 10^{-6}$ under $\mathcal{H}1$ hypothesis and attack *Pois. 120***

|     | TP rate | FP rate |
|-----|---------|---------|
| [9] | 96.4%   | 6.34%   |
| [3] | 34.5%   | 0.0%    |

For both the original and the modified algorithms, and for each type of attack, the number of watermarked images in which the detection is positive was computed. These values are denoted $TP_{Orig}$ and $TP_{Grubbs}$, and correspond to the TP rates respectively obtained in the original and the modified algorithm. In addition, we counted the number of images in which the modified detection scheme retrieves the watermark (TP), while the original scheme does not (FN); this number is denoted $\Delta_{TP}$. We also counted the number of images in which the opposite scenario arises: the original scheme retrieves the watermark, but the modified scheme does not; this number is denoted $\Delta_{FN}$. The obtained results are listed in Table 8.

As was observed previously in Fig. 6, results from Table 8 demonstrate weak robustness performances for [9] in comparison to [3]. Nevertheless, the use of Grubbs' test improves the detection performances in most cases, no matter how good is the robustness of the original method. In [3], the introduction of Gaussian blur (attack *Blur 3*) leads to strongly diverging results when using either the original or the modified detection scheme. This suspicious effect is further investigated in the next section.

Fig. 7 plots the detection gain ($\Delta_{TP}$, positive bars) and loss ($\Delta_{FN}$, negative bars) obtained in both experimented methods. The suspicious results obtained in [3] with attack *Blur 3* are omitted for readability purposes. Apart from the attack *Med. 5*, the proposed detection method performs better than the original detection methods and their fixed thresholds. Detection rates significantly improve, by up to 10% in [9] against the attack *Blur 3*.

**Table 8: Robustness to attacks (%) for dataset $\mathcal{D}_a$: original and modified schemes.**

|                   | Blur 3 | Pois. 120 | Pois. 140 | Med. 5 |
|-------------------|--------|-----------|-----------|--------|
| **Solachidis *et al.* [3]** |  |  |  |  |
| $TP_{Orig}$       | 78.8*  | 92.5      | 87.6      | 99.9   |
| $TP_{Grubbs}$     | 7.5*   | 96.4      | 94.5      | 98.2   |
| $\Delta_{TP}$     | 0.0*   | 4.0       | 7.2       | 0.0    |
| $\Delta_{FN}$     | 71.3*  | 0.0       | 0.0       | 1.7    |
| **Lin *et al.* [9]** |  |  |  |  |
| $TP_{Orig}$       | 20.5   | 25.1      | 12.0      | 95.2   |
| $TP_{Grubbs}$     | 30.7   | 34.5      | 18.1      | 98.1   |
| $\Delta_{TP}$     | 10.2   | 9.4       | 6.1       | 2.9    |
| $\Delta_{FN}$     | 0.0    | 0.0       | 0.0       | 0.0    |

* These unexpected results are further discussed in section 4.6

## 4.6 Investigating suspicious results

Some results obtained with algorithm [3] in previous Section raised suspicions. In particular, under the attack *Blur 3*, it is striking to notice that the original detection scheme retrieves 78.8% of the watermarks, while the modified scheme only detects 7.5% of them. This is especially surprising in regards to other attacks or algorithms where such an effect never occurs. To further investigate this specific scenario, we plotted in Fig. 8 the distribution of the CC returned by the original detection scheme (which is equal to the amplitude of the central peak of the cross-correlation data) in four scenarios: (1) on original un-watermarked images ($\mathcal{H}0$); (2) on watermarked images in the absence of any attack ($\mathcal{H}1'$); (3) on watermarked images after *Blur 3* attack ($\mathcal{H}1_{B3}$); and (4) in a variant of scenario $\mathcal{H}2$ which also features the *Blur 3* attack ($\mathcal{H}2_{B3}$).

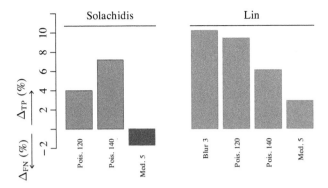

Figure 7: Contribution of Grubbs' test: $\Delta_{TP}$ denotes the percentage of images in which Grubbs' test is successfull contrary to the original detector; conversely, $\Delta_{FN}$ denotes the percentage of images in which Grubbs' test is unsuccessful contrary to the original detector.

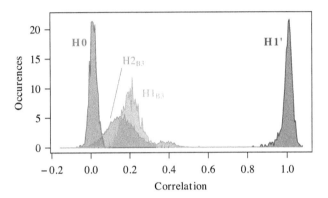

Figure 8: Distribution of the cross-correlation peaks: comparison between scenarios $\mathcal{H}0$, $\mathcal{H}1'$, $\mathcal{H}1_{B3}$ and $\mathcal{H}2_{B3}$.

In the absence of attacks ($\mathcal{H}0$ and $\mathcal{H}1'$), the distribution of the cross-correlation peaks are narrow and clearly disjoint, and the detection threshold (0.17) is located in between the two. The original detection scheme is thus correct for both of these scenarios. When the images are attacked ($\mathcal{H}1_{B3}$ and $\mathcal{H}2_{B3}$), these distributions are widening and shift towards the threshold, so that they strongly overlap. In this case, the advocated threshold (0.17) fails to distinguish between those images in which a watermark should be detected and those in which it should not. For this reason, the technique in [3] features a high FP rate. The use of 0.5 as a threshold may circumvent this issue, but then none of the watermarked and attacked images would be detected at all.

Practical experiments were conducted on dataset $\mathcal{D}_b$ under hypothesis $\mathcal{H}2_{B3}$. Results show that the original detection method in [3] presents a FP rate of 46.1%, while the proposed detection method never detects the wrong watermark. This tends to show that the suspicious results from Table 8 are more likely to be in favor of the proposed detection technique, which in this case takes the better decision to consider that the watermark cannot be retrieved.

## 4.7 Original versus modified algorithms: investigating the reasons for disagreement

With the exception of the suspicious results obtained under hypothesis $\mathcal{H}1_{B3}$, the other results – see Fig. 7 – show increased detection performances for most attacks when using the proposed detection method. One may wonder, however, under which circumstances exactly Grubbs' test disagrees with the original threshold-based detection method. Experimental results for scenarios $\mathcal{H}1$ and $\mathcal{H}2$ were further examined in two situations: ($i$) when Grubbs' test positively detects an outlier but the peak correlation is below the original detection threshold; ($ii$) when inversely, Grubbs' test does not detect any outlier but the peak correlation is above the original detection threshold.

In both situations ($i$) and ($ii$), the average, minimum and maximum amplitudes of the corresponding cross-correlation data were computed for each value of the correlation shift. The resulting data is plotted in Fig. 9. The dark blue curve represents the average value of the cross-correlation data (**A** in Fig. 9a). The average central peak is represented by a red round symbol (**D** in Fig. 9a). The amplitude range within which the central peak is comprised is delimited by two horizontal light red lines (**E** and **F** in Fig. 9a) that respectively cross the $y$-axis at the minimum and maximum values of the central peak. Finally, the light blue area delimited by the curves (**B** and **C** in Fig. 9a), represents the amplitude range that comprises the remaining cross-correlation data, which we call cross-correlation noise. In other words, **B** (resp. **C**) plots, in all shifting positions except the center, the minimum (resp. maximum) value amongst collected cross-correlation data. The same representation is used in Fig. 9b, 9c and 9d.

Two scenarios can be envisioned: either (1) the noise range (light blue area) and the peak range (light red area) do not overlap or (2) they do. In the first case, this would tend to show that a watermark can indeed be detected. In the second case, either the hypothesis that a watermark is present should be rejected, or the searched watermark presents bad auto-correlation properties, which is problematic and very likely to induce False Alarms.

Fig. 9a corresponds to 286 $\mathcal{H}1$ scenarios in which the modified algorithm [9] positively detects the watermark while the original algorithm does not. Out of the 1000 images of dataset $\mathcal{D}_a$, this occured 102 times under *Blur 3* attack, 29 times under *Med. 5* attack, 94 times under *Pois. 120* and 61 times under *Pois. 140*; in total, this sums up to 286 cases out of 4000. As can be seen in Fig. 9a, despite the fact that the amplitude of the cross-correlation peak is located below the original detection threshold, its values span a range that is clearly above and disjoint from the cross-correlation noise. The presence of a detection peak cannot be denied; therefore Grubbs' test takes the better decision to consider that a watermark is indeed found.

A similar scenario can be seen in Fig. 9b: the modified algorithm [3] performs better in 86 images out of 4000 (30 against *Pois. 120* attack, 56 against *Pois. 140* attack). Again, although it is less obvious than in Fig. 9a, the values of the cross-correlation peak and those of the cross-correlation noise are most of the time non-overlapping. The presence of a watermark is thus extremely likely, which is consistent with Grubbs' decision.

Conversely, the modified algorithm [3] does not detect any watermark in 772 images (742 against *Blur 3*, 2 against

*Pois. 120*, 2 against *Pois. 140* and 26 against *Med. 5*) while the original algorithm does. Fig. 9c represents the average, maximum and minimum values of the 770 corresponding cross-correlation data. Here, the dynamic of the cross-correlation noise is much larger relatively to the amplitude of the peak; for some correlation shifts, the maximum amplitude of the noise even exceeds the average amplitude of the peak. Moreover, the cross-correlation noise regularly exceeds the original detection threshold: cross-correlation peaks that should go undetected may therefore be detected which is likely to cause False Alarms. Again, this puts back into question the choice for the original detection threshold, as was already discussed in Section 4.6. In [9], the modified detection scheme never missed a watermark that was detected by the original detector.

Finally, the modified algorithm [3] was experimented under hypothesis $\mathcal{H}2$. Out of the 10000 detections, the original detection is positive in 3778 cases, that is 37.78% of False Alarms. In contrast, the proposed detection scheme is positive in 634 cases only, that is a reduction of 31.44% in FP rate. Fig. 9d plots a summary of the 3151 images in which the original detection is positive (thus erroneous) and the modified detection is not. Although less blatant here, the maximum amplitude of the cross-correlation noise regularly exceeds the original detection threshold. With Grubbs' test, this limited overlap is significant enough to correctly reject the hypothesis that the correct watermark is present.

## 4.8 Receiver Operating Characteristics

So far, results suggest that Grubbs' test for outlier is suited to the detection of peaks within cross-correlation data. Moreover, the significance level can be used to tune the accuracy of the detector, that is to (jointly) control the TP and FP rates. Here, it is proposed to plot the Receiver Operating Characteristic (ROC) of the modified detection scheme, for various values of $\alpha_G$, and to compare it to the ROC curve of the original algorithm [9].

The original detection CC was collected under two hypotheses: $\mathcal{H}0$ and $\mathcal{H}1$ (against *Pois. 120* attack). Their distribution, in either case, are not Gaussian. Rather, $\mathcal{H}0$'s distribution is best fitted to a skew-normal distribution with parameters $\Theta_{\mathcal{H}0} = \{\mu = -8.722 \times 10^{-3}, \sigma = 4.262 \times 10^{-2}, \xi = 1.054\}$, where $\xi$ is the skewness parameter. As for $\mathcal{H}1$ (*Pois. 120*), it is best fitted by a generalized skew-hyperbolic distribution with parameters $\Theta_{\mathcal{H}1} = \{\mu = -0.174, \delta = 0.050, \alpha = 858.3, \beta = 844.4\}$, where $\beta$ is the skewness parameter. Fig. 10 plots the distributions of the CC under both hypotheses (solid lines) as well as the corresponding fits (colored areas). Here, most detection methods – that often assume normal distribution of the CC – are likely not to estimate a proper detection threshold.

The obtained distributions for $\mathcal{H}0$ and $\mathcal{H}1$ were then used to plot the ROC curve in Fig. 11. For best understanding, the ROC curve is plotted twice: in Fig. 11a, it is plotted over a linear $x$-axis; in Fig. 11b, it is plotted in its entirety over a logarithmic $x$-axis. The solid green curve is drawn from experimental data (the solid curves from Fig. 10), while the dashed red curve is drawn from interpolated data (the fits from Fig. 10). The experimental operating point of the original detection scheme is schematized by a green diamond symbol; its interpolation from the fitted curves is schematized by a red square symbol (Fig. 11b). Their positions are matching in Fig. 11a.

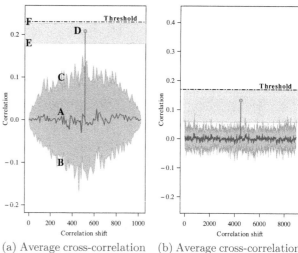

(a) Average cross-correlation when Grubbs' detection performs better than [9]

(b) Average cross-correlation when Grubbs' detection performs better than [3]

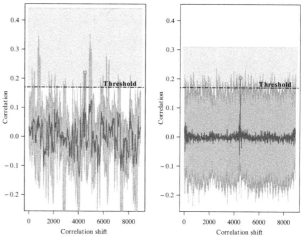

(c) Average cross-correlation when Grubbs' detection performs worse than [3]

(d) Average cross-correlation for [3] when testing wrong watermarks

**Figure 9: Average cross-correlation data in various scenarios. In (a) and (b) (respectively algorithms [9] and [3]), Grubbs' test outperforms the original algorithm. In (c), Grubbs' test fails to detect the watermark but the original algorithm [3] is successful. In (d), Grubbs' test avoids detecting wrong watermarks but the original algorithm [3] does not.**

The ROC curve of the modified scheme is plotted in blue with round symbols. Its values are based on experimental results only: it is not possible to interpolate neither FP nor TP rates for other values of $\alpha_G$ with Grubbs' test. As seen earlier, both TP and FP rates in the modified detection scheme increase with $\alpha_G$.

As can be seen from Fig. 11b, the ROC curve of the proposed method passes over the original curve for values of $\alpha_G$ below $10^{-6}$, that is the value which we used in the experiments. The optimal value for $\alpha_G$ is thus $10^{-6}$ as it provides the best TP rate with a null FP rate. Moreover, the

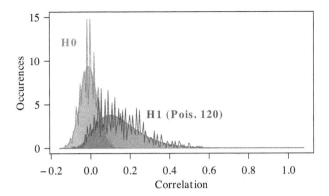

Figure 10: $\mathcal{H}0$ and $\mathcal{H}1$ (Poisson 120) distributions: histograms are superimposed on the corresponding skew-normal and generalized skew hyperbolic fits.

proposed method, $\alpha_G$ increases the TP rate by more than 11% (from 22.8% to 34.5%) in comparison to the original operating point.

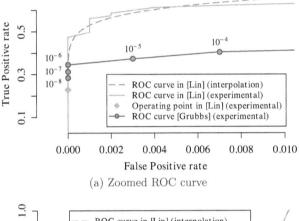

(a) Zoomed ROC curve

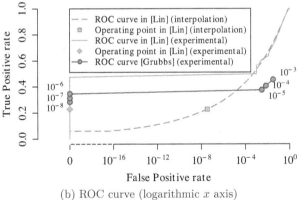

(b) ROC curve (logarithmic $x$ axis)

Figure 11: ROC curves computed on the initial algorithm in [9]. The experimental data are depicted by the solid green curves, the interpolated data by the dashed red curve, and the Grubbs detections are depicted by the blue symbols.

## 5. CONCLUSION

This work presents a prospective study on the possible use of outlier detection methods on correlation data for watermark detection without the need to select a threshold. It was shown that Grubbs' test (among other outlier detection methods) can be used to accurately determine whether the watermark is present within the tested content. Grubbs's test is virtually applicable on any correlation-based watermarking method, whatever the embedding domain, the embedding equation, etc. In this work, three algorithms from the literature [3, 10, 9] were adapted to incorporate Grubbs' test. The adaptation is straightforward and brings improvements in most cases. Specifically, our experiments showed that either the FP rate was reduced (in [3]), or the TP rate was increased (in [9]), without one affecting the other. Finally, we showed that varying the significance level in Grubbs' test allows fine tuning of both the False Positive rate and the True Positive rate.

## 6. REFERENCES

[1] Ingemar J. Cox, Matthew L. Miller, Jeffrey A. Bloom, Jessica Fridrich, and Ton Kalker. Digital Watermarking and Steganography. The Morgan Kaufmann Series in Multimedia Information and Systems, San Francisco, CA, USA, 2nd edition, 2007.

[2] Ante Poljicak, Midija Mandic, and Darko Agic. Discrete Fourier transform–based watermarking method with an optimal implementation radius. Journal of Electronic Imaging, 20(3):033008–1–8, July 2011.

[3] V Solachidis and I Pitas. Circularly symmetric watermark embedding in 2-D DFT domain. IEEE transactions on image processing : a publication of the IEEE Signal Processing Society, 10(11):1741–53, January 2001.

[4] Mauro Barni, Franco Bartolini, and Alessandro Piva. Improved wavelet-based watermarking through pixel-wise masking. IEEE transactions on image processing : a publication of the IEEE Signal Processing Society, 10(5):783–91, January 2001.

[5] Wei Liu, Lina Dong, and Wenjun Zeng. Optimum Detection for Spread-Spectrum Watermarking That Employs Self-Masking. IEEE Transactions on Information Forensics and Security, 2(4):645–654, December 2007.

[6] A Piva, M Barni, F Bartolini, and V Cappellini. Threshold Selection for Correlation-Based Watermark Detection. In Proc. COST254 Workshop on Intelligent Communications, pages 5—-6, 1998.

[7] Qiang Cheng and T.S. Huang. Robust optimum detection of transform domain multiplicative watermarks. IEEE Transactions on Signal Processing, 51(4):906–924, April 2003.

[8] Michael Arnold, Peter G. Baum, and Xiao-Ming Chen. Robust detection of audio watermarks after acoustic path transmission. In Proceedings of the 12th ACM workshop on Multimedia and security - MM&Sec '10, page 117, New York, New York, USA, 2010. ACM Press.

[9] WH Lin, SJ Horng, and TW Kao. An Efficient Watermarking Method Based on Significant Difference

of Wavelet Coefficient Quantization. IEEE Transactions on Multimedia, 10(5):746–757, August 2008.

[10] Roland Kwitt, Peter Meerwald, and Andreas Uhl. Blind DT-CWT domain additive spread-spectrum watermark detection. In 2009 16th International Conference on Digital Signal Processing, pages 1–8. IEEE, July 2009.

[11] D. M. Hawkins. Identification of Outliers. Biometrical Journal, 29(2):198–198, 1980.

[12] Victoria Hodge and Jim Austin. A Survey of Outlier Detection Methodologies. Artificial Intelligence Review, 22(2):85–126, October 2004.

[13] Frank E. Grubbs. Procedures for detecting outlying observations in samples. Technometrics, 11(1):1–21, 1969.

[14] B. Rosner. Percentage Points for a Generalized ESD Many-Outlier Procedure. Technometrics, 25(2):165–172, 1983.

[15] W. J. Dixon. Processing data for Outliers. Biometrics, 9(1):74—-89, 1953.

[16] Gary L. Tietjen and Roger H. Moore. Some Grubbs-Type Statistics for the Detection of Outliers. Technometrics, 14(3):583—-597, 1972.

[17] J. P. Lewis. Fast normalized cross-correlation. In Vision interface, pages 120–123, 1995.

[18] P Meerwald, C Koidl, and A Uhl. Attack on "Watermarking Method Based on Significant Difference of Wavelet Coefficient Quantization". IEEE Transactions on Multimedia, 11(5):1037–1041, August 2009.

[19] V. Barnett and T. Lewis. Outliers in Statistical Data. Wiley Series in Probability and Mathematical Statistics, John Wiley & Sons; Chichester, 1994.

[20] C Croarkin and P Tobias. NIST/SEMATECH e-handbook of statistical methods. Retrieved January, 1:2014, 2014.

# FastPass - Automated Border Control as Challenging Combination of Various Security Technologies

Markus Clabian
AIT Austrian Institute of Technology GmbH
Donau-City-Str.1
1220 Vienna, Austria
markus.clabian@ait.ac.at

## ABSTRACT

In this paper, we present the FastPass project - a new research approach to automated border control (ABC) systems. In the last two decennia various concepts of ABCs have been developed mainly driven by pure technological and industrial viewpoints. Those systems are nowadays tested and even employed in regular operation by many states and reveal several drawbacks. Various security technologies are used for such complex ABC solutions including biometrics, surveillance, certificate exchange, data protection, secure user interaction and information security. Hence, the FastPass project proposes a *multiple stakeholders driven approach* emphasizing user's needs and providing a deeper look into the security technologies to estimate the risk, challenges and opportunities of an automated approach. The FastPass project reconsiders these factors and proposes a reference architecture for all European border crossing points.

**Categories and Subject Descriptors:** J.7

**Keywords:** Automated border control; harmonization; reference architecture

## 1. INTRODUCTION

Increasing travel activities (645 Mio border crossings in Europe per year with an estimated increase of 80% at air borders until 2030) and decreasing public budgets poses a challenge to today's border control officers. Automation seems to be one option to mitigate this problem, however, first test installations and even operational installations show multiple difficulties associated with the fact that the redesign of a complex security process in a multi-stakeholder environment has to be accomplished.

One main aspect of border control is immigration control, consisting of the following steps (i) checking the travel document (ii) checking the identity of a person (iii) checking whether this person is eligible to enter the country (iv) checking, whether the person poses a potential threat, when entering the country.

Many different technologies are applied within an ABC. First the document is checked for electronic and optical features. Solutions employ RFID technology, lighting and camera technology as well as secure certificate checks with the IT backend-systems. Identity check needs biometric technologies such as acquisition and matching of faces, fingers and/or iris data. Eligibility is usually defined in legal frameworks that are implemented in process tools and are relatively fixed – additional checks with backend databases are performed. Threats associated with immigration of persons can usually be mitigated by surveillance technologies.

## 2. THE FASTPASS PROJECT

### 2.1 Main goals

The main goals of FastPass are (i) integration of the "smart border package" (entry-exit system and registered traveler programme) (ii) harmonization and standardization, (iii) innovative border crossing concepts, (iv) architecture based on innovative technologies, and (v) European cooperation.

### 2.2 Consortium

The partners of the consortium are representing the whole value chain of ABC systems, from component producers, hardware and software vendors, integrators (11 industry partners), research institutes (5) and universities (4), infrastructure operators (4) and border guard institutions (3). Legal, social and political research is an additional asset to a multi-perspective view on ABC-systems.

### 2.3 First outcomes

Stakeholder needs analysis leads to clear view about requirements of users (travelers and border guards) and non-users (from unawareness to non-acceptance). Analysis of the legal frameworks reveals the needed balance between privacy concerns and compliance with the Schengen acquis. Security analysis reveals potential risks which are answered by innovative methods for detection of (i) document fraud, (ii) attacks within the document scanning process, (iii) biometric spoofing and others. New advances in innovative processes and surveillance technology allow increased gate usage and shorter transmission times. Different ABC topologies can be combined and a reference design has been proposed, that shall be applicable for various types of border crossings at land, air and sea.

## 3. SUMMARY AND NEXT STEPS

We can show that ABC poses a challenging problem due to the combination of different security technologies. The technological solution has to be developed within a multi-stakeholder environment, where strong diverging requirements exist. Therefore, we propose a combination of heuristic and systematic innovation procedures to come up with a leading-edge technology that fulfills the needs and interests of multiple stakeholders.

## 4. ACKNOWLEDGMENTS

This project has received funding from the European Union's Seventh Framework Programme for research, technological development and demonstration under grant agreement no 312583.

*IH&MMSec'14*, June 11–13, 2014, Salzburg, Austria.
ACM 978-1-4503-2647-6/14/06.
http://dx.doi.org/10.1145/2600918.2600944

# Biometrics based Observer Free Transferable E-cash

Kamlesh Tiwari
Dept. of Computer Science and Engineering
Indian Institute of Technology Kanpur
ktiwari@cse.iitk.ac.in

Phalguni Gupta
Dept. of Computer Science and Engineering
Indian Institute of Technology Kanpur
pg@cse.iitk.ac.in

## ABSTRACT

This paper proposes a transaction strategy to implement transferable E-cash. It does not involve any third party observer at the time of transaction and possesses strong anonymity property. It uses biometric features of the legitimate holder of e-cash to progress the transaction. It works on the transfer of coin ownership and is built around the restrictive blinding and biometric digital signature scheme. Its mathematical model utilizes the hardness of discrete log problem and representation problem in groups. It guarantees anonymity and unlinkability for a genuine user and non repudiation to a fraudulent one.

## Categories and Subject Descriptors

K.4.4 [**Electronic Commerce**]: Cybercash, digital cash;
D.4.6 [**Security and Protection**]: Cryptographic controls;
K.6.5 [**Security and Protection**]: Authentication

## Keywords

Biometrics Features; E-cash; Transferability; Blind Signature; Double Spending; Representation problem; Anonymity; Coin Ownership Transfer

## 1. INTRODUCTION

Modern electronic payment system requires a new kind of realization of money, particularly in electronic form to improve user privacy and to reduce network usage. Connectivity requirement with the central server at the time of the payment is the prime criteria which classifies the electronic fund transfer into one of the two categories, called *online* and *offline*. In online fund transfer system, the buyer provides his account details along with the amount of payment to the merchant's point of sale device. These details are then sent to the bank along with payment order. The bank verifies the credential of the buyer and transfers the said amount from the payee's account to the seller's account. The physical money remains within the bank before and after the payment. The account information of the buyer is usually carried on a plastic card having a magnetic strip, that may or may not carry information of the available money in the account. There are two concerns in this system. First, the bank is required to be present online at the time of payment. If a connection with the server cannot be established then the user fails to make the desired transaction. Secondly, a bank can keep track all transactions, including amount of payment, buyer and seller details etc. which are susceptible to be used for any unwanted purpose and privacy compromise.

In offline electronic fund transfer system [34], the user carries digital e-cash which is analogous to physical paper money for buying commodities or services. Digital e-cash can be obtained from enabled banks after undergoing through a well defined *withdrawal* transaction. Neither the buyer nor the seller is required to establish any direct connection with the bank while *spending* digital e-cash. The seller may credit the received digital e-cash to his bank account by executing a *deposit* transaction at some later point of time, not necessarily immediately after receiving the payment. Like paper currency, e-cash also provides sense of possessing and privacy to expense. Critical properties of conventional paper currency such as (i) offline usability, i.e. ability to perform the desired transaction without any network connection (2) intracability, i.e. bank not being able to trace the expenditure history of the currency and (iii) transferability, i.e. enabling a merchant accepting the e-cash by selling his goods to spend again to another merchant, are the intensely desired from e-cash. These requirements are not obvious to achieve in case of e-cash.

Various models have been proposed to attain certain properties of conventional paper currency in e-cash such as Single-valued one time spendable coin, Single-valued multi-spendable coin [25], Single-valued one time spendable transferable coin [34, 22], etc. Single-valued one time spendable coin described in [9, 19] is shown in Figure. 1. The electronic money is realized in the form of virtual coins [26]. All coins are supposed to have same denomination that cannot be broken down or combined into other denomination. A person holds unit value coin; each being unique and differentiable from others. User has to undergo a *withdrawal* transaction with the bank to obtain an e-cash coin. The protocol ensures that the bank recognizes the customer well but he does not have sufficient parameters to identity the issued e-cash coin. Lack of e-cash coin identity limits the bank to keep track the spending history for genuine payments. Level of anonymity introduced in the system is called *weak* when var-

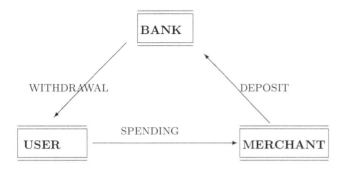

**Figure 1: Single valued coin based e-cash circulation cycle**

ious spendings of a user can be linked; otherwise it is strong. During the payment, the user has to follow a *spending* transaction at the point of sales with the merchant. During e-cash payments payer and payee naturally know each other's identity by having authentication mechanism; however any third party should not be able to know them for genuine payments. Mathematical model of the protocol ensures that there is no need of the bank to be present when the *spending* transaction executes. The merchant later submits the coin obtained from the user to the bank by executing a *deposit* transaction. In turn, the bank verifies the value deposited by the merchant and accepts the payment transcript. Double spending and colluding of merchants are two well defined challenges with the system. Double spending is the act of spending e-cash more than the allowed number of time (usually one) by the owner while colluding of merchants opens the possibility of more than one merchant cooperating to produce the fake double spent e-cash to defeat unforgeability. Genuine users are protected from false accusation of double spending by exculpability. Mathematical model of the e-cash system provides proofs to meet these challenges.

Often an e-cash coin once spent cannot be used by its receiver for making any further payment. To facilitate the transferability as similar to conventional paper money, few schemes have been suggested in literature which require the coin receiver to contact an observer to refresh the coin before spending. These schemes are as inconvenient as depositing the e-cash in the bank and asking for the new one. This has motivated us to device an observer free transferable e-cash solution. Transferable e-cash coin proposed in this paper is not required to deposit back in the bank after a single payment. The merchant, in turn on receiving such a coin, can spend the same to another merchant as a spender without refreshing it.

The proposed strategy utilizes the biometric characteristics of the parties involved in the transaction to secure the e-cash coin integrity. Physiological or behavioral characteristics uniquely describes a person and are hard to imitate by imposters. There exists personal recognition systems in literature which are based on single or a combination of biometric traits. Some of the well known biometric traits includes face [33, 38], fingerprint [18, 46, 51, 50], palmprint [3, 49, 48], ear [44], iris [40], knuckleprint [39, 4, 41] *etc.* Any biometric

system consists of four major phases; viz. data acquisition, preprocessing, feature extraction, and matching. In data acquisition phase, an image is captured by using suitable sensor. Preprocessing improves the suitability of image to the application. Features from the image called template are extracted and stored in database. When a query image comes for recognition, similar features are extracted and the degree of similarity/dis-similarity is estimated against template in the stored database. Matching decisions are based on a suitable threshold. These features can also be used for authentication of user's identity for e-cash coin by the bank, and for digital signature [32].

Various efficient biometric based cryptosystems have been proposed in literature. In [32] Davida et el have proposed an iris based cryptosystem which utilizes multiple iris scans to arrive at a canonical iris code with error correcting information which are used as biometric-key. In [36] Monrose et el have proposed an efficient voice based method to derive cryptographic key. In [24] an enhanced method has been proposed to generate strong key from biometric data. A detailed security analysis and survey of biometric cryptosystems has been discussed in [37].

This paper proposes a space efficient e-cash transaction strategy to support bounded transferability by developing the concept of coin ownership transfer. Advantage of the proposed protocol with respect to current solution is that it does not involve any third party observer during e-cash coin transaction and thereby, eliminates the risk of unwanted exposure of transaction details to protect user's privacy for genuine payment. Security analysis provides proof of strong security requirements that (i) e-cash spending of genuine user remains anonymous, (ii) identity of double spender gets exposed (non repudiation), (iii) colluding of merchants is not possible (unforgeability), (iv) bank fails to decide whether two different deposited e-cash coins are originally withdrawn by the same user (unlinkability). Biometrics authentication impacts to improve security during spending transaction and non-repudiation. The proposed protocol uses biometrics characteristics of the involved parties for digital signature to protect identity share of spending parties against tampering. The paper is organized as follows. Section 2 briefly highlights some of the well known work related to the problem. The proposed biometric based single use transferable coin transaction strategy has been described in Section 3. Next section discusses the security claims and identification of fraudulent user. Conclusions are given in the last section.

## 2. RELATED WORK

The concept of anonymous offline electronic cash has been introduced by Chaum in [19] which uses blind signatures and cut-and-choose methodology. Construction of off-line e-cash has been demonstrated in [20, 21] and more secure and efficient schemes have been proposed in [30]. Although these solutions guarantee unlinkability i.e. it is hard to determine whether two given e-cash coins are withdrawn by the same user and non-repudiation i.e. a user can not deny his genuine participation, but the construction is not space efficient.

A compact ways to represent e-cash using restrictive blinding has been described in [9, 10, 11, 12] by taking advantage of representation problem in groups. For a group $G_q$ of large prime order, consider a generator tuple $(g_1, g_2, ..., g_k)$ where $k \geq 2$ and $g_i \in G_q - \{1\}$ and $g_i \neq g_j$. Representation of any $x \in G_q$ is a tuple $(a_1, a_2, ..., a_k)$ such that $\prod_{i=1}^{k} g_i^{a_i} = x$

where $a_i \in \mathbb{Z}_q$ for $1 \leq i \leq k$. With generator-tuples of length $k$ there exist $q^{k-1}$ representations of $x \in G_q$. Therefore, probability of guessing a representation without knowing it is $1/q$ which is very low when $q$ is large. Assuming that it is infeasible to compute *discrete logarithm*[1] in $G_q$, there cannot exist a polynomial-time algorithm that provides a representation of $x$ with non-negligible probability of success. Also, there cannot exist a polynomial-time algorithm which can produce a number $x \in G_q$ and its two different representations for given generator tuple $(g_1, g_2, ..., g_k)$ with non-negligible probability of success. In [22], a method to store personal database has been presented using a blind signature scheme that computes bank's digital signature $\sigma_B(A) = (z, a, b, r) \in G_q \times G_q \times G_q \times \mathbb{Z}_q$ on $A \in G_q$ such that $g^r = a.h^{H(A,z,a,b)}$ and $A^r = b.z^{H(A,z,a,b)}$ where $H$ are publicly known multi-variable collision-untraceable hash function [2]. This paper also uses the same blind signature scheme.

In [9], has discussed that how a user with known bank parameters $g, g_1, g_2, h(= g^p), g_1^p, g_2^p$ can register its fabricated account number $I = g_1^u$ with the bank without exposing $u$. E-cash coin *withdrawal* transaction is initiated by the withdrawer user. After his identities are verified, the bank chooses a random challenge $w \in_R \mathbb{Z}_q$ to send $a = g^w$ and $b = (Ig_2)^w$ to the user who selects $s \in_R \mathbb{Z}_q^*$, and $x_1, x_2, v_1, v_2 \in_R \mathbb{Z}_q$ to form $A = (Ig_2)^s$, $B = g_1^{x_1} g_2^{x_2}$, $z = (Ig_2^p)$, $z' = z^s$, $a' = a^{v_1} g^{v_2}$, and $b' = b^{sv_1} A^{v_2}$ to send the value $c = H(A, B, z', a', b')/u \mod q$ to the bank. In turn, the bank provides $r = (cx + w) \mod q$ to the user and subsequently, debits the unit amount from the user's account. Its response satisfies two equations $g^r = h^c a$ and $(Ig_2)^r = z^c b$. The user computes $r' = (ru + v) \mod q$ to get digital signature of the bank on $(A, B0$ which is a tuple of the form $\sigma_B(A, B) = (z', a', b', r')$. To spend the coin, the user sends $A, B, \sigma_B(A, B)$ to merchant who in turn, sends a challenge $x = H_0(A, B, I_M, \text{time-stamp})$ and expects the response $r_1(= x(u_1 s) + x_1 \mod q)$ and $r_2(= xs + x_2 \mod q)$ from the user that satisfies $g_1^{r_1} g_2^{r_2} = A^x B$. This response proves that the user is the genuine bearer of e-cash as he only knows the representation of both $A$ and $B$. Buyers and sellers are required to know each other's identity during a transaction and for this purpose biometrics characteristics can be used to ensure the non-repudiation. The merchant can deposit the e-cash coin in the bank by sending the payment transcript consisting of $A, B, \sigma_B(A, B), r_1, r_2$ and transaction time-stamp. The bank, after successful verification of the equation $g_1^{r_1} g_2^{r_2} = A^x B$ and the signature on $(A, B)$, credits unit amount in the merchant's bank account. When $A$ happens to be a duplicate entry for the deposit database, bank can expose the double-spender by using $(x, r_1, r_2)$ of the new transcript and $(x', r_1', r_2')$ from the database by disclosing his account number as $I = g_1^{(r_1 - r_1')/(r_2 - r_2')}$. Values received by the bank during deposit neither contain coin identity nor withdrawing user's account information; therefore, the bank cannot keep track of the user's account with

respect to e-cash payments. All transactions involves only two parties which can be present face to face with an enabled device; therefore it does not require any external connection.

Randomized blinding and polynomials have been used in [26] to achieve multi-spendability. A compact representation of e-cash using pseudo-random variables has been proposed in [1, 13, 14, 6]. Scheme in [1] allows simultaneous withdrawal of $2^L$ coins such that the space requirement is proportional to $(L + k)$, rather than $(k.2^L)$. A scheme for transferable e-cash has been introduced in [47] by using an observer for coin refreshing. In [31], Jeong has described another approach to implement transferable e-cash using group signature scheme with observers.

Concept of conditional e-cash payments is presented in [45], where payment to the merchant becomes only valid when a trusted publisher (a third party) flags in its favor. In conditional payments, a payer obtains an electronic coin and anonymously transfers it to an anonymous payee. In this scheme, payer and payee need not to know each other during the payments. An improved conditional e-payment scheme is presented in [7]. Anonymous transferable conditional e-cash is presented in [52] by using Groth-Sahai proofs [29] and commuting signatures. Proofs provided in [23] states that the size of transferable e-cash coin grows as it passes by and an adversary having unbounded computation power can definitely recognize his own spend money.

First transferable e-cash scheme is proposed in [42] by using disposable zero knowledge authentication to prevent multiple use of same authentication. Anonymity is not confirmed because multiple spendings of the same user can be combined. [43] proposes a transferable and divisible e-cash system which allows its customer to subdivide their cash balance. The scheme requires smart-card equipped with Rabin scheme chip and a distributed database system for the bank and it allows the construction of universal electronic cash open. Another transferable e-cash scheme with reduced number of communication between the bank and the user is presented in [17] and more divisible e-cash schemes are presented in [2, 15]. A protocol based on [29] is proposed in [28] that involves an authority to revoke anonymity in fraud cases. Transferable e-cash scheme based on the work on randomization of Groth-Sahai proofs [5, 29, 27] is proposed in [8] which claims to achieve optimal anonymity by involving a trusted authority called judge who can trace coins and users.

Anonymity in transferable e-cash is studied in [16] and it defines two natural levels of anonymity calling as *full anonymity* (FA) and *perfect anonymity* (PA), and subsequently has proved that FA is possible but PA is not. It also defines two restricted PA properties and shows both of them can be reached.

# 3. PROPOSED BIOMETRIC BASED SINGLE-USE TRANSFERABLE E-COIN

This section describes the transaction strategy of the proposed transferable e-cash coin. By transaction, it is meant the way that one can withdraw/spend or deposit an e-cash coin. The chain of money handover starts from a bank, passing through a series of users and finally, ends by reaching back to the bank. Bounded transferability signifies that a newly withdrawn e-cash coin of user $\mathcal{U}_1$ can be in hand of at most $m$ users $\mathcal{U}_2, \mathcal{U}_3, ...\mathcal{U}_{m+1}$ before it is deposited back

---

[1]Discrete log problem [35]: For a group $G_q$ of large prime order, let $a, b \in G_q$ such that $a^i = b$ with $i \in \mathbb{Z}_q$. Then, for given $a$ and $b$ finding $i$ is discrete log problem. An algorithm to find $i$ in **polynomial time** is not known.

[2]For a pair of values $(A, B) \in G_q \times G_q$ Bank's signature $\sigma_B(A, B)$ can be similarly extended to consists of a tuple $(z, a, b, r) \in G_q \times G_q \times G_q \times \mathbb{Z}_q$ such that $g^r = a.h^{H(A,B,z,a,b)}$ and $A^r = b.z^{H(A,B,z,a,b)}$.

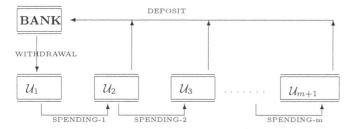

**Figure 2: Transferable coin withdrawal, spending and deposit transaction cycle**

to the bank for its redemption as shown in Figure. 2. A user $U_k$, $2 \leq k \leq m$, can transfer e-cash to the another user to buy goods or services, or he can deposit it to the bank. In our design, the digital representation of an $m$-transferable e-coin contains the following information.

1. **Coin Identity:** It is a large pseudo random number used to differentiate one coin from another. The withdrawing user $U_1$ randomly generates this identity number and gets it digitally signed by the bank executing restrictive blinding protocol. It ensures that the bank has no knowledge of this account number. The specific blind digital signature procedure ensures that the identity of $U_1$ is also embedded in this identity number of the e-coin.

2. **Coin ownership proof:** These set of parameters are provided by the spender of e-cash to the receiver so that the receiver can himself satisfy ownership challenge during his turn of spending.

3. **Spenders history:** This is an ordered list of secret sharing information collected incrementally from the users in transferability chain across the spending transactions. This information is useless till the e-cash transactions are genuine. But in case of unauthorized spendings, this information enables the bank to reveal the identity of a misbehaving user.

4. **Integrity proof:** A set of values is used to prove that the e-cash contents are not tampered.

Except coin identity, all other coin parameters keep updating as it passes from one user to another. Subsection 3.1 elaborates the initial security parameters published by bank, Next subsection specifies how a user acquires his bank account related parameters, Section 3.3 explains *withdrawal* and *spending* transaction procedure. *Deposit* transaction procedure is presented in Subsection 3.4.

## 3.1  Initial Public Parameters

During initialization, bank needs to register each user and has to provide user specific parameters for the secure e-cash transactions. In order to do so the bank chooses a large prime number $q$ and creates random parameters $g, g_1, g_2 \in G_q^*$ and $p \in \mathbb{Z}_q^*$ along with a re-hashing function $H$ over $\mathbb{Z}_q^*$. Keeping the value of $p$ secret, the bank publishes all other values and $g^p$ in public.

## 3.2  User-specific Account Parameters

Registration of the user with bank generates two parameters; first one is his unique bank account number and other one is the digital signature on a randomly chosen number of the user. Registration process is as follows, user $U_i$ picks a random number $u_i \in_R \mathbb{Z}_q^*$ such that $I_i(= g_1^{u_i})$ becomes a unique bank account number for the user $U_i$. User's account number is also used as his identity. Bank cannot guess $u_i$ from $I_i$ because of the hardness of discrete log problem. The user $U_i$ picks two more random numbers $v_1, v_2 \in_R \mathbb{Z}_q^*$ to form $B_i = g_1^{v1} g_2^{v2}$ and subsequently obtains a digital signature $\sigma_B(I_i, B_i)$ from the bank in blinded manner [22]. Values of $u_i, v_1, v_2$ are only known to the user $U_i$. One cannot compute these values by $I_i$ or $B_i$ because of the hardness of discrete log problem and success probability of guessing the values is very low.

## 3.3  Withdrawal/Spending Procedure

Transferable e-cash *withdrawal* procedure is executed between the bank and the first user while *spending* procedure is followed between any two users. During *withdrawal*, bank first verifies the account number of the user and subsequently issues e-cash coins against his available account balance. Bank identifies well to the user but, for the issued e-cash coin except that they are genuine it it not known to whom it was issued. Blind signature scheme in [10], is followed to issue e-cash coin. User with bank account number $I$ chooses a random number $s \in_R \mathbb{Z}_q^*$ to device the coin identity as $A = (Ig_2)^s$. The blind signature strategy followed as in [10] ensures that $s$ and $A$ remain unknown to the bank despite of user verification and digital signature $\sigma_B(A)$ on $A$. Advantage of this strategy is that the identity of the e-cash coin has its genuine holder's account number parameters embedded within it.

Two more parameters called *correction factor $C$* and *spending history $(R, T)$* are considered to make the coin transferable. Correction factor enables a receiving user to prove his ownership with the e-cash coin on his turn. Again, spending history maintains secret share of previous owners of the e-cash coin which helps the bank to identify a fraudulent user, if any, in case of double spending. For the initial user $U_0$ (which is bank), spending history parameters $R$ and $T$ contain null and $C$ is 1.

When a user $U_i$, $i \geq 2$ is asked to accept e-cash coin during *spending*, he generates a random number $x$ and asks from payee $U_{i-1}$ to provide two values $r_{(i-1)1}$ and $r_{(i-1)2}$ that can satisfy the equation $(A.C_{i-1})^x B_{i-1} = g_1^{r_{(i-1)1}} . g_2^{r_{(i-1)2}}$. Spending history parameters $R$ and $T$ are updated by appending $r_{(i-1)1}$ and $r_{(i-1)2}$ respectively. It can be noted that only a genuine holder of the e-cash user $U_{i-1}$ can provide $r_{(i-1)1}$ and $r_{(i-1)2}$ such that they satisfy the equation because of two reason such as the coin related secret parameters are only known to its genuine holder and second, coin parameters also embed holders secret within it. Confidentiality of the coin parameters disappoints an attacker to attempt for a replay or stolen data attack with biometric spoofs as it alone cannot succeed in e-cash coin payment in the absence of genuine coin parameters.

Now the e-cash receiving user knows some of the required coin parameters. But since his identity is not embedded in the coin, he needs a correction factor that enables him as a genuine bearer. In order to compute correction factor $C_i$, the user $U_{i-1}$ cooperates with $U_i$ who randomly gen-

· erates a secret $s_i \in_R \mathbb{Z}_q^*$ and sends $I_i^{s_i}$ with $g_2^{s_i}$ to payee $\mathcal{U}_{i-1}$, and in return $\mathcal{U}_{i-1}$ computes $C_i$ which is given by $C_i = (I_i^{s_i}.g_2^{s_i}.C_{i-1})/(I_{i-1}.g_2)^{s_{i-1}}$ and replies back to $\mathcal{U}_i$. It can be noted that the value of $s_{i-1}$ is a secret component of $\mathcal{U}_{i-1}$ only known him. Initially $C_1$ of user $\mathcal{U}_1$ is 1. Since $s_i$ is only known to user $\mathcal{U}_i$ for all $i$. Therefore $C_i$ can only be computed by $\mathcal{U}_{i-1}$ when $\mathcal{U}_i$ provides $I_i^{s_i}$ and $g_2^{s_i}$. One should be sure about $\mathcal{U}_i$ using $I_i$ because otherwise $\mathcal{U}_i$ needs to solve discrete log problem for using the obtained correction factor. To make the coin transferable but secure, its integrity proof is computed by taking digital signature using biometric features[3] $F_{i-1}$ of the user $\mathcal{U}_{i-1}$ on values $I_i, C_i, R, T, F_i$. Finally, the user $\mathcal{U}_i$ has the following set of values $\{A, s_i, \sigma_B(A), C_i, R, T, F_i, \delta_{\mathcal{U}_{i-1}}(I_i, C_i, R, T, F_i)\}$ as e-cash coin. Thus, withdrawal procedure can be depicted in Table 1 while spending procedure between $\mathcal{U}_{i-1}$ and $\mathcal{U}_i$, $2 \leq i \leq m+1$ is shown in Table 2.

**Table 1: Proposed Withdrawal Procedure**

| User $\mathcal{U}_1$ | Bank |
|---|---|
| User $\mathcal{U}_1$'s identity → | |
| Coin identity parameter $A$ → | |
| | ← Digital Signature on $A$ in blinded way |
| User's biometric features → | |
| | ← Biometric Digital Signature on initialised values |

**Table 2: Proposed Spending Procedure**

| User $\mathcal{U}_{i-1}$ | User $\mathcal{U}_i$ |
|---|---|
| User $\mathcal{U}_{i-1}$'s identity → | |
| Coin identity info. → | |
| Spender history & proof → | (Integrity check) |
| | ← Random Challenge |
| Coin ownership proof → | |
| | ← User $\mathcal{U}_i$'s identity share |
| Coin ownership transfer → | |

## 3.4 Deposit Procedure

When a user $\mathcal{U}_i$ wishes to convert e-cash coin into real money, he can submit this coin to the bank. The user $\mathcal{U}_i$ gets verified his own identity information using his biometric characteristics to the bank and subsequently submits the e-cash coin parameters $A, \sigma_B(A), R, T, F_i$ to the bank for verification and redemption. This transaction is not based on challenge response method.

Bank verifies its own digital signature $\sigma_B(A)$ on coin identification information $A$, and $F_i$ with user's biometric char-

---

[3]$\delta_{\mathcal{U}_k}(a_1, a_2, a_3, a_5, a_5)$ is the biometric key based digital signature of user $\mathcal{U}_k$ on values $a_1, a_2, a_3, a_5, a_5$, where $\mathcal{U}_0$ is bank

acteristics. After successful verification, the bank stores $(A, R, T, F_i)$ in its database and credits an amount equal to the face value of the coin (generally unit value) to the bank account of the user $\mathcal{U}_i$.

## 4. SECURITY ANALYSIS

This section produces critical security claims and their analysis. Claim 1 provides proof to show that e-cash spendings of a well behaved user remains anonymous to bank, whereas Claim 2 proves that the bank cannot decide whether two deposited e-cash coins have been actually withdrawn by same user. Claim 3 states that the bank account details of a user who makes double spending can be exposed by the bank. Claim 4 explains how the coin ownership transfer is secure and it prevents colluding of merchants. Finally it is shown that the identity share of various users in transferability chain during spending is protected against tampering.

**Claim** 1. E-cash spendings of a genuine user remain anonymous to bank.

PROOF. Even though the bank knows $R$ and $T$ but these values are constructed by secret share which are random number and cannot reveal the identity of the user. However, it is discussed later that if any fraudulent user spends twice the coin, he provides enough information to expose his identity. Therefore, a genuine spender remains anonymous. □

**Claim** 2. E-cash coins are unlinkabe.

PROOF. Unlinkability refers to the bank's inability to decide whether two different deposited coins are originally withdrawn by the same user or not. This property helps to protect the privacy of a genuine user. In the proposed withdrawal transaction scheme, the user himself generates the coin identity randomly and gets bank's digital signature on that in a blinded way. So the bank has no information about the identity of the coin with the user. Therefore, getting two such coin identities exposed to bank at the time of deposit, the bank cannot link them to conclude upon the similarity of withdrawing user. □

**Claim** 3. Double spender is identifiable at the bank.

PROOF. Since electronic data is easy to copy, it is suspected that a malicious user can always keep backup of the e-cash coin before the execution of spending procedure, and after the spending it, he can get the original values of the e-cash coin by restoring. When such a user tries to spend second time with the restored e-cash coin, this act of misbehavior is called double spending. It is an faulty behavior in context of e-cash.

In the case of malicious double spending by a user (say $\mathcal{U}_k$), the fraud would be exposed by the bank during the deposit procedure when the duplicate coin reaches to the bank. Assume that two users $\mathcal{U}_p$ and $\mathcal{U}_q$ wish to deposit coin parameters $(A, \sigma_B(A), R, T)$ and $(A, \sigma_B(A), R', T')$ with the bank. The scenario is illustrated in Figure 3.

Since these deposits happen at two different instant of time, one user (say $\mathcal{U}_p$) first deposits the coin in the bank. When another user $\mathcal{U}_q$ reaches the bank to deposit his coin, the bank can unfold all values of $(r_{11}, r_{21}, r_{31}, ..., r_{p1})$ and $(r_{12}, r_{22}, r_{32}, ..., r_{p2})$ from $R$ and $R'$ using modulo division operation. In the same way, the bank using $T$ and $t'$ to

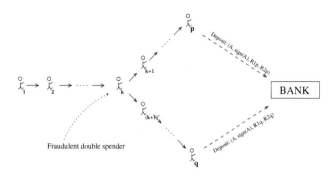

**Figure 3: Double spending scenario in transferable e-cash**

unfold values $(r'_{11}, r'_{21}, r'_{31}, ..., r'_{q1})$ and $(r'_{12}, r'_{22}, r'_{32}, ..., r'_{q2})$. A simple comparison can reveal position and secret share of the double spender. Out of these two sequences $(r_{11}, r_{21}, r_{31}, ..., r_{p1})$ and $(r'_{11}, r'_{21}, r'_{31}, ..., r'_{q1})$, the bank can observe that the prefix sequence $(r_{11}, r_{21}, r_{31}, ..., r_{(k-1)1})$ and $(r'_{11}, r'_{21}, r'_{31}, ..., r'_{(k-1)1})$ are same. After finding the value of $k$, it gets two sets of values $(r_{k1}, r_{k2})$ and $(r'_{k1}, r'_{k2})$. These values reveal the identity of the double spender as follows.

$$I_k = g_1^{(r_{k1} - r'_{k1})/(r_{k2} - r'_{k2})}.$$

Thus, the scheme achieves non repudiation. $\square$

**Claim** 4. Coin ownership transfer is secure and colluding is prevented.

PROOF. A user owning the coin carries the representation of e-coin which is not known to any one else. For the ownership transfer between $\mathcal{U}_{i-1}$ and $\mathcal{U}_i$, the secret part of e-coin representation $s_i$ for $\mathcal{U}_i$ is randomly generated by $\mathcal{U}_i$ and two parameters $I_i^{s_i}$ and $g_2^{s_i}$ are sent to the user $\mathcal{U}_{i-1}$. Since finding discrete log is hard, therefore, $\mathcal{U}_{i-1}$ cannot find $s_i$. But the user $\mathcal{U}_{i-1}$ can calculate $C_i$ by using his secret value $s_{i-1}$ and the received values. $\mathcal{U}_{i-1}$ provides $C_i$ and his digital signature on it to $\mathcal{U}_i$. Coin ownership transfer requires the secret values of the e-coin on both users ($\mathcal{U}_{i-1}$ and $\mathcal{U}_i$). Therefore, ownership is a mutual activity of two parties which cannot be carried out by a single individual. Further, since the construction restricts the involvement of more than two parties during coin ownership transfer, it is secure against colluding of merchants. $\square$

**Claim** 5. Identity share of previous spender is protected against tampering.

PROOF. Spenders history is an ordered list of secret sharing information of users in reusable chain of an e-coin across all spending. It is constructed in an incremental way as the e-coin passes from one user to another. This information enables the bank to reveal the identity of a user who is involved in unauthorized spending. To protect spending history from being tampered by its owner, the spender provides his digital signature on it. Therefore, any tampering makes the coin unusable for further spending. Spending transaction is designed in such a way that every user verifies not only the digital signature but also its incremental construction by the predecessor. $\square$

## 5. CONCLUSIONS

This paper has proposed an efficient and secure procedure for bounded transferable e-coin where there is no need of coin refreshing with either a bank or observer at intermediate places. The transaction strategy has used a biometric based digital signature and ensures anonymity, non-repudiation and unlinkability. E-cash is an offline digital cash. A user having the right kind of device can withdraw this money from the bank and he can later spend this for purchasing an item from a merchant in absence of bank or third party observer. At some later point of time, the merchant has to deposit the values obtained from the user to the bank for its redemption. The transaction is based on the concept of spending-ownership transfer. Representation of transferable e-cash involves identity of its owner and secret values known only to its owner. E-cash handover procedure between users ensures that a user having knowledge of coin representation can only remodel the coin's parameters to make spendable by its successive owner. Secondly, it guarantees anonymity, that is, the identity of the user should not be traceable by linking the withdrawal, spending and deposit transaction together in any way. It has been ensured that for a genuine payment, the bank fails to figure out who has made the payment and to whom. In addition, the bank fails to link two different payments to the same user; thereby protecting the user's identity.

## Acknowledgment

Authors like to acknowledge the support provided by the Department of Information Technology, Government of India to carry out this research work.

## 6. REFERENCES

[1] M. Au, W. Susilo, and Y. Mu. Practical compact e-cash. In *Information Security and Privacy*, pages 431–445, 2007.

[2] M. H. Au, W. Susilo, and Y. Mu. Practical anonymous divisible e-cash from bounded accumulators. In *Financial Cryptography and Data Security*, pages 287–301. 2008.

[3] G. Badrinath, K. Tiwari, and P. Gupta. An efficient palmprint based recognition system using 1d-dct features. In *Intelligent Computing Technology*, pages 594–601, 2012.

[4] G. S. Badrinath, A. Nigam, and P. Gupta. An efficient finger-knuckle-print based recognition system fusing sift and surf matching scores. In *International Conference on Information, Communications, and Signal Processing (ICICS)*, pages 374–387, 2011.

[5] M. Belenkiy, J. Camenisch, M. Chase, M. Kohlweiss, A. Lysyanskaya, and H. Shacham. Randomizable proofs and delegatable anonymous credentials. In *Advances in Cryptology-CRYPTO*, pages 108–125. 2009.

[6] P. Bichsel, J. Camenisch, G. Neven, N. Smart, and B. Warinschi. Get shorty via group signatures without encryption. *Security and Cryptography for Networks*, pages 381–398, 2010.

[7] M. Blanton. Improved conditional e-payments. In *Applied Cryptography and Network Security*, pages 188–206, 2008.

[8] O. Blazy, S. Canard, G. Fuchsbauer, A. Gouget, H. Sibert, and J. Traoré. Achieving optimal anonymity in transferable e-cash with a judge. In *Progress in Cryptology–AFRICACRYPT*, pages 206–223. 2011.

[9] S. Brands. An efficient off-line electronic cash system based on the representation problem. Technical report, CWI (Centre for Mathematics and Computer Science), Amsterdam, 1993.

[10] S. Brands. Untraceable off-line cash in wallet with observers. In *Advances in Cryptology - CRYPTO*, pages 302–318, 1994.

[11] S. Brands. Electronic cash on the internet. In *Proceedings of the Symposium on Network and Distributed System Security*, pages 64–84, 1995.

[12] S. Brands. Restrictive binding of secret-key certificates. In *Advances in Cryptology - EUROCRYPT*, pages 231–247, 1995.

[13] J. Camenisch, S. Hohenberger, and A. Lysyanskaya. Compact e-cash. *Advances in Cryptology - EUROCRYPT*, pages 566–566, 2005.

[14] J. Camenisch and M. Michels. Separability and efficiency for generic group signature schemes. In *Advances in Cryptology - CRYPTO*, pages 785–785, 1999.

[15] S. Canard and A. Gouget. Divisible e-cash systems can be truly anonymous. In *Advances in Cryptology-EUROCRYPT*, pages 482–497. 2007.

[16] S. Canard and A. Gouget. Anonymity in transferable e-cash. In *Applied Cryptography and Network Security*, pages 207–223, 2008.

[17] S. Canard, A. Gouget, and J. Traoré. Improvement of efficiency in (unconditional) anonymous transferable e-cash. In *Financial Cryptography and Data Security*, pages 202–214. 2008.

[18] R. Cappelli, M. Ferrara, and D. Maltoni. Fingerprint indexing based on minutia cylinder-code. *IEEE Transactions on Pattern Analysis and Machine Intelligence*, 33(5):1051–1057, 2011.

[19] D. Chaum. Blind signatures for untraceable payments. In *Advances in Cryptology - CRYPTO*, volume 82, pages 199–203, 1983.

[20] D. Chaum. Achieving electronic privacy. *Scientific American*, 267(2):96–101, 1992.

[21] D. Chaum, A. Fiat, and M. Naor. Untraceable electronic cash. In *Advances in Cryptology - CRYPTO*, pages 319–327, 1990.

[22] D. Chaum and T. Pedersen. Wallet databases with observers. In *Advances in Cryptology - CRYPTO*, pages 89–105, 1993.

[23] D. Chaum and T. P. Pedersen. Transferred cash grows in size. In *Advances in Cryptology-EUROCRYPT*, pages 390–407, 1993.

[24] Y. Dodis, R. Ostrovsky, L. Reyzin, and A. Smith. Fuzzy extractors: How to generate strong keys from biometrics and other noisy data. *SIAM Journal on Computing*, 38(1):97–139, 2008.

[25] N. Ferguson. Extensions of single-term coins. In *Advances in Cryptology - CRYPTO*, pages 292–301, 1994.

[26] N. Ferguson. Single term off-line coins. In *Advances in Cryptology - EUROCRYPT*, pages 318–328, 1994.

[27] G. Fuchsbauer. Commuting signatures and verifiable encryption. In *Advances in Cryptology–EUROCRYPT*, pages 224–245. 2011.

[28] G. Fuchsbauer, D. Pointcheval, and D. Vergnaud. Transferable constant-size fair e-cash. In *Cryptology and Network Security*, pages 226–247. 2009.

[29] J. Groth and A. Sahai. Efficient non-interactive proof systems for bilinear groups. In *Advances in Cryptology–EUROCRYPT*, pages 415–432. 2008.

[30] R. Hirschfeld. Making electronic refunds safer. In *Advances in Cryptology - CRYPTO*, pages 106–112, 1993.

[31] I. R. Jeong, D. H. Lee, and J. I. Lim. Efficient transferable cash with group signatures. In *Information Security*, pages 462–474. 2001.

[32] J. Jo, J. Seo, and H. Lee. Biometric digital signature key generation and cryptography communication based on fingerprint. In *Proceedings of the 1st annual international conference on Frontiers in algorithmics*, pages 38–49, 2007.

[33] S. Li and A. Jain. *Handbook of face recognition*. Springer-Verlag New York Inc, 2011.

[34] C. Ma and Y. Yang. Transferable off-line electronic cash. *Chinease Journal on Computers - Jisuanji Xuebao*, 28(3):301–308, 2005.

[35] K. McCurley. The discrete logarithm problem. In *Proceedings of Symposium in Applied Math*, volume 42, pages 49–74, 1990.

[36] F. Monrose, M. Reiter, Q. Li, and S. Wetzel. Using voice to generate cryptographic keys. In *A Speaker Odyssey - The Speaker Recognition Workshop*, pages 237–242, 2001.

[37] A. Nagar, K. Nandakumar, and A. Jain. Biometric template transformation: a security analysis. In *Proc. of Society of Photographic Instrumentation Engineers (SPIE) – Electronic Imaging, Media Forensics and Security*, volume 7541, 2010.

[38] A. Nigam and P. Gupta. Comparing human faces using edge weighted dissimilarity measure. In *International Conference on Control, Automation, Robotics and Vision (ICARCV)*, pages 1831–1836, 2010.

[39] A. Nigam and P. Gupta. Finger knuckleprint based recognition system using feature tracking. In *Chinese Conference on Biometric Recognition (CCBR)*, pages 125–132, 2011.

[40] A. Nigam and P. Gupta. Iris recognition using consistent corner optical flow. In *Asian Conference on Computer Vision (ACCV)*, pages 358–369, 2012.

[41] A. Nigam and P. Gupta. Quality assessment of knuckleprint biometric images. In *International Conference on Image Processing (ICIP)*, pages 4205–4209, 2013.

[42] T. Okamoto and K. Ohta. Disposable zero-knowledge authentications and their applications to untraceable electronic cash. In *Advances in Cryptology-CRYPTO*, pages 481–496, 1990.

[43] T. Okamoto and K. Ohta. Universal electronic cash. In *Advances in Cryptology-CRYPTO*, pages 324–337, 1992.

[44] S. Prakash and P. Gupta. An efficient ear recognition technique invariant to illumination and pose. *Telecommunication Systems*, pages 1–14, sep 2011.

[45] L. Shi, B. Carbunar, and R. Sion. Conditional e-cash. In *Financial Cryptography and Data Security*, pages 15–28. 2007.

[46] N. Singh, K. Tiwari, A. Nigam, and P. Gupta. Fusion of 4-slap fingerprint images with their qualities for human recognition. In *World Congress on Information and Communication Technologies (WICT)*, pages 925–930, 2012.

[47] H. Tewari, D. Mahony, and M. Peirce. Reusable off-line electronic cash using secret splitting. *Networks & Telecommunications Research Group, Computer Science Department, Trinity College, Dublin*, 2, 1998.

[48] K. Tiwari, D. K. Arya, G. Badrinath, and P. Gupta. Designing palmprint based recognition system using local structure tensor and force field transformation for human identification. *Neurocomputing*, 116:222–230, 2013.

[49] K. Tiwari, D. K. Arya, and P. Gupta. Palmprint based recognition system using local structure tensor and force field transformation. In *International Conference of Intelligence Computing (ICIC)*, pages 602–607, 2011.

[50] K. Tiwari, J. Mandal, and P. Gupta. Segmentation of slap fingerprint images. In *Emerging Intelligent Computing Technology and Applications*, pages 182–187, 2013.

[51] K. Tiwari, S. Mandi, and P. Gupta. A heuristic technique for performance improvement of fingerprint based integrated biometric system. In *Intelligent Computing Theories*, pages 584–592, 2013.

[52] J. Zhang, Z. Li, and H. Guo. Anonymous transferable conditional e-cash. In *Security and Privacy in Communication Networks*, pages 45–60. 2013.

# From StirMark to StirTrace: Benchmarking Pattern Recognition Based Printed Fingerprint Detection

Mario Hildebrandt
Otto-von-Guericke University of Magdeburg,
Dept. of Computer Science,
Research Group Multimedia and Security,
PO Box 4120, 39016 Magdeburg, Germany
hildebrandt@iti.cs.uni-magdeburg.de

Jana Dittmann
Otto-von-Guericke University of Magdeburg,
Dept. of Computer Science,
Research Group Multimedia and Security,
PO Box 4120, 39016 Magdeburg, Germany
dittmann@iti.cs.uni-magdeburg.de;
The University of Buckingham,
Buckingham, United Kingdom

## ABSTRACT

Artificial sweat printed fingerprints need to be detected during crime scene investigations of latent fingerprints. Several detection approaches have been suggested on a rather small test set. In this paper we use the findings from StirMark applied to exemplar fingerprints to build a new StirTrace tool for simulating different printer effects and enhancing test sets for benchmarking detection approaches. We show how different influence factors during the printing process and acquisition of the scan sample can be simulated. Furthermore, two new feature classes are suggested to improve detection performance of banding and rotation effects during printing. The results are compared with original existing detection feature space. Our evaluation based on 6000 samples indicates that StirTrace is suitable to simulate influence factors resulting into overall 195000 simulated samples. Furthermore, the original and our extended feature set show resistance towards image manipulations with the exception of scaling (to 50 and 200%) and cropping to 25%. The new feature space enhancement is capable for handling banding, rotation as well as removal of lines and columns and shearing artifacts, while the original feature space performs better for additive noise, median cut and stretching in X-direction.

## Categories and Subject Descriptors

I.5.2 [**Pattern Recognition**]: Design Methodology—*Classifier design and evaluation*

## Keywords

Recognition of Printed Fingerprints; Printer Simulation; Forensics

## 1. MOTIVATION

Printed fingerprints, artificial sweat printed fingerprints created with an ink-jet printer, pose a challenge for crime scene forensics, as described in [6]. Such artificial traces

might lead to mis-identifications and false accusations of innocent persons. Thus, it is necessary to recognize (detect or identify) such traces. The first detection approaches from [6] identify variations in printing results and derive the challenge to differentiate between legit and malicious traces. Further work uses pattern recognition techniques in combination with high resolution sensory achieving a more reliable detection of malicious traces as reported in [5]. However, the utilized test set is limited to only one printer and three substrates and the results are highly dependent on the dot size. Practically, tests are getting very complex in considering several different printer parameter variations and conditions such as printer and surface characteristics. To offer a more simple test approach, we suggest to extend the original test set $T_{orig}$ from [5] by means of simulation ($T_{sim}$) covering a broad spectrum of different circumstances for benchmarking the recognition performance. A similar approach is motivated for biometrics in [4] for benchmarking fingerprint matchers using StirMark [9]. This software is originally intended for benchmarking watermarking approaches towards image manipulations. Uhl et al. [4] use these image manipulation techniques to simulate various distortions, defects and challenges that might occur during the acquisition of exemplar fingerprints used in biometrics. Similar to that, we see it is of course possible to alter scans of printed fingerprints to simulate different contexts of printers and substrates. In Table 1 we show the purpose of each image manipulation technique in the context of printed fingerprints compared to Uhl et al. [4]. Motivated by [4] we propose the new tool **StirTrace**[1] by using and enhancing StirMark image manipulation techniques to the context of printed fingerprints (see more details in Section 3). To further **improve the detection performance**, we additionally suggest considering scaling functions to account for different dot sizes of amino acid residues during artificial sweat printing. Our feature set extension is designed to improve the detection performance for dot size variations by two feature classes a) determining the average area of each dot in relation to its enclosing circle and by b) extending the dot distance features using the nearest neighbor method. In particular 17 **new detection features** are introduced to handle **banding** and **rotation** artifacts (see Section 4). To test and compare recognition performances of printed fingerprint detectors with StirTrace enhanced test sets, we use a) the original feature set from

---

[1]Available at http://sourceforge.net/p/stirtrace/

| StirMark Bench-mark for max 572x572 pixel RGB images | Uhl et al.[4] | StirTrace for Printed fingerprint context for 1024x768 image size |
|---|---|---|
| Additive Noise | Noise caused by dust, sensor, systematic errors | Substrate and sensor noise |
| Median Cut Filtering | Smudgy fingerprints | Smudgy fingerprints/merging amino acid dots |
| Remove Lines and Columns | Acquisition errors | Printer characteristics |
| Rotation | Rotation during the acquisition | Rotation during the acquisition |
| Stretching in X-direction | Force on the finger during acquisition | Printer characteristics |
| Shearing in Y-direction | Force on the finger during acquisition (non-perpendicular to the contact area) | Printer characteristics |
| Small Random Distortions | Perturbations | Not applicable: causes large distortions of the trace leading to exclusions from expert examiners |

**Table 1: StirMark image manipulation techniques: purpose in [4] and in the context of printed fingerprints (from 7 we have selected 6 as appropriate)**

[5] and b) our enhanced feature space. Both feature sets are classified with MultilayerPerceptron [10], RotationForest [11] and Logistic Model Tree (LMT) [8] using the Weka data mining software [3]. Finally, the results from the original processing chain from [5] and our extension are compared within $T_{orig}$ and $T_{sim}$ (StirTrace enhanced StirMark simulations).

In summary, our evaluation uses test set $T_{orig}$ from [5] consisting of 3000 samples of printed fingerprints and 3000 samples of real latent fingerprints. The training of three selected machine learning algorithms from the Weka data mining software [3] is performed on 50% of the data set. The remainder is used for the testing in the original and StirTrace-altered representations. We compare the recognition accuracies of the original feature set with those of the extended feature set a) and b) for each test.

Our results indicate that StirTrace is suitable to simulate various image distortions and artifacts. From the overall analysis, all three classifiers show a good performance (see analysis of min, max, mean, standard deviation and median values in Table 3). Furthermore, both feature sets are very resistant towards image manipulations with the exception of cropping and significant rescaling (e.g. 50 and 200%). The new feature set is well able to handle banding and rotation as expected. Additionally, it is very robust towards the removal of lines and columns and shearing artifacts. The original feature set has the best performance for additive noise, median cut and stretching in X-direction. This paper is structured as follows: Section 2 briefly summarizes the state of the art of printed fingerprint recognition approaches. Our StirTrace based benchmarking approach is introduced in Section 3. The extended feature set for the detection of printed fingerprints is described in Section 4. We describe and discuss the experimental setup and the evaluation results in Section 5. Subsequently, the paper is concluded in Section 6.

## 2. STATE OF THE ART WITH STIRTRACE ENHANCEMENTS

In this section we briefly summarize how artificial sweat printed fingerprints are generated and which features can be used for detection. We show conceptually, how StirTrace can enhance existing data sets and how the new two features can enhance the detection process in the overall pipeline.

As described in [7], artificial sweat printed fingerprints can be produced by using either an acquired original latent fingerprint from a real subject, a captured fingerprint stored al-

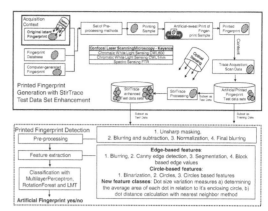

**Figure 1: Context of the robustness evaluation for the detection of printed fingerprints using StirTrace**

ready in databases or a computer-generated artificial fingerprint, e.g. created with SFinGe [1]. The fingerprint is usually pre-processed achieving better printing quality generating a printing sample for final printing with an artificial sweat enabled ink jet printer as shown in [5]. Figure 1 summarizes **firstly** the different original fingerprint sources and the overall process of printing[2]. Several contactless acquisition devices are known from the literature either suitable for original latent sample acquisition or for printed fingerprint acquisition (e.g. Confocal Laser Scanning Microscopy such as devices from Keyence, Chromatic White Light Sensing such as CWL600 or CWL1mm or spectral sensing FTR both offered for example from FRT (http://www.frt-gmbh.com/en, website request 7.1.2014)). In particular in [5] full original latent fingerprints from four subjects are captured with a CWL600 chromatic white light sensor. Further, as pre-processing methods a 16- to 8-bit conversion and a manual binarization is performed before the printing sample is printed with an ink-jet printer (Canon PIXMA iP4600 bubble-jet ink-jet) with an artificial sweat ink mixture. The printed fingerprint is afterward acquired with contactless sensory to build an artificial printed fingerprint test data set for testing detection methods. In [5] the Keyence VK-X110 CLSM with a lens magnification of 10 is used. Here, we now suggest enhancing the setup from [5] with **StirTrace** (see Section 3) to simulate different trace acquisition contexts, see in Figure 1 the part of the **Printed Fingerprint Generation** with **StirTrace Test Data Set Enhancement**. **Secondly**, the figure summarizes in the second part the overall **artificial sweat printed fingerprint detection pipeline** containing a set of pre-processing, feature extraction and classification methods. In [5] the **pre-processing** consists of four steps: 1. Unsharp masking (strong Gaussian blur (kernel size of 768x768 pixels, $\sigma = 19.2$)), 2. Subtraction of the blurred image from original intensity image, 3. Normalization of the 16 bit image to an 8 bit range, 4. Final blurring (kernel size of 9x9 pixel, $\sigma = 2$). The **feature extraction** from [5] uses edge- and circle-based features. The **edge-based features** are calculated within four processing steps: 1. Blurring (kernel size of 7x7 pixels, $\sigma = 2$), 2. Canny edge detection (threshold 1: 66, threshold 2: 33), 3. Segmentation into blocks with 10x10 pixels, 4. Calculation

---

[2]The visualization in Figure 1 was sketched by Jana Dittmann and is/will be part of different figures of several publications to visualize context aspects in different research fields of her research group.

of amount of edge pixels within each block by a thresholds $\tau$ block-based decision (5 and 50 % edges, resulting in 10 features). The **circle-based features** are calculated within three steps: 1. Otsu's Binarization, 2. Smallest enclosing circles determination, 3. Calculation of number of circles, mean and standard deviation of radii, the mean horizontal and vertical dot distance and probability density functions (15 features for each distribution) of dot radii, horizontal and vertical dot distances (only circles with distance not exceeding 150 $\mu m$ in measured direction and 300 $\mu m$ in other direction are regarded as neighbors). In total 50 circle-based features are determined. The **classification** from [5] covers different supervised learning approaches based on the Bayes theorem, support vector machines, perceptrons, rule based classifiers, trees, as well as ensemble classifiers (in particular the following: BayesNet, NaiveBayes, LibSVM, SMO, MultilayerPerceptron, Bagging, Dagging, RotationForest, OneR, Ridor, J48, LMT, RandomForest, REPTree). The best performances are reported in [5] for MultilayerPerceptron, RotationForest and LMT, which we have selected for our further investigations and experiments in Section 5. The final classification goal is to determine if the trace is an artificial fingerprint or not. In [5] a ten-fold stratified cross validation on the **Artificial Printed Fingerprint Test data sets** is performed. To determine robustness of the detection features, we propose to enhance the data set for testing with StirTrace called **StirTrace enhanced Test data sets**. For our training a subset from the original **Artificial Printed Fingerprint Test data** is used, see detailed training and test procedure in Section 5.

In addition to the test data set enhancements with StirTrace, in our investigations, we suggest enhancing the recognition performances of printed fingerprint detectors with **two new detection feature classes**, see feature extraction step in Figure 1 and further details in Section 4. The StirTrace enhanced test data set is tested with the original detection approach from [5] as well as with our additional two new detection feature classes.

# 3. STIRTRACE FOR SIMULATING DISTORTIONS AND PRINTER DIFFERENCES

The general idea of simulating characteristics of images as used for fingerprint images in [4] is also already considered in other evaluations, e.g. for the simulation of completely different fingerprint acquisition sensory for determining their particular quality [2]. We apply this kind of simulations to determine the robustness of a feature set for detecting artificial sweat printed fingerprints towards different distortions. Regarding the input signals, in StirMark the maximum size of input images seems to be limited by an internal buffer and does not allow processing of 24 bit RGB images exceeding 572x572 pixels. Due to this limitation and the need for simulating other artifacts we introduce within **StirTrace** an theoretically unlimited input signal size and select most relevant StirMark properties for our simulations. The laser intensity images are converted before processing into a bitmap file by reducing the bit depth from 16 to 8 bit per pixel after a min-max-normalization. In the experimental section we also compare the impact of this loss to the original findings in [5]. Table 2 summarizes the StirTrace properties containing 8 originally proposed features from StirMark, the proposed new image manipulation technique and our 65 utilized parameter settings. Our **additive noise** image manipulation

| StirTrace for Printed fingerprint context for arbitrary image sizes | Implementation and parametrization details |
|---|---|
| Additive Noise: Simulation of substrate and sensor noise | Derived from StirMark, (grayscale) noise levels: 3, 6, 9, 12, 15 |
| Median Cut Filtering: Simulation of smudgy fingerprints/merging amino acid dots | Derived from StirMark, Filter size (kernel size): 3, 5, 7, 9 |
| Remove Lines and Columns: Simulation of printer characteristics | Derived from StirMark, Removal of every 10th, 20th, 30th, ..., 100th line/column |
| Rotation: Simulation of rotation during the acquisition | Derived from StirMark, Rotation by -20, -15, -10, -5.5, -5, 7, 7.5, 13, 18, 20 degrees |
| Stretching in X-direction: Simulation of printer characteristics | Derived from StirMark, Parameter values: 1.035, 1.070, 1.105, 1.140, 1.175, 1.210, 1.280, 1.350 |
| Shearing in Y-direction: Simulation of printer characteristics | Derived from StirMark, Parameter values: 0.05, 0.10, 0.15, 0.20, 0.25, 0.30 |
| Rescaling: Simulation of printer/substrate characteristics (different size of amino acid depositions) | Derived from StirMark, Rescaling to 50%, 75%, 90%, 110%, 150%, 200% of the of the original size |
| Cropping: Simulation of sensor characteristics (different acquisition area) | Derived from StirMark, Cropping to 25%, 50%, 75% of the original size |
| Banding: Simulation of printing defects caused by blocked nozzles | Replacement of random lines (width 50 $\mu m$) with the median value of the image: probability of 0.5%, 1.0%, 2.5% for each line to be the beginning of a banding artifact |

Table 2: StirTrace image manipulation techniques: originally derived from StirMark and new proposed banding simulation, 65 different parametrization initializations considered in our experiments

technique operates slightly different in comparison to StirMark: it creates a grayscale noise pattern in contrast to RGB color noise as used by StirMark which is advantageous because we solely use grayscale images. Both techniques create a pattern of random Gaussian noise. It is expected that an increasing level of noise reduces the detection performance for printed fingerprints. Such noise can be caused by different substrates or the usage of non-optimal acquisition parameters. The **median cut** filtering is the application of a standard median filter. It usually results in a blurred image and the removal of very small artifacts. Especially for larger kernel sizes (filters) the detection accuracy might be affected by the removal of smaller dots of amino acid. The **removal of lines and columns** skips lines or columns of the image at a given constant frequency. Thus, it alters the dimensions of the image. This can simulate different distances of amino acid depositions without stretching the image in either direction. The simulation of the **rotation** of the sample is very important because such influences are likely to be present when acquiring the fingerprint samples. In contrast to StirMark, StirTrace replaces the resulting black areas after the rotation with the median value of the original image. The **stretching in X-direction** is used to simulate different printer characteristics, e.g. a different geometry of the print head which might cause different shapes of amino acid depositions. It is simulated by applying an Affine transformation with the following transformation matrix:

$$M = \begin{bmatrix} P_{sx} & 0 & 0 \\ 0 & 1 & 0 \end{bmatrix}$$

Here, $P_{sx}$ is the parameter determining the degree of stretching. The same technique is used to simulate the **shearing in Y-direction**, which might be caused by different original patterns or an inhomogeneous paper feed of the printer. It uses the following transformation matrix for the Affine transformation, whereas $P_{sy}$ is the parameter from Table 2 which determines the degree of shearing:

$$M = \begin{bmatrix} 1 & 0 & 0 \\ P_{sy} & 1 & 0 \end{bmatrix}$$

Similar to the rotation, resulting black areas are replaced with the median value of the image simulating a natural background to avoid influencing the feature extraction. The **rescaling** simulates different sizes of amino acid blocks which are reported for different printer models in [6]. The **cropping** simulates different acquisition areas of sensors. Especially microscopes are limited in their acquirable area of a trace by the utilized objective lens. For point sensors the number of acquired points influences the required time for digitizing the trace. Thus, it is important determining the minimum area, which is required for a reliable detection of printed fingerprints (50% in our tests in Section 5.2). Our new image manipulation technique is the simulation of **banding** artifacts: it replaces random sections of the trace with the median value of the image simulating blocked nozzles of the print head.

## 4. EXTENDED DETECTION FEATURE SET

In order to increase the robustness of the recognition of printed fingerprints we suggest extending the feature set from [5] by determining the degree of filling of each circle and the distances based on the nearest neighbor technique. Our motivation for using the **degree of filling** for each circle is based on our observation of nearly circular depositions of amino acid dots in samples of printed fingerprints. Thus, printed fingerprints should tend to high filling degree values. For determining the filling degree, we perform a flood fill operation on each blob starting from the center point of its enclosing circle. This operation fills all pixels of the blob and thus, determines the area covered by it. Afterward, we divide the covered area by the area within the enclosing circle. Subsequently, we determine the mean degree of filling for all circles within the sample to derive our new feature (**1: meanfill**). The primary advantage of this feature is the complete independence from the size of the amino acid depositions. Thus, this feature should be applicable to various printer models and only a small number of amino acid depositions are necessary for a reliable extraction of this feature. This is especially advantageous if banding artifacts are present within the sample. Our second feature set extension is motivated by the possibility of a rotation of the sample during the acquisition. The horizontal and vertical dot distance features from [6] are primarily motivated by the geometry of the print head and the paper feed of the printer. However, those features cannot account for any rotation of the sample. Thus, we additionally suggest determining the **distances of amino acid dots** by using the **nearest neighbor technique**, resulting in a rotation invariant feature. In particular we determine the distribution of the distances similar to the horizontal and vertical dot distance leading to 15 feature values (**2-16: nnpdf1-nnpdf15**) and the **average dot distance** (**17: nnmean**). In summary we extend the original feature set with 17 additional features.

## 5. EXPERIMENTS

In this section we describe our experimental setup and present our results for the original and our extended feature set based on the test set from [5] with our StirTrace test set simulations. The test goals are: $G_1$ - comparison of the original findings in [5] on 16-bit samples with the performance of the original and the extended feature set on 8-bit images without any StirTrace simulations, $G_2$ - analysis of the general robustness of detection within original and extended detection feature set in comparison to $G_1$ to single StirTrace manipulation effects influencing the classification accuracy of individual classifiers. We perform two evaluations, **Evaluation 1** for $G_1$ and **Evaluation 2** for $G_2$.

### 5.1 Experimental Setup

As already summarized, our experiments are performed on the data set from [5]. The samples are printed with Canon PIXMA iP4600 bubble-jet printer using the high quality and gray-scale print modes and captured using a Keyence VK-x110 confocal microscope with a 10x magnification (z-Pitch 1 $\mu m$, image size 1024x768 pixels, lateral resolution approx. 20000 ppi) from three different substrates (overhead foil, compact disc, hard disk platter). For each substrate, it contains 1000 samples of real latent fingerprints from 4 different test persons and 1000 corresponding printed fingerprints (resulting in 6000 overall test samples). The original samples for the printing process are acquired from a hard disk platter with 500 ppi using a chromatic white light sensor. Those images are binarized to avoid any half-toning patterns during the printing process. Afterward, the captured 16 bit intensity images from the confocal microscope are converted to 8 bit bitmap files. Furthermore, each image is accompanied by a file containing the original resolution of the scan sample.

**Training:** We use in $T_{orig_{training}}$ 3000 samples (1500 real and 1500 printed - 500 for each substrate) to train the three best performing classifiers from [5] (MultilayerPerceptron [10], RotationForest [11] and LMT [8] of the Weka data mining software [3]).

**Evaluation 1:** For $G_1$, firstly, with $T_{orig_{evaluation}}$, we compare the detection performance using a) the original feature set from [5] and b) the extended feature set from Section 4.

**Evaluation 2:** For $G_2$, by applying StirTrace to the evaluation test set $T_{orig_{evaluation}}$ of 3000 samples, 8 originally proposed StirMark and the one new image manipulation techniques are parameterized. This results in summary in $T_{sim_{evaluation}}$ in additional 65*3000=195000 samples.

In both evaluations, our performance measure is the achieved recognition accuracy which is an objective measure due to the same number of samples for each of the two classes of printed fingerprints and real fingerprints.

### 5.2 Experimental Results

**Evaluation 1:** In this section we firstly discuss our results for $G_1$ comparing the findings from [5] with the original ($FS_O$) and extended feature set ($FS_E$) based on 8 bit images. The $G_1$ results are summarized in Table 3 in the first row of results. For comparison, see the first cell of the last row of the statistics with the original error rates achieved in [5] with 16-bit images. From these results we see, that the conversion of the intensity data from 16 bit to 8 bit bitmap images increased the error from 0.5% as reported in Hildebrandt et al.[5] to 4.3333% using the same classifier, feature set and training set size. Of course, in contrast to [5], where a random split is used for creating the test and training set, we use the samples from two test subjects for training and from the other two subjects for testing, which might have an impact increasing the rate of error. Since we use the same samples for the StirTrace simulation, the recognition accuracy is still sufficient for a comparison of both feature sets towards their robustness. Nevertheless, in future work StirTrace should be also enhanced to handle 16 bit images and further evaluations should determine the cause for the increased error rate.

Furthermore, in respect to the 8 bit sample, the best performance is achieved using the RotationForest classifier for the

| Image Manipulation Technique | Parameter | Original Feature Set | | | Extended Feature Set | | |
|---|---|---|---|---|---|---|---|
| | | Multilayer-Perceptron | LMT | Rotation-Forest | Multilayer-Perceptron | LMT | Rotation-Forest |
| $T_{orig_{evaluation}}$ | - | 95.6667 | 92.2333 | **96.6000** | 93.9000 | 95.1667 | 96.4333 |
| Additive Noise | 3 | 96.1487 | 92.5299 | 96.6135 | 94.2895 | 95.2523 | **96.7131** |
| | 6 | 96.3000 | 93.1333 | **97.3667** | 94.7000 | 95.3667 | 96.5667 |
| | 9 | 97.1333 | 93.9667 | **97.4333** | 95.0333 | 95.5000 | 97.0000 |
| | 12 | 97.4333 | 94.8000 | **98.1333** | 95.5000 | 95.8667 | 96.8667 |
| | 15 | 97.7333 | 95.2667 | **98.1000** | 95.7667 | 95.7667 | 97.1000 |
| Median Cut Filtering | 3 | 96.7333 | 94.4667 | **97.7333** | 94.7000 | 95.4333 | 96.6667 |
| | 5 | **96.8333** | 95.8000 | 96.0333 | 94.8000 | 95.2333 | 95.6667 |
| | 7 | **94.4000** | 93.9000 | 93.4333 | 92.7667 | 92.8333 | 93.7000 |
| | 9 | 87.1000 | 87.8000 | 75.6000 | **88.0667** | 86.7333 | 87.2000 |
| Remove Lines | 10 | 96.0667 | 92.7667 | 96.5333 | 94.7667 | 96.3667 | **97.1000** |
| | 20 | 96.1667 | 92.5000 | **96.9333** | 94.5667 | 95.5333 | 96.7333 |
| | 30 | 95.7333 | 92.2667 | **96.4333** | 94.3667 | 95.2000 | 96.4000 |
| | 40 | 95.9333 | 91.6333 | 96.5000 | 94.0333 | 95.1333 | **96.7000** |
| | 50 | 96.0000 | 92.3667 | 96.2667 | 94.6000 | 95.0667 | **96.8000** |
| | 60 | 95.7333 | 92.3000 | 96.5667 | 93.8667 | 95.0667 | 96.5333 |
| | 70 | 95.9333 | 92.6333 | 96.5000 | 94.0333 | 95.1333 | **96.7000** |
| | 80 | 95.9000 | 92.4333 | 96.2667 | 94.0000 | 95.2333 | **96.7000** |
| | 90 | 96.1000 | 92.3000 | 96.5667 | 94.2000 | 95.1667 | **96.6667** |
| | 100 | 95.9333 | 92.3000 | 96.4667 | 93.9333 | 95.0667 | **96.5333** |
| Remove Columns | 10 | 95.8333 | 92.6333 | 96.2333 | 94.8333 | 95.9333 | **97.4000** |
| | 20 | 95.6000 | 92.3667 | 96.2667 | 94.5333 | 95.4333 | **96.7667** |
| | 30 | 95.8667 | 92.3333 | 96.8333 | 94.2333 | 95.5000 | **96.9000** |
| | 40 | 96.0333 | 92.1667 | 96.5667 | 94.0333 | 95.2000 | **96.8333** |
| | 50 | 95.7333 | 92.2667 | 96.4000 | 94.0333 | 95.2667 | **96.5667** |
| | 60 | 96.0000 | 92.3333 | 96.5333 | 94.0667 | 95.1667 | **96.5667** |
| | 70 | 96.0333 | 92.1667 | 96.5667 | 94.0333 | 95.2000 | **96.8333** |
| | 80 | 95.8667 | 92.2667 | **96.5667** | 94.0333 | 95.1333 | 96.4333 |
| | 90 | 95.3667 | 92.0667 | 96.2333 | 94.2333 | 94.9667 | **96.4000** |
| | 100 | 95.8333 | 92.3000 | 96.3000 | 94.1000 | 95.1667 | **96.4333** |
| Rotation | -20° | 97.7000 | 94.9667 | **98.2667** | 96.1000 | 96.6000 | 97.8333 |
| | -15° | 97.2333 | 94.5000 | **97.9000** | 96.1333 | 96.5000 | 97.7333 |
| | -10° | 96.8333 | 93.5333 | **97.4333** | 95.2667 | 96.0333 | 97.4000 |
| | -5.5° | 93.6333 | 84.7000 | 94.9000 | 94.3370 | 94.9667 | **96.7000** |
| | -5° | 94.7667 | 86.4667 | 95.9667 | 94.5333 | 95.2333 | **96.9333** |
| | 7° | 90.6667 | 83.9667 | 94.0333 | 94.3333 | 95.1000 | **97.0667** |
| | 7.5° | 94.5667 | 85.9333 | 95.4667 | 94.4667 | 95.0667 | **96.7000** |
| | 13° | 96.9333 | 94.1667 | 97.3667 | 95.7000 | 96.7000 | **97.4333** |
| | 18° | 97.3667 | 94.2667 | 96.5333 | 96.0000 | 96.9333 | **97.6667** |
| | 20° | 97.6667 | 94.7000 | **98.0667** | 96.0333 | 96.7000 | 97.3333 |
| Stretching in X-Direction | 1.035 | 95.9000 | 92.1000 | **96.4000** | 93.3667 | 94.4667 | 96.1333 |
| | 1.07 | 96.0000 | 92.3333 | **96.4667** | 93.0667 | 94.2667 | 95.6333 |
| | 1.105 | 95.8667 | 92.1000 | **96.4000** | 92.6333 | 93.7333 | 95.3000 |
| | 1.14 | 95.9000 | 92.2667 | **96.3000** | 92.2333 | 93.3333 | 94.8667 |
| | 1.175 | 95.9000 | 92.1667 | **96.2333** | 91.9667 | 93.0333 | 94.4333 |
| | 1.21 | 95.6000 | 91.9333 | **96.1000** | 91.5333 | 92.7667 | 94.2333 |
| | 1.28 | **95.8000** | 91.8667 | 95.6333 | 91.0667 | 92.2000 | 93.7333 |
| | 1.35 | 95.5000 | 91.7667 | **95.7000** | 90.2333 | 91.3333 | 93.5000 |
| Shearing in Y-Direction | 0.05 | 95.9000 | 91.5667 | 96.3667 | 94.1667 | 95.6000 | **96.5333** |
| | 0.1 | 94.4000 | 91.5000 | 96.1333 | 94.2667 | 95.0333 | **96.3333** |
| | 0.15 | 96.6667 | 92.7000 | 96.3667 | 95.1000 | 95.5667 | **96.7667** |
| | 0.2 | 97.1000 | 93.9667 | 97.2333 | 95.4667 | 96.0333 | **97.3000** |
| | 0.25 | 96.9000 | 94.1667 | 97.2000 | 95.9000 | 96.3000 | **97.3000** |
| | 0.3 | 97.4000 | 94.1000 | 97.2667 | 96.1000 | 96.7333 | **97.5333** |
| Rescaling | 50% | **79.3000** | 52.8000 | 50.0333 | 50.6000 | 54.1000 | 53.2333 |
| | 75% | 96.5333 | 91.7333 | 93.0000 | 96.2667 | **97.2667** | 92.1667 |
| | 90% | 96.4667 | 93.2000 | 97.3000 | 96.2000 | 97.4667 | **98.3000** |
| | 110% | **95.8333** | 91.9000 | 95.7000 | 91.6667 | 92.3667 | 94.1333 |
| | 150% | **95.9333** | 88.9667 | 94.3333 | 91.7667 | 82.0333 | 86.5667 |
| | 200% | **85.4667** | 72.4000 | 73.6333 | 68.8333 | 68.4333 | 77.1333 |
| Cropping | 25% | 58.1000 | 56.9667 | 49.8000 | 59.0667 | **64.7000** | 51.8667 |
| | 50% | **93.8333** | 89.1000 | 50.2333 | 83.7333 | 86.9333 | 64.3000 |
| | 75% | 97.0000 | 92.8333 | 92.8667 | 97.4333 | **98.4333** | 96.0667 |
| Banding | 0.5% | 97.0667 | 93.7333 | 97.5333 | 96.5333 | 96.7000 | **97.9667** |
| | 1% | 97.5533 | 94.4333 | 97.3333 | 97.9667 | 97.8000 | **98.2333** |
| | 2.5% | 96.7667 | 94.8333 | 94.8333 | **97.2333** | 96.9667 | 95.5333 |
| **Statistics** Performance of Multi-layerPerceptron in [5] based on 3000 training samples: 99.5% | Min | **58.1000** | 52.8000 | 49.8000 | 50.6000 | 54.1000 | 51.8667 |
| | Max | 97.7333 | 95.8000 | 98.2667 | 97.9667 | **98.4333** | 98.3000 |
| | Mean | **94.9270** | 90.8323 | 93.6199 | 92.5959 | 93.3715 | 94.0275 |
| | StDev | **5.4162** | 7.2300 | 10.3554 | 7.7438 | 7.3752 | 8.8960 |
| | Median | 95.9333 | 92.3167 | 96.4167 | 94.2781 | 95.2000 | **96.6667** |

Table 3: Results for evaluation 1 and 2 (highest recognition accuracy for each image manipulation technique and parameter in bold)

original feature set with 96.6% and for the extended feature set with 96.4333%.

**Evaluation 2** ($T_{sim_{Evaluation}}$): In Table 3, the last row *Statistics* shows a general robustness of detection within original and extended detection feature set. In comparison to $G_1$ all classifiers have an overall good robustness by achieving a median close to $G_1$ and higher max value than for $G_1$. The lowest values are achieved for cropping to 25% and large scaling (50 and 200%). From the overall analysis, all three classifiers show a good performance, see analysis of min, max, mean, standard deviation and median values. In comparison to $G_1$, the MultilayerPerceptron shows best min, mean and standard deviation for the original feature set and the RotationForest achieves best median with the extended feature set. In respect to the analysis of single StirTrace manipulation effects to classification results and individual classifier performance, the cropping and large re-scaling affects both feature sets showing lowest detection performances.

The new feature set is well able to handle banding and rotation as expected, e.g. for RotationForest with $FS_E$ the rotation classification accuracy is rather stable within the range between 96.7 and 97.8333% accuracy. Additionally the new feature set achieves also best classification results for the removal of lines and columns and shearing artifacts. Our extended feature set shows less performance for stretching of the image. The original feature set has best performance for additive noise, median cut and stretching in X-direction. In particular, the additive noise performance is increasing with increasing noise levels for both $FS_O$ and $FS_E$. This is caused by the removal of small artifacts due to the overlaid noise pattern. Here, in future work the influence of stronger noise patterns should be investigated. The best performance for simulated noise is achieved for $FS_O$ in combination with the RotationForest classifier. For Median Cut Filtering, the filtering decreases the performance for larger filter kernels. For smaller kernels the best performance is achieved based on $FS_O$. However, for a filter kernel size of 9x9 pixels $FS_E$ seems to be slightly more accurate. Nevertheless, even larger filter kernels should be investigated in future work.

## 6. CONCLUSION AND FUTURE WORK

In this paper we proposed applying image manipulation techniques to evaluate the robustness of the pattern recognition based detection of printed fingerprints. The StirTrace framework is motivated by StirMark. It is designed to overcome limitations of the original approach and to introduce the new manipulation technique to simulate banding artifacts. We extend the feature set from [5] to increase the robustness of the detection for rotation and banding effects using the degree of filling of the detected circles and distances based on the nearest neighbor technique.

Our evaluation results based on 6000 original and additional 195000 StirTrace simulated samples show that both feature sets are already very robust towards image manipulations. However, overall for additive noise, median cut and stretching in X-direction the original feature set performs slightly better than our extension for the evaluated techniques and parameters. As all three classifiers show a generally good performance, a classifier fusion should be studied in more detail in future work. Additionally, the feature space should be analyzed towards a reduction of dimensionality, e.g. by feature selection or a PCA. Moreover, additional parameter settings should be evaluated. Furthermore, StirTrace should be extended with a manipulation technique which solely increases the dot sizes. Moreover, the overall impact of the conversion from 16 to 8 bit color depth prior to the preprocessing from [5] should be investigated. The updated version of StirTrace already supports bit depths up to 32 bpp.

## Acknowledgments

The work in this paper has been funded in part by the German Federal Ministry of Education and Science (BMBF) through the Research Program under Contract No. FKZ: 13N10818.

## 7. REFERENCES

[1] R. Cappelli. Synthetic fingerprint generation. In D. Maltoni, D. Maio, A. Jain, and S. Prabhakar, editors, *Handbook of Fingerprint Recognition (Second Edition)*. Springer (London), 2009.

[2] R. Cappelli, M. Ferrara, and D. Maltoni. On the operational quality of fingerprint scanners. *Information Forensics and Security, IEEE Transactions on*, 3(2):192–202, 2008.

[3] M. Hall, E. Frank, G. Holmes, B. Pfahringer, P. Reutemann, and I. H. Witten. The weka data mining software: An update. *SIGKDD Explorations*, 11(1):10 – 18, 2009.

[4] J. Hämmerle-Uhl, M. Pober, and A. Uhl. Towards a standardised testsuite to assess fingerprint matching robustness: The stirmark toolkit - cross-feature type comparisons. In *Communications and Multimedia Security*, volume 8099 of *Lecture Notes in Computer Science*, pages 3–17. 2013.

[5] M. Hildebrandt, S. Kiltz, and J. Dittmann. Printed fingerprints at crime scenes: a faster detection of malicious traces using scans of confocal microscopes. In *Proc. SPIE 8665*, pages 866509–866509–12, 2013.

[6] M. Hildebrandt, S. Kiltz, J. Dittmann, and C. Vielhauer. Malicious fingerprint traces: a proposal for an automated analysis of printed amino acid dots using houghcircles. In *Proceedings of the thirteenth ACM multimedia workshop on Multimedia and security*, pages 33–40, 2011.

[7] S. Kiltz, M. Hildebrandt, J. Dittmann, C. Vielhauer, and C. Kraetzer. Printed fingerprints: a framework and first results towards detection of artificially printed latent fingerprints for forensics. In *Image Quality and System Performance VIII, Proceedings of SPIE Vol. 7867*, 2011.

[8] N. Landwehr, M. Hall, and E. Frank. Logistic model trees. *Machine Learning*, 95(1-2):161 – 205, 2005.

[9] F. Petitcolas, R. Anderson, and M. Kuhn. Attacks on copyright marking systems. In *Information Hiding*, volume 1525 of *Lecture Notes in Computer Science*, pages 218–238. 1998.

[10] M. Riedmiller. Advanced supervised learning in multi-layer perceptrons - from backpropagation to adaptive learning algorithms. *Computer Standards & Interfaces*, 16(3):265 – 278, 1994.

[11] J. J. Rodriguez, L. I. Kuncheva, and C. J. Alonso. Rotation forest: A new classifier ensemble method. *IEEE Trans. Pattern Anal. Mach. Intell.*, 28:1619 – 1630, 2006.

# Digital Crime Scene Analysis: Automatic Matching of Firing Pin Impressions on Cartridge Bottoms using 2D and 3D Spatial Features

Robert Fischer[1], Claus Vielhauer[1,2]

[1]Brandenburg University of Applied Sciences, Dept. of Informatics & Media,
PO Box 2132, 14737 Brandenburg, Germany
{robert.fischer,claus.vielhauer}@fh-brandenburg.de

[2]Otto-von-Guericke University of Magdeburg, Dept. of Computer Science, AMSL Research Group,
PO Box 4120, 39016 Magdeburg, Germany
claus.vielhauer@iti.cs.uni-magdeburg

## ABSTRACT

The examination of forensic toolmarks impressed on shot cartridges and bullets is a well known and broadly accepted forensic discipline. The underlying concept is based on two main hypotheses: every firearm owns unique toolmark characteristics which lead to consistent and reproducible impressions on cartridges and bullets. Furthermore, it is possible to differentiate between markings of two different firearms. The application of optical 2D and 3D sensing technologies for acquisition, as well as pattern recognition techniques for automated toolmark examination are currently emerging fields of research in the domain of digital crime scene analysis. In this paper we propose and evaluate a pattern recognition approach for automated firearm identification based on central-fire firing pin impressions. The entire pattern recognition chain is addressed, starting with a confocal microscope for optical data acquisition. The preprocessing covers image enhancement, as well as necessary registration and segmentation tasks for cartridge bottoms. Feature extraction involves 18 firing pin related features from 2D and 3D spatial domain. The classification accuracy is evaluated by using 10-fold stratified cross-validation. Our evaluation approach is two-fold, during the first part we examine how well it is possible to differentiate between two firearms of the same mark and model. During the second part the evaluation is extended to analyze the accuracy of discrimination using six different weapons, whereby each two guns are of the same model. The test set contains 72 cartridge samples including three different ammunition manufactures and six individual 9mm guns. Every possible combination of weapon model, instance and ammunition type is represented by four samples within the test set. Regarding the first evaluation goal a classification accuracy between 87.5% and 100% is achieved. For the second evaluation goal the achieved classification accuracy equates to 86.11%.

## Categories and Subject Descriptors

I.4 [**Image Processing and Computer Vision**]: I.4.1 [**Digitization and Image Capture**] Scanning, Segmentation, I.4.7 [**Feature Measurement**] Size and shape, Feature representation
I.5 [**Pattern Recognition**]: I.5.4 [**Applications**] Computer Vision

## General Terms

Algorithms, Measurement, Design, Experimentation

## Keywords

Ballistics, firearm identification, digital crime scene analysis, digitized forensics, image processing, pattern classification

## 1. INTRODUCTION

The manual examination of toolmarks impressed on shot cartridges and bullets plays a very important role in forensic examinations. These examinations comprise a sub-discipline of forensic ballistics and are generally known as inner ballistics. The main objective is to link a spent cartridge or bullet to a specific firearm, or exclude that a specific gun has provoked the markings. The underlying concept is based on two main hypotheses. Firstly, markings that are provoked by a weapon are consistent and reproducible. Secondly, it is possible to differentiate between the individual markings of two different weapons [1]. During the last decade, emerging technologies in the field of computer assisted forensic ballistic have led to two challenging developments. Firstly, large databases and therefore an increasing amount of reference material raise questions about the uniqueness of ballistic toolmarks and the so called 'ballistic fingerprint'. This was amongst others stated by Cork at al. [2]: "... uniqueness and reproducibility of firearms-related toolmarks has not yet been fully demonstrated." The second point comprises the simultaneous introduction of 3D sensing technique. This is by some considered as aggravation of the problem, by others it is considered as possible solution. For example M. Barrett's [3] appraisal: "... 3D technology gives ballistic examiners ability to solve more gun crimes." We acknowledge that a proof of uniqueness / reproducibility of firearm toolmarks can only be achieved empirically in the long run. This papers goal is to show potential and limits of the introduced feature set based on an initial dataset.

At the same time proprietary systems are introduced by private companies and law enforcement agencies. One of the first semi-automated systems based on 2D imaging is DRUGFIRE developed by the FBI since 1991 [2]. Another system based on 2D imaging is IBIS [2]. Further development led to a merge of these systems and the introduction of IBIS BulletTrax / BrassTrax [4] for automated ballistic examination. Other examples are ALIAS [3] and EvoFinder [5]. To the best of our knowledge, neither the applied algorithms itself, nor the selection of evaluated toolmarks, or applied pattern recognition techniques of these systems are generally disclosed to the public. Furthermore, we were not able to identify any public ballistic databases.

Consequently, the work presented in this paper aims at a scientifically reproducible study on the potential of a feature extraction and classification approach based on combined 2D and 3D features. We introduce a pattern recognition approach for automatic firearm identification based on firing pin impression characteristics on central-fire cartridges, addressing the entire pattern recognition pipeline. A confocal laser scanning microscope is used for the acquisition of 72 cartridge bottoms. The device simultaneously gathers color, laser-intensity and topography data, consequently resulting in three different datasets for each scan. Preprocessing is applied for the datasets, including image preprocessing and additional registration of the samples, regarding translation and rotation. Subsequently 18 features are extracted out of 2D as well as 3D spatial domain. The fused feature set is used for classification. Stratified cross-validation is applied for evaluating the classification accuracy of the proposed method. Our evaluation thereby is two-fold:

1.  Evaluating the achieved accuracy regarding discrimination of two firearms of same brand and model. ($E_1$)
2.  Evaluating the achieved accuracy regarding discrimination of six firearms, each two of same brand and model. ($E_2$)

Our test set contains cartridges shot by three different weapon systems, whereat two instances are used for each model. Cartridges from three different ammunition manufactures are included. Overall four samples of each possible combination are part of the test set, resulting in a total amount of 72 cartridges. Regarding the first evaluation goal accuracies from 87.5% to 100% are achieved. With respect to the second evaluation goal an overall accuracy of 86.11% is achieved by our proposed approach. Understanding and evaluation of potential evidence, as well as evaluation of automated systems for forensic examinations currently play an important role in of digital crime scene analysis.

Hereafter the paper is organized as follows; section two summarizes the state of the art regarding 2D, 3D and combined approaches. In section three detailed descriptions of the features and classification scenarios are given. Section four explains the experimental setup in detail, followed by the presentation and discussion of experimental results in section five. A conclusion and prospects for future work are given in the final section six.

## 2. STATE OF THE ART

The following section provides a brief summary of prior works in the field of automated ballistic examinations based on cartridge casings. Generally it is possible to differentiate between approaches based on 2D data, 3D data and combinations of both.

*2D acquisition* includes data gathering using for example ring-light-illuminated optical microscopes, or digital cameras. In 2000 Xin et al. [6] published an approach based on three features, the ratio between inner and outer firing pin circle, the firing pin diameter and a similarity measure, for comparison of 150 digitally acquired cartridge bottoms. The results are given as a best-hit-list with a likelihood of 88.0% for the matched specimen to appear in the top 5% of the list. Geradts et al. [7] published an approach based on log polar transformation and difference computation, the test set consists of 49 cartridges shot by 19 different firearms which are matched against a not further explained database. The authors state that it is possible to retrieve all images in the top 5% of the hit list. Another work was presented by Zhou et al. [8] using a test set of 150 samples with 10 different firearms. The firing pin center and radius, as well as texture characteristics of the breechface impression are utilized as features. Classification is done by using a support vector machine. According to the authors the system achieves an accuracy of 12.7% false acceptance rate and 1.7% false rejection rate. Donguang Li [9] suggested an approach based on a morphological gradient for rim-firing pin

mark identification and a neural network for classification. The presented system achieves a classification accuracy of 97.0% on a test set consisting of 150 rim-fire cartridges. Thumwarin [10] suggested a combination of log polar transform, a subsequent calculation of Fourier coefficients and utilization of Fisher's linear discriminant function to determine the similarity of different cartridge bottom images. The test set consists of 166 cartridges fired by six different firearms. The results are presented in subjective fashion, and in doing so no accuracy measures are provided by the authors. An extension of this work was published by Thumwarin et al. [11] in 2010. The before described approach is expanded by using a Wiener filter for handling noise and fluctuation of the toolmark impressions. Experimental evaluation is performed on a test set of 900 spent cartridges fired by six different weapons. The system achieves a correct classification rate of 87.53% with additional use of Wiener filter and 86.17% without. In 2010, Leng et al. [12] published an extension of the original [9] approach using a back-propagation neural network for classification. Though, there are no detailed descriptions of experimental setup or results given, the authors are stating that based on 50 cartridge samples an accuracy of 98% is indicated.

*3D acquisition* includes data gathering using for example line-scan imaging, laser conoscopic holography, photometric stereo, chromatic white light or confocal microscopy. One early suggestion for using surface profile measurements and additional topography information was made by Smith et al. [13]. The authors suggest the application of line-scan imaging for retrieving 2D spatial distributions of cylindrical objects. Bachrach et al. [14] seized this suggestion and presented a system for bullet identification based on line-scanning. The test set consists of six bullets shot by three different firearms of the same model. Regarding the worst case, the described evaluation indicates a discrimination ratio of 0.88 for the approach. In 2010 Senin et al. [15] presented an approach based on laser conoscopic holography and their idea of a 3D virtual comparison microscope. No experimental evaluation is presented in this work. Sakarya et al. [16] suggested a system based on photometric stereo for 3D surface extraction of cartridges. Furthermore, a combined examination of 2D and 3D data is motivated by the authors. Suapang et al. [17] introduced an acquisition system based on a CCD camera and a rotary device, which is able to acquire 2D images as well as line-scans of the specimens. Feature extraction is suggested as a combination of a Sobel filter for contour and edge detection and a subsequent FFT-based analysis. No detailed descriptions of the used test set or the achieved accuracy of the system are provided by the authors. Makrushin et al. [18] demonstrated the application of a chromatic white sensor (CWL) for acquiring the topography of cartridge bottoms. The firing pin dimension, depth, eccentricity and shape are suggested as feasible features. Even though no automatic classification is carried out, the utilization of the suggested feature set indicates a positive tendency regarding the used test set of 15 cartridges and three different firearms. In prior work [19] we examined the application of confocal laser scanning microscopy for the acquisition of cartridge bottoms. Based on an initial test set of 18 cartridges and using five features from 3D spatial domain the achieved classification accuracy equates to 78%.

Potential *combination of 2D and 3D* data acquisition / examination for forensic ballistics has been motivated in several of the aforementioned works. Furthermore, scientific challenges arise from the ongoing discussion about uniqueness of ballistic toolmarks. In this paper we introduce an automated comparison approach using firing pin impressions on cartridge bottoms.

# 3. PROCESSING CHAIN AND FEATURES

This section gives a general description of our processing pipeline and the utilized features. Detailed descriptions of each processing step are given in the fourth section. The overall processing chain in a simplified fashion is shown in Figure 1.

handling outliers and invalid measurement values. Subsequent data normalization results in a preprocessed topography image ($IP_{Topo}$). Preprocessing ($pre_2$) of the laser-intensity ($I_{Laser}$) and color ($I_{Color}$) data is done identically. An adaptive gamma-correction is applied, after that a median filter is used for handling

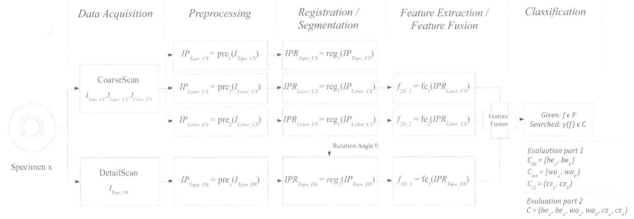

**Figure 1: Our proposed processing chain**

*Data Acquisition* is done using an out-of-the-box confocal laser scanning microscope, with yet no optimization for ballistic examinations. The microscope acquires 16bit laser-intensity ($I_{Laser}$), 24bit color ($I_{Color}$) and 32bit topography ($I_{Topo}$) data at once (see Figure 2). All three images are of the same size $X$ by $Y$. Due to the fact that high detail scans of large areas take much time and generate large amounts of data, a split-scan approach as introduced in [19] is applied to acquire two scans of each cartridge bottom as shown in Figure 1. After manually positioning the specimens at the motorized xy-table the first scan is a low-detail scan (*Coarse-scan CS*) of the entire cartridge bottom. Coarse-scans ($I_{Laser\_CS}$, $I_{Color\_CS}$, $I_{Topo\_CS}$) are used for later registration, extraction of coarse-scan features and localization of toolmarks. The second scan is a high-detail scan (*Detail-scan DS*) exclusively covering the firing pin impression area. For later extraction of 3D features we only use the topography dataset ($I_{Topo\_DS}$) from Detail-scans. Specimens remain untouched during both scans. See Figure 2 and 3 for examples of the acquired data.

**Figure 2: Coarse-scan; a)** $I_{Color\_CS}$ **b)** $I_{Laser\_CS}$ **c)** $I_{Topo\_CS}$
(3D visualization Keyence Analysis Software [24])

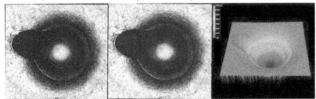

**Figure 3: Detail-scan firing pin a)** $I_{Color\_DS}$ **b)** $I_{Laser\_DS}$ **c)** $I_{Topo\_DS}$
(3D visualization Keyence Analysis Software [24])

*Preprocessing* of the individual images is slightly varying with respect to the data type. The preprocessing ($pre_1$) of topography data ($I_{Topo}$) starts with correcting the vertical alignment of the surface, this is done by subtracting the best fitting plane. Afterwards a Gaussian blur and a median filter are applied for

outliers and invalid values. The results are preprocessed laser-($IP_{Laser}$) and color-images ($IP_{Color}$).

*Registration* of the cartridge bottoms is required due to the fact that not all of the used features are invariant with respect to translation / rotation. For *translational registration* the outermost circle (outer edge of cartridge) is detected using a geometrical shape detection approach based on [20]. Given the outermost circle and using a margin value $m$ the translation is applied by shifting the original coordinate system $(O, X, Y)$ to a system $(O', X', Y')$. The resulting image is cropped to a size of $N$ by $N$, where $N$ is equal to the sum of the outer circle diameter and the used margin $m$. The *rotational registration* of the images is applied based on the center point of the ejector position. For now the ejector position is determined manually and marked for each sample. The angle $\theta$ between the outer circle center point and the ejector center point is determined and the coordinate system $(O', X', Y')$ is rotated by $\theta$ around the center point of the outer circle in order to rotate the ejector impression to 90° (12 o'clock position). The result is a coordinate system $(O'', X'', Y'')$ where all samples are registered with respect to translation and rotation. The rotation angle determined during Coarse-scan registration ($reg_1$) is afterwards used for rotational alignment of Detail-scans ($reg_2$).

*Segmentation* is based on four circles found on cartridge bottoms (circle detection on cartridge bottoms is addressed for example in [20, 22]). The *outer circle* represents the outer edge of the cartridge, the *primer circle* represents the outer primer edge and the *inner / outer firing pin circle* describe the outer / inner edge of the firing pin impression. Given these circles it is possible to determine, if a given point $P_{x,y}$ is located inside, outside, or on one of the circles. The result of registration and segmentation is an aligned image of each data type ($IPR_{Topo}$, $IPR_{Laser}$, $IPR_{Color}$).

*Feature Extraction* is applied considering the 18 features summarized in Table 1 (not ranked by importance). Feature level fusion results in a feature vector $f = (f_1, f_2, f_3, ..., f_{18})$ for each sample. Features 1-3 and 9 were introduced by Makrushin et al. [18] and feature 6 was suggested by Xin et al. [6]. The general idea for features 15-18 is based on line-scan imaging introduced by Smith et al. [13] and Bachrach et al. [14]. This approach was extended / customized for 3D imaging in [19]. Remaining features are introduced within this paper, as a suggested extension of prior approaches. A formal definition of all features is given in Table 2.

**Table 1: Overview and description of extracted features**

| # | Feature | Description | S | Data |
|---|---------|-------------|---|------|
| *2D Spatial Domain* | | | | |
| 1 | $FP\_CIRC$ | Circumference of outer firing pin circle | CS | $I_{Color}$, $I_{Laser}$ |
| 2 | $FP\_ECC\_OFC\_OC\_DIST$ | Eccentricity of outer firing pin circle - outer cartridge circle distance | CS | $I_{Color}$, $I_{Laser}$ |
| 3 | $FP\_ECC\_OFC\_OC\_ANGLE$ | Eccentricity of outer firing pin circle - outer cartridge circle angle | CS | $I_{Color}$, $I_{Laser}$ |
| 4 | $FP\_ECC\_OFC\_PC\_DIST$ | Eccentricity of outer firing pin circle - primer circle distance | CS | $I_{Color}$, $I_{Laser}$ |
| 5 | $FP\_ECC\_OFC\_PC\_ANGLE$ | Eccentricity of outer firing pin circle - primer circle angle | CS | $I_{Color}$, $I_{Laser}$ |
| 6 | $FP\_RATIO\_OFC\_IFC$ | Ratio between dimension inner and outer firing pin circle | CS | $I_{Color}$, $I_{Laser}$ |
| 7 | $FP\_ECC\_OFC\_IFC\_DIST$ | Eccentricity of outer / inner firing pin circle distance | CS | $I_{Color}$, $I_{Laser}$ |
| 8 | $FP\_ECC\_OFC\_IFC\_ANGLE$ | Eccentricity of outer / inner firing pin circle angle | CS | $I_{Color}$, $I_{Laser}$ |
| *3D Spatial Domain* | | | | |
| 9 | $FP\_MAX\_DEPTH$ | Maximum depth of firing pin impression | DS | $I_{Topo}$ |
| 10 | $FP\_AVG\_DEPTH$ | Average depth of firing pin impression | DS | $I_{Topo}$ |
| 11 | $FP\_HEIGHT\_OFC\_IFC$ | Maximum height difference inner and outer firing pin circle | DS | $I_{Topo}$ |
| 12 | $FP\_MAX\_STEEP\_OFC\_IFC$ | Maximum steepness of firing pin impression perimeter | DS | $I_{Topo}$ |
| 13 | $FP\_MIN\_STEEP\_OFC\_IFC$ | Minimum steepness of firing pin impression perimeter | DS | $I_{Topo}$ |
| 14 | $FP\_AVG\_STEEP\_OFC\_IFC$ | Average steepness of firing pin impression perimeter | DS | $I_{Topo}$ |
| 15 | $FP\_VERT\_PATH\_INC$ | Incremental vertical path-length of firing pin impression | DS | $I_{Topo}$ |
| 16 | $FP\_VERT\_PATH\_CUM$ | Cumulative vertical path-length of firing pin impression | DS | $I_{Topo}$ |
| 17 | $FP\_HORI\_PATH\_INC$ | Incremental horizontal path-length of firing pin impression | DS | $I_{Topo}$ |
| 18 | $FP\_HORI\_PATH\_CUM$ | Cumulative horizontal path-length of firing pin impression | DS | $I_{Topo}$ |

*Classification* in general can be comprehended as a function $\gamma$ which is trying to determine the class $c$ of a given feature vector $f$. In particular the sets of classes are determined by the six different firearms. We are using a *NearestNeighbor* (*NNge*) and a *BayesianNet* (*BN*) classifier from WEKA data mining software [21]. 10-fold stratified cross-validation is used for evaluating the classification accuracy. A more detailed description of the test set and the individual classes is given within the following section.

## 4. EXPERIMENTAL SETUP

*Test set.* Due to the lack of public ballistic databases we use a test set created within the scope of the project under support by German state-police of Saxony-Anhalt. Overall six 9mm firearms have been used, each two of them are of the same brand and model. The guns (two instances each) are a Walther P99 ($wa_a$, $wa_b$), a Ceska 75B ($cz_a$, $cz_b$) and a Beretta 92FS ($be_a$, $be_b$). Regarding evaluation goal $E_1$ there are three class sets: $C_{BE} = \{be_a, be_b\}$, $C_{WA} = \{wa_a, wa_b\}$ and $C_{CZ} = \{cz_a, cz_b\}$. With respect to evaluation goal $E_2$ the complete set of classes is: $C = \{be_a, be_b, wa_a, wa_b, cz_a, cz_b\}$. In prior work [19] we observed that the characteristics of firing pin impressions heavily depend on the type of ammunition used. Therefore, we use cartridges from three manufactures differing in color, reflection characteristics and mechanical resistance of the primer. The manufactures used are *S&B* (old version), *Geco* and *S&B* (new version).

*Data Acquisition* is done using a 5-fold magnification and a 10μm z-pitch for Coarse-scans (approx. dimension 11.5x12.5mm). The digital representation offers a dot-distance of 8.17μm which is equal to approx. 3000ppi. Detail-scans of firing pin impressions are covering an area of approx. 2.5x2.5mm acquired by using a 20-fold magnification and 0.5μm z-pitch. The dot-distance of the digital result equates to 1.3μm (approx. 18000ppi).

*Preprocessing* ($pre_1$) of topography data ($I_{Topo}$) starts with correcting the vertical alignment of the surface by subtracting the best fitting plane. Afterwards a Gaussian blur ($\sigma = 2.0$, $size = 7$) and a median filter ($size = 7$) are applied for handling sensor noise, outliers and invalid measurement values. Finally the data is normalized to the range $[0,1]$ resulting in the preprocessed topography image ($IP_{Topo}$). Preprocessing ($pre_2$) of laser-intensity ($I_{Laser}$) and color ($I_{Color}$) data is done identically. Adaptive gamma-correction is applied, a median filter ($size = 7$) is used for handling outliers / invalid values, results are preprocessed laser- ($IP_{Laser}$) and color images ($IP_{Color}$). Parameter values are derived from prior experiments with respect to subjective visual quality.

*Registration* of Coarse-scans is applied based on the outermost cartridge circle and the location of the ejector mark. Given the outermost circle $c_{Outer} = (c_x, c_y, c_r)$ and using a margin value of $m = 5$ the translation is applied: $x' = x - (c_r + m)$ and $y' = y - (c_r + m)$ shifting the original coordinate system $(O, X, Y)$ to the system $(O', X', Y')$. The margin is needed to preserve a gap between outer circle edge and image borders for later processing tasks. The image is cropped to a size of $N$ by $N$ where $N = 2c_r + m$. For registering the rotation the angle $\theta$ between ejector location and center point of the outer circle is determined. In order to shift the ejector point to $90°$ the entire image is rotated by $\theta$ around the outer circles center $c_{x,y}$. The coordinate systems point-of-origin is translated to $c_{x,y}$ after that the rotation is applied: $x'' = x' \cdot \cos\theta - y' \cdot \sin\theta$ and $y'' = x' \cdot \sin\theta + y' \cdot \cos\theta$. Finally the coordinate systems point-of-origin is translated back to its original position. The result is a coordinate system $(O'', X'', Y'')$ where all samples are aligned with respect to translation / rotation. Registration of Detail-scans is performed similar only difference being; instead of the outermost cartridge circle the outer firing pin circle is used for lateral alignment. The same rotation angle $\theta$ is used for alignment of rotation.

*Segmentation* is applied based on the positions of outer- ($c_{OC}$), primer- ($c_{PC}$), outer firing pin- ($c_{OFC}$) and inner firing pin-circle ($c_{IFC}$). Two functions are defined as shown in Table 2. The function $onCircle(c, I)$ determines all points of a given matrix $I$ which are located on a given circle $c$. The function $inCircle(c, I)$ returns all points of $I$ which are located within the diameter of $c$. Using this segmentation all subsequent operations can be limited to certain areas of the bottom e.g. the firing pin impression area.

*Feature Extraction* is based on formal dataset definitions, introduced features, as well as required functions and circles. We define four functions: $values(I)$ returns a set of all values of matrix $I$, $value(I, x, y)$ returns the value of matrix $I$ at position $x, y$ and the two functions $onCircle(c, I)$, $inCircle(c, I)$ as explained above. Using the functions all single feature results are calculated as shown in Table 2 and are afterwards concatenated to an 18-dimensional feature vector $f_n$ for each sample.

**Table 2: Definition of datasets, circles, functions and features**

| *Definitions* | $I \subset \mathbb{N} \times \mathbb{N} \times \mathbb{R}$ |
|---|---|
| | $p: p = (p_x, p_y, p_v) \in I$ |
| | $C \subset \mathbb{N} \times \mathbb{N} \times \mathbb{R}$ |
| | $c: c = (c_x, c_y, c_r) \in C$ |
| *Datasets* | $I_{Laser}, I_{Color}, I_{Topo}$ |

| Circles | $c_{OC} \in C$ : outer circle |
|---|---|
| | $c_{PC} \in C$ : primer circle |
| | $c_{OFC} \in C$ : outer firing pin circle |
| | $c_{IFC} \in C$ : inner firing pin circle |
| Functions | $values(I) = \{p_v : p \in I\}$ |
| | $value(I, x, y) = p_v, p \in I, p_x = x, p_y = y$ |
| | $onCircle(c, I) =$ |
| | $\{p : p \in I, (p_x - c_x)^2 + (p_y - c_y)^2 = rnd(c_r^2)\}$ |
| | $inCircle(c, I) =$ |
| | $\{p : p \in I, (p_x - c_x)^2 + (p_y - c_y)^2 < rnd(c_r^2)\}$ |

| | 2D Spatial Domain | |
|---|---|---|
| 1 | $FP\_CIRC$ | $2\pi c_{OC_r}$ |
| 2 | $FP\_ECC\_OFC\_OC\_DIST$ | $\sqrt{(c_{OC_x} - c_{OFC_x})^2 + (c_{OC_y} - c_{OFC_y})^2}$ |
| 3 | $FP\_ECC\_OFC\_OC\_ANGLE$ | $\dfrac{atan2((c_{OFC_y} - c_{OC_y}), (c_{OFC_x} - c_{OC_x})) \cdot 180}{\pi}$ |
| 4 | $FP\_ECC\_OFC\_PC\_DIST$ | $\sqrt{(c_{PC_x} - c_{OFC_x})^2 + (c_{PC_y} - c_{OFC_y})^2}$ |
| 5 | $FP\_ECC\_OFC\_PC\_ANGLE$ | $\dfrac{atan2((c_{OFC_y} - c_{PC_y}), (c_{OFC_x} - c_{PC_x})) \cdot 180}{\pi}$ |
| 6 | $FP\_RATIO\_OFC\_IFC$ | $c_{OFC_r} / c_{IFC_r}$ |
| 7 | $FP\_ECC\_OFC\_IFC\_DIST$ | $\sqrt{(c_{IFC_x} - c_{OFC_x})^2 + (c_{IFC_y} - c_{OFC_y})^2}$ |
| 8 | $FP_{ECC\_OFC\_IFC\_ANGLE}$ | $\dfrac{atan2((c_{OFC_y} - c_{IFC_y}), (c_{OFC_x} - c_{IFC_x})) \cdot 180}{\pi}$ |

| | 3D Spatial Domain | |
|---|---|---|
| 9 | $FP\_MAX\_DEPTH$ | $max(values(inCircle(c_{OFC}, I_{Topo})))$ |
| 10 | $FP\_AVG\_DEPTH$ | $avg(values(inCircle(c_{OFC}, I_{Topo})))$ |
| 11 | $FP\_HEIGHT\_OFC\_IFC$ | $max(values(onCircle(c_{OFC}, I_{Topo}))) - min(values(onCircle(c_{IFC}, I_{Topo})))$ |
| | $FP\_STEEP\_OFC\_IFC$ | $z_{OFC} = avg(values(onCircle(c_{OFC}, I_{Topo})))$ |
| | | $z_{IFC} = avg(values(onCircle(c_{IFC}, I_{Topo})))$ |
| | | $\Delta z = z_{OFC} - z_{IFC}, \Delta x, y = c_{OFC_{x,y}} - c_{IFC_{x,y}}$ |
| | | $x_{IFC_{1,2}} = c_{IFC_x} \pm c_{IFC_r}, y_{IFC_{3,4}} = c_{IFC_y} \pm c_{IFC_r}$ |
| | | $x_{OFC_{1,2}} = c_{OFC_x} \pm \sqrt{c_{OFC_r}^2 - \Delta y^2}$ |
| | | $y_{OFC_{3,4}} = c_{OFC_y} \pm \sqrt{c_{OFC_r}^2 - \Delta x^2}$ |
| | | $d_{1,2} = \mid x_{OFC_{1,2}} - x_{IFC_{1,2}} \mid, d_{3,4} = \mid y_{OFC_{3,4}} - y_{IFC_{3,4}} \mid$ |
| | | $\propto_{1,2,3,4} = \tan^{-1}\dfrac{d_{1,2,3,4}}{\Delta z}$ |
| 12 | $FP\_MAX\_STEEP\_OFC\_IFC$ | $max(\{\alpha_i \mid i = 1 \dots 4\})$ |
| 13 | $FP\_MIN\_STEEP\_OFC\_IFC$ | $min(\{\alpha_i \mid i = 1 \dots 4\})$ |
| 14 | $FP\_AVG\_STEEP\_OFC\_IFC$ | $avg(\{\alpha_i \mid i = 1 \dots 4\})$ |
| 15 | $FP\_VERT\_PATH\_INC$ | $\sum_{i = c_{OFC_x} - c_{OFC_r}}^{c_{OFC_x} + c_{OFC_r}} \mid value(I_{Topo}, c_{OFC_x}, i) - value(I_{Topo}, c_{OFC_x}, i - 1) \mid$ |
| 16 | $FP\_VERT\_PATH\_CUM$ | $\sum values(\{p : p_x = c_{OFC_x}, c_{OFC_y} - c_{OFC_r} \le p_y \le c_{OFC_y} + c_{OFC_r}\})$ |
| 17 | $FP\_HORI\_PATH\_INC$ | $\sum_{i = c_{OFC_y} - c_{OFC_r}}^{c_{OFC_y} + c_{OFC_r}} \mid value(I_{Topo}, i, c_{OFC_y}) - value(I_{Topo}, i - 1, c_{OFC_y}) \mid$ |
| 18 | $FP\_HORI\_PATH\_CUM$ | $\sum values(\{p : p_y = c_{OFC_y}, c_{OFC_x} - c_{OFC_r} \le p_x \le c_{OFC_x} + c_{OFC_r}\})$ |

*Classification* results are evaluated with respect to $E_1$ and $E_2$. Regarding evaluation goal $E_1$ the classification can be comprehended as a 2-class classification scenario. We perform a 10-fold stratified cross-validation using the features from Table 2

and the class sets introduced in test set section. True positives $TP$, false positives $FP$, true positive rate $TPR = TP/(TP + FN)$, false positive rate $FPR = FP/(FP + TN)$ and precision $P = TP/(TP + FP)$ are used as performance measures. During second evaluation $E_2$ we use all 72 test samples together in a 6-class classification scenario. Again we perform a 10-fold stratified cross-validation using the features from Table 2; also $TP$, $FP$, $TPR$, $FPR$ and $P$ are used for measuring classification performance. By using 10-fold cross-validation the classifiers are trained 10 times for each evaluation. The performance is calculated as mean of errors of the individual training cycles [23].

## 5. EXPERIMENTAL RESULTS

The results for $E_1$ are summarized in Table 3, Table 4 and Table 5. Regarding individualization of weapon model *Walther P99*; 100% correctly classified samples, $TPR$ and $P$ of 1 and $FPR$ of 0 are achieved by both classifiers (Table 3). Regarding the second weapon model *Ceska 75B* (Table 4), *NNge* classifier achieves 100% correctly classified samples, $TPR$, $P$ equates to 1 and $FPR$ equates to 0. The *BN* classifier misclassified one sample, this results in 95.83% correctly classified samples ($TPR$ 0.958, $FPR$ 0.042, $P$ 0.962). Classification results regarding the third weapon system *Beretta 92FS* are shown in Table 5. Again both classifiers show similar performance. Regarding *NNge* classifier the percentage of correctly classified samples is 87.5% ($TPR$ 0.875, $FPR$ 0.125, $P$ 0.878). For *BN* algorithm the percentage of correct classifications is 83.33% ($TPR$ 0.833, $FPR$ 0.167, $P$ 0.843).

**Table 3: Results $E_1$: individualization *Walther P99* (wa)**

| C | # | TP | FP | TPR | FPR | P |
|---|---|---|---|---|---|---|
| *NNge Classifier* | | | | | | |
| all | 24 | 24 | 0 | 1 | 0 | 1 |
| $wa_a$ | 12 | 12 | 0 | 1 | 0 | 1 |
| $wa_b$ | 12 | 12 | 0 | 1 | 0 | 1 |
| *Bayesian Net Classifier* | | | | | | |
| all | 24 | 24 | 0 | 1 | 0 | 1 |
| $wa_a$ | 12 | 12 | 0 | 1 | 0 | 1 |
| $wa_b$ | 12 | 12 | 0 | 1 | 0 | 1 |

**Table 4: Results $E_1$: individualization *Ceska 75B* (cz)**

| C | # | TP | FP | TPR | FPR | P |
|---|---|---|---|---|---|---|
| *NNge Classifier* | | | | | | |
| all | 24 | 24 | 0 | 1 | 0 | 1 |
| $cz_a$ | 12 | 12 | 0 | 1 | 0 | 1 |
| $cz_b$ | 12 | 12 | 0 | 1 | 0 | 1 |
| *Bayesian Net Classifier* | | | | | | |
| all | 24 | 23 | 1 | 0.958 | 0.042 | 0.962 |
| $cz_a$ | 12 | 12 | 1 | 1 | 0.083 | 0.923 |
| $cz_b$ | 12 | 11 | 0 | 0.917 | 0 | 1 |

**Table 5: Results $E_1$: individualization *Beretta 92FS* (be)**

| C | # | TP | FP | TPR | FPR | P |
|---|---|---|---|---|---|---|
| *NNge Classifier* | | | | | | |
| all | 24 | 21 | 3 | 0.875 | 0.125 | 0.878 |
| $be_a$ | 12 | 10 | 1 | 0.833 | 0.083 | 0.909 |
| $be_b$ | 12 | 11 | 2 | 0.917 | 0.167 | 0.846 |
| *Bayesian Net Classifier* | | | | | | |
| all | 24 | 20 | 4 | 0.833 | 0.167 | 0.843 |
| $be_a$ | 12 | 9 | 1 | 0.75 | 0.083 | 0.9 |
| $be_b$ | 12 | 11 | 3 | 0.917 | 0.25 | 0.786 |

The results for $E_2$ are summarized in Table 6. With respect to the complete test set of 72 samples the overall classification accuracy of the *NNge* classifier is 86.11% with 62 *TP* and 10 *FP*. Whereat *TPR* equates to 0.861, *FPR* is 0.028 and *P* equates to 0.865.

Regarding the *BN* algorithm a correct classification is attained in 83.33% of the cases (*TPR* 0.833, *FPR* 0.033, *P* 0.859). Breaking down the results as shown in Table 6 it can be seen, that classification results for individual weapons differ. Best results are achieved for $wa_b$ and $cz_a$ with a *TPR* of 1. The worst result is achieved for $cz_b$ with a *TPR* of 0.667 for *NNge* and 0.5 for *BN*.

**Table 6: Results $E_2$: individualization over entire test set**

| C | # | TP | FP | TPR | FPR | P |
|---|---|----|----|-----|-----|---|
| *NNge Classifier* | | | | | | |
| *all* | 72 | 62 | 10 | 0.861 | 0.028 | 0.865 |
| $wa_a$ | 12 | 11 | 0 | 0.917 | 0 | 1 |
| $wa_b$ | 12 | 12 | 0 | 1 | 0 | 1 |
| $cz_a$ | 12 | 12 | 1 | 1 | 0.017 | 0.923 |
| $cz_b$ | 12 | 8 | 2 | 0.667 | 0.033 | 0.8 |
| $be_a$ | 12 | 9 | 3 | 0.75 | 0.05 | 0.75 |
| $be_b$ | 12 | 10 | 4 | 0.833 | 0.067 | 0.714 |
| *Bayesian Net Classifier* | | | | | | |
| *all* | 72 | 60 | 12 | 0.833 | 0.033 | 0.859 |
| $wa_a$ | 12 | 11 | 0 | 0.917 | 0 | 1 |
| $wa_b$ | 12 | 12 | 1 | 1 | 0.017 | 0.923 |
| $cz_a$ | 12 | 12 | 2 | 1 | 0.033 | 0.857 |
| $cz_b$ | 12 | 6 | 0 | 0.5 | 0 | 1 |
| $be_a$ | 12 | 9 | 3 | 0.75 | 0.05 | 0.75 |
| $be_b$ | 12 | 10 | 6 | 0.833 | 0.1 | 0.625 |

# 6. CONCLUSION AND FUTURE WORK

In this work we proposed a new firearm identification method based on firing pin impressions on center-fire cartridges, a combined set of 18 features from 2D and 3D spatial domain, along with two different classifiers. For evaluating the performance of the method a 10-fold stratified cross-validation is used on a test set of 72 cartridge samples. Regarding individualization of two guns of the same brand and model correct classification rates from 87.5% to 100% are achieved. With respect to individualization over the entire test set with six individual guns our proposed approach achieves a correct classification rate of 86.11%. Compared to the state of the art the proposed approach achieves a similar level of accuracy to [8] with 12.7 false acceptance rate, [14] with a discrimination ratio of 0.88 or [11] with 87.53% correct classifications. In comparison to [19] the introduced extended feature vector increases the percentage of correct classifications from 78% to 86.11%, with a comparatively larger dataset. Compared to the results of the first two weapon systems the achieved classification performance for the *Beretta 92FS* is significantly poorer as shown in the results section.

Future work should address: an evaluation of the varying classification performance in relation to different guns, a ranking of the features with regards to their importance, a realization of automatic and robust ejector detection to address the currently required user interaction during registration stage, a sensor-specific de-noising, possible approaches for direct warping of 3D data, an extension of test- and feature set, as well as a combination of translation / rotation variant and invariant features.

# 7. ACKNOWLEDGMENTS

This work is supported by German Federal Ministry of Education and Science (BMBF) through research program under contract numbers FKZ: 13N10816 and 13N10818. The documents content is under sole responsibility of the authors. We would like to thank Jana Dittmann, Andrey Makrushin, Tobias Kiertscher and AMSL research group Magdeburg for all the interesting discussions and valuable comments. We also want to thank the German state-police of Saxony-Anhalt for providing the cartridge samples.

# 8. REFERENCES

[1] Uchiyama, Tsuneo: "Toolmark Reproducibility on Fired Bullets and Expended Cartridge Cases", AFTE Journal, Vol. 40, No. 1, 2008

[2] Cork, D.; Rolph, J.; Meieran, E.; Petrie, C.: "Ballistic Imaging - Accuracy and Technical Capability of a National Ballistics Database", National Research Council, ISBN: 0-309-11725-9, 2008

[3] Barret, M.; Warren, G.: "Portable Forensic Ballistic Examination Instrument: Advanced Ballistics Analysis System (ALIAS)", AFTE Journal, Vol. 43 No. 1, 2011

[4] Dillon, Jr. John H.: "BulletTRAX-3D, MatchPoint Plus and the Firearms Examiner / Forensic Technology WAI Inc", Sci. rep., 2005

[5] EvoFinder Europe, http://www.evofinder.com, checked: 23.04.2014

[6] Xin, L.; Zhou J.: "A Cartridge Identification System for Firearm Authentication", Signal Processing Proceedings, 2000. WCCC-ICSP 2000. 5th Int. Conference on , vol.2, no., pp.1405,1408, 2000

[7] Geradts, Z.; Bijhold, J.; Hermsen, R.; Murtagh, F.: " Image matching algorithms for breech face marks and firing pins in a database of spent cartridge cases of firearms", For. Sci. Int., Volume 119, Issue 1, 1 June 2001, Pages 97-106, ISSN 0379-0738

[8] Zhou, J.; Xin, L.; Gao, D.; Zhang, C: "Automated cartridge identification for firearm authentication", Computer Vision and Pattern Recognition, 2001. CVPR 2001. Proc. of the 2001 IEEE Computer Society Conf. on , vol.1, no., pp.I-749,I-754 vol.1, 2001

[9] Li, D.: "Ballistics Projectile Image Analysis for Firearm Identification", IEEE Trans. o. Image Proc., pp: 2857 -2865, 2006

[10] Thumwarin, P., "An Automatic System for Firearm Identification," Communications and Information Technologies, 2008. ISCIT 2008. International Symposium on, pp.100,103, 21-23 Oct. 2008

[11] Thumwarin, P.; Prasit, C.; Matsuura, T., "Firearm identification based on rotation invariant feature of cartridge case", SICE Annual Conference, 2008 , pp.45-49, 20-22 Aug. 2008

[12] Leng, J.; Huang, Z.; Li, D.: "Feature extraction and classification of cartridge images for ballistics identification" In Proceedings of the 23rd int. conf. on Ind. Eng., Volume Part III (IEA/AIE'10) Springer-Verlag, Berlin, Heidelberg, 331-340, 2010

[13] Smith, C.L.; Robinson, M.; Evans, P.: "Line-scan imaging for the positive identification of ballistics specimens", Security Technology, 2000. Proc. IEEE 34th Annual 2000 International Carnahan Conference on, pp. 269 -275, 2000

[14] Bachrach, B.: "Development of a 3D-Based Automated Firearms Evidence Comparison System", J. of For. Sci., vol.47, no. 6, pp. 1253-1264, 2002

[15] Senin, N.; Groppetti, R.; Garofano, L.; Fratini, P.; Pierni, M.: "Three-Dimensional Surface Topography Acquisition and Analysis for Firearm Identification", J. of For. Sci., 51: 282–295, 2006

[16] Sakarya, U; Murat, U; Erol, L.: "Three-dimensional surface reconstruction for cartridge cases using photometric stereo", For. Sci. Int., Vol. 175, Issues 2–3, 5, pp. 209-217, 2008

[17] Suapang, P.; Yimmun. S.; Chumnan, N.: "Tool and Firearm Identification System Based on Image Processing", Control, Automation and Systems (ICCAS), 11th International Conference on, pp.178,182, 26-29 Oct. 2011

[18] Makrushin, A.; Hildebrandt, M.; Dittmann, J.; et al.: "3D imaging for ballistics analysis using chromatic white light sensor", Proc. of SPIE 8290, 3DIP, 2012

[19] Fischer, R.; Vielhauer, C.: "Forensic ballistic analysis using a 3D sensor device", In Proceedings of the on Multimedia and security (MM&Sec '12), ACM, NY, USA, pp. 67-76, 2012

[20] Fischer, R.; Vielhauer, C.; Hildebrandt, M.; et al.: "Ballistic examinations based on 3D data: a comparative study of probabilistic Hough Transform and geometrical shape determination for circle-detection on cartridge bottoms", Proc. of SPIE 86650F, 2013

[21] Hall, M.; Frank, E.; Holmes, G.; et al.: "The WEKA data mining software: An update", SIGKDD Exp., vol.11, no.1, pp. 10 –18, 2009

[22] Speck, C.: „Automatisierte Auswertung forensischer Spuren auf Patronenhülsen", Institut für Mess- und Regelungstechnik Universität Karlsruhe, Dissertation, 2009 (German)

[23] Duda, R.; Hart, P.; Stork, G.: "Pattern Classification (2nd Edition)", Wiley-Interscience, ISBN: 0471056693, 2009

[24] Keyence Corp., http://www.keyence.com/, checked: 23.04.2014

# Video Steganalysis Based on Subtractive Probability of Optimal Matching Feature

Yanzhen Ren
Computer Science
Department
Key Laboratory of Aerospace
Information Security and
trusted computing Ministry of
Education
Wuhan University
Wuhan, China
renyz@whu.edu.cn

Liming Zhai
Computer Science
Department
Key Laboratory of Aerospace
Information Security and
trusted computing Ministry of
Education
Wuhan University
Wuhan, China
zhailiminghn@163.com

Lina Wang
Computer Science
Department
Key Laboratory of Aerospace
Information Security and
trusted computing Ministry of
Education
Wuhan University
Wuhan, China
lnwang@whu.edu.cn

Tingting Zhu
Information security
department
Naval university of engineering
Wuhan, China
zlztt1688@sina.com.cn

## ABSTRACT

This paper presents a novel motion vector (MV) steganalysis method. MV-based steganographic methods exploit the variability of MV to embed messages by modifying MV slightly. However, we have noticed that the modified MVs after steganography cannot follow the optimal matching rule which is the target of motion estimation. It means that steganographic methods conflict with the basic principle of video compression. Aiming at this difference, we proposed a steganalysis feature based on Subtractive Probability of Optimal Matching(SPOM), which statistics the MV's Probability of the Optimal matching (POM) around its neighbors, and extract the classification feature by subtracting the POM of the test video and its recompressed video. Experiment results show that the proposed feature is sensitive to MV-based steganography methods, and outperforms the other methods, especially for high temporal activity video.

## 1. INTRODUCTION

Steganography is a technology of sending secret messages under the covert channel of normal objects, such as digital images and videos. Steganalysis is the art to attack steganography by identifying suspected cover objects. In recent years, with the widespread of networked multimedia applications, such as IPTV, Video Conference, and Video on Demand, etc., compressed video streams which can easily

achieve a large hiding capacity become a new covert channel for steganography. A lot of video steganography algorithms and tools emerged[9, 5, 8, 16, 1, 2, 4]. Unlike traditional video steganography, which uses the spatial or frequency coefficients of video frames for embedding secret messages, the MV-based schemes adopt MVs as the information carrier to achieve covert communication. There are two benefits of MV-based steganography method. The first is that the statistical characteristics of the spatial or frequency coefficients of video frames will not be changed, thus the methods is secure to the traditional steganalysis methods. The second is that the degradation of the visual quality will be very little. Owing to these two reasons, several MV-based steganographic algorithms have been proposed in the last few years (e.g., [8, 1, 2, 4, 16, 5]).

Kutter et al.[8] firstly proposed a MV-based steganlography method, selected MVs whoes magnitudes are non-zero and embedded secret message by modifying the LSBs of those MVs' horizontal or vertical components. Xu et al.[1] suggested embedding the data in the MVs which magnitudes are above a predefined threshold. Fang and Chang[2] designed a method adjusting MVs' phase angles by modifying MV's magnitude. In order to reduce the negative effects of coding efficiency. Aly[4] selected the candidate subset of motion vectors which have smaller prediction errors to hide information. Cao et al.[16] choose the optimal or suboptimal MVs according to the embedded information, and wet-paper coding algorithm was adopted to enhance the security of steganography. Jing et al.[5] choose a small part of motion vectors to modify to resist the steganalysis method in[19]. All MV-based steganography methods above share some features in common, i.e., they first select a subset of MVs following a predefined selection principle, then do the embedding operations by modifying the MV's magnitude to meet consistent with the secret information.

To attack the MV-based steganography, Su et al.[19] firstly proposed a MV-steganalystic method based on the statistical analysis of relative properties between neighboring MVs. A feature classification technique is adopted to determine the existence of hidden messages. Cao *et al.*[17] considered the tendency of MV's reversion, designed a recompression calibration-based approach to estimate the cover video, and proposed a steganalysis method which adopts MV reversion-based features derived from the differences between the original and the calibrated videos. Deng *et al.*[18] presented a MV recovery algorithm based on local-polynomial kernel regression model, and proposed statistical features based on calibration distance histogram for steganalysis. The methods in [19] and [18] are based on the correlation which exists between the neighboring MVs, but for videos which have high temporal activity, the correlated characteristic is not obvious, and the steganalysis method will work ineffectively.

Most of the steganalysis features proposed in the literatures(e.g., [17, 18, 19]) are all based on the statistic characters of the MV's magnitude. However, MV is an intermediate variable in video compression, which magnitude is not unique, thus the steganalysis features based on MV's magnitude are not stable. In this paper, we change the direction to look for the steganalysis feature. We have noticed that those MVs modified by MV-based steganographic methods don't follow the optimal matching rules which are the aim of motion estimation in general video compression. It means that steganographic methods conflict with the basic encoding principles. Based on this idea, we proposed a feature by measuring MVs' optimal matching characteristics to complete steganalysis.

The rest of the paper is organized as follows: In Section II, we introduce the basic concepts of motion estimation in video compression, and present the optimal matching characteristics of MVs in cover and stego video. The implementation of our proposed steganalysis method is described in Section III. In Section IV,comparative experiments are carried out to show the performance of the proposed method. Finally, concluding remarks are given in Section V with some considerations about future research.

## 2. THE OPTIMAL MATCHING CHARACTERISTICS OF MVS

### 2.1 Motion Estimation

Motion vector is generated by motion estimation (ME) in video compression. Most video encoding standards, such as MPEG-2, MPEG-4, H.263, H.264, H.265, etc., implement video compression by removing both the spatial and temporal redundancy[12]. The goal of motion estimation is to reduce the temporal redundancy of video, and its basic idea is to predict the current coded frame by one or more prior coded frames due to the high correlation of neighbored video frames. The schematic diagram of motion estimation is shown in Figure 1. To encode the current macro-block (MB) of size $m \times m$, the encoder adopts one prior coded frame R as the reference, and search for the best matching block $R_B$ within a searching area $R_s$ as $B$'s reference block. As result, the motion vector $mv_B$ represents the spatial displacement offset between $B$ and $R_B$, and the Prediction Error (PE) which is the pixel difference between $B$ and $R_B$ is further coded and transmitted.

To search for the best matching block, Full search (FS) algorithm gives the global optimum solution by exhaustively

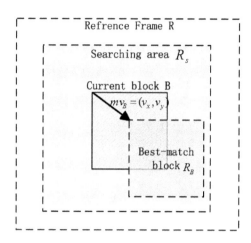

**Figure 1: Schematic Diagram of Motion Estimation**

testing all the candidate blocks within the searching area. To lower the huge computational complexity of FS, many fast block-matching algorithms (BMAs) have been proposed and applied to the video compression standards, such as Three-step Search (TSS), Four-step Search(FSS), Diamond Search(DS), etc.[6]. These fast BMAs exploit different searching patterns and searching strategies to find the optimum motion vector which drastically reduce the number of search points as compared with the FS algorithm. To measure the prediction error between the target and candidate blocks, several matching criteria have been used, such as Mean Squared Error (MSE), Sum of Absolute Differences (SAD), Mean Absolute Difference (MAD)[14], etc. Where SAD is commonly used and computed as:

$$SAD(B, R_B) = \sum_{1 \leq i,j \leq m} |B(i,j) - R_B(i,j)| \qquad (1)$$

Where $B(i,j)$ and $R_B(i,j)$ are luminance values of current coded block B and reference block $R_B$. The purpose of BMAs is to find an optimal matching block which makes SAD or MAD to be minimum.

### 2.2 The optimal matching characteristics of MVs in cover and stego video

For cover video which is compressed by normal video encoder and not modified by MV-based steganography methods, its MVs are generated by motion estimation and its reference block should be the best matching block among its neighbors. For stego video which MVs are modified to embed secret message, the MV will shift from the optimal matching location. In order to maintain the visual quality and avoid distortion drift, the steganography methods need to modify the reference block accordingly, thus the new reference block will not be the best matching block among its neighbors. Figure 2 shows an example of MV steganography to explain the opinion simply. The original MV is $mv(v_x, v_y)$, which is the best matching MV within its neighbors. When $mv$ is modified to $mv'(v_{x-1}, v_{y-1})$ by steganography method shown in Figure 2(b), we can see that the new MV $mv'$ will not be the best matching MV within its neighbors.

The optimal matching properties of MVs in cover video and stego video will be analyzed in this section. Without loss of generality, given an inter-Macro Block (MB) $B(i, j)$ in a video frame, while $(i, j)$ are the coordinates of $B$'s left-upper point. $B$'s MV in compressed stream is $mv(v_x, v_y)$, where $v_x$ is the horizontal value of MV, and $v_y$ is the vertical value of MV. The corresponding reference MB is $R_B(i + v_x, j + v_y)$ in reference frame $R$. To measure the optimal matching properties of MVs, we will give some definitions as follows:

*Definition 1.* MV's neighborhood Set $N_{n \times n}$. For $mv(v_x, v_y)$, given a neighborhood range $n \times n$, where $n = 2k + 1, k \geq 1$, given a MV set

$$\mathbb{C} = mv(v_x + d_x, v_y + d_y) | - k \leq d_x \leq k, -k \leq d_y \leq k$$

$\mathbb{C}$ is called $mv$'s neighborhood Set $N_{n \times n}$. Figure 3 shows the example of $N_{5 \times 5}$.

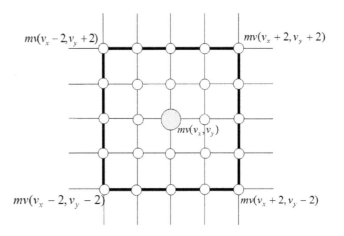

**Figure 3: The example of MV neighborhood Set $N_{5 \times 5}$**

*Definition 2.* Optimal matching. For $mv(v_x, v_y)$ and its reference block $R_B$, given a MV neighborhood set $N_{n \times n}$. For arbitrary $mv_i \in N_{n \times n}$, its corresponding reference MB is $R_i$ $(1 <= i <= n^2)$, and the set of neighborhood reference MB is $R_{round}$. If $SAD(B, R_B) = MIN_{R_i \in R_{round}}(SAD(B, R_i))$, where function $MIN_r(x)$ means the minimum value of $x$ in range $r$, then we called $mv$ is the optimal matching, otherwise, $mv$ is not optimal matching.

*Definition 3.* Probability of optimal matching (POM). Given a video segment $V$, the number of MVs in $V$ is $N_{mv}$, and the number of MVs which are optimal matching is $N_{om}$, then the POM of $V$ is $P_V = N_{om}/N_{mv}$.

*Definition 4.* Calibrated Video. Calibration is a procedure of video recompression. Given a compressed video segment V, decompressed V to spatial domain and gained the YUV sequence Vseq, then compress Vseq again without any embedding to get the compressed video segmen $\hat{V}$. $\hat{V}$ is named as the calibrated video of $V$.

*Definition 5.* Subtractive probability of optimal matching (SPOM). Given a test video segment $V$, $\hat{V}$ is the calibrated video of $V$. The POM of $V$ is $P_{test}$, and the POM of $\hat{V}$ is $P_{cab}$, then the SPOM of $V$ is $P_{err}$, which is the subtraction of $P_{cab}$ and $P_{test}$, i.e. $P_{err} = P_{cab} - P_{test}$.

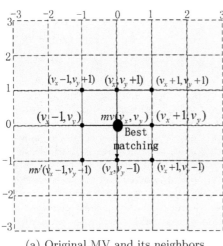

(a) Original MV and its neighbors

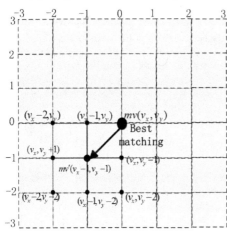

(b) Modified MV and its neighbors

**Figure 2: Example of MV steganography**

For cover video, the MVs are selected by motion estimation to search for the best matching MV. If MVs are selected by Full search algorithm, all MVs should be optimal matching, and the POM of those cover videos should be one. However this situation is too idealistic. All the video encoders used actually employ fast Block Matching Algorithms (BMAs) to search MV, and a little amount of points are checked. In this situation, POM of those cover video cannot reach one. We had done experiment on nine standard video sequences to test POM of cover videos and stego videos, the sequences are selected from Xiph[15] and described in Table 1. Table 2 shows POM of cover videos which are encoded by X264[13] and JM18.0[10] respectively on different neighborhood Set. Table 3 shows POM of the stego videos which all MVs are modified randomly by 1/4 pixels, and the videos are encoded by X264[13] and JM18.0[10]. The result in Table 2 shows that POM of cover videos compressed by different encoder are all larger than 50%, and The result in Table 3 shows that POM of stego videos are smaller and lower than their cover videos obviously. It can be found that POM should be a good feature to distinguish cover video and MV-based stego video.

#### Table 1: Description of Video Sequence

| Video Sequence | Frame size | Frame Number | Camera motion | Object motion |
|---|---|---|---|---|
| Bus | 352x288 | 150 | Panning | Translation(fast) |
| Flower | 352x288 | 250 | Panning | Translational |
| Foreman | 352x288 | 300 | Panning | Translation(fast) |
| Coastguard | 352x288 | 300 | panning | Translation (slow) |
| Container | 352x288 | 300 | panning | Translation (slow) |
| Mother | 352x288 | 300 | neglible | Translation (slow) |
| Stefan | 352x288 | 300 | Panning | Translational |
| Soccer | 352x288 | 600 | Panning(fast) | Translation(fast) |
| Football | 352x288 | 360 | Panning(fast) | Translation(fast) |

#### Table 2: POM of Cover Videos

| Video Sequence | X.264 encoder $N_{3\times3}$ | $N_{5\times5}$ | $N_{9\times9}$ | JM18.0 Encoder $N_{3\times3}$ | $N_{5\times5}$ | $N_{9\times9}$ |
|---|---|---|---|---|---|---|
| Bus | 62.46% | 61.04% | 60.64% | 61.75% | 61.53% | 60.46% |
| Flower | 64.82% | 63.65% | 63.35% | 62.83% | 61.79% | 61.65% |
| Foreman | 57.25% | 54.18% | 53.31% | 58.77% | 57.65% | 57.24% |
| Coastguard | 63.50% | 62.47% | 63.50% | 61.46% | 60.79% | 60.15% |
| Container | 67.46% | 65.75% | 65.72% | 66.59% | 65.77% | 64.61% |
| Mother | 52.47% | 52.16% | 51.99% | 55.65% | 54.87% | 54.13% |
| Stefan | 64.45% | 63.78% | 62.97% | 61.87% | 61.43% | 60.99% |
| Soccer | 51.62% | 51.54% | 51.24% | 53.86% | 52.71% | 52.15% |
| Football | 53.75% | 53.25% | 52.47% | 55.65% | 54.73% | 54.02% |
| **Average** | **59.75%** | **58.65%** | **58.35%** | **59.83%** | **59.10%** | **58.38%** |

For the actual steganography methods described in literatures [e.g.,[8, 1, 2, 4, 16, 5]], the modified rate of MVs cannot be 100%, thus the POM of the stego videos cannot be so small as Table 3. For example, the methods in [8] selected MVs which magnitude is non-zero and embedded secret message by modifying LSBs of those MVs' horizontal or vertical components. Even if all MVs are non-zero, and the modified rate of the method in [8] is nearly 50% when each MV is embedded. Figure 4(a) shows the POM of the videos on different embedding rate by methods described in [8], while embedding rate means the proportion

#### Table 3: POM of Stego Videos (All MVs are Modified)

| Video Sequence | X.264 encoder $N_{3\times3}$ | $N_{5\times5}$ | $N_{9\times9}$ | JM18.0 Encoder $N_{3\times3}$ | $N_{5\times5}$ | $N_{9\times9}$ |
|---|---|---|---|---|---|---|
| Bus | 2.98% | 2.44% | 2.37% | 1.85% | 1.37% | 1.29% |
| Flower | 2.88% | 1.98% | 1.90% | 1.73% | 1.44% | 1.09% |
| Foreman | 3.67% | 3.10% | 2.96% | 2.57% | 2.28% | 1.97% |
| Coastguard | 3.88% | 3.33% | 2.99% | 2.84% | 2.58% | 2.29% |
| Container | 2.62% | 2.48% | 2.06% | 2.54% | 2.46% | 2.02% |
| Mother | 3.35% | 3.10% | 2.82% | 2.99% | 2.49% | 2.11% |
| Stefan | 2.66% | 2.22% | 2.03% | 1.86% | 1.60% | 1.16% |
| Soccer | 3.16% | 2.95% | 2.65% | 2.79% | 2.37% | 2.07% |
| Football | 1.46% | 1.03% | 1.01% | 0.96% | 0.85% | 1.76% |
| **Average** | **2.96%** | **2.51%** | **2.31%** | **2.24%** | **2.00%** | **1.75%** |

of the number of embedding bits and the number of non-zero MVs. When embedding rate is zero, it means that the video is cover video, and when embedding rate is 100%, it means all the non-zero MVs in the video are embedded by LSB method and almost half non-zero MVs should be modified. From Figure 4(a) we can find that POM of varied cover videos are different greatly, but for one specific video, the POM on different embedding rate is liner to embedding rate nearly. Therefore, if we can get the POM of the video's cover video, we can steganalysis the video accurately.

Calibration [7] is a well known image steganalytic concept which estimates the macroscopic properties of the cover from the stego image. For compressed video, MV is an intermediate referenced data, the video frame is resumed by MV and its corresponding PE jointly. The recovered frame of MV-based stego video has little distortion from its original cover video, and the MVs of the recompressed video are selected by motion estimation, thus POM of calibrated video can be taken as the estimation of its cover video. This idea had been verified by the experiment results shown in Figure 4(b), where the x-axis is the calibrated videos which are recompressed by videos on varied embedding rate (cover videos' embedding rate is zero ). Figure 4(b) shows that POM of calibrated videos on different embedding rate are almost near to its cover video's.

For a test video, we can adopt its SPOM feature between the test video and its calibrated video to check whether the video is steoganographied. Figure 4(c) shows SPOM of the test video sequences in Table 1, we can find that SPOM of cover video is almost near to zero, and SPOM of stego video is linear to its embedding rate. Therefore SPOM can classify the cover video and stego video effectively. Based on this feature, we propose our steganalyzer in next section and compare its performance with the other methods in section IV.

### 3. PROPOSED STEGANALYZER

Based on the fact that MV's POM in stego video is lower than its original cover video's, and the POM of calibrated video is almost similar to cover video, we proposed a MV-based steganlyzer which classify the video by the SPOM feature of test video. The framework of our steganlyzer is shown in Figure 5, and the procedure is described as follows.

For a given test video $V$, firstly, calculate the POM of $V$ $P_{test}$ as described in Section II. Then Decode V to spatial

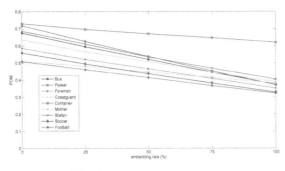

(a) POM of video sequences

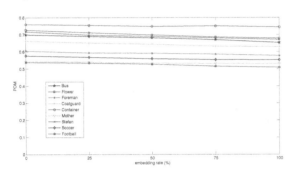

(b) POM of calibrated video sequences

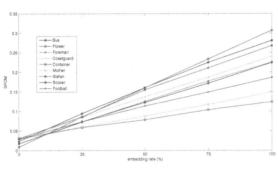

(c) SPOM of video sequences

**Figure 4: The POM and SPOM feature of standard video sequences**

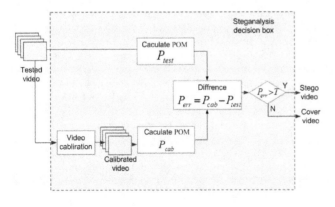

**Figure 5: Proposed framework for steganalysis**

domain and encode it again to get the calibrated video $\hat{V}$, and calculate the POM value of $\hat{V}$'s $P_{cab}$. Calculate the subtraction of $P_{cab}$ and $P_{test}$ to get $V$'s steganalysis feature $P_{err}$, $P_{err} = P_{cab} - P_{test}$. Finnaly, given an experienced threshold $T$, if $P_{err} > T$, then judge the test video as stego video, otherwise, the test video is classified as cover video.

## 4. EXPERIMENTS

To evaluate the performance of our proposed feature, we apply the proposed steganalytic algorithm to the standard video sequences, and compared its performance with the methods state-in-art. Besides, the performance under high temporal activity videos are also evaluated.

### 4.1 Experiment Setup

#### 4.1.1 Test Sequences

A video database of 47 CIF video sequences in 4:2:0 YUV format is used for experiments which are selected from Xiph[15] and TNT[11], with a special emphasis on the dynamic components in the videos, such as camera motion and moving objects. The frame rate of the video sequences is 30 fps. Since the length of sequences is varied and most of them have 300 frames, then we divide each sequence into non-overlapping sub-sequences with 100 frames and the total number of sub-sequences sums up to 162. The experiments of these sub-sequences are carried on compressed video sequences in H.264 compressed by X264 [13] encoder, and decoded by FFmepg H.264 decoder[3].

#### 4.1.2 Steganographic Methods

Our experiments focus on attacking three MV-based steganographic methods, i.e. Xu et al.'s [1], Aly's [4], Cao et al.'s [16] methods, and which are referred to as Xu, Aly, and Cao. These targets are implemented using X264 [13] encoder. As the message bits are embedded into MVs, the embedding strength in the experiment is measured by the average embedded bits per inter-frame (bpf). The MV's modified step is 1/4 pixel and embedded in a random embedding range from -3/4 to 3/4 pixels.

#### 4.1.3 The threshold T

the value of T in our method is gainned by training method. 1/3 video sequences (15 YUV sequence consisting of 52 subsequence) are randomly selected. All subsequences are compressed by X264 encoder with standard settings to produce the class of cover videos. At the same time, all subsequences are embedded with the method in [1] at different embedding strength, including 50 bpf, 100 bpf, 200 bpf. When T = 0.036, the true negative rate and true positive rate of the method can be reached a good tradeoff, both of them can be reached to 92.80%, thus we adopt T as 0.036 in the experiment.

#### 4.1.4 The detected range of the Neighborhood

We have made experiments on $N_{3\times3}$, $N_{5\times5}$, $N_{9\times9}$, the result shows that the increasing of the detected range have got small upgrade for detection accuracy. From table 2 and table 3 we can learn that the range of the Neighborhood has little affect on the POM of the test videos.Thus in this experiment, we adopt $N_{5\times5}$ , it can get a good tradeoff between detected accuracy and computational complexity.

## 4.2 Performance Results

In this experiment, besides our proposed features, Su *et al.*'s [19], Cao *et al.*'s [17], and Deng *et al.*'s[18] steganalytic features are leveraged for comparison, and they are referred to as Su2011, Cao2012, and Deng2012. We evaluate the performance using true positive (TP) and true negative (TN), where TP is the occurrence that a stego video is classified as stego, TN is the occurrence that a cover video is calssified as cover. The performances of the steganalyzers with varied embedding strengths are tested, and the corresponding results are recorded in Table 4.

Table 4: Performance Comparsion within Su2011's, Cao2012's, Deng2012's and Our Proposed Method

| | bpf | Su2011 | | Cao2012 | | Deng2012 | | Our proposed | |
|---|---|---|---|---|---|---|---|---|---|
| | | TP | TN | TP | TN | TP | TN | TP | TN |
| Xu | 50 | 58.4 | 54.6 | 88.5 | 86.7 | 88.3 | 94.9 | 92.8 | 92.8 |
| | 100 | 76.1 | 76.2 | 90.7 | 88.1 | 87.5 | 93.4 | 100 | 92.8 |
| | 200 | 84.5 | 95.3 | 95.4 | 89.7 | 92.1 | 92.7 | 100 | 92.8 |
| | 300 | 97.5 | 95.6 | 99.3 | 95.2 | 95.7 | 92.1 | 100 | 92.8 |
| Aly | 50 | 59.1 | 52.3 | 79.5 | 80.2 | 90.7 | 87.6 | 94.2 | 92.8 |
| | 100 | 72.3 | 63.6 | 84.6 | 81.2 | 91.3 | 91.7 | 100 | 92.8 |
| | 200 | 81.3 | 77.4 | 91.5 | 85.9 | 94.8 | 92.1 | 100 | 92.8 |
| | 300 | 94.5 | 93.1 | 98.1 | 91.3 | 96.5 | 93 | 100 | 92.8 |
| Cao | 50 | 53.4 | 52.8 | 76.9 | 78.5 | 90.5 | 86.4 | 91.5 | 92.8 |
| | 100 | 65 | 55.4 | 79.8 | 75.8 | 92 | 87.9 | 100 | 92.8 |
| | 200 | 79.1 | 76.9 | 88.1 | 85.1 | 94.7 | 91.8 | 100 | 92.8 |
| | 300 | 90.7 | 89.3 | 93 | 90.7 | 93.1 | 90.6 | 100 | 92.8 |
| Average | | 76 | 73.5 | 89.2 | 85.7 | 92.3 | 91.2 | 98.2 | 92.8 |
| Feature dimension | | 12 | | 15 | | 3 | | 1 | |

In comparison with the detection performance of Su2011's, Cao2012's and Deng2012's steganalyzers, our proposed features have better performance. Since that the classification in our method is judged by comparing with one fixed threshold T, thus, TN of our method is the same in varied embedding strength, and TP for varied test sample is different. The average TP of our proposed method is 98.2%. When embedding strength is higher than 100bpf, TP of our proposed method is 100%. The dimension of steganalysis features in Su2011's, Cao2012's and Deng2012's is 12, 15, and 3 respectively, in our method, only 1 feature is needed, it means that the feature we proposed is sensitive to MV-based steganography methods.

The detector receiver operating characteristic (ROC) curves of these seganalyzers for different steganography are shown in Figure 6, where the embedding strength is 50bpf. Figure 6(a) is the ROC for stego video by Xu's method, and Figure 6(b) is the ROC for stego video by Cao's method. We can find that the performance of our method is better than the comparing methods for the same steganography method.

The computational complexity of the proposed method is not very high. To extract the feature, each video should be recompressed once, and each inter-frame should be decoded and the POM should be calculated for each MV, The computational complexity of the method is less than the complexity to recompress the video twice. The experiment results show that the averge time consumed to get the SPOM of a CIF video of 300 frame is almost 20 seconds. To improve the com-

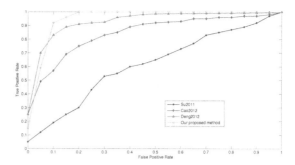

(a) Steganography method is Xu's

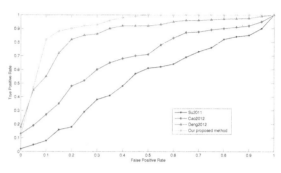

(b) Steganography method is Cao's

Figure 6: ROC curves of steganalyzers using Su2011's, Cao2012's and Deng2012's and our proposed features on 50bpf

putational efficiency, some new high-performance computing technologies, such as parallel computing or cloud computing can be adopted.

## 4.3 Discussion

The classification features of literature methods are based on the correlation among adjacent MVS, thus the detection accuracy strongly depends on the video's content. For example, the methods in [19] is based on the spatial correlation and temporal correlation of the motion vectors in video streams. Experiments results show that the correlation strength is relevant to the video content. When there has fast-moving object in the scene, the correlation in spatial domain is strong. However, when there is a low motion object in the scene or the adjacent scenes has little difference, the correlation in temporal domain is stronger than spatial domain. In a video sequence with many scenes, it is difficult to evaluate the differences in strength of correlation. For some high temporal activity videos, such as Highway, Tempete, etc. [15], the correlation among adjacent MVs is weak, and the performance of literature methods will be dropped.

For our proposed method, the classification feature is based on the basic principle of MV's generation. The optimal matching characteristic is constant for all kinds of compressed video. When MV is modified, its optimal matching characteristic will be destroyed, even for the video of weak correlation among adjacent MVS, our method is still effective. To prove this opinion, we have done experiments on high temporal activity videos to compare the performance of our proposed method and the literature methods.

Four video sequences are selected from Xiph[11] and TNT[14] in the 4:2:0 YUV, and the detailed description of the video sequences is given in Table 5.

**Table 5: Description of the High Temporal Activity Video Sequences**

| Video Sequence | Frame size | Number of frames | Camera motion | Object motion |
|---|---|---|---|---|
| Soccer | 352x288 | 300 | Panning(fast) | Translation(fast) |
| Highway | 352x288 | 360 | Panning | Translation(fast) |
| Tempete | 352x288 | 260 | Zooming | Translation(fast) |
| Ice | 352x288 | 480 | Static | Translation(fast) |

The cover and stego videos of Table 5 are compressed by X264[13], and the stego videos are produced by the steganography of Xu's [1] to embed random messages, the embedding strength is 300bpf. The experiment results are shown in Table 6. Since that TP of the comparing steganalysis methods are all 100% in this situation, we only show TN of each methods. From Table 6, we can find that the average of TN in our method is 92.6%, others' are lower than 42.1%.

**Table 6: TN of Su2011's, Cao2012's, Deng2012's and Our Proposed Method(300bpf, Target Method is Xu's)**

| Video Sequence | Su2011 TN | Cao2012 TN | Deng2012 TN | Our proposed TN |
|---|---|---|---|---|
| Soccer | 18.2 | 27.6 | 32.6 | 92.8 |
| Higway | 25.6 | 31.7 | 44 | 94.5 |
| Tempete | 28.7 | 39.7 | 46.2 | 91.7 |
| Ice | 26.2 | 35.1 | 45.7 | 91.3 |
| Average | 24.7 | 33.5 | 42.1 | 92.6 |

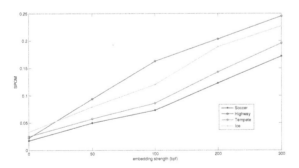

**Figure 7: SPOM of high temporal activity video sequences**

Figure 7 shows the SPOM features of the video sequences in Table 6 under varied embedding strength. For an embedding strength of 300bpf, the value of each video's SPOM is larger than T obviously, and TN of our proposed method depends only on the embedding strength. When embedding strength is under 25 bpf, the performance of our method needs further improvement.

# 5. CONCLUSION AND FUTURE WORK

In this paper, we proposed a novel MV-steganalytic method which is based on the optimal matching characteristic in compressed video by calculating the feature of MVs' Subtractive Probability of Optimal Matching (SPOM). Experiment results show that the feature is stable and sensitive to distinguish the cover and MV-based stego video. There are three advantages of the feature. Firstly, based on the common principle of MV's generation, the feature can be applicable for a variety of video compression standards which select the optimal matching MV to reduce the video's temporal redundancy, including MPEG-2, MPEG-4, H.263, H.264, H.265, etc. Secondly, the feature is independence on the correlation of adjacent MV, thus the feature has less relationship with the content of the video. Especially for high temporal activity videos, the feature has better classification capability than literature methods. Thirdly, the feature is comparing the relationship between the MV and its neighbors, instead of comparing the value of the MV and recovered MV (eg. [17, 18]), thus it has little dependence on the recovery accuracy of calibration algorithm, and especially suitable for the video encoding standards with variable block size motion estimation, such as H.264, H.265.

However, the detection performance of our proposed method under very low embedding strength (for example: 25bpf) is not satisfactory and should be improved further. Meanwhile, although the method can gain a good performance aginst the MV-based steganographic method in literatures, it only takes account of MV's POM feature for a local range. For some future steganographic methods which can guarantee locally optimal matching character, the proposed method should be improved, and the megered feature of local feature and global feature will be successed. Therefore, in our future work, we will combine the SPOM feature with the correlation character of the adjacent MVs to attack the steganographic methods which will be emerged in future.

# 6. ACKNOWLEDGEMENTS

This research was supported by the National Natural Science Foundation of China (NSFC) under the grant No. 61373169, 61272451 and 61272453.

# 7. REFERENCES

[1] C.XU, X.PING, AND T.ZHANG. Steganography in compressed video stream. *IEEE First International Conference on Innovative Computing, Information and Control* (2006), 269–272.

[2] D.FANG, AND L.CHANG. Data hiding for digital video with phase of motion vector. *Proc. Int. Symposium on Circuit and Systems (ISCAS)* (2006), 1422–1425.

[3] FFMPEG. *FFmpeg 264 decoder.* http://ffmpeg.org/. *@Online.*

[4] H.A.ALY. Data hiding in motion vectors of compressed video based on their associated prediction error. *IEEE Transactions on Information Forensics and Security 1* (6 2011), 14–18.

[5] H.JING, X.HE, Q.HAN, AND X.M.NIU. Motion vector based information hiding algorithm for h.264/avc against motion vector steganalysis. *4th Asian Conference on Intelligent Information and Database Systems* (2012), 78–83.

[6] H.Y.C.TOURAPIS, AND A.M.TOURAPIS. Fast motion estimation within the h.264 codec. *International Conference on Multimedia and Expo 3* (2003), 517–520.

[7] J.FRIDRICH. Feature-based steganalysis for jpeg images and its implications for future design of steganographic schemes. *Proc.IH'04, Lecture Notes in Computer Science 3200/2005* (2004), 67–81.

[8] M.KUTTER, F.JORDAN, AND T.EBRAHIMI. Proposal of a watermarking technique for hiding/retrieving data in compressed and decompressed video. *Technical Report M2281, ISO/IEC document, JTCI/ SC29/ WG11* (1997).

[9] STEGO, M. *MSU :: MSU Graphics Media Lab.* http://compression.ru/video/stego-video/index-en.html. *@Online.*

[10] SUEHRING, K. *H.264/AVC JM Reference Software Download.* http://iphome.hhi.de/suehring/tml/download/. *@Online.*

[11] TNT. *Tnt.uni Video Test Media.* ftp://ftp.tnt.uni-hannover.de/pub/svc/testsequences/. *@Online.*

[12] T.WIEGAND, G.J.SULLIVAN, G.BJONTEGAARD, AND A.LUTHRA. Overview of the h.264/avc video coding standard. *IEEE Trans. CircuitsSyst. VideoTechnol 13* (2003), 560–576.

[13] VIDEOLAN. *VideoLAN x264, the best H.264/AVC encoder.* http://www.videolan.org/developers/x264.html. *@Online.*

[14] XIAOZHONG, X., AND YUN, H. Improvements on fast motion estimation strategy for h.264/avc. *IEEE Transactions on Circuits and Systems for Video Technology 18,* 3 (2008), 285–293.

[15] XIPH. *Xiph.org :: Derf's Test Media Collection.* http://media.xiph.org/video/derf/. *@Online.*

[16] Y.CAO, X.F.ZHAO, AND D.G.FENG. Video steganography with perturbed motion estimation. *13th International Conference on Information Hiding* (May 2011).

[17] Y.CAO, X.F.ZHAO, AND D.G.FENG. Video steganalysis exploiting motion vector reversion-based features. *IEEE Signal Process Lett.19* (2012), 35–38.

[18] Y.DENG, Y.WU, AND L.ZHOU. Digital video steganalysis using motion vector recovery-based features. *Applied Optics 51,* Issue 20 (2012), 4667–4677.

[19] Y.T.SU, C.Q.ZHANG, AND C.T.ZHANG. A video steganalytic algorithm against motion-vector-based steganography. *Signal Processing* (2011), 1901–1909.

# Adaptive Steganalysis Against WOW Embedding Algorithm

**Weixuan Tang**
School of Information Science
and Technology
Sun Yat-sen University
Guangzhou, P.R. China
tweix@mail2.sysu.edu.cn

**Haodong Li**
School of Information Science
and Technology
Sun Yat-sen University
Guangzhou, P.R. China
lihaod@mail2.sysu.edu.cn

**Weiqi Luo** [*]
School of Software
Sun Yat-sen University
Guangzhou, P.R. China
weiqi.luo@yahoo.com

**Jiwu Huang**
College of Information
Engineering
Shenzhen University
Shenzhen, P.R. China
jwhuang@szu.edu.cn

## ABSTRACT

WOW (Wavelet Obtained Weights) [5] is one of the advanced steganographic methods in spatial domain, which can adaptively embed secret message into cover image according to textural complexity. Usually, the more complex of an image region, the more pixel values within it would be modified. In such a way, it can achieve good visual quality of the resulting stegos and high security against typical steganalytic detectors. Based on our analysis, however, we point out one of the limitations in the WOW embedding algorithm, namely, it is easy to narrow down those possible modified regions for a given stego image based on the embedding costs used in WOW. If we just extract features from such regions and perform analysis on them, it is expected that the detection performance would be improved compared with that of extracting steganalytic features from the whole image. In this paper, we first proposed an adaptive steganalytic scheme for the WOW method, and use the spatial rich model (SRM) based features [4] to model those possible modified regions in our experiments. The experimental results evaluated on 10,000 images have shown the effectiveness of our scheme. It is also noted that our steganalytic strategy can be combined with other steganalytic features to detect the WOW and/or other adaptive steganographic methods both in the spatial and JPEG domains.

## Categories and Subject Descriptors

I.4 [**Image Processing and computer vision**]

---

[*]Corresponding author

## Keywords

Adaptive Steganography; WOW; Adaptive Steganalysis; S-RM; Texture Complexity

## 1. INTRODUCTION

Steganaography has improved greatly with the development of steganalysis. LSB (Least Significant Bit) replacement is the simplest steganography. Though it can easily cheat our human eyes, it brings some artifacts into resulting images, and thus it is easy to be detected even at a low embedding rate using some steganalytic methods, such as the Chi-squared attack [13] and regular/singular groups (RS) analysis [3]. A minor modification to LSB replacement called LSB matching is proposed to avoid such obvious artifacts, and has been proved to be a more secure method compared to the LSB replacement. Subsequently, some steganographic methods have been proposed to improve the embedding efficiency and/or capacity, for instance LSB matching revisited [9] and PVD (pixel value difference) based method [14].

All the above-mentioned methods can be regarded as non-adaptive methods, since the locations of modified pixels with these methods are mainly dependent on a pseudorandom number generator. Their security performances against some advanced steganalytic features such as SPAM [10] , SRM [4], PSRM [6] or LBP based method [12] are still far from satisfactory, especially when the embedding rate is high. To improve the security, some adaptive embedding methods have been proposed. The basic idea of such adaptive methods is that preferentially modifying those complex textural regions that are hard to model, while keeping those smooth and flat regions as they are when performing data hiding. For instance, Luo *et al.* proposed an edge adaptive image steganography [8] based on LSB matching revisited. Recently, Pevny *et al.* proposed a novel strategy for adaptive steganography [11]. The strategy firstly builds a distortion function in the spatial domain to assign pixel costs by measuring the impact of changing each pixel in a feature space under investigation, and then combines with the advanced Syndrome-Trellis Codes (STCs) coding technique [2] to minimize the expected distortion for all pixels in an image. Based on this strategy, two modern steganographic methods *i.e.* HUGO [11] and WOW [5] have been proposed. The main difference of the two methods is the design of distortion function. The SPAM feature [10] model is used in HUGO, while for WOW, three directional wavelet filters have been used for obtaining the embedding costs for each pixel. Based on the results in [5], the WOW embedding algorithm achieves the best security performance in spatial domain evaluated by the modern steganalytic high-dimensional rich models SRM [4].

In this paper, we propose an adaptive steganalytic strategy for the WOW embedding algorithm. Based on our experiments, we found that like other adaptive steganograhic methods, most embedding changes would be highly concentrated on those complex textural or "noisy" regions using the WOW. In such a way, the visual quality of the resulting stego images and the security against some typical steganalytic methods are improved significantly compared with those non-adaptive ones, since embedding changes in the "noisy" regions are insensitive to our eyes and those regions are relatively difficult to model. However, this advantage would inevitably lead to a loophole in the WOW embedding algorithm. That is, it is possible to narrow down those suspicious regions (*i.e.* in those "noisy" regions) for a given questionable image. Even though those suspicious regions may be difficult to model, the relative modification rates (*i.e.* the number of modified pixels after data hiding over the number of pixels in the suspicious regions) would be increased significantly. Therefore, it is expected that the detection performance may be improved if the steganalytic features are extracted from those possible modified regions rather than the whole image like the typical steganalytic methods, and this is the main idea of the proposed steganalytic strategy.

The rest of this paper is arranged as follows. Section 2 describes how to narrow down the suspicious regions, Section 3 describes the proposed adaptive steganalytic strategy; Section 4 shows the experimental results. Finally, the concluding remarks and future works are given in Section 5.

## 2. LOCATION OF SUSPICIOUS REGIONS

In this Section, we firstly give a brief overview of the WOW embedding algorithm, and then propose a method to locate those suspicious regions based on the embedding costs used in WOW.

The WOW embedding algorithm works as follows. Firstly, three directional filters (denoted $K^{(k)}, k = 1, 2, 3$ using Daubechies 8 wavelets) are performed on the cover image $X$ to obtain the LH, HL and HH directional residuals $R^{(k)} = K^{(k)} * X$, respectively. Here, the $*$ denotes the convolution mirror-padded operation. And then the embedding suitability $\xi_{ij}^{(k)}$ for each pixel can be obtained by measuring the difference between $R^{(k)}$ and the same residual after changing only one pixel at $ij$ (denoted $R_{[ij]}^{(k)}$) by the wavelet coefficient itself.

$$\xi_{ij}^{(k)} = |R^{(k)}| * |R^{(k)} - R_{[ij]}^{(k)}| \tag{1}$$

| (a) Cover Image | (b) Modifications |

**Figure 1: Illustration of cover image and the modifications after using the WOW with 0.4bpp**

Then the embedding costs $\rho_{ij}$ are computed by aggregating three suitability $\xi_{ij}^{(k)}$, $k = 1, 2, 3$ by

$$\rho_{ij}^{(p)} = (\sum_{i=1}^{3} |\xi_{ij}^{(k)}|^p)^{-1/p}), p = -1 \tag{2}$$

Finally, the STCs is applied to minimize the following distortion function and get the resulting stego image $Y$.

$$D(X, Y) = \sum_{i=1}^{n_1} \sum_{j=1}^{n_2} \rho_{i,j}(X, Y_{i,j}) |X_{i,j} - Y_{i,j}| \tag{3}$$

where $n_1 \times n_2$ denotes the dimension of cover image $X$; $\rho_{i,j}$ denote the costs of changing pixel $X_{ij}$ to $Y_{ij}$, the WOW limits the embedding changes to $\pm 1$.

Usually, the $\rho_{i,j}^{(-1)}$ is smaller for those pixels located at the regions with more textural complexity, and thus the modifications after minimizing the above distortion function with STCs would be concentrated on textural regions, just as illustrated in Fig. 1. Since the textural regions are relatively difficult to model compared with smooth/flat regions, and the use of STCs can significantly reduce the embedding changes compared with typical methods, such as LSB Matching, the WOW is currently the most secure steganography in spatial domain.

Please note that in all universal steganalytic methods such as [4] and [12], features are extracted from the whole image, meaning that the contribution for every pixel in an image is assumed the same. Based on above analysis, however, we found that most embedding changes with the WOW embedding algorithm would be highly located at the textural regions, while lots of smooth and flat regions would not change at all. The typical universal methods may not be suitable for such adaptive methods. If we can firstly remove those smooth and flat regions, just consider those suspicious regions that are probably changed with WOW embedding algorithm, it is expected that the steganalysis performance would be better. Therefore, how to narrow down the suspicious regions is one of the key issues in the proposed steganalytic strategy. Fortunately, the embedding costs $\rho_{ij}^{(-1)}$ used in the WOW can help us deal with the problem effectively.

For a given stego image $Y$, we try to locate those possible modified pixels based on the embedding costs calculated

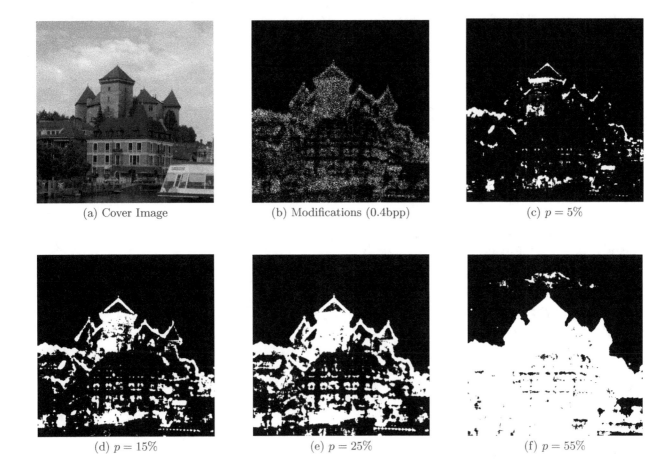

(a) Cover Image     (b) Modifications (0.4bpp)     (c) $p = 5\%$

(d) $p = 15\%$     (e) $p = 25\%$     (f) $p = 55\%$

**Figure 2: Illustrations of modifications and the locations of those selected pixels at different parameter $p$**

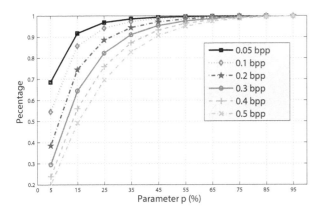

**Figure 3: The percentages of modified pixels located at selected pixels with increasing the parameter $p$**

from $Y$ [1]. According to the adaptive rule of WOW, the smaller the $\rho_{ij}$ is, the higher probability the pixel $(i, j)$ would be modified. To test the effectiveness of using $\rho_{ij}$ for locating those modified pixels, we firstly sort the $\rho_{ij}$ from the small-

---

[1] Although the cover image $X$ is not available, we can obtain the approximative $\rho_{ij}$ from the stego image Y, since the difference between $X$ and $Y$ is very small.

est to largest, and then we just select a small proportion $p$ of pixels with smaller embedding costs, where $p \in (0, 1]$ denotes the proportion of selected pixels in an image; and calculate the percentage that the number of modified pixels located at the selected pixels over all modified pixels. An example is shown in Fig. 2. It is observed that the selected pixels (see Fig. 2(c)-(f)) can estimate the location of modified pixels (see Fig. 2(b)) effectively. In this example, the corresponding percentages are $23.85\%, 59.78\%, 83.94\%$ and $100\%$ for $p = 5\%, 15\%, 25\%$ and $55\%$, respectively, which means that $45\% = 1 - 55\%$ of pixels in this image would not change at all when the embedding rate is 0.4bpp.

Obviously, the percentage depends on the embedding rate, the parameter $p$, and image content itself. To provide more convincing results, we show the average results evaluated on 10,000 images from BOSSBase ver. 1.01 [1]. In this experiment, the embedding rates are ranging from 0.05bpp to 0.5bpp, and $p$ is ranging from 5% to 95% with a step 10%. The results are shown in Fig. 3. It is observed that the percentages would increase with increasing the proportion $p$ for the six embedding rates. When $p$ becomes 35%, all percentages are larger than 82%, and they are larger than 95% when $p$ increases to 55%, which means that most modified pixels are concentrated on those pixels with small embedding costs. Therefore, it is possible to remove lots of unchanged pixels based on the embedding cost.

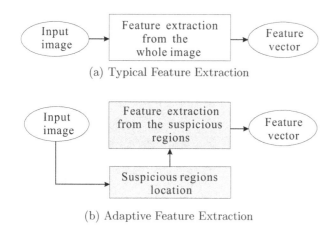

(a) Typical Feature Extraction

(b) Adaptive Feature Extraction

**Figure 4: Comparison of the typical steganalytic feature extraction and the proposed adaptive strategy**

## 3. THE PROPOSED ADAPTIVE STEGANALYTIC STRATEGY

As described in previous Section 2, we found that lots of pixels with larger embedding costs would not changes at all with the WOW embedding algorithm. It is expected that their contributions to steganalysis would be low. Thus the proposed adaptive steganalytic strategy for WOW is illustrated in Fig. 4. It is observed that the main difference between the proposed strategy and the typical one is that we just focus on those probably modified pixels (with a proportion $p$) according to the embedding costs for feature extraction. In such a case, the typical strategy can be regarded as a special case of our strategy when $p = 100\%$.

Please note that there is an important parameter $p$ (the proportion of image pixels that we selected for analysis, where $p \in (0, 1]$) in the proposed strategy. Based on our experiments, it would affect the detection performances significantly. The reason is that when the $p$ is smaller, the selected pixels may not be sufficient for extracting effective features. However, the relative modified rate (i.e. the number of modified pixels over the number of selected pixels) would become larger. Please refer to the average relative modified rates evaluated on BOSSBase [1] in Table 1. It is observed that for a given embedding rate, the relative modified rates will decrease with increasing the parameter $p$. For instance, when embedding rate is 0.05 bpp, the relative modified rate for $p = 5\%$ is over 14 times ($\approx 11.73/0.83$) of that for $p = 100\%$ (i.e. original method), while the number of selected pixels is just $5/100$ of the original one in this case. Since both the number of selected pixels and the relative modified rates would affect the detection performances, we should carefully select the parameter $p$. In the following Section 4, some experimental results would be given to show how the parameter $p$ affects the detection performances.

## 4. EXPERIMENTAL RESULTS

In the experiments, 10,000 original images with size of $512 \times 512$ are from BOSSBase ver. 1.01 [1]. The spatial rich model (SRM) based features [4] is used for feature extraction, and the ensemble classifier [7] is used in the training and testing stages, and the detection performance is quanti-

**Table 1: The relative modified rates for different parameters $p$ and embedding rates**

| Embedding rate | $p = 5\%$ | $p = 25\%$ | $p = 55\%$ | $p = 100\%$ |
|---|---|---|---|---|
| 0.05 bpp | 11.73% | 3.22% | 1.50% | 0.83% |
| 0.10 bpp | 20.33% | 6.85% | 3.26% | 1.80% |
| 0.20 bpp | 31.20% | 14.26% | 7.13% | 3.97% |
| 0.30 bpp | 38.04% | 21.27% | 11.31% | 6.36% |
| 0.40 bpp | 42.95% | 27.52% | 15.72% | 8.93% |
| 0.50 bpp | 46.71% | 32.93% | 20.92% | 11.67% |

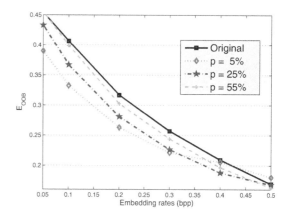

**Figure 5: The detection error $E_{OOB}$ with increasing the embedding rates from 0.05 to 0.50 bpp**

fied using the ensemble's "out-of-bag" error $E_{OOB}$ as it did in [5]. Two following experiments have been carried out.

### 4.1 Experiment #1

In this experiment, we fix the parameter $p$ with three different values, i.e. 5%, 25%, 55%, and we try to compare the average detection errors with the original SRM method [4] (i.e. $p = 100\%$). The embedding rates of 0.05, 0.10, 0.20, 0.30, 0.40 and 0.50 bpp, have been evaluated, respectively. The experimental results are shown in Fig. 5.

From Fig. 5, it is observed that the proposed strategy with the three different parameters outperforms the original SRM in almost all cases (except for a case of $p = 5\%$ and the embedding rate is 0.50bpp), especially when the embedding rate is low, such as lower than 0.30 bpp. On average, we obtain an improvement of around 3.7%, 2.5% and 0.9% for $p = 5\%, 35\%$ and 55%, respectively.

### 4.2 Experiment #2

In this experiment, we fix the embedding rate with 0.05, 0.10, 0.20, 0.30, 0.40 and 0.50 bpp, respectively, and compare the average detection error with different parameter $p$, which ranging from 5% to 95% with a step 10%. We try to analyze the best parameter $p$ for a given embedding rate. The experimental results are shown in Fig. 6.

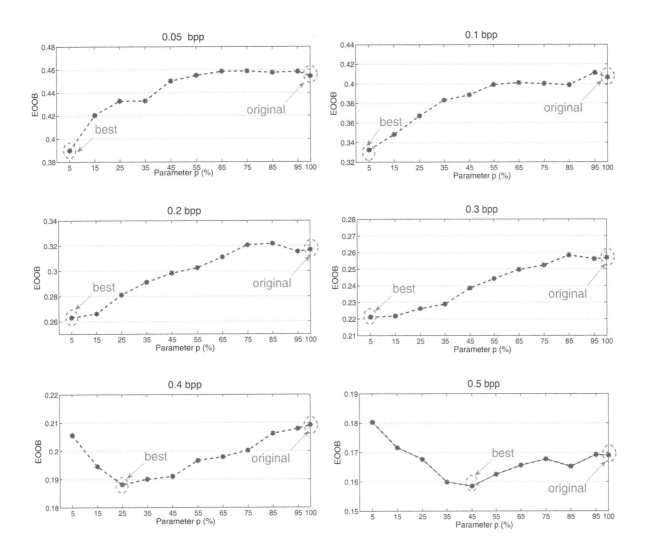

**Figure 6: The detection error $E_{OOB}$ with increasing the parameter $p$ from 5% to 95%**

**Table 2: Average detection improvements with different parameters $p$**

| Embedding rate | $p \in$ $\{5\%, \ldots 55\%\}$ | $p \in$ $\{5\%, \ldots 95\%\}$ | $p \in$ Best one |
|---|---|---|---|
| 0.05 bpp | 2.42% | 1.29% | 6.46% |
| 0.10 bpp | 3.68% | 2.36% | 7.42% |
| 0.20 bpp | 3.31% | 1.97% | 5.38% |
| 0.30 bpp | 2.67% | 1.72% | 3.57% |
| 0.40 bpp | 1.49% | 1.14% | 2.11% |
| 0.50 bpp | 0.23% | 0.22% | 1.05% |

From Fig. 6, it is also observed that the proposed strategy works better than the original method in most cases. As highlighted in the Fig. 6, however, the best parameter $p$ is different for different embedding rates. For instance, the best $p$ is 5% when the embedding rate is 0.05, 0.10, 0.20 and 0.30 bpp. While it increases to 25% and 45% when the embedding rate increases to 0.40 and 0.50 bpp, respectively.

For a given stego image, the best parameter $p$ is not available since the embedding rate is unknown. Thus, we need to restrict the range of selected $p$. Two different ranges are considered here: Range #1: from 5% to 55% (in this case, over 95% modified pixels would be located at the selected pixels based on the results shown in Fig.3) with a step 10%; Range #2: from 5% to 95% with a step 10%. Then the average improvements and the best improvements are shown in Table 2. Both Fig. 6 and Table 2 show that we can obtain better detection results with smaller $p$ (*e.g.* in range # 1) when the embedding rate is less than 0.5 bpp.

## 5. CONCLUDING REMARKS

Based on our experiments and analysis, we found that the modified pixels after using the adaptive WOW steganography would highly located at those textural/noisy regions that are difficult to model and insensitive to our human eyes. This embedding property can significantly improve the security performance against typical steganalysis as well as the visual quality of the resulting stego images compared with the non-adaptive steganography. However, it may be a loophole for the detector, since it is possible to narrow down the suspicious regions for steganalysis. In this paper, we propose an adaptive steganalytic strategy for the WOW embedding algorithm based on this loophole. The proposed strategy tries to restrict the feature extraction on those pixels with low embedding costs rather than the whole image. The experimental results evaluated on 10,000 images show that the proposed strategy can improve the effectiveness of the typical steganalysis, such as SRM, especially when the embedding rate is low than 0.40 bpp.

Please note that the proposed strategy is flexible. In the next step, we would extend other steganalytic features such as PSRM [6] and LBP based features [12] in our strategy, and evaluate whether or not the proposed strategy still works for other steganography, such as edge adaptive method [8] and HUGO [11]. Besides, the relationship between the parameter $p$ and the detection performance needs further analysis. Furthermore, we would further analyze the common loophole of the adaptive steganogrpahy, and propose an improved adaptive steganalytic strategy.

## 6. ACKNOWLEDGMENTS

This work is supported by National Science & Technology Pillar Program (2012BAK16B06), NSFC (U1135001, 61332012, 61272191), the funding of Zhujiang Science and technology (2011J2200091), and the Guangdong NSF (S2013010012039).

## 7. REFERENCES

[1] P. Bas, T. Filler, and T. Pevny. Break our steganographic system. In *Information Hiding*, volume 6958 of *Lecture Notes in Computer Science*, pages 59–70. Springer Berlin Heidelberg, 2011.

[2] T. Filler, J. Judas, and J. Fridrich. Minimizing additive distortion in steganography using syndrome-trellis codes. *IEEE Trans. on Information Forensics and Security*, 6(3):920–935, 2011.

[3] J. Fridrich, M. Goljan, and R. Du. Detecting LSB steganography in color, and gray-scale images. *IEEE Multimedia*, 8(4):22–28, Oct. 2001.

[4] J. Fridrich and J. Kodovsky. Rich models for steganalysis of digital images. *IEEE Trans. on Information Forensics and Security*, 7(3):868–882, Jun. 2011.

[5] V. Holub and J. Fridrich. Designing steganographic distortion using directional filters. In *2012 IEEE International Workshop on Information Forensics and Security(WIFS)*, pages 234–239, 2012.

[6] V. Holub, J. Fridrich, and T. Denemark. Random projections of residuals as an alternative to co-occurrences in steganalysis. *IEEE Trans. on Information Forensics and Security*, 8(12):1996–2006, 2013.

[7] J. Kodovsky, J. Fridrich, and V. Holub. Ensemble classifiers for steganalysis of digital media. *IEEE Trans. on Information Forensics and Security*, 7(2):432–444, 2012.

[8] W. Luo, F. Huang, and J. Huang. Edge adaptive image steganography based on LSB matching revisited. *IEEE Trans. on Information Forensics and Security*, 5(2):201–214, Jun. 2010.

[9] J. Mielikainen. LSB matching revisited. *IEEE Signal Processing Letters*, 13(5):285–287, May 2006.

[10] T. Pevny, P. Bas, and J. Fridrich. Steganalysis by subtractive pixel adjacency matrix. *IEEE Trans. on Information Forensics and Security*, 5(2):215–224, 2010.

[11] T. Pevny, T. Filler, and P. Bas. Using high-dimensional image models to perform highly undetectable steganography. In *Information Hiding*, volume 6387 of *Lecture Notes in Computer Science*, pages 161–177. Springer Berlin Heidelberg, 2010.

[12] Y. Q. Shi, P. Sutthiwan, and L. Chen. Textural features for steganalysis. In *Information Hiding*, volume 7692 of *Lecture Notes in Computer Science*, pages 63–77. Springer Berlin Heidelberg, 2013.

[13] A. Westfeld and A. Pfitzmann. Attacks on steganographic systems. In *Information Hiding*, volume 1768 of *Lecture Notes in Computer Science*, pages 61–76. Springer Berlin Heidelberg, 2000.

[14] D.-C. Wu and W.-H. Tsai. A steganographic method for images by pixel-value differencine. *Pattern Recognition Letters*, 24:1613–1626, Jun. 2003.

# Predictable Rain? Steganalysis of Public-Key Steganography using Wet Paper Codes

Matthias Carnein
Dept. of Information Systems
University of Münster
Leonardo-Campus 3
48149 Münster, Germany
matthias.carnein@wwu.de

Pascal Schöttle
Dept. of Information Systems
University of Münster
Leonardo-Campus 3
48149 Münster, Germany
pascal.schoettle@wwu.de

Rainer Böhme
Dept. of Information Systems
University of Münster
Leonardo-Campus 3
48149 Münster, Germany
rainer.boehme@wwu.de

## ABSTRACT

Symmetric steganographic communication requires a secret stego-key pre-shared between the communicating parties. Public-key steganography (PKS) overcomes this inconvenience. In this case, the steganographic security is based solely on the underlying asymmetric encryption function. This implies that the embedding positions are either public or hidden by clever coding, for instance using Wet Paper Codes (WPC), but with public code parameters. We show that using WPC with efficient encoding algorithms may leak information which can facilitate an attack. The public parameters allow an attacker to predict among the possible embedding positions the ones most likely used for embedding. This approach is independent of the embedding operation. We demonstrate it for the case of least significant bit (LSB) replacement and present two new variants of Weighted Stego-Image (WS) steganalysis specifically tailored to detect PKS using efficient WPC. Experiments show that our WS variants can detect PKS with higher accuracy than known methods, especially for low embedding rates. The attack is applicable even if a hybrid stegosystem is constructed and public-key cryptography is only used to encapsulate a secret stego-key.

## Categories and Subject Descriptors

I.4.9 [**Computing Methodologies**]: Image Processing and Computer Vision – *Applications*; C.2.0 [**General**]: Security and Protection

## General Terms

Security, Algorithms, Theory

## 1. INTRODUCTION

Steganography enables hidden communication between two parties without allowing a third party to notice the hidden communication. To do so, a sender typically embeds

hidden messages in a digital medium by slightly modifying parts of the medium. The security of steganography solely depends on the detectability of an embedded message, regardless of whether an attacker is able to read the hidden message. Many steganographic methods require a secret stego-key, shared between the communicating parties. Public-key steganography (PKS) is an approach to allow hidden communication without a shared secret between the sender and the recipient [24]. This is possible by using asymmetric cryptography to encrypt a message before embedding. One way to implement this requires that the positions of the elements used for embedding are publicly known [2], by which the security of this communication only depends on the strength of the cryptographic system [11]. It is often taken for granted that indistinguishability from a random bit sequence is sufficient to achieve steganographic security. Although this is indeed a necessary condition, an attacker can still analyse the local neigbourhood of likely embedding positions to obtain information about the plausibility of the position's value and therefore indications on whether any embedding has taken place.

Even though public embedding positions allow communication without a shared stego-key, they give an attacker a starting point to mount an attack by contrasting the set of elements that might carry a hidden message and those that do not [7, 13]. To prevent this, it is possible to extend PKS by using Wet Paper Codes (WPC) [11, 16]. WPC let steganographic schemes use embedding positions that are not shared with the recipient and are therefore also unknown to an attacker [13]. To apply WPC, both parties have to use the same parameters for embedding and extraction. Since in PKS the communicating parties cannot share a secret stego-key, these code parameters must be public [11].

In this paper, we analyse how public code parameters can be utilized to attack PKS using WPC by identifying more likely embedding positions. We follow an early approach presented by Böhme [4] and calculate the change probability for every element of an object from public parameters. We explore why these probability patterns exist and explain theoretically how they arise. Furthermore we propose an approach that uses this information in order to extend existing steganalysis methods for attacking PKS using WPC.

Our approach is exemplified for hidden messages that are embedded with LSB replacement. We use the information about likely embedding positions by extending Weighted Stego-Image (WS) steganalysis, the state-of-the-art approach to estimate the hidden payload length of messages embedded with random uniform LSB replacement. We propose two extensions of this method to make it applicable for attacking PKS using WPC. First, we use a method presented by Schöttle et. al. [23] and sort the stego object according to its most likely embedding positions. This allows the application of WS steganalysis for initial sequential embedding, originally proposed by Ker [17]. Second, we build on Weighted WS steganalysis and assign a distinct weight to each element of the stego object based on its embedding probability.

Our results show that the calculation of a change probability for every element allows us to identify likely embedding positions if time-efficient encoding algorithms are used. This works exceptionally well in the somewhat artificial situation when a sender does not impose restrictions on possible embedding positions, e.g., based on their predictability, but considers all elements. However, even when restrictions are applied, the approach remains possible. Both proposed extensions of WS steganalysis outperform the current detectors for uniform random LSB replacement when applied to attack PKS using WPC, especially for low embedding rates. We also find that weighting the stego elements gives better results than sorting them.

This paper is organized as follows: Section 2 presents the notation and introduces the relevant concepts of WPC, PKS, and WS steganalysis. Section 3 describes how probability patterns can be generated and proposes two extensions of WS steganalysis tailored to attack PKS using WPC. Section 4 assesses the performance of the proposed estimation of embedding positions and evaluates the detection performance of the proposed extensions. Finally, Section 5 concludes with a summary of the results and discusses their implications.

## 2. RELATED WORK

### 2.1 Notation

Matrices and vectors are denoted by boldface symbols. Covers are objects without any embedded messages. Using the notation of [6], a cover is denoted by $x^{(0)}$ using $n$ implicitly to describe its length. After embedding a message $m$ of length $q$, the resulting stego object is denoted by $x^{(m)}$. A stego object with embedding rate $p = q/n$ is denoted by $x^{(p)}$. Symbol $\bar{x}$ denotes an integer value $x$ with the LSB flipped: $\bar{x} = x + (-1)^x$. This notation is also applicable to vectors and matrices, by changing the LSBs of every element. In addition, $\hat{x}^{(0)}$ is the estimated cover, calculated from the stego object $x^{(p)}$, e.g., by estimating the original value of each element by using a weighted average of the adjacent elements. Our approach determines probability patterns by calculating embedding probabilities $p_i$ for every element in a cover $x^{(0)}$. Probability patterns are observable probability characteristics of certain elements when using fixed parameters, in particular irregular distributed embedding probabilities. These patterns can be used to weight the elements of a cover, denoted as $\omega_i$. A stego object sorted from its most probable to least probable embedding position is written as $y^{(p)}$. Even though the described methods are in principle applicable to all digital media, we focus on greyscale images for simplicity.

### 2.2 Wet Paper Codes

Wet Paper Codes, as first proposed by Fridrich et. al. [15], enable steganographic schemes where a sender is able to select possible embedding position without sharing this selection with the recipient. Their name is a metaphor for a piece of paper that was exposed to rain and got partially wet. A sender is only able to hide a message in dry elements of the paper. During transmission, the wet spots dry out, so that the recipient cannot identify the embedding positions. WPC allow the recipient to read the message without the knowledge of possible embedding positions. A sender can therefore use private selection rules to embed messages. This is supposed to increase the security of steganographic schemes. A detailed description of WPC can be found in [11].

WPC can be seen as a generalization of the selection channel as introduced by Anderson [1]. They embed the message as the syndrome of a linear code [13]. Assuming the sender and recipient share a secret stego-key, they can use this key to generate a shared binary matrix $D$ with $q$ rows and $n$ columns. Furthermore, a public function transforms a cover $x^{(0)}$ or stego image $x^{(m)}$ into a binary vector $b^{(0)}$ or $b^{(m)}$, respectively. The sender embeds the message into the cover such that the resulting binary vector satisfies:

$$Db^{(m)} = m. \tag{1}$$

This matrix product is called the syndrome of $b^{(m)}$. To read the message, a recipient calculates the syndrome of $b^{(m)}$ using the shared matrix as well as the binary vector of the stego image. To determine which embedding changes are necessary in order to embed a message, a sender can rewrite this equation to (2) by using a change vector $v$, which indicates whether the corresponding element in the cover needs to be changed in order to satisfy Equation (1).

$$Dv = m - Db^{(0)} \tag{2}$$

This system of linear equations consists of $q$ equations and $n$ variables. The sender selects $k$ possible embedding positions, the 'dry' pixels, resulting in unknown variables. Note that the recipient does not have to know the value of $k$. The remaining $n - k$ known variables correspond to the 'wet' pixels that cannot be used to embed a message. By removing all columns from $D$ and all elements from $v$ that correspond to these 'wet' pixels, this equation can be rewritten as

$$Hv = m - Db^{(0)}, \tag{3}$$

where $H$ consists of the columns of $D$ corresponding to the changeable pixels in the cover and $v$ is reduced to hold the values of all 'dry' pixels [13].

This system can be solved for $v$, for example, by using Gaussian elimination. Assuming the maximum message length is sent, the complexity of Gaussian elimination is $\mathcal{O}(k^3)$. One approach to reduce the complexity is the structured Gaussian elimination, where the cover is divided into several subsets. The message is then successively embedded into these subsets using Gaussian elimination. A drawback of this approach is that the probability of successfully embedding an entire message is reduced due to the increased number of systems of linear equations, each with a non-zero probability of being singular [13].

An elegant and efficient approach to embed a message using WPC is the matrix LT process [14, 16]. The matrix LT process transforms an under-determined system of linear equations into upper triangle form by permuting its rows and columns. It uses an iterative process, selecting a column with Hamming-weight one in each iteration. This means a column $j$ with only a single value $H_{i,j} = 1$. It then permutes

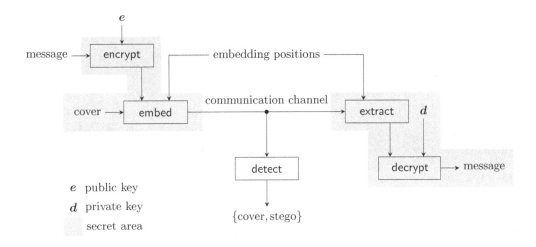

$e$    public key

$d$    private key

     secret area

Figure 1: Block diagram of public-key steganography

the columns and rows of the system so that $H_{1,1} = 1$ and $H_{i,1} = 0$ for $i > 1$. In the next iteration the first row and column are ignored, and the rows and columns are permuted such that $H_{2,2} = 1$ and $H_{i,2} = 0$ for $i > 2$ [8]. Given that there will always be a column with Hamming-weight one, this process will transform the system into upper triangle form, which can be efficiently solved using back-substitution [16]. Algorithm 1 gives the pseudo code for the matrix LT process. To increase the probability of a column with Hamming-weight one in every iteration, the columns of the matrix $\boldsymbol{H}$ can be generated so that their Hamming-weights follow the Robust Soliton distribution (RSD)[1] [20]. This is supposed to make the system of linear equations sparsely populated while remaining solvable. The matrix $\boldsymbol{H}$, however, is not directly generated, but derived from the columns of $\boldsymbol{D}$ that correspond to the 'dry' pixels. Both communicating parties therefore generate the shared Matrix $\boldsymbol{D}$ following the RSD. The columns of matrix $\boldsymbol{H}$ then inherit the distribution of the corresponding columns in matrix $\boldsymbol{D}$ [11].

WPC are a first approach that utilizes encoding in connection with steganography. This approach has been further developed, for example, leading to the widely used syndrome trellis codes [10].

## 2.3   Public-Key Steganography

Steganography uses cryptographic keys to ensure that only authorized parties are able to identify and read hidden messages [6]. Many steganographic methods depend on a shared stego-key between the sender and the recipient. An approach to overcome this restriction is public-key steganography [2].

PKS uses asymmetric encryption in order to avoid a shared secret between the sender and the recipient [11]. To do so, it uses pairs of public and private keys. While the sender holds a private key $\boldsymbol{d}$, there exists a corresponding public key $\boldsymbol{e}$. The public key is used to encrypt a message $\boldsymbol{m}$, i.e., $\boldsymbol{e}(\boldsymbol{m}) = \boldsymbol{m}'$ and the private key is able to decrypt such an encrypted message, i.e., $\boldsymbol{d}(\boldsymbol{m}') = \boldsymbol{m}$ [21].

In PKS, this principle is used to construct a steganographic scheme [11]. Before embedding a message, a sender encrypts the message using the public key of the recipient and embeds the message in publicly available embedding positions [2].

On receipt of a medium the recipient reads the message along the public embedding path and decrypts it using the corresponding private key. This enables the sender to determine whether a hidden message has been embedded into the medium [2]. Figure 1 shows a block diagram of PKS. As long as the encryption function produces uniform i.i.d. ciphertexts, an attacker is not able to distinguish between a random bit-sequence and an encrypted message [21].

Even though an attacker is not able to identify an encrypted message due to the apparently random ciphertexts, the public embedding positions can be used as a starting point to mount an attack on the communication [11]. The attacker can search for traces that indicate the embedding of a bit sequence. These are best exploited when the attacker has knowledge about embedding probabilities of the medium.

Anderson and Petitcolas [2] mention a possible approach for using PKS as key distribution scheme in order to initiate conventional steganographic communication:

> 'the value encrypted under a public key could be a control block consisting of a session key [...], and the session key would drive a conventional steganographic scheme.' [2, p. 480]

This method has its roots in cryptography where it is known as a key encapsulation scheme [9]. The idea is to use asymmetric cryptography only to exchange a symmetric key, which then enables symmetric encryption. In general, a similar approach can be applied in steganography, allowing the exchange of a secret stego-key. This approach reduces the message length sent under public parameters considerably. It must be noted, however, that encapsulating a conventional stego-key of 64–128 bits requires a much larger payload because the key must be encrypted with the public key of the recipient. In a scenario where both parties rely on steganographic communication, we assume a reasonably secure public-key cryptosystem. With the recent revelations, a careful steganographer would be wary of elliptic curve cryptography, which promises shorter minimum message sizes, and consider a system based on RSA with a key size of at least 2048 bits. Its ciphertext is in the order of 2048 bits, independent of the plaintext size. Assuming that the cover image is a greyscale image of size $128 \times 128$ pixels, this payload will be $p = 0.13$. Even if the size of the image is increased

---

[1]See Appendix A for an explanation of the RSD.

to $512 \times 512$ pixels, the payload of approximately $p = 0.078$ lies in a range where modern detectors may catch it.

An approach to avoid attacks on PKS is to use, quoting the authoritative textbook,

> 'selection channels that are completely random implemented using wet paper codes.' [11, p. 184]

This would allow a sender to embed the message in secret embedding positions so that an attacker cannot use this information. Since there is no shared secret between the sender and the recipient in PKS, both cannot generate the matrix $\boldsymbol{D}$ based on a shared key. To allow the use of WPC, this matrix (or its seed) can be made public [11, p. 184]. This allows every party to extract the encrypted message, but without revealing the exact embedding positions. Only the owner of the private key is able to decrypt and read the message [11]. Even though the author does not specifically propose the matrix LT process in order to embed messages in PKS, it is by far the most efficient approach when embedding with WPC, and the only improvement to Gaussian elimination that retains a sufficient probability of solving the system of linear equations. This extension of PKS is supposed to enable steganographic communication, now quoting original research work,

> 'without revealing any information about the placement of the embedding changes.' [16, p. 216]

Our contribution challenges this view.

## 2.4 Weighted Stego-Image Steganalysis

Weighted Stego-Image steganalysis, as presented by Fridrich and Goljan [12], is a quantitative steganalytic method targeting LSB replacement. It uses a so called Weighted Stego-Image $\boldsymbol{x}^{(p,\lambda)}$, which is a weighted average between the stego image and the stego image with every element's LSB flipped. Following [18] and [6], we define $\boldsymbol{x}^{(p,\lambda)}$ as:

$$\boldsymbol{x}^{(p,\lambda)} = \lambda \overline{\boldsymbol{x}}^{(p)} + (1 - \lambda) \boldsymbol{x}^{(p)}, \tag{4}$$

where $\lambda$ describes the weighting and $\overline{\boldsymbol{x}}^{(p)}$ denotes the stego image with every element's LSB flipped.

Theorem 1 in [12] states that the Euclidean distance between $\boldsymbol{x}^{(p,\lambda)}$ and $\boldsymbol{x}^{(0)}$ is minimized for $\lambda = q/(2n)$. As the cover is unknown to an attacker, she has to estimate it from the stego image. This can be achieved by using a linear filter, i.e., a weighted average of the local neighborhood. An example for such a filter is presented by Ker and Böhme using a filter of the form (5). The performance of these filters has mainly been evaluated experimentally and needs further research [6, 18].

$$\begin{matrix} -\frac{1}{4} & \frac{1}{2} & -\frac{1}{4} \\ \frac{1}{2} & 0 & \frac{1}{2} \\ -\frac{1}{4} & \frac{1}{2} & -\frac{1}{4} \end{matrix} \tag{5}$$

We can use twice the Euclidean distance as an estimator for the embedding rate, using Equation (6). By differentiating the Euclidean distance for $\lambda$, we can estimate $p$ using Equation (7) [12].

$$\hat{p} = 2 \arg\min_{\lambda} \sum_{i=1}^{n} \left( x_i^{(p,\lambda)} - \hat{x}_i^{(0)} \right)^2 \tag{6}$$

$$= \frac{2}{n} \sum_{i=1}^{n} \left( x_i^{(p)} - \hat{x}_i^{(0)} \right) \left( x_i^{(p)} - \overline{x}_i^{(p)} \right) \tag{7}$$

Several approaches to improve this method have been made. Most notably is Weighted WS steganalysis which adds element weights to the stego image [12]. This second weighting takes differences in local predictability into account. Elements which can be estimated with high confidence contribute more to the estimation than elements where errors are expected:

$$\hat{p} = 2 \sum_{i=1}^{n} w_i \left( x_i^{(p)} - \hat{x}_i^{(0)} \right) \left( x_i^{(p)} - \overline{x}_i^{(p)} \right), \tag{8}$$

using $\sum_{i=1}^{n} w_i = 1$ [12].

Both basic methods assume that changes in the cover are spread uniformly [18]. Ker [17] proposes a variant tailored to initial sequential embedding. He decomposes Equation (6) into two parts, reflecting that embedding changes only occur in the first elements. The first elements are therefore weighted using $\lambda = 1/2$ while the remaining elements are weighted with $\lambda = 0$. Note that in this scenario any change to the weighting, e.g., based on local predictability, will degrade the estimation. This is the case because it is certain that the first elements contain the hidden message. The resulting estimator (Eq. (9)) is minimized for the point where the embedding ends, i.e., $l = q$ [17].

$$E(l) = \sum_{i=1}^{l} \left( \frac{1}{2} \left( x_i^{(p)} + \overline{x}_i^{(p)} \right) - \hat{x}_i^{(0)} \right)^2 + \sum_{i=l+1}^{n} \left( x_i^{(p)} - \hat{x}_i^{(0)} \right)^2 \tag{9}$$

This approach outperforms the previously introduced detectors when applied to initial sequential embedding [17]. However, it is not possible to obtain a closed form by differentiating Equation (9). To overcome this, Ker proposes the recursive function in Equation (10).

$$e_0 = 0$$
$$e_l = e_{l-1} + \left( \frac{1}{2} \left( x_{l-1}^{(p)} + \overline{x}_{l-1}^{(p)} \right) - \hat{x}_{l-1}^{(0)} \right)^2 - \left( x_{l-1}^{(p)} - \hat{x}_{l-1}^{(0)} \right)^2 \tag{10}$$

This is possible because Equation (10) satisfies $E(l) = e_l + \sum_{i=1}^{n}(x_i^{(p)} - \hat{x}_i^{(0)})^2$. Since the last term is constant it can be ignored to find the minimum of Equation (10).

The approach presented in [23] utilizes this method to make WS steganalysis applicable for naive adaptive embedding, where the sender embeds a message only in the $q$ elements she considers to be most secure [22]. By reordering the stego image according to the criterion used for locating these elements, this kind of embedding reduces to initial sequential.

There exist further specializations of WS steganalysis, for example with bias correction [6, 18] or tailored to JPEG covers [5]. To the best of our knowledge none of these extensions take information about the encoding process into account to create an improved detector. This is the starting point for our approach which considers information that can be derived from the encoding process of WPC.

# 3. CONTRIBUTION

In this section we discuss how the public parameters in PKS can be utilized to mount an attack on PKS using WPC. We first present a general approach on how to estimate likely embedding positions by estimating probability patterns, following the early ideas presented in [4]. We further explore why these patterns exist and present a theoretical explanation on how they arise. Then we explain how to use this information in order to attack PKS using WPC. To do so, we extend WS steganalysis and make it applicable for WPC with public parameters. In a first approach we build on a method presented in [23]. In addition, we present a new attack that enables us to utilize the embedding patterns to attack WPC in PKS.

## 3.1 Estimating embedding positions

To use WPC without a shared key, the sender and recipient are required to use the same parameters to generate the matrix $D$ [11]. The public matrix, however, determines a large part of the system of linear equations that needs to be solved in order to make the necessary embedding changes [13]. This knowledge gives an attacker information about the embedding process and can be used as a starting point to mount an attack. A first approach to utilize this information is motivated in [4] by using the public parameters to determine probable embedding positions. To use the metaphor of a piece of paper exposed to rain [13], an attacker does not predict where the rain hit the paper but, which of the 'dry' positions were most likely used for embedding.

To estimate the embedding positions, an attacker may embed multiple messages using the same public parameters. By observing the necessary embedding changes in the medium, it is possible to calculate an embedding probability for every element in the cover. This approach is enabled due to the public matrix $D$ as well as the information that can be derived from its dimensions. While the number of columns in $D$ indicates the length $n$ of the cover, the number of rows corresponds to the message length $q$. The message and the cover are secret and unknown to an attacker. Embedding probabilities therefore have to be calculated using random messages and random covers. This means an attacker can generate random messages of length $q$ and embed them into random covers of length $n$, using the public matrix.

### 3.1.1 Without the Use of a Selection Rule

First we discuss the generating process of these embedding probabilities if the sender does not use a selection rule and thus, all elements can be used for embedding. To determine the embedding changes, the system of linear equations (3) must be solved. As discussed in Section 2.2, an elegant and efficient approach to solve the system is the matrix LT process [11, 16]. Preliminary results reported in [4] indicate that for a fixed matrix $D$, probability patterns can be observed after embedding multiple messages. This means that certain elements of the cover are more likely used for embedding than others.

Without the use of a (random or adaptive) selection rule, the embedding probabilities can be determined with almost perfect accuracy. The reason for this can be seen from

looking at the pseudo code for the matrix LT process in Algorithm 1. The algorithm is perfectly deterministic and thus, with the same input matrix $D$ the same output, i.e., the same embedding positions will be produced.

To understand why these probability patterns exist, one has to understand the selection of pivot elements during the solving process. The solution of the system of linear equations indicates the necessary embedding changes in the cover. Only elements that correspond to columns that are used during the solving process are therefore subject to change and might carry a hidden message bit. When using the matrix LT process to solve the system of linear equations, the pivot columns are selected based on their column sum. This selection is biased towards sparsely populated columns (lines 3–5 in Algorithm 1).

---

**Algorithm 1:** Matrix LT process to solve $Hv = z$ [11]

1  $j = 1$ and $t = 0$;
2  **while** $j \leq q$ & $(\exists j' \geq j, \sum_{i>j} H[i,j'] = 1)$ **do**
3  | swap rows $j$ and $i_j$;
4  | swap $z[i]$ and $z[i_j]$;
5  | swap columns $v[j]$ and $v[j']$;
6  | $t = t + 1$;
7  | $\tau[t]$;
8  | $j = j + 1$;

9  **if** $j \leq q$ **then**
10 | failure;
11 $v[j] = 0$ for $q < j \leq k$;

    // back substitution
12 **while** $t > 0$ **do**
13 | $v \leftarrow \tau[t](v)$;
14 | $t = t - 1$;

---

The consequence of this can be best understood when using a simple example and looking at the relationship between the embedding probabilities and the matrix $D$. Figure 2 shows the embedding process of 1000 random messages of length $q = 2$ in random covers of length $n = 5$. Figure 2(a) shows an example of matrix $D$ where filled rectangles denote ones and empty rectangles zeros. The histogram in Figure 2(b) shows the observed change probability for every element. It becomes obvious that only the elements with index two and four are changed in order to embed a message. This indicates that the matrix LT process is biased towards sparsely populated columns. In this example, the fourth column is always selected as the first pivot column because it is the first and only column with column sum one. During the matrix LT process, the first and fourth column are therefore swapped. The process continues by neglecting the first column and row, searching another column with a Hamming-weight of one. Since this applies to all the remaining columns, the first one is selected in order to solve the system. This is the second column in the example. After this, the message is embedded and no further changes are required. This example shows that for a fixed matrix $D$, the selection of columns during the matrix LT process happens in a deterministic order. As no selection rule is used, the elements corresponding to these columns are always used to carry a message bit. These elements can therefore be exactly identified by an attacker.

### 3.1.2 With the Use of a Selection Rule

Using a selection rule reduces this effect because only selected elements may be changed. The attacker still has to solve the system of linear equations in (3). But now, she has to use random selection rules and thus, the input to Algorithm 1 changes with every simulated embedding. This leads to different embedding positions in every iteration, as in each iteration different elements may not be used. The selection during the solving process seems still biased towards sparsely populated columns, though. This enables an attacker to express a change probability for every element.

Instead of the random selection rules suggested in [11], a sender could also use an adaptive selection rule and thus select embedding positions that are supposedly harder to detect. We conjecture that if this adaptive selection rule is publicly known, an attacker could use this knowledge to even better estimate the most likely embedding positions.

### 3.1.3 Gaussian Elimination

The Gaussian elimination is not biased towards sparsely populated columns. The process instead focusses on the first columns of the matrix. Without using a selection rule, most of the first columns of the matrix are used to solve the system. Only the corresponding elements may therefore contain the hidden message. When using a selection rule, this pattern again diminishes. Assuming that this selection happens randomly, the embedding probability for all used elements is approximately the same. Since the embedding probabilities for all elements are reduced equally, this does not allow the generation of embedding patterns.

A third approach to embed a message using WPC is the structured Gaussian elimination as presented in [15]. For this approach the cover is split into subsets. In each of the subsets a part of the message is embedded using Gaussian elimination. As expected, each subset shows a similar pattern as the Gaussian elimination. Since most elements hold the same probability when using Gaussian elimination, they hold similar probabilities when repeating the process for several subsets. Structured Gaussian elimination uses several elements per subset as a buffer to increase the probability that a message can be successfully embedded. These buffer elements hold slightly lower embedding probabilities. Since the remaining elements have similar embedding probabilities, this knowledge can hardly be utilized for an attack.

These results show that PKS using WPC can be attacked when the matrix LT process is used. This is the case because certain columns of the public matrix are selected more likely to solve the system of linear equations. When using Gaussian elimination, columns are uniformly selected, leading to equal change probabilities. The following section presents an approach on how to use these patterns by extending an already existing attack on LSB replacement to make it applicable for PKS using WPC.

## 3.2 Extending Weighted Stego-Image Steganalysis

As shown in the previous section, the proposed estimation of embedding positions only depends on the publicly available matrix. It is therefore independent from the used embedding method. This enables an attacker to use the estimation in order to extend already existing steganographic attacks on embedding methods and make them applicable for PKS using WPC. This section proposes an extension of WS steganalysis to attack PKS using WPC when LSB replacement is used to embed a message. Although LSB replacement is clearly insecure and should not be used in practice, it is a good candidate to demonstrate our attack because it is best understood and reliable steganalysis benchmarks are readily available.

In the following we propose two extensions of WS steganalysis: The first one builds on the approach of WS steganalysis for naive adaptive embedding as proposed in [23]. The second approach uses the element weights in Weighted WS steganalysis. We call these two WS variants Sorted WS and Probability WS, respectively.

### 3.2.1 Sorting the Stego Image

The first possibility we discuss to extend WS steganalysis for PKS using WPC is to sort the stego image according to its most probable embedding positions. To determine the embedding probability for each element, we use the method presented in Section 3.1. We then sort the elements of the stego image $x^{(p)}$ according to theses probabilities in descending order to estimate the ordered stego image $\hat{y}^{(p)}$. Assuming the attacker is able to identify each embedding position correctly, the first $p \cdot n$ elements of $y^{(p)} = (y_1^{(1)}, \ldots, y_{p \cdot n}^{(1)}, y_{p \cdot n+1}^{(0)}, \ldots, y_n^{(0)})$ contain the hidden message [23]. This will, again, reduce the embedding to initial sequential embedding, allowing the use of the specialized WS steganalysis approach as proposed in [17].

For a correctly ordered image, all elements containing a hidden message are placed at the beginning. Only the first elements of the ordered image are therefore weighted using $\lambda = 1/2$. Thus, we get the estimator corresponding to Equation (9) as:

$$E(l) = \sum_{i=1}^{l} \left( \frac{1}{2} \left( y_i^{(p)} + \overline{y}_i^{(p)} \right) - \hat{y}_i^{(0)} \right)^2 + \sum_{i=l+1}^{n} \left( y_i^{(p)} - \hat{y}_i^{(0)} \right)^2. \quad (11)$$

As described in Section 2.4, this determines the point where embedding ends and therefore the payload length [17]. Again, we use the recursive function (Eq. (10)) of Ker to reduce the complexity. As we work with a sorted stego image here, we will refer to this method as *Sorted WS* in the following.

As discussed in Section 3.1, it is only possible to determine exact embedding positions when no selection rule is used. Considering that WPC allow secret selection rules, it is likely that a sender will use this possibility. When using such a constraint on possible embedding positions, it is only possible to calculate embedding probabilities. When sorting the stego image according to these probabilities, it is therefore likely that not all embedding positions are correctly ordered. This leaves 'gaps' in the first $p \cdot n$ elements, i.e., elements that do not contain a hidden message. Since WS steganalysis for sequential embedding expects a continuous payload at the beginning of an image, it handles these 'gaps' poorly and tends to underestimate the payload length [23].

### 3.2.2 Weighting the Stego Image

Our second approach to make WS steganalysis applicable for PKS using WPC is to extend Weighted WS steganalysis. Weighted WS steganalysis introduces element weights to the stego image in order to respect different levels of uncertainty

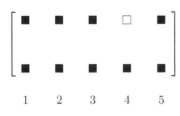

(a) Visualization of matrix $D$

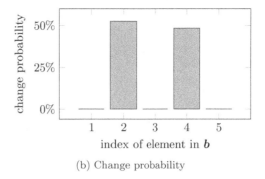

(b) Change probability

Figure 2: Visualization of connection between matrix LT process and observed probability patterns

when estimating the original elements in the cover [6]. The weighting $w_i$ describes the predictability of every element. This weighting can be used to utilize the information about likely embedding positions.

To estimate the embedding rate we use the same approach as Weighted WS steganalysis. As outlined in Section 2.4, this enables us to estimate half the embedding rate. This estimation holds true when using a normalized weighting for every element [12]. We can therefore use this weighting to incorporate the embedding probabilities. In a first step we calculate the embedding probability $p_i$ for every element using the approach presented in Section 3.1. This allows to replace the weighting $w_i$ of Weighted WS steganalysis with a normalized weighting $\omega_i$, based on the change probability. This focuses on more likely embedding positions and therefore relevant parts of the stego image. Using this approach, the embedding rate can be estimated by using Equation (12). By differentiating for $\lambda$, we can develop a first estimator for the embedding rate using Equation (13) and the normalized weighting $\omega_i = p_i / \left( \sum_{i=1}^n p_i \right)$.

$$\hat{p}' = 2 \arg \min_\lambda \sum_{i=1}^n \omega_i \left( x_i^{(p,\lambda)} - \hat{x}_i^{(0)} \right)^2 \qquad (12)$$

$$= 2 \sum_{i=1}^n \omega_i \left( x_i^{(p)} - \hat{x}_i^{(0)} \right) \left( x_i^{(p)} - \overline{x}_i^{(p)} \right), \qquad (13)$$

However, it has to be considered that the embedding rate is only estimated for elements with a positive weight. Elements with an assigned weighting of zero, i.e., elements that are never changed during the embedding process are not considered. This leads to an over-estimation, since only elements are considered that are likely to contain a hidden message. To estimate the embedding rate for the entire object, one can translate the estimation using:

$$\hat{p} = \frac{\hat{p}' \cdot |\omega'|}{|\omega|}, \qquad (14)$$

with $\omega' = \{\omega_i \in \omega | \omega_i > 0\}$ and $\omega = \{\omega_1, \ldots, \omega_n\}$. As we replace the weights of Weighted WS with the change probabilities, we will refer to this method as *Probability WS* in the following.

A drawback of this approach is that we replace the weighting based on the local predictability with our calculated embedding probabilities. We therefore neglect the knowledge about local predictability. To join both approaches we could combine both weightings, assigning a higher weighting to elements that can be predicted with high confidence and that

are likely to carry a hidden message. Although this approach works well for messages that are embedded uniformly over all elements, it collapses when the sender embeds the message adaptively into elements that are harder to predict. Adaptive embedding, however, is one of the main reasons to use WPC. We therefore do not further evaluate this approach, but focus on a single (additional) weighting based on the change probabilities.

## 4. EXPERIMENTAL RESULTS

This section evaluates the performance of our proposed methods. We first investigate how accurately we can estimate the embedding positions. We then apply this knowledge to attack PKS using WPC when using LSB replacement as proposed in Section 3.2. We use the full BOSSBase [3] image database with 10 000 grayscale images and embed random messages of different lengths using LSB replacement[2]. To accelerate the calculation of embedding patterns, we crop the images to a size of $128 \times 128$ pixels. Steganalysis is generally more difficult in smaller images due to the square root law [19], but the relative performance differentials are unlikely to be affected by smaller test images. Furthermore we use the matrix LT process to solve the system of linear equations. Matrix $D$ is generated from a random key using $c = 0.1$ and $\delta = 0.4$ as parameters for the RSD.

### 4.1 Estimating Embedding Positions

We analyse how accurately embedding positions can be estimated by calculating a change probability for every element. To do so, we embed 1000 random messages of length $q = 500$ in random covers of length $n = 1500$ without using any 'wet' pixels and observe the embedding changes. The results show that the change probability of exactly $q$ elements is approximately 50% while the remaining elements are never used to embed a message. This shows that for each embedding process the very same elements are used to hold a message. On average the elements are changed for every second embedding, since in every second case an element already holds the desired value.

WPC enable using a secret selection rule. It is therefore likely that a sender will use such a selection rule to select possible embedding positions. Repeating the experiment, using a selection rule which randomly selects 50% 'wet' pixels, it becomes obvious that the probability patterns diminish, but remain visible. In our example, a quarter of the elements

---

[2]Note that we exclude the image borders from embedding and detection attempts to eliminate boundary conditions.

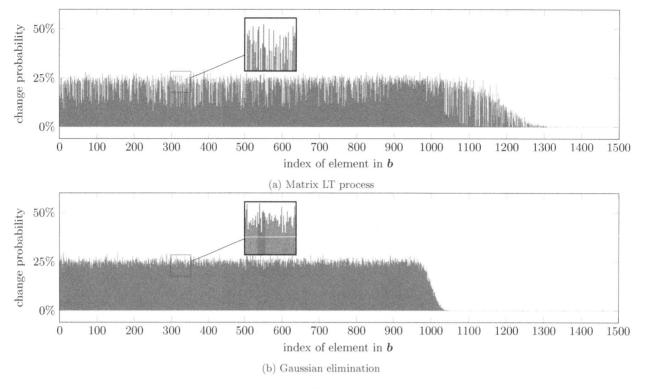

(a) Matrix LT process

(b) Gaussian elimination

Figure 3: Change probabilities for a fixed matrix $\boldsymbol{D}$, using 50% random 'wet' pixels, generated by 1000 embedding iterations

are never used to embed a message. The remaining elements hold a distinct change probability, which indicates how often each element is used during the embedding process. Figure 3(a) shows the observed change probabilities when using the matrix LT process and a random selection rule. The magnification of some of the probability peaks illustrates inconsistent change probabilities. The results show that we cannot determine the exact embedding positions, but are able to calculate a probability for every element to identify more likely embedding positions in the cover. These results show that even though WPC allow a secret selection rule, the attacker can use the public parameters of PKS to estimate where embedding changes are more likely to happen. This gives him a starting point to mount an attack on PKS using WPC.

While the matrix LT process is a very elegant and efficient method for solving the system of linear equations, other approaches exist, e.g., Gaussian elimination. To analyse the probability patterns when using Gaussian elimination, we repeat the experiments using a matrix $\boldsymbol{D}$ with equal probability for ones and zeros and solving the system of linear equation using Gaussian elimination. The results show that the first elements of the cover are always used to hold the hidden message when no selection rule is applied. Similar to the matrix LT process, an attacker is able to exactly identify the embedding positions. However, when using a selection rule, all elements that are used to embed a message are used equally likely. Figure 3(b) shows the observed change probability when using Gaussian elimination and a selection rule that randomly selects 50% 'wet' pixels. When looking at the magnified probability peaks it shows more consistent change probabilities across all elements. The results show that an attacker is not able to identify more likely embedding

positions. This supports the suggestions made in Section 3.1 that these patterns arise in an effort to solve the system more efficiently.

## 4.2 Estimating the Embedding Rate

This section examines the accuracy of the proposed specializations of WS steganalysis. We first assume that an attacker has knowledge about the number of possible embedding positions $k$ by using a fixed amount of $k = 50\%$ 'dry' pixels. Figure 5(a) shows the mean absolute error (MAE), $|p - \hat{p}|$, of the estimated embedding rate for 10000 stego images for different embedding rates $p$. It has to be considered that the payload estimation for covers depends on the public embedding rate and therefore slightly varies depending on the corresponding probability patterns. To evaluate the performance for covers we therefore calculate the average of all considered embedding rates as the estimation. It is visible that weighting the stego image by embedding probabilities clearly outperforms the current detectors for all evaluated embedding rates. Ordering the stego image according to these probabilities works well for small embedding rates, but quickly loses accuracy when using larger embedding rates. This observation is similar to the results of [23].

In practice, an attacker has no information about the number of possible embedding positions. Since this information is crucial for the calculation of probability patterns, we need to estimate it. We propose to estimate the embedding rate by attacking every stego image multiple times under different assumptions about $k$. In a first approach we used the maximum estimation of all attacks. However, we found that a better estimation can be made when using the point where both proposed methods estimate a similar embedding rate. Figure 4(a) shows the estimation of the embedding rate of

$p = 0.1$ with 50% 'dry' pixels under different assumptions about $k$. It shows that the most accurate estimation is the point where both approaches estimate a similar embedding rate, even if the assumption about $k$ is incorrect. We therefore exploit this observation and stick to this tactic in the following. Figure 4(b) shows the influence of this estimation on the performance of the detectors. It can be seen that the reduced knowledge of the attacker has very little influence on the detection performance and leads to similar mean absolute errors. In many cases the estimation of the amount of 'dry' pixels even leads to slightly better results. This can be explained by Figure 4(a), as the estimation of the embedding rate is better where the two methods coincide, than it is for the assumption of the real amount of 'dry' pixels.

Using this knowledge we can estimate the embedding rate by finding the point where the distance between Sorted WS and Probability WS is minimal. We denote these assumptions over $k$ as $\boldsymbol{k}$. In our experiments we attack the stego images using the assumptions $\boldsymbol{k} = \{10\%, 20\%, \ldots, 100\%\}$. To retain solvability, we only use assumptions greater than the actual embedding rate. The used embedding rate is public due to the size of matrix $\boldsymbol{D}$. Figure 5(b) shows the MAE of the same experiment with an unknown, random amount of 'dry' pixels. It can be seen that all methods still perform well for small embedding rates, but lose accuracy for higher embedding rates. For larger embedding rates, Sorted WS benefits from using the minimal distance between both methods as it reduces the estimation error. The good estimation performance for smaller payloads suggests that the attack is also applicable when a hybrid stegosystem is constructed and PKS is only used for a key encapsulation, as described in Section 2.3.

These results show a good estimation of the embedding rate for our specialized methods. However, as already discussed, the payload length is public due to the size of the public matrix. It is therefore more important to identify stego images reliably. To evaluate the performance of such detectors, we use a recipient operating characteristics (ROC) curve. A ROC curve compares the false positive rate to the detection rate for a varying threshold [6]. Figure 6(a) and Figure 6(b) show the empirical ROC curves, again for $k = 50\%$ and for an unknown amount of 'dry' pixels, respectively. In both cases our specialized methods clearly outperform the existing unspecialized methods and allow a more reliable detection of stego images.

When comparing different estimators, it is helpful to use a single value that expresses their steganalytic performance. An example for such a metric is the equal error rate (EER). It expresses the error rate for the point where the probability for a missed detection equals the false positive rate. A smaller value indicates a better detector. Table 1 shows the EERs for our experiment. The result underlines the good performance for our estimators for various embedding rates. For almost all evaluated embedding rates our detectors lead to a better performance. For large embedding rates, this advantage slowly diminishes.

## 5. DISCUSSION AND CONCLUSION

In this paper we assume that an attacker makes use of all knowledge available to her and thus tries to predict which of the 'dry' pixels have more likely been modified during embedding with WPC. More specifically, we develop an approach to attack PKS using WPC by determining probability patterns that can be calculated from public parameters. We investigate, formalise and quantify an early approach proposed in [4] and observe the change probability for every element when using fixed parameters. We are able to use this approach to calculate embedding probabilities for every element in a stego image based on these public parameters. We investigate why these probability patterns arise and state that the proposed calculation of embedding probabilities is independent of the embedding method. We are therefore able to use the information about more likely embedding positions to extend known attacks on embedding methods to make them applicable for PKS using WPC. This possibility is illustrated by extending WS steganalysis to attack the use of LSB replacement in PKS with WPC. More specifically, we propose two extension of WS Steganalysis. The first approach sorts the elements of the suspect image according to their embedding probabilities. This places likely embedding positions at the beginning, which allows to run WS steganalysis for initial sequential embedding. We further propose to use the knowledge of embedding probabilities as element weights in Weighted WS steganalysis.

Our results indicate that the probability patterns arise when using the matrix LT process in an attempt to solve a system of linear equations more efficiently than with Gaussian elimination. Solving this system determines the necessary embedding changes when using WPC. We show that an attacker is able to identify the exact embedding positions when no selection rule is used. While these patterns diminish when using a selection rule, it is still possible to calculate an embedding probability for each element. This is in contrast to the assumption that the use of WPC does not reveal any information about the placement of embedding changes. These patterns do not occur when using other algorithms to solve the system, e.g., when using the computationally more complex Gaussian elimination.

We investigate our specialised WS detector on a large dataset. The results show that both proposed methods outperform current unspecialized methods when using a fixed number of possible embedding positions. Both methods show better results in estimating the embedding rate as well as better classification of stego objects and covers. Since the number of possible embedding positions is typically unknown, we further present an approach to estimate the embedding rate without any further knowledge about the amount of embedding positions. Our experiments show that the point where both proposed methods estimate a similar embedding rate is a good estimator for the actual embedding rate. We therefore estimate the embedding rate under different assumptions about the amount of 'dry' pixels. We then exploit the fact that both proposed methods' estimates converges to each other and use the point where the distance between the estimated embedding rates is minimal. Interestingly, this trick gives an even more accurate estimator than if we have the real amount of 'dry' pixels available as side-information.

Although the proposed approach is specifically targeted at the use of WPC, the main weakness arises from its public parameters and the efficient solver. It is likely that further steganographic coding schemes are also vulnerable when used in PKS. Future research may therefore investigate the implications of the proposed attack on other steganographic schemes as well as efficient countermeasures. We do not rule out the possibility that a similar approach may be used to attack the widely used syndrome trellis codes [10]. While

| $p$ | Probability WS | Sorted WS | Unweighted WS | Weighted WS |
|-------|----------------|-----------|---------------|-------------|
| 0.005 | 0.37 | 0.38 | 0.48 | 0.47 |
| 0.010 | 0.34 | 0.36 | 0.46 | 0.44 |
| 0.025 | 0.29 | 0.31 | 0.41 | 0.37 |
| 0.050 | 0.24 | 0.27 | 0.33 | 0.27 |
| 0.100 | 0.17 | 0.21 | 0.23 | 0.15 |
| 0.150 | 0.14 | 0.17 | 0.16 | 0.10 |
| 0.200 | 0.10 | 0.14 | 0.12 | 0.07 |

Table 1: EER of the ROC curves of 10000 covers and 10000 stego images, embedding rate $p$ and estimated amount of 'dry' pixels

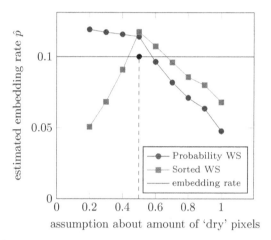

(a) Assumptions about $k$, with actual $k = 50\%$ and $p = 0.1$

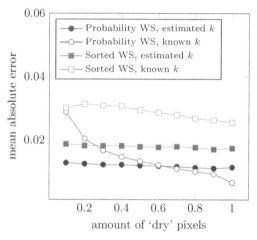

(b) Attacks with and without knowledge of $k$, $p = 0.01$

Figure 4: Comparison of the performance of Probability WS and Sorted WS

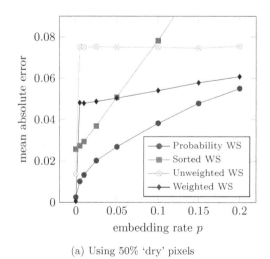

(a) Using 50% 'dry' pixels

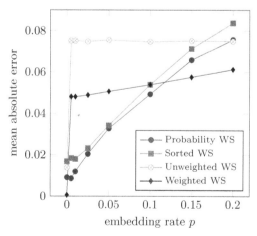

(b) Unknown amount of 'dry' pixels

Figure 5: Mean absolute error for the estimated embedding rate $\hat{p}$

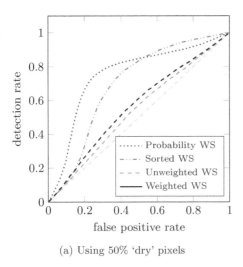

(a) Using 50% 'dry' pixels

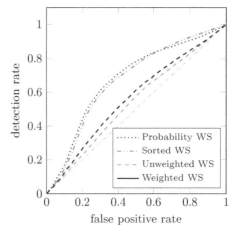

(b) Unknown amount of 'dry' pixels

Figure 6: Empirical ROC curves for $p = 0.01$

LSB replacement is (hopefully) rarely used in practice, the method is well understood and serves as a starting point. Our work illustrates the possibility to extend known targeted attacks to make them more accurate against PKS using WPC. The generalization to other embedding operations and feature-based detectors is left for future work. Other open research directions are the possibility to extract the embedding probabilities by theoretical means instead of numerical simulation; to combine the estimation of embedding probabilities with knowledge about a selection rule; and finally, to find an approach to solve the PKS problem efficiently without leaking compromising patterns to the steganalyst.

Closing with the metaphor of Wet Paper Codes: although the presented method is not able to predict the rain, it can predict the most likely *hideouts in the storm*. The results show that for certain combinations of building blocks, the prediction of these hideouts can be sufficient information to significantly reduce the security of PKS using WPC.

## Acknowledgments

This work has been partially supported by a grant of Deutsche Forschungsgemeinschaft (DFG). The quantitative experiments were carried out on the University of Münster's central high-performance computing cluster Palma.

## 6. REFERENCES

[1] R. J. Anderson. Stretching the limits of steganography. In R. J. Anderson, editor, *Information Hiding (1st International Workshop)*, volume 1174 of *Lecture Notes in Computer Science*, pages 39–48. Springer-Verlag, Berlin Heidelberg, 1996.

[2] R. J. Anderson and F. A. P. Petitcolas. On the limits of steganography. *IEEE Journal on Selected Areas in Communications*, 16(4):474–481, 1998.

[3] P. Bas, T. Filler, and T. Pevný. Break our steganographic system — the ins and outs of organizing BOSS. In T. Filler, T. Pevný, S. Craver, and A. Ker, editors, *Information Hiding (13th International Workshop)*, volume 6958 of *Lecture Notes in Computer Science*, pages 59–70, Berlin Heidelberg, 2011. Springer-Verlag.

[4] R. Böhme. Wet paper codes for public key steganography? Unpublished rump session talk at the 7th Information Hiding workshop, Presentation slides available at `http://www1.inf.tu-dresden.de/~rb21/publications/Boehme2005_IHW_RumpSession.pdf` (last accessed: April 2014), 2005.

[5] R. Böhme. Weighted stego-image steganalysis for JPEG covers. In K. Solanki, editor, *Information Hiding (10th International Workshop)*, volume 5284 of *Lecture Notes in Computer Science*, pages 178–194, Berlin Heidelberg, 2008. Springer-Verlag.

[6] R. Böhme. *Advanced Statistical Steganalysis*. Springer-Verlag, Berlin Heidelberg, 1st edition, 2010.

[7] R. Böhme and A. Westfeld. Exploiting preserved statistics for steganalysis. In J. Fridrich, editor, *Information Hiding (6th International Workshop)*, volume 3200 of *Lecture Notes in Computer Science*, pages 82–96. Springer-Verlag, Berlin Heidelberg, 2004.

[8] I. Cox, M. Miller, J. Bloom, J. Fridrich, and T. Kalker. *Digital Watermarking and Steganography*. Morgan Kaufmann, Burlington, MA, 2nd edition, 2007.

[9] R. Cramer and V. Shoup. A practical public key cryptosystem provably secure against adaptive chosen ciphertext attack. In H. Krawczyk, editor, *Advances in Cryptology – CRYPTO '98*, volume 1462 of *Lecture Notes in Computer Science*, pages 13–25, Berlin Heidelberg, 1998. Springer-Verlag.

[10] T. Filler, J. Judas, and J. Fridrich. Minimizing additive distortion in steganography using syndrome-trellis codes. *IEEE Transactions on Information Forensics and Security*, 6(3):920–935, 2011.

[11] J. Fridrich. *Steganography in Digital Media. Principles, Algorithms, and Applications*. Cambridge University Press, New York, NY, USA, 1st edition, 2009.

[12] J. Fridrich and M. Goljan. On estimation of secret message length in LSB steganography in spatial domain. In E. J. Delp and P. W. Wong, editors, *Security, Steganography, and Watermarking of Multimedia Contents VI*, volume 5306 of *Proceedings of SPIE*, pages 23–34, San Jose, CA, 2004. SPIE.

[13] J. Fridrich, M. Goljan, P. Losiněk, and D. Soukal. Writing on wet paper. *IEEE Transactions on Signal Processing*, 53(10):3923–3935, 2005.

[14] J. Fridrich, M. Goljan, P. Losiněk, and D. Soukal. Writing on wet paper. In E. J. Delp and P. W. Wong, editors, *Security, Steganography and Watermarking of Multimedia Contents VII*, volume 5681 of *Proceedings of SPIE*, pages 328–340. SPIE, San Jose, CA, 2005.

[15] J. Fridrich, M. Goljan, and D. Soukal. Perturbed quantization steganography with wet paper codes. In *Proceedings of the ACM workshop on Multimedia and Security (MM&Sec)*, pages 4–15, New York, NY, 2004. ACM Press.

[16] J. Fridrich, M. Goljan, and D. Soukal. Efficient wet paper codes. In M. Barni, J. Herrera-Joancomartí, S. Katzenbeisser, and F. Pérez-González, editors, *Information Hiding (7th International Workshop)*, volume 3727 of *Lecture Notes in Computer Science*, pages 204–218. Springer-Verlag, Berlin Heidelberg, 2005.

[17] A. D. Ker. A weighted stego image detector for sequential LSB replacement. In *Third International Symposium on Information Assurance and Security*, pages 453–456. IEEE Computer Society, 2007.

[18] A. D. Ker and R. Böhme. Revisiting weighted stego-image steganalysis. In E. J. Delp, P. W. Wong, J. Dittmann, and N. D. Memon, editors, *Security, Forensics, Steganography, and Watermarking of Multimedia Contents X*, volume 6819 of *Proceedings of SPIE*, page 681905, San Jose, CA, 2008. SPIE.

[19] A. D. Ker, T. Pevný, J. Kodovský, and J. Fridrich. The square root law of steganographic capacity. In *Proceedings of the ACM workshop on Multimedia and Security (MM&Sec)*, pages 107–116, New York, NY, USA, 2008. ACM Press.

[20] M. Luby. LT codes. In *Proceedings of the 43rd Annual IEEE Symposium on Foundations of Computer Science, FOCS 2002*, pages 271–280. IEEE Computer Society, 2002.

[21] B. Schneier. *Applied cryptography: protocols, algorithms, and source code in C*. John Wiley & Sons, Inc., New York, NY, 2nd edition, 1995.

[22] P. Schöttle and R. Böhme. A game-theoretic approach to content-adaptive steganography. In M. Kirchner and D. Ghosal, editors, *Information Hiding (14th International Workshop)*, volume 7692 of *Lecture Notes in Computer Science*, pages 125–141. Springer-Verlag, Berlin Heidelberg, 2012.

[23] P. Schöttle, S. Korff, and R. Böhme. Weighted stego-image steganalysis for naive content-adaptive embedding. In *Proceedings of the IEEE International Workshop on Information Forensics and Security (WIFS)*, pages 193–198. IEEE, 2012.

[24] L. von Ahn and N. J. Hopper. Public-key steganography. In C. Cachin and J. L. Camenisch, editors, *Proceedings of EUROCRYPT*, volume 3027 of *Lecture Notes in Computer Science*, pages 323–341, Berlin Heidelberg, 2004. Springer-Verlag.

# APPENDIX

## A. ROBUST SOLITON DISTRIBUTION

The Robust Soliton distribution is a discrete probability distribution introduced by Luby [20]. It is an extension of the Ideal Soliton distribution (ISD) $\rho(i)$. It is defined as follows [20]:

$$\rho(i) = \begin{cases} \frac{1}{q} & i = 1 \\ \frac{1}{i(i-1)} & i = 2, \ldots, q \end{cases} \tag{15}$$

The RSD is defined as the normalized sum of the ISD and $\tau(i)$ [11, 20]:

$$\mu(i) = \frac{\rho(i) + \tau(i)}{\eta} \tag{16}$$

$$\tau(i) = \begin{cases} \frac{T}{iq} & i = 1, \ldots \lfloor q/T \rfloor - 1 \\ \frac{T \log(T/\delta)}{q} & i = \lfloor q/T \rfloor \\ 0 & i = \lfloor q/T \rfloor + 1, \ldots, q \end{cases} \tag{17}$$

with $\eta = \sum_{i=1}^{q} (\rho(i) + \tau(i))$ and $T = c \log(q/\delta) \sqrt{q}$ [11, 20].

Generating matrix $\boldsymbol{D}$ according to this distribution is supposed to make the resulting system of linear equations sparse while remaining solvable [11]. Figure 7 shows the distribution of the RSD for parameter $\delta = 0.5$, $c = 0.1$ and $q = 100$. While the high probabilities for low Hamming-weights are supposed to make the matrix sparse, the high probability for Hamming-weight 18 is supposed to ensure that the system remains solvable [11].

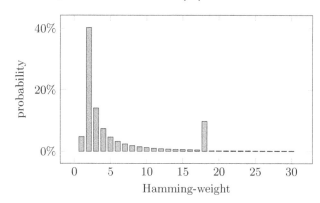

Figure 7: Robust Soliton distribution for $\delta = 0.5$, $c = 0.1$ and $q = 100$

# Steganographic Key Leakage Through Payload Metadata

Tomáš Pevný
Agent Technology Group
CTU in Prague
Prague 16627, Czech Republic
pevnak@gmail.com

Andrew D. Ker
Department of Computer Science
University of Oxford
Oxford OX1 3QD, UK
adk@cs.ox.ac.uk

## ABSTRACT

The only steganalysis attack which can provide absolute certainty about the presence of payload is one which finds the embedding key. In this paper we consider refined versions of the key exhaustion attack exploiting metadata such as message length or decoding matrix size, which must be stored along with the payload. We show simple errors of implementation lead to leakage of key information and powerful inference attacks; furthermore, complete absence of information leakage seems difficult to avoid. This topic has been somewhat neglected in the literature for the last ten years, but must be considered in real-world implementations.

## Categories and Subject Descriptors

D.2.11 [**Software Engineering**]: Software Architectures—*Information hiding*; H.1.1 [**Models and Principles**]: Systems and Information Theory—*Information theory*

## Keywords

Steganographic Security; Key Leakage; Brute-force Attack; Bayesian Inference

## 1. INTRODUCTION

A steganographic object does not only contain its covert payload: it will also contain a small amount of metadata about the payload. Typically this will be the length of the payload and/or some parameters that tell the recipient how to decode it: otherwise, the embedder is forced to use a fixed coding method which cannot exploit better embedding efficiency available for lower payloads, or adapt the embedding method to the cover. Does this metadata leak information about the embedding key? In this paper we consider details of implementation which are typically elided in the literature, and this paper is aimed at real-world practitioners [12]. We show how easy it is to make mistakes, with examples of a historic steganography scheme that does make obvious

*IH&MMSec'14,* June 11–13, 2014, Salzburg, Austria.
Copyright 2014 ACM 978-1-4503-2647-6/14/06 ...$15.00.
http://dx.doi.org/10.1145/2600918.2600921.

mistakes, and hypothetical implementations where the mistakes are more subtle. Indeed, it seems surprisingly difficult to avoid information leakage altogether.

In this paper we do not consider *statistical* steganalysis: a highly-refined discipline (particularly for still, grayscale, images) which can detect even small payloads with surprising accuracy. But the level of reliability is never certainty and never enough, for example, to convince a criminal court. The authors believe that steganalysis with false positive rates below, say, $10^{-9}$ is an important area for research, but no current statistical steganalysis method meets such a standard. (Even if one did, we would have no way to prove it.)

Instead, we turn to the older *brute force* attack, which tries all possible embedding keys in turn. Such attacks are certainly plausible, we argue more so than in traditional cryptography, and are the only methods by which one could truly pronounce guilt with certainty. The brute force attack is not, of course, new, but we suggest that the embedding metadata provides a way to speed up and refine exhaustion attacks, which can be mitigated (but perhaps not prevented) by careful implementation.

### 1.1 Typical Extraction Procedure

Consider a typical steganographic *extraction* process:

(i) The *embedding key* is derived from a password, using a key derivation function (KDF): $k = \text{KDF}(p)$.

(ii) The embedding key locates and decodes a small block of metadata, the *decoding parameters*.

(iii) The decoding parameters and the embedding key are used to extract the *payload*.

In step (i) we distinguish a *password* $p$, the secret shared between the sender and receiver which we expect to have only a moderate amount of entropy (e.g. one of a few million possible words and modified words), from the quasi-cryptographic key $k$ that parameterizes the extraction. In contemporary security systems, the relatively small entropy of passwords is often a weakness because it permits a brute-force attack [8]. Ideally, the sender and receiver would share a 64- or 128-bit secret key, but the practicalities of covert communication make this unlikely: if they can share such keys at will, they may have no need for steganography at all. Perhaps a protocol could be used to exchange embedding keys, but at the moment public-key steganography protocols have enormous computational costs [12].

By *(de)coding parameters* we mean the information necessary to en/decode the payload: it might simply be the payload length; in syndrome coding methods it will determine the parity-check matrix size [3] (the contents of the matrix will probably derive from the embedding key); in adaptive embedding methods it may determine the parameters of the trellis [4]. Most research literature assumes that decoding parameters are somehow already known to the receiver, e.g. YASS [22], or provide only simulators that do not encode a real message, e.g. UNIWARD [9] and HUGO [17].

In the real world, decoding parameters must be embedded in step (ii), using a fixed code, and stored securely using the embedding key (for example as a cryptographic key), otherwise the system does not survive Kerckhoffs' Principle. For example, OutGuess [19] has a header containing a 16-bit field storing payload length (in bytes); F5 [23] uses 8 bits to store the dimension of the Hamming code used in matrix embedding [3] and 23 bits to store payload length (in bytes); JpHide&Seek [15] stores the message length (in bytes) in 24 bits encrypted by the same password as the payload.

The distinction between steps (ii) and (iii) is important. Having step (iii) depend on the output of (ii) allows the embedder to vary the encoding parameters according to the payload size or cover characteristics. For example, using random linear codes, smaller relative payloads can be embedded with higher embedding efficiency by choosing codes with higher dimension [7]. Or in the paradigm of distortion minimization using syndrome trellis codes, the width of the generator matrix must be adjusted according to the inverse payload size, to approach the rate-distortion bound [9]. Without transmitting decoding parameters, the encoder would be unable to adjust their embedding to make the best use of the particular cover and payload combination.

In this paper, in sections 2–4, we examine increasingly refined versions of exhaustion attacks attempting to use step (ii) to determine the embedding key. We will assume that the embedder has created multiple stego images using the same key (with different payloads); this seems highly realistic in a covert communication scenario.

## 1.2 Prior Art on Brute Force

Recovering the embedding key seems to have received relatively little attention in the literature. Probably the first work was [20], which tried to detect the use of steganography on the internet. Downloaded images were first scrutinised by statistical steganalysis based on the $\chi^2$-test, and if deemed suspicious the hidden content was further verified by guessing the embedding key from a dictionary. A key was deemed possible if it extracted a header compatible with known embedding algorithms. The approach resembles the Intersection Attack we present in section 3, but it only uses one stego image; contrary to this prior art, we can often determine the embedding key uniquely.

Ref. [6] used a statistical approach, generating the embedding path from each stego key. The attack, targeting OutGuess and F5, assumed that pixels/coefficients carrying the payload have different statistical properties from those that do not. A $\chi^2$-test is used to measure this difference. Such an attack will not work directly with modern content-adaptive embedding schemes, which use all pixels with some probability, but could perhaps be adapted to them: it was demonstrated in [21] that knowledge of the embedding path makes them more vulnerable to modified weighted stego-image steganalysis [13] in the limited case of LSB Replacement.

## 2. RECOGNISABLE PLAINTEXT

An important concept in cryptography is the *recognisable plaintext*: the assumption that an attacker can tell when they have found the correct decryption key, by verifying the decoded plaintext in some way. Ciphertext-only attacks (as opposed to those with a known plaintext-ciphertext pair) are impossible without this assumption. The same assumption is plausible in steganography, for much the same reasons: if the payload has meaning, it most likely also has redundancy or structure, for which an attacker can look. Given this assumption, the simplest attack on steganography is:

**The Exhaustion Attack.** The attacker tests every possible key $k$, or alternatively every possible password $p$, decoding the plaintext and checking for known structure.

### 2.1 Countermeasures

Recognisable plaintext is a genuine problem for steganography, particularly if it is more difficult to convey good passwords in a covert communication setting than in traditional cryptography. Compressing redundancy, or encrypting plaintext with the embedding key, provides no additional security because a Kerckhoffs' attacker can reverse it.

One countermeasure is to ensure that the keyspace is at least 64 bits: in modern times, there is no excuse for using a 32-bit embedding key, because 32-bit keyspaces can be exhausted. Unfortunately this still allows an attacker possessing a suitably generous dictionary to attack the passwords instead. Increases in computational power were supposed to benefit cryptographers (who can increase key sizes with polynomially more work) more than cryptanalysts (who are forced into near-exponentially more work), but humans' ability to remember passwords has not kept pace [8].

We could borrow a technique from entity authentication mechanisms, and ensure that the KDF is slow to compute, for example by iterating a cryptographic hash at least $10^5$ times [10]. This slows down the embedder, extractor, and attacker equally. However, slow KDFs can be defeated by attackers with plenty of parallel computational resources, and the key dictionary can be derived offline unless the keys are also salted [16] (and with what? – perhaps a sequence number, but this is vulnerable to prediction and fragile under desynchronization). Similarly, but less sensibly, we could try to ensure that the decoding process itself is very slow.

The best that we can suggest is a separate password encrypting the payload itself; a similar approach is assumed in [5]. Although doubling the password requirement, it squares the brute-force work for an attacker, who must exhaust for each embedding key and then again to recognise plaintexts.

## 3. IMPOSSIBLE PARAMETERS

Even a separate encryption password or a completely unrecognisable plaintext may not protect against exhaustion. We make the same observation as Provos [20]: that most embedding keys will imply decoding parameters which are not possible, and these can be discarded. With multiple images embedded under the same key, we can use:

**The Intersection Attack.** The attacker maintains a list of all possible keys $k$, or passwords $p$. For each image received, they remove all keys which produce impossible decoding parameters.

Consider the OutGuess [19] algorithm: it uses 16 bits to store the length of the payload. Its capacity can be estimated as half the number of non-zero, non-one, non-DC, discrete cosine transform (DCT) coefficients. It is easy to compare the message length extracted from the header with the capacity (which is not changed by embedding) and, if exceeded, the key can be discarded. For incorrect keys, we expect to read uniformly distributed lengths of less than $2^{16}$ bytes, most of which will be too long for the stego image.

For F5 the same attack is slightly more difficult, because the embedding process reduces the capacity. However, the capacity can never be less than the number of nonzero AC coefficients, since if F5 changes a coefficient to zero it re-embeds using another; thus we obtain an upper bound on the capacity of the cover from the stego object. Furthermore, its implementation has even key higher leakage, because it also stores the parameters of the Hamming code. As well as discarding impossible message lengths, we can also verify that the Hamming coding is compatible with the message length and capacity. A similar mechanism can be expected for embedding algorithms using syndrome trellis codes.

This attack can be extremely powerful: when proportion $\alpha$ of all possible keys give rise to possible decoding parameters, after $n$ images there will be on average only $\alpha^n$ possible keys left. Put another way, we expect the entropy of the keyspace to decrease linearly with $n$.

## 3.1 Experiment

The Intersection Attack is demonstrated using set of approximately 9000 images, where every image contains a payload of random length (uniformly chosen up to capacity) embedded using OutGuess with the same password 'Neil'. All images were JPEG images downloaded from one user of the photo-sharing site Flickr. We simulate a steganalyst with a list of more than 2 million passwords downloaded from [1] (the searchable keyspace therefore has an entropy of approximate 21 bits). The experiment was repeated each time with up to 50 images embedded with the same key, and after each image the steganalyst removes passwords implying a message length not compatible with capacity. The average- and worst-case (over 1000 repetitions) entropy of the remaining keyspace (the binary logarithm of the number of possible passwords) at each stage is shown in Figure 1. The results demonstrate key leakage, but not as much as we had expected: this is because the OutGuess implementation does not decode all parameter blocks to uniformly random payloads: some keys imply consistently small payloads, regardless of image, and cannot be eliminated. Thus 50 images are not sufficient to determine the password uniquely.

## 3.2 Countermeasures

Implementations which allow the Intersection Attack are flawed, but it can be tricky to remove the flaw entirely. The first step is to use the correct length of field: for example, if payload length can never be more than (say) $2^{23}$ bits (1 bit per pixel of an 8 megapixel image) then only 23 bits should be used to store payload length; if they must be padded to 32 bits, the other nine bits should be random and discarded by the extractor.

However, this still leaves plenty of impossible parameters for smaller images, and the exponential power of the Intersection Attack can exploit even small gaps. We propose a simple padding scheme that makes all parameter blocks possible: if the number to be stored (payload size, matrix parameters, etc.) lies in the range $0 \ldots (N-1)$, encrypt us-

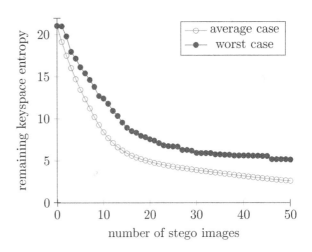

**Figure 1: Entropy of keyspace after the Intersection Attack.**

ing $k$ a uniformly-chosen random integer with the correct value (mod $N$).

It is not always easy to choose such an $N$. If we are storing a payload size, ideally $N$ should be the maximum capacity of the cover. But $N$ has to be recoverable by the receiver, so that they can perform the same modular reduction. Unfortunately, for many embedding schemes the capacity is lower after embedding (e.g. F5 as we previously stated [5]). The sender may be forced to predict a *lower* bound based on the capacity of the *stego object* and use that $N$ instead, which in turns limits their own capacity meaning that maximum-size payloads cannot be embedded. However, maximum-size payloads are more vulnerable to statistical steganalysis, so perhaps this does not matter. Analogous problems may arise in storing coding parameters such as matrix or trellis sizes.

Even random padding that makes all decoding parameters possible may leak information, if the parameters are not equally likely. This is the subject of the following section.

## 4. PAYLOAD SIZE ESTIMATION

We try to use some techniques from statistical steganalysis to strengthen the brute-force attack. Most embedding methods are vulnerable to *quantitative steganalysis*, which attempts to estimate the payload length (or its proxy, number of embedding changes) from a stego image: a form of regression. Most steganalysis classifiers can be converted to regressors [18]. Even though the estimates are subject to error, they make certain keys more likely than others.

For now, we will assume that the decoding parameters simply specify the payload length; we will revisit this in subsection 4.3. We assume that the regressor outputs an estimate of the payload length $y$ and, by empirical simulation, we can obtain an estimate of the distribution of the estimate conditional on the true payload length $x$ (typically by fitting the estimation error to a distribution, preferably one with heavy tails [2]). We denote this distribution $P(y|x)$. Each possible embedding key $k$ decodes a parameter block specifying that the payload length is $x(k)$. Now we can perform:

**Bayesian Key Inference.** If $p(k)$ represents the prior probability that the key is $k$, then the posterior $p(k|y)$ after one observation of a stego image with estimated payload $y$

is given by

$$p(k|y) = \frac{\mathrm{P}\big(y|x(k)\big)p(k)}{\sum_{k'} \mathrm{P}\big(y|x(k')\big)p(k')} \propto \mathrm{P}\big(y|x(k)\big)p(k).$$

We can ignore the denominator, because it is constant in $k$, and rescale the distribution (if necessary) at the end. Iterating for multiple observations $y_1, \ldots, y_n$, the unscaled posterior can therefore be written

$$\log p(k|y_1, \ldots, y_n) = \log p(k) + \sum_{i=1}^{n} \log \mathrm{P}\big(y_i|x(k)\big).$$

Regardless of the prior, this means that all keys can be scored by their log-likelihood.

We briefly analyse the performance of this algorithm (proof omitted). Let $S$ denote the score for the true key $k$, and $S'$ the score of an incorrect key $k'$. Then

$$\mathrm{E}[S] = n \int \mathrm{P}\big(y|x(k)\big) \log \mathrm{P}\big(y|x(k)\big) \, \mathrm{d}y,$$

and if $\tilde{\mathrm{P}}(y)$ represents the unconditional output of the regressor, the mixture over all true payloads (which may very well be uniform random) then

$$\mathrm{E}[S'] = n \int \mathrm{P}\big(y|x(k)\big) \log \tilde{\mathrm{P}}(y) \, \mathrm{d}y.$$

Thus the separation of the scores of true and false keys is linear in $n$, governed by the Kullback-Leibler divergence

$$\mathrm{D}_{KL}\Big(\mathrm{P}\big(y|x(k)\big) \,\|\, \tilde{\mathrm{P}}(y)\Big), \qquad (1)$$

which is larger when the regressor is more accurate, and (assuming independent scores between images) its variance is $O(n)$. This implies that the probability of the correct key will soon dominate the others.

## 4.1 Experiment

Bayesian Key Inference was evaluated using the same image set as in subsection 3.1. In each repetition we randomly picked 10 images (embedding using the same key) over which to perform Bayesian inference. The remaining 8990 images were split into two sets: 66% of them were used to train a linear quantitative steganalyzer by ordinary least-square regression on Cartesian-calibrated PF-584 features [14] the remaining 34% were used to estimate the quantitative steganalyzer's error, which was fitted to a Gaussian distribution to create $\mathrm{P}(y|x)$.

Figure 2 shows the entropy of the keyspace (the posterior key distribution) after applying the attack. We observe significantly faster convergence than for the Intersection Attack; at most eight images was sufficient to determine the correct password uniquely. Although the Gaussian model for regressor error is probably optimistic, it does not seem to hurt the accuracy of inference unless we care about the precise posterior probabilities; on the other hand, it could easily be swapped for a heavier-tailed distribution.

## 4.2 Countermeasures

To our knowledge, such an attack has not previously been described. It exploits an implementation rather than the method for putting the bits into the cover, and such topics have received relatively little attention in the literature.

It seems difficult to prevent this attack in any situation where the number of possible keys or passwords is exhaustible

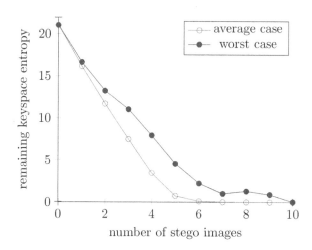

**Figure 2: Entropy of keyspace after Bayesian Key Inference using message length metadata.**

and a quantitative steganalyzer exists, but we suggest that some countermeasures may be possible. The exponential power of Bayesian Key Inference relies on the following observation: if $x_i(k)$ the payload size implied by key $k$ in image $i$, and if $k'$ is an incorrect guess for the true embedding key $k$ then

$$|x_i(k') - x_i(k)| \text{ is independent of } |x_j(k') - x_j(k)| \qquad (2)$$

for $i \neq j$. In other words, a key which is a 'near miss' for image $i$ is unlikely also to be a 'near miss' for other images $j$, so the likelihood of incorrect keys diminishes very quickly.

If $b(k)$ specifies some sequence of bits from the stego image, depending on the key $k$, we have implicitly assumed that $x(k) = D_k(b(k))$ or $x(k) = D_k(b(k)) \pmod{N}$, where $D_k(-)$ is some cryptographic decryption. It is precisely this cryptographic property that gives (2). Is it possible to mitigate the effect, introducing strong covariance between $|x_i(k') - x_i(k)|$ and $|x_j(k') - x_j(k)|$? One simple proposal to avoid (2) is

$$x(k) = b + k \pmod{N} \qquad (3)$$

for some block $b$ at fixed location.

We can measure the amount of leaked information using a similar experiment simulating an OutGuess-like embedding. The message length is stored in 16 bits, so the effective key space for one-time pad is $\mathcal{K} = \{0, 1, \ldots, 2^{16} - 1\}$. Background bits $b$ are read from some fixed positions. The inference is done only against $\mathcal{K}$, and it is assumed that the capacity is $\frac{1}{16}M$ bytes, where $M$ is the number of useable coefficients (recall that OutGuess reserves approximately 50% of them for statistical restoration). The number of images available for key-breaking was increased to 50, since we expect the inference to be weaker.

The results are summarised in Figure 3. Comparing to the previous case, the inference is much weaker: the keyspace was not very large to begin with, but only approximately half of its entropy is lost.

It is counter-intuitive to use a weak encoding such as (3), and indeed it does leak information. Although the payload size is secured by the one-time pad of modular addition, multiple images with similar payloads and the same embedding key will all have similar values stored in the block: this allows an attacker an easy target for statistical attacks. It

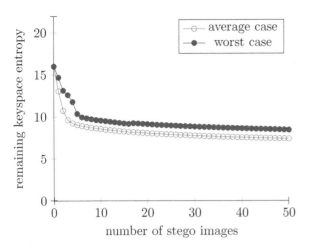

**Figure 3: Entropy of keyspace after Bayesian Key Inference, where message length is protected by a one-time pad.**

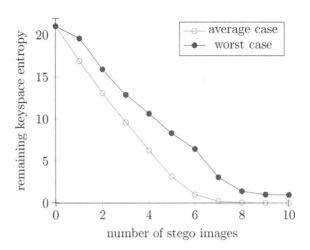

**Figure 4: Entropy of keyspace after Bayesian Key Inference using the dimension of the code.**

would appear that (2) forces such a weakness, because then

$$x_i(k) \approx x_j(k) \text{ implies } x_i(k') \approx x_j(k')$$

for every $k'$. We leave open the question as to whether there is a clever solution which prevents exponential key leakage from multiple stego images but does not introduce statistical dependence between those images.

### 4.3 Extension

Having read the preceding sections, any sensible steganographer should learn the lesson: do not embed the payload size at all. There is no absolute need for it, since the end-of-payload can be marked by an escape code, and the rest discarded after extraction. However, the same inference technique works even if the decoding parameters do not specify the payload precisely, as long as they imply some range of possible payloads. This is usually the case.

For example, take F5, which uses a Hamming syndrome code to increase embedding efficiency. For any integer $m$, it embeds $m$ bits into blocks of size $2^m - 1$ while making at most one change. Thus larger $m$ gives higher embedding efficiency but lower payload rates, and the embedder chooses the largest $m$ such that the desired payload will fit. The only embedding parameter that must be communicated to the receiver is $m$, which we shall assume is perfectly padded so that the Intersection Attack is also impossible.

Even though the parameter block does not store the payload length, Bayesian inference is still possible. Each key $k$ implies a value of $m$, which in turn implies a bound on the number of embedding changes in the image as follows. If the image has $M$ usable locations then there can be at most $M/(2^m - 1)$ blocks used, so at most $M/(2^m - 1)$ embedding changes. And there cannot be much fewer than $M/(2^{m+1} - 1)$ changes, otherwise the payload size is (very likely) small enough that a larger value of $m$ would have been used by the embedder. Given an estimator for the number of changes (e.g. [18]), we can assume a uniformly random number of changes $x$ between these two limits, and still compute

$$P(y|m) = \sum_x P(y|x)P(x|m).$$

The conditional distribution $P(y|m)$ is flatter than the plain output of a regressor $P(y|x)$, so the divergence (1) is smaller, but inference can still happen and should still converge exponentially fast (reduce entropy linearly) if different keys imply independent decodings of $m$.

### 4.4 Experiment

We simulated the above scenario, using the estimator of the message length from subsection 4.1. Assuming Hamming codes used in F5, the probability of code parameter $m$, when the estimated length of the message is $\hat{y}$ and number of non-zero DCT coefficients is $M$ is

$$P(y|m) = \int_{\frac{M(m-1)}{2^{m-1}-1}}^{\frac{Mm}{2^m-1}} \mathcal{N}(y \,|\, \hat{y}, \sigma^2) \, \mathrm{d}y, \tag{4}$$

where $\sigma^2$ is the estimated variance of the estimator. For every key, we assumed the most efficient code parameter

$$m = \max \left\{ m \Big| y \leq \frac{Mm}{2^m - 1}, m \in 1, 2, \ldots, 8 \right\}. \tag{5}$$

Figure 4 shows the results, which are surprisingly powerful considering that the payload is only determined very approximately by the code parameters. At most 10 images were sufficient to determine the correct password uniquely.

### 5. CONCLUSION

This paper aims to bring steganography a little further from the laboratory into the real world [12], by focusing on the somewhat-neglected topic of key exhaustion, an attack that is likely to be practical. It is easy to dismiss as an 'implementation issue', but we have shown that it is difficult to include embedding parameters that are not subject to some kind of inference. Other key attacks [21, 6] could potentially be combined with the ideas presented here, but at present they are already sufficiently powerful for most purposes, reducing the potential keyspace in our experiments from 2 million down to a few hundred, or even down to one, given a few images embedded with the same key.

The entire attack could be avoided if the keyspace were 64 bits, and not derived from any password, because it would not be exhaustible. Furthermore, no two covers should ever be embedded using the same key [11]. But the real world may preclude these good practices. Certainly, steganographers should avoid including the payload length in any kind of header, if possible. It is telling that most (perhaps all) widely-available steganography software makes this mistake. Any embedding parameters must be properly padded so that all decoded parameters are *possible*, but we have shown that this does not make them equally likely. Storing embedding parameters cryptographically is the root cause of the exponential power of inference attacks, because it makes incorrect key guesses independent over different images. Although we have suggested an alternative, it unlocks statistical attacks.

The alternative is to embed no metadata at all, use an escape code as an end-of-payload marker, and accept that embedding parameters must be fixed (or derived solely from the stego image). This reduces vulnerability to exhaustion, but probably makes statistical steganalysis more effective because of the suboptimal codes. Indeed, we conjecture that the embedder may be forced to choose between more susceptibility to exhaustion attacks or more susceptibility to statistical steganalysis.

## Acknowledgments

This work was supported by European Office of Aerospace Research and Development under the research grant numbers FA8655-11-3035 and FA8655-13-1-3020. The U.S. Government is authorized to reproduce and distribute reprints for Governmental purposes notwithstanding any copyright notation there on. The views and conclusions contained herein are those of the authors and should not be interpreted as necessarily representing the official policies, either expressed or implied, of EOARD or the U.S. Government.

## 6. REFERENCES

[1] Free list of 2 million popular ASCII passwords. http://dazzlepod.com/site_media/txt/passwords.txt.

[2] R. Böhme and A. D. Ker. A two-factor error model for quantitative steganalysis. In *Security, Steganography, and Watermarking of of Multimedia Contents VIII*, volume 6072 of *Proc. SPIE*, pages 59–74. SPIE, 2006.

[3] R. Crandall. Some notes on steganography. *Steganography Mailing List*, 1998. available from http://os.inf.tu-dresden.de/~westfeld/crandall.pdf.

[4] T. Filler, J. Judas, and J. Fridrich. Minimizing additive distortion in steganography using syndrome-trellis codes. *IEEE Trans. Information Forensics and Security*, 6(3):920–935, 2011.

[5] J. Fridrich, M. Goljan, and D. Hogea. Steganalysis of JPEG images: Breaking the F5 algorithm. In *Proc. 5th Information Hiding Workshop*, volume 2578 of *LNCS*, pages 310–323. Springer, 2002.

[6] J. Fridrich, M. Goljan, and D. Soukal. Searching for the stego key. In *Security, Steganography, and Watermarking of Multimedia Contents VI*, volume 5306 of *Proc. SPIE*, pages 70–82, 2004.

[7] J. Fridrich, M. Goljan, and D. Soukal. Wet paper codes with improved embedding efficiency. *IEEE Trans. Information Forensics and Security*, 1(1):102–110, 2006.

[8] D. Goodin. Why passwords have never been weaker and crackers have never been stronger.

http://arstechnica.com/security/2012/08/passwords-under-assault/, 2012.

[9] V. Holub and J. Fridrich. Digital image steganography using universal distortion. In *Proc. 1st ACM Workshop on Information Hiding and Multimedia Security*, pages 59–68. ACM, 2013.

[10] B. Kaliski. *PKCS #5: Password-Based Cryptography Specification Version 2.0*. Request for Comments 2898. Internet Engineering Task Force, 2000. http://www.ietf.org/rfc/rfc2898.txt.

[11] A. D. Ker. Locating steganographic payload via WS residuals. In *Proc. 10th ACM Workshop on Multimedia and Security*, pages 27–32. ACM, 2008.

[12] A. D. Ker, P. Bas, R. Böhme, R. Cogranne, S. Craver, T. Filler, J. Fridrich, and T. Pevný. Moving steganography and steganalysis from the laboratory into the real world. In *Proc. 1st ACM Workshop on Information Hiding and Multimedia Security*, pages 45–58. ACM, 2013.

[13] A. D. Ker and R. Böhme. Revisiting weighted stego-image steganalysis. In *Security, Forensics, Steganography, and Watermarking of Multimedia Contents X*, volume 6819 of *Proc. SPIE*, pages 0501–0517. SPIE, 2008.

[14] J. Kodovský and J. Fridrich. Calibration revisited. In *Proc. 11th ACM Workshop on Multimedia and Security*, pages 63–74. ACM, 2009.

[15] A. Latham. Implementation of the JPHide and JPSeek algorithms ver 0.3 (released August 1999). http://linux01.gwdg.de/~alatham/stego.html.

[16] R. Morris and K. Thompson. Password security: A case history. *Communications of the ACM*, 22:594–597, 1979.

[17] T. Pevný, T. Filler, and P. Bas. Using high-dimensional image models to perform highly undetectable steganography. In *Proc. 12th Information Hiding Conference*, volume 6387 of *LNCS*, pages 161–177. Springer, 2010.

[18] T. Pevný, J. Fridrich, and A. D. Ker. From blind to quantitative steganalysis. *IEEE Trans. Information Forensics and Security*, 7(2):445–454, 2012.

[19] N. Provos. Defending against statistical steganalysis. In *Proc. 10th Conference on USENIX Security Symposium - Volume 10*, SSYM, pages 323–335. USENIX Association, 2001.

[20] N. Provos and P. Honeyman. Detecting steganographic content on the internet. Technical Report CITI Technical Report 01-11, University of Michigan, 2001.

[21] P. Schottle, S. Korff, and R. Böhme. Weighted stego-image steganalysis for naive content-adaptive embedding. In *IEEE International Workshop on Information Forensics and Security (WIFS 2012)*, pages 193–198, 2012.

[22] K. Solanki, A. Sarkar, and B. Manjunath. YASS: Yet another steganographic scheme that resists blind steganalysis. In *Proc. 9th Information Hiding Conference*, volume 4567 of *LNCS*, pages 16–31. Springer, 2007.

[23] A. Westfeld. F5 – a steganographic algorithm. In *Proc. 4th Information Hiding Workshop*, volume 2137 of *LNCS*, pages 289–302. Springer, 2001.

# Video Steganography with Perturbed Macroblock Partition

Hong Zhang
State Key Laboratory of
Information Security
Institute of Information
Engineering, Chinese
Academy of Sciences
Beijing, 100093, P.R.China
zhanghong@iie.ac.cn

Yun Cao[*]
State Key Laboratory of
Information Security
Institute of Information
Engineering, Chinese
Academy of Sciences
Beijing, 100093, P.R.China
caoyun@iie.ac.cn

Xianfeng Zhao
State Key Laboratory of
Information Security
Institute of Information
Engineering, Chinese
Academy of Sciences
Beijing, 100093, P.R.China
zhaoxianfeng@iie.ac.cn

Weiming Zhang
School of Information Science
and Technology
University of Science and
Technology of China
Hefei, 230026, P.R.China
zhangwm@ustc.edu.cn

Nenghai Yu
School of Information Science
and Technology
University of Science and
Technology of China
Hefei, 230026, P.R.China
ynh@ustc.edu.cn

## ABSTRACT

In this paper, with a novel data representation named macroblock partition mode, an effective steganography integrated with H.264/AVC compression is proposed. The main principle is to improve the steganographic security in two directions. First, to embed messages, an internal process of H.264 compression, i.e., the macroblock partition, is slightly perturbed, hence the compression compliance is ensured. Second, to minimize the embedding impact, a high efficient double-layered structure is deliberately designed. In the first layer, the syndrome-trellis codes (STCs) is utilized to perform adaptive embedding, and the costs in visual quality and compression efficiency are both considered to construct the distortion model. In the second layer, facilitated by the wet paper codes (WPCs), an expected 3-bit per change gain in embedding efficiency is obtained.

## Categories and Subject Descriptors

D.2.11 [**SOFTWARE ENGINEERING**]: Software Architectures—*Information hiding*; H.5.1 [**INFORMATION INTERFACES AND PRESENTATION**]: Multimedia Information Systems—*Video*

## Keywords

Information hiding; video; steganography; H.264/AVC

---

[*]The corresponding author.

## 1. INTRODUCTION

Modern steganography is the art and science of concealing the existence of the secret information into certain digital media. The hidden information should be undetectable, that is, the modified content should be perceptually and statistically (with respect to certain features) similar to its original unaltered counterpart [6].

This paper aims to design a novel steganographic methodology using digital videos as the cover media. Since digital video is one of the most influential media in our daily life, video transmission plays an ideal cloak of secret communication and provides sufficient payload capacity. The raw video is essentially a series of successive still images captured by optical devices. For the purpose of economical storage and efficient transmission, a variety of video compression technologies have been developed. It has been about 20 years since the MPEG (Motion Picture Expert Group) standard was established in 1993 [12] and MPEG-2 in 1995. Then in the pursuit of a better compression performance, H.264/AVC is developed [16] and has become one of the most commonly practiced video coding standard since 2003.

In most early video steganography, embedding is designed to take place prior to compression, and is applied directly to individual frame. However, such methodology is rarely adopted not only to avoid information lost caused by compression, but also to reduce the risk of being detected by highly-developed image-oriented steganalysis. As current video coding standards usually consist of several crucial processes, e.g., motion estimation, transformation, quantization and entropy coding, recent researches suggest to combine compression and information hiding together by directly manipulating certain coding process [15].

It is noticed that many recent high performance video steganography are inclined to utilizing the motion information, i.e., the motion vector (MV), as the data representation [10, 1, 11, 3, 4]. Although MV-based schemes have many advantages as high capacity and low quality degradation, it has a few inherent vulnerabilities which have already facilitated many targeted attacks. For instance, Zhang *et al.*

suggest that, if the embedding process can be modeled as an additive independent noise signal to the horizontal and vertical components, the statistical analysis of relative properties can be used to reveal the existence of hidden messages [19, 14]. Cao *et al.* implement video calibration for steganalysis and pointed out that, if a certain MV has been changed for embedding, the changed MV will show an inclination to revert to its prior value during re-compression [2]. Xu *et al.* make a point that in certain embedding scenarios, the mutual constraints of MVs will be destroyed [17] upon which they propose a steganalysis.

Faced with the situation stated above, we are motivated to search for other data representations to provide equivalent or even higher levels of steganographic security. Fortunately, with H.264, new opportunities for steganography can be found. As one distinguishing characteristic, H.264 allows each inter-macroblock to be further partitioned into smaller blocks of different sizes for inter-prediction. Correspondingly, an alternative data representation named "partition mode" (PM) is defined and chosen as the secret information carrier.

*Definition 1.* (**Partition Mode**). After partitioning macroblock (MB) into smaller blocks, the resultant partition form is defined as MB's partition mode.

The reasons for our choice are listed below. First, compression is an information-reducing process, the information required for MB partition can be exploited as the "side information" to help constructing a good distortion model for adaptive embedding. Second, other than MB partition, crucial processes, e.g., motion estimation, transformation, quantization, entropy coding, are not affected. Consequently, very limited losses of visual quality and coding efficiency would occur. Last but not least, to the best of our knowledge, no effective targeted-steganalyzer is found. The reliability of existing steganalytic models are likely to deteriorate when embedding with PM.

The prototype of PM-based data hiding schemes can be traced back to Kapotas and Skodras's work [13] which hides the scene change information by sequentially forcing the encoder to choose particular PMs. Similarly, Yang *et al.* suggest to make use of only sub-MB (with the size of 8 × 8) partitions [18]. Our studies show that, the existing schemes have several issues of concern. To start with, the existing schemes choose PMs arbitrarily which should be considered a serious violation of the coding principle, and the sequential embedding manner might drop the coding performance. Secondly, as analyzed in 4.3, the achieved embedding efficiency is not satisfactory. Consequently, steganalytic results in 4.4.3 demonstrated that the security level is affected to a certain degree.

In this paper, with the help of STCs [8] and WPCs [9], a ZZW-like [20] double-layered structure is designed to perform adaptive embedding during the process of MB partition. In the $1^{st}$ channel, each PM is assigned a distortion scalar considering the factors of visual quality and coding efficiency. For the purpose of introducing the minimal embedding impact with the given payload, syndrome-trellis coding is performed to determine the candidate set of MBs whose PM should be modified. Then the $2^{nd}$ channel can be built upon the coding results, and WPCs are used to embed additional messages. According to the analysis in 3.1, with the designed structure, an expected 3-bit per change gain

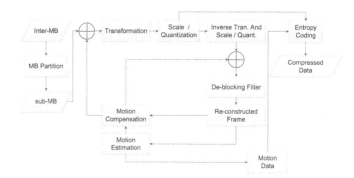

**Figure 1: Structure of inter-MB coding.**

in embedding efficiency is obtained compared to the STCs used. Moreover, by virtue of the STCs, the steganographer is free to design different distortion functions for different purposes without sharing it with the recipient. The experimental results demonstrate that, the proposed scheme can achieve satisfactory levels of coding performance and steganographic security with adequate payloads.

The rest of the paper is structured as follows. In section 2, the basic concepts of the MB partition and the problem of distortion minimization are introduced. In section 3, the perturbed MB partition technique is presented, and we give detailed description of the double-layered embedding structure together with the analysis of embedding efficiency. In section 4, comparative experiments are conducted to show the performance of our scheme with special attention paid to the security evaluation. Finally in section 5, concluding remarks are given with some future research directions.

## 2. PRELIMINARIES AND NOTATIONS

### 2.1 MB Partition and Partition Mode

Like the other state-of-art video coding standards, H.264 reduces the temporal redundancy between frames by block based inter prediction. To be more specific, Figure 1 depicts the structure according to which an inter-MB is processed. At the very beginning, the currently coded frame is divided into non-overlapping 16 × 16 (in pixels) MBs. Then each MB is further partitioned into smaller blocks. After that, motion estimation is invoked for each block, and only the calculated MV along with the difference between blocks need to be further coded, e.g., DCT, quantization, and entropy coding.

As shown in Figure 2, H.264 supports seven different block sizes in inter prediction mode. As a result, there exists a two-level hierarchy inside the MB partition and the corresponding PMs can be further divided into two levels.

*Definition 2.* (**level-1 and level-2 PMs**). After partitioning a certain MB into smaller blocks, the resultant PM is called a **level-1 PM**, if only block sizes of 16 × 16, 16 × 8 or 8 × 16 are comprised, or a **level-2 PM**, if block sizes equal to or smaller than 8 × 8 are comprised.

Figure 3 gives examples of all level-1 PMs and some level-2 PMs. It is observed that, actually, one level-2 PM is comprised of four sub-PMs corresponding to its four 8 × 8 sub-MBs, and can be denoted by $\mathbf{P} = (\mathbf{p}_1, \mathbf{p}_2, \mathbf{p}_3, \mathbf{p}_4)$.

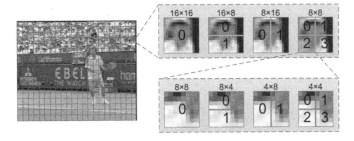

Figure 2: MB Partition.

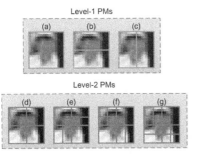

Figure 3: Examples of level-1 and level-2 PMs.

The PM decision is a trade-off between the visual quality and the coding efficiency. In this paper, we use

$$J(\mathbf{P}') = \beta SSD(\mathbf{P}') + \lambda R(\mathbf{P}') \quad (1)$$

to measure the cost of partitioning a certain MB in the form of $\mathbf{P}'$, where $SSD$ is sum of the squared differences between the original and the reconstructed MBs, $R$ reflects the number of bits associated with $\mathbf{P}'$, $\beta$ and $\lambda$ are weighting coefficients. Then a decision is made via

$$\mathbf{P} = \arg \min_{\mathbf{P}' \in \mathcal{J}} J(\mathbf{P}'), \quad (2)$$

where $\mathcal{J}$ is the set of all possible PMs.

## 2.2 Framework of Distortion Minimization

Without loss of generality, here we use a single inter-frame $\mathbb{F}$ with $n$ inter-MBs as the cover. After MB partitions, the associated PMs are recorded as

$$\mathbb{P} = Partition(\mathbb{F}) = (\mathbf{P}_1, \ldots, \mathbf{P}_n). \quad (3)$$

Since the MBs' PMs are used as the data representation, $\mathbb{F}$ can be represented by $\mathbb{P}$. With a given relative payload $\alpha$, a $\alpha n$-bit message $\mathbf{m}$ is expected to be embedded by introducing modifications to some PMs in $\mathbb{P}$, and the resultant stego frame is expressed as $\mathbb{P}' = (\mathbf{P}'_1, \ldots, \mathbf{P}'_n)$. In this paper, the modifications are assumed to be mutually independent, and let every $\mathbf{P}_i$ be assigned a scalar $\gamma_i$ expressing the distortion of replacing it with $\mathbf{P}'_i$, the overall embedding impact can be measured by the sum of per-element distortions

$$D(\mathbb{P}, \mathbb{P}') = \sum_{i=1}^{n} \gamma_i [\mathbf{P}_i \neq \mathbf{P}'_i], \quad (4)$$

here the Iverson bracket $[I]$ is defined to be 1 if the logical expression $I$ is true and 0 otherwise.

Table 1: Binary codes of sub-PMs

| sub-PM | Binary code |
| --- | --- |
| One $8 \times 8$ block | 00 |
| Two $8 \times 4$ blocks | 01 |
| Two $4 \times 8$ blocks | 10 |
| Four $4 \times 4$ blocks | 11 |

In order to achieve a minimal distortion with the given payload, a flexible coding method named STCs can be leveraged to guide the embedding process. In fact, STCs are a kind of syndrome coding with which the embedding and extraction can be formulated as

$$\text{Emb}(\mathbb{P}, \mathbf{m}) = \arg \min_{\mathcal{P}(\mathbb{P}') \in \mathcal{C}(\mathbf{m})} D(\mathbb{P}, \mathbb{P}'), \quad (5)$$

$$\text{Ext}(\mathbb{P}') = \mathbb{H}\mathcal{P}(\mathbb{P}'). \quad (6)$$

Here, $\mathcal{P} : \mathcal{J} \to \{0, 1\}$ can be any parity check function, and $\mathcal{P}(\mathbb{P}) = (\mathcal{P}(\mathbf{P}_1), \ldots, \mathcal{P}(\mathbf{P}_n))^T$. $\mathbb{H}$ is a parity-check matrix of the code $\mathcal{C}$, and $\mathcal{C}(\mathbf{m})$ is the coset corresponding to syndrome $\mathbf{m}$. In more detail, $\mathbb{H} \in \{0, 1\}^{\alpha n \times n}$ is formed from a sub-matrix $\hat{\mathbb{H}} \in \{0, 1\}^{h \times w}$, where $h$ (called the *constraint height*) is a design parameter that affects the algorithm speed and efficiency and $w$ is dictated by $\alpha$ [8].

## 3. PERTURBED MACROBLOCK PARTITION

In the proposed scheme, message embedding is implemented ultimate in the form of PM modification. We call our method perturbed macroblock partition (PMP) because during inter-frame coding the encoder (the process of MB partition) is slightly perturbed according to the coding result of the designed embedding structure.

### 3.1 The Double-layered Embedding Structure

Inspired by the ZZW construction [20], a double-layered structure is designed to offer two channels for embedding. With the $1^{st}$ channel, the STCs is used to fulfill adaptive embedding. Then with the $2^{nd}$ channel, WPCs is used to embed additional messages.

Under the designed structure, only level-2 PMs comprised of four sub-PMs are utilized. According to the mapping defined in Table 1, each sub-PM is assigned a 2-bit code, thus a level-2 PM can be expressed as an 8-bit vector. For example, the PM (e) in Figure 3 can be expressed as "00100100" and (g) "11001011".

Suppose the steganographer uses a cover $\mathbb{P}$ comprised of $n$ PMs which is written as a binary matrix of the size $n \times 8$

$$
\begin{aligned}
\mathbf{P}_1 &= & p_{1,1} & \quad p_{1,2} & \cdots & \quad p_{1,8} \\
\mathbf{P}_2 &= & p_{2,1} & \quad p_{2,2} & \cdots & \quad p_{2,8} \\
\vdots & & \vdots & \quad \vdots & \vdots \quad \vdots & \quad \vdots \\
\mathbf{P}_n &= & p_{n,1} & \quad p_{n,2} & \cdots & \quad p_{n,8},
\end{aligned} \quad (7)
$$

and the two embedding channels is constructed as follows.

$1^{st}$ **embedding channel**: A parity check function $\mathcal{P} : \mathcal{J}_2 \to \{0, 1\}$ is used to compress $\mathbb{P}$ into the $1^{st}$ channel $\mathbf{x} = (x_1, x_2, \ldots, x_n)$, where $\mathcal{P}$ is defined as

$$\mathcal{P}(\mathbf{P}) = \oplus_{i=1}^{8} p_i, \quad (8)$$

$\mathcal{J}_2$ is the set of all possible level-2 PMs and $x_i = \mathcal{P}(\mathbf{P}_i)$.

Given a relative payload $\alpha$, the constructed STCs is used to embed $\alpha n$ message bits into the $1^{st}$ channel, and the number of bits flipped is recorded as $r$.

$2^{nd}$ **embedding channel**: Take the first 7 bits from each PM, and write them as

$$
\begin{aligned}
\tilde{\mathbf{P}}_1 &= & p_{1,1} & & p_{1,2} & & ... & & p_{1,7} \\
\tilde{\mathbf{P}}_2 &= & p_{2,1} & & p_{2,2} & & ... & & p_{2,7} \\
\vdots & & \vdots & & \vdots & & \vdots & & \vdots \\
\tilde{\mathbf{P}}_n &= & p_{n,1} & & p_{n,2} & & ... & & p_{n,7}.
\end{aligned}
\tag{9}
$$

If $x_i \in \mathbf{x}$ needs to be flipped, any bit in $\mathbf{P}_i$ is allowed to be flipped. As a result, $\tilde{\mathbf{P}}_i$ can be mapped into any 3-bit vector by $\mathbb{H}_h \tilde{\mathbf{P}}_i^T$, where $\mathbb{H}_h$ is the parity check matrix of the [7, 4] Hamming code. Then a wet paper channel can be constructed as

$$
\mathbf{y} = (\tilde{\mathbf{P}}_1 \mathbb{H}_h^T, \tilde{\mathbf{P}}_2 \mathbb{H}_h^T, ..., \tilde{\mathbf{P}}_n \mathbb{H}_h^T),
\tag{10}
$$

and $3r$ additional message bits are expected to be embedded via wet paper coding [1].

With $n$ level-2 PMs, totally $\alpha n + 3r$ message bits are expected to be embedded at the cost of $r$ PM modifications, Correspondingly, the achieved embedding efficiency can be calculated as

$$
e_{\mathrm{PMP}} = \frac{\alpha n + 3r}{r} = e_{\mathrm{STCs}} + 3.
\tag{11}
$$

It is noticed that, compared to the pure STCs, an expected 3-bit per change gain is obtained.

### 3.2 Distortion Definition

Under the framework described in 2.2, with every $\mathbf{P}_i \in \mathbb{P}$ be assigned a scalar $\gamma_i$ expressing its embedding impact, the overall embedding impact can be measured by the sum of per-element distortions. Then the formulation of the scalar $\gamma_i$ has become the chief problem of the adaptive steganography designing.

Suppose that after the $1^{st}$ channel embedding, the $t^{th}$ bit $x_t$ needs to be flipped. According to (8), this can be achieved by flipping any bit within $\mathbf{P}_t$. However, the steganographer is not free to choose which bit to flip since it is determined by the wet paper and Hamming coding result. In other words, it is possible for $\mathbf{P}_t$ to be changed into any PM in the set $\mathcal{K}_t = \{\mathbf{P} | |w(\mathbf{P}_t) - w(\mathbf{P})| = 1\}$, where $w(\mathbf{P})$ is the Hamming weight of $\mathbf{P}$.

Since the PM modification is uncontrollable, the embedding impact of $\mathbf{P}_i$ should be measured by the maximum cost of replacing it with any PM in $\mathcal{K}_i$. Therefore $\gamma_i$ is defined as

$$
\gamma_i = \max\{J(\mathbf{P}_i) - J(\mathbf{P}) | \mathbf{P} \in \mathcal{K}_i\}.
\tag{12}
$$

### 3.3 Communication with Single Inter-frame

To better explain how the double-layered embedding structure is applied, this subsection gives detailed description of the communication with single inter-frame.

Suppose the steganographer has one frame $\mathbb{F}$ to be compressed in the inter-mode, and wants to communicate the message $\mathbf{m}$, then the PMP embedding process is carried out in the following 3 steps:

---

**Pre-macroblock partition**: Apply macroblock partition to $\mathbb{F}$. Meanwhile, record all the level-2 PMs $\mathbb{P} = (\mathbf{P}_1, ..., \mathbf{P}_n)$ and compute the associated distortion scales $\Gamma = (\gamma_1, ..., \gamma_n)$ using (12).

**Double-layered embedding**: Perform the double-layered embedding process to determine which PMs in $\mathbb{P}$ have to be changed and how the modifications should apply. With $\alpha$ denotes the relative payload, $\hat{\mathbb{H}}$ denotes a sub-matrix and $K$ the seed of a pseudo-random number generator, the details are given in **Algorithm 1**.

---

**Algorithm 1** Double-layered embedding with single inter-frame

**Require:** Input $\mathbb{P}$, $\Gamma$, $\alpha$, $\hat{\mathbb{H}}$, $K$ and $\mathbf{m}$
**Ensure:** Output $\mathbb{P}'$ and $r$
1: compress $\mathbb{P}$ into the $1^{st}$ channel buffer $\mathbf{x}$ using (8);
2: generate the STCs' parity check matrix $\mathbb{H}_s$ with $\alpha$ and $\hat{\mathbb{H}}$;
3: perform syndrome coding to embed $\alpha n$ message bits by modifying $\mathbf{x}$ to $\mathbf{x}'$;
4: record the number of flipped bits in $\mathbf{x}$ as $r$ and the indexes of changed positions as $(I_1, ..., I_r)$ ;
5: construct the $2^{nd}$ channel buffer $\mathbf{y}$ with $\mathbb{P}$ and $\mathbb{H}_h$ using (10);
6: generate the WPCs' parity check matrix $\mathbb{H}_w \in \{0, 1\}^{3r \times 3n}$ with the seed $K$;
7: perform wet paper coding to embed $3r$ message bits by modifying $\mathbf{y}$ to $\mathbf{y}'$;
8: **for** $i = 1$ to $r$ **do**
9:     calculate the index $j$ of the bit to be flipped in $\mathbf{P}_{I_i}$;
10:     change $\mathbf{P}_{I_i}$ into $\mathbf{P}'_{I_i}$ by flipping $p_{I_i,j}$;
11: **end for**

---

**Perturbed macroblock partition**: Perform macroblock partitions to $\mathbb{F}$ according to the modified PMs.

Then further encoding processes are continued to generate the compressed stego frame $\mathbb{F}'$. Note that before $\mathbb{F}'$ is emitted, the steganographer has to share some parameters with the intended recipient as the secret key including $\alpha$, $\hat{\mathbb{H}}$, $K$ and $r$.

As to the recipient, he will first decompress the received stego frame $\mathbb{F}'$ to get $\mathbb{P}' = (\mathbf{P}'_1, ..., \mathbf{P}'_n)$, then extract the secret messages as described in **Algorithm 2**.

---

**Algorithm 2** Extraction with single inter-frame

**Require:** Input $\mathbb{P}'$, $\alpha$, $\hat{\mathbb{H}}$, $K$, and $r$
**Ensure:** Output $\mathbf{m}$
1: compress $\mathbb{P}'$ into the $1^{st}$ channel buffer $\mathbf{x}'$ using (8);
2: generate the STCs' parity check matrix $\mathbb{H}_s$ with $\alpha$ and $\hat{\mathbb{H}}$;
3: $\mathbf{m}_1 \Leftarrow \mathbb{H}_s \mathbf{x}'^T$;
4: construct the $2^{nd}$ channel buffer $\mathbf{y}'$ with $\mathbb{P}'$ and $\mathbb{H}_h$ using (10);
5: generate the WPCs' parity check matrix $\mathbb{H}_w \in \{0, 1\}^{3r \times 3n}$ with $K$;
6: $\mathbf{m}_2 \Leftarrow \mathbb{H}_w \mathbf{y}'^T$;
7: $\mathbf{m} \Leftarrow [\mathbf{m}_1 \ \mathbf{m}_2]$

---

### 3.4 Communication with Video Sequence

One dominant advantage of video data as the cover object is its huge capacity. But for security reasons, each inter-

---

[1] For conciseness and without loss of generality, we assume that the capacity of the wet paper channel equals to its dry-spot number.

frame offers a very limited capacity. So the payloads have to be shared in practice.

In order to communicate message **m** with a relatively large size, suppose the steganographer always has sufficient covers $\mathbb{V} = (\mathbb{F}_1, \mathbb{F}_2, \ldots)$ and has shared $\alpha$, $\hat{\mathbb{H}}$ and $K$ to the recipient as the secret key. Note that in order to generate the WPCs' parity check matrix, the recipient has to be informed of the message length. As a solution to this problem, for the $i^{th}$ frame to be compressed in the inter-mode, the number of flipped bits in its $1^{st}$ channel $r_i$ is stored as a binary vector with a fixed length $l$ and embedded with message bits alternately. For example, when embedding with $\mathbb{F}_i$, $r_{i+1}$ is assessed in advance and then embedded into $\mathbb{F}_i$'s $2^{nd}$ channel with other message bits. Specific to $\mathbb{F}_1$, only a $l$-bit vector indicating $r_2$ is embedded into its $2^{nd}$ channel without any message bits.

## 4. PERFORMANCE EXPERIMENTS

### 4.1 Experiment Setup

Our experimental environment is based on the H.264/AVC reference encoder software JM 18.5, created by the joint video team (JVT). The baseline profile is used in compression which supports only I and P frames. To implement the PMP scheme, with the relative payload $\alpha$ set to $1/2$ and constraint height $h$ set to 7, a good STCs listed in [7] is used to perform the $1^{st}$ channel embedding. Besides, Yang *et al.*'s method is also implemented for comparison. As shown in Figure 4, 14 standard CIF sequences in the 4:2:0 YUV format are selected for tests. The frame size varies from 90 to 376 at the frame rate of 30 frame per second. All sequences are compressed by the standard encoder (referred to as STD) to produce the class of clean videos. On the other hand, for Yang's method and PMP, all sequences are subjected to compression with random messages embedded to create the class of stego videos, and the achieved embedding strength vary from 80 to 200 bits per inter-frame.

### 4.2 Impacts on Coding Performance

The embedding impacts on coding performance is evaluated from two aspects, i.e., the visual quality and compression efficiency, which are measured by PSNR and the average bit-rate respectively. Corresponding results are recorded in Table 2. What's more, we take a closer look at one specific sequence "stefan.yuv" and plot the dynamic changes in PSNR and the percentage of bit-rate increase compared to the STD along frames in Figure 5 and Figure 6. It is observed that, both Yang's and our PMP scheme affect the visual quality very slightly, and PMP outperforms its competitor for it introduces less bit-rate increases.

### 4.3 Embedding Efficiency

With PMP, as discussed in 3.1, an expected 3-bit per change gain in embedding efficiency is obtained compared to the pure STCs.

With Yang's method, the encoder is forced to partition a sub-MB choose a particular sub-PM according to the 2-bit to be embedded. Since each sub-PMs has a 1 in 4 chance of not being changed, the corresponding embedding efficiency can be calculated as

$$e_{\text{Yang's}} = \frac{2}{1/4 \times 0 + 3/4 \times 1} = \frac{8}{3}. \quad (13)$$

Table 2: Test results. (SN (Sequence Name), FN (Frame Number), EM (Embedding Method), SP (Secret Payload (kbit)), PSNR (dB), BR (Bit-Rate (kbit/s)), EE (Embedding Efficiency)).

| SN | FN | EM | SP | PSNR | BR | EE |
|---|---|---|---|---|---|---|
| stefan | 90 | STD | N/A | 36.684 | 1415.47 | N/A |
| | | Yang's | 14.42 | 36.713 | 1441.87 | 2.67 |
| | | PMP | 14.42 | 36.684 | 1420.38 | 5.96 |
| foreman | 300 | STD | N/A | 37.166 | 532.08 | N/A |
| | | Yang's | 24.71 | 37.169 | 541.07 | 2.67 |
| | | PMP | 24.71 | 37.165 | 535.73 | 6.14 |
| city | 300 | STD | N/A | 35.795 | 477.26 | N/A |
| | | Yang's | 23.90 | 35.809 | 485.27 | 2.67 |
| | | PMP | 23.90 | 35.800 | 478.75 | 5.97 |
| bus | 150 | STD | N/A | 35.980 | 1443.11 | N/A |
| | | Yang's | 24.87 | 35.985 | 1460.57 | 2.67 |
| | | PMP | 24.87 | 35.977 | 1447.25 | 5.92 |
| crew | 300 | STD | N/A | 38.066 | 1105.52 | N/A |
| | | Yang's | 44.37 | 38.071 | 1123.10 | 2.67 |
| | | PMP | 44.37 | 38.068 | 1112.09 | 6.28 |
| coastguard | 300 | STD | N/A | 35.694 | 1338.14 | N/A |
| | | Yang's | 43.94 | 35.700 | 1352.65 | 2.67 |
| | | PMP | 43.94 | 35.693 | 1343.35 | 6.19 |
| ice | 240 | STD | N/A | 40.734 | 440.66 | N/A |
| | | Yang's | 21.01 | 40.747 | 450.98 | 2.67 |
| | | PMP | 21.01 | 40.737 | 443.67 | 5.92 |
| football | 260 | STD | N/A | 37.155 | 1715.63 | N/A |
| | | Yang's | 42.74 | 37.163 | 1734.74 | 2.67 |
| | | PMP | 42.74 | 37.160 | 1723.93 | 6.10 |
| soccer | 300 | STD | N/A | 36.835 | 816.81 | N/A |
| | | Yang's | 30.83 | 36.848 | 829.31 | 2.67 |
| | | PMP | 30.83 | 36.840 | 821.94 | 6.03 |
| harbour | 300 | STD | N/A | 35.515 | 1747.95 | N/A |
| | | Yang's | 62.20 | 35.509 | 1765.33 | 2.67 |
| | | PMP | 62.20 | 35.511 | 1751.91 | 6.11 |
| tempete | 260 | STD | N/A | 36.063 | 1502.69 | N/A |
| | | Yang's | 50.01 | 36.068 | 1518.96 | 2.67 |
| | | PMP | 50.01 | 36.061 | 1506.37 | 6.14 |
| walk | 376 | STD | N/A | 38.614 | 1074.30 | N/A |
| | | Yang's | 47.36 | 38.620 | 1090.28 | 2.67 |
| | | PMP | 47.36 | 38.610 | 1078.33 | 6.10 |
| flower | 250 | STD | N/A | 36.051 | 1947.45 | N/A |
| | | Yang's | 45.24 | 36.049 | 1964.67 | 2.67 |
| | | PMP | 45.24 | 36.053 | 1952.32 | 6.06 |
| mobile | 300 | STD | N/A | 35.227 | 1919.92 | N/A |
| | | Yang's | 59.93 | 35.243 | 1938.90 | 2.67 |
| | | PMP | 59.93 | 35.235 | 1925.34 | 6.06 |

Figure 4: Sequences used.

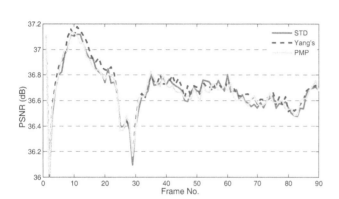

Figure 5: Dynamic changes in PSNR.

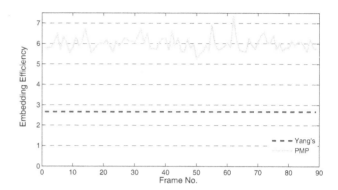

Figure 7: Dynamic changes in embedding efficiency.

After embedding with different sequences, the achieved average embedding efficiencies are recorded in Table 2, and the dynamic changes along frames of "stefan.yuv" are plotted in Figure 7.

## 4.4 Steganalysis

### 4.4.1 Steganalytic Features

To the best of our knowledge, no effective steganalysis against PM-based schemes is proposed so far. In order to test the steganographic security of the PM-based schemes, the idea of "video calibration" is adopted to design a targeted steganalytic feature set. For those MV-based schemes, it is proved that the modified MVs have the inclination to revert during recompression [2]. Analogically, we wonder whether the PMs have such inclination which can be used to reveal the fact of embedding. To test this idea, a 20-d feature vector is designed as follows:

Considering only sub-PMs are indeed modified, we pay attention to the changes in sub-PMs before and after recompression. According to Table 1, we define 4 states corresponding to the 4 different sub-PMs, i.e., $s_0$, $s_1$, $s_2$ and $s_3$. Note that, it is also possible that recompression turns some level-2 PMs into level-1 ones, so a state $s_4$ is defined to cover any other states. We write an imperfect transition probability matrix $\mathbb{M}$ to describe the state transitions before and after recompression as

$$
\begin{matrix}
Pr(0,0) & Pr(0,1) & Pr(0,2) & Pr(0,3) & Pr(0,4) \\
Pr(1,0) & Pr(1,1) & Pr(1,2) & Pr(1,3) & Pr(1,4) \\
Pr(2,0) & Pr(2,1) & Pr(2,2) & Pr(2,3) & Pr(2,4) \\
Pr(3,0) & Pr(3,1) & Pr(3,2) & Pr(3,3) & Pr(3,4)
\end{matrix} \tag{14}
$$

where $Pr(i,j)$ denotes the probability of $s_i$ to $s_j$ state transition, and compose all the elements in $\mathbb{M}$ into a 20-d fea-

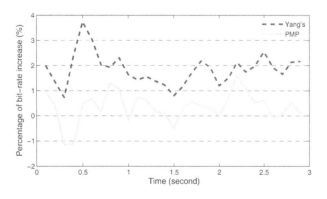

Figure 6: Dynamic changes in percentage of bit-rate increase.

**Table 3: Steganalysis Results (%).**

| | STMB | | MVRB | |
|---|---|---|---|---|
| | TN | TP | TN | TP |
| Yang's | 61.0 | 72.0 | 50.2 | 53.7 |
| PMP | 40.5 | 76.0 | 52.3 | 53.1 |

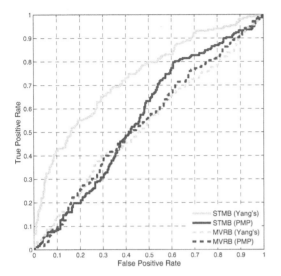

**Figure 8: ROC curves of the used steganalyzers.**

ture vector for steganalysis. The obtained features are then named STMB (state transition matrix-based) features.

In addition, Cao *et al*'s MVRB (motion vector reversion-based) features [2] are also leveraged to test whether detectable changes in MV domain are introduced.

### 4.4.2 Training and Classification

In our steganalysis, 9 pairs of compressed sequences (clean and stego) are randomly selected for training purposes, and the remaining 5 are left for testing. A fixed 8-frame sliding window is used to scan each sequence without overlapping, and the steganalytic features are extracted from the frames within the window. The classifier is implemented using Chang's support vector machine (SVM) [5] with the polynomial kernel.

### 4.4.3 Steganalytic Results

The true negative (TN) rates, true positive (TP) rates are computed by counting the number of detections in the test sets. The performances of the steganalyzers with two feature sets are tested, and results are recorded in Table 3. Besides, the detector receiver operating characteristic (ROC) curves of the two steganalyzers are plotted in Figure 8.

It is observed that with the considered embedding strength, the MVRB features cannot reliably detect the PM-based schemes, and PMP outperforms its competitor when attacked by the targeted steganalyzer with STMB features. We can infer that, arbitrary and sequential PM modifications may cause serious deviations from the optimal coding results, which may facilitate targeted attacks.

## 5. CONCLUSIONS AND FUTURE WORK

This paper presents a video steganography tightly combined with H.264 compression. A novel data representation called PM is defined and utilized to convey secret messages. To perform data hiding, optimized perturbations are introduced to the process of MB partition under a high efficient double-layered structure. Experimental results show that, satisfactory levels of coding performance and security are achieved with adequate payloads.

In the near future, the PMP scheme would be further optimized by testing on different distortion functions and embedding structures. Meanwhile, attempts of further steganalysis are to be carried out under more complicated steganalytic models to ensure security.

## 6. ACKNOWLEDGMENTS

The work on this paper was supported by the NSF of China under 61303259, 61170281 and 61303254, the Strategic Priority Research Program of the Chinese Academy of Sciences under XDA06030600, and the IIE's Research Project on Cryptography under Y3Z0012102.

## 7. REFERENCES

[1] H. Aly. Data hiding in motion vectors of compressed video based on their associated prediction error. *IEEE Transactions on Information Forensics and Security*, 6(1):14–18, 2011.

[2] Y. Cao, X. Zhao, and D. Feng. Video steganalysis exploiting motion vector reversion-based features. *IEEE Signal Processing Letters*, 19(1):35–38, 2012.

[3] Y. Cao, X. Zhao, D. Feng, and R. Sheng. Video steganography with perturbed motion estimation. In *Proc. 13th Information Hiding Conf.*, volume 6958 of *Lecture Notes in Computer Science*, pages 193–207, 2011.

[4] Y. Cao, X. Zhao, F. Li, and N. Yu. Video steganography with multi-path motion estimation. In *Proc. SPIE, Media Watermarking, Security, and Forensics*, volume 8665, pages 86650K–86650K–6, 2013.

[5] C. Chang and C. Lin. Libsvm – a library for support vector machines, 2013.

[6] I. Cox, M. Miller, J. Bloom, J. Fridrich, and T. Kalker. *Digital Watermarking and Steganography, 2nd ed.* Morgan Kaufmann Publishers Inc., San Francisco, CA, USA, 2008.

[7] T. Filler, J. Judas, and J. Fridrich. Minimizing embedding impact in steganography using trellis-coded quantization. In *Proceedings SPIE, Electronic Imaging, Security and Forensics of Multimedia XII*, volume 7541, pages 1–14, 2010.

[8] T. Filler, J. Judas, and J. Fridrich. Minimizing additive distortion in steganography using syndrome-trellis codes. *Information Forensics and Security, IEEE Transactions on*, 6(3):920–935, 2011.

[9] J. Fridrich, M. Goljan, and D. Soukal. Perturbed quantization steganography with wet paper codes. In *Proceedings of the 2004 workshop on Multimedia & security*, MM&Sec'04, pages 4–15, 2004.

[10] Y. Guo and F. Pan. Information hiding for h.264 in video stream switching application. In *Proc. IEEE Int. Conference on Inform. Theory and Inform. Security*, pages 419–421, 2010.

[11] B. Hao, L. Zhao, and W. Zhong. A novel steganography algorithm based on motion vector and matrix encoding. In *Proc. IEEE 3rd International Conference on ICCSN*, pages 406–409, 2011.

[12] ISO. *Information technology-Coding of moving pictures and associated audio for digital storage media at up to about 1,5 Mbit/s-Part 1:System*. Int. Organization for Standardization, Geneva, Switzerland, 1993.

[13] S. Kapotas and A. Skodras. A new data hiding scheme for scene change detection in h.264 encoded video sequences. In *Multimedia and Expo, 2008 IEEE International Conference on*, pages 277–280, 2008.

[14] Y. Su, C. Zhang, and C. Zhang. A video steganalytic algorithm against motion-vector-based steganography. *Signal Process.*, 91(8):1901–1909, 2011.

[15] Y. Tew and K. Wong. An overview of information hiding in h.264/avc compressed video. *IEEE Trans. Circuits Syst. Video Technol.*, 2013.

[16] T. Wiegand, G. J. Sullivan, G. Bjontegaard, and A. Luthra. Overview of the h.264/avc video coding standard. *IEEE Trans. Circuits Syst. Video Technol.*, 13(7):560–576, Jul. 2003.

[17] X. Xu, J. Dong, W. Wang, and T. Tan. Video steganalysis based on the constraints of motion vectors. In *Proc. IEEE International Conference on Image Processing*, 2013.

[18] X. Yang, L. Zhao, and K. Niu. An efficient video steganography algorithm based on sub-macroblock partition for h.264/avc. *Advanced Materials Research*, pages 5384–5389, 2012.

[19] C. Zhang, Y. Su, and C. Zhang. A new video steganalysis algorithm against motion vector steganography. In *Proc. 4th International Conference on Wireless Communications, Networking and Mobile Computing*, pages 1–4, 2008.

[20] W. Zhang, X. Zhang, and S. Wang. Maximizing steganographic embedding efficiency by combining hamming codes and wet paper codes. In *Proc. 10th Information Hiding Conf.*, volume 5284 of *Lecture Notes in Computer Science*, pages 60–71, 2008.

# Capacities and Capacity-Achieving Decoders for Various Fingerprinting Games

Thijs Laarhoven
Eindhoven University of Technology
P.O. Box 513, 5600 MB
Eindhoven, The Netherlands
mail@thijs.com

## ABSTRACT

Combining an information-theoretic approach to fingerprinting with a more constructive, statistical approach, we derive new results on the fingerprinting capacities for various informed settings, as well as new log-likelihood decoders with provable code lengths that asymptotically match these capacities. The simple decoder built against the interleaving attack is further shown to achieve the simple capacity for unknown attacks, and is argued to be an improved version of the recently proposed decoder of Oosterwijk et al. With this new universal decoder, cut-offs on the bias distribution function can finally be dismissed.

Besides the application of these results to fingerprinting, a direct consequence of our results to group testing is that (i) a simple decoder asymptotically requires a factor 1.44 more tests to find defectives than a joint decoder, and (ii) the simple decoder presented in this paper provably achieves this bound.

## Categories and Subject Descriptors

E.4 [**Data**]: Coding and Information Theory;
G.3 [**Math. of Computing**]: Probability and Statistics

## General Terms

Design, Security, Theory

## Keywords

Fingerprinting, traitor tracing, collusion-resistance, information theory, log-likelihood ratios, group testing.

## 1. INTRODUCTION

To protect copyrighted content against unauthorized redistribution, distributors may embed watermarks or fingerprints in the content, uniquely linking copies to individual users. Then, if an illegal copy of the content is found, the distributor can extract the watermark from the copy and com-

*IH&MMSec'14*, June 11–13, 2014, Salzburg, Austria.
Copyright 2014 ACM 978-1-4503-2647-6/14/06 ...$15.00.
http://dx.doi.org/10.1145/2600918.2600925.

pare it to the database of watermarks, to determine which user was responsible.

To combat this solution, pirates may try to form a coalition of several colluders, each owning a differently watermarked copy of the content, and perform a collusion attack. By comparing their different versions of the content, they will detect differences in their copies which must be part of the watermark. They can then create a new pirate copy, where the resulting watermark matches the watermark of different pirates in different segments of the content, making it hard for the distributor to find the responsible users. Fortunately, under the assumption that if the pirates don't detect any differences (because they all received the same version) they output this watermark (known in the literature as the Boneh-Shaw marking assumption [5]), it is still possible to find all colluders using suitable fingerprinting codes.

### 1.1 Model

The above fingerprinting game is often modeled as the following two-person game between the distributor $\mathcal{D}$ and the coalition of pirates $\mathcal{C}$. The set of colluders is assumed to be a random subset of size $|\mathcal{C}| = c$ from the complete set of $n$ users $\mathcal{U}$, and the identities of these colluders are unknown to the distributor. The aim of the game for the distributor is ultimately to discover the identities of the colluders, while the colluders want to stay hidden. The game consists of the following three phases: (i) the distributor uses an *encoder* to generate the fingerprints; (ii) the colluders employ a *collusion channel* to generate the pirate output, and (iii) the distributor uses a *decoder* to map the pirate output to a set of accused users.

#### Encoder.

First, the distributor generates a fingerprinting code $\mathcal{X}$, consisting of $n$ code words $\boldsymbol{X}_1, \ldots, \boldsymbol{X}_n$ from $\{0,1\}^{\ell}$.[1] The $i$th entry of code word $j$ indicates which version of the content is assigned to user $j$ in the $i$th segment. The parameter $\ell$ is referred to as the code length, and the distributor would like $\ell$ to be as small as possible.

A common restriction on the encoding process is to assume that $\mathcal{X}$ is created by first generating a probability vector $\boldsymbol{P} \in [0,1]^{\ell}$ by choosing each entry $P_i$ independently from a certain distribution function $F$, and then generating $\mathcal{X}$ according to $\mathbb{P}(X_{j,i} = 1) = P_i$. This guarantees that watermarks of different users $j$ are independent, and that wa-

---

[1]More generally $\mathcal{X}$ is a code with code words of length $\ell$ from an alphabet $\mathcal{Q}$ of size $q \geq 2$, but in this paper we restrict our attention to the binary case $q = 2$.

termarks in different positions $i$ are independent. Schemes that satisfy this assumption are sometimes called *bias-based schemes*, and the encoders discussed in this paper also belong to this category.

### Collusion channel.

After generating $\mathcal{X}$, the entries are used to select and embed watermarks in the content, and the content is sent out to all users. The colluders then get together, compare their copies, and use a certain collusion channel or pirate attack $\boldsymbol{\theta}$ to select the pirate output $\boldsymbol{Y} \in \{0, 1\}^{\ell}$. If the pirate attack behaves symmetrically both in the colluders and in the positions $i$, then the collusion channel can be modeled by a vector $\boldsymbol{\theta} \in [0, 1]^{c+1}$, consisting of entries $\theta_z = f_{Y|Z}(1|z)$ indicating the probability of outputting a 1 when the pirates received $z$ ones and $c - z$ zeroes. Some common attacks $\boldsymbol{\theta}$ are described in Section 2.3.

### Decoder.

Finally, after the pirate output has been generated and distributed, we assume that the distributor intercepts it and applies a decoding algorithm to the pirate output $\boldsymbol{Y}$, the code $\mathcal{X}$ and the (secret) bias vector $\boldsymbol{P}$ to compute a set $\mathcal{C}' \subseteq \mathcal{U}$ of accused users. This is commonly done by assigning *scores* to users, and accusing those users whose score exceeds some predefined threshold $\eta$. The distributor wins the game if $\mathcal{C}'$ is non-empty and contains only colluders (i.e. $\emptyset \neq \mathcal{C}' \subseteq \mathcal{C}$) and loses if this is not the case, which could be because an innocent user $j \notin \mathcal{C}$ is falsely accused (a false positive error), or because no guilty users are accused (a false negative error). We often write $\varepsilon_1$ and $\varepsilon_2$ for upper bounds on the false positive and false negative probabilities respectively.

## 1.2 Related work

Work on the above bias-based fingerprinting game started in 2003, when Tardos proved that any fingerprinting scheme must satisfy $\ell \propto c^2 \ln n$, and that a bias-based scheme is able to achieve this optimal scaling in $\ell$ [38]. He proved the latter by providing a simple and explicit construction with a code length of $\ell = 100c^2 \ln(n/\varepsilon_1)$, which is known in the literature as the Tardos scheme.

### Improved constructions.

Later work on the constructive side of fingerprinting focused on improving upon Tardos' result by sharpening the bounds [3, 35], optimizing the distribution functions [27], improving the score function [36], tightening the bounds again with this improved score function [18, 22, 28, 34, 36, 37], optimizing the score function [29], and again tightening the bounds with this optimized score function [16, 30] to finally end up with a sufficient asymptotic code length of $\ell \sim 2c^2 \ln n$ for large $n$. This construction can be extended to larger alphabets, in which case the code length scales as $\ell \sim 2c^2 \ln(n)/(q-1)$. Other work on practical constructions focused on joint decoders, which are computationally more involved but may work with shorter codes [24, 25, 31], and side-informed fingerprinting games [7, 10, 21, 29], where estimating the collusion channel $\boldsymbol{\theta}$ was considered to get an improved performance.

Recently Abbe and Zheng [1] showed that, in the context of fingerprinting [24], if the set of allowed collusion channels satisfies a certain one-sidedness condition, then a decoder that achieves capacity against the information-theoretic worst-case attack is a universal decoder achieving capacity against arbitrary attacks. The main drawback of using this result is that the worst-case attack is hard to compute, but this does lead to more insight why e.g. Oosterwijk et al. [30] obtained a universal decoder by considering the decoder against the 'interleaving attack', which is known to be the asymptotic worst-case attack.

### Fingerprinting capacities.

At the same time, work was also done on establishing bounds on the fingerprinting capacity $C$, which translate to lower bounds on the required asymptotic code length $\ell$ through $\ell \gtrsim C^{-1} \log_2 n$ for large $n$. For the binary case Huang and Moulin [11, 12, 13, 14, 25] and Amiri and Tardos [2] independently derived asymptotics for the fingerprinting capacity for arbitrary attacks as $C \sim (2c^2 \ln 2)^{-1}$, corresponding to a minimum code length of $\ell \sim 2c^2 \ln n$. Huang and Moulin [14] further showed that to achieve this bound, an encoder should use the arcsine distribution $F^*$ for generating biases $p$:

$$F^*(p) = \frac{2}{\pi} \arcsin \sqrt{p}. \qquad (0 < p < 1) \qquad (1)$$

These capacity-results were later generalized to the $q$-ary setting [4, 15] showing that a $q$-ary code length of $\ell \sim 2c^2 \ln(n)/(q-1)$ is asymptotically optimal.

### Dynamic fingerprinting.

There has also been some interest in a variant of the above fingerprinting game where several rounds of the two-player game between the distributor and the coalition are played sequentially. This allows the distributor to adjust the encoding and decoding steps of the next rounds to the knowledge obtained from previous rounds. Many of the bias-based constructions can also be used effectively in this dynamic setting [17, 20, 21] with equivalent asymptotics for the required code length, but allowing the distributor to trace all colluders even if the collusion channel is not symmetric in the colluders, and leading to significantly smaller first order terms than in the 'static' setting. These bias-based dynamic schemes may even be able to compete with the celebrated scheme of Fiat and Tassa [9].

### Group testing.

Finally, a different area of research closely related to fingerprinting is that of group testing, where the set of $n$ users corresponds to a set of $n$ items, the set of $c$ colluders corresponds to a subset of $c$ defective items, and where the aim of the distributor is to find all defective items by performing group tests. This game corresponds to a special case of the fingerprinting game, where the pirate attack is fixed in advance (and possibly known to the distributor) to (a variant of) the 'all-1 attack'. In this game it is significantly easier to find all pirates/defectives; it is known that a joint decoder asymptotically requires only $\ell \sim c \log_2 n$ tests [33], while simple decoders exist requiring as few as $\ell \sim ec \ln n$ tests to find all defectives [6]. Recent work has shown that applying results from fingerprinting to group testing may lead to improved results compared to what is known in the group testing literature [19, 23].

**Table 1:** Asymptotics for tight lower bounds on $L = \ell / \ln n \cong C^{-1} / \ln 2$, based on the simple and joint capacities, with different amounts of side information (see Section 2.2). The proposed simple decoders are shown to match these bounds, and we conjecture that the proposed joint decoders are also asymptotically optimal.

|  | Fully informed | | Partially informed | |
| --- | --- | --- | --- | --- |
|  | Simple | Joint | Simple | Joint |
| Interleaving atk. | $2c^2$ | $2c^2$ | $2c^2$ | $2c^2$ |
| All-1 attack | $2.08c$ | $1.44c$ | $1.83c\sqrt{c}$ | $1.32c\sqrt{c}$ |
| Majority voting | $3.14c$ | $1.44c$ | $2.41c\sqrt{c}$ | $1.20c\sqrt{c}$ |
| Minority voting | $2.08c$ | $1.44c$ | $0.66c\sqrt{c}$ | $0.43c\sqrt{c}$ |
| Coin-flip attack | $8.33c$ | $4.48c$ | $5.18c\sqrt{c}$ | $2.32c\sqrt{c}$ |

## 1.3 Contributions

In this work we first extend the work of Huang and Moulin [14] by deriving explicit asymptotics for the simple and joint capacities of various fingerprinting games with different amounts of side-information. Table 1 summarizes tight lower bounds on the code length constant for various informed settings obtained via the capacities. These asymptotics can be seen as our 'targets' for the second part of this paper, which describes decoders with provable bounds on $\ell$ and $\eta$ that asymptotically achieve these capacities. In fact, if the collusion channel that the decoder was built against matches the attack used by the pirates, then the proof that the resulting simple decoders achieve capacity is remarkably simple and holds for arbitrary attacks.

*Capacity-achieving simple decoding without cut-offs.*

Similar to Oosterwijk et al. [29, 30], who studied the decoder built against the interleaving attack because that attack is in a sense optimal, we then turn our attention to the simple decoder designed against the interleaving attack, and argue that it is an improved version of Oosterwijk et al.'s universal decoder. To provide a sneak preview of this result, the new score function is the following:

$$g(x, y, p) = \begin{cases} \ln\left(1 + \frac{p}{c(1-p)}\right) & x = y = 0 \\ \ln\left(1 - \frac{1}{c}\right) & x \neq y \\ \ln\left(1 + \frac{1-p}{cp}\right) & x = y = 1 \end{cases} \quad (2)$$

This decoder is shown to achieve the uninformed simple capacity, and we argue that with this decoder (i) the Gaussian assumption always holds (and convergence to the normal distribution is much faster), and (ii) no cut-offs on the bias distribution function $F$ are ever needed anymore.

*Joint log-likelihood decoders.*

Since it is not hard to extend the definition of the simple decoder to joint decoding, we also present and analyze joint log-likelihood decoders. Analyzing these joint decoders turns out to be somewhat harder due to the 'mixed tuples', but we give some motivation why these decoders seem to work well. We also conjecture that the joint decoder tailored against the interleaving attack achieves the joint uninformed capacity, but proving this result is left for future work.

*Applications to group testing.*

Since the all-1 attack in fingerprinting is equivalent to a problem known in the literature as group testing [21, 23], some of our results can also be applied to this area. In fact, we derive two new results in the area of group testing: (i) any simple-decoder group testing algorithm requires at least $\ell \sim \log_2(e)^2 c \ln n \approx 2.08c \ln n$ group tests to find $c$ defective items hidden among $n$ items, and (ii) the decoder discussed in Section 4.1 provably achieves this optimal scaling in $\ell$. This decoder was previously considered in [23], but no provable bounds on the (asymptotic) code lengths were given there.

## 1.4 Outline

The outline of the paper is as follows. Section 2 first describes the various different models we consider in this paper, and provides a roadmap for Sections 3 and 4. Section 3 discusses capacity results for each of these models, while Section 4 discusses decoders which aim to match the lower bounds on $\ell$ obtained in Section 3. Finally, in Section 5 we conclude with a brief discussion of the most important results and remaining open problems.

## 2. DIFFERENT MODELS

Let us first describe how the results in Sections 3 and 4 are structured according to different assumptions, leading to different models. Besides the general assumptions on the model discussed in the introduction, we further make a distinction between models based on (1) the computational complexity of the decoder, (2) the information about $\boldsymbol{\theta}$ known to the distributor, and (3) the collusion channel used by the pirates. These are discussed in Sections 2.1, 2.2 and 2.3 respectively.

### 2.1 Decoding complexity

Commonly two types of decoders are considered, which use different amounts of information to decide whether a user should be accused or not.

1. **Simple decoding**: To quote Moulin [25, Section 4.3]: *"The receiver makes an innocent/guilty decision on each user independently of the other users, and there lies the simplicity but also the suboptimality of this decoder."* In other words, the decision to accuse user $j$ depends only on the $j$th code word of $\mathcal{X}$, and not on other code words from $\mathcal{X}$.

2. **Joint decoding**: In this case, the decoder is allowed to base the decision whether to accuse a user on the entire code $\mathcal{X}$. Such decoders may be able to obtain smaller code lengths than possible with the best simple decoders.

Using more information generally causes the time complexity of the decoding step to go up, so usually there is a trade-off between a shorter code length and a faster decoding algorithm.

### 2.2 Side-informed distributors

We consider three different scenarios with respect to the knowledge of the distributor about the collusion channel $\boldsymbol{\theta}$. Depending on the application, different scenarios may apply.

1. **Fully informed**: Even before $\mathcal{X}$ is generated, the distributor already knows exactly what the pirate attack

$\boldsymbol{\theta}$ will be. This information can thus be used to optimize both the encoding and decoding phases. This scenario applies to various group testing models, and may apply to dynamic traitor tracing, where after several rounds the distributor may have estimated the pirate strategy.

2. **Partially informed**: The tracer does not know in advance what collusion channel will be used, so the encoding is aimed at arbitrary attacks. However, after obtaining the pirate output $\boldsymbol{y}$, the distributor does learn more about $\boldsymbol{\theta}$ before running an accusation algorithm, e.g. by estimating the attack based on the available data. So the encoding is uninformed, but we assume that the decoder is informed and knows $\boldsymbol{\theta}$. Since the asymptotically optimal bias distribution function $F$ in fingerprinting is known to be the arcsine distribution $F^*$, we will assume that $F^*$ is used for generating biases. This scenario is similar to EM decoding [7, 10].

3. **Uninformed**: In this case, both the encoding and decoding phases are assumed to be done without prior knowledge about $\boldsymbol{\theta}$, so also the decoder should be designed to work against arbitrary attacks. This is the most commonly studied fingerprinting game.

For simplicity of the analysis, in the partially informed setting we assume that the estimation of the collusion channel is precise, so that $\boldsymbol{\theta}$ is known exactly to the decoder. This assumption may not be realistic, but at least we can then obtain explicit expressions for the capacities, and get an idea of how much estimating the strategy may help in reducing the code length. This also allows us to derive explicit lower bounds on $\ell$: even if somehow the attack can be estimated correctly, then the corresponding capacities tell us that we will still need at least a certain number of symbols to find the pirates.

## 2.3 Common collusion channels

As mentioned in the introduction, we assume that collusion channels satisfy the marking assumption, which means that $\theta_0 = 0$ and $\theta_c = 1$. For the remaining values of $z \in \{1, \ldots, c-1\}$ the pirates are free to choose how often they want to output a 1 when they receive $z$ ones. Some commonly considered attacks are listed below.

1. **Interleaving attack**: The coalition randomly selects one of its members and outputs his symbol. This corresponds to $(\boldsymbol{\theta}_{\text{int}})_z = z/c$. This attack is known to be asymptotically optimal (from the point of view of the colluders) in the uninformed max-min fingerprinting game [14].

2. **All-1 attack**: The pirates output a 1 whenever they can, i.e., whenever they have at least one 1. This translates to $(\boldsymbol{\theta}_{\text{all1}})_z = 1\{z > 0\}$. This attack is of particular interest due to its relation with group testing.

3. **Majority voting**: The colluders output the most common symbol among their received symbols. This means that $(\boldsymbol{\theta}_{\text{maj}})_z = 1\{z > c/2\}$.

4. **Minority voting**: The traitors output the symbol which they received the least often (but received at least once). For $1 \leq z \leq c-1$, this corresponds to $(\boldsymbol{\theta}_{\text{min}})_z = 1\{z < c/2\}$.

5. **Coin-flip attack**: If the pirates receive both symbols, they flip a fair coin to decide which symbol to output. So for $1 \leq z \leq c-1$, this corresponds to $(\boldsymbol{\theta}_{\text{coin}})_z = \frac{1}{2}$.

For even $c$, defining $\theta_{c/2}$ in a consistent way for majority and minority voting is not straightforward. For simplicity, in the analysis of these two attacks we will therefore assume that $c$ is odd. Note that in the uninformed setting, we do not distinguish between different collusion channels; the encoder and decoder should then work against arbitrary attacks.

## 2.4 Roadmap

The upcoming two sections about capacities (Section 3) and decoders (Section 4) are structured according to the above classification, where first the decoding complexity is chosen, then the side-information is fixed, and finally different attacks are considered. For instance, to find the joint capacity in the fully informed game one has to go to Section 3.2.1, while the new simple uninformed decoder can be found in Section 4.1.3.

## 3. CAPACITIES

In this section we establish lower bounds on the code length of any valid decoder, by inspecting the information-theoretic capacities of the various fingerprinting games. We will use some common definitions from information theory, such as the binary entropy function $h(x) = -x \log_2 x - (1 - x) \log_2(1 - x)$, the relative entropy or Kullback-Leibler divergence $d(x \| y) = x \log_2(x/y) + (1 - x) \log_2((1 - x)/(1 - y))$, and the mutual information $I(X; Y) = \sum_{x,y} \mathbb{P}(x, y) \log_2(\mathbb{P}(x, y)/\mathbb{P}(x)\mathbb{P}(y))$. The results in this section build further upon previous work on this topic by Huang and Moulin [14].

## 3.1 Simple capacities

For simple decoders, we assume that the decision whether to accuse user $j$ is based solely on $\boldsymbol{X}_j$, $\boldsymbol{Y}$ and $\boldsymbol{P}$. Focusing on a single position, and denoting the random variables corresponding to a colluder's symbol, the pirate output, and the bias in this position by $X_1$, $Y$ and $P$, the interesting quantity to look at [11] is the mutual information $I(X_1; Y | P = p)$. This quantity depends on the pirate strategy $\boldsymbol{\theta}$ and on the bias $p$. To study this mutual information we will use the following equality [14, Equation (61)],

$$I(X_1; Y | P = p) = p\,d(a_1 \| a) + (1 - p)\,d(a_0 \| a), \quad (3)$$

where $a, a_0, a_1$ are defined as

$$a = \sum_{z=0}^{c} \binom{c}{z} p^z (1 - p)^{c-z} \theta_z, \quad (4)$$

$$a_0 = \sum_{z=0}^{c-1} \binom{c-1}{z} p^z (1 - p)^{c-z-1} \theta_z, \quad (5)$$

$$a_1 = \sum_{z=1}^{c} \binom{c-1}{z-1} p^{z-1} (1 - p)^{c-z} \theta_z. \quad (6)$$

Note that given $p$ and $\boldsymbol{\theta}$, the above formulas allow us to compute the associated mutual information explicitly.

### 3.1.1 Fully informed

In the fully informed setting we are free to choose $F$ to maximize the capacity, given a collusion channel $\boldsymbol{\theta}$. When the attack is known to the distributor in advance, there is no reason to use different values of $p$; the distributor should always use the value of $p$ that maximizes the mutual information payoff $I(X_1; Y | P = p)$. Given an attack strategy $\boldsymbol{\theta}$, the capacity we are interested in is thus

$$C^s(\boldsymbol{\theta}) = \max_p I(X_1; Y | P = p). \tag{7}$$

For general attacks finding the optimal value of $p$ analytically can be hard, but for certain specific attacks we can investigate the resulting expressions individually to find the optimal values of $p$ that maximize the mutual information. This leads to the following results for the five attacks listed in Section 2.3. Proofs will appear in the full version.

THEOREM 1. *The simple informed capacities and the corresponding optimal values of $p$ for the five attacks of Section 2.3 are:*

$$C^s(\boldsymbol{\theta}_{int}) \sim \frac{1}{2c^2 \ln 2}, \qquad p_{int}^s = \frac{1}{2}, \tag{S1}$$

$$C^s(\boldsymbol{\theta}_{all1}) \sim \frac{\ln 2}{c}, \qquad p_{all1}^s \sim \frac{\ln 2}{c}, \tag{S2}$$

$$C^s(\boldsymbol{\theta}_{maj}) \sim \frac{1}{\pi c \ln 2}, \qquad p_{maj}^s = \frac{1}{2}, \tag{S3}$$

$$C^s(\boldsymbol{\theta}_{min}) \sim \frac{\ln 2}{c}, \qquad p_{min}^s \sim \frac{\ln 2}{c}, \tag{S4}$$

$$C^s(\boldsymbol{\theta}_{coin}) \sim \frac{\ln 2}{4c}, \qquad p_{coin}^s \sim \frac{\ln 2}{2c}. \tag{S5}$$

Since fully informed protection against the all-1 attack is equivalent to noiseless group testing, and since the code length $\ell$ scales in terms of the capacity $C$ as $\ell \geq C^{-1} \log_2 n$, we immediately get the following corollary.

COROLLARY 1. *Any simple group testing algorithm for $c$ defectives and $n$ total items requires an asymptotic number of group tests $\ell$ of at least*

$$\ell \sim \frac{c \ln n}{\ln(2)^2} \approx 2.08 c \ln n. \tag{8}$$

Note that this seems to contradict earlier results of [19], which suggested that under a certain Gaussian assumption, only $\ell \sim 2c \ln n$ tests are required. This apparent contradiction is caused by the fact that the Gaussian assumption in [19] is not correct in the regime of small $p$, for which those results were derived. In fact, the distributions considered in that paper roughly behave like binomial distributions over $\ell$ trials with probability of success of $O(1/\ell)$, which converge to Poisson distributions. Numerical inspection shows that the relevant distribution tails are indeed not very Gaussian and do not decay fast enough. Rigorous analysis of the scores in [19] shows that an asymptotic code length of about $3c \ln n$ is sufficient when $p \sim \ln(2)/c$, which is well above the lower bound of Corollary 1. Details can be found in the full version.

### 3.1.2 Partially informed

If the encoder is uninformed, then the best he can do against arbitrary attacks (for large $c$) is to generate biases using the arcsine distribution $F^*$. So instead of computing the mutual information in one point $P = p$, we now average over different values of $p$ where $p$ follows the arcsine

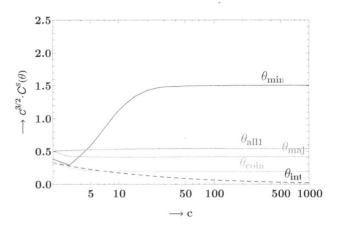

**Figure 1: The partially informed simple capacity (multiplied by $c^{3/2}$) as a function of $c$ for different pirate attacks. From top to bottom these curves correspond to minority voting, the all-1 attack, majority voting, the coin-flip attack, and the interleaving attack. Except for the interleaving attack, for which the capacity scales as $c^{-2}$ (the dashed line), these capacities all seem to scale as $c^{-3/2}$.**

distribution. So the capacity we are interested in is given by

$$C^s(\boldsymbol{\theta}) = \mathbb{E}_p I(X_1; Y | P = p) = \int_0^1 \frac{I(X_1; Y | P = p)}{\pi \sqrt{p(1-p)}} \, dp. \tag{9}$$

The resulting integrals are hard to evaluate analytically, even for large $c$, although for some collusion channels we can use Pinsker's inequality (similar to the proof of [14, Theorem 7]) to show that $C^s(\boldsymbol{\theta}) = \Omega(c^{-3/2})$. And indeed, if we look at the numerics of $c^{3/2} C^s(\boldsymbol{\theta})$ in Figure 1, it seems that the partially informed capacity usually scales as $c^{-3/2}$. As a consequence, even if the attack can be estimated exactly, then still a code length of the order $\ell \propto c^{3/2} \ln n$ is required to get a scheme that works. Note that for the interleaving attack, the capacity scales as $c^{-2}$.

### 3.1.3 Uninformed

For the uninformed fingerprinting game, where both the encoder and decoder are built to work against arbitrary attacks, we are interested in the following max-min game:

$$C^s = \max_F \min_{\boldsymbol{\theta}(F)} \mathbb{E}_p I(X_1; Y | P = p). \tag{10}$$

Huang and Moulin [14, 15] previously solved this uninformed game for asymptotically large coalition sizes $c$ as follows.

PROPOSITION 1. *[15, Theorem 3] The simple uninformed capacity is given by*

$$C^s \sim \frac{1}{2c^2 \ln 2}, \tag{11}$$

*and the optimizing encoder $F$ and collusion channel $\boldsymbol{\theta}$ achieving this bound for large $c$ are the arcsine distribution $F^*$ and the interleaving attack $\boldsymbol{\theta}_{int}$.*

Note that while for the interleaving attack the capacity is the same (up to order terms) for each of the three side-informed cases, for the four other attacks the capacity gradually increases from $O(c^{-2})$ to $O(c^{-3/2})$ to $O(c^{-1})$ when the distributor is more and more informed.

## 3.2 Joint capacities

If the computational complexity of the decoder is not an issue, joint decoding may be an option. In that case, the relevant quantity to examine is the mutual information between the symbols of all colluders, denoted by $X_1, \ldots, X_c$, and the pirate output $Y$, given $P$: $I(X_1, \ldots, X_c; Y | P = p)$ [14]. Note that $Y$ only depends on $X_1, \ldots, X_c$ through $Z = \sum X_i$, so $I(X_1, \ldots, X_c; Y | P = p) = I(Z; Y | P = p)$. To compute the joint capacities, we use the following convenient explicit formula [14, Equation (59)]:

$$\frac{1}{c} I(Z; Y | P = p) = \frac{1}{c} \left[ h(a) - a_h \right], \quad (12)$$

where $h(p) = -p \log_2 p - (1 - p) \log_2 (1 - p)$ is the binary entropy function, and $a_h$ is defined as

$$a_h = \sum_{z=0}^{c} \binom{c}{z} p^z (1 - p)^{c-z} h(\theta_z). \quad (13)$$

### 3.2.1 Fully informed

In the fully informed setting, the capacity is again obtained by considering the mutual information and maximizing it as a function of $p$:

$$C^j(\boldsymbol{\theta}) = \frac{1}{c} \max_p I(Z; Y | P = p). \quad (14)$$

Computing this is very easy for the all-1 attack, the majority voting attack and the minority voting attack, since one can easily prove that the joint capacity is equal to $\frac{1}{c}$ whenever the collusion channel is deterministic, e.g. when $\theta_z \in \{0, 1\}$ for all $z$. Since the capacity for the interleaving attack was already known, the only non-trivial case is the coin-flip attack. A proof of the following theorem can be found in the full version.

THEOREM 2. *The joint informed capacities and the corresponding optimal values of $p$ for the five attacks of Section 2.3 are:*

$$C^j(\boldsymbol{\theta}_{int}) \sim \frac{1}{2c^2 \ln 2}, \qquad p^j_{int} = \frac{1}{2}, \qquad (J1)$$

$$C^j(\boldsymbol{\theta}_{all1}) = \frac{1}{c}, \qquad p^j_{all1} \sim \frac{\ln 2}{c}, \qquad (J2)$$

$$C^j(\boldsymbol{\theta}_{maj}) = \frac{1}{c}, \qquad p^j_{maj} = \frac{1}{2}, \qquad (J3)$$

$$C^j(\boldsymbol{\theta}_{min}) = \frac{1}{c}, \qquad p^j_{min} = \frac{1}{2}, \qquad (J4)$$

$$C^j(\boldsymbol{\theta}_{coin}) \sim \frac{\log_2(5/4)}{c}, \qquad p^j_{coin} \sim \frac{\ln(5/3)}{c}. \qquad (J5)$$

Recall that there is a one-to-one correspondence between the all-1 attack and group testing, so the result above establishes firm bounds on the asymptotic number of group tests required by any probabilistic group testing algorithm. This result was already known, and was first derived by Sebő [33, Theorem 2].

### 3.2.2 Partially informed

For the partially informed capacity we again average over the mutual information where $p$ is drawn at random from

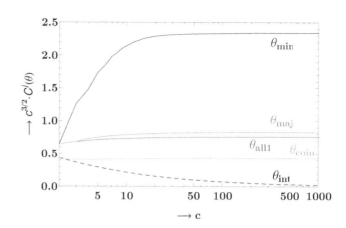

**Figure 2: The partially informed joint capacity, as a function of $c$, for different attacks. From top to bottom these are minority voting, majority voting, the all-1 attack, the coin-flip attack and the interleaving attack. Except for the interleaving attack, these capacities all seem to scale as $c^{-3/2}$.**

the arcsine distribution $F^*$. Thus the capacity is given by

$$C^j(\boldsymbol{\theta}) = \frac{1}{c} \mathbb{E}_p I(Z; Y | P = p). \quad (15)$$

Exact results are again hard to obtain, but we can at least compute the capacities numerically to see how they behave. Figure 2 shows the capacities of the five attacks of Section 2.3. Although the capacities are higher for joint decoding than for simple decoding, the joint capacities of all attacks but the interleaving attack also scale as $c^{-3/2}$.

### 3.2.3 Uninformed

Finally, if we are working with joint decoders which are supposed to work against arbitrary attacks, then we are interested in the following max-min mutual information game:

$$C^j = \max_F \min_{\boldsymbol{\theta}(F)} \mathbb{E}_p \frac{1}{c} I(Z; Y | P = p). \quad (16)$$

This joint capacity game was previously solved by Huang and Moulin [14] who showed that also in the joint game, the interleaving attack $\boldsymbol{\theta}_{\mathrm{int}}$ and the arcsine distribution $F^*$ together form a saddle-point solution to the uninformed fingerprinting game.

PROPOSITION 2. *[14, Theorem 6, Corollary 7] The joint uninformed capacity is given by*

$$C^j \sim \frac{1}{2c^2 \ln 2}, \quad (17)$$

*and the optimizing encoder $F$ and collusion channel $\boldsymbol{\theta}$ achieving this bound for large $c$ are the arcsine distribution $F^*$ and the interleaving attack $\boldsymbol{\theta}_{int}$.*

## 4. DECODERS

After deriving "targets" for our decoders in the previous section, this section discusses decoders that aim to match these bounds. We will follow the score-based framework introduced by Tardos [38], which was later generalized to joint decoders by Moulin [25]. For simple decoding, this means that a user $j$ receives a score $S_j$ of the form

$$S_j = \sum_{i=1}^{\ell} S_{j,i} = \sum_{i=1}^{\ell} g(X_{j,i}, y_i, p_i), \quad (18)$$

where $g$ is called the score function. User $j$ is then accused if $S_j > \eta$ for some threshold $\eta$.

For joint decoding, scores are assigned to tuples $T = \{j_1, \ldots, j_c\}$ of $c$ distinct users according to

$$S_T = \sum_{i=1}^{\ell} S_{T,i} = \sum_{i=1}^{\ell} g(X_{j_1,i}, \ldots, X_{j_c,i}, y_i, p_i). \quad (19)$$

In this case, a tuple of users is accused if the joint tuple score exceeds some other threshold $\eta$. Note that this accusation algorithm is not exactly well-defined, since it is possible that a user appears both in a tuple that is accused and in a tuple that is not accused. For the analysis we will assume that the scheme is only successful if the single tuple consisting of all colluders has a score exceeding $\eta$ and no other tuples have a score exceeding $\eta$, in which case all users in the guilty tuple are accused.

## 4.1 Simple decoders

Several different score functions for the simple decoder setting were considered before, but in this work we will restrict our attention to the following log-likelihood scores, which perform well and turn out to be easy to analyze:

$$g(x, y, p) = \ln \left( \frac{\mathbb{P}_g(x, y|p)}{\mathbb{P}_i(x, y|p)} \right). \quad (20)$$

Here $\mathbb{P}_g(x, y|p) = \mathbb{P}(X_{j,i} = x, Y_i = y | P_i = p, j \in \mathcal{C})$ corresponds to the probability of seeing the pair $(x, y)$ when user $j$ is guilty, and $\mathbb{P}_i(x, y|p)$ corresponds to the same probability under the assumption that $j$ is innocent. Using this score function $g$, the complete score of a user is the logarithm of a Neyman-Pearson score over the entire codeword:

$$S_j = \sum_{i=1}^{\ell} \ln \left( \frac{\mathbb{P}_g(x_{j,i}, y_i|p_i)}{\mathbb{P}_i(x_{j,i}, y_i|p_i)} \right) = \ln \left( \frac{\mathbb{P}_g(\boldsymbol{x}_j, \boldsymbol{y}|\boldsymbol{p})}{\mathbb{P}_i(\boldsymbol{x}_j, \boldsymbol{y}|\boldsymbol{p})} \right). \quad (21)$$

Such Neyman-Pearson scores are known to be optimally discriminative to decide whether to accuse a user or not. Log-likelihood scores were previously considered in the context of fingerprinting in e.g. [24, 32].

### 4.1.1 Fully informed

For the central theorem below, we will make use of the following function $M$, which is closely related to the moment generating functions of scores in one position $i$ for innocent and guilty users. This function is defined as

$$M(t) = \sum_{x,y} \mathbb{P}_i(x, y|p)^{1-t} \mathbb{P}_g(x, y|p)^t \quad (22)$$

and it satisfies $M(t) = \mathbb{E}_i e^{t S_{j,i}} = \mathbb{E}_g e^{(t-1) S_{j,i}}$ and $M(0) = M(1) = 1$.

THEOREM 3. Let $p$ and $\boldsymbol{\theta}$ be fixed and known to the distributor. Let $\gamma = \ln(1/\varepsilon_2)/\ln(n/\varepsilon_1)$, and let the threshold $\eta$ and code length $\ell$ be defined as

$$\eta = \ln \left( \frac{n}{\varepsilon_1} \right), \qquad \ell = \frac{\sqrt{\gamma}(1 + \sqrt{\gamma})}{-\ln M(1 - \sqrt{\gamma})} \ln \left( \frac{n}{\varepsilon_1} \right). \quad (23)$$

Then with probability at least $1 - \varepsilon_1$ no innocent users are accused (regardless of which collusion channel was used), and with probability at least $1 - \varepsilon_2$ a colluder is caught (if the collusion channel is indeed $\boldsymbol{\theta}$).

PROOF. For innocent users $j$, we would like to prove that $\mathbb{P}_i(S_j > \eta) \leq \varepsilon_1/n$, where $S_j$ is the user's total score over all positions. If this can be proved, then it follows that with probability at least $(1 - \varepsilon_1/n)^n \geq 1 - \varepsilon_1$ no innocent users are accused. Using the Markov inequality for $e^{\alpha S_j}$ with $\alpha > 0$ and optimizing over $\alpha$, we see that the optimum lies close to $\alpha = 1$. For simplicity we choose $\alpha = 1$ which, combined with the given value of $\eta$, leads to the following bound:

$$\mathbb{P}_i(S_j > \eta) = \min_{\alpha > 0} \mathbb{P}_i(e^{\alpha S_j} > e^{\alpha \eta}) \leq \min_{\alpha > 0} \frac{\mathbb{E}_i(e^{\alpha S_j})}{e^{\alpha \eta}} \quad (24)$$

$$= \min_{\alpha > 0} \frac{\prod_{i=1}^{\ell} \mathbb{E}_i(e^{\alpha S_{j,i}})}{e^{\alpha \eta}} = \min_{\alpha > 0} \frac{M(\alpha)^{\ell}}{(n/\varepsilon_1)^{\alpha}} \leq \frac{M(1)^{\ell}}{n/\varepsilon_1} = \frac{\varepsilon_1}{n}. \quad (25)$$

For guilty users, we would like to prove that for an arbitrary guilty user $j$, we have $\mathbb{P}_g(S_j < \eta) \leq \varepsilon_2$. Again using Markov's inequality (but now with a more sophisticated exponent $\beta = \sqrt{\gamma}$) we get

$$\mathbb{P}_g(S_j < \eta) \leq \min_{\beta > 0} \frac{\mathbb{E}_g(e^{-\beta S_j})}{e^{-\beta \eta}} = \min_{\beta > 0} \frac{\prod_{i=1}^{\ell} \mathbb{E}_g(e^{-\beta S_{j,i}})}{e^{-\beta \eta}} \quad (26)$$

$$= \min_{\beta > 0} \frac{M(1 - \beta)^{\ell}}{e^{-\beta \eta}} \leq \frac{M(1 - \sqrt{\gamma})^{\ell}}{e^{-\sqrt{\gamma} \eta}} = \varepsilon_2, \quad (27)$$

where the last equality follows from the definitions of $\ell$ and $\eta$ of (23). □

Compared to previous papers analyzing provable bounds on the error probabilities, the proof of Theorem 3 is remarkably short and simple. The only problem is that the given expression for $\ell$ is not very informative as to how $\ell$ scales for large $n$. The following corollary answers this question, by showing how $\ell$ scales for small $\gamma$.

COROLLARY 2. If $\gamma = o(1)$ then $\ell$ achieves the optimal asymptotic scaling (achieves capacity) for arbitrary $p$:

$$\ell = \frac{\log_2 n}{I(X_1; Y | P = p)} [1 + O(\sqrt{\gamma})], \quad (28)$$

PROOF. First, let us study the behavior of $M(1 - \sqrt{\gamma})$ for small $\gamma$, by computing the first order Taylor expansion of $M(1 - \sqrt{\gamma})$ around $\gamma = 0$:

$$M(1 - \sqrt{\gamma})$$

$$= \sum_{x,y} \mathbb{P}_g(x, y|p) \exp \left( -\sqrt{\gamma} \ln \left( \frac{\mathbb{P}_g(x, y|p)}{\mathbb{P}_i(x, y|p)} \right) \right) \quad (29)$$

$$\overset{(a)}{=} \sum_{x,y} \mathbb{P}_g(x, y|p) \left( 1 - \sqrt{\gamma} \ln \left( \frac{\mathbb{P}_g(x, y|p)}{\mathbb{P}_i(x, y|p)} \right) + O(\gamma) \right) \quad (30)$$

$$= 1 - \sqrt{\gamma} \sum_{x,y} \mathbb{P}_g(x, y|p) \ln \left( \frac{\mathbb{P}_g(x, y|p)}{\mathbb{P}_i(x, y|p)} \right) + O(\gamma) \quad (31)$$

$$= 1 - \sqrt{\gamma} I(X_1; Y | P = p) \ln 2 + O(\gamma). \quad (32)$$

Here $(a)$ follows from the fact that if $\mathbb{P}_g(x, y|p) = 0$, the factor $\mathbb{P}_g(x, y|p)$ in front of the exponentiation would already cause this term to be 0, while if $\mathbb{P}_g(x, y|p) > 0$, then also $\mathbb{P}_i(x, y|p) > 0$ and thus the ratio is bounded and does not depend on $\gamma$. Substituting the above result in the original equation for $\ell$ we thus get the result of (28):

$$\ell = \frac{\sqrt{\gamma}(1+\sqrt{\gamma})}{-\ln M(1-\sqrt{\gamma})} \ln\left(\frac{n}{\varepsilon_1}\right) \tag{33}$$

$$= \frac{\sqrt{\gamma}(1+\sqrt{\gamma})}{\sqrt{\gamma}I(X_1;Y|P=p)\ln 2 + O(\gamma)} \ln\left(\frac{n}{\varepsilon_1}\right) \tag{34}$$

$$= \frac{\log_2 n}{I(X_1;Y|P=p)}[1+O(\sqrt{\gamma})]. \tag{35}$$

Since the capacities tell us that $\ell/\log_2(n) \gtrsim I(X_1;Y|P=p)^{-1}$, it follows that $\ell$ asymptotically achieves capacity. $\quad\square$

Since this construction is asymptotically optimal regardless of $p$, in the fully informed setting we can now simply optimize $p$ (using Theorem 1) to get the following results.

COROLLARY 3. *Using the values for $p$ of Theorem 1, the asymptotics for $\ell$ for the five attacks of Section 2.3 are:*

$$\ell(\boldsymbol{\theta}_{int}) = 2c^2\ln(n)\left[1+O(\sqrt{\gamma})\right], \tag{36}$$

$$\ell(\boldsymbol{\theta}_{all1}) = \frac{c}{\ln(2)^2}\ln(n)\left[1+O(\sqrt{\gamma})\right], \tag{37}$$

$$\ell(\boldsymbol{\theta}_{maj}) = \pi c\ln(n)\left[1+O(\sqrt{\gamma})\right], \tag{38}$$

$$\ell(\boldsymbol{\theta}_{min}) = \frac{c}{\ln(2)^2}\ln(n)\left[1+O(\sqrt{\gamma})\right], \tag{39}$$

$$\ell(\boldsymbol{\theta}_{coin}) = \frac{4c}{\ln(2)^2}\ln(n)\left[1+O(\sqrt{\gamma})\right]. \tag{40}$$

Since the all-1 attack is equivalent to group testing, we mention this result separately, together with a more explicit expression for $g$.

COROLLARY 4. *Let $\boldsymbol{\theta}=\boldsymbol{\theta}_{all1}$ and let $p\approx\ln(2)/c$ be fixed. Then the log-likelihood score function $g$ is given by[2]*

$$g(x,y) = \begin{cases} +1 & (x,y)=(0,0) \\ -1+O(1/c) & (x,y)=(0,1) \\ -\infty & (x,y)=(1,0) \\ +c & (x,y)=(1,1) \end{cases} \tag{41}$$

*Using this score function in combination with the parameters $\eta$ and $\ell$ of Theorem 3, we obtain a simple group testing algorithm with an asymptotic number of group tests of*

$$\ell \sim \frac{c\ln n}{\ln(2)^2} \approx 2.08c\ln n, \tag{42}$$

*thus achieving the simple group testing capacity.*

### 4.1.2 Partially informed

Since the score functions from Section 4.1.1 achieve capacity for each value of $p$, using this score function we also trivially achieve the partially informed capacity when the arcsine distribution is used. Estimates of these capacities, and thus the resulting code lengths, can be found in Section 3.1.2.

### 4.1.3 Uninformed

We now arrive at what is arguably one of the most important results of this paper. Just like Oosterwijk et al. [29], who specifically studied the score function $h$ tailored against

the interleaving attack, we now also take a closer look at the log-likelihood score function designed against the interleaving attack. [3] Working out the details, this score function is of the form:

$$g(x,y,p) = \begin{cases} \ln\left(1+\frac{p}{c(1-p)}\right) & x=y=0 \\ \ln\left(1-\frac{1}{c}\right) & x\neq y \\ \ln\left(1+\frac{1-p}{cp}\right) & x=y=1 \end{cases} \tag{43}$$

The first thing to note here is that if we denote Oosterwijk et al.'s [30] score function by $h$, then $g$ satisfies

$$g(x,y,p) = \ln\left(1+\frac{h(x,y,p)}{c}\right). \tag{44}$$

If $h(x,y,p)=o(c)$, then by Tayloring the logarithm around $c=\infty$ we see that $g\approx h/c$. Since scaling a score function by a constant does not affect its performance, this implies that $g$ and $h$ are then equivalent. Since for Oosterwijk et al.'s score function one generally needs to use *cut-offs* on $F$ that guarantee that $h(x,y,p)=o(c)$ (cf. [16]), and since the decoder of Oosterwijk et al. is known to asymptotically achieve the uninformed capacity, we immediately get the following result.

PROPOSITION 3. *The score function $g$ of (43) asymptotically achieves the uninformed simple capacity when the same cut-offs on $F$ as those in [16] are used.*

So optimizing the decoder so that it is resistant against the interleaving attack again leads to a decoder that is resistant against arbitrary attacks.

### Cutting off the cut-offs.

Although Proposition 3 is already a nice result, we can do even better. We can prove a stronger statement, which shows one of the reasons why the log-likelihood decoder is probably more practical than the decoder of Oosterwijk et al.

THEOREM 4. *The score function $g$ of (43) achieves the uninformed simple capacity when **no cut-offs** are used.*

PROOF SKETCH. First note that in the limit of large $c$, the cut-offs of Ibrahimi et al. converge to 0. So for large $c$, the difference between not using cut-offs and using cut-offs is negligible, as long as the contribution of the tails of $p$ near 0 or 1 to the distribution of user scores is negligible. Since with this score function $g$, all moments of both innocent and guilty user scores are finite (arbitrary powers of logarithms always lose against the $1/\sqrt{p(1-p)}$ of the arcsine distribution and the decreasing width of the interval between 0 and the cut-off), the tails indeed decay exponentially. So also without cut-offs this score function asymptotically achieves the uninformed simple capacity. $\quad\square$

---

[2]To be precise: $g(0,1)=c\log_2(2-2^{1/c})$, and for convenience we have scaled $g$ by a factor $c\ln 2$.

[3]Considering the interleaving attack for designing a universal decoder is further motivated by the results of Abbe and Zheng [1, 24], who showed that under certain conditions, the worst-case attack decoder is a universal capacity-achieving decoder. The interleaving attack is theoretically not the worst-case attack for finite $c$, but since it is known to be the asymptotic worst-case attack, the difference between the worst-case attack and the interleaving attack vanishes for large $c$.

Note that the same result does not apply to the score function of Oosterwijk et al. [30], for which the tails of the distributions are not Gaussian enough to omit the use of cut-offs. The main difference is that for small $p$, the score function $h$ of [29] scales as $1/p$ (which explodes when $p$ is really small), while the log-likelihood decoder $g$ then only scales as $\ln(1/p)$ which is much smaller.

*All roads lead to Rome.*

Let us now mention a third way to obtain a capacity-achieving uninformed simple decoder which is again very similar to the two decoders above. To construct this decoder, we use a Bayesian approximation of the proposed empirical mutual information decoder of Moulin [25], and again plug in the asymptotic worst-case attack, the interleaving attack.

THEOREM 5. *Using Bayesian inference with an a priori probability of guilt of* $\mathbb{P}(j \in \mathcal{C}) = \frac{c}{n}$, *the empirical mutual information decoder tailored against the interleaving attack can be approximated with the following score function:*

$$m(x,y,p) = \begin{cases} \ln\left(1 + \frac{p}{n(1-p)}\right) & x = y = 0 \\ \ln\left(1 - \frac{1}{n}\right) & x \neq y \\ \ln\left(1 + \frac{1-p}{np}\right) & x = y = 1 \end{cases} \quad (45)$$

PROOF SKETCH. For now, let $p$ be fixed. The empirical mutual information decoder assigns a score $S_j$ to a user $j$ using

$$S_j = \sum_{x,y} \hat{\mathbb{P}}(x,y) \ln\left(\frac{\hat{\mathbb{P}}(x,y)}{\hat{\mathbb{P}}(x)\hat{\mathbb{P}}(y)}\right) = \sum_{i=1}^{\ell} \ln\left(\frac{\hat{\mathbb{P}}(x_{j,i},y_i)}{\hat{\mathbb{P}}(x_{j,i})\hat{\mathbb{P}}(y_i)}\right) \quad (46)$$

where $\hat{\mathbb{P}}(\cdot)$ denotes the empirical estimate of $\mathbb{P}(\cdot)$ based on the data $\boldsymbol{x}, \boldsymbol{y}, \boldsymbol{p}$. For large $\ell$, these estimates will converge to the real probabilities, so we can approximate $S_j$ by

$$S_j \approx \sum_{i=1}^{\ell} \ln\left(\frac{\mathbb{P}(x_{j,i},y_i)}{\mathbb{P}(x_{j,i})\mathbb{P}(y_i)}\right) = \sum_{i=1}^{\ell} m(x_{j,i},y_i,p_i). \quad (47)$$

Here $\mathbb{P}(X_{j,i})$ and $\mathbb{P}(y_i)$ can be easily computed, but for computing $\mathbb{P}(X_{j,i},y_i)$ we need to know whether user $j$ is guilty or not. Using Bayesian inference, we can write

$$\mathbb{P}(x,y) = \mathbb{P}_g(x,y)\mathbb{P}(j \in \mathcal{C}) + \mathbb{P}_i(x,y)\mathbb{P}(j \notin \mathcal{C}). \quad (48)$$

Assuming an a priori probability of guilt of $\mathbb{P}(j \in \mathcal{C}) = c/n$, we can work out the details to obtain

$$m(x,y,p) = \ln\left(1 + \frac{c}{n}\left[\frac{\mathbb{P}_g(x,y)}{\mathbb{P}_i(x,y)} - 1\right]\right). \quad (49)$$

Filling in the corresponding probabilities for the interleaving attack, we end up with the score function of (45). □

For values of $p$ with $o(1) < p < 1 - o(1)$, this decoder is again equivalent to both the log-likelihood score function $g$ and Oosterwijk et al.'s score function $h$.

## 4.2 Joint decoders

For the joint decoding setting, scores are assigned to tuples of $c$ users, and again higher scores correspond to a higher probability of being accused. The most natural step from the simple log-likelihood decoders to joint decoders seems to be to use the following joint score function:

$$g(x_1,\ldots,x_c,y,p) = \ln\left(\frac{\mathbb{P}_{g^c}(x_1,\ldots,x_c,y|p)}{\mathbb{P}_{i^c}(x_1,\ldots,x_c,y|p)}\right). \quad (50)$$

Here $\mathbb{P}_{g^c}(\cdot)$ is under the assumption that in this tuple *all users are guilty*, while for $\mathbb{P}_{i^c}(\cdot)$ we assume that *all users are innocent*. Note that under the assumption that the attack is colluder-symmetric, the score function only depends on $z = \sum_{i=1}^{c} x_i$:

$$g(x_1,\ldots,x_c,y,p) = g(z,y,p) = \ln\left(\frac{\mathbb{P}_{g^c}(z,y|p)}{\mathbb{P}_{i^c}(z,y|p)}\right). \quad (51)$$

### 4.2.1 Fully informed

To analyze the joint decoder, we again make use of the moment generating function for the score assigned to tuples of $c$ innocent users. This function is now defined by

$$M(t) = \sum_{z,y} \mathbb{P}_{i^c}(z,y|p)^{1-t}\mathbb{P}_{g^c}(z,y|p)^t \quad (52)$$

and it satisfies $M(t) = \mathbb{E}_{i^c}e^{tS_{j,i}} = \mathbb{E}_{g^c}e^{(t-1)S_{j,i}}$ and $M(0) = M(1) = 1$. Using similar techniques as in Section 4.1.1, we obtain the following result.

THEOREM 6. *Let $p$ and $\boldsymbol{\theta}$ be fixed and known to the distributor. Let $\gamma = \ln(1/\varepsilon_2)/\ln(n^c/\varepsilon_1)$, and let the threshold $\eta$ and code length $\ell$ be defined as*

$$\eta = \ln\left(\frac{n^c}{\varepsilon_1}\right), \qquad \ell = \frac{\sqrt{\gamma}(1+\sqrt{\gamma})}{-\ln M(1-\sqrt{\gamma})}\ln\left(\frac{n^c}{\varepsilon_1}\right). \quad (53)$$

*Then with probability at least $1 - \varepsilon_1$ all all-innocent tuples are not accused, and with probability at least $1 - \varepsilon_2$ the single all-guilty tuple is accused.*

PROOF SKETCH. The proof is very similar to the proof of Theorem 3. Instead of $n$ innocent and $c$ guilty users we now have $\binom{n}{c} < n^c$ all-innocent tuples and just 1 all-guilty tuple, which changes some of the numbers in $\gamma$, $\eta$ and $\ell$. We again apply the Markov inequality with $\alpha = 1$ for innocent tuples and $\beta = \sqrt{\gamma}$ for guilty tuples, to obtain the given expressions for $\eta$ and $\ell$. □

Note that Theorem 6 does not prove that we can actually find the set of colluders with high probability, since mixed tuples consisting of both innocent and guilty users also exist, and these may or may not have a score exceeding $\eta$. This does prove that with high probability we can find a set $\mathcal{C}'$ of $c$ users, for which (i) all tuples not containing these users have a score below $\eta$, and (ii) the tuple containing exactly these users has a score above $\eta$. Regardless of what the scores for mixed tuples are, with probability at least $1 - \varepsilon_1 - \varepsilon_2$ such a set consists and contains at least one colluder. Furthermore, if this set $\mathcal{C}'$ is unique, then with high probability this is exactly the set of colluders. But there is no guarantee that it is unique without additional proofs. This is left for future work.

To further motivate why using this joint decoder may be the right choice, the following proposition shows that at least the scaling of the resulting code lengths is optimal. Note that the extra $c$ that we get from $\ln(n^c) = c \ln n$ can be combined with the mutual information $I(\cdot)$ to obtain $\frac{1}{c}I(\cdot)$, which corresponds to the joint capacity.

PROPOSITION 4. *If $\gamma = o(1)$ then the code length $\ell$ of Theorem 6 scales as*

$$\ell = \frac{\log_2 n}{\frac{1}{c}I(Z;Y|P=p)}\left[1 + O(\sqrt{\gamma})\right], \qquad (54)$$

*thus asymptotically achieving the optimal code length (up to first order terms) for arbitrary values of $p$.*

Since the asymptotic code length is optimal regardless of $p$, these asymptotics are also optimal when $p$ is optimized to maximize the mutual information in the fully informed setting.

Finally, although it is hard to estimate the scores of mixed tuples with this decoder, just like in [31] we expect that the joint decoder score for a tuple is roughly equal to the sum of the $c$ individual simple decoder scores. So a tuple of $c$ users consisting of $k$ colluders and $c - k$ innocent users is expected to have a score roughly a factor $k/c$ smaller than the expected score for the all-guilty tuple. So after computing the scores for all tuples of size $c$, we can get rough estimates of how many guilty users are contained in each tuple, and for instance try to find the set $\mathcal{C}'$ of $c$ users that best matches these estimates. There are several options for post-processing that may improve the accuracy of using this joint decoder, which are left for future work.

### 4.2.2 Partially informed

As mentioned in Proposition 4, the code length is asymptotically optimal regardless of $p$, so the code length in the partially uninformed setting is also asymptotically optimal. Asymptotics on $\ell$ can thus be obtained by combining Proposition 4 with the results of Section 3.2.2.

### 4.2.3 Uninformed

Note that if the above joint decoder turns out to work well, then we can again plug in the interleaving attack to get something that might just work well against arbitrary attacks. While we cannot prove that this joint decoder is optimal, we can already see what the score function would be, and conjecture that it works against arbitrary attacks.

CONJECTURE 1. *The joint log-likelihood decoder against the interleaving attack, with the score function $g$ defined by*

$$g(z,y,p) = \begin{cases} \ln(1 - \frac{z}{c}) - \ln(1-p) & (y=0) \\ \ln(\frac{z}{c}) - \ln(p) & (y=1) \end{cases} \qquad (55)$$

*works against arbitrary attacks and asymptotically achieves the joint capacity of the uninformed fingerprinting game.*

A further study of this universal joint decoder is left as an open problem.

## 5. DISCUSSION

Let us now briefly discuss the results from Sections 3 and 4, their consequences, and some directions for future work.

### *Informed simple decoding.*

For the setting of simple decoders, we derived explicit asymptotics on the informed capacities for various attacks, which often scale as $\Theta(c^{-1})$. We further showed that log-likelihood scores provably match these bounds for large $n$, regardless of $\boldsymbol{\theta}$ and $p$. Because these decoders are optimal for any value of $p$, they are also optimal in the partially

informed setting, where different values of $p$ are used. If the encoder uses the arcsine distribution to generate biases, we showed that these capacities generally seem to scale as $\Theta(c^{-3/2})$, which is roughly 'halfway' between the fully informed and uninformed capacities.

### *Uninformed simple decoding.*

Although log-likelihood decoders have already been studied before in the context of fingerprinting, the main drawback was always that to use these decoders, you would either have to fill in (and know) the exact pirate strategy, or compute the worst-case attack explicitly. So if you are in the simple uninformed setting where you don't know the pirate strategy and where the worst-case attack is not given by a nice closed-form expression [14, Fig. 4b], how can you construct such decoders for large $c$? The trick seems to be to just fill in the *asymptotic* worst-case attack, which Huang and Moulin showed is the interleaving attack [14], and which is much simpler to analyze. After previously suggesting this idea to Oosterwijk et al., we now used the same trick here to obtain two other capacity-achieving score functions using two different methods (but each time filling in the interleaving attack). So in total we now have three different methods to obtain (closed-form) capacity-achieving decoders in the uninformed setting:

- Using Lagrange-multipliers, Oosterwijk et al. [29] obtained:

$$h(x,y,p) = \begin{cases} +\frac{p}{1-p} & x = y = 0 \\ -1 & x \neq y \\ +\frac{1-p}{p} & x = y = 1 \end{cases} \qquad (56)$$

- Using Neyman-Pearson-based log-likelihood scores, we obtained:

$$g(x,y,p) = \begin{cases} \ln\left(1 + \frac{p}{c(1-p)}\right) & x = y = 0 \\ \ln\left(1 - \frac{1}{c}\right) & x \neq y \\ \ln\left(1 + \frac{1-p}{cp}\right) & x = y = 1 \end{cases} \qquad (57)$$

- Using a Bayesian approximation of the empirical mutual information decoder of Moulin [25], we obtained:

$$m(x,y,p) = \begin{cases} \ln\left(1 + \frac{p}{n(1-p)}\right) & x = y = 0 \\ \ln\left(1 - \frac{1}{n}\right) & x \neq y \\ \ln\left(1 + \frac{1-p}{np}\right) & x = y = 1 \end{cases} \qquad (58)$$

For $o(1) < p < 1 - o(1)$ and large $c, n$, these score functions are equivalent up to a scaling factor:

$$h(x,y,p) \sim c \cdot g(x,y,p) \sim n \cdot m(x,y,p), \qquad (59)$$

and therefore all three are asymptotically optimal. So there may be many different roads that lead to Rome, but they all seem to have one thing in common: to build a universal decoder that works against arbitrary attacks, one should build a decoder that works against the asymptotic worst-case pirate attack, the interleaving attack. And if it does work against this attack, then it probably works against any other attack as well.

*Joint decoding.*

Although deriving the joint informed capacities is much easier than deriving the simple informed capacities, actually building decoders that provably match these bounds is a different matter. We conjectured that the same log-likelihood scores achieve capacity when a suitable accusation algorithm is used, and we conjectured that the log-likelihood score built against the interleaving attack achieves the uninformed joint capacity, but we cannot prove any of these statements beyond reasonable doubt. For now this is left as an open problem.

*Group testing.*

Since the all-1 attack is equivalent to group testing, some of the results we obtained also apply to group testing. The joint capacity was already known [33], but to the best of our knowledge both the simple capacity (Corollary 1) and a simple decoder matching this simple capacity (Corollary 4) were not yet known before. Attempts have been made to build efficient simple decoders with a code length not much longer than the joint capacity [6], but these do not match the simple capacity. Future work will include computing the capacities and building decoders for various noisy group testing models, where the marking assumption may not apply.

*Dynamic fingerprinting.*

Although this paper focused on applications to the 'static' fingerprinting game, the construction of [20] can trivially be applied to the decoders in this paper as well to build efficient dynamic fingerprinting schemes. Although the asymptotics for the code length in this dynamic construction are the same, (i) the order terms are significantly smaller in the dynamic game, (ii) one does not need the assumption that the pirate strategy is colluder-symmetric, and (iii) one does not necessarily need to know (a good estimate of) $c$ in advance [20, Section V]. An important open problem remains to determine the dynamic uninformed fingerprinting capacity, which may prove or disprove that the construction of [20] is optimal.

*Further generalizations.*

While this paper already aims to provide a rather complete set of guidelines on what to do in the various different fingerprinting games (with different amounts of side-information, and different computational assumptions on the decoder), there are some further generalizations that were not considered here due to lack of space. We mention two in particular:

- **Larger alphabets**: In this work we focused on the binary case of $q = 2$ different symbols, but it may be advantageous to work with larger alphabet sizes $q > 2$, since the code length decreases linearly with $q$. For the results about decoders we did not really use that we were working with a binary alphabet, so it seems a straightforward exercise to prove that the $q$-ary versions of the log-likelihood decoders also achieve capacity. A harder problem seems to be to actually compute these capacities in the various informed settings, since the maximization problem then transforms from a one-dimensional optimization problem to a $(q-1)$-dimensional optimization problem.

- **Tuple decoding**: As in [31], we can consider a setting in between the simple and joint decoding settings, where decisions to accuse are made based on looking at tuples of users of size at most $t$. Tuple decoding may offer a trade-off between the high complexity, low code length of a joint decoder and the low complexity, higher code length of a simple decoder, and so it may be useful to know how the capacities scale in the region $1 < t < c$.

## 6. ACKNOWLEDGMENTS

The author is very grateful to Pierre Moulin for his insightful comments and suggestions during the author's visit to Urbana-Champaign that inspired work on this paper. The author would also like to thank Teddy Furon for pointing out the connection between decoders designed against the interleaving attack and the results of Abbe and Zheng [1], and for finding some mistakes in a preliminary version of this manuscript. Finally, the author thanks Jeroen Doumen, Jan-Jaap Oosterwijk, Boris Škorić, and Benne de Weger for valuable discussions and comments.

## 7. REFERENCES

[1] E. Abbe and L. Zheng. Linear universal decoding for compound channels. *IEEE Transactions on Information Theory*, 56(12):5999–6013, 2010.

[2] E. Amiri and G. Tardos. High rate fingerprinting codes and the fingerprinting capacity. In *20th ACM-SIAM Symposium on Discrete Algorithms (SODA)*, pages 336–345, 2009.

[3] O. Blayer and T. Tassa. Improved versions of Tardos' fingerprinting scheme. *Designs, Codes and Cryptography*, 48(1):79–103, 2008.

[4] D. Boesten and B. Škorić. Asymptotic fingerprinting capacity for non-binary alphabets. In *13th Conference on Information Hiding (IH)*, pages 1–13, 2011.

[5] D. Boneh and J. Shaw. Collusion-secure fingerprinting for digital data. *IEEE Transactions on Information Theory*, 44(5):1897–1905, 1998.

[6] C.-L. Chan, S. Jaggi, V. Saligrama, and S. Agnihotri. Non-adaptive group testing: explicit bounds and novel algorithms. In *IEEE International Symposium on Information Theory (ISIT)*, pages 1837–1841, 2012.

[7] A. Charpentier, F. Xie, C. Fontaine, and T. Furon. Expectation maximization decoding of Tardos probabilistic fingerprinting code. In *SPIE Proceedings*, volume 7254, 2009.

[8] T. M. Cover and J. A. Thomas. *Elements of Information Theory (2nd Edition)*. Wiley Press, 2006.

[9] A. Fiat and T. Tassa. Dynamic traitor tracing. *Journal of Cryptology*, 14(3):354–371, 2001.

[10] T. Furon and L. Pérez-Freire, EM decoding of Tardos traitor tracing codes. In *ACM Symposium on Multimedia and Security (MM&Sec)*, pages 99–106, 2009.

[11] Y.-W. Huang and P. Moulin. Capacity-achieving fingerprint decoding. In *IEEE Workshop on Information Forensics and Security (WIFS)*, pages 51–55, 2009.

[12] Y.-W. Huang and P. Moulin. Saddle-point solution of the fingerprinting capacity game under the marking

assumption. In *IEEE International Symposium on Information Theory (ISIT)*, pages 2256–2260, 2009.

[13] Y.-W. Huang and P. Moulin. Maximin optimality of the arcsine fingerprinting distribution and the interleaving attack for large coalitions. In *IEEE Workshop on Information Forensics and Security (WIFS)*, pages 1–6, 2010.

[14] Y.-W. Huang and P. Moulin. On the saddle-point solution and the large-coalition asymptotics of fingerprinting games. *IEEE Transactions on Information Forensics and Security*, 7(1):160–175, 2012.

[15] Y.-W. Huang and P. Moulin. On fingerprinting capacity games for arbitrary alphabets and their asymptotics. In *IEEE International Symposium on Information Theory (ISIT)*, pages 2571–2575, 2012.

[16] S. Ibrahimi, B. Škorić, and J.-J. Oosterwijk. Riding the saddle point: asymptotics of the capacity-achieving simple decoder for bias-based traitor tracing. *Cryptology ePrint Archive*, 2013.

[17] T. Laarhoven, J.-J. Oosterwijk, and J. Doumen. Dynamic traitor tracing for arbitrary alphabets: divide and conquer. In *IEEE Workshop on Information Forensics and Security (WIFS)*, pages 240–245, 2012.

[18] T. Laarhoven and B. de Weger. Discrete distributions in the Tardos scheme, revisited. In *1st ACM Workshop on Information Hiding and Multimedia Security (IH&MMSec)*, pages 13–18, 2013.

[19] T. Laarhoven. Efficient probabilistic group testing based on traitor tracing. In *51st Annual Allerton Conference on Communication, Control and Computing (Allerton)*, 2013.

[20] T. Laarhoven, J. Doumen, P. Roelse, B. Škorić, and B. de Weger. Dynamic Tardos traitor tracing schemes. *IEEE Transactions on Information Theory*, 59(7):4230–4242, 2013.

[21] T. Laarhoven. Dynamic traitor tracing schemes, revisited. In *IEEE Workshop on Information Forensics and Security (WIFS)*, pages 191–196, 2013.

[22] T. Laarhoven and B. de Weger. Optimal symmetric Tardos traitor tracing schemes. *Designs, Codes and Cryptography*, 71(1): 83–103, 2014.

[23] P. Meerwald and T. Furon. Group testing meets traitor tracing. In *IEEE International Conference on Acoustics, Speech and Signal Processing (ICASSP)*, pages 4204–4207, 2011.

[24] P. Meerwald and T. Furon. Toward practical joint decoding of binary Tardos fingerprinting codes. *IEEE Transactions on Information Forensics and Security*, 7(4):1168–1180, 2012.

[25] P. Moulin. Universal fingerprinting: capacity and random-coding exponents. *arXiv:0801.3837v3 [cs.IT]*, 2011.

[26] J. Neyman and E. S. Pearson. On the problem of the most efficient tests of statistical hypotheses. *Philosophical Transactions of the Royal Society A: Mathematical, Physical and Engineering Sciences*, 231:289–337, 1933.

[27] K. Nuida, M. Hagiwara, H. Watanabe, and H. Imai. Optimization of Tardos's fingerprinting codes in a viewpoint of memory amount. In *9th Conference on Information Hiding (IH)*, pages 279–293, 2007.

[28] K. Nuida, S. Fujitsu, M. Hagiwara, T. Kitagawa, H. Watanabe, K. Ogawa, and H. Imai. An improvement of discrete Tardos fingerprinting codes. *Designs, Codes and Cryptography*, 52(3):339–362, 2009.

[29] J.-J. Oosterwijk, B. Škorić, and J. Doumen. Optimal suspicion functions for Tardos traitor tracing schemes. In *1st ACM Workshop on Information Hiding and Multimedia Forensics (IH&MMSec)*, pages 19–28, 2013.

[30] J.-J. Oosterwijk, B. Škorić, and J. Doumen. A capacity-achieving simple decoder for bias-based traitor tracing schemes. *Cryptology ePrint Archive*, 2013.

[31] J.-J. Oosterwijk, J. Doumen, and T. Laarhoven. Tuple decoders for traitor tracing schemes. In *SPIE Proceedings*, volume 9028, 2014.

[32] L. Pérez-Freire and T. Furon. Blind decoder for binary probabilistic traitor tracing codes. In *IEEE Workshop on Information Forensics and Security (WIFS)*, pages 46–50, 2009.

[33] A. Sebő. On two random search problems. *Journal of Statistical Planning and Inference*, 11:23–31, 1985.

[34] A. Simone and B. Škorić. Accusation probabilities in Tardos codes: beyond the Gaussian approximation. *Designs, Codes and Cryptography*, 63(3):379–412, 2012.

[35] B. Škorić, T. U. Vladimirova, M. U. Celik, and J. C. Talstra. Tardos fingerprinting is better than we thought. *IEEE Transactions on Information Theory*, 54(8):3663–3676, 2008.

[36] B. Škorić, S. Katzenbeisser, and M. U. Celik. Symmetric Tardos fingerprinting codes for arbitrary alphabet sizes. *Designs, Codes and Cryptography*, 46(2):137–166, 2008.

[37] B. Škorić and J.-J. Oosterwijk. Binary and $q$-ary Tardos codes, revisited. *Designs, Codes and Cryptography*, 2013.

[38] G. Tardos. Optimal probabilistic fingerprint codes. In *35th ACM Symposium on Theory of Computing (STOC)*, pages 116–125, 2003.

# Notes on Non-Interactive Secure Comparison in "Image Feature Extraction in the Encrypted Domain with Privacy-Preserving SIFT"

Matthias Schneider
Computer Vision Laboratory
ETH Zurich, Switzerland
schneider@vision.ee.ethz.ch

Thomas Schneider
Engineering Cryptographic Protocols Group
TU Darmstadt, Germany
thomas.schneider@ec-spride.de

## ABSTRACT

Protocols for secure comparison are a fundamental building block of many privacy-preserving protocols such as privacy-preserving face recognition or privacy-preserving fingerprint authentication. So far, all existing secure comparison protocols that have been used in practical implementations require interaction.

In recent work, Hsu et al. (IEEE Transactions on Image Processing 2012) propose protocols for privacy-preserving computation of the scale-invariant feature transform (SIFT) in the encrypted domain. Their fundamental building block is a new protocol for performing secure comparisons under additively homomorphic encryption that requires no interaction.

In this paper we present potential for optimization and shortcomings of their secure comparison protocol. More specifically, we show that it 1) allows optimizations by shifting computation from the server to the user, 2) removes the gain that the user has in outsourcing computations to the server, and most importantly is 3) either computationally intractable for the server or insecure. As alternatives we propose to use either interactive comparison protocols or non-interactive somewhat or fully homomorphic encryption.

## Categories and Subject Descriptors

F.1.2 [**Modes of computation**]: Interactive and reactive computation—*cryptographic protocols*

## Keywords

Signal Processing in the Encrypted Domain; Homomorphic Encryption; Privacy-preserving Comparison

## 1. INTRODUCTION

Privacy-preserving protocols allow to process sensitive data, signals and multimedia content under encryption, cf. [EPK+07]. A fundamental primitive in many such protocols are protocols for secure comparison that allow two parties to compare their inputs in a privacy-preserving way, e.g., [Yao86, Fis01, BK04, DGK08b, DGK08a, KSS09]. As many privacy-preserving protocols are based

on additively homomorphic encryption, secure comparison protocols have been adapted to use ciphertexts as inputs and outputs, e.g., in protocols for privacy-preserving face recognition [EFG+09, SSW09], privacy-preserving fingerprint authentication [BBC+10], or processing encrypted floating point signals [FK11].

All such secure comparison protocols over ciphertexts known so far require interaction between the parties. An intuitive reason for this is that additively homomorphic encryption allows only to perform linear operations (i.e., addition or multiplication by a constant) under encryption, whereas comparison is an inherently non-linear operation. Hence, secure comparison of encrypted values is often considered to be an expensive operation, see e.g., [EPK+07, EBVL12].

One possibility to avoid interaction is to use fully homomorphic encryption schemes that allow both addition and multiplication under encryption. Such schemes were recently introduced by Gentry [Gen09a, Gen09b] and many optimizations and alternative schemes have been proposed, e.g., [DGHV10, SS11, BV11b, BV11a, CNT12, BGV12, GHS12a, GHS12b]. Although first implementations of fully homomorphic encryption have emerged, e.g., [SV10, GH11, LNV11, GHS12c], these implementations are currently not efficient enough to be used in larger privacy-preserving applications.

Recently, a system for privacy-preserving computation of the scale-invariant feature transform (SIFT) in the encrypted domain has been proposed in [HLP12]. Their fundamental building block is a new protocol for performing secure comparisons under *additively homomorphic encryption* that requires *no interaction*.

*Our Contributions.* In §3 of this paper we present potential for optimization and shortcomings of [HLP12] which are also present in earlier versions of that article [HLP10, HLP11]. More precisely, the non-interactive protocol for secure comparison of additively homomorphically encrypted values proposed in these works 1) allows optimizations by shifting computation from the server to the user, 2) removes the gain that the user has in outsourcing computations to the server, and most importantly is 3) either computationally intractable for the server or insecure. In §4, we summarize alternative solutions from the literature.

*Outline.* In §2 we give necessary preliminaries and summarize the comparison protocol of [HLP12] and its application for privacy-preserving SIFT. As our contributions we present potential for optimization and shortcomings of the protocol in §3 and give alternative solutions from the literature in §4. We conclude in §5.

## 2. BACKGROUND ON HSU ET AL.'S COMPARISON PROTOCOL

We first summarize the additively homomorphic encryption scheme of Paillier in §2.1, the protocol for privacy-preserving SIFT of [HLP12] in §2.2, and their non-interactive secure comparison protocol in §2.3.

### 2.1 Additively Homomorphic Encryption

The protocols of [HLP12] are based on the additively homomorphic cryptosystem of Paillier [Pai99] as described next.

The encryption of a message $m \in Z_N^*$ using randomness $r \in_R Z_N^*$ is computed as $E(m, r) = g^m r^N \mod N^2$, where the public key consists of $g \in Z_{N^2}^*$ and an RSA modulus $N = pq$, where $p$ and $q$ are large primes. Early versions of the paper [HLP10,HLP11] recommended to use 100 bit primes $p, q$ which is too small to provide security in practice. The journal version [HLP12, Sect. VI] proposes to use 1 000 bit primes which is in accordance with the 1 024 bits proposed in current recommendations for key lengths[1].

The cryptosystem is additively homomorphic, i.e., it allows to add two messages under encryption:

$$E(m_1, r_1) \cdot E(m_2, r_2) \mod N^2 = g^{m_1+m_2}(r_1 r_2)^N \mod N^2$$
$$= E(m_1 + m_2 \mod N, r_1 r_2 \mod N^2).$$

(**Note** that for addition of messages the randomness is multiplied.)

It is also possible to multiply an encrypted message with a constant $a$:

$$E(m, r)^a \mod N^2 = g^{am} r^{aN} \mod N^2$$
$$= E(am \mod N, r^a \mod N^2).$$

(**Note** that for multiplying the message with $a$ the randomness gets raised to the $a$-th power.)

Informally speaking, the semantic security of the Paillier cryptosystem implies that it is not possible to infer any information about the encrypted plaintext from seeing the ciphertext and the public key only. In particular, it is not possible to compare two ciphertexts when knowing only the public key.

The cryptosystem can also be extended to have a larger plaintext-space and optimized such that encryption costs about one modular exponentiation [DJ01].

### 2.2 Privacy-Preserving SIFT

The authors of [HLP12] propose to use the Paillier cryptosystem for privacy-preserving SIFT. Here, the user wants to outsource the computation of the SIFT algorithm on an image to the server in such a way that the server does not learn any information about the image. In the first step, the server applies the Difference-of-Gaussian (DoG) transform in the encrypted domain: First, he receives from the client the pixel-wise encrypted image $I_e(x, y) = E(I(x, y), r_{x,y})$ for all pixels $(x, y)$ of the image $I(x, y)$, where $r_{x,y}$ is a randomly chosen value used for encryption. Afterwards, the DoG filter $G_{\text{Diff}}(u, v, \rho = (\rho_i, \rho_j))$, defined as the scaled difference of two Gaussian kernels at scales $\rho_i$ and $\rho_j$ with DoG filter coefficients eventually rounded to integer values (cf. Eq. (9) in [HLP12]), is applied to the encrypted image by computing

$$\text{DoGImg}_e(x, y, \rho) = \prod_{u,v} I_e(x-u, y-v)^{G_{\text{Diff}}(u,v,\rho)} \mod N^2$$
$$= E(\text{DoGImg}(x, y, \rho), R_\rho)$$

(cf. Eq. (11) and Eq. (12) in [HLP12]).

[1] http://keylength.com

The resulting randomness is $R_\rho = \prod_{u,v} r_{x-u,y-v}^{G_{\text{Diff}}(u,v,\rho)}$ (cf. Eq. (13) in [HLP12]). Afterwards, the server should detect local extrema of these transformed images in the encrypted domain. For this, the authors of [HLP12] propose a secure comparison protocol described next.

### 2.3 The Comparison Protocol of Hsu et al.

To allow the server to compare two ciphertexts $E(m_1, r_1)$ and $E(m_2, r_2)$, the authors of [HLP12] propose the following protocol: First, the server reveals to the user the random values $r_1$ and $r_2$. As the server does not know these random values, he reveals to the user the sequence of operations that he has applied to the initial ciphertexts obtained by the user. This allows the user to compute the random values (cf. notes in §2.1 above). Afterwards, the user chooses an increasing sequence of random thresholds $T_i \in Z_N$ and encrypts them using the same random values $r_1$ and $r_2$. He sends $E(T_i, r_1)$ and $E(T_i, r_2)$ to the server. Now, the server computes the distance $a_{k_1}$ between the first encrypted message and the closest encrypted threshold with index $t_{k_1}$ as

$$(a_{k_1}, t_{k_1}) = \arg\min_{\text{Inc},i} \left( E(m_1, r_1)g^{\text{Inc}} - E(T_i, r_1) \right). \quad (1)$$

The authors of [HLP12] propose to compute this by repeatedly multiplying $E(m_1, r_1)$ with $g$ until after $a_{k_1} = \text{Inc}$ times this value is equal to the encrypted threshold with index $t_{k_1} = i$. After having computed $a_{k_2}$ and $t_{k_2}$ in a similar way, it is possible to determine whether $m_1 < m_2$ or not. To speed up computations, the server (or the user) could also pre-compute a lookup table, but this essentially shifts the computations from the online phase into a setup phase.

## 3. NOTES ON HSU ET AL.'S COMPARISON PROTOCOL

The comparison protocol of [HLP12] has potential for optimization and shortcomings as described next.

### 3.1 Potential for Optimization and Alternatives

To allow the user to compute the random values $r_1$ and $r_2$, the server needs to reveal to the user the exact sequence of operations and parameters that he has applied to the ciphertexts. For example, in the setting of privacy-preserving SIFT, the server reveals the Gaussian coefficients $G_{\text{Diff}}(x, y, \rho)$ (cf. [HLP12, Fig. 3]). Hence, the user knows all operations that the server has performed before the comparison and hence can apply the operations himself to the plaintexts before sending the encrypted values to the server. This allows to shift computation from the server to the user, but can increase the amount of data sent from the user to the server. As performing operations on plaintexts is substantially faster than on ciphertexts, this is a viable solution for many applications, cf. [Ker11]. Wagner et al. [WRM+10] have even shown that variations of SIFT features can efficiently be computed in real time on mobile devices facing limited computational resources. In this case, the encrypted feature descriptors rather than the image data would have to be transmitted from the client to the server. Computing the SIFT descriptors in the plaintext domain would also allow to overcome most of the simplifications of PPSIFT over SIFT, e.g., rounding of Gaussian coefficients [HLP12, Eq. (9)], four restrictive gradient directions [HLP12, Sect. IV.C], no accurate keypoint localization [Low04, Sect. 4]. Furthermore, shifting the feature computation from the server to the client side even allows to approach the problem of secure image retrieval without the Paillier-based privacy-preserving SIFT evaluation of [HLP12]. Instead, a visual words representation of the query image based on SIFT features can be used along with more efficient cryptographic techniques such as random permutations or order preserving encryption as proposed in [LVSW09,LSVW09]. For this, additional computational effort is required on the client side as the SIFT features of the query image have to be quantized with respect to a codebook first. The codebook can be computed, e.g., by hierarchically clustering the SIFT descriptors of the remote server database into a vocabulary tree. To the best of our knowledge, a detailed performance comparison between the techniques proposed in [LVSW09,LSVW09] and the protocol of [HLP12] has not been published yet (we will show later in §3.3 that the protocol of [HLP12] is either completely impractical or insecure).

## 3.2 High Computational Effort for the User

Now, as the user knows the operations that the server wants to apply under encryption, he could perform these operations by himself as well: he performs the computations in the plaintext domain and afterwards generates a fresh encryption of the result (which costs about one modular exponentiation [DJ01]), i.e., instead of re-computing the same random value for the encrypted thresholds (cf. §2.3), he chooses a new random value for the encryption and the encrypted thresholds. For example, in the setting of privacy-preserving SIFT, the user could use the Gaussian coefficients to apply the Gaussian filter himself and afterwards generate a fresh encryption of the filtered image which is sent to the server. In fact, the computational effort for applying the operation on the plaintexts is smaller than computing the random values (cf. notes in §2.1 above): adding two plaintexts requires one modular addition (instead of a modular multiplication for computing the randomness) and multiplying a plaintext with a constant requires one modular multiplication (instead of a substantially more expensive modular exponentiation). Hence, in the proposed comparison protocol, the client has no advantage in outsourcing all computations done before the comparison to the server any more.

## 3.3 Infeasible Computational Effort for the Server or Insecurity

Next we show that the protocol is either computationally infeasible or insecure, depending on the size of the encrypted values.

*Infeasible computational effort for large values.* For sufficiently large encrypted values, we show that the amount of computation that the server needs to perform to evaluate Eq. (1) is not feasible when the security parameters are chosen according to today's recommendations. Assuming that 10 thresholds are chosen at random and the primes $p, q$ have 1000 bits (as recommended in [HLP12, Sect. VI]). Then, the plaintext space $Z_N$ has about $2^{2000}$ elements and the distance to the next threshold is on average $2^{2000}/(2 \cdot 10) > 2^{1995}$. Today's fastest supercomputer, the IBM Sequoia, has a performance of 16.32 petaflops, i.e., it can perform $16.32 \cdot 10^{15}$ floating point operations per second. Even when assuming that one step in the computation of Eq. (1) could be performed at the time of a single floating point operation, this would require more than $2^{1995}/(16.32 \cdot 10^{15}) > 2^{1941}$ seconds which is far beyond the lifetime of our universe. Note that using more thresholds would also increase the communication in the setup phase and essentially shifts computations from the server to the user: Even with $2^{80}$ thresholds, which results in 1000 YottaBytes ($= 1000 \cdot 10^{24}$ Bytes) of initial communication (this is more than the total amount of information stored on the Internet today), the distance to the next threshold would still be more than $2^{1919}$ operations which remains computationally infeasible.

*Insecurity for small values.* We have shown above that the comparison protocol is computationally infeasible when the encrypted values are large, i.e., taken from the entire plaintext space. When the encrypted values are taken from a smaller domain, the complexity of the protocol can be reduced, but this completely breaks security as we show next. Indeed, in the usage scenario for the SIFT application the image space, i.e., the range for the representation of pixel values, is between 0 and 255 in [HLP12], which is much smaller than the plaintext space of the cryptosystem. (There is some rescaling applied for the Gaussian filter, but the image space still remains much smaller than the plaintext space. More concretely, the authors of [HLP12] propose to use a scaling factor $s = 2^{24}$ such that the largest value would be at most $255 \cdot 2^{24} < 2^{32}$ which is relatively small.) Now, the thresholds can also be taken from the same subspace s.t. the entire range in between thresholds will also be just a subset of the ciphertext space (because the same randomness is used for encrypting the thresholds). This smaller image space makes the comparison protocol computationally feasible, but completely insecure. As the same encrypted thresholds are used for comparison, it is in fact possible for a curious server to completely break the security of the proposed comparison protocol as follows: First, the server computes the distance between the two encrypted messages $m_1$ and $m_2$ to their next threshold using Eq. (1) twice. Afterwards, he substitutes in this equation $E(m_1, r_1)$ and $E(T_i, r_1)$ with the two encrypted thresholds to compute their distance. Adding these three distances yields the distance between $m_1$ and $m_2$. This information is not to be revealed in secure protocols for comparison which are described below. Hence, substantially improving the computational complexity of the protocol while attaining security is an important open problem, cf. [HLP12, Sect. VII].

Another observation made as early as in [RAD78] is that any homomorphic cryptosystem that allows non-interactive comparisons of ciphertexts and reveals the result of this comparison in the clear is insecure, as it allows the adversary to decrypt a given ciphertext using a binary search strategy.

## 4. ALTERNATIVE SECURE COMPARISON PROTOCOLS

As shown in §3, the non-interactive solution based on additively homomorphic encryption proposed in [HLP12] has several shortcomings and hence cannot be used in practice (unless short key lengths are used [HLP10,HLP11] which undermine security). Currently, there is no solution available that is both 1) non-interactive and 2) requires only additively homomorphic encryption. The only solution known so far is to drop one of the requirements, i.e., either drop 1) and keep 2) by using interactive protocols (§4.1), or keep 1) and drop 2) by using more powerful but slower somewhat or fully homomorphic encryption (§4.2).

### 4.1 Interactive Protocols using Additively Homomorphic Encryption

Existing and provably secure protocols for secure comparisons can be used instead, e.g., [BK04,DGK08b,DGK08a,KSS09]. Such protocols have been adapted to compare values encrypted with an additively homomorphic encryption scheme, e.g., in protocols for privacy-preserving face recognition [EFG+09,SSW09] or privacy-preserving fingerprint authentication [BBC+10]. However, these secure comparison protocols would require interaction between the user and the server which should be avoided in the framework of [HLP12], cf. footnote on page 3 of their paper. We propose a non-interactive solution next.

Another approach that minimizes the interaction between the user and the server is to outsource computations not only to a single server but to two (or more) non-colluding servers among which an interactive secure computation protocol is run. This approach was taken in many applications, e.g., [FPRS04, BLW08, BCD+09], and can result in very efficient solutions.

## 4.2 Non-Interactive Comparison using Somewhat or Fully Homomorphic Encryption

For a non-interactive solution, fully-homomorphic encryption schemes could be used as described in §1. Boolean circuits for secure comparison can be built with logarithmic multiplicative-depth[2], e.g., the circuit described in [GSV07] has multiplicative depth $\lceil \log_2 \ell \rceil$ for comparing $\ell$-bit values. Hence, it is also possible to use somewhat homomorphic encryption schemes, e.g., [Gen09b, DGHV10, BV11b, BV11a], that allow a fixed number of multiplications of ciphertexts. In contrast to fully-homomorphic encryption schemes, these schemes do not require an expensive bootstrapping step and hence can be implemented more efficiently, cf. [LNV11]. The authors of [LNV11] report on practical implementation results for the somewhat homomorphic encryption scheme of [BV11b] where parameters are chosen to allow up to 15 multiplications, i.e., it can be used to non-interactively compare numbers of of up to $2^{15} = 32\,768$ bits which is sufficient for the privacy-preserving SIFT application of [HLP12] where numbers fit into the plaintext space with $|N| = |p| + |q| = 2\,000$ bits. The performance reported in [LNV11, Tab. 2] is in the order of few seconds per operation which makes non-interactive secure comparison feasible. However, this solution requires that the inputs are given as encrypted bits. To decompose encrypted integers into encrypted bits can be done using an interactive bit decomposition protocol, e.g., [DFK+06, ST06], or using fully homomorphic encryption.

## 5. CONCLUSION

In this paper we showed potential for optimization and shortcomings of the non-interactive comparison protocol using additively homomorphic encryption of [HLP12]. One solution to get a practical protocol is to use short keys, as proposed in earlier versions of the paper [HLP10, HLP11], but this does not provide enough security. For keys of reasonable size the protocol gets only computationally feasible when the encrypted values and thresholds are from a small domain, but then the protocol is insecure. In order to get a secure *and* computationally feasible solution that can be implemented in a real system, we propose to drop one of the requirements and use either interactive comparison protocols or more powerful, but still computationally feasible somewhat or fully homomorphic encryption. Finding a solution that is secure, computationally feasible, non-interactive, and uses only *additively* homomorphic encryption remains an open research problem. An interesting direction for future work might be to consider also secure computation of other descriptors, e.g., BRIEF [CLSF10] or SURF [BTG06], and compare their performance with secure computation of SIFT.

## Acknowledgments

We thank the anonymous reviewers of IH&MMSec'14 for their helpful comments. The second author was supported by the German Federal Ministry of Education and Research (BMBF) within EC SPRIDE, by the Hessian LOEWE excellence initiative within CASED, and by the European Union Seventh Framework Program (FP7/2007-2013) under grant agreement n. 609611 (PRACTICE).

---

[2]The multiplicative depth of a circuit is its maximum number of multiplications (AND gates) on any path from an input to an output.

## 6. REFERENCES

[BBC+10] Mauro Barni, Tiziano Bianchi, Dario Catalano, Mario Di Raimondo, Ruggero Donida Labati, Pierluigi Failla, Dario Fiore, Riccardo Lazzeretti, Vincenzo Piuri, Fabio Scotti, and Alessandro Piva. Privacy-preserving fingercode authentication. In *ACM Workshop on Multimedia and Security (MM&Sec'10)*, pages 231–240. ACM, 2010.

[BCD+09] Peter Bogetoft, Dan L. Christensen, Ivan Damgård, Martin Geisler, Thomas P. Jakobsen, Mikkel Krøigaard, Janus D. Nielsen, Jesper B. Nielsen, Kurt Nielsen, Jakob Pagter, Michael I. Schwartzbach, and Tomas Toft. Secure multiparty computation goes live. In *Financial Cryptography and Data Security (FC'09)*, volume 5628 of *Lecture Notes in Computer Science*, pages 325–343. Springer, 2009.

[BGV12] Zvika Brakerski, Craig Gentry, and Vinod Vaikuntanathan. (Leveled) fully homomorphic encryption without bootstrapping. In *Innovations in Theoretical Computer Science (ITCS'12)*, pages 309–325. ACM, 2012.

[BK04] Ian F. Blake and Vladimir Kolesnikov. Strong conditional oblivious transfer and computing on intervals. In *Advances in Cryptology – ASIACRYPT'04*, volume 3329 of *Lecture Notes in Computer Science*, pages 515–529. Springer, 2004.

[BLW08] Dan Bogdanov, Sven Laur, and Jan Willemson. Sharemind: A framework for fast privacy-preserving computations. In *European Symposium on Research in Computer Security (ESORICS)*, volume 5283 of *Lecture Notes in Computer Science*, pages 192–206. Springer, 2008.

[BTG06] Herbert Bay, Tinne Tuytelaars, and Luc Gool. SURF: Speeded up robust features. In *European Conference on Compute Vision (ECCV'06)*, volume 3951 of *Lecture Notes in Computer Science*, pages 404–417. Springer, 2006.

[BV11a] Zvika Brakerski and Vinod Vaikuntanathan. Efficient fully homomorphic encryption from (standard) LWE. In *Foundations of Computer Science (FOCS'11)*, pages 97–106. IEEE, 2011.

[BV11b] Zvika Brakerski and Vinod Vaikuntanathan. Fully homomorphic encryption from ring-LWE and security for key dependent messages. In *Advances in Cryptology – CRYPTO'11*, volume 6841 of *Lecture Notes in Computer Science*, pages 505–524. Springer, 2011.

[CLSF10] Michael Calonder, Vincent Lepetit, Christoph Strecha, and Pascal Fua. BRIEF: Binary robust independent elementary features. In *European Conference on Compute Vision (ECCV'10)*, volume 6314 of *Lecture Notes in Computer Science*, pages 778–792. Springer, 2010.

[CNT12] Jean-Sébastien Coron, David Naccache, and Mehdi Tibouchi. Public key compression and modulus switching for fully homomorphic encryption over the integers. In *Advances in Cryptology – EUROCRYPT'12*, volume 7237 of *Lecture Notes in Computer Science*, pages 446–464. Springer, 2012.

[DFK+06] Ivan Damgård, Matthias Fitzi, Eike Kiltz, Jesper Buus Nielsen, and Tomas Toft. Unconditionally secure constant-rounds multi-party computation for equality, comparison, bits and exponentiation. In *Theory of Cryptography Conference (TCC)*, volume 3876 of *Lecture Notes in Computer Science*, pages 285–304. Springer, 2006.

[DGHV10] Marten van Dijk, Craig Gentry, Shai Halevi, and Vinod Vaikuntanathan. Fully homomorphic encryption over the integers. In *Advances in Cryptology – EUROCRYPT'10*, volume 6110 of *Lecture Notes in Computer Science*, pages 24–43. Springer, 2010.

[DGK08a] Ivan Damgård, Martin Geisler, and Mikkel Krøigaard. A correction to "efficient and secure comparison for on-line auctions". Cryptology ePrint Archive, Report 2008/321, 2008.

[DGK08b] Ivan Damgård, Martin Geisler, and Mikkel Krøigaard. Homomorphic encryption and secure comparison. *Journal of Applied Cryptology*, 1(1):22–31, 2008.

[DJ01] Ivan Damgård and Mats Jurik. A generalisation, a simplification and some applications of Paillier's probabilistic public-key system. In *Public-Key Cryptography (PKC'01)*, Lecture Notes in Computer Science, pages 119–136. Springer, 2001.

[EBVL12] Zekeriya Erkin, Michael Beye, Thijs Veugen, and Reginald L. Lagendijk. Privacy-preserving content-based recommender system. In *ACM Workshop on Multimedia and Security (MM&Sec'12)*, pages 77–84. ACM, 2012.

[EFG+09] Zekeriya Erkin, Martin Franz, Jorge Guajardo, Stefan Katzenbeisser, Inald Lagendijk, and Tomas Toft. Privacy-preserving face recognition. In *Privacy Enhancing Technologies (PET'09)*, volume 5672 of *Lecture Notes in Computer Science*, pages 235–253. Springer, 2009.

[EPK+07] Zekeriya Erkin, Alessandro Piva, Stefan Katzenbeisser, Reginald L. Lagendijk, Jamshid Shokrollahi, Gregory Neven, and Mauro Barni. Protection and retrieval of encrypted multimedia content: When cryptography meets signal processing. *EURASIP Journal on Information Security*, 2007.

[Fis01] Marc Fischlin. A cost-effective pay-per-multiplication comparison method for millionaires. In *Cryptographer's Track at RSA Conference (CT-RSA'01)*, volume 2020 of *Lecture Notes in Computer Science*, pages 457–472. Springer, 2001.

[FK11] Martin Franz and Stefan Katzenbeisser. Processing encrypted floating point signals. In *ACM Workshop on Multimedia and Security (MM&Sec'11)*, pages 103–108. ACM, 2011.

[FPRS04] Joan Feigenbaum, Benny Pinkas, Raphael Ryger, and Felipe Saint-Jean. Secure computation of surveys. In *EU Workshop on Secure Multiparty Protocols (SMP)*. ECRYPT, 2004.

[Gen09a] Craig Gentry. *A fully homomorphic encryption scheme*. PhD thesis, Stanford University, 2009.

[Gen09b] Craig Gentry. Fully homomorphic encryption using ideal lattices. In *Symposium on Theory of Computing (STOC'09)*, pages 169–178. ACM, 2009.

[GH11] Craig Gentry and Shai Halevi. Implementing Gentry's fully-homomorphic encryption scheme. In

*Advances in Cryptology – EUROCRYPT'11*, volume 6632 of *Lecture Notes in Computer Science*, pages 129–148. Springer, 2011.

[GHS12a] Craig Gentry, Shai Halevi, and Nigel P. Smart. Better bootstrapping in fully homomorphic encryption. In *Public Key Cryptography (PKC'12)*, volume 7293 of *Lecture Notes in Computer Science*, pages 1–16. Springer, 2012.

[GHS12b] Craig Gentry, Shai Halevi, and Nigel P. Smart. Fully homomorphic encryption with polylog overhead. In *Advances in Cryptology – EUROCRYPT'12*, volume 7237 of *Lecture Notes in Computer Science*, pages 465–482. Springer, 2012.

[GHS12c] Craig Gentry, Shai Halevi, and Nigel P. Smart. Homomorphic evaluation of the AES circuit. In *Advances in Cryptology – CRYPTO'12*, volume 7417 of *Lecture Notes in Computer Science*, pages 850–867. Springer, 2012.

[GSV07] Juan Garay, Berry Schoenmakers, and José Villegas. Practical and secure solutions for integer comparison. In *Public Key Cryptography (PKC'07)*, volume 4450 of *Lecture Notes in Computer Science*, pages 330–342. Springer, 2007.

[HLP10] Chao-Yung Hsu, Chun-Shien Lu, and Soo-Chang Pei. Homomorphic encryption-based secure SIFT for privacy-preserving feature extraction, July 12, 2010. Technical Report No. TR-IIS-10-006.

[HLP11] Chao-Yung Hsu, Chun-Shien Lu, and Soo-Chang Pei. Homomorphic encryption-based secure SIFT for privacy-preserving feature extraction. In *IS&T/SPIE Media Watermarking, Forensics, and Security*, volume 7880, pages 788005–1–788005–17, 2011.

[HLP12] Chao-Yung Hsu, Chun-Shien Lu, and Sao-Chang Pei. Image feature extraction in encrypted domain with privacy-preserving SIFT. *IEEE Transactions on Image Processing*, 21(11):4593–4607, November 2012.

[Ker11] Florian Kerschbaum. Automatically optimizing secure computation. In *Computer and Communications Security (CCS'11)*, pages 703–714. ACM, 2011.

[KSS09] Vladimir Kolesnikov, Ahmad-Reza Sadeghi, and Thomas Schneider. Improved garbled circuit building blocks and applications to auctions and computing minima. In *Cryptology And Network Security (CANS'09)*, volume 5888 of *Lecture Notes in Computer Science*, pages 1–20. Springer, 2009.

[LNV11] Kristin Lauter, Michael Naehrig, and Vinod Vaikuntanathan. Can homomorphic encryption be practical? In *ACM Cloud Computing Security Workshop (CCSW'11)*, pages 113–124. ACM, 2011.

[Low04] David G. Lowe. Distinctive image features from scale-invariant keypoints. *International Journal of Computer Vision*, 60(2):91–110, 2004.

[LSVW09] Wenjun Lu, Ashwin Swaminathan, Avinash L. Varna, and Min Wu. Enabling search over encrypted multimedia databases. In *Media Forensics and Security*, volume 7254 of *SPIE Proceedings*, page 725418. SPIE, 2009.

[LVSW09] Wenjun Lu, Avinash L. Varna, Ashwin Swaminathan, and Min Wu. Secure image retrieval through feature protection. In *IEEE International*

*Conference on Acoustics, Speech, and Signal Processing (ICASSP)*, pages 1533–1536. IEEE, 2009.

[Pai99]    Pascal Paillier. Public-key cryptosystems based on composite degree residuosity classes. In *Advances in Cryptology – EUROCRYPT'99*, volume 1592 of *Lecture Notes in Computer Science*, pages 223–238. Springer, 1999.

[RAD78]   Ronald Rivest, Len Adleman, and Michael Dertouzos. On data banks and privacy homomorphisms. In *Foundations of Secure Computation*, pages 169–177. Academic Press, 1978.

[SS11]     Peter Scholl and Nigel P. Smart. Improved key generation for Gentry's fully homomorphic encryption scheme. In *IMA International Conference on Cryptography and Coding*, volume 7089 of *Lecture Notes in Computer Science*, pages 10–22. Springer, 2011.

[SSW09]   Ahmad-Reza Sadeghi, Thomas Schneider, and Immo Wehrenberg. Efficient privacy-preserving face recognition. In *International Conference on Information Security and Cryptology (ICISC'09)*, volume 5984 of *Lecture Notes in Computer Science*, pages 229–244. Springer, 2009.

[ST06]     Berry Schoenmakers and Pim Tuyls. Efficient binary conversion for paillier encrypted values. In *Advances in Cryptology – EUROCRYPT*, volume 4004 of *Lecture Notes in Computer Science*, pages 522–537. Springer, 2006.

[SV10]     Nigel P. Smart and Fre Vercauteren. Fully homomorphic encryption with relatively small key and ciphertext sizes. In *Public Key Cryptography (PKC'10)*, volume 6056 of *Lecture Notes in Computer Science*, pages 420–443. Springer, 2010.

[WRM$^+$10]  Daniel Wagner, Gerhard Reitmayr, Alessandro Mulloni, Tom Drummond, and Dieter Schmalstieg. Real-time detection and tracking for augmented reality on mobile phones. *IEEE Transactions on Visualization and Computer Graphics*, 16(3):355–368, 2010.

[Yao86]    Andrew C. Yao. How to generate and exchange secrets. In *IEEE Symposium on Foundations of Computer Science (FOCS'86)*, pages 162–167. IEEE, 1986.

# Distributional Differential Privacy for Large-Scale Smart Metering

Márk Jelasity
University of Szeged, Hungary and MTA-SZTE
Research Group on Artificial Intelligence

Kenneth P. Birman
Cornell University, Ithaca, NY, USA

## ABSTRACT

In smart power grids it is possible to match supply and demand by applying control mechanisms that are based on fine-grained load prediction. A crucial component of every control mechanism is monitoring, that is, executing queries over the network of smart meters. However, smart meters can learn so much about our lives that if we are to use such methods, it becomes imperative to protect privacy. Recent proposals recommend restricting the provider to differentially private queries, however the practicality of such approaches has not been settled. Here, we tackle an important problem with such approaches: even if queries at different points in time over statistically independent data are implemented in a differentially private way, the parameters of the distribution of the query might still reveal sensitive personal information. Protecting these parameters is hard if we allow for *continuous monitoring*, a natural requirement in the smart grid. We propose novel differentially private mechanisms that solve this problem for sum queries. We evaluate our methods and assumptions using a theoretical analysis as well as publicly available measurement data and show that the extra noise needed to protect distribution parameters is small.

## 1. INTRODUCTION

By deploying smart meters within individual homes and offices, it becomes possible to continuously measure, predict, and even control the consumption of power by the household. This could save money for consumers and for power producers, while also reducing unnecessary generation. An important component of any complete control solution that employs a network of smart meters is to monitor aggregate (predicted) consumption. Monitoring creates a challenge, however: we also need to ensure the privacy of the data, which can reveal the individual habits of the inhabitants of a home, reveal times when there is no one at home, the location of individuals within the home, or in extreme cases even very fine grained information such as which show is being watched on TV [1]. Our premise in this paper is that in an ideal system, personal data should be protected not only from eavesdroppers, but even from the utility itself.

The privacy protection problem has been well studied. The essential requirement is to calculate aggregation queries without revealing any individual records. Achieving this is non-

trivial if the measurements are distributed: the meters should not trust one-another with sensitive data, nor can the network be trusted [2]. In addition, we must also make sure that the computed query results do not leak too much information about individual measurements either. The intent of the differential privacy model is to address this problem [3]. Differentially private query results contain a carefully designed amount of noise that masks the influence of any individual data record.

Unfortunately, supporting an unlimited number of queries introduces a further complication. Even if we implement a distributed differentially private mechanism, the stream of the query results still has a potential to leak information about the constant parameters of the distribution of the measurements in an individual home. That is, *existing techniques do not prevent information leakage about static properties* of the household, despite the fact that those static properties indirectly influence individual readings. This is a problem, because static properties that might be teased out over a period of time could still reveal sensitive information. Examples include the number of inhabitants, behavioral patterns and habits, the list of devices in the home, and so on.

In this paper we focus on solving the problem of protecting the privacy of distribution parameters even when an unlimited number of queries are allowed. Our main contribution takes the form of novel distributed differentially private mechanisms for sum queries that protect not only the individual records but also the parameters of individual energy consumption patterns. We evaluate our methods and assumptions using a theoretical analysis and publicly available measurement data. We believe ours is the first solution in which it is possible to monitor the network for an unlimited time while still achieving provable guarantees of differential privacy that extend to static aspects of personal information.

## 2. BACKGROUND AND RELATED WORK

It is possible to control energy consumption using smart devices with approaches ranging from purely local scheduling methods [4], to central control schemes that do nothing to protect privacy, to global self-organization without central control [5]. We are interested in the latter style of solutions. These typically start with a global aggregation component, and then use the output from the aggregation step as input to a control loop or a decision mechanism. As our global aggregation function, we focus on the sum function, which turns out to be a surprisingly powerful primitive both in and of itself, and for calculating more complex statistics [6, 7].

Preserving privacy in this context has been studied extensively. Cryptographic techniques have been proposed to perform computations in individual homes [8], for example, for the purposes of policy based billing. Our area of interest, aggregate computing, has also been addressed. One part of the problem is to be able to collaboratively compute the sum of a set of values distributed over a network without any node revealing its value to any other node. Techniques for achieving this are known [2], and have typically been based on secret sharing schemes [9, 10].

The other part of the problem is to make sure that the computed aggregate query cannot be used to infer much information about individual records. *Differential privacy* (see also Section 5) is a framework for protecting data, whereby noise is judiciously introduced to the query result to mask the contribution and hence content of individual records [3]. Distributed implementations have been proposed that—on top of some secret sharing scheme for secure multi-party computations—also implement noise generation in a distributed way [11, 12]. We build on this work in that we will assume that an implementation of a distributed differentially private mechanism is available for computing sum queries and for generating Gaussian and Laplacian noise, and we will use these as black box components to implement our distributional differentially private schemes.

Our main focus here is on the problems that arise from the repeated computation of the sum query (as opposed to the single-shot approach of previous techniques). In fact there has been prior work on very closely related questions [13, 14]. However, previously proposed approaches make very different kinds of assumptions than we do both about how the data is generated and exactly what needs to be protected. We revisit previous work in this area in Section 5.

## 3. PROBLEM STATEMENT

Let us assume that we have $n$ smart meters. At a given time $t$, let the database containing the readings of the smart meters be $D(t) = (x_1(t), \ldots, x_n(t))$. These readings can correspond to actual power consumption at time $t$, aggregated power consumption in a short time interval before $t$, or predicted consumption in a short time interval after $t$. Since all these cases result in similar distributions, our discussion covers all these cases. Let us consider the series of databases $D_1, D_2, \ldots$, where $D_j = D(t_0 + j \cdot \delta)$. That is, the databases are defined as snapshots taken at regular time intervals starting at time $t_0$. Let us introduce the notation $D_j = (x_{1j}, \ldots, x_{nj})$.

The database $D_j$ is distributed in that the smart meters do not upload their output to a central location. For the present paper, details of the distributed communication are irrelevant to the analysis: instead, we assume that there is a secure privacy preserving mechanism in place to compute the sum query of the readings, such as those discussed in [11, 12]. These mechanisms can deal not only with computing the sum query, but also with adding the necessary noise to it to achieve differential privacy in a fully distributed way. With this in mind, for the remainder of the treatment we will build on the primitives of summation and the addition of certain noise terms, noting that the actual implementation is intended to be fully distributed.

We assume that the databases are generated by some probability distribution, that is, we model each measurement $x_{ij}$ as a random variable. We elaborate on this model in Section 4. The utility wishes to carry out a series of queries $M_j(D_j)$, with $j = 1, 2, \ldots$. Although the answers should become available to the utility in a timely manner, the computation must not reveal any of the individual values $x_{ij}$. In addition, the utility should not learn about the parameters of the underlying probabilistic models. As mentioned before, we focus on the sum query $M_j = \sum_{i=1}^{n} x_{ij}$.

## 4. A GENERATIVE PROBABILISTIC MODEL

Our model is shown in Figure 1(a). Variable $M_j$ is the query result that is obtained over database $D_j$. In this model, we assume that the distribution of the variables $x_{ij}$ depends on a set of global external parameters $\phi_j$ for all databases $j = 1, 2, \ldots$, and a set of internal smart meter parameters $\theta_i$ for all smart meters $1 \le i \le n$.

Parameters $\phi_j$ are common to all meters but depend on the time when the snapshot was taken. These include weather conditions, the day of week, public holidays, and the time of day as well. We assume that parameters $\phi_j$ are publicly known, and also that within a database $D_i$ the values $x_{ij}$ depend on each other only through the common parameters $\phi_j$. This means that if the common parameters are known (as we have just assumed) then within any database $D_j$ all variables $x_{ij}$ are independent. Note that here we introduced a simplification by not considering any further structure, such as geography, that could result in parameters that are shared by a subset of meters. Every parameter is either fully local to a meter, or common to all meters.

Parameters $\theta_i$ are internal to smart meter $i$. As expressed by the plate model, these parameters are static during the observation of the meters. That is, these parameters are constant, but unknown. They describe, for example, the set of appliances in the home, and the stable habits, behavioral patterns, and preferences (that is, the personal profile) of the inhabitants. We want to make sure that the static parameters $\theta_i$ are also protected by a differentially private mechanism, in addition to the individual readings in the databases.

Note that—to simplify our discussion—we made the assumption that at any point in time the system follows some single underlying probabilistic model, but that the variables at different points in time are independent if the static parameters of the model are known. As it will be evident later, our approach to protect the static parameters $\theta_i$ is completely insensitive to this assumption but, in the lack of extra measures, the privacy of the individual readings $x_{ij}$ could weaken if consecutive readings are correlated.

To characterize autocorrelation, we examined the publicly available SMART∗ dataset [15]. The dataset contains power consumption measurements in five second intervals in three homes that are called home A, B and C. The interval covered by the dataset spans from the 15th of April until the 5th of July, 2012. Due to the relatively limited amount of data that covers a relatively short amount of time, we considered only the time of day as a global parameter. Based on the available data, we tested the assumption of independence by extracting several time series that correspond to the same value of the global parameter, namely the time of day. More precisely, we divided the time into 30 minute intervals and aggregated the consumption in them. We then created a series using the values corresponding to the same time of day in the series of days that are covered in the dataset. Let such a series be denoted by $x_{ij}^t$ where $i \in \{A, B, C\}$ selects the home, $j$ selects the day, and $t$ defines the time of day.

Figure 2 shows autocorrelation plots for the series $(x_{Aj})_{j=1}^{88}$, with $t \in \{\text{midnight}, 7\text{am}, 6\text{pm}\}$ (for homes B and C the plots are similar). The choice of $t$ is arbitrary, but other values result in similar results. The data covers 88 consecutive days. We used 50 samples to calculate the approximation for each time lag to make sure the variance of the approximations is the same. Patterns in these graphs would indicate significant autocorrelation. None are evident, but notice that the confidence band is far from perfect, in that the underlying distribution is not normal (see Section 6.2).

While proposing a full control strategy is outside the scope of this paper, note that the above observation does not mean that control mechanisms that operate with a control period shorter than one day are impossible. Recall that we target communities with large numbers of consumers. In such a setting, we could introduce an increased amount of noise carefully calculated based on the observed correlations so as to protect $x_{ij}$. As we will see, the noise we need to add to each query has a small expected value independent of network

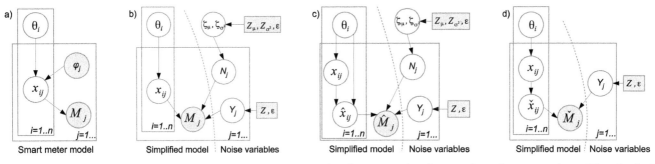

a) Smart meter model    b) Simplified model : Noise variables    c) Simplified model : Noise variables    d) Simplified model : Noise variables

Figure 1: Probabilistic models of smart meter data and privacy mechanisms using plate notation. The shaded variables are known. The rest of the variables need privacy protection. a: our model of smart meters; b: model when $x_{ij}$ is normally distributed; c: $x_{ij}$ is not normally distributed and $\hat{x}_{ij}$ is normally distributed; d: arbitrarily distributed $x_{ij}$ and $\check{x}_{ij} \sim \text{Bernoulli}(x_{ij})$.

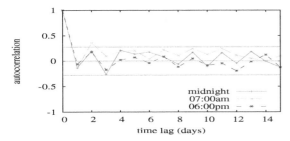

Figure 2: Autocorrelation plot of the time series of 30 minute measurement intervals at the same time of day during the days covered by the data. The 95% confidence interval assuming random data with normal distribution is shown.

size; but in a large network an increased (but still constant) amount of noise is still suitable. Also, to stabilize control, the provider might choose to sample the large network with each query. This also reduces correlation as a side-effect through the increased period of reading a particular meter. Moreover, sampling itself fits into our model, as taking a random subset simply introduces another private parameter: the probability whether the given meter is included or not.

## 5. DISTRIBUTIONAL PRIVACY

Let us now introduce the notion of differential privacy for general queries [16]. Let $M$ be an algorithm producing an answer to a query issued on any possible database $D \in \mathcal{D}$. While operating on a fixed database $D$, algorithm $M$ will also introduce random noise, thereby randomizing its output. That is, for a fixed database $D$, $M(D)$ will be a random variable. Let the distance function $d : \mathcal{D} \times \mathcal{D} \mapsto \mathbb{N}$ be defined as the number of records in which two given databases differ. Without loss of generality, we assume that all the databases contain the same number of records.

*Definition 1. ($\varepsilon$-differential privacy)* Let $M$ be a randomized mechanism acting on databases. $M$ is *$\varepsilon$-differentially private* iff for any two fixed databases $D$ and $D'$ such that $d(D, D') = 1$, and for any output $M$, we have

$$P(D|M) \leq P(D'|M) \cdot \exp(\varepsilon). \qquad (1)$$

We expressed the traditional definition in a Bayesian style. This definition is equivalent to the usual definition [16] if the prior distribution over the databases is uniform (any possible database is equally likely, that is, $P(D) = P(D')$).

One possible way to achieve differential privacy of the sum query in a database $D_i$ is by adding noise to the output of the query calibrated according to the *sensitivity* of the query [17].

In other words, we can return

$$M_j = M(D_j) = Y_j + \sum_{i=1}^{n} x_{ij}, \qquad (2)$$

where $Y_j$ is an appropriate random variable. A common choice for the distribution of $Y_j$ is $Y_j \sim \text{Laplace}(0, Z/\varepsilon)$, where $Z$ is a constant representing the *global sensitivity* of the sum function [3, 17]:

*Definition 2. (global sensitivity [17])* The *global sensitivity* $Z_f$ of $f : \mathcal{D} \mapsto \mathbb{R}$ is given by

$$Z_f = \max_{D, D': \, d(D, D') = 1} |f(D) - f(D')| \qquad (3)$$

We can apply this approach if there is a global upper bound on the values $x_{ij}$, since the global sensitivity of the sum is bounded by the maximal value of any addend. Such a bound can be assumed to exist in our application domain.

Now, we can turn to our goal, that is, to release $M_j$, $j = 1, 2, \ldots$. One possible approach would be to follow the work of Dwork et al [13], where the notion of event level privacy in *growing* databases is defined. Roughly speaking, the idea there is that two series are adjacent if they differ in one element. This is almost the same notion as the adjacency of databases, except that the static databases are now replaced by data streams. With this in mind, we could define a notion of adjacency of two series of databases by requiring that exactly one pair of databases is adjacent, and the rest of the pairs are identical (where identical time points define the pairs). We could then release $M_j$, $j = 1, 2, \ldots$, if the series is differentially private in terms of this adjacency definition. Indeed, the series $M_j$, $j = 1, 2, \ldots$ is $\varepsilon$-differentially private if all queries $M_j$ are because of the *parallel composition* [18] of the queries (each query is run on a separate subset of the union of the available data).

As noted in the introduction, however, this form of protection is inadequate because it overlooks a potentially important form of leakage. Intuitively, even if all individual queries $M_j$ are protected by adding noise, the parameters $\theta_i$ are still not protected if we can observe an unlimited number of query results. To see this, consider that if the global parameters $\phi_j$ are in fact constant (do not depend on $j$), then all variables $M_j$ will have an identical distribution that can be recovered with an arbitrary precision after performing a sufficient number of measurements. This is because (as evident from Figure 1(a)) in this case all variables $x_{ij}$ will have the same distribution for all $j$. In the case of the sum query, and if the sensitivity mechanism is applied, this distribution can be determined from equation (2). Since $Z$ and $\varepsilon$ are known, as are the $\phi_j$, the unknown parameters are $\theta_i$. This means that approximating the query distribution could lead to information leakage about the private parameters $\theta_i$ of the smart meters.

If the global external parameters $\phi_j$ are time-varying, then the parameters $\theta_i$ would be more secure, since in that case the shape of the distribution of the queries will be more complex (it will become a mixture distribution determined by the distribution of $\phi_j$). An adversary interested in $\theta_i$ will therefore attempt to limit itself to considering only subsets of the readings that share the same external parameters, since that way approximating $\theta_i$ is easier. In other words, a constant $\phi_j$ is the worst case for privacy. The considerations above motivate the following definition of adjacency.

*Definition 3.* (*distributional adjacency*) Let us assume the probabilistic model in Figure 1(a). Consider two series of databases $(D_j)_{j=1}^{\infty}$ and $(D'_j)_{j=1}^{\infty}$ that were generated by the model. The two series are *distributionally adjacent* iff $\theta_i = \theta'_i$ for all but one index $1 \leq k \leq n$, for which $\theta_k \neq \theta'_k$, and all the other variables that do not depend on $\theta_k$ are the same.

The intuition behind the definition is simple. When monitoring smart meters, distributional adjacency captures the situation when we are collecting smart metering data in a set of homes that differs in exactly one element (we replace one home with another one), but otherwise everything remains exactly the same including all the readings in the rest of the homes. Based on this notion of adjacency, we define distributional differential privacy.

*Definition 4.* (*distributional $\varepsilon$-differential privacy*) Let $M$ be a randomized mechanism acting on databases. Let us assume the probabilistic model in Figure 1(a). $M$ is *distributionally $\varepsilon$-differentially private* iff for any two fixed and distributionally adjacent database series $(D_j)_{j=1}^{\infty}$ with parameters $\theta = (\theta_1, \ldots, \theta_n)$ and $(D'_j)_{j=1}^{\infty}$ with parameters $\theta' = (\theta'_1, \ldots, \theta'_n)$, and for any query output series $(M_j)_{j=1}^{\infty}$

$$P(\theta \,|\, (M_j)_{j=1}^{\infty}) \leq P(\theta' \,|\, (M_j)_{j=1}^{\infty}) \cdot \exp(\varepsilon). \qquad (4)$$

# 6. ACHIEVING DISTRIBUTIONAL PRIVACY

Here, we provide techniques to achieve distributional privacy that differ in their assumptions about the available knowledge and the distribution of $x_{ij}$. First, let us ignore the parameter $\phi_j$ in the model in Figure 1(a). As we argued before, this is the worst case from the point of view of privacy, since the adversary has a noise-free sample of the distribution of the query. Besides, in a real system an adversary can collect samples that belong to the same value of $\phi_j$; recall that the value of $\phi_j$ is known publicly.

## 6.1 Readings with Gaussian distributions

We provide an example where distributional $\varepsilon$-differential privacy can be achieved. Let us assume that measurement $x_{ij}$ has a Gaussian distribution: $x_{ij} \sim \mathcal{N}(\theta_i)$ for all $j$, where $\theta_i = (\mu_i, \sigma_i^2)$. In this case, assuming the model in Figure 1(a) (without $\phi_j$), we know that $\sum_{i=1}^{n} x_{ij} \sim \mathcal{N}(\sum_{i=1}^{n} \mu_i, \sum_{i=1}^{n} \sigma_i^2)$. In other words, the sum query that we are interested in has a Gaussian distribution as well. Many other distributions have a similar property, for example, the binomial or the Poisson distributions. The class of *stable* distributions also has this property. This class covers many practical distributions including normal and power-law distributions [19]. Most importantly, in this case the distribution of the query is simple and it has only a few parameters that depend on the parameters of the distributions of the individual measurements.

Observe that by returning an infinite series of query results the mechanism essentially returns the sum query over the parameters of the distributions $\theta_i$. We never obtain the exact parameter set of the query distribution (the sum of $\theta_i$), but instead we can draw an unlimited number of samples from this distribution. Even so, let us make the very conservative

assumption that eventually the adversary learns the exact parameters in this case; doing so only makes it harder to achieve distributional privacy.

To make the solution distributionally private, we can apply, among other options, a sensitivity-based approach to the parameter space. That is, we can add independent noise $N_j \sim \mathcal{N}(\zeta_\mu, \zeta_{\sigma^2})$, which results in the query distribution

$$N_j + \sum_{i=1}^{n} x_{ij} \sim \mathcal{N}(\zeta_\mu + \sum_{i=1}^{n} \mu_i, \zeta_{\sigma^2} + \sum_{i=1}^{n} \sigma_i^2), \qquad (5)$$

where $\zeta_\mu$ and $\zeta_{\sigma^2}$ are constants that are drawn from the distribution $\text{Laplace}(0, Z_\mu/\varepsilon)$ and $\text{Laplace}(0, Z_{\sigma^2}/\varepsilon)$, respectively, where $Z_\mu$ and $Z_{\sigma^2}$ are the global sensitivities of the sum queries $\sum_{i=1}^{n} \mu_i$ and $\sum_{i=1}^{n} \sigma_i^2$, respectively. Constants $\zeta_\mu$ and $\zeta_{\sigma^2}$ are drawn at the beginning of collecting the query results and are not changed later. This, similarly to traditional differential privacy, results in a noisy result; but this time this noise will be applied to the parameters of the distributions, and not the data.

Indeed—under the assumption that the adversary will eventually learn from the infinite series of query results the exact parameters $(\sum_{i=1}^{n} \mu_i, \sum_{i=1}^{n} \sigma_i^2)$—distributional privacy (Definition 4) becomes simply an instance of differential privacy (Definition 1) with the database being the distribution parameters $(\mu_i, \sigma_i^2)$, $i = 1, \ldots, n$ over which a differentially private sum query is run. This proves that the mechanism in equation (5) is distributionally $\varepsilon$-differentially private.

Finally, to also achieve the differential privacy of the data in each individual database in time, we introduce the usual noise term, as mentioned previously in equation (2):

$$M_j = N_j + Y_j + \sum_{i=1}^{n} x_{ij}, \qquad (6)$$

where $Y_j \sim \text{Laplace}(0, Z/\varepsilon)$ and $Z$ is the global sensitivity of the sum query. This will not change distributional differential privacy, since adding additional independent noise will never weaken the privacy of any scheme. Also, note that $Z \geq Z_\mu$. The resulting model is illustrated in Figure 1(b).

We stress that in this example we assumed that an unlimited number of samples are available from the same query distribution, and so the parameters of the query distribution can be recovered to an arbitrary precision. Nonetheless, we were able to achieve distributional differential privacy due to the special property of Gaussian distributions.

## 6.2 Realistic distributions

The distribution of the readings is not normal (and not even stable) in practice. Indeed, Figure 3 (left) illustrates the probability density of power consumption as a function of the time of day in home A in the SMART* dataset [15]. For this plot we aggregated the consumption in 5 minute intervals and produced a scatterplot based on the days that are covered in the dataset. These plots (and related work [20]) suggest that the distribution of power consumption at a certain time of day is a mixture distribution. In a mixture distribution the variables that select the components of the mixture are those internal variables that are not constant during the observation period (for example, whether the owner is on a holiday or not, whether there are guests in the home, whether the air conditioning is on, etc.).

In the case of mixture distributions, the number of parameters of the distribution of the query will grow with the number of readings used to answer the query, unlike in the case of stable distributions mentioned in Section 6.1. This creates a new challenge to distributional privacy, particularly given our assumption that the adversary can recover the exact parameters of the query distribution using the unlimited

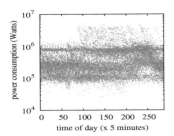
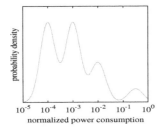

**Figure 3:** Left: scatter plot to illustrate the observed probability density of energy consumption as a function of time of day, based on 5 minute intervals during the days covered by the data. Right: probability density for modeling power consumption prediction. This is a lognormal mixture distribution over the $[0, 1]$ interval.

number of query samples. In practice an additional source of uncertainty regarding the parameters of the distribution is the limited number of samples available; a topic we do not exploit in this paper.

## 6.3  Transformation to Gaussian distributions

Our first approach to tackling arbitrary distributions converts the meter readings' distributions to Gaussian. The main advantage of this approach is that we can theoretically guarantee distributional privacy for arbitrary distributions for the case of the sum query, while introducing negligible extra noise. However, we need to assume that the local parameters $\theta_i$ are known locally by meter $i$. This assumption is reasonable, since the local meter has full access to local consumption data and hence can easily approximate the distribution. Further, if we aggregate predicted consumption, then the parameters are fully determined by the local meter.

The idea is that, based on the knowledge of $\theta_i$ and $x_{ij}$, the local meter $i$ will generate a variable $\hat{x}_{ij}$ that has a Gaussian distribution with the same expectation and standard deviation as $x_{ij}$ and is maximally correlated with $x_{ij}$. After this, the query is calculated using $\hat{x}_{ij}$ instead of $x_{ij}$ using the same noise variables as in equation (6):

$$\hat{M}_j = N_j + Y_j + \sum_{i=1}^{n} \hat{x}_{ij}, \qquad (7)$$

while keeping $x_{ij}$ private. Applying the same reasoning as in Section 6.1, it is clear that the method is distributionally differentially private. Instead of a Gaussian distribution, any other stable distribution can be used, as mentioned in Section 6.1, depending on the shape of the distribution to be approximated.

The resulting probabilistic model is illustrated in Figure 1(c). Let us elaborate on how $\hat{x}_{ij}$ is computed. Let $(\mu_i, \sigma_i^2)$ be the expectation and variance of $x_{ij}$, and let $\mathcal{X}(x) = P(x_{ij} \leq x)$ be the distribution function of $x_{ij}$. We know that $\mathcal{X}(\cdot)$ and $(\mu_i, \sigma_i^2)$ are known locally. Let

$$\hat{x}_{ij} = \mathcal{N}^{-1}(\mathcal{X}(x_{ij}); \mu_i, \sigma_i^2), \qquad (8)$$

in other words, we compute $\hat{x}_{ij}$ in such a way that it corresponds to the same quantile according to $\mathcal{N}(\cdot; \mu_i, \sigma_i^2)$ as $x_{ij}$ according to $\mathcal{X}(\cdot)$. (To simplify the discussion, without loss of generality, we assumed that $\mathcal{X}(\cdot)$ is continuous.)

It is obvious that the expectation and variance of $M_j$ and $\hat{M}_j$ are the same since $x_{ij}$ and $\hat{x}_{ij}$ have the same expectation and variance by design for all $(i, j)$, the readings $x_{ij}$ are independent (and hence the transformed readings $\hat{x}_{ij}$ are independent as well), and $M_j$ and $\hat{M}_j$ are defined by the same linear function of the readings. Furthermore, the distribu-

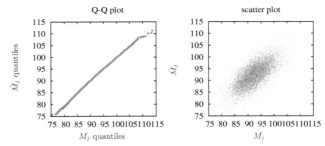

**Figure 4:** Q-Q plot (left) and scatter plot (right) based on 10,000 observations. The correlation coefficient is $0.7$.

tions of $M_j$ and $\hat{M}_j$ will be very similar. This is because $\hat{M}_j$ is normally distributed, while $M_j$ is the sum of many similar variables, so it is also likely to be normally distributed.

To examine the distribution of $(M_j, \hat{M}_j)$ empirically, we model the distribution of $x_{ij}$ at time $j$ for all $i$ using the mixture distribution in Figure 3 (right). This distribution is an approximation of the distribution in home A at noon (Figure 3 (left)). We assume that there are 1000 meters (i.e., $i = 1, \ldots, 1000$). We empirically generate 10,000 independent samples of $(M_j, \hat{M}_j)$. The quantile-quantile (Q-Q) plot in Figure 4 clearly shows that $M_j$ is almost exactly normal. In addition, the scatter plot in Figure 4 shows a high correlation. Overall, we can conclude that in a realistic setting the proposed transformation preserves most of the original information while providing full distributional privacy.

## 6.4  Transformation to Bernoulli distributions

Our second approach to tackle arbitrary distributions is based on converting the meter readings' distributions to a Bernoulli distribution. The main advantage of this approach is that we will *not* assume that the local parameters $\theta_i$ are known locally by meter $i$. Also, we will theoretically prove that this approach will protect the privacy of $\theta_i$, with the exception of the expected value $E(x_{ij})$. The approach is also very simple to implement. However, this approach introduces a higher level of noise, as we will see.

Let us assume that the distribution of the reading $x_{ij}$ is arbitrary, but the values are bounded. Without loss of generality, let $0 \leq x_{ij} \leq 1$. Let us introduce a new variable $\check{x}_{ij}$ for all readings $x_{ij}$ where $\check{x}_{ij} \sim \text{Bernoulli}(x_{ij})$.

We calculate the query over the new variables $\check{x}_{ij}$ while the variables $x_{ij}$ are kept private. Since $E(\check{x}_{ij}|x_{ij}) = x_{ij}$, we know that $E(\check{x}_{ij}) = E(E(\check{x}_{ij}|x_{ij})) = E(x_{ij})$, which means that, due to the linearity of expectation and the construction of $\check{x}_{ij}$, $E\left[\sum_{i=1}^{n} \check{x}_{ij}\right] = E\left[\sum_{i=1}^{n} x_{ij}\right]$. That is, using variables $\check{x}_{ij}$ results in the same expected query value for the sum query and, in fact, for any linear query. The same observations hold also if we consider index $j$ and fix $i$. Further, and most importantly, the series $(\check{x}_{ij})_{j=1}^{\infty}$ carries no information about the parameters of the distribution of $x_{ij}$ other than the expected value, since all the values are 0 or 1, and they are drawn independently.

As a practical technique, we propose to return the query

$$\check{M}_j = Y_j + \sum_{i=1}^{n} \check{x}_{ij}. \qquad (9)$$

Here—as before—$Y_j \sim \text{Laplace}(0, Z/\varepsilon)$ and $Z$ is the global sensitivity of $\sum_{i=1}^{n} \check{x}_{ij}$. Clearly, due to the Bernoulli distribution of $\check{x}_{ij}$ we have $Z = 1$. Since the authors are not aware of any closed form for the convolution of multiple Bernoulli distributions with different parameters, the Bernoulli variables are not made distributionally private here. However, since these variables only reveal the expectation of the common distribution of the masked variables $x_{ij}$, we protect most of the fine structure of the local distribution. The resulting probabilistic model is illustrated in Figure 1(d).

Let us examine exactly how much noise we introduced. Our first intuition is that in a usual setting this noise is in the same order of magnitude as the noise introduced by sampling $x_{ij}$ using parameters $\theta_i$. Additionally, this noise will also decrease in a relative sense as the number of smart meters increases. More precisely, the variance of the distribution Bernoulli($p$) is $p(1-p)$. This is maximal if $p = 0.5$. Now, under the probabilistic model we work with this means that

$$\text{stdev}\left[\sum_{i=1}^{n} \tilde{x}_{ij}\right] = \sqrt{\sum_{i=1}^{n} x_{ij}(1 - x_{ij})} \leq \frac{\sqrt{n}}{2} \qquad (10)$$

since the variables are independent. The worst case of $\sqrt{n}/2$ is given when $x_{ij} = 0.5$ for all $i$.

This noise, however, is not necessarily extra noise from the point of view of the application. For example, if the variables $x_{ij}$ are statistical predictions then the question is the ratio of the expected noise that originates from the uncertainty in the prediction and the extra noise due to converting the variables. To examine this case, as in Section 6.3, we again model the distribution of the prediction using the mixture distribution in Figure 3. As before, the consumption values are normalized to the interval $[0, 1]$. Setting $n = 1000$ and taking 10,000 samples of $\sum_{i=1}^{1000} \tilde{x}_{ij}$ we find the empirical standard deviation to be 9.15. At the same time, $\text{stdev}(\sum_{i=1}^{1000} x_{ij}) = 4.82$, which gives the ratio of 1.9. This ratio is constant as a function of $n$, and both standard deviations are $O(\sqrt{n})$. For the sake of completeness, for $n = 1000$, the upper bound of standard deviation is $\sqrt{1000}/2 = 15.81$. We achieve a variance of 9.15 due to the strong asymmetry of the original distribution.

## 7. CONCLUSIONS

We proposed novel techniques to implement distributed sum queries in a privacy preserving way. We believe that our work is the first to offer practical options for achieving full privacy covering both individual readings and hidden static parameters. The key insight was that if the individual meter readings (or predictions) are normally distributed then the sum query will also be normally distributed. This allows us to apply differentially private techniques on the distribution parameters. Since normality is not always satisfied, we proposed techniques to transform the distributions. We argued that the extra noise due to these techniques is small. In a full practical implementation of our distributed sum queries the noise terms we identified and the sum itself can be computed in a distributed and private way, a problem known to be tractable [11,12]. A full control solution based on the monitoring approach described here is the subject of our ongoing research.

## 8. ACKNOWLEDGMENTS

This work was supported, in part, by grants from the US NSF, from the ARPAe "GENI" program at DOE, and from the EU and the European Social Fund through project FuturICT.hu (grant no .: TAMOP-4.2.2.C-11/1/KONV-2012-0013). M. Jelasity was supported by the Fulbright Program and the Bolyai Scholarship of the Hungarian Acad. Sci.

## 9. REFERENCES

[1] Rouf, I., Mustafa, H., Xu, M., Xu, W., Miller, R., Gruteser, M.: Neighborhood watch: security and privacy analysis of automatic meter reading systems. In: Proc. 2012 ACM Conf. on Comp. and Comm. Security (CCS'12), ACM (2012) 462–473

[2] Clifton, C., Kantarcioglu, M., Vaidya, J., Lin, X., Zhu, M.Y.: Tools for privacy preserving distributed data mining. SIGKDD Explor. Newsl. **4**(2) (2002) 28–34

[3] Dwork, C.: A firm foundation for private data analysis. Commun. ACM **54**(1) (January 2011) 86–95

[4] Barker, S., Mishra, A., Irwin, D., Shenoy, P., Albrecht, J.: Smartcap: Flattening peak electricity demand in smart homes. In: IEEE Intl. Conf. on Pervasive Computing and Comm. (PerCom). (2012) 67–75

[5] Beal, J., Berliner, J., Hunter, K.: Fast precise distributed control for energy demand management. In: IEEE Sixth Intl. Conf. on Self-Adaptive and Self-Organizing Systems (SASO). (2012) 187–192

[6] Blum, A., Dwork, C., McSherry, F., Nissim, K.: Practical privacy: the sulq framework. In: Proc. 24th ACM SIGMOD-SIGACT-SIGART Symp. on Principles of Database Systems (PODS'05), ACM (2005) 128–138

[7] Zhang, J., Zhang, Z., Xiao, X., Yang, Y., Winslett, M.: Functional mechanism: regression analysis under differential privacy. Proc. VLDB Endow. **5**(11) (July 2012) 1364–1375

[8] Rial, A., Danezis, G.: Privacy-preserving smart metering. In: Proc. 10th annual ACM workshop on Privacy in the electronic society (WPES'11), ACM (2011) 49–60

[9] Maurer, U.: Secure multi-party computation made simple. Discrete Applied Math. **154**(2) (2006) 370–381

[10] Yao, A.C.C.: How to generate and exchange secrets. In: Proc. 27th Annual Symposium on Foundations of Comp. Sci. (FOCS). (October 1986) 162–167

[11] Ács, G., Castelluccia, C.: I have a dream! (differentially private smart metering). In: Information Hiding. LNCS 6958. Springer (2011) 118–132

[12] Dwork, C., Kenthapadi, K., McSherry, F., Mironov, I., Naor, M.: Our data, ourselves: Privacy via distributed noise generation. In: Advances in Cryptology - EUROCRYPT 2006. LNCS 4004. Springer (2006) 486–503

[13] Dwork, C., Naor, M., Pitassi, T., Rothblum, G.N.: Differential privacy under continual observation. In: Proc. 42nd ACM symposium on Theory of computing (STOC'10), ACM (2010) 715–724

[14] Ny, J.L., Pappas, G.J.: Differentially private filtering. Technical Report 1207.4305, arxiv.org (2012)

[15] Barker, S., Mishra, A., Irwin, D., Cecchet, E., Shenoy, P., Albrecht, J.: Smart*: An open data set and tools for enabling research in sustainable homes. In: Proc. 2012 Workshop on Data Mining Applications in Sustainability (SustKDD 2012). (August 2012)

[16] Dwork, C.: Differential privacy. In: Automata, Languages and Programming (ICALP). LNCS 4052. Springer (2006) 1–12

[17] Dwork, C., McSherry, F., Nissim, K., Smith, A.: Calibrating noise to sensitivity in private data analysis. In: Theory of Cryptography. LNCS 3876. Springer (2006) 265–284

[18] McSherry, F.D.: Privacy integrated queries: an extensible platform for privacy-preserving data analysis. In: Proc. 2009 ACM SIGMOD Intl. Conf. on Mgmt. of Data (SIGMOD'09), ACM (2009) 19–30

[19] Nolan, J.P.: 1. In: Stable Distributions - Models for Heavy Tailed Data. Birkhauser (2013) to appear.

[20] Barker, S., Kalra, S., Irwin, D., Shenoy, P.: Empirical characterization and modeling of electrical loads in smart homes. In: The Fourth Intl. Green Computing Conf. (IGCC'13). (2013)

# Influence of Data Granularity on Nonintrusive Appliance Load Monitoring

Günther Eibl
Josef Ressel Center for User-Centric Smart Grid
Privacy, Security and Control
Salzburg University of Applied Sciences
Urstein Sued 1, Puch/Salzburg, Austria
guenther.eibl@en-trust.at

Dominik Engel
Josef Ressel Center for User-Centric Smart Grid
Privacy, Security and Control
Salzburg University of Applied Sciences
Urstein Sued 1, Puch/Salzburg, Austria
dominik.engel@en-trust.at

## ABSTRACT

Decreasing time resolution is the simplest possible privacy enhancing technique for energy consumption data. However, its impact on privacy analyses of load signals has never been studied systematically. Non-intrusive appliance load monitoring algorithms (NIALM) have originally been designed for energy disaggregation for subsequent energy feedback. However, the information on appliance use may also be misused for the extraction of personal information. In this work, the effect of decreasing the time resolution in the usual first step, namely edge detection, is studied. It is shown that event values can be estimated rather reliably, but the detection rate of events significantly decreases with increasing measurement time interval.

## Categories and Subject Descriptors

I.5 [**Pattern Recognition**]: Design Methodology—*Pattern analysis*

## General Terms

Privacy

## Keywords

Privacy enhancement; smart metering; data representation; load disaggregation; edge detection

## 1. INTRODUCTION

There is a lot of public concern and discussions on the privacy impact of smart metering. However, the discussion is led without knowing the extent of personal information that can be read out of smart meter load profiles. Even more so, there is nearly a complete lack of knowledge about how the amount of personal information relates to the measured time interval. For example, in many European countries, it is planned, that people can opt-in for delivering their load

data in 15 minute time intervals. To our knowledge, no one has tried to assess the amount of personal information that can be extracted on 15 minute time interval load profiles.

Note that the decrease in time resolution can be viewed as the most straightforward and simplest privacy enhancing technology (PET), cf. [3]. The goal of this work is making a first step towards the study of its actual impact. This work is a first step, because we focus on determining appliances. The main reasoning behind this approach is that activities of persons in the house trigger appliances that sum up to the total load. The activities themselves are already personal information of which some general habits could be deduced. However, such an analysis of general habits is out of scope of this work.

Information on the appliances are usually extracted from the load profiles by means of so-called 'non-intrusive appliance load monitoring analysis" (NIALM). There is a lot of literature on NIALM algorithms ([5, 15, 2, 1, 14, 8, 6, 13]). The goal of these algorithms is the disaggregation of the total load into the individual appliances loads, e.g., for sake of providing energy feedback to the end-user. From the privacy viewpoint, such NIALM analyses can be seen as a first step of attacking methods, which aim at the unauthorized extraction of personal information.

There are only a few papers treating the technical details of privacy implications of smart metering. In [9], load data were recorded with parallel video data which were processed into activity logs. A NIALM analysis was done yielding the input for subsequent behavior-extraction routines. Extracted behaviors include, e.g., presence, sleep cycles or meal times. In [12] the load profile is divided into so-called power segments using a density based clustering technique. These power segments are described by features such as start time, average power and duration. It is illustrated how such power events could be used for answering several privacy questions. In [4], it is shown that under ideal conditions load curves can be used to identify the currently viewed TV-program.

In this work, the impact of reducing the time granularity on the first part of typical low-frequency NIALM algorithms, namely edge detection ([5, 9, 1, 2, 8, 13]) is studied. In Section 2.1, event detection is described as part of low frequency NIALM analyses. In Section 2.2 the investigated edge detection methods are reviewed. After describing the experimental setup in Section 3, the performance of different edge detection methods is compared in Section 4.1. The core Section 4.2 of this work describes the effect of the time reso-

| Time | 1s | 3s | 15s | 20s | 1min |
|------|-----|------|------|------|------|
| Paper | [12, 11, 2, 1] | [8, 6] | [9] | [14] | [13] |

Table 1: Time Granularities of low-frequency NIALM-studies

lution on the detection of events. Finally, Section 5 contains conclusion and outlook.

## 2. EVENT DETECTION METHODS

Event detection methods are the typical first analysis step in low frequency NIALM algorithms. Decreasing the performance of event detection is a countermeasure against a possible NIALM-privacy-attack and increase privacy. After discussing why event detection is such a useful first step of NIALM analysis, the event detection methods that are investigated in the experimental part are described.

### 2.1 Event Detection as Part of NIALM

NIALM approaches are divided broadly into two kinds of methods: high frequency methods look at the waveform of appliances or study transients or higher order harmonics. While high-frequency methods usually need a sampling in the range of kHz, low-frequency methods typically analyze load profiles which are sampled using time intervals in the order of seconds (see Table 1).

Since in this work the time granularity is decreased for privacy purposes, the focus is laid on low-frequency instead of high frequency NIALM methods. Supervised low frequency methods usually consist of several blocks: edge detection, cluster analysis and finding pairs of on-and off clusters for the determination of the duration of an appliance. Edges are sharp increases or decreases of the load signal due to turning on or off an appliance. More generally, edges arise due to the change from one state to another state of an appliance when modeled as a finite state machines (FSM). NIALM algorithms commonly use edges instead of the absolute values for two reasons: First, using absolute values in the presence of unknown appliances, these unknown appliances could be described as a combination of other known appliances. Second, there are adverse cases where a small change in the measured power would result in a big change in the configuration of used appliances, which is an implausible result [5]. Since edge detection is a common first step of a NIALM algorithm, if a decrease of time resolution is able to negatively influence edge detection, the subsequent part of the NIALM algorithm is expected to suffer significantly as well. Considering a possible abuse of NIALM algorithms the diminished disaggregation ability is beneficial from the privacy perspective. For sake of completeness it is noted that the use of edges is common but not mandatory, e.g., in [12] shape features are used instead of edges.

### 2.2 Investigated Event Detection Methods

In this section event detection methods used in the experimental part are reviewed. A main assumption of this work is the modeling of appliances as finite state machines (FSMs) having different power values for different states. In this work an event $e = (t_e, \Delta P_e)$ is a transition between two such states which is represented by its onset time $t_e$ and

the difference between the two power levels of the states $\Delta P_e$. Many appliances have only two states and can simply only be turned on or off. Correspondingly, events for which the signal increases ($\Delta P > 0$) are called on-events because they should typically arise from turning on such an onoff-appliance. Analogously, events for which the signal decreases are called off-events.

The most straightforward method detects an edge, if the backward difference $\Delta P_i = P_i - P_{i-1}$ between consecutive points exceeds a threshold. Each detected edge is considered to be an event $e = (t_i, \Delta P_i)$. This method can be classified as one that focuses on the transition between two levels of a signal [10]. If the transition needs several time intervals, this method divides the transition between two levels in several edges having smaller values than the transition which is usually an unwanted behavior.

The drawback of the backward difference method can be accommodated by merging of subsequent occurring edges stemming from backward differences into a single event [1]. The value of the event is the sum of the individual edge values which can be both positive and negative. The time where the event occurs is defined as the onset time, i.e., the time of the first edge contributing to the event.

Another method proposed in [5] is called 'transient passing edge detection." As its names suggests it is a method focusing on the power levels of the two transition states instead of the transition itself. A transition is defined as being not steady. In the first step the method finds the steady subsequences of the signal. This is done using a sliding window approach where a point is considered part of a steady subsequence, if the range of it and the next $n - 1$ does not exceed a given threshold. The whole signal is thus divided into consecutive steady parts $st$ and transitions $tr$. For the description of the event, all subsequences $(st_i, tr_{i+1}, st_{i+2})$ are considered. The onset-time $t_{e_i}$ for the description of the event is the last time point of the first steady part $st_i$. The transition value $\Delta P_i$ is the difference between the median of the values of the first steady part $st_i$ and the median of the values of the consecutive steady part $st_{i+1}$. Taking the median value over the whole steady part leads to a greater robustness in the determination of the event value $\Delta P_i$.

## 3. EXPERIMENTAL SETUP

The experiments were done using a so-called low frequency dataset of the publicly available REDD-dataset [7]. This dataset consists of measurements of the apparent power for 6 different houses. Measurements are available for the main circuits mains1 and mains2, and for subcircuits like for example kitchen outlets and measurements of individual appliances.

Although the decrease of the time granularity seems straightforward (integrating over the period), it is in fact not. There are several possibilities. First, considering a time interval, different statistics could be computed for this interval. The most straightforward statistic is the average load value which should be enough for most practical solutions such as normal billing or time-of-use billing. However, for some reasons, e.g., pricing based on the maximum load or for control reasons, the maximum load needed during the time interval, could be another useful number. Other statistics as for example the standard deviation of the load values, are also possible but will not be considered further. Finally, there is still the possibility of simple sampling, i.e., taking the load value at the specific point in time.

In the subsequent experiments, three variants are considered: (i) taking the average load in a time interval, (ii) taking the maximum load in a time interval and (iii) sampling at time points.

In order to account for noise, for all methods, events $e$ with a value $\Delta P$ smaller than a threshold of 20 Watt are discarded. The same threshold was used for the detection of the stable parts of transient edge detection. The minimal required number of steady points $n$ in transient passing was set to 3 which has good detection properties at reasonable stability.

## 4. RESULTS

In this section, different edge detection methods are compared with respect to their ability to detect events in smart meter load profiles. Then the effect of the decrease of time resolution on the events found is described.

### 4.1 Event detection

Since the results are based on the events found, the performance of the event detection methods is assessed for the highest available time resolution of 3 seconds first. A value of 20W was used as threshold for the removal of events occurring due to noise. If the threshold is set too low, additional edges can occur which tends to happen for high-power devices. For low-power devices such as lighting, a noise threshold that is in turn too high can lead to a loss of events. Therefore, the tradeoff between noise removal and the detection of events from low-power devices has to be considered.

The form of the load consumption of appliances can be quite complex. As an example, the load consumed for a full run of the dishwasher is shown in Figure 1. Since the

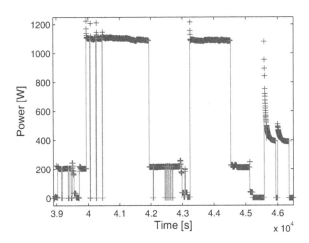

**Figure 1: Dishwasher events, marked as "+", detected using transient detection at the highest time resolution**

dishwasher's load profile has such a rich structure with long and short on-durations at different power levels and power levels that are decreasing, it was chosen for demonstration of effects of different edge detection settings and of the change

of time granularity. Simpler devices for heating are usually purely ohmic and show high power values. These are the appliances whose load profiles have the highest similarity to a rectangular profile.

As expected, the simple backward difference yields more, but disturbing, events and can therefore not be recommended (compare Figures 1 and 2).

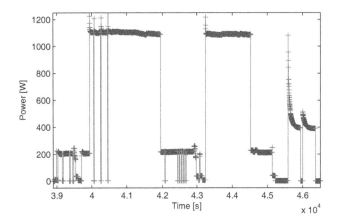

**Figure 2: Dishwasher events, marked as "+", detected using backward differences at the highest time resolution. Too many events are detected (compare with Figure 1).**

Generally, in terms of detecting appliances, both transient passing and edge merging give good and very similar results. There are also only tiny differences due to the use of the different variants of decreasing the time resolution. The correctness of the edges found was visually verified for all appliances. Additionally, the edge values of all appliances are shown in Figure 3. It can be seen that for all appliances rather distinct edge values can be found. The expected strong similarity of the absolute values of the on-events and the off-events leads to the symmetric look of Figure 3. More importantly, this figure suggests that some appliances such as washerDryer3 should be easily distinguishable from others. Other appliances such as kitchen outlets 2 and 4 are expected to be hardly distinguishable from others. For another class of appliances such as the dishwasher only some levels are distinguishable from the events of other appliances. The fact that the result of edge detection enables to formulate such an expected behavior shows the value of edge detection for a possibly privacy invading analysis of load profiles.

### 4.2 Effect of Decrease of Time Resolution

In this section, the influence of time granularity $\Delta t$ on the events found above is studied. First, transient passing using the averaging statistic is studied. As can be seen in Figure 4 with increasing the time interval fewer edges are detected. Especially short-lived states cannot be detected anymore. The edges that are still detected have surprisingly stable heights $\Delta P$.

Another remarkable point is that already with a time interval of 5 minutes, nearly the whole finer structure cannot be seen any more. These results can also be seen for the mains signals which was calculated as the sum of the

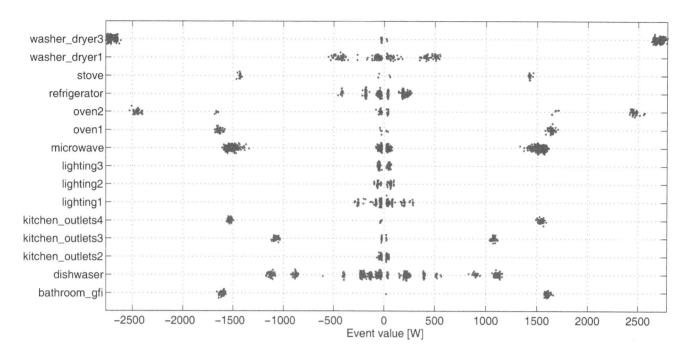

**Figure 3: All events found at the highest time resolution, detected using transient detection. The symmetry of the figure stems from the strong similarity of the absolute values of on-events and their corresponding off-events.**

mains1 and the mains2 signals. Using a 5 minute interval mostly privacy-irrelevant refrigerator events remain.

Possible effects on the decrease in privacy due to the decrease in time resolution can already be estimated. Since the edge heights are rather stable it seems reasonable that the edges of different appliances can still be distinguished at higher time intervals. However, the detection rate of appliances is diminished. In summary, the effect of a decrease in time resolution means that single events cannot be detected reliably. However, for the identification of habits, the detection of each single event is not necessary.

Comparing the different edge detection and time decrease variants, the following behavior could be seen: For high time resolution, edge merging and transient passing lead to nearly identical results, however, for lower time resolutions transient passing seems to better preserve the edge values. The results of both transient passing and edge merging are quite insensitive to the kind of statistic. Although still leading worse results, it should be noted that the performance of the backward difference method is better with taking the max statistic or with sampling than with taking the average statistic where extensive smearing of edge values occurs.

## 5. CONCLUSION AND OUTLOOK

The impact of decreasing the time resolution on privacy analysis of load signals obtained from smart metering to date has not been studied systematically. Based on the reasoning that knowledge about appliance use can be used as a first step in a privacy attack, the influence of the time interval on edge detection methods has been studied.

Three edge detection methods were investigated: the transient passing method [5], merging of backward differences and simple backward differences. Based on experiments with the REDD-data [7] the simple backward difference cannot be recommended as an edge detection tool in this setting leading to too many edges.

The decrease of the measurement time interval as a privacy enhancing operation has the effect that edge detection still works in the sense that edge heights can be detected in a stable manner. Privacy is enhanced in a way that not every edge is detected. The longer the time interval the fewer edges can be detected. Already with 5 minute intervals, for most of the appliances, the number of detected edges is significantly decreased. A potential privacy consequence would state that not every single event but rather regular habits can be detected.

This work constitutes the first, descriptive assessment of the effect of a decrease of data granularity on smart meter privacy focusing on the detection of appliance use. Next logical steps include the development of quantifiable performance indicators, e.g., based on the result of subsequent pattern recognition algorithms. Using these performance indicators the difference of the effect on different appliances should be described and visualized in a way that is also understandable for non-experts. Furthermore, when appropriate datasets are available, personal information such as activities or habits should be considered in addition to appliance usage.

## 6. ACKNOWLEDGMENTS

The financial support by the Austrian Federal Ministry of Economy, Family and Youth and the Austrian National Foundation for Research, Technology and Development is gratefully acknowledged. Funding by the Austrian Research Promotion Agency (FFG) under Bridge Project 832082 is gratefully acknowledged.

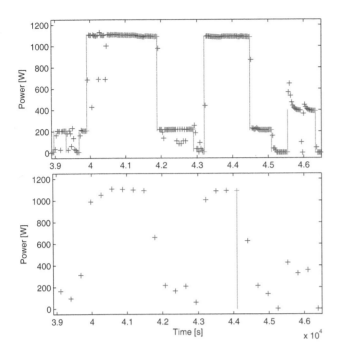

Figure 4: Dishwasher events, marked as "+", detected for $\Delta t = 30s$ (top) and 5 minutes (bottom).

# 7. REFERENCES

[1] M. Baranski and J. Voss. Genetic algorithm for pattern detection in nialm systems. In *IEEE International Conference on Systems, Man and Cybernetics*, 2004.

[2] D. C. Bergman, D. Jin, J. Juen, N. Tanaka, C. Gunter, and A. Wright. Distributed non-intrusive load monitoring. In *Proceedings of the IEEE/PES Conference on Innovative Smart Grid Technologies (ISGT 2011), Anaheim, CA, USA*, 2011.

[3] D. Engel. Wavelet-based load profile representation for smart meter privacy. In *Proc. IEEE PES Innovative Smart Grid Technologies (ISGT'13)*, pages 1–6, Washington, D.C., USA, Feb. 2013.

[4] U. Greveler, B. Justus, and D. Löhr. Multimedia content identification through smart meter power usage profiles. In *Proceedings of the 2012 International Conference on Information and Knowledge Engineering (IKE'12)*, Las Vegas, USA, 2012.

[5] G. Hart. Nonintrusive appliance load monitoring. *Proceedings of the IEEE*, 80(12):1870–1891, Dec. 1992.

[6] H. Kim, M. Marwah, M. Arlitt, G. Lyon, and J. Han. Unsupervised disaggregation of low frequency power measurements. In *The 11th SIAM International Conference on Data Mining*, pages 747–758, 2011.

[7] J. Kolter and M. Johnson. Redd: A public data set for energy disaggregation research. In *Workshop on Data Mining Applications in Sustainability (SIGKDD)*, pages 1–6, 2011.

[8] J. Z. Kolter and T. Jaakkola. Approximate inference in additive factorial hmms with application to energy disaggregation. *Journal of Machine Learning Research - Proceedings Track*, 22:1472–1482, 2012.

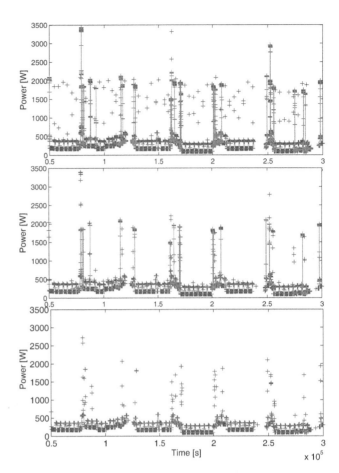

Figure 5: Mains events, marked as "+", detected with $\Delta t = 3s$ (top), 60s (middle) and 5min (bottom).

[9] M. Lisovich, D. Mulligan, and S. Wicker. Inferring personal information from demand-response systems. *IEEE Security & Privacy*, 8(1):11–20, 2010.

[10] M. A. Little and N. S. Jones. Generalized methods and solvers for noise removal from piecewise constant signals, background theory. In *Proceedings of the Royal Society A: Mathematical, Physical and Engineering Science*, volume 467, pages 3088–3114, 2011.

[11] A. Marchiori, D. Hakkarinen, Q. Han, and L. Earle. Circuit-level load monitoring for household energy management. *IEEE Pervasive Comp.*, 10:40–48, 2011.

[12] A. Molina-Markham, P. Shenoy, K. Fu, E. Cecchet, and D. Irwin. Private memoirs of a smart meter. In *Proceedings of the 2nd ACM Workshop on Embedded Sensing Systems for Energy-Efficiency in Building*, BuildSys '10, pages 61–66, New York, NY, USA, 2010.

[13] O. Parson, S. Ghosh, M. Weal, and A. Rogers. Non-intrusive load monitoring using prior models of general appliance types. In *Twenty-Sixth Conference on Artificial Intelligence (AAAI-12)*, 2012.

[14] E. Vogiatzis, G. Kalogridis, and S. Z. Denic. Real-time and low cost energy disaggregation of coarse meter data. In *4th IEEE PES Innovative Smart Grid Technologies Europe (ISGT Europe)*, 2013.

[15] M. Zeifman and K. Roth. Nonintrusive appliance load monitoring: Review and outlook. *IEEE Transactions on Consumer Electronics*, 57:76–84, 2011.

# Architecture-Driven Smart Grid Security Management

**Markus Kammerstetter**
Institute of Computer Aided
Automation
Automation Systems Group
International Secure Systems
Lab
Vienna University of
Technology
mk @ iseclab.org

**Lucie Langer**
Safety and Security
Department
Austrian Institute of
Technology
lucie.langer @ ait.ac.at

**Florian Skopik**
Safety and Security
Department
Austrian Institute of
Technology
florian.skopik @ ait.ac.at

**Wolfgang Kastner**
Institute of Computer Aided
Automation
Automation Systems Group
Vienna University of
Technology
k @ auto.tuwien.ac.at

## ABSTRACT

The introduction of smart grids goes along with an extensive use of ICT technologies in order to support the integration of renewable energy sources. However, the use of ICT technologies bears risks in terms of cyber security attacks which could negatively affect the electrical power grid. These risks need to be assessed, mitigated and managed in a proper way to ensure the security of both current and future energy networks. Existing approaches have been either restricted to very specific components of the smart grid (e.g., smart meters), or provide a high-level view only. We therefore propose an architecture-driven security management approach for smart grids which goes beyond a mere abstract view without focusing too much on technical details. Our approach covers architecture modeling, risk identification and assessment as well as risk mitigation and compliance checking. We have proven the practical usability of this process together with leading manufacturers and utilities.

## Categories and Subject Descriptors

C.2 [**Computer-Communication Networks**]: General—
*Security and protection*; H.4 [**Information Systems Applications**]: Miscellaneous; K.6.5 [**Management of Computing and Information Systems**]: Security and Protection

## Keywords

Smart Grid, Security, Security Management, Risks

## 1. INTRODUCTION

While traditionally electrical power grids adhered to the producer-consumer model, in modern smart grids everyone can become an energy producer – by leveraging green energy produced through solar panels, wind turbines or heating and biogas plants, consumers turn into "prosumers". For traditional large-scale utilities and energy producers, this has introduced a massive drawback: due to decentralized energy production, energy networks can no longer be centrally controlled. The solution is to upgrade existing power grids to smart grids by establishing an ICT network in parallel to the electrical power grid. While this brings advantages with respect to energy efficiency, green energy harvesting and consumer freedom, it also introduces ICT security risks in critical infrastructures that may cause disastrous effects.

As manufacturers of smart grid components move from pure electrical systems to the development of complex ICT systems, and though security may be an important target for them, market pressure and a lack of security experience may force them to roll out insecure products. Utilities, on the other hand, need to rely on manufacturers that their smart grid devices are secure in order to run this critical infrastructure. To lower the risks involved, proper risk management needs to be put in place. However, existing ICT-related risk management processes are not directly applicable to the smart grid domain as the technology and the security requirements are significantly different. On the other hand, readily available smart grid security guidelines such as the Protection Profiles [3, 4] developed by the German Federal Office for Information Security (BSI) merely focus on smart metering and thus do not map to the entire smart grid architectures deployed.

We decided to take a different approach. Instead of focusing on a single technological component, we model European smart grid architectures by using the Smart Grid Architecture Model (SGAM) [17]. Based on well-established sources of ICT-related security threats, we created a catalog for ICT security threats to the smart grid, which can be applied to components in the SGAM model. In this work, we show how our approach can be practically used for smart grid risk management, including risk assessment, mitigation and compliance checking. As our approach has been developed in conjunction with leading smart grid manufacturers and utilities, we believe that it has a strong practical impact.

In summary, the main contributions of our work are:
- an SGAM-based smart grid model representing both current and near-future European smart grid architectures,
- a comprehensive catalog of cyber security threats for smart grids, and
- a practical risk assessment approach able to bridge the gap between a high-level architectural view and specific technical security measures.

The remainder of this paper is organized as follows. Section 2 outlines existing work on smart grid security and risk assessment. Section 3 describes the five steps of our smart grid risk management approach, which is subsequently evaluated in Section 4. Section 5 concludes the paper and identifies potential areas for future work.

## 2. RELATED WORK

Smart grid technologies have received major attention in both academia and industry in recent years. Various works discuss the basics of the smart grid, such as its structure, application, and potential impact [1, 18]. Others cover established and recently developed technical standards [5]. The European Union plans to replace traditional electricity meters with smart meters to a large extent until 2020, which draws major attention to various security and privacy aspects of this technology [8, 15]. Therefore, the U.S. NIST and European ENISA have released numerous guidelines on how to secure smart grid architectures [12, 6]. Although these documents build a solid basis, they do not show the complete picture. NIST, for instance, focuses on technologies employed in U.S. smart grids, and both guidelines give quite high-level recommendations only. Similarly, the BSI Protection Profiles [3, 4] do not provide a holistic approach either. Instead, they focus on smart metering only (which is only one building block of a smart grid), and their target of evaluation is a very specific smart metering implementation that does not reflect deployed smart metering systems.

The electric grid is perhaps the most critical infrastructure today, and thus safety, i.e., reliability and availability, is a top priority. Potential vulnerabilities of smart metering systems – and the grid in general – are widely discussed topics [9, 8, 22]. As a consequence, many research works focus on quite small (technical) parts of the overall smart grid architecture. For instance, data communication security controls (e.g., cryptographic functions such as encryption, message authentication codes, and digital signatures) provide standard security services in terms of confidentiality, integrity, and accountability of messages and their origin [5]. Others deal with effective key distribution [21] and management for devices with very limited computational power [9] to enable efficient encryption of meter readings and access control (similar to Pay-TV access control systems [21]). Yan et al., Mohan et al. and Vigo et al. provide an overview of security mechanisms for smart grids and smart meters [23, 10, 20].

While their work provides an overview of how security mechanisms should be realized, in our approach, we focus on the security mechanisms that are either implemented currently or will be part of near-future implementations.

The Smart Grid Coordination Group formed by the European standards organizations CEN, CENELEC and ETSI has provided a comprehensive framework on smart grids in response to the EU Smart Grid Mandate M/490 [16]. As part of that framework, the "Smart Grid Information Security (SGIS)" report defines five SGIS *Security Levels* to assess the criticality of smart grid components. Additionally, five SGIS *Risk Impact Levels* are defined that can be used to classify inherent risks in order to assess the importance of every asset of the smart grid provider. The assessment is carried out under the assumption that no security controls whatsoever are in place. Compared to the work carried out by the SGIS group within M/490, our main goal was to develop a practical risk assessment approach for smart grid systems that are currently deployed or will be deployed in the near future. Our approach should be readily applicable by utilities in contrast to more formal approaches as suggested for example in [13, 19].

## 3. SMART GRID RISK MANAGEMENT APPROACH

Most efforts on smart grid security either deal with threats and vulnerabilities on an abstract, high architectural level, or focus on very specific technical aspects, e.g., encryption or authentication, without considering the overall picture.

**Figure 1: Architecture-driven Smart Grid Risk Management Approach**

Our proposed smart grid risk management approach therefore aims at bridging the gap between a high-level architectural view and specific technical security measures. For that purpose, it employs a five-step cyclic process model depicted in Fig. 1, which consists of the following phases:

I. Architecture Modeling
II. Risk Identification
III. Risk Assessment
IV. Risk Mitigation
V. Compliance Checking

First, it allows DSOs (distribution systems operators) to map their deployed components to the standard architecture model SGAM. This phase is crucial to get a holistic view on the deployed components and their underlying technologies in a standardized and structured manner. The second phase subsequently enables a sophisticated risk identification and a later risk assessment. Based on the concrete technologies employed, specific technical controls (in addition to organizational measures) can be applied to mitigate the identified risk. If, for instance, the architectural model reveals insufficiently secured communication lines, potential technical mitigation measures are to use stronger authentication and encryption methods. Eventually, in the fifth phase, compliance to technological guidelines, regulations and corporate strategy needs to be ensured in order to avoid undesired secondary effects of mitigation measures. The whole model, from phase I to V, is cyclic since every mitigation action will eventually cause adaptations of the architecture, which need to be reflected in the model maintained in phase I. Following these phases, our approach is able to provide concrete technical solutions without losing a connection to the overall picture. In the following paragraphs, we explain each phase more closely.

## 3.1 Architecture Modeling using SGAM

In order to model smart grid architectures, we employ the Smart Grid Architecture Model (SGAM) [17]. The SGAM model was originally intended to identify standardization gaps in smart grid standardization processes. The model is structured in zones and domains. The *zones* are derived from hierarchical automation system models that classify systems into Field, Process and Station towards Operation, Enterprise and Market level [14]. The *domains* reflect power-grid-specific domains ranging from the Customer, Distributed Energy Resources (DER), Distribution and Transmission to the Generation domain. In contrast to the NIST Smart Grid Framework [11], SGAM features a dedicated DER domain, in which small distributed generators with their special infrastructure find their place. Finally, in the third dimension, SGAM has *interoperability layers* that highlight different aspects of networked smart grid systems from hard- and software components over communication links and protocols up to functional and business layers. We used SGAM as a means for visualizing and comparing different smart grid automation architectures and depicting existing and near-future smart grid architectures (see Fig. 2). A more detailed description of our architecture model can be found in [7].

## 3.2 Risk Identification

In order to identify risks that can occur within smart grid environments, we compiled a threat catalog focusing on technical threats. Since the threat catalog should build upon a well-established source of ICT-related security threats, we used the IT Baseline Protection Catalogs [2] as our main source. Threats quoted in the smart-grid-specific Protection Profiles [3, 4] were also taken into account. We focused on technical threats and thus omitted organizational threats or force majeure. All remaining threats were checked for their generic applicability in smart grid environments and filtered accordingly. As some of the threats in the BSI Catalogs are very specific while others are more generic, we adapted the threats to the smart grid scenario and merged them into a practically usable threat catalog comprising 31 threats (see Table 1). These threats were subsequently interpreted in the smart grid context and grouped into the following clusters:

- Authentication / Authorization

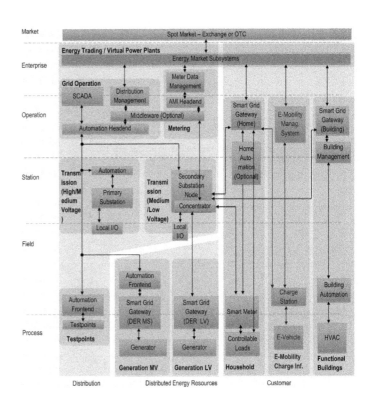

**Figure 2: Proposed Architecture Model**

- Confidentiality
- Integrity / Availability
- Internal / External Interfaces
- Maintenance / System Status
- Missing / Inadequate Security Controls

Since the threats in the threat catalog are kept in a generic form, there is no need to adapt the threat catalog in case the smart grid architecture model (see Section 3.1) changes.

## 3.3 Risk Assessment

In the next phase, the threats identified in phase II are applied to the architecture components which have been defined in phase I. For each component and threat, we evaluated both the likelihood as well as the impact of a threat to occur. Both probability and impact were measured on a five-level scale ranging from very low (level 1) to very high (level 5), depending on the frequency and range of successful attacks. However, while this could be exercised on all smart grid components in the SGAM model, it would quickly become impractical due to the high number of elements in the threat matrix. For this reason, we decided to cluster smart grid components into the following building blocks (cf. Figure 2:

- Functional Buildings
- E-Mobility & Charge Infrastructure
- Customer Premises
- Generation Low Voltage
- Generation Medium Voltage
- Test Points
- Transmission (High/Medium Voltage)
- Transmission (Medium/Low Voltage)
- Grid Operation

| Threat Category | Threat |
|---|---|
| *Authentication / Authorization* | Defective or missing authentication or inappropriate handling of authentication data |
| | Defective authorization |
| *Confidentiality* | Defective key management |
| | Disclosure of sensitive data |
| | Insecure encryption methods or parameters |
| *Integrity / Availability* | Outage or disruption of IT systems |
| | Outage or disruption of networks or network components |
| | Outage or disruption of supply networks |
| | Tampering with devices |
| | Tampering with data |
| | Loss or corruption of data due to physical factors |
| | Loss or corruption of data due to misuse or negligence |
| | Fee fraud |
| *Internal / External Interfaces* | Illegal physical interfaces |
| | Illegal logical interfaces |
| | Incompatibilities between systems or (network) components |
| *Maintenance / System Status* | Operation of unregistered or insecure components or components which provide unnecessary services |
| | Missing or inadequate maintenance |
| | Insufficient anomaly detection |
| | Insufficient dimensioning |
| | Security issues during software migration |
| | Insufficient monitoring and controlling capabilities |
| | Faulty use or administration of IT systems |
| | Faulty time synchronization |
| | Faulty data synchronization |
| | Uncontrolled cascading effects |
| *Missing / Inadequate Security Controls* | Defective or missing security controls in networks |
| | Defective or missing security controls in software products |
| | Software vulnerabilities or bugs |
| | Use of insecure protocols |
| | Failure or disruption of safety controls |

Table 1: Threat Catalog

- Metering

In case of considerably different smart grid architectures and models, these building blocks might differ and would need to be adapted accordingly. However, in the common case there is no need for adaptation due to the generic form of the threats and building blocks.

Severity

| Probability | 1 | 1,5 | 2 | 2,5 | 3 | 3,5 | 4 | 4,5 | 5 |
|---|---|---|---|---|---|---|---|---|---|
| 1 | 1 | 1,5 | 2 | 2,5 | 3 | 3,5 | 4 | 4,5 | 5 |
| 1,5 | 1,5 | 2,25 | 3 | 3,75 | 4,5 | 5,25 | 6 | 6,75 | 7,5 |
| 2 | 2 | 3 | 4 | 5 | 6 | 7 | 8 | 9 | 10 |
| 2,5 | 2,5 | 3,75 | 5 | 6,25 | 7,5 | 8,75 | 10 | 11,25 | 12,5 |
| 3 | 3 | 4,5 | 6 | 7,5 | 9 | 10,5 | 12 | 13,5 | 15 |
| 3,5 | 3,5 | 5,25 | 7 | 8,75 | 10,5 | 12,25 | 14 | 15,75 | 17,5 |
| 4 | 4 | 6 | 8 | 10 | 12 | 14 | 16 | 18 | 20 |
| 4,5 | 4,5 | 6,75 | 9 | 11,25 | 13,5 | 15,75 | 18 | 20,25 | 22,5 |
| 5 | 5 | 7,5 | 10 | 12,5 | 15 | 17,5 | 20 | 22,5 | 25 |

Figure 3: Assessing the Risk Potential

The result is a risk matrix showing the risk potential for all building blocks in the modeled smart grid environment. Depending on its value (i.e., probability level multiplied by impact level), the risk potential has been defined as low (green), medium (yellow) and high (red), see Fig. 3. This approach allowed us to identify potentially high risks in European smart grids. For high-risk domains it is advisable to identify the individual smart grid components causing the high risk potential, therefore, we are currently performing technical security audits (see Section 4).

## 3.4 Risk Mitigation

Based on the risks identified in phase II and assessed in phase III of our smart grid risk management approach, mitigation strategies are subsequently developed in phase IV. The goal of the mitigation strategies is to either decrease the probability of a successful attack, or to alleviate its impact, possibly also both at the same time. We are currently identifying suitable mitigation actions for the individual risks by addressing each of the 31 threats individually. For each threat, generic measures are first defined (such as introducing a Public Key Infrastructure to counter risks that emerge from insecure handling of cryptographic keys). Subsequently, specific measures for the individual architecture building blocks (see Section 3.3) are identified. We are focusing on mitigation actions suitable for establishing a basic level of protection in order to ensure a broad application among the utilities. Additionally, advanced controls for a higher security level are defined, which can be implemented by utilities with more mature security management processes.

## 3.5 Compliance Check

In order to maintain a high level of the overall smart grid system security, it is important to include automated security compliance checks. These checks should be run against all infrastructure components. Depending on the component type, the tool should check whether the device configuration (such as the firmware version or the currently deployed configuration file) adheres to the latest protection and mitigation strategies. If not, the tool can identify specific components that need to be updated accordingly. Since a single vulnerable component in the smart grid can compromise overall system security, it is highly important that all deployed system components are known to the automated checking tool. We thus advise utilities to include the tool setup into the regular deployment processes.

## 4. EVALUATION AND DISCUSSION

The following section describes the findings we came up with when applying our five-step risk management approach together with distribution systems operators, and comments on the necessity of complementing the theoretical approach with practical security audits.

**Risk Landscape.** The risk management approach outined in Section 3 allowed us to identify areas (i.e. architecture components) in European smart grids which show high risk potential in terms of cyber attacks. Specifically, our analysis showed that there are significant risks in the Functional Buildings, Customer Premises and Grid Operation domains. Regarding centralized components such as the Grid Operation and SCADA system, the probability of a security breach is relatively low as an outside attacker typically has no physical access to these components. Moreover, protection mechanisms are not prone to cost pressure on this level. However, once an attacker manages to get access to these systems, the negative impact will eventually be high; for instance, shutting down a primary substation node could affect whole city districts.

In contrast, security breaches targeted on decentralized components, which are deployed typically in the Functional Buildings and Customer Premises domain, are much more likely as attackers can easily get hold of these components. Attacks on these components are facilitated by the fact that the Smart Grid Gateways are accessible via Internet, and a lack of software security or a misconfiguration may be easily exploited. While the probability of an attack is high, the impact is expected to be limited at first. This may however turn out wrong as soon as a successful smart meter mass attack is published on the Internet, potentially leading to unanticipated cascading effects in the power grid. Thus, not only the probability, but also the impact of a successful attack occurring within the so-called "last mile" are possibly high, which explains the high risk potential.

Our analysis showed that a general risk affecting most of the architecture domains is a lack of secure authentication methods. A potential consequence is that system components accept malicious data or control commands from unauthorized sources, which could have strong negative impacts on grid stability. We therefore recommend broad use of standardized authentication mechanisms such as digital certificates, role-based access control, and two-way authentication for remote maintenance access points.

**Security Audits.** For high risk domains, it is advisable to identify the individual smart grid components causing the high risk potential. For these components, individual technical security audits should be performed by independent auditors in order to assess the technical risks and their reasons. According to the risk potential, we suggest two types of security audits.

The first type of security audit is a typical network and lightweight software security audit. For the chosen smart grid component (i.e. a smart meter), it focuses on network and communication security. Similarly, the lightweight software security audit analyzes how the component's software implementation reacts on security test inputs such as maliciously modified network communication or test input generated through fuzz testing. However, the monitoring of the component's software is limited to the communication with the device. For instance, if a test case leads to an unexpected device response or a crash, a potential vulnerability is identified, but it is not further investigated due to the limited technical access on the device hard- and software internals. The audit is thus feasible with limited resources such as limited time or device access.

The second type of security audit is an in-depth hard- and software security audit starting at the point where the first audit type ends. The audit includes a low level hard- and software security analysis including hardware disassembly, physical port accesses as well as both static and dynamic software analysis. In comparison to the lightweight audit, this type of analysis is extremely powerful and can uncover a wide range of vulnerabilities. Besides, it is also possible to demonstrate proof-of-concept attacks and estimate the severity of these attacks on a larger scale. The drawback of the analysis type is the high effort with respect to analysis time and costs as well as the requirement of a dedicated test system that can be physically dissembled and possibly damaged in course of the analysis.

For instance, our analysis showed that smart meters have a high risk potential, mainly due to the easy physical accessibility by attackers as well as the severity of potential large-scale attacks. Due to the requirement of a testbed, we set out to create a security test system comprising a smart meter, a PLC Data Concentrator as well as a Headend system. On this test system, we are currently performing lightweight analyses on the components. Due to the high risk potential, the smart meter is also subject to an in-depth hardware and software security audit. This allows us to get a spot sample of how secure these systems are currently, and to develop tailored mitigation strategies.

## 5. CONCLUSION AND FUTURE WORK

We have presented an architecture-driven approach for smart grid risk management capable of bridging the gap between a high-level architectural view and specific technical security measures. Our approach cannot replace a risk analysis per se, as technical smart grid implementations and employed products differ significantly between users such as utilities or energy providers. It is, however, the first step in a utility-centric smart grid risk analysis that needs to include low-level technical implementation specifics as well, and may help users to identify areas with high risk potential, and to focus the mitigation actions on them.

Future smart grids will integrate a wide variety of different technologies. Therefore, the crucial challenges are to make sure that cybersecurity and interoperability requirements are satisfied. We argue that these issues can only be solved by a national smart grid reference architecture. Such a reference architecture would specify the minimum security requirements for the individual components and make sure that devices are carefully designed in accordance with them. At the same time, seamless interoperability would be ensured by defining appropriate interfaces. Individual implementations could still be derived from the reference architecture by instantiating specific domains.

Currently, there are no obligations for device vendors and utility providers to stick to the recommendations and guidelines published by existing standardization bodies. Therefore, a corresponding legal and regulatory framework should ensure that the minimum requirements defined by the reference architecture are followed. On the other hand, it must be ensured that the reference architecture is not only followed due to legal obligation, but rather broadly accepted by the different stakeholders. Therefore, all relevant stakeholders must be adequately involved in the process of establishing the reference architecture from the very beginning.

## 6. ACKNOWLEDGEMENT

This work has been partly funded by the project $(SG)^2$ under national FFG grant number 836276 through the KIRAS security research program run by FFG and BMVIT.

## 7. REFERENCES

[1] S. M. Amin and B. F. Wollenberg. Toward a smart grid: power delivery for the 21st century. *IEEE Power and Energy Magazine*, 3(5):34–41, Sept. 2005.

[2] BSI. IT Baseline Protection Catalogs. http://www.bsi.bund.de/gshb, 2013.

[3] BSI. Protection Profile for the Gateway of a Smart Metering System. BSI-CC-PP-0073, 2013.

[4] BSI. Protection Profile for the Security Module of a Smart Metering System (Security Module PP). BSI-CC-PP-0077, 2013.

[5] R. DeBlasio and C. Tom. Standards for the smart grid. In *IEEE Energy 2030 Conference*, pages 1–7, 2008.

[6] ENISA. Appropriate security measures for smart grids. http://www.enisa.europa.eu/activities/Resilience-and-CIIP/critical-infrastructure-and-services/smart-grids-and-smart-metering/appropriate-security-measures-for-smart-grids, December 2012.

[7] M. Kammerstetter, L. Langer, F. Skopik, F. Kupzog, and W. Kastner. Practical risk assessment using a cumulative smart grid model. In *3rd International Conference on Smart Grids and Green IT Systems (SMARTGREENS), April 3-4 2014, Barcelona, Spain*, 2014. To appear.

[8] H. Khurana, M. Hadley, N. Lu, and D. A. Frincke. Smart-grid security issues. *IEEE Security & Privacy*, 8(1):81–85, 2010.

[9] A. R. Metke and R. L. Ekl. Security technology for smart grid networks. *IEEE Transactions on Smart Grid*, 1(1):99–107, 2010.

[10] A. Mohan and H. Khurana. Towards addressing common security issues in smart grid specifications. In *Resilient Control Systems (ISRCS), 2012 5th International Symposium on*, pages 174–180, 2012.

[11] NIST. NIST Special Publication 1108R2 - NIST Framework and Roadmap for Smart Grid Interoperability Standards, Release 2.0, 2013.

[12] NIST. NISTIR 7628 - Guidelines for Smart Grid Cybersecurity, 2013.

[13] P. Ray, R. Harnoor, and M. Hentea. Smart power grid security: A unified risk management approach. In *Security Technology (ICCST), 2010 IEEE International Carnahan Conference on*, pages 276–285, 2010.

[14] T. Sauter, S. Soucek, W. Kastner, and D. Dietrich. The evolution of factory and building automation. In *IEEE Magazine on Industrial Electronics*, pages 35–48, 2011.

[15] F. Skopik and L. Langer. Cyber security challenges in heterogeneous ict infrastructures of smart grids. *Journal of Communications*, 8(8):463–472, 2013.

[16] Smart Grid Coordination Group, CEN-CENELEC-ETSI. Reports in response to smart grid mandate m/490. http://www.cencenelec.eu/standards/sectors/SmartGrids/Pages/default.aspx, 2012. [Online; accessed 16-October-2013].

[17] Smart Grid Coordination Group, CEN-CENELEC-ETSI. Smart grid reference architecture. http://ec.europa.eu/energy/gas_electricity/smartgrids/doc/xpert_group1_reference_architecture.pdf, 2012. [Online; accessed 15-October-2013].

[18] L. H. Tsoukalas and R. Gao. From smart grids to an energy internet: Assumptions, architectures and requirements. In *DRPT*, pages 94–98, 2008.

[19] P. Varaiya, F. Wu, and J. Bialek. Smart operation of smart grid: Risk-limiting dispatch. *Proceedings of the IEEE*, 99(1):40–57, 2011.

[20] R. Vigo, E. Yuksel, and C. Ramli. Smart grid security a smart meter-centric perspective. In *Telecommunications Forum (TELFOR), 2012 20th*, pages 127–130, 2012.

[21] S.-Y. Wang and C.-S. Laih. Efficient key distribution for access control in pay-tv systems. *IEEE Transactions on Multimedia*, 10(3):480–492, 2008.

[22] D. Wei, Y. Lu, M. Jafari, P. Skare, and K. Rohde. An integrated security system of protecting smart grid against cyber attacks. In *Innovative Smart Grid Tech.*, pages 1–7, Jan. 2010.

[23] Y. Yan, Y. Qian, H. Sharif, and D. Tipper. A survey on cyber security for smart grid communications. *Communications Surveys Tutorials, IEEE*, 14(4):998–1010, 2012.

# Audio Source Authentication and Splicing Detection Using Acoustic Environmental Signature

Hong Zhao
Department of Electrical and
Electronic Engineering
South University of Science
and Technology of China
Shenzhen, China
zhao.h@sustc.edu.cn

Yifan Chen
Department of Electrical and
Electronic Engineering
South University of Science
and Technology of China
Shenzhen, China
chen.yf@sustc.edu.cn

Rui Wang
Department of Electrical and
Electronic Engineering
South University of Science
and Technology of China
Shenzhen, China
wang.r@sustc.edu.cn

Hafiz Malik
Department of Electrical and
Computer Engineering
University of
Michigan–Dearborn
MI, USA, 48128
hafiz@umich.edu

## ABSTRACT

Audio splicing is one of the most common manipulation techniques in the audio forensic world. In this paper, the magnitudes of acoustic channel impulse response and ambient noise are considered as the environmental signature and used to authenticate the integrity of query audio and identify the spliced audio segments. The proposed scheme firstly extracts the magnitudes of channel impulse response and ambient noise by applying the spectrum classification technique to each suspected frame. Then, correlation between the magnitudes of query frame and reference frame is calculated. An optimal threshold determined according to the statistical distribution of similarities is used to identify the spliced frames. Furthermore, a refining step using the relationship between adjacent frames is adopted to reduce the false positive rate and false negative rate. Effectiveness of the proposed method is tested on two data sets consisting of speech recordings of human speakers. Performance of the proposed method is evaluated for various experimental settings. Experimental results show that the proposed method not only detects the presence of spliced frames, but also localizes the forgery segments. Comparison results with previous work illustrate the superiority of the proposed scheme.

## Categories and Subject Descriptors

K.4.4 [**Electronic Commerce**]: Intellectual Property; Security

## General Terms

Algorithms, Security, Authentication

*IH&MMSec'14*, June 11 - 13 2014, Salzburg, Austria
Copyright 2014 ACM 978-1-4503-2647-6/14/06...$15.00.
http://dx.doi.org/10.1145/2600918.2600933.

## Keywords

Audio Forensics; Acoustic Environmental Signature; Splicing Detection; Room Impulse Response

## 1. INTRODUCTION

Digial media (audio, video, and image) has become a dominant evidence in litigation and criminal justice, as it can be easily obtained by smart phones and carry-on cameras. For the admissability of the evidence in a court of law, integrity authentication of the evidentiary recording is required to avoid misjudgement or excessive punishment. This requirement becomes a challenging task, especially without *auxiliary data*, such as *digital watermarks* or *fingerprints*. This is common situation, especially if the media is only available in a compressed format. The availability of powerful, sophisticated, low-cost and easy-to-use digital media manipulation tools has rendered authentication of the integrity of digital media even more difficult.

*Audio splicing* is one of the most popular and easy-to-do attack, where target audio is assembled by splicing segments from multiple audio recordings captured in environments. Therefore, audio splicing detection has become an attractive research area. A method based on higher-order time-differences and correlation analysis has been proposed by Cooper [3] to detect traces of "*butt-splicing*" in digital recordings. Another audio splicing detection scheme is based on the analysis of high-order singularity of wavelet coefficients [2], where singular points detected by wavelet analysis is classified as forged. Experimental results show that the best detection rate of this scheme on WAV format audios is less than 94% and decreases significantly with the reduction of sampling rate. Pan *et al.* [13] have also proposed a time-domain method based on higher-order statistics to detect traces of splicing. The proposed method uses differences in the local noise levels in an audio signal for splice detection. Although, it works well on simulated spliced audio, which is generated by a pure clean audio and noise audio, the efficiency of this scheme in practical application is not clear. This is because noise-level based features can be easily counterfeited. Another popular audio splicing detection method is to utilize the electric network frequency (ENF) [12]. The discontinuity introduced by splicing is detected via analysis of magnitude and phase of ENF. However, this scheme is not applicable to the audios recorded by battery-powered devices (e.g. mobile phones), where ENF does not exist. Audio forensics based on the double compression detection [1] can reveal the trace of splicing if the segments are pre-compressed by different algorithms. However, the existence of double compression does not guarantee that the audio is tampered. Because the audio is usually recompressed or transcoded for legal purposes. Therefore, robust audio splicing detection is still an open issue.

The primary purpose of this paper is to develop a novel digital audio forensics technique, in particular audio splicing detection and localization. Here we exploit specific artifacts introduced at the time of recording as an intrinsic signature and for audio recording integrity authentication. The magnitudes of acoustic channel impulse response and ambient noise are used to model intrinsic acoustic environment signature and used it for splicing detection and splicing location identification. Both the acoustic channel impulse response and the ambient noise are jointly considered to achieve this objective. In this scheme, each query audio is divided into overlapping frames. For each frame, the magnitudes of channel impulse response and ambient noise are jointly estimated as an intrinsic signature by applying the spectrum classification technique. The correlation of signatures between the query frame and *reference frame* is calculated and classified by using a pre-determined optimal threshold. The spliced frame can be detected and localized if the correlation with the reference frame is less than the threshold. A refining step is further considered to reduce the detection and localization errors. The performance of the proposed scheme is tested using two data sets: (1) TIMIT database; (2) Real world audio recordings. Experimental results show that the proposed system can successfully identify the spliced frames in uncompressed audio recordings. In addition, performance of the proposed method is also compared against existing state-of-the-art work [13]. The detection performance is also superior to the existing methods.

Compared with the existing literatures, the contribution of this paper includes: 1) Environment dependent signatures are exploited for audio splicing detection; 2) Similarity between adjacent frames is proposed to reduce the detection and localization errors.

## 2. AUDIO SIGNAL MODELING AND SIGNATURE ESTIMATION

When audio/speech is recorded by a microphone positioned at a distance away from the speaker, the observed audio/speech will be contaminated due to the propagation through the acoustic channel between the speaker and the microphone, and the ambience noise. A simplified model is defined as,

$$y(t) = h_{RIR}(t) * s(t) + \eta(t) \qquad (1)$$

where $s(t)$, $h_{RIR}(t)$, and $\eta(t)$ represent the clean speech, room impulse response (RIR) and ambience noise, respectively.

$h_{RIR}(t)$ is uniquely determined when the environmental setting is fixed and $\eta(t)$ is a environment-related information. Both of them are referred to *environmental signature*. In this paper, we shall use the environmental signature to authenticate the integrity of captured audios. Blind estimation of the environmental signature [7] from signal channel audio will be introduced in the following section.

### 2.1 Environmental Signature Estimation

A brief overview of room impulse response (RIR), $h_{RIR}(t)$, estimation in the frequency domain presented in [7] is provided next.

The Short Time Fourier Transform (STFT) representation of (1) can be expressed as:

$$Y(k,l) = S(k,l) \times H(k,l) + V(k,l) \qquad (2)$$

where $Y(k,l)$, $S(k,l)$, $H(k,l)$ and $V(k,l)$ are the STFT coefficients(in the $k^{th}$ frequency bin and the $l^{th}$ frame) of $y(t)$, $s(t)$, $h_{RIR}(t)$ and $\eta(t)$, respectively. Power spectrum of the noisy observation $y(t)$ is expressed as,

$$
\begin{aligned}
|Y(k,l)|^2 = \ & |S(k,l)|^2 \times |H(k,l)|^2 + |V(k,l)|^2 + \\
& 2 \times |S(k,l)| \times |H(k,l)| \times |V(k,l)| \times \cos\theta
\end{aligned}
$$
$$(3)$$

where $\theta = \angle S(k,l) + \angle H(k,l) - \angle V(k,l)$. Dividing both sides of Eq.(3) by $|S(k,l)|^2 \times |H(k,l)|^2$ and transforming the resulting expression using logarithm operation results in:

$$\log|Y(k,l)| - \log|S(k,l)| = \log|H(k,l)| + \log\varepsilon(k,l) \qquad (4)$$

where

$$\varepsilon = \sqrt{(\xi^{-1} + 2\xi^{-0.5}\cos\theta + 1)}, \qquad (5)$$

and

$$\xi = \frac{|S(k,l)|^2 \times |H(k,l)|^2}{|V(k,l)|^2}, \qquad (6)$$

Gaubitch *et al.* in [7] has shown the way to extract $\log|H(k,l)|$ and $\log\varepsilon(k,l)$ from the noisy observation $|Y(k,l)|$, separately. However, in the application of audio forensics, the background noise provides useful information and its effectiveness has been experimentally verified in [8, 15] and [16]. In our scheme, the acoustic distortion (convolutional and additive distortion), also referred as the environmental signature, is jointly estimated.

Given the knowledge of the magnitude spectrum of the clean signal, $S(k,l)$, the log-spectrum magnitude of acoustic distortion can be estimated as,

$$\underline{H}(k) = \frac{1}{L} \sum_{l=1}^{L} \left(\log|Y(k,l)| - \log|S(k,l)|\right) \qquad (7)$$

where, $\underline{H}(k)$ is the estimated RIR contaminated by ambient noise. In practice, $S(k,l)$ is not available and can be approximated via a statistical model, such as the *Gaussian Mixture Model (GMM)*. The approximation of the clean log-spectrum, $\hat{S}(k,l)$, can be found in [7]. Then the estimated environmental signature $\underline{\hat{H}}(k)$ can be obtained.

## 3. APPLICATIONS TO AUDIO FORENSICS

A novel audio forensics framework based on estimated acoustic impulse response from input audio recording is proposed here. To this end, we consider two applications of estimated acoustic impulse response to audio forensic: (i) *audio source authentication* that refers as to determine whether the query audio/speech is captured in a specific environment or location as claimed; and (ii) *splicing detection* that refers as to determine whether the query audio/speech is original or assembled using multiple samples recorded in different environments and detects splicing locations (in case of forged audio).

### 3.1 Audio Source Authentication

In practice, the crime scene is usually secured and kept intact for possible further investigation. Under this circumstance, it is possible to rebuild the acoustic environmental setting, including the location of microphone and sound source, furniture arrangement, etc. The forensic expert can capture *sufficient* audio samples and use them to extract reference acoustic environment signature and compare them with the signature extracted from the query audio recording. Correlation between signatures extracted from the query audio and the reference audio are used to determine whether the query audio is made in the claimed environment or not.

To determine whether the query audio is recorded in the claimed environment, the correlation between the estimated environmental signatures, $\hat{\underline{H}}_q(k)$ and $\hat{\underline{H}}_{Ref}(k)$, which are extracted from the query audio and recaptured reference audio, is calculated as follows,

$$
\begin{aligned}
\rho &= \mathcal{NCC}(\hat{\underline{H}}_q, \hat{\underline{H}}_{Ref}) \\
&= \frac{\sum_{k=1}^{K}(\hat{H}_q(k) - \mu_q)(\hat{H}_{Ref}(k) - \mu_{Ref})}{\sqrt{\sum_{k=1}^{K}(\hat{H}_q(k) - \mu_q)^2}\sqrt{\sum_{k=1}^{K}(\hat{H}_{Ref}(k) - \mu_{Ref})^2}}
\end{aligned}
\tag{8}
$$

where $\mu_q$ and $\mu_{Ref}$ are the means of $\hat{\underline{H}}_q(k)$ and $\hat{\underline{H}}_{Ref}(k)$, respectively, and $\rho \in [-1, 1]$.

The distribution of correlation coefficient, $\rho$, is used for binary hypothesis testing, that is, to determine whether *the query audio and recaptured reference audio are from the same environment or not*. To make this decision, correlation coefficient is compared against the decision threshold, $T$. The Neyman-Person criterion [14] is used to compute the optimal decision threshold, $T$, which requires knowledge of the distribution of $\rho$. In the next, the optimal threshold is determined according to the statistical modeling technique.

The acoustic signatures extracted from the query audio and the reference audio, made in the same environment, are expected to be highly correlated. Similarly, correlation between $\hat{\underline{H}}_q(k)$ and $\hat{\underline{H}}_{Ref}(k)$ estimated from the query audio and the reference audio where both are made in two different environments is expected to be close to zero. To model distribution of $\rho_i$, we consider the same acoustic environment case first, that is, for identical acoustic environments, correlation coefficient, $\rho_i$, is very close to the extreme value (maximum value) of interval $[-1, 1]$. Thus, we model $\rho$ using the extreme value distribution. The *Probability Density Function (PDF)* of *extreme value distribution* is expressed as [9],

$$
f_e(\rho|\mu_e, \delta_e) = \delta_e^{-1} \exp\left[\frac{\rho - \mu_e}{\delta_e} - \exp\left(\frac{\rho - \mu_e}{\delta_e}\right)\right]
\tag{9}
$$

where $\mu_e$ and $\delta_e$ represent the location and scale parameter, respectively. The parameters, $\mu_e$ and $\delta_e$, can be estimated via maximum likelihood estimation [5].

Similarly, if the query audio and the recaptured audio are made in two different environments correlation coefficient $\rho_i$ is close to zero, and expected to obey a *heavy-tailed* distribution. To this end, distribution of $\rho(i)$ is modeled using *Generalized Gaussian* [4] distribution. Motivation behind considering generalized Gaussian model here is due to the fact that thicker tails will lead to more conservative error estimates. The *PDF* of *Generalized Gaussian* distribution is given as follows,

$$
f_g(\rho|\alpha_g, \beta_g, \mu_g) = \frac{1}{2\alpha_g \Gamma(1/\beta_g)} \exp\left[-\left(\frac{|\rho - \mu_g|}{\alpha_g}\right)^{\beta_g}\right]
\tag{10}
$$

where $\alpha_g$, $\beta_g$, and $\mu_g$ represent the scale, shape and mean parameters, respectively. The details of parameters estimation can be found in [4]

It can be observed from Fig. 2 that, the true distributions fit the models quite well. With these distributions, binary hypothesis testing based on optimal threshold, $T$, contributes to the following two types of errors:

- **Type I Error:** Labeling an authentic audio as a *forged*. The probability of Type I Error is called as *False Positive Rate (FPR)*, which is defined as,

$$
\begin{aligned}
FPR_T &= \int_{-\infty}^{T} f_e(\rho|\hat{\mu}_e, \hat{\delta}_e)\mathrm{d}x \\
&= 1 - \exp\left[-\exp\left(\frac{T - \hat{\mu}_e}{\hat{\delta}_e}\right)\right]
\end{aligned}
\tag{11}
$$

- **Type II Error:** Labeling a forged audio as *authentic*. The probability of Type II Error is called as *False Negative Rate (FNR)*, which is defined as,

$$
\begin{aligned}
FNR_T &= \int_{T}^{\infty} f_g(\rho|\hat{\alpha}_g, \hat{\beta}_g, \hat{\mu}_g)\mathrm{d}x \\
&= 1 - \mathcal{F}_g(T)
\end{aligned}
\tag{12}
$$

where, $\mathcal{F}_g$ is the *Cumulative Distribution Function(CDF)* of $f_g(\rho|\hat{\alpha}_g, \hat{\beta}_g, \hat{\mu}_g)$.

Then, the optimal decision boundary $T$ can be determined by minimizing the combination effect of these errors as follows,

$$
T := \arg\min_{T \in [-1,1]} [\lambda \times FPR_T + (1 - \lambda) \times FNR_T]
\tag{13}
$$

where $\lambda \in [0, 1]$ is the control factor chosen by the forensic expert according to the practical applications.

When $T$ is available, it is then used to determine whether the query audio is authentic or forged using the following hypothesis to design the following binary hypothesis testing rule,

$$
\begin{aligned}
\rho < T : & \quad \text{Forged} \\
\rho \geq T : & \quad \text{As Claimed}
\end{aligned}
\tag{14}
$$

## 3.2 Audio Splicing Detection and Localization

In this section, we will extend the method proposed in Section 3.1 for audio splicing detection. To illustrate audio splicing process, an audio clips was assembled from three segments, $Seg1$, $Seg2$, and $Seg3$ consisting of $M_1$, $M_2$, and $M_3$ frames, respectively. Here, audio segments $Seg1$ and $Seg3$ are recorded in acoustic environment $A$ and audio segment $Seg2$ is recorded in environment $B$. Shown in Fig. 1 is temporal plot of the resulting audio. It can be observed that splicing did not introduce any visual artifacts in the resulting audio. It should be noted that Fig. 1 is the simplified example and can be easily extended to a general case, which an audio is spliced by multiple segments.

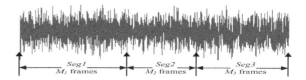

**Figure 1: Shown is the plot of the spliced audio obtained assembled from three segments, $Seg1$, $Seg2$, and $Seg3$ consisting of $M1$, $M2$, and $M3$ frames, respectively.**

To detect splicing in the query audio, acoustic environment signature estimated from the query audio can be used. One of the constraint in case of splicing detection is that forensic analyst does not have access to the reference audio. In other words, due to the lack of reference audio the forensic analyst has to rely on blind detection. In addition, forensic analyst also has no knowledge of $M_1$, $M_2$ and $M_3$. To get around these limitations, we proposed to use the first frame of the query audio as the reference frame and for splicing detection.

$$\rho_i = \begin{cases} 1, & i = 1 \\ \mathcal{NCC}(\underline{\hat{H}}_q^{(1)}, \underline{\hat{H}}_q^{(i)}), & 1 < i \leq M \end{cases} \quad (15)$$

where $\underline{\hat{H}}_q^{(i)}$ is the estimated channel response of the $i^{th}$ frame from the query audio, $M$ is the length of query audio, here, equaling to $M_1 + M_2 + M_3$.

However, it has been observed that splicing detecting using temporal variation of the acoustic signature with respect to the first frame as a reference frame results in $\rho_i$ being sensitive to the noise. To get around this issue, following post-processing based on temporal smoothing is applied on estimated acoustic signature,

$$\dot{\rho}_i = \begin{cases} \dfrac{1}{i} \sum_{j=1}^{i} \mathcal{NCC}(\hat{\underline{H}}_q^{(j)}, \hat{\underline{H}}_q^{(i)}), & \text{if } \dot{\rho}_{i-1} > T, 2 \leq i \leq M_T \\ \dfrac{1}{M_T} \sum_{j=1}^{M_T} \mathcal{NCC}(\hat{\underline{H}}_q^{(j)}, \hat{\underline{H}}_q^{(i)}), & \text{otherwise} \end{cases}$$
$$(16)$$

where

$$M_T = \min_{i \in [1, M_1 + M_2 + M_3]} \{i \mid \dot{\rho}_i < T\} \quad (17)$$

For the audio forensics applications, where binary decision (*Forged vs Authentic*) is only needed, the final result can be determined according to the following binary hypothesis testing rule,

$$\begin{aligned} D_b > T_r : & \quad \text{Forged} \\ D_b \leq T_r : & \quad \text{Authentic} \end{aligned} \quad (18)$$

$$D_b = \frac{\#\{\dot{\rho}_i \mid \dot{\rho}_i < T\}}{M_1 + M_2 + M_3} \quad (19)$$

where $T_r$ is a predefined rate, $0 < T_r < 1$ and $\#\{\cdot\}$ represents the cardinality of a set.

Here, (18) states that if the ratio of suspected audio frames exceeds a predefined threshold, the query audio will be classified as a *forged* audio. Furthermore, forensic expert may also be interested in determining splicing locations in the query audio. The splicing locations determined by simply checking if $\dot{\rho}_i < T$ satisfies or not. In other words, all frames satisfying $\dot{\rho}_i < T$ condition may be labeled as tampered. It has been observed that this framework for localizing forgery locations in audio requires *an accurate* estimate of the impulse response, $\hat{\underline{H}}_q(k)$. Any distortions in the estimated signature, $\hat{\underline{H}}_q(k)$, will result in a substantial number of false alarms. Local correlation between the estimated signatures from adjacent frames is used to make forgery localization approach robust to estimation errors.

The improved algorithm is heavily dependent on an assumption that *if the current frames is forged, the adjacent frames have a significatively high probability of being labeled as forged also*. This is a reasonable assumption because tampering usually occurs in many consecutive frames instead of a few scattered frames. The proposed refining algorithm robust to estimation distortion in the acoustic signature has following two major steps:

1. Detect the given suspected frames by simply checking if $\dot{\rho}_i < T$ satisfied or not; If $\dot{\rho}_i < T$, $p_i = 1$, which indicates the current frame may be forged. Otherwise, $p_i = 0$.

2. Refining the results using neighborhood similarity score as follows,

$$\text{If } \frac{\sum_{k=i-W/2}^{k=i+W/2} p_k - p_i}{W} > R_s, \text{ the } i^{th}\text{ frame is spliced.}$$
$$(20)$$

where, $W$ and $R_s$ represent the window size ($W$=3 or 5) and similarity score threshold ($R_s \in [0.7, 0.9]$), respectively. Eq.(20) means, for $i^{th}$ suspected frame, if most of its adjacent frames are also suspected frames, it has significantly high probability of being labeled as a forged frame.

Next section provides performance analysis of the proposed method on synthetic and real-world recordings.

## 4. PERFORMANCE EVALUATION

The effectiveness of the proposed methodology is evaluated using two data sets: synthetic data and real world human speech. Details for the data sets used, the experimental setup and the experimental results are provided below.

### 4.1 Data Set and Experimental Setting

Firstly, the speech data of TIMIT corpus [6] was used to train the clean log-spectrum and generate the synthetic data. TIMIT consists of 6300 sentences: ten sentences spoken by each of 438 male and 192 female speakers. The data set is divided into a training set (462 speakers) and a test set (168 speakers) with entirely different sentence contents. For training, the entire training set was processed using Hanning windowed frames(128 ms for each) with overlapping rate of 50%. 12 RASTA-MFCCs of each frame was calculated and used to train the GMM with 512 mixtures. For test, synthetic room response generated by source-image method [10] for a rectangular room is convolved with the test speech. Each time, all the parameters used for room response simulation were randomly selected to generate the RIRs of different environments.

For the second data set, a real world data set consists of 60 speech recording was used (used in [11]). The speeches were recorded in four different environments: (1) outdoor; (2) small office; (3) stairs; (4) restroom. In each recording environment, each of the three speakers (one male $S_1$, two females $S_2$ and $S_3$) read five different texts. The audio was originally recorded with 44.1 kHz sampling frequency, 16 bits/sample resolution, and then downsampled to 16 kHz.

### 4.2 Experimental Results

#### 4.2.1 Results on Synthetic Data

In this section, synthetically generated reverberant data were used to verify the effectiveness of the proposed algorithm. For the beginning, the optimal threshold $T$ can be determined from the synthetic data as follow. The randomly generated RIRs $H_A$ and $H_B$ were convolved to the test data set, respectively, resulting in two simulated synthetic data sets from two virtual environments $A$ and $B$. Then, the environmental signatures estimated from the synthetic speeches in environments $A$ and $B$ are represented as $\hat{\underline{H}}_{A,i}$ and $\hat{\underline{H}}_{B,i}$, respectively where $0 < i \leq N_t$, $N_t$ denotes total number of testing speeches. The distributions of intra-correlation coefficient, $\rho_{A,i \to A,j} = \mathcal{NCC}(\hat{\underline{H}}_{A,i}, \hat{\underline{H}}_{A,j}), i \neq j$ and inter-correlation coefficient $\rho_{A,i \to B,k} = \mathcal{NCC}(\hat{\underline{H}}_{A,i}, \hat{\underline{H}}_{B,k})$, were shown in Fig. 2. The optimal threshold $T$ for these distributions is determined as 0.3274 by setting $\lambda = 0.5$, which results in the minimal overall error of 2.23%.

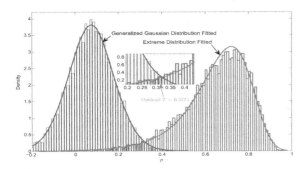

Figure 2: Shown are the plots of the true and the fitted distribution of $\rho_{A,i \to A,j}$ and $\rho_{A,i \to B,k}$ and the optimal decision threshold, $T = 0.3274$

Shown in Fig.3 is the plot of the ROC curve of True Positive Rate (TPR, which represents the probability of that the query audio is classified as *forged*, when in fact it is) vs False Positive Rate (FPR, which represents the probability of that query audio is labeled as authentic, when in fact it is) on the test audio set. It can be observed from Fig. 3 that the proposed audio source authentication scheme has almost perfect detection performance when the recaptured reference audios were available.

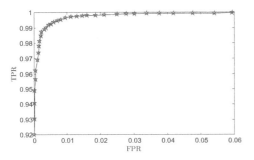

Figure 3: Shown is the ROC curve of the proposed audio source authentication scheme.

Furthermore, with the help of an optimal threshold $T$, performance of the proposed splicing detection algorithm is also evaluated on synthetic data. Two randomly selected speeches from the test set were convolved with $H_A$ and $H_B$, resulting in two reverberant speeches $RS_A$ and $RS_B$. And $RS_B$ was inserted into a random location within $RS_A$. It can be observed from Fig. 4 that the proposed forgery detection and localization algorithm has successfully detected and localized the inserted audio segment, $RS_B$ with 100% accuracy.

### 4.2.2  Results on Real World Data

Effectiveness of the proposed audio splicing detection method has also been verified on real-world speech data.

Shown in Fig. 5 are the detection results of the proposed scheme on real world recordings created by inserting speech recording of the $1^{st}$ speaker in the $1^{st}$ environment (red part in Fig. 5(a)) at middle of speech recording of $2^{nd}$ speaker in the $3^{rd}$ environment (blue parts in Fig. 5(a)). The resulting audio is analyzed using proposed splicing detection and localization method. It can be observed from that the proposed scheme is capable of detecting/localizing the inserted frames, even for frame sizes of $2s$ and $1s$. Similar results were obtained for other tested speech and omitted for the sack of limited space.

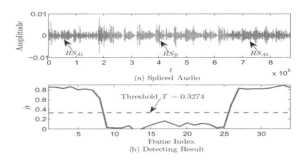

Figure 4: Forgery detection and localization results (with frame size = 3s).

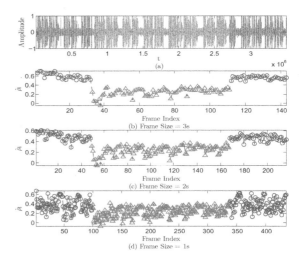

Figure 5: Detecting performance of the proposed scheme on real-world data with various frame size: (a)3s, (b)2s, and (c):1s. Blue circles and red triangles represent the frames from E1S1 and E3S2, respectively

In our next experiment, detection accuracy of the proposed scheme for real-world data set is evaluated. Shown in Fig. 6 are the resulting ROC curves computed at different frame sizes with over 50 runs. It can be observed from Fig. 6 that the overall detection accuracies improves for larger frame size. This is not a surprising observation as larger frame size results in more accurate and stable estimation of environment signature. Detection performance in the presence of ambient noise can improved by using larger frame size but at the cost of lower the forgery localization accuracy.

### 4.2.3  Comparison Results with Previous Works

In our last set of experiments, performance of the proposed framework is compared with the existing splicing detection scheme [13], which uses inconsistency in local noise levels estimated from the query audio for splicing detection.

To this end, forged(or spliced) audio recording is generated by splicing audio recordings made in two different environments. More specifically, speech recording of $3^{rd}$ speaker made in $3^{rd}$ environment (E3S3) is inserted at the middle of speech recording of $1^{st}$ speaker made in $1^{st}$ environment (E1S1). Shown in Fig. 7(a) is time-domain plot of the spliced audio assembled from E1S1 (blue) and E3S3 (red). It can be observed from Fig.7(a) that both original recordings, e.g., E1S1 and E3S3, contain same background noise level. Shown in Fig. 7(b) and Fig. 7(c) are plots of frame-level detection performance of the proposed scheme and Pan's scheme

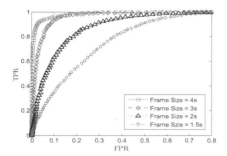

**Figure 6: Shown are the ROC curves of the proposed scheme on real-world data with various frame sizes.**

[13], respectively. It can be observed from Fig. 7(b)&(c) that the proposed scheme is capable of not only detects the presence of inserted frames but also localize these frames. On the other hand, Pan's scheme is unable to detect or localize the inserted frames. Inferior performance of Pan's scheme can be attributed to the fact that it only depends on the local noise level for forgery detection, which is almost same in the forged audio used for analysis.

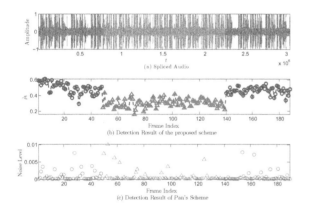

**Figure 7: Shown is the detection performance of the proposed scheme and Pan's scheme [13] (Frame size = 2s) .**

## 5. CONCLUSION

In this paper, a novel method for audio splicing detection and localization is proposed. The magnitude of acoustic channel impulse response and ambient noise are considered to model intrinsic acoustic environment signature. The performance of the proposed scheme is evaluated on two data sets with numerous experimental settings. Experimental results validate effectiveness of the proposed scheme for both forgery detection and localization. Performance of the proposed scheme is also compared with existing state of the art for audio splicing detection [13]. Performance comparison indicates that the proposed scheme outperforms selected state of the art [13].

## 6. ACKNOWLEDGMENT

This work is supported by 2013 Guangdong Natural Science Funds for Distinguished Young Scholar (S2013050014223), and NPST program by King Saud University under grant number 12-INF2634-02.

## 7. REFERENCES

[1] T. Bianchi, A. D. Rosa, M. Fontani, G. Rocciolo, and A. Piva. Detection and classification of double compressed MP3 audio tracks. In *Proceedings of the first ACM workshop on Information hiding and multimedia security*, pages 159–164, 2013.

[2] J. Chen, S. Xiang, W. Liu, and H. Huang. Exposing digital audio forgeries in time domain by using singularity analysis with wavelets. In *Proceedings of the first ACM workshop on Information hiding and multimedia security*, pages 149–158, 2013.

[3] A. J. Cooper. Detecting butt-spliced edits in forensic digital audio recordings. In *Proceedings of Audio Engineering Society 39th Conf., Audio Forensics: Practices and Challenges*, 2010.

[4] J. A. Dominguez-Molina, G. González-Farías, R. M. Rodríguez-Dagnino, and I. C. Monterrey. A practical procedure to estimate the shape parameter in the generalized gaussian distribution. *technique report I-01-18_eng.pdf, available through http://www.cimat.mx/reportes/enlinea/I-01-18_eng.pdf*, 1, 2001.

[5] S. R. Eddy. Maximum likelihood fitting of extreme value distributions. unpublished work, citeseer.ist.psu.edu/370503.html, 1997.

[6] J. S. Garofolo, L. F. Lamel, W. M. Fisher, J. G. Fiscus, D. S. Pallett, N. L. Dahlgren, and V. Zue. *TIMIT Acoustic-Phonetic Continuous Speech Corpus*. Linguistic Data Consortium, Philadelphia, 1993.

[7] N. D. Gaubitch, M. Brooks, and P. A. Naylor. Blind channel magnitude response estimation in speech using spectrum classification. *IEEE Transations Acoust, Speech, Signal Processing*, 21(10):2162–2171, 2013.

[8] S. Ikram and H. Malik. Digital audio forensics using background noise. In *Proceedings of IEEE Int. Conf. on Multimedia and Expo*, pages 106–110, 2010.

[9] S. Kotz and S. Nadarajah. *Extreme value distributions*. World Scientific, 2000.

[10] E. A. Lehmann and A. M. Johansson. Diffuse reverberation model for efficient image-source simulation of room impulse responses. *IEEE Transactions on Audio Speech and Language Processing*, 18(6):1429–1439, 2010.

[11] H. Malik. Acoustic environment identification and its application to audio forensics. *IEEE Transactions on Information Forensics and Security*, 8(11):1827–1837, 2013.

[12] D. Nicolalde and J. Apolinario. Evaluating digital audio authenticity with spectral distances and ENF phase change. In *IEEE International Conference on Acoustics, Speech and Signal Processing*, pages 1417–1420, Taipei, Taiwan, 2009.

[13] X. Pan, X. Zhang, and S. Lyu. Detecting splicing in digital audios using local noise level estimation. In *Proceedings of IEEE Int. Conf. on Acoustics, Speech, and Signal Processing (ICASSP'12)*, pages 1841–1844, Kyoto, Japan, 2012.

[14] H. Poor. *An Introduction to Signal Detection and Estimation*. Springer-Verlag, Berlin, Germany, $2^{nd}$ edition, 1994.

[15] H. Zhao and H. Malik. Audio forensics using acoustic environment traces. In *Proceedings of the IEEE Statistical Signal Processing Workshop (SSP'12)*, pages 373–376, Ann Arbor, MI, 2012.

[16] H. Zhao and H. Malik. Audio recording location identification using acoustic environment signature. *IEEE Transactions on Information Forensics and Security*, 8(11):1746–1759, 2013.

# A Universal Image Forensic Strategy Based on Steganalytic Model

Xiaoqing Qiu
School of Information Science
and Technology
Sun Yat-sen University
Guangzhou, P.R. China
qiuxq3@mail2.sysu.edu.cn

Haodong Li
School of Information Science
and Technology
Sun Yat-sen University
Guangzhou, P.R. China
lihaod@mail2.sysu.edu.cn

Weiqi Luo[*]
School of Software
Sun Yat-sen University
Guangzhou, P.R. China
weiqi.luo@yahoo.com

Jiwu Huang
College of Information
Engineering
Shenzhen University
Shenzhen, P.R. China
jwhuang@szu.edu.cn

## ABSTRACT

Image forensics have made great progress during the past decade. However, almost all existing forensic methods can be regarded as the specific way, since they mainly focus on detecting one type of image processing operations. When the type of operations changes, the performances of the forensic methods usually degrade significantly. In this paper, we propose a universal forensics strategy based on steganalytic model. By analyzing the similarity between steganography and image processing operation, we find that almost all image operations have to modify many image pixels without considering some inherent properties within the original image, which is similar to what in steganography. Therefore, it is reasonable to model various image processing operations as steganography and it is promising to detect them with the help of some effective universal steganalytic features. In our experiments, we evaluate several advanced steganalytic features on six kinds of typical image processing operations. The experimental results show that all evaluated steganalyzers perform well while some steganalytic methods such as the spatial rich model (SRM) [4] and LBP [19] based methods even outperform the specific forensic methods significantly. What is more, they can further identify the type of various image processing operations, which is impossible to achieve using the existing forensic methods.

## Categories and Subject Descriptors

I.4 [**Image Processing and computer vision**]

*Corresponding author

*IH&MMSec'14,* June 11–13, 2014, Salzburg, Austria.
Copyright 2014 ACM 978-1-4503-2647-6/14/06 ...$15.00.
http://dx.doi.org/10.1145/2600918.2600941.

## Keywords

Universal Forensics; Tampering Detection; Steganalysis

## 1. INTRODUCTION

Nowadays, with the powerful and user-friendly digital image editing software such as PhotoShop and GIMP, it becomes easy to modify digital images without leaving any perceptible artifacts. Once such tools are abused for those forgers, it would lead to some potential serious moral, ethical and legal consequences. Therefore, digital image forensics [21] have become an important issue and have attracted increasingly attention.

Up to now, many forensic methods have been proposed for different forensic scenes, such as exposing splicing images [18, 5], identifying image compression history [3, 13], detecting some image processing operations [14, 20, 23], and so on. However, most exiting methods just consider only one type of image processing operations, and these methods are difficult to be extended for other image operations. For example, a set of features proposed for identifying JPEG compression may not be suitable for identifying image splicing, re-sampling, and/or blurring operations. Moreover, most forensic methods usually assume that the questionable image has been processed by a specific image processing operation or not, and they aim to make a binary decision. In most forensic cases, however, such an assumption is not very reasonable since no prior information is available for a given image. If the suspicious image may be performed with several possible operations, all specific forensic methods become poor or even useless. Therefore, a universal forensic strategy is needed in this case. To our best knowledge, none related literatures have been reported previously.

In this paper, we try to find a universal strategy for detecting various types of image processing operations. We begin with studying the common artifacts introduced by different types of image processing operations, and found that any processing would inevitably modify many image pixels and destroy some inherent statistics within an original image, which is quite analogous to image steganography. Based on

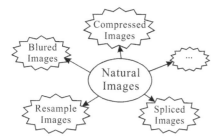

**Figure 1: Identification of image processing operations based on natural image model**

this analysis, we propose a forensic strategy via borrowing some powerful features from universal steganalysis. Unlike the typical forensic methods, the proposed strategy is universal in two senses. First of all, without changing the features, it can be widely used to identify those images modified by different kinds of operations from original ones. Secondly, the proposed strategy can also be used to further identify the types of the operations. In the experiments, we tested six typical kinds of image processing on 1050 natural images downloaded from the First IFS-TC Image Forensics Challenge [1]. The experimental results have shown the superiority of the proposed strategy compared with those specific forensic methods.

The rest of this paper is organized as follows. Section 2 analyzes the universal image forensics from the view of steganalysis; Section 3 describes the proposed universal strategy based on steganalytic model; Section 4 shows the experimental results and discussions. Finally, the concluding remarks and future works will be given in Section 5.

## 2. UNIVERSAL IMAGE FORENSICS FROM THE VIEW OF STEGANALYSIS

To develop a universal forensic method for detecting various image processing operations, such as lossy compression, region blurring, re-sampling, splicing, and so on, we should concentrate on the common artifacts left by various operations rather than some specific artifacts introduced by a certain operation as it did in most previous forensic methods. One of the options is to model the inherent statistical properties of original natural images, the common objects that various operations would perform on. As illustrated in Fig. 1, if such an ideal model is available, it is possible to identify various image processing operations since different operations usually modify the model in different manners and/or strengths in the corresponding feature space.

As we know, there are many inherent statistical properties within natural images, and some properties may be useful in our forensic scene. For instance, as illustrated in Fig. 2, the adjacent pixel values in spatial domain as well as their corresponding DCT frequency coefficients are highly correlated. However, any image processing operation would inevitably modify some pixels values within an image. As a result, the correlations among those modified pixels and their neighbors would be changed or even broken. If such correlated properties can be well studied and modeled, it is expected that those modifications in an image can be detected effectively. Therefore, our key issue is how to model the inherent correlations within natural images.

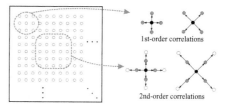

(a) Spatial correlations

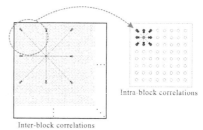

(b) Frequency correlations

**Figure 2: Illustration of the correlations in spatial and frequency domain within a natural image**

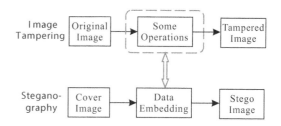

**Figure 3: Illustration of the relationship between image tampering and steganography**

Fortunately, some powerful statistical features can be borrowed from another research field - steganalysis, which aims to expose those stego images with hidden messages embedded by steganography. As illustrated in Fig. 3, if the operation of data embedding in steganography is regarded as a specific type of image tampering [1], then the tasks of image forensics and steganalysis become exactly the same, namely, differentiating those natural images (*i.e.* cover images) from the tampered ones (*i.e.* stego images). Please note that most typical image processing operations would change the inherent properties (such as the correlations and so on) more severely comparing with the data embedding operation. The reasons are list as follows.

- In the modern steganography such as HUGO [16] and WOW [6], the embedding changes are mainly located at the textural/noisy regions that are difficult to model. However, both textural and smooth regions within a natural image would be modified a lot for most image processing operations, such as JPEG compression, blurring, and median filtering.

- Both the number and the magnitude of modified pixel values in most image processing operations are much

---

[1]Note that both operations would modify many pixel values, and destroy some inherent correlations in original images.

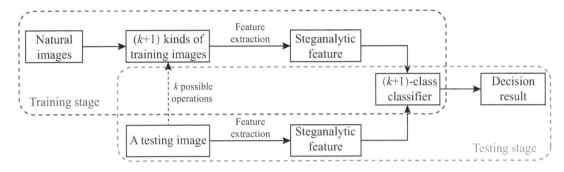

Figure 4: The diagram of the proposed strategy

larger than those in steganography. For most steganography, the modification magnitude is usually limited in $\pm 1$ for every pixel value, and the modification rate is typically less than 9% (around 0.4bpp using the WOW embedding algorithm [6]) for the secure embedding [2]. Based on our experiments on 1050 natural images in dataset [1], however, the average modification rates for JPEG compression, gamma correction, median filtering, and Gaussian filtering are 36.55%, 48.71%, 35.84%, and 37.93%, respectively, all are more than three times over the secure limit (*i.e.* 9% modification rate).

- No obvious visual artifacts would be introduced into those stego images. However, some image contents would be changed significantly for some tampering operations, such as copy-paste tampering, image splicing and in-painting.

Based on the above analysis, it is expected that some steganalytic features which can effectively model those inherent correlation properties within natural images would be also promising in image forensics.

## 3. THE PROPOSED STRATEGY

In this section, we will propose a universal image forensic strategy based on steganalytic model. First of all, we should analyze what kind of steganalytic features is suitable in the proposed strategy. It is known that the steganalytic methods can be divided into two different types, *i.e.* targeted and universal methods [11]. Targeted steganalytic methods require the knowledge of the targeted steganography. It may become useless for other steganographic ones, which is similar to those existing image forensic methods being effective to detect the corresponding image operations. Unlike the targeted steganalytic methods, universal steganalytic methods try to model some inherent statistical properties within natural images, and extract the steganalytic features without any information about the targeted steganography. Therefore, those universal steganalytic features should be considered in the proposed strategy. Besides, the supervised learning is needed to train a binary or multi-class classifier, which depends on the the number of possible image processing operations under investigation.

The proposed strategy is illustrated in Fig. 4. Assume the number of possible image processing operations is $k$ for a given testing image, where $k \geq 1$. In the training stage, we first collect sufficient natural images, and we create the corresponding $k + 1$ kinds of images (including the class of original natural images themselves) using the $k$ possible operations respectively, and then we extract the steganalytic features from every training image. Finally, we can train a $(k+1)$-class classifier. In the testing stage, the steganalytic features of the testing image are extracted and then are fed to the obtained classifier to get the decision results.

## 4. EXPERIMENTAL RESULTS

In the experiments, we use the image database from the first IEEE IFS-TC image forensics challenge [1], which consists of 1050 authentic and 1050 tampered images in PNG format. The original images are captured by different digital cameras with various scenes, their sizes are varying from $480 \times 640$ to $4288 \times 4752$. The tampered images are obtained via different manipulation techniques such as copy-paste, image in-painting and splicing using some image editing software such as GIMP, Adobe Photoshop *etc.* Some tampered image examples in the database are shown in Fig. 5. We have highlighted the tampered regions of these images. Please note that those tampered images are very realistic without any obvious artifacts.

We use the ensemble classifier for classification just as it did in [10]. 50% of the authentic images and 50% of the tampered images are randomly selected to train the classifier, and the detection accuracy is obtained by evaluating the remaining images in the testing stage. Please note that we repeat the training and testing 10 times and show the average results in the following tables in subsection 4.1-4.3.

### 4.1 Detection of Image Splicing

In this subsection, we try to evaluate the performances of six typical universal steganalytic methods (including three kinds of steganalytic features for spatial domain, *i.e.* SRM [4], LBP [19], and SPAM [15]; three kinds of steganalytic features for JPEG domain, *i.e.* CF* [10], CC-CHEN [2, 9], and CC-PEV [17, 9]) and two specific forensic methods for splicing detection (*i.e.* He [5], Shi [18]).

After splicing operation, the resulting images usually are stored in JPEG format. To evaluate the robustness against JPEG compression, all the images are JPEG compressed with a quality factor randomly selected from 75 to 95 with a step of 5. The detection accuracies for those splicing images

[2]Usually, the higher the embedding rate, the better the steganalytic performances. Based on the results shown in [6], when the embedding rate is smaller than 0.4bpp, the security of WOW is still acceptable evaluated on the state-of-the-art steganalytic SRM model [4].

Figure 5: Some tampered images in the dataset [1]

Table 1: Average detection accuracies(%) for those splicing image before and after JPEG compression with different quality factors (QF). The best result is marked with an asterisk "*" in each case.

| Feature Set | Spatial Steganalysis | | | JPEG Steganalysis | | | Specific Forensics | |
|---|---|---|---|---|---|---|---|---|
| | SRM[4] | LBP[19] | SPAM[15] | CF*[10] | CC-Chen[2, 9] | CC-PEV[17, 9] | He[5] | Shi[18] |
| QF=75 | **88.37*** | 86.94 | 81.05 | 86.12 | 82.74 | 78.70 | 86.83 | 73.54 |
| QF=80 | **89.35*** | 88.47 | 82.60 | 87.23 | 83.96 | 80.69 | 86.82 | 74.25 |
| QF=85 | **91.22*** | 90.57 | 83.92 | 90.19 | 84.96 | 81.67 | 87.98 | 77.05 |
| QF=90 | **92.92*** | 92.89 | 86.50 | 90.98 | 86.58 | 82.74 | 90.47 | 79.73 |
| QF=95 | **94.76*** | 94.36 | 88.52 | 92.16 | 90.50 | 86.94 | 92.84 | 85.32 |
| Without Compression | **97.70*** | 95.31 | 91.35 | 91.93 | 89.91 | 88.79 | 93.34 | 90.45 |

before and after JPEG compression are given in Table 1. From Table 1, three important properties can be observed.

- The detection accuracies of all the methods would increase with increasing the quality factors.

- Though the image splicing operation is performed in the spatial domain, the JPEG steganalytic methods can also achieve satisfactory results since the spatial modifications would probably destroy the inherent correlations among the adjacent DCT coefficients just as illustrated in Section 2.

- Overall, both spatial and JPEG steganalytic methods can detect image splicing, and their detection performances are similar or even much better than the two specific forensic methods, *i.e.* He [5] and Shi [18], especially when the quality factor is high. Among the eight methods, the spatial steganalytic SRM [4] performs the best in all cases.

### 4.2 Detection of Image Processing Operations

In this subsection, we try to determine whether or not a questionable image has been previously performed with a given image processing operation, including gaussian blurring, gamma correction, lossy JPEG compression, median filtering, and re-sampling.

For each of 1050 authentic images in the database [1], we create five different images with a random parameter selected in Table 2. Besides the two good steganalytic methods for image splicing detection (*i.e.* SRM [4] and LBP [19]) as shown in Table 1, other five forensic methods including AR[3] [7], CE [20], JPA [12], and PPI [14] have been included in the experiment for comparative studies. For each type of image processing operations, therefore, we obtain six different classifiers using the above mentioned methods, and then

we use the resulting classifiers to conduct the testing. The average detection accuracies are shown in Table 3.

From Table 3, it is observed that SRM [4] and LBP [19] usually perform the best or nearly the best in most cases (except for detecting gamma correction with the LBP [19]), which means that both the steganalytic features can be regarded as universal features for detecting different image processing operations. For those specific forensic methods, although their detection performances for the corresponding operations are good (see the underlined values in Table 3), their performances are rather poor for other operations. For instance, the method AR [7] can effectively detect the Gaussian blurring and median filtering with both accuracies larger than 97.5%, while it fails to detect gamma correction and the corresponding accuracy drops to 53.11% which is close to the random guessing.

### 4.3 Identification of Image Processing Operations

In this subsection, we try to identify the type of several possible operations previously used for a given questionable image. Six typical operations including image splicing in subsection 4.1 and five operations in subsection 4.2 are considered in this experiment. The test images are created similarly as described in subsection 4.1 and subsection 4.2. For each of the 1050 authentic images, therefore, we obtain six different types of tampered images.

Ensemble classifier is used for this multi-class classification via pairwise coupling method [8], which means that each pairwise comparison obtains a binary classifier to make a prediction, and then all the predictions are combined to make a final decision based on the majority voting. In our experiments, the two advanced steganalytic features *i.e.* S-RM [4] and LBP [19] have been evaluated with the proposed strategy, and the confusion matrices are shown in Table 4 and Table 5, respectively. It is observed that both methods can effectively identify the type of image processing operations for a given image, especially the SRM [4]. On average,

---

[3]The method AR [7] can be used for detecting both Gaussian blurring and median filtering operations effectively.

**Table 2: Parameters of different types of image processing operations**

| Type of Image Processing Operations | Parameters |
|---|---|
| Gaussian Blurring | hsize: $3 \times 3$, $5 \times 5$, $7 \times 7$, $9 \times 9$; *sigma*: 1.0, 2.0 |
| Gamma Correction | $\gamma$: 0.5, 0.6, 0.7, 0.8, 0.9, 1.2, 1.4, 1.6, 1.8, 2.0 |
| JPEG Compression | QF: 75, 76, 77, ..., 95 |
| Median Filtering | R: $3 \times 3$, $5 \times 5$, $7 \times 7$, $9 \times 9$ |
| Re-sampling | Up sampling: 1, 3, 5, 10, 20, 30, ..., 90 (%)<br>Down sampling: 1, 3, 5, 10, 15, 20, 25, 30, 35, 40, 45 (%)<br>Rotation angle: 1, 3, 5, 10, 15, 20, 25, 30, 35, 40, 45 (degrees) |

**Table 3: Average detection accuracies(%) for identifying original images and those images after a given type of image processing operations. The best result is marked with an asterisk "*" in each case, and the underlined values denote the accuracies using the specific methods detecting the corresponding type of operations.**

| Feature Set | Gaussian Blurring | Gamma Correction | JPEG Compression | Median Filtering | Re-sampling |
|---|---|---|---|---|---|
| AR [7] | <u>98.17</u> | 53.11 | 65.26 | <u>97.86</u> | 77.56 |
| CE [20] | 69.41 | <u>96.31</u>* | 60.41 | 82.57 | 54.55 |
| JPA [12] | 89.80 | 50.82 | <u>99.18</u> | 82.69 | 65.10 |
| PPI [14] | 52.79 | 50.28 | 82.91 | 52.49 | <u>86.39</u> |
| SRM [4] | 99.98* | 96.09 | 99.55 | 99.75 | 98.90* |
| LBP [19] | 99.90 | 83.64 | 99.87* | 99.81* | 97.91 |

**Table 6: Average accuracies (%) along the diagonal direction in the corresponding confusion matrix for the specific forensic methods.**

| Feature Set | AR[7] | CE[20] | JPA[12] | PPI[14] | He[5] |
|---|---|---|---|---|---|
| Accuracy | 53.60 | 37.91 | 38.74 | 20.68 | 90.83 |

the detection accuracies along the diagonal direction in the two confusion matrices are 96.89% and 92.42%, respectively. For the comparison purpose, we also show the average results for the other five specific forensic methods in Table 6. From Table 6, it is observed that the detection performances of most specific methods are rather poor. Please note that the result using the method [5] is still satisfactory, since it tries to detect image splicing based on the Markov features from adjacent DCT and DWT frequency coefficients. Thus, this method can also be regarded as a universal steganalytic method.

## 5. CONCLUDING REMARKS

In this paper, we propose a universal image forensic strategy based on steganalytic model. The main contribution of this paper is that we find that various image processing operations would inevitably modify many pixel values without considering some inherent statistical properties within natural image, such as the highly correlations among adjacent pixels, which is very similar to the data embedding operation in steganography. Based on such analysis, we build a bridge between two different research issues *i.e.* digital image forensics and steganalysis, and proposed a universal forensic strategy based on steganalytic model. The experimental results show that the proposed strategy with those universal steganalytic features usually performs well. Especially for some advanced steganalytic features such as SRM [4] and LBP [19], the proposed strategy can effectively determine whether or not a questionable image has been performed with a given type of image processing operation, their detection performances are even much better than those state-of-the-art specific forensic methods. Fur-

thermore, the proposed strategy can further identify the type of various typical image processing operations, which has not been considered in previous forensic methods.

In the next step, more image processing operations and universal steganalytic features will be included in our experiments. Furthermore, we will extend the proposed strategy to determine the order of image processing operations [22].

## 6. ACKNOWLEDGMENTS

This work is supported by National Science & Technology Pillar Program (2012BAK16B06), NSFC (U1135001, 61332012, 61272191), the funding of Zhujiang Science and technology (2011J2200091), and the Guangdong NSF (S2013010012039).

## 7. REFERENCES

[1] Images corpus of the 1st IEEE IFS-TC image forensics challenge. Available at: http://ifc.recod.ic.unicamp.br/fc.website/index.py?sec=5.

[2] C. Chen and Y. Q. Shi. JPEG image steganalysis utilizing both intrablock and interblock correlations. In *Proc. IEEE Int. Symposium on Circuits and Systems*, pages 3029–3032, May 2008.

[3] C. Chen, Y. Q. Shi, and W. Su. A machine learning based scheme for double JPEG compression detection. In *Proc. 19th Int. Conf. on Pattern Recognition*, pages 1–4, Dec. 2008.

[4] J. Fridrich and J. Kodovský. Rich models for steganalysis of digital images. *IEEE Trans. Information Forensics and Security*, 7(3):868–882, 2011.

[5] Z. He, W. Lu, W. Sun, and J. Huang. Digital image splicing detection based on markov features in DCT and DWT domain. *Pattern Recognition*, 45(12):4292–4299, 2012.

[6] V. Holub and J. Fridrich. Designing steganographic distortion using directional filters. In *Proc. IEEE Int. Workshop on Information Forensics and Security*, pages 234–239, 2012.

**Table 4:** Confusion matrix for identifying the operation types using the SRM features [4]. Please note that the asterisk "*" here denotes that the corresponding accuracy is less than 1%.

| Actual \ Predicted | Original | Gaussian Blurring | Gamma Correction | JPEG Compression | Median Filtering | Re-sampling | Splicing |
|---|---|---|---|---|---|---|---|
| Original | **96.28** | * | 1.94 | * | * | * | 1.24 |
| Gaussian Blurring | * | **99.54** | * | * | * | * | * |
| Gamma Correction | 5.37 | * | **93.19** | * | * | * | * |
| JPEG Compression | * | * | * | **99.03** | * | * | * |
| Median Filtering | * | * | * | * | **98.76** | * | * |
| Re-sampling | * | * | * | * | * | **97.49** | * |
| Splicing | 2.69 | * | * | 2.57 | * | * | **93.96** |

**Table 5:** Confusion matrix for identifying the operation types using the LBP features [19]. Please note that the asterisk "*" here denotes that the corresponding accuracy is less than 1%.

| Actual \ Predicted | Original | Gaussian Blurring | Gamma Correction | JPEG Compression | Median Filtering | Re-sampling | Splicing |
|---|---|---|---|---|---|---|---|
| Original | **86.11** | * | 11.47 | * | * | 1.16 | 1.24 |
| Gaussian Blurring | * | **99.54** | * | * | * | * | * |
| Gamma Correction | 20.03 | * | **78.29** | * | * | * | * |
| JPEG Compression | * | * | * | **99.58** | * | * | * |
| Median Filtering | * | * | * | * | **99.26** | * | * |
| Re-sampling | 1.01 | * | * | * | * | **96.68** | * |
| Splicing | 3.03 | * | 2.08 | 6.16 | * | * | **87.46** |

[7] X. Kang, M. Stamm, A. Peng, and K. Liu. Robust median filtering forensics based on the autoregressive model of median filtered residual. In *Proc. Asia-Pacific Signal and Information Processing Association Annual Summit and Conference*, pages 1–9, Dec. 2012.

[8] S. Knerr, L. Personnaz, and G. Dreyfus. Single-layer learning revisited: a stepwise procedure for building and training a neural network. In *Neurocomputing*, volume 68 of *NATO ASI Series*, pages 41–50. Springer, 1990.

[9] J. Kodovský and J. Fridrich. Calibration revisited. In *Proc. 11th ACM Workshop on Multimedia and Security*, pages 63–74, 2009.

[10] J. Kodovský, J. Fridrich, and V. Holub. Ensemble classifiers for steganalysis of digital media. *IEEE Trans. Information Forensics and Security*, 7(2):432–444, 2012.

[11] B. Li, J. He, J. Huang, and Y. Q. Shi. A survey on image steganography and steganalysis. *Journal of Information Hiding and Multimedia Signal Processing*, 2(2):142–172, 2011.

[12] W. Luo, J. Huang, and G. Qiu. JPEG error analysis and its applications to digital image forensics. *IEEE Trans. Information Forensics and Security*, 5(3):480–491, 2010.

[13] W. Luo, Y. Wang, and J. Huang. Detection of quantization artifacts and its applications to transform encoder identification. *IEEE Trans. Information Forensics and Security*, 5(4):810–815, 2010.

[14] B. Mahdian and S. Saic. Blind authentication using periodic properties of interpolation. *IEEE Trans. Information Forensics and Security*, 3(3):529–538, 2008.

[15] T. Pevný, P. Bas, and J. Fridrich. Steganalysis by subtractive pixel adjacency matrix. *IEEE Trans.*

*Information Forensics and Security*, 5(2):215–224, 2010.

[16] T. Pevný, T. Filler, and P. Bas. Using high-dimensional image models to perform highly undetectable steganography. In *Information Hiding*, volume 6387 of *Lecture Notes in Computer Science*, pages 161–177. Springer, 2010.

[17] T. Pevný and J. Fridrich. Merging markov and DCT features for multi-class JPEG steganalysis. In *Proc. SPIE, Security, Steganography, and Watermarking of Multimedia Contents IX*, volume 6505, page 650503, 2007.

[18] Y. Q. Shi, C. Chen, and W. Chen. A natural image model approach to splicing detection. In *Proc. 9th ACM Workshop on Multimedia and Security*, pages 51–62, 2007.

[19] Y. Q. Shi, P. Sutthiwan, and L. Chen. Textural features for steganalysis. In *Information Hiding*, volume 7692 of *Lecture Notes in Computer Science*, pages 63–77. Springer, 2013.

[20] M. Stamm and K. Liu. Blind forensics of contrast enhancement in digital images. In *Proc. 15th IEEE Int. Conf. on Image Processing*, pages 3112–3115, 2008.

[21] M. Stamm, M. Wu, and K. Liu. Information forensics: An overview of the first decade. *IEEE Access*, 1:167–200, 2013.

[22] M. C. Stamm, X. Chu, and K. Liu. Forensically determining the order of signal processing operations. In *Proc. IEEE Int. Workshop on Information Forensics and Security*, pages 162–167, 2013.

[23] H. Yuan. Blind forensics of median filtering in digital images. *IEEE Trans. Information Forensics and Security*, 6(4):1335–1345, 2011.

# Automatic Location of Frame Deletion Point for Digital Video Forensics

Chunhui Feng, Zhengquan Xu, Wenting Zhang, Yanyan Xu
Wuhan University
LIESMARS
Wuhan, P. R. China
86-27-68779508
{feng, xuzq, zwt910118, xuyy}
@whu.edu.cn

## ABSTRACT

Detection of frame deletion is of great significance in the field of video forensics. Several approaches have been presented through analyzing the side effect caused by frame deletion. However, most of the current approaches can detect the existence of frame deletion but not the exact location of it. In this paper, we present a method which can directly locate the frame deletion point. Through the analysis of the distinguishing fluctuation feature of motion residual caused by frame deletion compared to interference frames and ordinary video content jitter in tampered video sequence, an algorithm based on the total motion residual of video frame is proposed to detect the frame deletion point. Moreover, an initiative processing procedure for frame motion residual and an adaptive threshold detector are introduced so that the robustness of the detection can be markedly improved. Experimental results show that the proposed algorithm is effective in generalized scenarios such as different encoding settings, rapid or slow motion sequences and multiple group of picture deletion. It also has a high performance that the true positive rate reaches 90% and the false alarm rate is less than 0.8%.

## Categories and Subject Descriptors

H.4 [**Information Systems Applications**]: Miscellaneous

## General Terms

Algorithms, Performance, Reliability, Security

## Keywords

Video forensics; frame deletion point detection; fluctuation feature; intra-prediction-elimination processing

## 1. INTRODUCTION

Malicious manipulation of visual media may cause serious legal and social problems. Synthesized photos or videos could be used as fake evidence in court, misleading or inflammatory news report, or counterfeit proof for defrauding the insurance

compensation and so on. Some efforts have been made in the digital watermarking to detect the manipulation of visual media[3], [6]. While the major drawback of this approach is that a watermark must be embedded at precisely the time of recording, which would limit this approach to specially equipped digital cameras[10]. Different from digital watermarking, digital forensics explores the intrinsic features[13] in the media left by acquisition devices or manipulation acts without using any pre-embedded signal. It is a new research field rising in the last decade, and a promising tool in the authentication field of digital visual media. A large part of the research activities in this field are devoted to the analysis of still images. However, scientific research has been recently focusing on the forensics issues related to video signals because of their peculiarities and the wide range of possible alterations that can be applied to them[1], [16], [18], [19], [4], [14]. A typical video manipulation act is to delete a number of frames of the sequence, so that certain fact can be concealed. For instance, a video forger may cut several frames of the football additional penalty reference video to hide the actual foul scene; tampered surveillance video could be used as the alibi of the criminal by deleting the frames of his appearance. Situations above make the detection of frame deletion very important.

Lately, several approaches have been presented for detecting frame deletion. The most fundamental work was done by Wang and Farid[17]. They pointed out that after frame deletion, periodical spikes of the relocated I-frame (RI) will be observed on the mean motion residual sequence. Meanwhile, the magnitude of the Fourier transformation of the sequence can be inspected for peaks in the middle frequency. Based on[17], Stamm *et al.*[12] proposed an automatic solution for detecting the mean motion residual spikes of RI. It also expanded the work in an adaptive group of picture (GOP)-length structure[8] situation. Other than analyzing the specific change of one specific feature, Tamer[15] used four discriminative features in a machine learning process for detecting the existence of frame deletion. Based on a similar experimental setup to that reported in [12], the detection accuracy is improved, and the method is applicable for both variable and constant bitrate coding modes. In [2], Chao *et al.* proposed different schemes for detecting frame insertion and deletion based on the optical flow consistency.

However, most existing algorithms have one common character which leads to their common limitations. They detect the existence of frame deletion by analyzing the side effect of it. Namely, the artifacts of RI. While the artifacts of RI are effective in some cases, they are not in the following situations. First, When the frame number of the video is limited and the GOP-length is relatively long (in common settings of H.264 compression, the GOP-length is between 25~250), spikes of RI will be sparse, and the resulting representation is noisy and periodicity estimation is inaccurate[11]; Second, in frames with rapid motion content, artifacts of RI will become quite weak or even disappeared. Third, when one or more GOPs are deleted and the GOP structure of the recompression is the same with the first compression, I-frames in the first compression wouldn't be relocated, thus the artifacts do not exist. Last, when a non-tampered video is recompressed with a different GOP structure, relocation of I-frames also happens, namely the artifacts of RI do not necessarily imply frame deletion but also recompression. In summary, the artifacts of RI are greatly influenced by encoding parameters such as GOP-length, motion strength of the video content, or the position of the deleted frames; and since artifacts of RI could only indicate the existence of frame deletion, these methods couldn't be used for locating the exact frame deletion point (DP).

In this paper, we explore the statistical character of DP itself so that the detection doesn't depend on the side effect of frame deletion, and DP can be directly located as well. First we show that in the mean motion residual statistic, DP and RI have similar spikes. Therefore RI is considered as interference which needs to be eliminated. Secondly, we differentiate DP from RI by calculating the fluctuation strength of frame motion residual, where DPs still manifest spikes while RIs are submerged in adjacent frames. However, this phenomenon is quite unstable and depends on the content of the video. Therefore in the third, we propose an initiative processing procedure to make the temporal difference between frames fully exposed, so that the above mentioned feature can be essentially enhanced. Using the enhanced feature, an adaptive threshold detection method is proposed to automatically locate DPs of the tampered video.

The rest of the paper is organized as follows. In Section 2, our novel detection algorithm is presented. The experimental results and discussions are provided in Section 3, and the conclusion is drawn in Section 4.

## 2. PROPOSED DETECTION SCHEME

In this section, the inner statistical difference of DP and its interference frames is firstly discussed before we quantify this difference to obtain a fluctuation feature. After that, we show how the fluctuation feature is disturbed by the general video coding strategy. Then, an initiative processing procedure is proposed to eliminate the disturbance so that the proposed feature is essentially enhanced. In the end, we present an adaptive threshold detection method based on the enhanced feature to automatically detect the candidate location of DP.

### 2.1 Statistical Difference of DP and the Interference Frames

Intuitively, since several frames are cut, the temporal difference of DP and its reference frame becomes larger, therefore the most straightforward character of DP is a larger motion residual.

It is evident that frames with rapid motion content also have large motion residual. However, after extensive observation, we find that the differences of mean motion residual of adjacent quick motion frames are relatively continuous within a short period of time (Figure 1 (a)). This is because moving objects in the physical world do not have such sudden acceleration within one frame interval (usually 1/24 second) [21] in most cases. Whereas for DP, the temporal motion could be several times larger than adjacent

frames, thus the mean motion residual of DP shows an obvious increase. See Figure 1 (b).

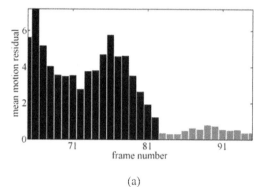

(a)

(b)

**Figure 1 Comparison of the mean motion residual of DP and ordinary frames in quick motion area. Frames in quick motion area are marked black and frames in slow motion area are marked grey. (a) Ordinary frames in quick and slow motion area; (b) DP in quick and slow motion area.**

However, in the tampered sequences, there are still no lack of other interference frames which have similar statistical characters with DP. Such as RI, frames with sudden lighting change, frames with sudden zooming, to name a few. Between them, RI is the most common hence the most inevitable interference. Because both frame deletion and change of GOP-length in the recompression could cause the appearance of RI. From Figure 2 we can see that both DP and RI manifest similar spikes in the mean motion residual histogram.

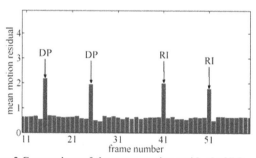

**Figure 2 Comparison of the mean motion residual of DP and RI. The first two spikes are the DPs, and the next two spikes are RIs.**

Nevertheless, the internal statistical characters of RI and DP are actually different, which can be used for distinguishing the two of them.

The formation of the mean motion residual spikes of RI has already explained by Wang[17]: due to the motion compensation strategy, the lossy compression artifacts propagate through each individual GOP. Therefore each P-frame is correlated to its neighboring P- or I-frame within one GOP. After frame deletion and recompression, original I-frame is relocated as a P-frame in another GOP, the correlation of the artifacts becomes weaker; thus the motion residual increases. Since compression artifacts are the result of the independent quantization[7] which fluctuate on the edge of each coding block, it can be concluded that the distribution of the increased motion residual of RI is relatively uniform.

As for DP, the distribution of the residual won't be as uniform as RI. Since the frame rate of general video is usually more than 24 frames per second, if a digital forger want to delete only 1 second of the video content, 24 frames need to be deleted at least. It means the temporal content difference between DP and its reference frame is the accumulation of 24 normal frames. Therefore, the increase of the mean motion residual of DP is mostly caused by the sudden change of the video content between frames. Since the movement of natural objects is quite random, the distribution of motion residual of DP won't be as uniform as that of compression artifacts. Figure 3 shows the distribution of the motion residual of RI and DP. It can be seen that when the mean motion residual of DP approximates RI, the fluctuation is much stronger in DP.

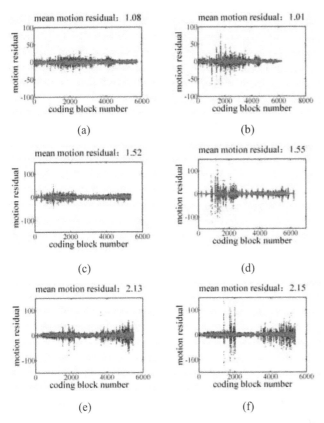

(a)      (b)

(c)      (d)

(e)      (f)

**Figure 3. Motion residual distribution of RI and DP. (a), (c), (e) is the motion residual distribution of RI, while (b), (d), (f) is the motion error distribution of DP with approximate mean motion residual values.**

## 2.2 Quantification of the Fluctuation Character

For comparing the aforementioned characters more formally, we propose a texture descriptor based algorithm to quantify the fluctuation strength of the frame motion residual. Note that in this paper, we constrain the video compression to be performed according to the baseline profile for H.264 standard. The quantification algorithm is firstly applied on the coding block level, the intermediate results are calculated using the relative smoothness descriptor[5]. See (2.1) - (2.5).

$$e_n = e_{n,1}, e_{n,2}, L, e_{n,C} \quad n \in [1, N] \tag{2.1}$$

$$s_n = \sigma(e_n) \tag{2.2}$$

$$s = s_1, s_2 L, s_N \tag{2.3}$$

$$R = 1 - \frac{1}{1 + \sigma^2} \tag{2.4}$$

$$r = R(s) \tag{2.5}$$

Where $e_n$ denotes the motion residual of each pixel in $n$-th coding block, and constant $C$ is 16 since one coding block of H.264 video is $4 \times 4$ pixel; $N$ denotes the number of coding blocks of inter-coded MBs in one frame; $s_n$ is the standard deviation of the $n$-th coding block; $R$ is the texture descriptor relative smoothness which measures the signal intensity contrast, and in this paper it is used to reflect the fluctuation strength of the frame motion residual.

Figure 4 compares the mean value and the fluctuation strength calculated by the proposed algorithm of the frame motion residual of a tampered video sequence. It can be observed that in the mean motion residual histogram, DP and RI both show obvious spikes; while in the fluctuation strength histogram, DP still shows prominent spikes while RI is greatly reduced and cannot be distinguished from neighboring frames. Therefore, we intended to use this fluctuation feature to locate DP while eliminating the interference of RI.

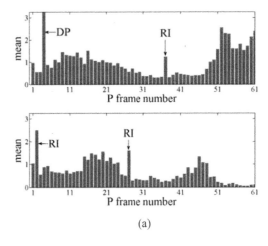

(a)

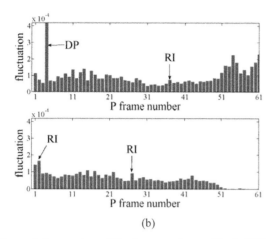

(b)

**Figure 4. Comparison of the frame motion residual of DP and RI under different statistics. (a) The mean motion residual histogram of a video sequence with 1 DP and 3 RIs; (b) The fluctuation strength histogram of the same sequence.**

## 2.3 Disturbance of the Fluctuation Feature

However, after extensive experiments, we find that the feature discussed above is not very stable. Visually distinguishable spikes of DP is merely 60%, and the height of the spikes varies with the content of the video.

Upon further analysis, we find that the uncertainty is the result of the general video encoding strategy. As discussed above, the unique fluctuation feature of DP comes from the temporal difference between frames. Whereas in H.264 and previous encoding strategy, macroblocks (MBs) of P-frames will be coded in intra mode which uses spatial prediction in strong motion area for improving the coding efficiency[9]. Therefore the prediction residual of a P-frame can be expressed as

$$PE = P_M + P_S \qquad (2.6)$$

Where $P_M$ is the motion prediction residual of inter-coded MBs and $P_S$ the spatial prediction residual of intra-coded MBs.

Denote $\gamma$ the motion strength of DP; as $\gamma$ increases, the encoding bitrate of inter prediction will exceeds intra prediction, thus more MBs will be encoded in intra modes[20]. Namely $P_S$ increases and $P_M$ decreases. Therefore the temporal difference of the entire frame cannot be fully reflected by motion residual, thus the robustness of the fluctuation feature of DP is weakened.

In addition, if the coding strategy uses adaptive GOP-length structure, when $\gamma$ exceeds the decision threshold[8], DP will be coded as I-frame with intra-coded MBs only, it means $P_M$=0, thus

$$PE = P_S. \qquad (2.7)$$

DP will also be coded as I-frame when multiple GOPs are deleted and the GOP-length of the first compression is equal to that of the second compression. In these cases, no motion residual could be acquired therefore it is impossible to locate DP by analyzing the temporal difference between frames.

## 2.4 Intra-Prediction-Elimination Processing for Enhanced Feature Abstraction

Based on the discussions above, we develop a simple yet effective initiative Intra-Prediction-Elimination (IPE) procedure to eliminate the spatial prediction to ensure that $P_S = 0$, therefore the prediction residual becomes:

$$PE = P_M. \qquad (2.8)$$

In this way, the interference of intra MBs will be removed, while the temporal difference of each frame can be completely reflected by motion residual.

Given a H.264 sequence under estimation, the IPE procedure is carried out as follows:

1. Using the open source H.264/MPEG-4 AVC compression library x264[22] to generate a modified encoder which disables the intra prediction modes, so that the coding mode determination is restricted within inter prediction encoding modes.

2. Recompress the test video again using the modified encoder, while turning off the adaptive GOP-length option and setting the GOP-length to its maximum value (250). In this way, all MBs in P-frames are inter-coded; and if DP is encoded as I-frame in the tampered video, the recompression process will encode DP as P-frame with only inter-mode MBs again. (Except for DPs with sequential numbers of multiples of 251)

3. Change the GOP-length to another value other than 250, such as 200, and generate another version of the processed video. In the second step, DP could be just recompressed as I-frames in the position of the multiples of 251, therefore in the third step, we change the IDR interval so that all the I-frames (except the first frame) in the first version could be compressed as P-frames again.

After applying the initiative procedure on the test sequences, the proportion of visually distinguishable spikes of DP in the fluctuation histogram is markedly increased.

In this paper, for videos that have been processed by the IPE procedure, we define the increases in the fluctuation strength histogram as the Enhanced Fluctuation Feature (EFF), and it is expected that the EFF can be used for locating DP in both quick and slow motion videos with different encoding parameter settings.

## 2.5 Measuring the EFF

The detection method aims at abstracting frames with strong EFF as DPs, and eliminating interference frames with weak EFF as background noise. As discussed above, the most evident interferences are frames in quick motion areas and the RI; the former are relatively continuous in both mean and fluctuation statics; while the spikes of RI are greatly reduced or totally submerged in adjacent frames in the fluctuation histogram, it could also be seen as continuous with its neighboring frames.

Therefore we propose an adaptive threshold strategy to measure the EFF within the range of $2N+1$ adjacent frames. For a certain frame under estimation, if the EFF exceeds certain threshold THR_R in the range of its $2N$ neighbors, it will be located as the candidate of DP.

Moreover, we found that in the extremely slow motion area, the EFF of DP becomes quite low, while increases of RIs emerge again. This is because the motion residual fluctuation is decreased as the motion strength decreases, while the lossy compression artifacts are not influenced by frame motion. Thus we set another threshold THR_M to eliminate frames in the very slow area, in which the detection method is not applicable.

The adaptive threshold algorithm is proposed as follows. Firstly, for the $k$-th frame, the mean value of the fluctuation strength of its adjacent $2N$ frames is calculated as

$$\overline{r}(k) = \frac{\sum_{i=1}^{N} r(k+i) + r(k-i)}{2N} \qquad (2.9)$$

Where $r(k)$ is calculated by (2.5), and $N$ is the window length for determine the number of the adjacent frames. The EFF of $k$-th frame is measured as

$$y(k) = \frac{r(k)}{\overline{r}(k)} - 1. \qquad (2.10)$$

The motion strength of $k$-th frame is denoted as $a(k)$, where

$$a(k) = mean(|e(k)|). \qquad (2.11)$$

and $|e(k)|$ denotes the absolute value of the matrix of motion residual of $k$-th frame. The mean motion strength of the neighboring frames is $\overline{a}(k)$,

$$\overline{a}(k) = \frac{\sum_{i=1}^{N} a(k+i) + a(k-i)}{2N}. \qquad (2.12)$$

If $y(k) > \text{THR\_R I } \overline{a}(k) > \text{THR\_M}$ , then the $k$-th frame is located as DP.

It can be seen from the above equations that there are three parameters needs to be determined for the detection algorithm, namely $N$, THR_R and THR_M. Since the motion strength may vary greatly in one sequence, $N$ cannot be chosen too large or too small so that the motion strength around the tested frame could be properly tracked, and the EFF could be thereby correctly obtained. After choosing the optimum value of $N$, the rest of the two thresholds can be further determined by experiments.

## 3. EXPERIMENTAL RESULTS AND DISCUSSIONS

This section evaluates the performance of the proposed deletion algorithm. First we simulate the frame deletion process to generate numerous tampered videos before the IPE procedure is applied. Then, we use a subset of the processed sequences to determine the window-length N and the thresholds THR_R and THR_M. The experiment results and discussions are drawn in the last.

## 3.1 Frame Deletion Simulation and IPE Processing

Compared to former work that detect the frame deletion[17], [12], [15], the number of the test video sequences is greatly expanded in our work, and sequences with both quick and slow motion characters are adopted in the dataset. Note that the detection algorithm isn't applicable to sequences with scene cut or shot cut, therefore the content of the test sequences are mostly continuous.

The simulated tampered videos are originated from 130 raw yuv sequences. Among them, 30 standard yuv sequences in the CIF format were downloaded from [23], and 100 sequences with the same format were recorded and decompressed by group members of our laboratory. While the downloaded sequences are mostly taken from sceneries with slow and uniform motion, the recorded sequences are taken from the highway and a football game which contains both quick and slow motion content.

The simulation procedure of the of video tampering is conducted as follows: First, original yuv files are encoded using the default parameter set of the x264 encoder to simulate the authentic videos; then decompress these videos; for each decompressed video, we generate 6 versions of tampered videos, each of which have 3 frame deletion points, and the frame deletion number for each version of each deletion point is 5, 10, 15, 20, 25, 30, respectively. Therefore, the total number of one group of the tampered videos is $130 \times 6 = 780$ , and the number of DPs is $780 \times 3 = 2340$ . We generate two groups of tampered videos: one is encoded using fixed GOP-length, and another is encoded by adaptive GOP-length structure.

After generating the tampered sequences, the IPE procedure is followed. We vary the encoding parameters of the reformed encoder to analyze that if they have any influence on the detection results. Therefore each of the tampered video groups is further divided into 6 processed video groups, namely CBR encoding strategy with bitrate of 500, 1000, 2000 and VBR with quantization parameter of 35, 25, and 15.

## 3.2 Threshold Determination

After generating the processed video set, we use a subset to determine the optimum window size $N$, fluctuation threshold THR_R and motion strength threshold THR_M to get the proper True Positive Rate (TPR) and False Alarm Rate (FAR).

The window size $N$ is firstly selected. The test video subset is chosen as CBR encoding of bitrate=2000 and the VBR encoding of quantization parameter=15, with the frame deletion number of 5, 10, 25. The thresholds THR_R and THR_M are set to fixed value of 1.2 and 0.4. From Table 1 we can see that for having the rational TPR and FAR, window size $N$ should be selected as 3.

**Table 1. Detection results of different window size $N$. br is short for bitrate, and qp is short for quantization parameter.**

| br 2000 | TPR | | | FAR | | |
|---|---|---|---|---|---|---|
| | $N=2$ | $N=3$ | $N=4$ | $N=2$ | $N=3$ | $N=4$ |
| cut 5 | 0.8078 | 0.8125 | 0.6129 | 0.0103 | 0.0095 | 0.0105 |
| cut 10 | 0.9148 | 0.9023 | 0.729 | 0.0099 | 0.0091 | 0.0095 |
| cut 25 | 0.9307 | 0.9382 | 0.8097 | 0.0107 | 0.0096 | 0.0093 |
| qp 15 | TPR | | | FAR | | |
| | $N=2$ | $N=3$ | $N=4$ | $N=2$ | $N=3$ | $N=4$ |
| cut 5 | 0.8171 | 0.8123 | 0.6409 | 0.0108 | 0.0092 | 0.0102 |
| cut 10 | 0.9128 | 0.9083 | 0.759 | 0.0109 | 0.0097 | 0.0097 |
| cut 25 | 0.9286 | 0.9329 | 0.8098 | 0.0104 | 0.0091 | 0.0101 |

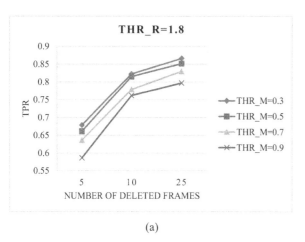

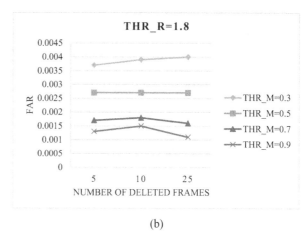

(a)

(b)

**Figure 5. Detection results of different motion strength threshold THR_M.**

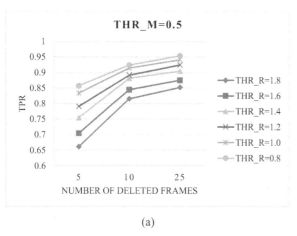

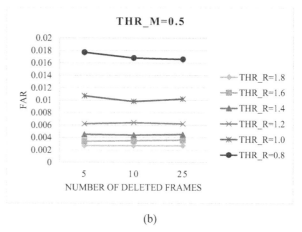

(a)

(b)

**Figure 6. Detection results of different fluctuation threshold THR_R.**

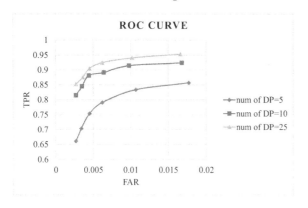

**Figure 7. ROC curve under different THR_R and different number of deleted frames.**

Then, set the window size and threshold THR_R to fixed value of 3 and 1.8 to for the selection of motion strength threshold THR_M. From Figure 5 it can be seen that when THR_M=0.5, the TPR is almost the highest while the FAR stays moderate. Therefore THR_M is selected 0.5.

The last step is to determine THR_R. Set the window size and threshold THR_M to fixed value of 3 and 0.5, then vary THR_R

from 0.8 to 1.8 with the step size of 0.2. The detection results are illustrated in Figure 6. For having the relatively high TPR and low FAR, THR_R is selected as 1.2.

Figure 7 is a ROC curve which illustrates the performance of the proposed detection algorithm under different THR_R and different number of deleted frames. It can be observed that the detection performance gets better as the number of deleted frames increases.

In summary, for having a relatively high TPR with a relatively low FAR, the window size $N$ is selected as 3, and the thresholds are chosen as THR_M=0.5 and THR_R=1.2.

## 3.3 Experiment Results and Discussions

Using the selected window size and thresholds, the detection results under different encoding parameters and different number of deleted frames are shown in Figure 8. In Figure 8, the horizontal axis is the number of deleted frames, and the vertical axis represents the corresponding TPR or FAR. Figure 8 (a), (b), (c), (d) are the detection results of the tampered video set of adaptive GOP-length, and the encoding parameters of IPE processing are set as CBR and VBR in different qualities. It is observed from Figure 8 (a), (c) that the relationship of TPR and the frame deletion number is basically

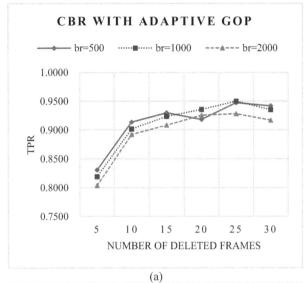

(a)

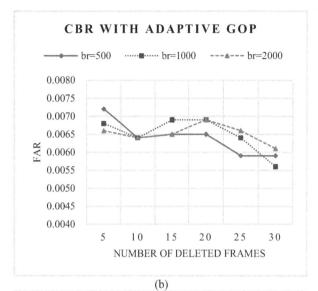

(b)

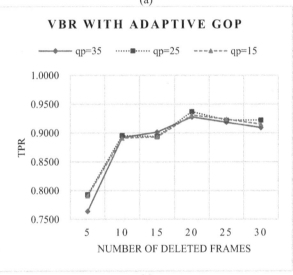

(c)

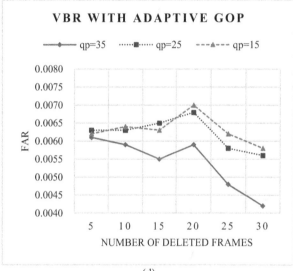

(d)

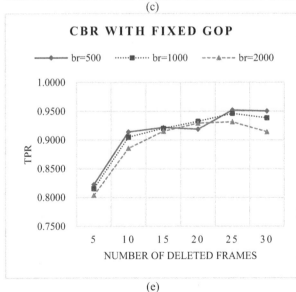

(e)

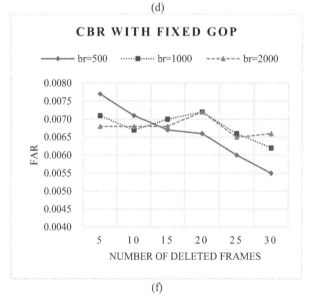

(f)

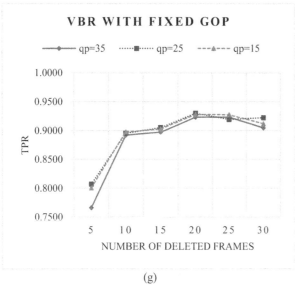

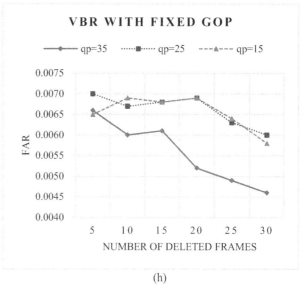

(g)                                                                      (h)

**Figure 8. Detection result of the tampered video with fixed and adaptive GOP-length structures. (a), (b), (c), (d) are the detection results of the tampered video set with adaptive GOP-length; (e), (f), (g), (h) are the results of the tampered video set with fixed GOP-length structure.**

proportional; the TPR lowers as the bitrate increases while the TPR has no obvious relation with the quantization parameters (Figure 8 (c)). When the frame deletion number is only 5, TPR is around 80%; when the frame deletion number is 10, TPR reaches 90%. From Figure 8 (b), (d), we can see that the mean value of the FAR is around 0.6%, and in a declining trend as the frame deletion number increases. Figure 8 (e), (f), (g), (h) are the results of the tampered video set with fixed GOP-length structure. No significant difference can be observed from the detection results of the adaptive GOP-length, which means the GOP structure has little influence on the performance of the proposed detection method.

By manually examining the falsely detected positives in the tampered sequences, we found that most of them are frames with sudden lighting change or automatic lens zoom. These types of frames could be further processed by the image enhancing techniques, so that the lighting or the focal length could be adjusted into similar status with neighboring frames. In this way, the temporal difference of these frames would be reduced, and the FAR could be further lowered.

Chao *et al.* [2] also proposed a detection method for locating DP. They used a different test dataset with slow motion content, and the highest precision rate is 85.67% while the frame deletion number is up to 100. In the future we plan to use a similar experimental set up for a formal comparison of [2] and our proposed detection algorithm.

## 4. CONCLUSIONS

Video forensics for locating the exact position of DP is a challenging task. In this paper, we present a method to detect it. Under the premise that RI is the interference of the detection of DP, we find that the fluctuation character of the motion residual is different between DP and RI. Therefore we use the texture descriptor relative smoothness to quantify this character for abstracting the distinguishing fluctuation feature of DP. Visually observed results show that in the fluctuation histogram, DP has obvious spikes while RI is submerged in its neighboring frames. However, since the unique fluctuation feature of DP is caused by the temporal content difference between frames, the intra

prediction coding strategy will lower the robustness of the feature. Therefore, we proposed an initiative IPE processing procedure to recompress the video under estimation by a modified encoder which disables the intra prediction modes. In this way the temporal motion is fully exposed by motion residual and the robustness of the fluctuation feature is essentially enhanced. Using the enhanced feature EFF, we propose an adaptive threshold detection method for locating the frame deletion point. The test video dataset contains a large number of video sequences with both quick and slow motions. Experiment results show that the detection algorithm is quite effective for locating the frame deletion point in the videos of different motion characters and different encoding structures; and the detection results of TPR is up to 90% while the FAR is lower than 0.8%. In the future, we intend to exclude the minor interference frames of sudden lighting change and zooming for further reducing the FAR; and integrate more features (such as the frame motion vector) to have a more robust feature vector for further increasing the TPR.

## 5. ACKNOLEDGEMENTS

This work is supported by the Major State Basic Research Development Program (No. 2011CB302200) and the National Natural Science Foundation of China (No. 41371402).

## 6. REFERENCES

[1]  P. Bestagini, M. Fontani, S. Milani *et al*. An Overview on Video Forensics. *2012 Proceedings of the 20th European Signal Processing Conference*, Bucharest, Romania, August 27 - 31, 2012.

[2]  J. Chao, X. Jiang, and T. Sun. A Novel Video Inter-frame Forgery Model Detection Scheme Based on Optical Flow Consistency. *Digital Forensics and Watermarking*, LNCS 7809: 267–281, 2013.

[3]  I. J. Cox, M. L. Miller, and J. A. Bloom. Digital Watermarking. San Francisco, CA: Morgan Kaufmann, 2002.

[4]  W. Chen and Y.Q. Shi. Detection of Double MPEG Compression Based on First Digit Statistics. *Digital Watermarking*, 2009, 5450: 16-30.

[5] R. C. Gonzalez and R. E. Woods. Digital Image Processing. (2nd ed.) Prentice-Hall, New Jersey (2002): 793

[6] S. Katzenbeisser and F. A. P. Petitcolas. Information Hiding Techniques for Steganography and Digital Watermarking. Norwood, MA: Artec House, 2000.

[7] W. Luo, Z. Qu, J. Huang, and G. Qiu. A Novel Method for Detecting Cropped and Recompressed Image Block. *IEEE International Conference on Acoustics, Speech and Signal Processing*, 2: II-217 - II-220.

[8] J. Lee, I. Shin, and H. Park. Adaptive Intra-Frame Assignment and Bit-Rate Estimation for Variable GOP Length in H.264. *IEEE Transactions on Circuits and Systems for Video Technology*, 16(10): 1271 – 1279, 2006.

[9] J. Ostermann, J. Bormans, P. List, *et al*. Video Coding with H.264/AVC: Tools, Performance, and Complexity. *IEEE Transactions on Circuits and Systems for Video Technology*, 15(7): 7 – 28, 2005.

[10] A. C. Popescu and H. Farid. Statistical Tools for Digital Forensics. *Information Hiding*, LNCS 3200: 128-147, 2005.

[11] D. V. Pad́ın, M. Fontani, T. Bianchi, *et al*. Detection of video double encoding with GOP size estimation. *The IEEE International Workshop on Information Forensics and Security*, 2-5, 2012.

[12] M. C. Stamm, W. S. Lin, and K. J. R. Liu. Temporal Forensics and Anti-Forensics for Motion Compensated Video. *IEEE Transactions on Information Forensics and Security*, 7(4): 1315 – 1329, 2012.

[13] A. Swaminathan, M. Wu, and K. J. R. Liu. Digital Image Forensics via Intrinsic Fingerprints. *IEEE Transactions on Information Forensics and Security*, 3(1): 101 – 117, 2008.

[14] Y. Su, J. Zhang, and J. Liu. Exposing Digital Video Forgery by Detecting Motion-compensated Edge Artifacts. *International Conference on Computational Intelligence and Software Engineering*: 1-4, 2009.

[15] T. Shanableh. Detection of Frame Deletion for Digital Video Forensics. *Digital Investigation*, 10(4): 350-360, 2013.

[16] W. Wang and H. Farid. Exposing Digital Forgeries in Interlaced and Deinterlaced Video. *IEEE Transactions on Information Forensics and Security*, 2(3): 438 – 449, 2007.

[17] W. Wang and Hany Farid. Exposing Digital Forgeries in Video by Detecting Double MPEG Compression. *MM&Sec '06 Proceedings of the 8th workshop on Multimedia and security*, 2006: 37-47.

[18] Weihong Wang and Hany Farid. Exposing Digital Forgeries in Video by Detecting Duplication. *MM&Sec '07 Proceedings of the 9th workshop on Multimedia and security*, 2007: 35-42.

[19] W. Wang, H. Farid. Exposing Digital Forgeries in Video by Detecting Double Quantization. *MM&Sec '07 Proceedings of the 9th workshop on Multimedia and security*, 2009: 39-48.

[20] H.264 / MPEG-4 Part 10 White Paper. Prediction of Intra Macroblocks; Prediction of Inter Macroblocks in P- slices.

[21] http://en.wikipedia.org/wiki/Frame_rate

[22] http://www.videolan.org/developers/x264.html

[23] http://trace.eas.asu.edu/yuv/

# Robust Palmprint Verification using Sparse Representation of Binarized Statistical Features: A Comprehensive Study

R. Raghavendra
Norwegian Biometrics Laboratory
Gjøvik University College
2812 Gjøvik, Norway
raghavendra.ramachandra@hig.no

Christoph Busch
Norwegian Biometrics Laboratory
Gjøvik University College
2812 Gjøvik, Norway
christoph.busch@hig.no

## ABSTRACT

This paper proposes a new scheme for robust palmprint verification using sparse representation of Binarized Statistical Image Features (BSIF). Since palmprint comprises of rich set of features including principal lines, ridges and wrinkles, the use of appropriate texture descriptor is expected to accurately capture these information. To this extent, we explore the BSIF texture descriptor which codes each pixel of the given palmprint image in terms of binary strings based on the filter response. The BSIF learns the filter basis from the natural images by exploring statistical independence. We then use the Sparse Representation Classifier (SRC) on these BSIF features to perform the subject verification. Extensive experiments are carried out on three different large scale publically available palmprint databases. We then present an extensive analysis by comparing the proposed scheme with five different contemporary state-of-the-art schemes that reveals the outstanding performance.

## Categories and Subject Descriptors

D.4.6 [**Security and Protection**]: Access controls, Authentication

## General Terms

Biometrics, Pattern recognition

## Keywords

Biometrics, palmprint recognition, statistical features, Sparse Representation

## 1. INTRODUCTION

Biometric based identity solutions have gained paramount interest to deal with increased demand of security requirements. The idea of the biometric system is to identify/verify the subject of interest based on physical or behavioral characteristics. Among the available biometric characteristics,

the palmprint recognition has been studied from past decade has revealed their applicability for the biometric application. The palmprint contains a rich set of texture features like principal lines (palm creases), wrinkles and ridges are unique and effectively captured using many low cost sensors with a very low resolution imaging of 75 dpi [18]. Further, recent work [19] has demonstrated the anti-spoofing nature of the palmprints that places the palmprint recognition as a reliable biometric characteristic.

Palmprint samples (or images) can be captured in either contact or contactless fashion. In case of a contact based palmprint capture process a subject will place the hand in contact with the sensor which is mounted with the pegs so that hand can be properly fixed to capture the images. While in case of contactless palmprint acquisition, the subject will place the palm at a distance without any pegs to hold the fingers and hand. Thus, the contactless palmprint acquisition exhibits more challenges due to their sensitivity to rotation and translation. Irrespective of the way one can interact with the sensor, the palmprint can be captured in both visible spectrum and and multiple other spectra. The advantage of using multiple spectra is that, one can not only capture the palmprint pattern but also the palm vein pattern that is visible in Near Infrared (NIR) spectrum.

The available techniques for the robust palmprint recognition can be coarsely classified into four types which include: (1) Line and Minutiae based methods (2) Texture based methods (3) Appearance based methods and (4) Hybrid schemes. The core idea of the line and minutiae based methods is to extract the features based on the principal lines and minutiae points that are present in the palmprint. However, success of these approaches will depend upon the resolution of the captured palmprint that typically demands very high resolution of at least 500 dpi [2]. The principal lines can be extracted using either templates [20] or using edge detection schemes for instance Sobel edge detector [4]. However the minutiae points are detected by finding the endings and bifurcation point of the ridges[2]. The texture based schemes involves in extracting the global patterns of lines, ridges and wrinkles that constitute for the robust palmprint recognition. Among the available texture extraction schemes the use of Local Binary Patterns (LBP) [15], Gabor Transform [13], Palmcode [10] , Fusion code [8], Competitive code [16] and Contour Code [7] have shown to perform accurately even on the very low resolution palmprint images. There exists a wide spectrum of appearance based techniques that includes Principal Component Analysis [1], Linear Discriminant Analysis (LDA) [17], Independent Component Analy-

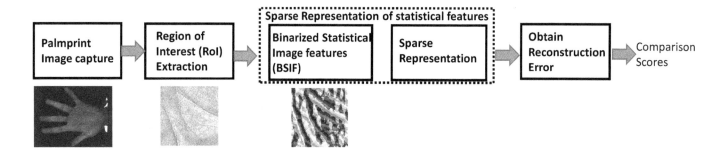

Figure 1: Block diagram of the proposed method

sis (ICA) [1], kernel based approaches like Kernel Discriminant Analysis (KDA) [13], kernel PCA (KPCA) [3] and generative model based approaches namely PCA Mixture model(PCAMM) and ICA Mixture Model (ICAMM) [14]. The hybrid scheme involves in combining more than one of the above mentioned schemes so that it can address short comings of individual schemes. When compared to all four different types of schemes, the hybrid schemes appears to be more robust and accurate for the palmprint recognition.

In this work, we present a new scheme for palmprint verification using sparse representation of Binarized Statistical Image Features (BSIF). The BSIF [6] is basically a texture descriptor similar to the LBP but the difference is the way the filters are learned. In case of BSIF, filters are leaned on the natural images while in LBP filters are manually predefined. Given, the palmprint image, the BSIF feature will compute the binary string by performing convolution with filters. We then use the Sparse Representation Classifier [11] on the obtained BSIF features to perform subject verification. Thus following are the main contribution of this paper: (1) Introducing BSIF as a possible feature extraction scheme for robust palmprint verification (2) Extensive experiments on three different palmprint databases namely: PolyU contact palmprint database [20] with 356 subjects, IIT Delhi contactless palmprint database with 236 subjects and Multispectral palmprint PolyU database [19] with 500 subjects. (3) Comprehensive analysis by comparing the proposed scheme with five different state-of-the-art contemporary schemes based on LBP [15], Palmcode [10], Fusion code[8], Gabor transform with KDA [13] and Gabor transform with sparse representation [12].

The rest of the paper is structured as follows: Section 2 disusses the proposed scheme for robust palmprint recognition, Section 3 discusses the experimental setup, protocols and results and Section 4 draws the conclusion.

## 2. PROPOSED METHOD

Figure 1 shows the block diagram of the proposed scheme for robust palmprint recognition that can be structured in two main steps.

## 2.1 Region of Interest (RoI) extraction

The main idea of the RoI is to extract the significant region from the palmprint that constitutes for the rich set of features such as principal lines, ridges and wrinkles by compensating for rotation and translation. The accurate extraction of RoI plays a crucial role in improving the performance of the overall palmprint recognition. In this work,

we have employed the algorithm proposed in [14] which is based on aligning the palmprint by computing center of mass and also by locating the valley regions. We carried out this RoI extraction scheme only on PolyU palmprint database as the other two databases (MSPolyU and IITD) have the RoI images are already available.

## 2.2 Sparse Representation of binarized statistical features

The idea of the BSIF is to represent each pixel as a binary code obtained by computing its response to a filter that are learned using the statistical properties of the natural images. The crucial part of the BSIF depends on exploring the statistical independence among the learnt filters. Thus, learning process is a crucial step in accurately constructing the filters which in turn characterizes the image to have BSIF descriptor.

In this work, we have employed the open-source filters [6] that are learnt using 50000 image patterns randomly sampled from thirteen different natural images [5]. The learning process to construct these statistically independent filters involves three main steps (1) Mean subtraction of each patches (2) Dimensionality reduction using Principle Component Analysis (PCA) (3) Estimation of statistically independent filters (or basis) using Independent Component Analysis (ICA). Thus, given the palmprint image patch $I_P(m,n)$ and a filter $F_i$ of same size then, filter response is obtained as follows [6]:

$$r_i = \sum_{m,n} I_P(m,n) W_i(m,n) \tag{1}$$

Where $m$ and $n$ denotes the size of the palmprint image patch and $W_i$, $\forall i = \{1, 2, \ldots, n\}$ denotes the number of linear filters whose response can be computed together and binarized to obtain the binary string as follows [6]:

$$b_i = \begin{cases} 1, & \text{if } r_i > 0 \\ 0, & \text{otherwise} \end{cases} \tag{2}$$

Finally, the BSIF features are obtained as the histogram of pixel's binary codes that can effectively characterize the texture components in the palmprint image. In order to effectively evaluate the BSIF descriptor for palmprint verification one needs to consider two important factors which include filter size and length of bit strings. In this work, we have evaluated 8 different filter sizes such as $3 \times 3$, $5 \times 5$, $7 \times 7$, $9 \times 9$, $11 \times 11$, $13 \times 13$, $15 \times 15$ and $17 \times 17$ and with five different bit lengths such as 5,6,7,8 and 9. Finally,

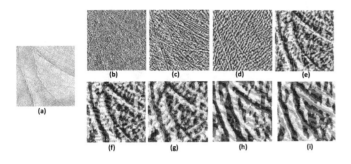

**Figure 2: Qualitative Results of BSIF with different path size and fixed bit length of 8 bits (a) Input palmprint image (b)** $3 \times 3$ **(c)** $5 \times 5$ **(d)** $7 \times 7$ **(e)** $9 \times 9$ **(f)** $11 \times 11$ **(g)** $13 \times 13$ **(h)** $15 \times 15$ **(i)** $17 \times 17$

we selected the filter of size $17 \times 17$ with 8 bit length by considering its accuracy based on our experiments.

Figure 2 shows the qualitative results on the example palmprint with varying filter size with fixed bit length of 8. It is interesting to observe here that, as the filter size increases the distinctive information about the coarse palm lines also increases. This further justifies our choice on employing the large filter size of $17 \times 17$ that was also found experimentally.

After obtaining the BSIF features, we perform the sparse representation on features that can be summarized in the following steps:

1. Given the reference palmprint samples, we first extract the BSIF features and form the matrix $T_r$ for all $C$ classes as follows:

$$T_r = [T_{r1}, T_{r2}, \ldots, T_{rC}] \in \Re^{N \times (n_u.C)} \quad (3)$$

Where, $n_u$ denotes the number of reference samples for each class and $N$ indicates the dimension of the BSIF features obtained on $n_u$ reference samples from $C$ classes.

2. Given the test sample $T_e$ obtain the BSIF features that can be considered as a linear combination of the training vectors as:

$$T_e = T_r \alpha \quad (4)$$

Where,

$$\alpha = [\alpha_1, \ldots, \alpha_{1n_u}|, \alpha_2, \ldots, \alpha_{2n_u}|, \ldots, |\alpha_{C1}, \ldots, \alpha_{Cn_u}] \quad (5)$$

3. solve $l_1$ minimization problem [11] as follows:

$$\hat{\alpha} = \arg \min_{\alpha' \in \Re^N} \|\alpha'\|_1 \qquad T_e = T_r \alpha' \quad (6)$$

4. Calculate the residual as follows:

$$r_c(y) = \|T_e - \Pi_C(\alpha')\|_2 \quad (7)$$

5. Finally, obtain the comparison score as the residual errors to compute the performance of the over all system.

In the following section we discuss the results obtained using the proposed scheme.

# 3. EXPERIMENTS AND RESULTS

Extensive experiments are carried out on three different large scale publicly available palmprint databases such as: (1) PolyU palmprint database[20] (2) IIT Delhi palmprint database [9] and (3) Multispectral palmprint PolyU database [19]. All the experimental results are presented in terms of Equal Error Rate (EER) and we also present the statistical validation of the results with 90% confidence interval [13].

## 3.1 Assessment Protocol

This section describes the evaluation protocol adopted in this work on three different palmprint databases.

### 3.1.1 PolyU palmprint database

This database comprises of 352 subjects such that each subject has 10 samples collected in two different sessions. For our experiments, we consider all 10 samples from the first session as reference and all samples from the second session as probe samples.

### 3.1.2 IIT Delhi palmprint database

This database consists of 235 subjects with both left and right palmprint samples. Each subject has 5 samples captured independently from both left and right palmprints. In order to evaluate this database, we consider four samples as the reference and remaining one sample as the probe sample. We repeat this selection of reference and probe samples using leaving-one-out cross validation with k = 10 and finally we present the result by averaging the performance over all 10 runs.

### 3.1.3 Multi-Spectral PolyU palmprint database

This database consists of 500 subjects whose palmprint samples are captured in two different session in four different spectrum : blue, red, green and Near Infrared (NIR). Each session has 6 samples per subject, thus we select samples from first session as reference samples while we select second session samples as probe. We repeat this procedure for all four spectral bands and results are presented independently.

## 3.2 Results and discussion

This section will present the quantitative results on the proposed palmprint recognition scheme on three different publically available database. Further, we also present the comprehensive comparison of the proposed scheme with five well adopted state-of-the-art palmprint recognition schemes.

Figure 3 shows the qualitative results of the proposed scheme along with the five different state-of-the-art schemes employed in this work. While Table1-Table3 shows the quantitative results that we obtained on three different databases and five different state-of-the-art schemes employed in the work.

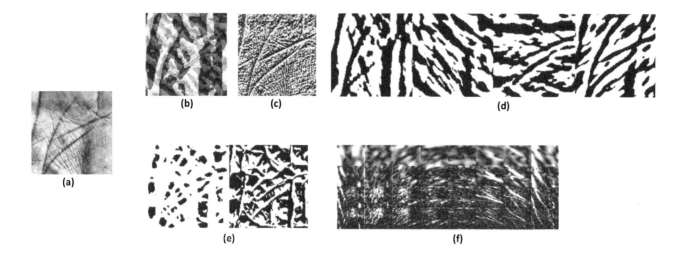

Figure 3: Illustration of (a) Palmprint sample (b) BSIF (c) LBP (d) Palmcode (e) Fusion code (f) Log-Gabor (LG) transform

| Methods | EER (%) with 90% confidence Interval |
|---------|---------|
| Proposed scheme | **6.19 [5.09; 7.29]** |
| LG-SRC[12] | 7.67 [6.47; 8.87] |
| LG-KDA [13] | 7.96 [6.56; 9.36] |
| Palm Code [10] | 14.66 [13.26; 16.06] |
| Fusion Code [8] | 14.51 [13.21; 15.81] |
| LBP-SRC [15] | 46.22 [43.84; 48.62] |

Table 1: Performance of the proposed method on PolyU palmprint database

| IIT Delhi DB | Methods | EER (%) 90% Confidence Interval |
|---------|---------|---------|
| Left Hand | Proposed Scheme | **0.42 [0.32;0.52]** |
| | Gabor-SRC [12] | 1.23 [0.93; 1.53] |
| | Gabor-KDA [13] | 2.34 [1.54; 3.14] |
| | Palmcode [10] | 2.67 [1.97; 9.37] |
| | Fusion Code [8] | 2.34 [1.54; 3.14] |
| | LBP-SRC[15] | 10.41 [8.81;12.10] |
| Right Hand | Proposed Scheme | **1.31 [0.91; 1.71]** |
| | Gabor-SRC[12] | 1.42 [1.02; 1.82] |
| | Gabor-KDA[13] | 7.82 [6.42; 9.22] |
| | Palmcode[10] | 3.41 [2.91; 3.91] |
| | Fusion Code [8] | 3.39 [2.89; 3.89] |
| | LBP-SRC [15] | 13.38 [11.49; 15.28] |

Table 2: Performance of the proposed method on IIT Delhi palmprint database

Table 1 shows the quantitative results obtained on PolyU palmprint database using our proposed scheme along with five different state-of-the-art scheme. Here, it can be observed that, the proposed scheme has shown the best performance with the lowest EER of 6.19%. Thus, these quantitative results justifies the efficacy of the proposed BSIF-SRC scheme over state-of-the-art schemes on PolyU palmprint database.

| Spectrum | Methods | EER (%) 90% Confidence Interval |
|---------|---------|---------|
| Blue | Proposed Scheme | **0** |
| | Gabor-SRC [12] | 0 |
| | Gabor-KDA [13] | 0.7 [0.55; 1.25] |
| | Palmcode [10] | 0.2 [0.1; 0.3] |
| | Fusion Code [8] | 0.4 [0.28; 0.68] |
| | LBP-SRC [15] | 9.76 [8.36; 11.16] |
| Green | Proposed Scheme | 0 |
| | Gabor-SRC [12] | **0** |
| | Gabor-KDA [13] | 0.40 [0.3; 0.5] |
| | Palmcode [10] | 0.41 [0.21; 0.61] |
| | Fusion Code [8] | 0.67 [0.38; 0.96] |
| | LBP-SRC [15] | 17.75 [15.58; 19.92] |
| Red | Proposed Scheme | 0 |
| | Gabor-SRC [12] | **0** |
| | Gabor-KDA [13] | 0.40 [0.3; 0.5] |
| | Palmcode [10] | 0 |
| | Fusion Code [8] | 0.21 [0.03; 0.38](0.17) |
| | LBP-SRC [15] | 14.78 [13.58; 15.98] |
| NIR | Proposed Scheme | 0 |
| | Gabor-SRC [12] | **0** |
| | Gabor-KDA [13] | 0.70 [0.4; 1.0] |
| | Palmcode [10] | 0 |
| | Fusion Code [8] | 0.2 [0.02;0.38] |
| | LBP-SRC [15] | 14.78 [13.38; 16.18] |

Table 3: Performance of the proposed method on MS PolyU palmprint database

Table 2 shows the performance of the proposed scheme on IIT Delhi contactless palmprint database independently for left and right hand. Here also it can be observed that, the proposed scheme using BSIF-SRC has shown the best performance with EER = 0.42% on left hand and EER = 1.31% on right hand palmprint.

Table 3 shows the quantitative performance of the proposed scheme on multi-spectral palmprint database. Here, we present the results independently for each spectral bands that shows the best performance of the proposed scheme with an outstanding performance with the EER = 0%.

Thus from the above experiments, it can be observed that, the proposed scheme has shown the best performance when compared with five well established state-of-the-art schemes for the palmprint recognition. Further, the performance achieved using the proposed scheme on three different databases justifies its robustness and applicability for the palmprint recognition.

## 4. CONCLUSION

In this work, we have proposed a new scheme for robust palmprint recognition based on the sparse representation of Binarized Statistical Image Features (BSIF). The BSIF features are obtained by convolving each pixel of the palmprint image with a set of filters that are learned using small set of natural images. The response of these filters can be represented as a binary string that describes the pixel neighborhood. Extensive experiments carried out on three different large scale publicly available databases shows the outstanding performance of the proposed scheme. The performance of the proposed scheme is compared with five well established state-of-the-art schemes. The obtained results justify that, the proposed scheme has emerged as an efficient and robust tool for accurate palmprint recognition.

## 5. ACKNOWLEDGMENT

This work was funded by the EU $7^{th}$ Framework Program (FP7) under grant agreement $n^o$ 284862 for the large-scale integrated project FIDELITY.

## 6. REFERENCES

[1] T. Connie, A. Teoh, M. Goh, and D. Ngo. Palmprint recognition with pca and ica. In *proceedings of Image and vision, Palmerston North, New Zealand*, pages 232–277, 2003.

[2] J. Dai and J. Zhou. Multifeature-based high-resolution palmprint recognition. *Pattern Analysis and Machine Intelligence, IEEE Transactions on*, 33(5):945–957, 2011.

[3] M. Ekinci and M. Aykut. Gabor-based kernel pca for palmprint recognition. *Electronics Letters*, 43(20):1077–1079, 2007.

[4] C. Han, H. Cheng, C. Lin, and K. Fan. Personal authentication using palmprint features. *Pattern Recognition*, 37(10):371–381, 2003.

[5] A. Hyvèarinen, J. Hurri, and P. O. Hoyer. *Natural Image Statistics*, volume 39. Springer, 2009.

[6] J. Kannala and E. Rahtu. Bsif: Binarized statistical image features. In *Pattern Recognition (ICPR), 2012 21st International Conference on*, pages 1363–1366. IEEE, 2012.

[7] Z. Khan, A. Mian, and Y. Hu. Contour code: Robust and efficient multispectral palmprint encoding for human recognition. *IEEE International Conference on Computer Vision*, pages 1935–1942, 2011.

[8] A. Kong, D. Zhang, and M. Kamel. Palmprint identification using feature-level fusion. *Pattern Recognition*, 39(3):478–487, 2006.

[9] A. Kumar. Incorporating cohort information for reliable palmprint authentication. In *Computer Vision, Graphics & Image Processing, 2008. ICVGIP'08. Sixth Indian Conference on*, pages 583–590. IEEE, 2008.

[10] A. Kumar and H. Shen. Palmprint identification using palm codes, 3rd int. In *Conference on mage and Graphics, ICIG20, Hong Kong*, pages 258–261.

[11] J. Mairal, F. Bach, J. Ponce, and G. Sapiro. Online learning for matrix factorization and sparse coding. *The Journal of Machine Learning Research*, 11:19–60, 2010.

[12] R. Raghavendra and C. Busch. Novel image fusion scheme based on dependency measure for robust multispectral palmprint recognition. *Pattern recognition*, 44(6):2505 – 2221, 2014.

[13] R. Raghavendra, B. Dorizzi, A. Rao, and G. H. Kumar. Designing efficient fusion schemes for multimodal biometric system using face and palmprint. *Pattern Recognition*, 44(5):1076–1088, 2011.

[14] R. Raghavendra, A. Rao, and G. Hemantha. A novel three stage process for palmprint verification. In *International Conference on Advances in Computing, Control, Telecommunication Technologies*, pages 88–92, 2009.

[15] X. Wang, H. Gong, H. Zhang, B. Li, and Z. Zhuang. Palmprint identification using boosting local binary pattern. In *Pattern Recognition, 2006. ICPR 2006. 18th International Conference on*, volume 3, pages 503–506. IEEE, 2006.

[16] J. Wei, W. Jia, H. Wang, and D.-F. Zhu. Improved competitive code for palmprint recognition using simplified gabor filter. In *Emerging Intelligent Computing Technology and Applications*, pages 371–377. 2009.

[17] X. Wu, D. Zhang, and K. Wang. Fisherpalms based palmprint recognition. *Pattern recognition letters*, 24(15):2829–2838, 2003.

[18] D. Zhang. *Palmprint Authentication*. Springer-verlag edition, 2004.

[19] D. Zhang, Z. Guo, G. Lu, Y. L. L.Zhang, and W. Zuo. Online joint palmprint and palmvein verification. *Expert Systems with Applications*, 38(3):2621–2631, 2011.

[20] D. Zhang, W.-K. Kong, J. You, and M. Wong. Online palmprint identification. *Pattern Analysis and Machine Intelligence, IEEE Transactions on*, 25(9):1041–1050, 2003.

# GSHADE: Faster Privacy-Preserving Distance Computation and Biometric Identification

Julien Bringer
Morpho
julien.bringer@morpho.com

Hervé Chabanne
Morpho, Télécom ParisTech
chabanne@telecom-paristech.fr

Mélanie Favre
Morpho
melanie.favre@morpho.com

Alain Patey
Morpho, Télécom ParisTech
patey@telecom-paristech.fr

Thomas Schneider
Engineering Cryptographic Protocols Group
TU Darmstadt, Germany
thomas.schneider@ec-spride.de

Michael Zohner
Engineering Cryptographic Protocols Group
TU Darmstadt, Germany
michael.zohner@ec-spride.de

## ABSTRACT

At WAHC'13, Bringer et al. introduced a protocol called SHADE for secure and efficient Hamming distance computation using oblivious transfer only. In this paper, we introduce a generalization of the SHADE protocol, called GSHADE, that enables privacy-preserving computation of several distance metrics, including (normalized) Hamming distance, Euclidean distance, Mahalanobis distance, and scalar product. GSHADE can be used to efficiently compute one-to-many biometric identification for several traits (iris, face, fingerprint) and benefits from recent optimizations of oblivious transfer extensions. GSHADE allows identification against a database of 1 000 Eigenfaces in 1.28 seconds and against a database of 10 000 IrisCodes in 17.2 seconds which is more than 10 times faster than previous works.

## General Terms

Algorithms, Security

## Keywords

Signal Processing in the Encrypted Domain; Privacy, Biometrics; Oblivious Transfer

## 1. INTRODUCTION

Secure Two-Party Computation (S2PC), introduced in the eighties by Yao [45] and Goldreich-Micali-Wigderson (GMW) [21] enables two parties to interactively compute a function on their private inputs without revealing any information other than what can be inferred from the function output. A natural field of application for S2PC is privacy-preserving biometric identification, *e.g.*, [3,5,9,10,18,28,35,

38, 41–43]. In this setting, a client $\mathcal{C}$, who holds a fresh biometric sample of a person, and a server $\mathcal{S}$, who holds a database of biometric data, want to determine whether there is a biometric reference for $\mathcal{C}$ in the database of $\mathcal{S}$. $\mathcal{C}$ wants to prevent $\mathcal{S}$ from learning the query sample, since it would allow $\mathcal{S}$ to track the person from which the sample was taken. $\mathcal{S}$, on the other hand, wants to prevent $\mathcal{C}$ from learning information about the contents of his database. We describe more detailed examples later in §1.3.

Privacy-preserving biometric identification has been researched very extensively in the last years. While the first protocols were based on (additively) homomorphic encryption schemes only (e.g., [18,38]), it was soon demonstrated that protocols which use generic secure computation techniques such as Yao's garbled circuits protocol [45] achieve a better performance and allow the extension to a richer set of functionalities. These protocols either combine homomorphic encryption with generic secure computation protocols, e.g., [3,5,25,28,41], or exclusively use generic secure computation protocols, e.g., [10,27,35].

A recent development in the area of secure computation is the design of efficient protocols that are based on oblivious transfer (OT) [40]. Although efficient constructions for OT have been known for several years, in particular OT extension [30] which allows to base OT on symmetric cryptographic primitives, OT was regarded as an expensive primitive. However, efficient implementations of OT, e.g., [12,27], have shown that OT can be performed at very low cost and have renewed the interest in protocols using OT. An example can be seen in the field of private set-intersection, where an OT-based solution was presented recently [17] that outperforms prior approaches based on homomorphic encryption [14] and generic secure computation [26]. Another example, from the field of biometric identification, is the SHADE (for Secure HAmming DistancE computation) protocol [9], which allows secure computation of the Hamming distance using OT only. In parallel to these applications of OT, even more efficient OT protocols have been developed recently that further improve the computation and communication complexity of OT extension [1,32].

*IH&MMSec'14,* June 11–13, 2014, Salzburg, Austria.
Copyright 2014 ACM 978-1-4503-2647-6/14/06 ...$15.00.
http://dx.doi.org/10.1145/2600918.2600922.

## 1.1 Our Contributions

In this paper, we build on recent developments in the area of efficient OT and develop a generic framework for secure biometric identification, called GSHADE (Generalized SHADE). GSHADE allows the efficient computation of various distance measures such as the (normalized) Hamming distance, the Euclidean distance, the scalar product, and the Mahalanobis distance using OT only. Furthermore, GSHADE can be combined with generic secure computation techniques and hence can be used to efficiently compute a rich set of functionalities that are based on distance measures. We evaluate the efficiency of GSHADE both theoretically and experimentally and compare it to related work.[1] Overall, GSHADE allows a factor of 10 to 20 improvement in runtime compared to the best previous solutions. A brief summary of the runtimes and communication complexities of GSHADE for different biometric identification schemes (described in §4), in combination with the generic secure computation protocol of Golreich-Micali-Wigderson (GMW),[2] is depicted in Tab. 1.

## 1.2 Setting

In our setting, a server $S$ and a client $C$ want to securely compute 1-vs-$N$ biometric identification. The actual inputs and possible outputs are given in Fig. 1. The privacy requirements of S2PC imply that one party does not get more information about the other party's inputs than what can be deduced from its own inputs and outputs. This is formally expressed using a simulation game, see [24] for more details. In this work, we focus on *semi-honest* (also called *passive* or *honest but curious*) adversaries. In this model, privacy of the inputs is ensured against parties that do not cheat but try to infer additional information from the observed messages. In particular, this model guarantees that even an insider that is able to access the communication records of the secure computation is unable to obtain additional information about the inputs. The semi-honest model is sufficient for many applications [6, 7] and allows to construct highly efficient protocols.

## 1.3 Example Use Cases

We emphasize the importance of our GSHADE protocol for biometric identification by giving a non-exhaustive list of use cases to which our solution can be applied.

**Anonymous Biometric Access Control.** Our first use case deals with biometric access control to, for instance, a company building. The employer $S$ wants to ensure that only the registered (and biometrically enrolled) employees are allowed to enter the building. We can use privacy-preserving biometric identification based on our solution to prevent the employer from tracking his employees' activities.

**Biometric Anonymous Credentials.** In this example, we have three parties: a client $C$, a service provider $P$, and a biometric data server holder $S$. $S$ can be, for instance, a government that holds a database of all people satisfying a given criterion (*e.g.*, be over 21). To access the services of $P$, $C$ identifies against the database of $S$. If $C$ was successfully identified, $S$ gives him a token to present to $P$ to prove that

---

Inputs:

- Client $C$ inputs a biometric acquisition $X$
- Server $S$ inputs $N$ biometric data items $Y^1, \ldots, Y^N$

**Possible Outputs (given to $S$ and/or $C$):**

- A yes/no answer (Is $X$ close enough to one of the $Y^i$s?)
- The index and/or distance of the closest match
- The $Y^i$s that are sufficiently close to $X$
- An identification score
- All distances between $X$ and the $Y^i$s
- ...

Figure 1: Secure Two-party Computation of Biometric Identification.

---

he fulfills the requirements. In the whole process, $C$ reveals his identity neither to $P$ nor to $S$.

**Secure Biometric Database Intersection.** In our third example, we consider two law enforcement agencies that want to identify the suspects they have in common or that want to determine whether a suspect is registered in a given database. For privacy and security reasons, the involved parties want to keep the data that is not in the intersection secret. Our solution can be adapted to this use case by letting the client input a list of biometric data.

## 1.4 Outline

The remainder of this paper is organized as follows. We describe preliminaries for this work in §2, including main techniques for S2PC, the state of the art in privacy-preserving biometric identification, and the original SHADE protocol. We introduce GSHADE, our generalization of the SHADE protocol for computing several distance metrics, in §3 and describe its applications to biometric identification in §4. We give implementation results and compare the performance of GSHADE to the state of the art in §5 and conclude in §6.

## 2. PRELIMINARIES

In this section, we summarize the properties of and techniques used for secure two-party computation (§2.1), distance metrics for biometric identification (§2.2), the state of the art in privacy-preserving biometric identification (§2.3), and the original SHADE protocol (§2.4). More details on S2PC can for instance be found in [24], while a deeper study of its application to biometric identification can be found in [8].

## 2.1 Secure Two-Party Computation (S2PC)

Several techniques can be applied to realize Secure Two-Party Computation (S2PC), most prominently Yao's garbled circuits protocol [45] and the protocol of Goldreich-Micali-Wigderson (GMW) [21] that both use oblivious transfer [19, 40]; or alternatively (additively) homomorphic en-

---

[1]Our GSHADE implementation is available online at http://encrypto.de/code/GSHADE.

[2]Alternatively, Yao's garbled circuits protocol could be used.

| Application | SCiFi Faces [38] | IrisCodes [16] | FingerCodes [31] | Eigenfaces [44] |
|---|---|---|---|---|
| Distance Computation using GSHADE | | | | |
| Metric | Hamming Distance | Normalized Hamming Distance | Euclidean Distance | Scalar Product + Euclidean Distance |
| Time in sec. (LAN/WiFi) | 0.9 / 1.4 | 8.8 / 14.3 | 5.1 / 10.3 | 1.0 / 2.8 |
| Communication in MB | 4.3 | 51.3 | 48.9 | 15.1 |
| Post-Processing using GMW | | | | |
| Method | Comparison | Comparison | Closest Match | Closest Match |
| Time in sec. (LAN/WiFi) | 0.09 / 0.27 | 0.3 / 1.4 | 1.6 / 4.1 | 4.0 / 13.1 |
| Communication in MB | 1.9 | 5.1 | 18.6 | 68.5 |

Table 1: Empirical performance of GSHADE for 1-vs-$5\,000$ biometric identification schemes. Details on the choice of parameters are given in Tab. 2.

cryption, e.g., [13]. In the following, we give a short summary of each of these techniques.

**Oblivious Transfer.** A 1-out-of-2 oblivious transfer (OT) [19,40], denoted by $OT^\ell$, is a two-party protocol where one party (the sender) inputs two $\ell$-bit strings $x_0, x_1 \in \{0,1\}^\ell$ and the other party (the receiver) inputs a bit $b$. At the end of the protocol, the receiver obtains $x_b$ but learns no information about $x_{1-b}$ whereas the sender learns no information about $b$. OT protocols can be built from public key cryptography, e.g., [36]. For a large number of OTs, OT extension [30] can be used that extends a few base OTs to many OTs using only efficient symmetric cryptographic primitives. Recent work of [32] further improved the communication complexity of OT extension and [1] provides even more efficient protocols for the correlated OT functionality, where the sender inputs only a single value $\Delta$ together with a correlation function $f$ s.t. at the end of the protocol, the sender obtains $x_0 \in_R \{0,1\}^\ell$ and $x_1 = f_\Delta(x_0)$ as output and the receiver obtains $x_b$.

**Yao's Garbled Circuits Protocol.** A garbled circuit [45] is an encrypted version of the binary circuit representing the function to be evaluated securely. In Yao's protocol, one party (the sender) generates the garbled circuit by building the binary circuit, choosing a pair of encryption keys for every wire of the circuit, and encrypting the output wire keys using the keys of the input wires. The sender then sends the garbled circuit and the input keys that correspond to his inputs to the second party (the receiver). The receiver obtains the keys corresponding to his inputs by engaging in an oblivious transfer with the sender. Using the obtained input keys, the receiver can then decrypt the garbled circuit to obtain the result while learning no intermediary information. See [27] for a more detailed description.

Yao's protocol relies mostly on symmetric cryptography and is best suited for functions that can efficiently be represented as binary circuits and in environments that have a high communication latency. However, Yao's protocol has a high communication complexity and requires the function and input sizes to be known in advance to allow precomputation. Yao's garbled circuits protocol has been implemented in the FastGC framework [27].

**GMW Protocol.** Similar to Yao's protocol, the GMW protocol [21] also uses a binary circuit representation of the function, but performs the secure evaluation on shares rather than using encrypted gates. The parties first secret-share their inputs using a XOR secret sharing scheme. To evaluate an XOR gate, the parties simply XOR the shares of the input wires. To evaluate an AND gate, the parties perform an

oblivious transfer, where one party pre-computes all possible outputs of the gate and the other party obliviously obtains the output that corresponds to its input shares. To obtain the output of the circuit, the parties exchange the shares of the output wires.

As shown in [1,12,42], the GMW protocol allows the precomputation of all symmetric cryptographic operations before the function or the inputs to the function are known and requires less communication per AND gate than Yao's garbled circuits protocol. However, the GMW protocol requires a number of communication rounds that is linear in the depth of the circuit. The GMW protocol has been implemented in [12] and further optimized for the two-party case in [1,42].

**Homomorphic Encryption.** A public-key encryption is homomorphic if it is possible to compute over encrypted data without the knowledge of the secret key. Although fully homomorphic encryption (*i.e.*, a cryptosystem that is homomorphic for any operation) has been introduced in 2009 [20], it is not yet practical. Most implemented proposals therefore use additively homomorphic encryption schemes, such as Paillier [39] or Damgård-Geisler-Krøigaard (DGK) [15].

Homomorphic encryption is more suited for arithmetic circuits and the ciphertexts can be re-used for several instances of secure computation, which reduces the communication complexity. However, homomorphic encryption requires computationally expensive public-key operations that scale very inefficiently for larger security parameters.

## 2.2 Distance Metrics

In the following, we summarize some distance metrics that are used in biometric identification schemes. In §2.3 we will describe which distance is used by which biometric identification scheme and in §3 we will show that each of these distances can be computed efficiently with our generalized SHADE protocol.

**Hamming Distance (HD).** The Hamming distance between two $\ell$-bit vectors $X = (x_1, \ldots, x_\ell)$ and $Y = (y_1, \ldots, y_\ell)$ is computed as $HD(X,Y) = \sum_{i=1}^\ell x_i \oplus y_i$.

**Normalized Hamming Distance (NHD).** The normalized Hamming distance between a $\ell$-bit vector $X = (x_1, \ldots, x_\ell)$ with $\ell$-bit mask $M = (m_1, \ldots, m_\ell)$ and a vector $Y = (y_1, \ldots, y_\ell)$ with mask $M' = (m'_1, \ldots, m'_\ell)$ is computed as $NHD(X,M;Y,M') = \frac{\sum_{i=1}^\ell (m_i m'_i (x_i \oplus y_i))}{\sum_{i=1}^\ell (m_i m'_i)}$.

**Scalar Product (SP).** The scalar product between two $K$-dimensional vectors $X = (X_1, \ldots, X_K)$ and $Y = (Y_1, \ldots, Y_K)$ is computed as $SP(X,Y) = \sum_{i=1}^K X_i Y_i$.

**Squared Euclidean Distance (ED).** The squared Euclidean distance between two $K$-dimensional vectors $X = (X_1, \ldots, X_K)$ and $Y = (Y_1, \ldots, Y_K)$ is computed as $\mathrm{ED}(X, Y) = \sum_{i=1}^{K}(X_i - Y_i)^2 = \sum_{i=1}^{K}((X_i)^2 - 2X_iY_i + (Y_i)^2)$.

**Squared Mahalanobis Distance (MD).** The squared Mahalanobis distance between two $K$-dimensional vectors $X = (X_1, \ldots, X_K)$ and $Y = (Y_1, \ldots, Y_K)$ is computed as $\mathrm{MD}(X, Y) = (X - Y)^T M (X - Y)$, where $M$ is a positive semi-definite matrix (which might be the inverse of the covariant matrix of a sample set). The Mahalanobis distance can be used for instance for hand shape, keystroke, or signature recognition [34].

## 2.3 Privacy-Preserving Biometric Identification

Several different schemes for privacy-preserving biometric identification using S2PC have been proposed. Most schemes focused on face [18, 38, 41], fingerprint [3, 5, 28, 43], or iris [5, 10, 35] recognition which we summarize next. We provide more details on the underlying algorithms in §4.

**Privacy-preserving face recognition.** Privacy-preserving face recognition has been realized based on two different recognition algorithms: Eigenfaces used in [18, 41, 42] and the SCiFI algorithm used in [9, 27, 38, 42].

In protocols based on the Eigenfaces algorithm [44], the parties have to perform a projection (matrix-vector or scalar products), compute the Euclidean distance, and compare the resulting distance to a threshold. Erkin et al. [18] suggest to employ additively homomorphic encryption for the whole protocol. Sadeghi et al. [41] showed that a hybrid solution gives better performances, using additively homomorphic encryption for projection and distance computation, then garbled circuits for comparisons. Schneider et al. [42] use GMW, which allows to pre-compute all cryptographic operations and thereby achieves a fast online phase.

The SCiFI algorithm [38] is a face recognition algorithm that is based on the Hamming distance and was specifically designed to yield an efficient privacy-preserving protocol. Originally, Osadchy et al. [38] used additively homomorphic encryption and subsequently Huang et al. [27] and Schneider et al. [42] showed that using Yao's garbled circuits respectively GMW results in better performances. The SHADE protocol of Bringer et al. [9] is an even more efficient construction based on oblivious transfer (cf. §2.4 for details).

**Privacy-preserving fingerprint recognition.** Secure fingerprint recognition has been considered using two main solutions. The FingerCodes technique [31] relies on Euclidean distance and has been proposed in [3, 5, 28], which use additively homomorphic encryption for Euclidean distance and several solutions for comparison/identification operations. Use of minutiae-based fingerprint recognition [34] has been envisioned in [5, 43], but we do not further discuss it in this paper as it does not fit our protocol.

**Privacy-preserving iris recognition.** Iris recognition using IrisCodes [16] requires secure evaluation of normalized Hamming distances and has first been considered by Blanton et al. [5] using homomorphic encryption, then by Luo et al. [35] and Bringer et al. [10] using Yao's garbled circuits.

## 2.4 Secure Hamming Distance Computation (SHADE)

The SHADE protocol [9] allows efficient secure Hamming distance computation using oblivious transfer. In the fol-

lowing we describe the original SHADE protocol and its extension to the 1-vs-$N$ case.

**The SHADE Protocol.** The SHADE protocol was first intended for secure computation of Hamming distances. For $\mathcal{S}$ and $\mathcal{C}$ with $\ell$-bit inputs $Y$ and $X$ the protocol works as follows. $\mathcal{S}$ and $\mathcal{C}$ perform $\ell$ $\mathrm{OT}^{\lceil \log_2(\ell+1)\rceil}$ where, in the $i$-th OT, $\mathcal{S}$ chooses a random $r_i \in_R \mathbb{Z}_{\ell+1}$ and inputs $(r_i + y_i, r_i + (y_i \oplus 1))$ and $\mathcal{C}$ inputs $y_i$ as choice bit and receives $t_i = r_i + (x_i \oplus y_i)$. $\mathcal{S}$ then sums up the random masks and outputs $R = \sum_{i=1}^{\ell} r_i$ and $\mathcal{C}$ sums up the received values and outputs $T = \sum_{i=1}^{\ell} t_i$. Note that we have $T - R = \sum_{i=1}^{\ell}(r_i + (x_i \oplus y_i)) - \sum_{i=1}^{\ell} r_i = \sum_{i=1}^{\ell} x_i \oplus y_i = \mathrm{HD}(X, Y)$.

**SHADE for the 1-vs-$N$ Case.** SHADE was observed to be efficiently extendable to the 1-vs-$N$ case, where $\mathcal{S}$ holds $N$ $\ell$-bit values $Y^1, \ldots, Y^N$ and $\mathcal{C}$ holds a single $\ell$-bit value $X$. The only additional overhead for the extended protocol is longer bit strings in the oblivious transfers. More detailed, in the $i$-th OT, the parties perform $\ell$ $\mathrm{OT}^{N\lceil \log_2(\ell+1)\rceil}$ where $\mathcal{S}$ inputs $(r_i^1 + x_i^1 || \ldots || r_i^N + x_i^N, r_i^1 + \bar{x}_i^1 || \ldots || r_i^N + \bar{x}_i^N)$ and $\mathcal{C}$ inputs $y_i$ and receives $t_i = (r_i^1 + (x_i^1 \oplus y_i) || \ldots || r_i^N + (x_i^N \oplus y_i))$. In the final step, the parties can again simply compute and output $R^1, \ldots, R^N$ and $T^1, \ldots, T^N$, where $R^b = \sum_{i=1}^{\ell} r_i^b$ and $T^b = \sum_{i=1}^{\ell} t_i^b$, for $1 \le b \le N$.

# 3. OUR GENERALIZED SHADE (GSHADE) PROTOCOL

In this section we describe our generalized SHADE protocol, called GSHADE, which allows to compute different distances (§3.1). We describe how to combine GSHADE with comparison or minimum protocols (§3.2), outline how to efficiently extend it to 1-vs-$N$ matching (§3.3) and how to base it on the more efficient correlated OT functionality (§3.4). We give applications of GSHADE to biometric identification with new adaptations for IrisCodes and Eigenfaces later in §4.

## 3.1 The GSHADE Protocol

We observe that the original SHADE protocol extends to the family $\mathcal{F}^{GSHADE}$ of functions that can be expressed as $f(X, Y) = f_X(X) + \Sigma_{i=1}^{n} f_i(x_i, Y) + f_Y(Y)$, where $X = (x_1, \ldots, x_n) \in \{0, 1\}^n$ is the input of $\mathcal{C}$ and $Y$ is the input of $\mathcal{S}$. (The set $\mathsf{S}$ to which $Y$ belongs does not impact the protocol.) In particular, several metrics used for biometric matching are included in this family of functions:

**Hamming Distance** $X = (x_1, \ldots, x_\ell)$ and $Y = (y_1, \ldots, y_\ell)$ are $n = \ell$-bit vectors. We have $f_X = f_Y = 0$ and $f_i(x_i, Y) = x_i \oplus y_i$, for $i = 1, \ldots, n$.

**Scalar Product** $X = (X_1, \ldots, X_K)$ with $X_i = (x_{K(i-1)+1}, \ldots, x_{K(i-1)+\ell})$ and $Y = (Y_1, \ldots, Y_K)$ with $Y_i = (y_{K(i-1)+1}, \ldots, y_{K(i-1)+\ell})$ are $n = K \times \ell$-bit-integer vectors. We have $f_X = f_Y = 0$ and $f_{K \cdot (i-1)+j}(x_{K(i-1)+j}, Y) = 2^{j-1} \cdot x_{K(i-1)+j} \cdot Y_i$, for $i = 1, \ldots, K$ and $j = 1, \ldots, \ell$.

**Squared Euclidean Distance** $X = (X_1, \ldots, X_K)$ with $X_i = (x_{K(i-1)+1}, \ldots, x_{K(i-1)+\ell})$ and $Y = (Y_1, \ldots, Y_K)$ with $Y_i = (y_{K(i-1)+1}, \ldots, y_{K(i-1)+\ell})$ are $n = K \times \ell$-bit-integer vectors. We have $f_X(X) = \Sigma_{i=1}^{K}(X_i)^2$, $f_Y(Y) = \Sigma_{i=1}^{K}(Y_i)^2$ and $f_{K \cdot (i-1)+j}(x_{K(i-1)+j}, Y) = -2^j \cdot x_{K(i-1)+j} \cdot Y_i$, for $i = 1, \ldots, K$ and $j = 1, \ldots, \ell$.

**Squared Mahalanobis Distance** We assume that $M = (M_{uv})_{u,v=1,\ldots,K}$ is known by both parties, and not a private input of either party.[3] $X = (X_1, \ldots, X_K)$ with $X_i = (x_{K(i-1)+1}, \ldots, x_{K(i-1)+\ell})$ and $Y = (Y_1, \ldots, Y_K)$ with $Y_i = (y_{K(i-1)+1}, \ldots, y_{K(i-1)+\ell})$ are $n = K \times \ell$-bit-integer vectors. We have $f_X(X) = X^T M X$, $f_Y(Y) = Y^T M Y$, $f_{K \cdot (i-1)+j}(x_{K(i-1)+j}, Y) = -2^j \cdot x_{K(i-1)+j} \cdot \sum_{v=1}^{K} M_{i,v} Y_v$, for $i = 1, \ldots, K$, $j = 1, \ldots, \ell$.

In Fig. 2, we describe the generalized SHADE protocol. Note that $m$ is such that the output of $f(X, Y)$ belongs to $\mathbb{Z}_m$. For instance, if $f$ is the Hamming distance between two $\ell$-bit vectors, we set $m = \ell + 1$.

---

**Inputs:**

- $\mathcal{C}$ inputs a $n$-bit string $X = (x_1, \ldots, x_n)$
- $\mathcal{S}$ inputs $Y \in \mathtt{S}$

**Outputs:**

- $\mathcal{S}$ obtains $R \in_R \mathbb{Z}_m$
- $\mathcal{C}$ obtains $T = R + f(X, Y)$

**Protocol:**

1. $\mathcal{S}$ chooses $n$ random values $r_1, \ldots, r_n \in_R \mathbb{Z}_m$.

2. For each $i = 1, \ldots, n$, $\mathcal{S}$ and $\mathcal{C}$ engage in a $\mathrm{OT}^{\lceil \log_2(m) \rceil}$ where

   - $\mathcal{S}$ acts as the sender and $\mathcal{C}$ as the receiver.
   - $\mathcal{C}$'s selection bit is $x_i$.
   - $\mathcal{S}$'s input is $(r_i + f_i(0, Y), r_i + f_i(1, Y))$.
   - The output obtained by $\mathcal{C}$ is consequently $t_i = r_i + f_i(x_i, Y)$.

3. $\mathcal{C}$ computes and outputs $T = \Sigma_{i=1}^{n} t_i + f_X(X)$.

4. $\mathcal{S}$ computes and outputs $R = \Sigma_{i=1}^{n} r_i - f_Y(Y)$.

---

**Figure 2: Generalized SHADE (GSHADE) protocol.**

**Correctness.** Since $r_1, \ldots, r_n$ are picked uniformly at random over $\mathbb{Z}_m$, then, for fixed $X$ and $Y$, $R = \sum_{i=1}^{n} r_i - f_Y(Y)$ is distributed uniformly over $\mathbb{Z}_m$ and the output of $\mathcal{S}$ is correct. Moreover, we have $T - R = \sum_{i=1}^{n}(t_i - r_i) + f_X(X) + f_Y(Y) = \sum_{i=1}^{n} f_i(x_i, Y) + f_X(X) + f_Y(Y) = f(X, Y)$. Thus, $T = R + f(X, Y)$ and the output of $\mathcal{C}$ is correct. $\square$

**Security.** The proof of security of GSHADE is similar to that of SHADE [9]. We give a proof sketch against static semi-honest adversaries next. Security is proven by simulation in the OT-hybrid setting, where OTs are simulated by

a trusted oracle. We recall that each simulator is provided with the input and output of the corrupted party.

*Case 1 – $\mathcal{S}$ is corrupted.* Since $\mathcal{S}$ receives no messages beyond those in OT, its view can be perfectly simulated.

*Case 2 – $\mathcal{C}$ is corrupted.* Given $\mathcal{C}$'s output $T$ and input $X$, $\mathcal{C}$'s view can be perfectly simulated by sending random values $t'_1, \ldots, t'_{n-1} \in_R \mathbb{Z}_m$ and $t'_n = T - \sum_{i=1}^{n-1} t'_i - f_X(X)$ to $\mathcal{C}$ in the OTs. $\square$

## 3.2 Adding Comparison or Minimum

In some use-cases of privacy-preserving biometric identification, it is required that the parties learn whether the distance is lower than a certain threshold (comparison) or the index of the closest match (minimum). For these protocols, we require a secure comparison or minimum operation after the distance calculation, which keeps the resulting distance secret. Using GSHADE does not improve comparison or minimum operations. However, if one runs GSHADE, the masked results can easily be used as input to a secure comparison or minimum protocol. Several protocols are possible, depending on the actual desired output. We refer the reader to the papers mentioned in §2.3 for an overview. Note that for Yao's garbled circuits protocol and the GMW protocol, we have to build a circuit which first reconstructs $f(X, Y) = T - R$ and subsequently computes the desired functionality. In our experiments in §4 we use the GMW protocol for the comparison or minimum operations.

## 3.3 Adaptation to the 1-vs-$N$ case

Analogue to the original SHADE protocol, the GSHADE protocol can be efficiently extended to the 1-vs-$N$ biometric identification, where the client has one input $X$ and the server has $N$ inputs $Y^1, \ldots, Y^N$ and they want to compute all the distances $f(X, Y^b)$, for $b = 1, \ldots, N$. The protocol is modified in the following way

1. $\mathcal{S}$ generates $n \cdot N$ random values $r_{b,i} \in_R \mathbb{Z}_m$, for $b = 1, \ldots, N$.

2. For each $i = 1, \ldots, n$, $\mathcal{S}$ and $\mathcal{C}$ engage in a $\mathrm{OT}^{N \lceil \log_2(m) \rceil}$ where

   - $\mathcal{S}$ acts as the sender and $\mathcal{C}$ as the receiver.
   - $\mathcal{C}$'s selection bit is $x_i$.
   - $\mathcal{S}$'s input is $(r_{1,i} + f_i(0, Y^1) || \ldots || r_{N,i} + f_i(0, Y^N), r_{1,i} + f_i(1, Y^1) || \ldots || r_{N,i} + f_i(1, Y^N))$.
   - The output obtained by $\mathcal{C}$ is $(t_{1,i} || \ldots || t_{N,i}) = (r_{1,i} + f_i(x_i, Y^1) || \ldots || r_{N,i} + f_i(x_i, Y^N))$.

3. $\mathcal{C}$ computes and outputs $T^1 = \Sigma_{i=1}^{\ell} t_{1,i} + f_X(X), \ldots, T^N = \Sigma_{i=1}^{\ell} t_{N,i} + f_X(X)$

4. $\mathcal{S}$ computes and outputs $R^1 = \Sigma_{i=1}^{n} r_{1,i} - f_Y(Y^1), \ldots, R^N = \Sigma_{i=1}^{n} r_{N,i} - f_Y(Y^N)$

Note that the number $n$ of OTs remains unchanged compared to the 1-vs-1 case and only the length of the inputs grows linearly with the number of database entries $N$. As the protocol is essentially a parallel execution of the basic GSHADE protocol, but using OTs with longer strings, correctness and security carry over from GSHADE (cf. §3.1).

---

[3] This assumption is reasonable, for instance, if MD is used instead of ED in the Eigenfaces protocol (see §4.4). Indeed, the matrix $M$ would only disclose statistical information about the projection space, which is not very sensitive, whereas the Eigenfaces basis gives information about real biometric data (they can reveal "average" faces) and should be kept private, as it is the case in our protocol.

### 3.4 Using Correlated OTs

As described in §2.1, the *correlated* OT (C-OT) extension protocol of [1] has an even lower communication complexity than generic OT extension. Here, the sender obtains one randomly chosen value as output and inputs a correlation that determines the second value. This functionality was initially used for Yao's protocol with the free-XOR technique [33] where for each wire $w$ one key $k_w^0$ is chosen randomly and the other key is correlated with $k_w^1 = k_w^0 \oplus \Delta$, where $\Delta$ is a fixed offset. In the following we show how GSHADE can be based on C-OT instead of OT. Here we assume that $m$ is a power of 2 (we discuss the case where $m$ is not a power of 2 in Appendix A). The GSHADE protocol can be rewritten as follows:

1. For each $i = 1, \ldots, n$, $\mathcal{S}$ and $\mathcal{C}$ engage in a C-OT$^{\lceil \log_2(m) \rceil}$ where

   - $\mathcal{C}$ acts as the receiver with selection bit $x_i$.
   - $\mathcal{S}$ acts as the sender with input $\Delta_i = f_i(1, Y) - f_i(0, Y)$.
   - The correlation function is $f_{\Delta_i}(\cdot) = \cdot + \Delta_i$.
   - The output obtained by $\mathcal{S}$ is $\rho_i \in_R \mathbb{Z}_m$.
   - The output obtained by $\mathcal{C}$ is $\tau_i = \rho_i - f_i(0, Y) + f_i(x_i, Y)$.

2. $\mathcal{C}$ computes and outputs $T = \sum_{i=1}^n \tau_i + f_X(X)$.

3. $\mathcal{S}$ computes and outputs $R = \sum_{i=1}^n (\rho_i - f_i(0, Y)) - f_Y(Y)$.

**Correctness.** During the $i^{th}$ C-OT, $\mathcal{C}$ obtains $\rho_i = \rho_i - f_i(0, Y) + f_i(0, Y)$ if $x_i = 0$, or $\rho_i + \Delta_i = \rho_i + f_i(1, Y) - f_i(0, Y)$ if $x_i = 1$. Thus, $\mathcal{C}$ always obtains $\tau_i = \rho_i + f_i(x_i, Y) - f_i(0, Y)$. Regarding final outputs, $T - R = \sum_{i=1}^n (\tau_i - \rho_i + f_i(0, Y)) + f_X(X) + f_Y(Y) = \sum_{i=1}^n (\rho_i + f_i(x_i, Y) - f_i(0, Y) - \rho_i + f_i(0, Y)) + f_X(X) + f_Y(Y) = \sum_{i=1}^n f_i(x_i, Y) + f_X(X) + f_Y(Y) = f(X, Y)$. Thus, $R \in_R \mathbb{Z}_m$ and $T = R + f(X, Y)$ and the protocol is correct. $\square$

**Security.** Security is proven in a similar way as for the OT-based GSHADE protocol described in §3.1. We still give a proof sketch against static semi-honest adversaries. Here, we assume that C-OTs are simulated by a trusted oracle.
*Case 1 – $\mathcal{S}$ is corrupted.* Given $\mathcal{S}$'s output $R$ and input $Y$, $\mathcal{S}$'s view can be perfectly simulated by sending random values $\rho_1', \ldots, \rho_{n-1}' \in_R \mathbb{Z}_m$ and $\rho_n' = R - \sum_{i=1}^{n-1} \rho_i' + \sum_{i=1}^n f_i(0, Y) + f_Y(Y)$ to $\mathcal{C}$ in the C-OTs.
*Case 2 – $\mathcal{C}$ is corrupted.* Given $\mathcal{C}$'s output $T$ and input $X$, $\mathcal{C}$'s view can be perfectly simulated by sending random values $\tau_1', \ldots, \tau_{n-1}' \in_R \mathbb{Z}_m$ and $\tau_n' = T - \sum_{i=1}^{n-1} \tau_i' - f_X(X)$ to $\mathcal{C}$ in the C-OTs. $\square$

This adaptation is also compatible with the 1-vs-$N$ version of GSHADE described in §3.3. Using the C-OT extension protocol of [1] allows to reduce the asymptotic communication complexity by a factor of two compared to using the original OT extension of [30], cf. [1].

## 4. APPLICATIONS

We demonstrate several applications where the GSHADE protocol can be used for secure and efficient distance computations: the SCiFI (§4.1) and Eigenfaces (§4.4) protocol for face recognition, the IrisCodes (§4.2) protocol, and the FingerCodes (§4.3) protocol. In Tab. 2 we summarize the parameters for the distances used, the number of OTs $n$, and the length of the OTs' outputs. Note that the parameters in Tab. 2 include optimizations proposed in previous works.

### 4.1 SCiFI

In the setting of face recognition using SCiFI [38], biometric vectors are $\ell = 900$-bit binary vectors that are compared using Hamming distance. One can simply apply the original SHADE protocol of [9] which is a special case of our GSHADE protocol. The authors of [38] point out that the Hamming distances in the SCiFI protocol never exceeded 180. Thus, we decrease the range of Hamming distances from $\mathbb{Z}_{901}$ to $\mathbb{Z}_{181}$. Therefore, in case of SCiFI, we have to perform $n = \ell = 900$ OTs on $\lceil \log_2 181 \rceil N = 8N$-bit strings.

### 4.2 IrisCodes

IrisCodes [16] are 512-byte representations of iris images made of a template and a mask of $\ell = 2048$-bit each. The mask signifies reliable bits of the iris template, *i.e.*, a mask bit set to 1 indicates that the corresponding template bit is reliable, while a mask bit set to 0 indicates an erasure (due to eyelids, eyelashes, blurs,... ). IrisCodes can be compared using normalized Hamming distance (NHD).

One can see that normalized Hamming distance does not exactly match the family $\mathcal{F}^{GSHADE}$. However, if we adopt the convention that a template bit which is associated to a 0 in the mask is also set to 0, which is not restrictive, numerator ($num$) and denominator ($den$) of normalized Hamming distance both match the family. We integrate both template and mask to the input vector. Let $n = 2\ell$, $f^{num}(X, Y) = \sum_{i=1}^{\ell} x_{\ell+i} \cdot y_{\ell+i} \cdot (x_i \oplus y_i)$ and $f^{den}(X, Y) = \sum_{i=1}^{\ell} x_{\ell+i} \cdot y_{\ell+i}$. For $i = 1, \ldots, \ell$, let $f_i^{den}(x_i, Y) = 0$, $f_{i+\ell}^{den}(x_{i+\ell}, Y) = x_{i+\ell} \cdot y_{i+\ell}$ and let $f_i^{num}$ and $f_{i+\ell}^{num}$ be defined as in Tab. 3. Our convention enforces that $(x_{i+\ell} = 0 \implies x_i = 0)$ (and same for $Y$), for each $i = 1, \ldots, \ell$. If both inputs $X$ and $Y$ respect this convention, then one can easily check that $f^{num}(X, Y) = \sum_{i=1}^n f_i^{num}(x_i, Y)$ and $f^{den}(X, Y) = \sum_{i=1}^n f_i^{den}(x_i, Y)$.

| $y_i$ | \multicolumn{2}{c}{0} | \multicolumn{2}{c}{1} |
|---|---|---|---|---|
| $y_{i+\ell}$ | 0 | 1 | 0 | 1 |
| $f_i^{num}(0, Y)$ | 0 | 0 | – | 1 |
| $f_i^{num}(1, Y)$ | 0 | 1 | – | 0 |
| $f_{i+\ell}^{num}(0, Y)$ | 0 | 0 | – | -1 |
| $f_{i+\ell}^{num}(1, Y)$ | 0 | 0 | – | 0 |

**Table 3: Definition of $f_i^{num}$ and $f_{i+\ell}^{num}$, for $i \in [1, \ell]$.**

Outputting the numerator and the denominator does not satisfy complete privacy requirements, if one wants to securely evaluate the normalized Hamming distance. Nevertheless, our goal is to apply GSHADE to biometric identification. Thus, instead of outputting NHD, we output the result of $\text{NHD}(X, Y) \overset{?}{<} t$, which can be rewritten as $f^{num}(X, Y) \overset{?}{<} t \cdot f^{den}(X, Y)$, where $0 < t < 1$ is a threshold. Thus, one runs GSHADE on both $f^{num}$ and $f^{den}$. $\mathcal{C}$ obtains $T^{num} = f^{num}(X, Y) + R^{num}$ and $T^{den} = f^{den}(X, Y) + R^{den}$ while $\mathcal{S}$ holds masks $R^{num}$ and $R^{den}$ (see Fig. 2). If $t$ is known by $\mathcal{C}$, then $\mathcal{C}$ includes $T^{num}$ and $t \cdot T^{den}$ and $\mathcal{S}$ inputs $R^{num}$ and $t \cdot R^{den}$ to a protocol that first pairwise subtracts inputs and then compares the results. If $t$ is not known by $\mathcal{C}$,

| Protocol | Operation | $n$ | $\lceil \log_2(m) \rceil$ |
|---|---|---|---|
| SCiFI [38] | Hamming Distance | 900 | 8 |
| IrisCodes [5] | Normalized Hamming Distance | $2\,048 + 2\,048$ | $31 + 11$ |
| FingerCodes [28] | Euclidean Distance | $640 \times 8 = 5\,120$ | 16 |
| Eigenfaces (projection) [18, 25, 41, 42] | Scalar Product | $10\,304 \times 8 = 82\,432$ | $12 \times 30 = 360$ |
| Eigenfaces (distance) [18, 25, 41, 42] | Euclidean Distance | $12 \times 30 = 360$ | 50 |

**Table 2: Parameters used in our experiments ($n$: number of OTs, $\mathbb{Z}_m$: range of OT inputs).**

this secure protocol should first include a secure multiplication step or GSHADE should be run on $t \cdot f^{den}$.

When actually running this protocol, we suggest to run $n$ OTs for both $f^{num}$ and $f^{den}$, where the first $\ell$ OTs only concern $f^{num}$ while the last $\ell$ OTs concatenate contributions to both $f^{num}$ and $f^{den}$. Thus, complexity (before comparison) is $\ell \times \mathrm{OT}^{\lceil \log_2(\ell) \rceil} + \ell \times \mathrm{OT}^{2\lceil \log_2(\ell) \rceil}$ in the 1-vs-1 case or $\ell \times \mathrm{OT}^{N\lceil \log_2(\ell) \rceil} + \ell \times \mathrm{OT}^{2N\lceil \log_2(\ell) \rceil}$ in the 1-vs-$N$ case.

## 4.3 FingerCodes

Fingerprint recognition via FingerCodes [31] uses a global representation (unlike the more standard minutiae-based recognition protocols that describe local features) of biometric data as integer vectors. Comparison between two biometric data samples is then simply done using Euclidean distance. As mentioned in §3.1, one can directly apply GSHADE to securely evaluate this metric. In general, without experimental optimizations, one has to perform $n = K\ell$ OTs on $N(2\ell + \lceil \log_2(K) \rceil)$-bit inputs. Two different sets of parameters for FingerCodes were suggested: [3, 5] use $K = 16$-dimensional vectors of $\ell = 7$-bit elements and perform the comparison on 19-bit results while [28] uses $K = 640$-dimensional vectors of $\ell = 8$-bit elements and performs the comparison on 16-bit results. Consequently, for the parameters of [3, 5] we have to perform $n = K\ell = 112$ OTs on $19N$-bit strings, and for the parameters of [28] we have to perform $n = 5\,120$ OTs on $16N$-bit strings. For our experiments in Tab. 1 we choose the parameters of [28].

## 4.4 Eigenfaces

In the setting of face recognition using Eigenfaces [44], the client holds a face image $X = (x_1, \ldots, x_{K'})$ with $\ell$-bit elements and the server holds an average face image $\Psi = (\psi_1, \ldots, \psi_{K'})$, a set of Eigenfaces $(U^1, \ldots, U^K)$, with $U^j = (u_1^j, \ldots, u_{K'}^j)$ for $j = 1, \ldots, K$, and a database of $N$ projected faces $Y^1, \ldots, Y^N$. The identification protocol consists of three phases:

1. Projection: The average face image $\Psi$ is subtracted from $X$. The result is projected on the Eigenfaces basis. Thus, one gets $\bar{X} = (\bar{x}_1, \ldots, \bar{x}_K)$, with $\bar{x}_j = \mathrm{SP}(X - \Psi, U^j)$, for $j = 1, \ldots, K$.

2. Distance: The Euclidean distances $d_j = \mathrm{ED}(\bar{X}, Y^i)$ are computed, for $i = 1, \ldots, N$.

3. Comparison: The distances $d_i$ are compared to thresholds and an identification result is output (see §3.2).

We suggest to use our GSHADE protocol to securely compute the first two steps, in the following way:

**Projection.** The operation consists of a subtraction then a scalar product and thus belongs to the family of functions that can be computed using GSHADE. Since $\mathcal{C}$ uses the

same input for all $K$ projections, one can use the 1-vs-$K$ variant described in §3.3. Thus, $\mathcal{C}$ gets $T = \bar{X} + R = (\bar{x}_1 + r_1, \ldots, \bar{x}_K + r_K)$ and $\mathcal{S}$ gets $R = (r_1, \ldots, r_K)$, where the $r_i$s are random masks in $\mathbb{Z}_p$, where $p = 2^{2\ell + \lceil \log_2 K' \rceil}$. Note that here we compute this step as $\bar{x}_j = \mathrm{SP}(X, U^j) - \mathrm{SP}(\Psi, U^k)$, i.e., $-\mathrm{SP}(\Psi, U^j)$ is computed on the server's side as part of $f_Y$ (with notations of §3.1).

**Distance.** Here $\mathcal{C}$ and $\mathcal{S}$ use the GSHADE protocol a second time in the 1-vs-$N$ variant, where the computed function is $(T; R, Y) \mapsto \mathrm{ED}(T - R, Y)$, which is included in $\mathcal{F}^{GSHADE}$.

For the parameters used in [18, 25, 41, 42], the projection is computed on $K' = 10\,304$-dimensional vectors with $\ell = 8$-bit elements and yields a 30-bit result on a $K = 12$-dimension plane. The Euclidean distance is then computed on $K = 12$-dimensional vectors with 30-bit elements and results in a 50-bit value. Thus, we have to perform $82\,432$ OTs on 360-bit elements and 360 OTs on $50N$-bit elements. Notice that the cost of the projection phase is independent of the size of the database $N$.

We emphasize that GSHADE can be applied to other privacy-preserving biometric recognition protocols that follow the same architecture as Eigenfaces, such as Fisherfaces [4], where the difference mostly lies in the algorithm to choose the basis (in the case of Fisherfaces, Linear Discriminant Analysis instead of Principal Component Analysis for Eigenfaces) and thus does not impact the identification protocol.

## 5. PERFORMANCE EVALUATION

In this section we evaluate the performance of GSHADE. We discuss the use of quantized inputs in §5.1, asymptotic complexities are studied in §5.2 and our experimental results are described and compared to the state of the art in §5.3.

## 5.1 Quantization

Our GSHADE protocol relies on the fact that inputs are binary vectors, either originally binary or by binarizing vectors of integers. However, it is often the case that the coordinates of feature vectors used for, e.g., face recognition are real or floating point numbers. It must be validated that the same protocols can be used on integer or binary inputs without loss of accuracy. Erkin et al. [18] showed, from experiments on the AT&T [2] database, that integers can be used as inputs to the Eigenfaces protocol (by multiplying original inputs by $1\,000$) without reliability losses and parameters used in [18] are chosen accordingly.

The performance of GSHADE is directly related to the size of the inputs, but also to the size of the outputs ($\lceil \log_2(m) \rceil$ in Tab. 2). We ran experiments to show that the outputs' size could be further reduced without impacting accuracy. Our biometric experiments have been conducted on the AT&T [2] and Multi-PIE [11, 22] (restricted to frontal images taken using camera 05_1) databases, using the Python Face Recognition Library [23, 29]. We took 30 eigenfaces (instead of 12 for [18]) and showed that the size of the projected faces could be reduced to $30 \times 13 = 390$-bit vectors, which is comparable to the parameters of [18]. However, our analysis showed that squared Euclidean distances can be reduced to 26-bit (for the AT&T database) or 24-bit integers (for the Multi-PIE database), which is about half the size used in [18, 25, 41, 42]. Using these parameters would allow to further decrease the communication complexity of GSHADE by about a factor of two without any loss in correctness, accuracy, or security. However, aiming at fairness in our comparison to other protocols, experiments described in §5.3 were run with the same parameters as in [18, 25, 41, 42].

## 5.2 Asymptotic Performance Comparison

In the following we compare the asymptotic performance of the GSHADE protocol when computing various distances to related work. The parameters that affect the performance of GSHADE are the number of OTs and the length of strings that are transferred obliviously. In the following, $\kappa$ is the symmetric security parameter and $\rho$ is the asymmetric security parameter (in our experiments in §5.3 we set $\kappa = 80$ and $\rho = 1\,024$).

In Tab. 4, we summarize the asymptotic computation and communication complexities when computing different distance metrics using GSHADE with those of secure distance computation protocols in related work (§2.3). For each solution, we outline the technique that is used, i.e., homomorphic encryption (HE), garbled circuits (GC), GMW, or GSHADE, the computation complexity of $S$ (which dominates the one of $C$) and the overall communication. Note that the complexities only include the distance computation excluding later computation steps such as minimum, greater than, and so on. However, each of the solutions can be extended by a generic secure computation protocol to obtain the desired functionality. We obtain the computation complexity for HE by counting the number of modular exponentiations and for GC, GMW, and GSHADE by counting the number of symmetric cryptographic operations. For GC we determine the communication complexity as the size of the garbled circuit ($3\kappa$ bits per non-linear gate using the free XOR [33] and garbled row reduction [37] techniques) plus the number of input keys of the server ($\kappa$ bits per $S$'s input bit). We neglect the inputs of $C$ as these do not depend on the database size $N$. For GMW, the communication complexity is two symmetric keys per non-linear gate (see complexity analysis in [1, 42]). The complexity of GSHADE takes into account the C-OT technique of [1]: communication complexity for $n \times C - OT^{\ell}$ is $n \times (\ell + \kappa)$ bits and computation complexity is $3n + 2n\ell/o$ symmetric operations, where $o$ is the output size of the PRF (pseudo-random function) used by the C-OT (see [1]). The HE-based protocols of [3, 5, 18, 25, 28, 38] to compute the Hamming distance, scalar product, and Euclidean distance use Paillier's additively homomorphic encryption [39], so ciphertexts have size $2\rho$ bits. For GSHADE and HE we include in Tab. 4 some communication that does not depend on $N$, but that might be dominant when $N$ is not too large (e.g., for a few dozens or hundreds of entries).

**Computation.** For the Hamming distance and normalized Hamming distance, where the HE, GC, and GMW techniques have a computation complexity that is linear in $N\ell$, GSHADE achieves a computation complexity linear in $(N\ell \log_2 \ell)/o$. Considering that the output size of the PRF $o$ is in the order of some hundred bits (e.g., 128, 192, or 256), while $\log_2 \ell$ is much smaller (e.g., about 10 for SCiFI and IrisCodes), the computation complexity of GSHADE is considerably smaller than that of the previous techniques, especially compared to HE based solutions because of the cost of asymmetric operations. For the scalar product and Euclidean distance, GMW requires $\mathcal{O}(NK\ell^2)$ symmetric cryptographic operations while GSHADE requires $\mathcal{O}(NK\ell^2/o)$ and hence GSHADE has a smaller computation complexity by around a factor of $o$. The HE-based schemes, on the other hand, achieve a performance of $NK$ asymmetric cryptographic operations, compared to $4NK\ell^2/o$ symmetric cryptographic operations in GSHADE. However, asymmetric cryptographic operations, i.e., modular exponentiations, are usually several orders of magnitudes slower than symmetric cryptographic operations such as AES or SHA, especially when increasing the security parameter. We provide concrete performance numbers in our experiments in §5.3.

**Communication.** For all distances, we can observe that GSHADE requires transmitting some orders of magnitude less data than the generic secure computation protocols (GC or GMW). When comparing the communication complexity of GSHADE to HE-based protocols, on the other hand, the communication complexity of GSHADE depends highly on the bit length $\ell$. For the Hamming distance and normalized Hamming distance, the communication complexity of GSHADE grows with $\mathcal{O}(N\ell \log_2 \ell)$ while the communication complexity of HE-based protocols grows with $2N\rho$. In biometric identification protocols that use (normalized) Hamming distance the bitlength is relatively large (e.g., $\ell \in \{900, 2\,048\}$) s.t. $\ell \log_2 \ell > 2\rho$ and the communication complexity of GSHADE is higher than that of HE-based protocols. This is also the case for the scalar product and Euclidean distance where the communication complexity of GSHADE grows with $2NK\ell^2$ which is higher than the $2N\rho$ of HE-based protocols. Still, in our experiments in §5.3 GSHADE requires less than three times more communication than HE-based protocols.

## 5.3 Experimental Performance Comparison

In the following, we experimentally compare the performance of GSHADE to that of related work on the Eigenfaces and IrisCodes applications.

**Experimental Setup.** For all schemes, we compare the overall run-time and estimated communication complexity. We measured the complexity for our GSHADE protocol and compare it to the numbers reported in related work. We do not claim that we provide a fair comparison, since the results were measured on different machines and using different programming languages. Moreover, most implementations are not publicly available. We rather intend for the experiments to support the asymptotic complexities summarized in Tab. 4. However, we argue that the orders of magnitude improvements that we obtain are too significant to be explained by the use of different programming languages, libraries, or hardware alone. Note that, other than some related works, we only give the overall complexities and do not divide them into pre-computation and online phase. We

| Distance Metric | Technique | Computation of $\mathcal{S}$ | Communication [bits] |
|---|---|---|---|
| Hamming Distance | HE [38] | $N\ell$ asym | $2(N+\ell)\rho$ |
| | GC [27] | $4N\ell$ sym | $4N\ell\kappa$ |
| | GMW [42] | $4N\ell$ sym | $2N\ell\kappa$ |
| | **GSHADE (§3)** | $(2N\ell \log_2 \ell)/o + 3\ell$ sym | $\ell(N \log_2 \ell + \kappa)$ |
| Normalized Hamming Distance | HE [5] | $N\ell$ asym | $(2N+\ell)\rho$ |
| | GC [10, 35] | $16N\ell$ sym | $14N\ell\kappa$ |
| | **GSHADE (§3)** | $(8N\ell \log_2 \ell)/o + 6\ell$ sym | $2\ell(2N \log_2 \ell + \kappa)$ |
| Scalar Product / Euclidean Distance | HE [3, 5, 18, 25, 28] | $NK$ asym | $2(N+K)\rho$ |
| | GMW [42] | $8NK\ell^2$ sym | $4NK\ell^2\kappa$ |
| | **GSHADE (§3)** | $(2NK\ell(2\ell + \log_2 K))/o + 3K\ell$ sym | $K\ell(2N\ell + N \log_2 K + \kappa)$ |

Table 4: Asymptotic complexities for different 1-vs-$N$ distance metrics with bit length $\ell$, PRF output size $o$, vector dimension $K$, symmetric security parameter $\kappa$, and asymmetric security parameter $\rho$.

point out that, since the only cryptographic protocol that we use is OT, we can pre-compute all required cryptographic operations and thereby achieve a very efficient online phase, as demonstrated in [12,42]. We implemented our GSHADE protocol using the correlated OT extension from the C++ OT library of [1]. For evaluating the comparison and minimum circuits, we use the C++ GMW implementation of [12] with optimizations of [42] and the random OT extension protocol of [1]. We chose the GMW framework of [12] as it is implemented in the same programming language and is also extensively based on OT. However, as GSHADE is independent of the generic secure computation protocol, we could alternatively use Yao's garbled circuits protocol, e.g., as implemented in [27]. For the WiFi experiments in Tab. 1 we limit the bandwidth between the PCs using the `tc` command. In order to allow comparison with previous works we also use short-term security parameters, i.e., symmetric security parameter $\kappa = 80$ and asymmetric security parameter $\rho = 1\,024$. We run our experiments on two 3.2 GHz Intel i5-4570 CPUs with 8 GB RAM each running Ubuntu 12.04 that are connected via Gigabit LAN.

### 5.3.1 SCiFI

The SCiFI protocol for face-recognition was specifically designed to be computed in a privacy-preserving fashion and has been implemented using various secure computation protocols. While the seminal work of [38] introduced the SCiFI algorithm and used homomorphic encryption to perform face-recognition, [27] and [42] improved on its performance by expressing the SCiFI functionality as binary circuit and evaluate it using Yao's garbled circuits protocol and the GMW protocol, respectively. The original SHADE protocol [9] improved on the performance of both when securely computing the Hamming distance. In the following we compare the performance of GSHADE, which in the case of SCiFI is the same as the SHADE protocol. We depict our results in Tab. 5.

From our results we can observe that the (G)SHADE protocol outperforms previous protocols both in communication and computation. Additionally, compared to the GMW implementation of [42], the performance of (G)SHADE scales better with increasing database size, resulting in an increasing runtime advantage of factor 4-5 and a communication advantage of factor 14 for 50 000 elements.

### 5.3.2 IrisCodes

We perform the IrisCode experiments using the same parameters as [5], where the iris codes $X, Y^1, \ldots, Y^N$ and masks $M, M'^1, \ldots, M'^N$ are 2 048-bit long and $\mathcal{S}$ holds thresholds $t^1, \ldots t^N$. The protocol of [5] uses DGK [15] to compute the numerator $A_j = |M \wedge M'^i \wedge (X \oplus Y^i)|$ and the denominator $B_i = |M \wedge M'^i|$ of the normalized Hamming distance and the product $B_i t^i$ and performs the comparison $A_i \overset{?}{<} t^i B_i$ using garbled circuits. The protocol of [5] also proposes to let the server rotate his codes $Y^i$ and masks $M'^i$ left and right by $c$ different offsets (thus creating $2c$ rotated vectors, in addition to the original $Y^i$) and perform the comparison on each rotated value. If any of the distances with a rotated version of $Y^i$ is below the threshold, the protocol outputs a match for $Y^i$, which can be done by evaluating a circuit consisting of $2c$ OR-gates. For our experiments, we set the number of rotations to $c = 0$, since performing $c$ rotations essentially adds the same performance overhead for both, the protocol of [5] and GSHADE, as increasing the database size $N$ by factor $2c + 1$.

Performances of GSHADE applied to IrisCode identification are depicted in Tab. 6. We observe that the performance of GSHADE for biometric IrisCode identification is acceptable overall, but as shown in Tab. 1 it is the slowest among all biometric identification protocols we tested. This low performance can be explained by the high amount of single-bit operations that are required to process the data in the OTs. While other applications process the data byte-wise or, in the case of SCiFI, require only few bitwise operations, the IrisCode application makes an extensive use of bitwise operations, thereby becoming far less efficient than other applications. However, we stress that a more careful implementation of bit operations as well as pre-computing required inputs would further decrease the runtime of GSHADE. In particular, all the values $f_i(0, Y^j)$ and $f_i(1, Y^j)$ can be computed once, when a data $Y^j$ is added to the database, and stored with the database, instead of computing them online.

As shown in Tab. 6, the communication complexity of GSHADE is around 3 times higher compared to the homomorphic encryption based protocol of [5]. However, the overall computation time is much lower for GSHADE than for [5]: GSHADE is about 35 times faster for $N = 320$ and 12 times faster for $N = 10\,000$. Note that this improvement by more than one order of magnitude is significant and does not result from using different hardware.

| Protocol (Techniques) | N = 100 | | | | N = 320 | | | N = 50,000 | |
|---|---|---|---|---|---|---|---|---|---|
| | [38] (HE) | [27] (GC) | [42] (GMW) | **Ours** (GSHADE +GMW) | [27] (GC) | [42] (GMW) | **Ours** (GSHADE +GMW) | [42] (GMW) | **Ours** (GSHADE +GMW) |
| Programming Language | Java | Java | C++ | C++ | Java | C++ | C++ | C++ | C++ |
| Time in sec. | 244 | 8.8 | 0.3 | **0.2** | 42.9 | 0.5 | **0.3** | 46.0 | **9.9** |
| Communication in MB | 7.3 | 2.6 | 1.7 | **0.2** | 8.3 | 5.7 | **0.5** | 886.5 | **63.4** |

Table 5: Performances of privacy-preserving SCiFI identification protocols.

| Protocol (Techniques) | N = 320 | | N = 10 000 | |
|---|---|---|---|---|
| | [5] (HE+GC) | **Ours** (GSHADE+GMW) | [5] (HE+GC) | **Ours** (GSHADE+GMW) |
| Programming Language | C | C++ | C | C++ |
| Time in sec. | 17.6 | **0.5** | 212.6 | **17.2** |
| Communication in MB | 1.7 | **4.9** | 37.6 | **87.5** |

Table 6: Performances of privacy-preserving IrisCode identification protocols.

### 5.3.3 FingerCodes

For privacy-preserving FingerCode identification, we compare GSHADE to [28], which uses Paillier encryption to compute the Euclidean distance and garbled circuits to find the minimum. The results of this comparison are depicted in Tab. 7. Note that we excluded the backtracking step of [28] in the evaluation, which can be added if necessary.

While our protocol only slightly improves the communication complexity, the runtime improvements are significant, i.e., do not only result from choosing a different programming language. Our protocol improves the runtime by factor 500 for $N = 128$ elements and by factor 700 for $N = 1 024$ elements.

### 5.3.4 Eigenfaces

Secure computation of face recognition using Eigenfaces has been initially proposed based on homomorphic encryption [18] and subsequently the runtime has been improved by using a combination of homomorphic encryption and garbled circuits [25, 41] and using the GMW protocol [42]. These works use the same parameters summarized in Tab. 2 and we give a performance comparison with our protocol in Tab. 8.

We observe that GSHADE achieves a very efficient runtime and achieves a speedup of factor 20 over the GMW-based protocol of [42] and even factor 66 to 100 over the HE-based protocols of [18,25]. Note that these runtime improvements of orders of magnitude are significant and hence do not only result from using different programming languages and hardware. The communication complexity of GSHADE is several times lower than that of the GMW-based solution and even comparable to the HE-based protocols.

## 6. CONCLUSION

We described an efficient protocol called GSHADE to securely evaluate several distance metrics ((normalized) Hamming distance, Euclidean distance, scalar product, Mahalanobis distance) and showed that it can be used for efficient privacy-preserving biometric identification of several biometric traits (iris, face, fingerprint) and protocols (SCiFI, Eigenfaces, Fisherfaces, FingerCodes, IrisCodes). GSHADE is based on oblivious transfer and benefits from recently proposed optimizations for oblivious transfer extensions. Our performance analysis shows that, depending on the traits, GSHADE can be used for privacy-preserving identification against up to several thousand database items per second.

We believe that GSHADE can be used for several applications in signal processing, pattern recognition, or image processing that require privacy. Finding further applications of GSHADE is an interesting topic for future research.

## Acknowledgements

This work was supported by the German Federal Ministry of Education and Research (BMBF) within EC SPRIDE, by the Hessian LOEWE excellence initiative within CASED, and by the European Union Seventh Framework Programme (FP7/2007-2013) under grant agreement n. 609611 (PRACTICE). This work has been partially funded by the European FP7 FIDELITY project (SEC-2011-284862). The opinions expressed in this document only represent the authors' view. They reflect neither the view of the European Commission nor the view of their employer. This work has also been partially funded by the ANR SecuLar project. The first four authors are with Identity and Security Alliance (The Morpho and Télécom ParisTech Research Center).

## 7. REFERENCES

[1] G. Asharov, Y. Lindell, T. Schneider, and M. Zohner. More efficient oblivious transfer and extensions for faster secure computation. In *Computer and Communications Security (CCS)*, pages 535–548. ACM, 2013. Code available at http://encrypto.de/code/OTExtension.

[2] AT&T Laboratories Cambridge. The database of faces. http://www.cl.cam.ac.uk/research/dtg/attarchive/facedatabase.html.

[3] M. Barni, T. Bianchi, D. Catalano, M. Di Raimondo, R. Donida Labati, P. Failla, D. Fiore, R. Lazzeretti, V. Piuri, F. Scotti, and A. Piva. Privacy-preserving fingercode authentication. In *ACM workshop on Multimedia and Security (MMSEC)*, pages 231–240. ACM, 2010.

[4] P. N. Belhumeur, J. P. Hespanha, and D. J. Kriegman. Eigenfaces vs. Fisherfaces: Recognition

|  | $N = 128$ | | $N = 1024$ | |
|---|---|---|---|---|
| Protocol (Techniques) | [28] (HE+GC) | **Ours** (GSHADE+GMW) | [28] (HE+GC) | **Ours** (GSHADE+GMW) |
| Programming Language | Java | C++ | Java | C++ |
| Time in sec. | 148.2 | **0.3** | 1114.3 | **1.6** |
| Communication in MB | 2.2 | **1.8** | 17.5 | **13.8** |

Table 7: Performances of privacy-preserving FingerCode identification protocols.

|  | $N = 320$ | | | | $N = 1000$ | | |
|---|---|---|---|---|---|---|---|
| Protocol (Techniques) | [18] (HE) | [25] (HE+GC) | [42] (GMW) | **Ours** (GSHADE +GMW) | [25] (HE+GC) | [42] (GMW) | **Ours** (GSHADE +GMW) |
| Programming Language | C++ | Python | C++ | C++ | Python | C++ | C++ |
| Time in sec. | 40 | 79.6 | 17.7 | **0.6** | 139.6 | 26.3 | **1.3** |
| Communication in MB | 7.3 | 9.2 | 291.1 | **7.7** | 17 | 446.0 | **9.4** |

Table 8: Performances of privacy-preserving Eigenfaces identification protocols.

using class specific linear projection. In *European Conference on Computer Vision (ECCV)*, volume 1064 of *LNCS*, pages 43–58. Springer, 1996.

[5] M. Blanton and P. Gasti. Secure and efficient protocols for iris and fingerprint identification. In *European Symposium on Research in Computer Security (ESORICS)*, volume 6879 of *LNCS*, pages 190–209. Springer, 2011.

[6] D. Bogdanov, R. Talviste, and J. Willemson. Deploying secure multi-party computation for financial data analysis. In *Financial Cryptography (FC)*, volume 7397 of *LNCS*, pages 57–64. Springer, 2012.

[7] P. Bogetoft, D. L. Christensen, I. Damgård, M. Geisler, T. P. Jakobsen, M. Krøigaard, J. D. Nielsen, J. B. Nielsen, K. Nielsen, J. Pagter, M. I. Schwartzbach, and T. Toft. Secure multiparty computation goes live. In *Financial Cryptography (FC)*, volume 5628 of *LNCS*, pages 325–343. Springer, 2009.

[8] J. Bringer, H. Chabanne, and A. Patey. Privacy-preserving biometric identification using secure multiparty computation: An overview and recent trends. *IEEE Signal Processing Magazine*, 30(2):42–52, 2013.

[9] J. Bringer, H. Chabanne, and A. Patey. SHADE: Secure HAmming DistancE computation from oblivious transfer. In *Workshop on Applied Homomorphic Cryptography (WAHC)*, volume 7862 of *LNCS*, pages 164–176. Springer, 2013.

[10] J. Bringer, M. Favre, H. Chabanne, and A. Patey. Faster secure computation for biometric identification using filtering. In *IAPR International Conference on Biometrics (ICB)*, pages 257–264. IEEE, 2012.

[11] Carnegie Mellon University. The CMU Multi-PIE face database. http://www.multipie.org.

[12] S. G. Choi, K.-W. Hwang, J. Katz, T. Malkin, and D. Rubenstein. Secure multi-party computation of Boolean circuits with applications to privacy in on-line marketplaces. In *Cryptographers' Track at the RSA Conference (CT-RSA)*, volume 7178 of *LNCS*, pages 416–432. Springer, 2012. Code available at http://www.ee.columbia.edu/~kwhwang/projects/gmw.html.

[13] R. Cramer, I. Damgård, and J. B. Nielsen. Multiparty computation from threshold homomorphic encryption. In *EUROCRYPT*, volume 2045 of *LNCS*, pages 280–300. Springer, 2001.

[14] E. D. Cristofaro and G. Tsudik. Practical private set intersection protocols with linear complexity. In *Financial Cryptography (FC)*, volume 6052 of *LNCS*, pages 143–159. Springer, 2010.

[15] I. Damgård, M. Geisler, and M. Krøigaard. Efficient and secure comparison for on-line auctions. In *Australasian Conference on Information Security and Privacy (ACISP)*, volume 4586 of *LNCS*, pages 416–430. Springer, 2007.

[16] J. Daugman. How iris recognition works. *IEEE Transactions on Circuits and Systems for Video Technology*, 14(1):21–30, 2004.

[17] C. Dong, L. Chen, and Z. Wen. When private set intersection meets big data: An efficient and scalable protocol. In *Computer and Communications Security (CCS)*, pages 789–800. ACM, 2013.

[18] Z. Erkin, M. Franz, J. Guajardo, S. Katzenbeisser, I. Lagendijk, and T. Toft. Privacy-preserving face recognition. In *Privacy Enhancing Technologies Symposium (PETS)*, volume 5672 of *LNCS*, pages 235–253. Springer, 2009.

[19] S. Even, O. Goldreich, and A. Lempel. A randomized protocol for signing contracts. In *CRYPTO*, pages 205–210. Springer, 1982.

[20] C. Gentry. Fully homomorphic encryption using ideal lattices. In *Symposium on Theory of Computing (STOC)*, pages 169–178. ACM, 2009.

[21] O. Goldreich, S. Micali, and A. Wigderson. How to play any mental game or a completeness theorem for protocols with honest majority. In *Symposium on Theory of Computing (STOC)*, pages 218–229. ACM, 1987.

[22] R. Gross, I. Matthews, J. F. Cohn, T. Kanade, and S. Baker. Multi-PIE. *Image Vision and Computing*, 28(5):807–813, 2010.

[23] M. Günther, R. Wallace, and S. Marcel. An open source framework for standardized comparisons of face recognition algorithms. In *Benchmarking Facial Image*

Analysis Technologies (BeFIT), volume 7585 of *LNCS*, pages 547–556. Springer, 2012.

[24] C. Hazay and Y. Lindell. *Efficient Secure Two-Party Protocols - Techniques and Constructions*. Information Security and Cryptography. Springer, 2010.

[25] W. Henecka, S. Kögl, A.-R. Sadeghi, T. Schneider, and I. Wehrenberg. TASTY: Tool for Automating Secure Two-partY computations. In *Computer and Communications Security (CCS)*, pages 451–462, 2010.

[26] Y. Huang, D. Evans, and J. Katz. Private set intersection: Are garbled circuits better than custom protocols? In *Network and Distributed System Security Symposium (NDSS)*. The Internet Society, 2012.

[27] Y. Huang, D. Evans, J. Katz, and L. Malka. Faster secure two-party computation using garbled circuits. In *USENIX Security Symposium*. USENIX Association, 2011.

[28] Y. Huang, L. Malka, D. Evans, and J. Katz. Efficient privacy-preserving biometric identification. In *Network and Distributed System Security Symposium (NDSS)*. The Internet Society, 2011.

[29] Idiap Research Institute. Face recognition library. https://pypi.python.org/pypi/facereclib.

[30] Y. Ishai, J. Kilian, K. Nissim, and E. Petrank. Extending oblivious transfers efficiently. In *CRYPTO*, volume 2729 of *LNCS*, pages 145–161. Springer, 2003.

[31] A. K. Jain, S. Prabhakar, L. Hong, and S. Pankanti. FingerCode: A filterbank for fingerprint representation and matching. In *Computer Vision and Pattern Recognition (CVPR)*, pages 187–193. IEEE, 1999.

[32] V. Kolesnikov and R. Kumaresan. Improved OT extension for transferring short secrets. In *CRYPTO*, volume 8043 of *LNCS*, pages 54–70. Springer, 2013.

[33] V. Kolesnikov and T. Schneider. Improved garbled circuit: Free XOR gates and applications. In *International Colloquium on Automata, Languages and Programming (ICALP)*, volume 5126 of *LNCS*, pages 486–498. Springer, 2008.

[34] S. Z. Li and A. K. Jain, editors. *Encyclopedia of Biometrics*. Springer, 2009.

[35] Y. Luo, S.-C. S. Cheung, T. Pignata, R. Lazzeretti, and M. Barni. An efficient protocol for private iris-code matching by means of garbled circuits. In *International Conference on Image Processing (ICIP)*, pages 2653–2656. IEEE, 2012.

[36] M. Naor and B. Pinkas. Efficient oblivious transfer protocols. In *Symposium On Discrete Algorithms (SODA)*, pages 448–457. ACM/SIAM, 2001.

[37] M. Naor, B. Pinkas, and R. Sumner. Privacy preserving auctions and mechanism design. In *Conference on Electronic Commerce (EC)*, pages 129–139. ACM, 1999.

[38] M. Osadchy, B. Pinkas, A. Jarrous, and B. Moskovich. SCiFI - a system for secure face identification. In *IEEE Symposium on Security and Privacy (S&P)*, pages 239–254. IEEE, 2010.

[39] P. Paillier. Public-key cryptosystems based on composite degree residuosity classes. In *EUROCRYPT*, volume 1592 of *LNCS*, pages 223–238. Springer, 1999.

[40] M. O. Rabin. *How to exchange secrets with oblivious transfer*, TR-81 edition, 1981. Aiken Computation Lab, Harvard University.

[41] A.-R. Sadeghi, T. Schneider, and I. Wehrenberg. Efficient privacy-preserving face recognition. In *International Conference on Information Security and Cryptology (ICISC)*, volume 5984 of *LNCS*, pages 229–244. Springer, 2009.

[42] T. Schneider and M. Zohner. GMW vs. Yao? Efficient secure two-party computation with low depth circuits. In *Financial Cryptography (FC)*, volume 7859 of *LNCS*, pages 275–292. Springer, 2013.

[43] S. F. Shahandashti, R. Safavi-Naini, and P. Ogunbona. Private fingerprint matching. In *Australasian Conference on Information Security and Privacy (ACISP)*, volume 7372 of *LNCS*, pages 426–433. Springer, 2012.

[44] M. Turk and A. Pentland. Eigenfaces for recognition. *Journal of Cognitive Neuroscience*, 3(1):71–86, 1991.

[45] A. C.-C. Yao. How to generate and exchange secrets (extended abstract). In *Foundations of Computer Science (FOCS)*, pages 162–167. IEEE, 1986.

# APPENDIX

## A. CORRELATED OBLIVIOUS TRANSFER

In [1], Asharov *et al.* introduce a protocol that implements the correlated OT (C-OT) functionality. They describe it in a version that is adapted to Yao's protocol, *i.e.*, where the correlation function is an exclusive-OR. The generic version of their protocol can be used with any correlation function as long as the outputs lie in $\{0,1\}^l$ (or $\mathbb{Z}_{2^l}$), for some integer $l$. However, if the outputs of C-OT are integers from $\mathbb{Z}_m$, where $m \in \mathbb{N}$ is not a power of 2, the protocol cannot be applied directly. In particular, we need a hash function $H : \{0,1\}^* \to \mathbb{Z}_m$ that can be modeled as a random oracle. The protocol described in [1, Sec. 5.4] should then be modified as follows:

- $\mathcal{S}$ sends $y_j = f_{\Delta_j}(H(\mathbf{q}_j)) - H(\mathbf{q}_j \oplus \mathbf{s})$, for every $j = 1, \ldots, n$.

- For every $1 \le j \le n$, $\mathcal{R}$ outputs $H(\mathbf{t}_j)$ if $r_j = 0$ or $y_j + H(\mathbf{t}_j)$ if $r_j = 1$.

However, it is not practical to deal with such hash functions in actual implementations. Consequently, if the modulus $m$ can be adapted, it is preferable to use a larger modulus $m' = 2^{\lceil \log_2(m) \rceil}$ and apply the protocol. This is the case for the biometric recognition protocols dealt with by GSHADE, since the modulus $m$ is such that all distances lie in $\mathbb{Z}_m$ and taking a larger modulus $m' > m$ would not change correctness, because all distances obviously also lie in $\mathbb{Z}_{m'}$. Also notice that taking a modulus equal to $m' = 2^{\lceil \log_2(m) \rceil}$ does not degrade communication complexity and that the choice of the modulus does not impact security.

# Author Index